Fortran 90

Loren P. Meissner
University of San Francisco

PWS Publishing Company
I(T)P **An International Thomson Publishing Company**
Boston • Albany • Bonn • Cincinnati • Detroit • London • Madrid • Melbourne
Mexico City • New York • Paris • San Francisco • Singapore • Tokyo • Toronto • Washington

PWS PUBLISHING COMPANY
20 Park Plaza, Boston, MA 02116-4324

I(T)P™
International Thomson Publishing
The trademark ITP is used under license.

For more information, contact:

PWS Publishing Co.
20 Park Plaza
Boston, MA 02116

International Thomson Publishing Europe
Berkshire House I68-I73
High Holborn
London WC1V 7AA
England

Thomas Nelson Australia
102 Dodds Street
South Melbourne, 3205
Victoria, Australia

Nelson Canada
1120 Birchmont Road
Scarborough, Ontario
Canada M1K 5G4

International Thomson Editores
Campos Eliseos 385, Piso 7
Col. Polanco
11560 Mexico D.F., Mexico

International Thomson Publishing GmbH
Königswinterer Strasse 418
53227 Bonn, Germany

International Thomson Publishing Asia
221 Henderson Road
#05-10 Henderson Building
Singapore 0315

International Thomson Publishing Japan
Hirakawacho Kyowa Building, 31
2-2-1 Hirakawacho
Chiyoda-ku, Tokyo 102
Japan

Sponsoring Editor: Jonathan Plant
Production Editor: Kathleen Wilson
Manufacturing Coordinator: Lisa Flanagan
Associate Developmental Editor: Mary Thomas
Assistant Editor: Ken Morton
Editorial Assistant: Lai Wong
Marketing Manager: Nathan Wilbur
Interior Design: Sue Caffey/Kirby Lozyniak
Cover Design: Marshall Henrichs
Cover Printer: Henry Sawyer Co.
Printer & Binder: R.R. Donnelley & Sons

Library of Congress Cataloging-in-Publication Data

Meissner, Loren P.
Fortran 90 / Loren P. Meissner.
p. cm.
Includes index.
ISBN 0-534-93372-6
1. FORTRAN 90 (Computer Program Language) I. Title.
QA76.73.F25M435 1994
005.13'3—dc20 94-40209
CIP

Printed and bound in the United States of America by Courier Westford, Inc.
1 2 3 4 5 6 7 8 9 10—99 98 97 96 95

Contents

Part II CONTROL

Part III DATA OBJECTS

Part IV PROGRAMS AND SUBPROGRAMS

Preface

This book is intended for introductory courses in Fortran programming offered in the fields of science, engineering, applied mathematics, and statistics. Fortran has traditionally been the language of choice for creating programs for engineering and large-scale scientific applications. Development of the Fortran 90 standard — with new capabilities for structured types and recursion, internal procedures, whole-array operations, and object encapsulation — is driving renewed interest in Fortran for business and educational programs. This book helps ease the transition from previous versions of Fortran to the new world of Fortran 90 programming.

Migrating from traditional Fortran to the modern Fortran 90 dialect is a bit like moving back to the town where you grew up, and finding that it is no longer the sleepy little village you remember from your childhood. Your old Fortran programming habit patterns still work, but as you begin to understand the newer ways of doing things you feel less and less affection for the old ways. A few major examples:

- With `implicit none` and other new safety features, you may find that the Fortran compiler detects a much larger proportion of your syntax errors than before.
- Using the improved `do` construct (with `exit`) and the new `case` construct to supplement Fortran 77's `if-then-else`, you will probably find yourself programming without statement labels.
- You will find that assumed-shape dummy argument arrays can make array handling in procedures nearly painless.
- You will be able to replace many loop operations with whole array and array section notation.
- You will come to appreciate the smooth interface between a program unit and the internal procedures that it contains or the modules that it imports.

According to the traditional Fortran view, variables (including arrays) are simply collections of bits whose properties are determined locally and independently in each program unit. Fortran 90 permits you to view a variable as an *object* whose data type and other attributes are permanently attached to it — an object that can be manipulated in ways appropriate to its data type and dimensions.

Whither Fortran?

The role of Fortran among programming languages has changed drastically over the past couple of decades. At the time Fortran 77 was standardized, Fortran was the leading general-purpose programming language for most computer applications, with exceptions in a few specialized areas such as accounting and computer operating systems. Surveys at academic and research institutions showed 35 to 40 percent preference levels for Fortran, with the next highest competitor typically at 20 to 25 percent.

Perhaps the 1977 revision of the Fortran standard was too conservative. Whatever the reason, the upstart Pascal, with its modern data structures and control structures, elbowed Fortran aside in the early 1980s and became the primary academic programming language. Meanwhile C, and more recently C++ with its superior encapsulation and information hiding features, replaced Fortran as the preferred language for operating systems and many other applications.

For engineering and large-scale scientific applications, however, Fortran has retained its traditional niche. Anyone who wants to do "number crunching" — to get a lot of numerical answers quickly and efficiently — still turns to Fortran. Fortran is ideally suited to optimization, especially for array processing with modern parallel architectures. Comprehensive software libraries for scientific, statistical, and mathematical applications are available for use with Fortran. In today's academic curriculum, Fortran appears most often in service courses for science, engineering, applied mathematics, and statistics.

The Fortran 90 Language

Immediately upon completion of the Fortran 77 language standard, the standards establishment started a radical modernization program. In 1990, after 13 years, this effort finally bore fruit.

Fortran 90 is a truly modern programming language, and yet it maintains full compatibility with Fortran 77. The new language includes structured types and recursion, considered essential even for simple programming tasks. Internal procedures are present, limited to a single nesting level. Fortran's statement format is now comparable to that of other modern languages. (Nevertheless, for compatibility, the old punched-card oriented form is accepted as an alternative. You can still read your old "dusty decks" directly into Fortran 90 — if you can find a card reader.)

Added features make Fortran 90 highly suitable for the scientific application areas that are Fortran's stronghold.

- Whole-array operations and flexible precision specification enhance the usefulness of the language in scientific, statistical, and mathematical areas.
- Allocatable arrays and strongly typed pointers manage heap storage.
- Bit operations are based on an existing standard, US MIL-STD 1753; packed logical arrays are recognized as an alternative.

- Modules with "public" and "private" accessibility attributes permit information hiding. A module can encapsulate data, new data types, and operations — including generic (polymorphic) operations — on the new types.

A careful review of Fortran 90 confirms its sound design. This version of the language deserves to expand beyond the strictly scientific applications niche, and to regain some of its former popularity as a general purpose language.

Even as acceptance of the new version grows, further revision is already contemplated. A varying-length character string capability has been developed as a possible standard extension module. Several new standardization projects are building on Fortran 90, including at least two parallel processing syntax projects and a Fortran-UNIX™ language compatibility effort.

Obsolete Features.

In the Fortran 90 standard, the following nine features are stigmatized as "obsolescent" — although they are retained in the language standard to maintain compatibility with previous versions — and superior replacements are identified.

1. arithmetic `if`,
2. real `do` variables and real do parameters,
3. shared `do` termination, and terminal statements other than `continue` or `end do`,
4. branching to an `end if` statement from outside the `if` block,
5. alternate `return` (statement label arguments),
6. the `pause` statement,
7. the `assign` and assigned `go to` statements,
8. assigned `format` statement,
9. the *c*H (Hollerith) edit descriptor.

Some of these features are hardly mentioned in this text; the others are relegated to Appendix D ("Obsolete Fortran Features"). Appendix D also describes some features that are not on the official list, but for which superior replacements are available.

How This Text is Organized

This book is about the Fortran 90 language and its applications. It is not about algorithms and data structures, although it includes a number of examples (such as sorting procedures and linked lists) that illustrate those subjects.

The text attempts to be both comprehensive and pedagogically sound. All aspects of the language are fully covered, although some obscure features are relegated to appendices. The descriptions are self-contained, and the material follows a logical and deliberate progression.

The vocabulary and terminology are very close to those of the official Fortran 90 standard. The `implicit none` directive is introduced at the beginning and used consistently in the Fortran program examples. Array dimensions and string lengths are consistently declared as named constants. Intrinsic function references are accompanied by `intrinsic` declarations, and dummy arguments have declared `intent` attributes. Dummy argument arrays are of the assumed-shape class.

The Prologue

With the first part written in narrative form, the Prologue that precedes Chapter 1 raises issues as they would naturally occur to a group of people designing a Fortran program. For programming novices, the Prologue provides a quick overview of Fortran programming. For readers experienced in another language (or in traditional Fortran), it gives a quick introduction to the new look and feel of modern Fortran syntax.

The Prologue describes statement form, assignment, list-directed input and output, repetition (indexed `do`) and branching (`if-then-else`), internal procedures, and the programming environment. This rudimentary set of features is sufficient for writing simple but useful Fortran programs.

Parts I to IV

Chapters 1 through 9 cover all essential Fortran features step by step. Careful attention has been given to the sequence of topics. An introduction to each Part describes and motivates the Fortran concepts discussed therein.

Advanced, Optional, and Obsolete Features.

Fortran 90 is a large language, and this is a large textbook. Some guidance is given in the headings concerning topics that could most easily be omitted from an initial study of the language.

Advanced topics:

Features that almost every serious Fortran user will eventually need to know about, but which might well be omitted from an introductory course, include

- Complex data type
- Expressions in initialization and specification statements
- `Merge`, the `where` statement, and the `where` construct
- Logical data type
- Lower array bounds
- Stride (increment) in array sections
- Array and structure constructors
- Pointers
- Data type encapsulation
- Optional and keyword arguments
- File input and output

Optional topics:

Features that are essential in some specific applications areas, but can be completely ignored by many other users, are marked optional. Some of these appear as parts of advanced topics. These are

- Attribute-oriented declarations (except for arrays)
- `kind` (variant hardware representations of data)
- Recursive procedures
- Construct names
- `do while`
- The `cycle` statement
- Vector subscripts
- Non-ASCII character sets
- Nonallocated pointer targets
- User-defined generic procedures
- Pointers as dummy arguments
- Procedure names as arguments
- Implementation of arguments
- Direct acess, unformatted, internal, and namelist input and output

Obsolete Features.

Features of traditional Fortran that are no longer essential are described in Appendix D to permit reading and understanding of existing programs. Use of these features in new programs is not recommended.

Supplements

A handy Reference Guide for students, included with each copy of this textbook, summarizes the essentials of Fortran 90 syntax and contains a complete list of intrinsic functions and subroutines in the Fortran library.

An Instructor's Manual, available from the publisher, contains suggestions for using the text as well as complete solutions to the exercises. Included with the Instructor's Manual is a diskette containing all of the program examples from the text (as ASCII text files), along with sample input data.

Acknowledgements

The four principal reviewers of the manuscript for this text, Graham Barber, Lawrence Genalo, Jeanne Martin, and John Prentice, made a multitude of very helpful suggestions and corrections to the draft manuscript. John Prentice also proposed a number of the scientific and engineering examples and exercises. Brian Smith and John Reid suggested programming techniques that appear in some of the examples.

Many of the array examples in Chapter 5, the suggested module applications in Chapter 7, and the intrinsic library function descriptions in Appendix A are adapted from the Fortran 90 standard document (international standard ISO/IEC 1539:1991). The array examples (from Appendix C.13 of the standard document), and in particular the Ising model (on which Example 5.45 is based), were originally propounded by Alan Wilson. Material from ISO/IEC 1539:1991 is used with the permission of the International Standards Organization.

Examples 7.13 (Quicksort), 8.14 (Keyword Arguments), and 8.15 (Optional Arguments) are adapted from *Programmer's Guide to Fortran 90*, by Brainerd, Goldberg, and Adams (McGraw-Hill, 1990), and are used with permission.

The program Explore in Section 1.6, Exercise 2 is abstracted and adapted from the program `f90_utility`, written by Malcolm Cohen and Robert Iles (© 1991, Numerical Algorithms Group, Oxford, UK), and is used with permission.

Some material in this textbook is adapted from *Fortran 77*, by Loren P. Meissner and Elliott I. Organick (Addison-Wesley, 1980). A careful analyst could trace some paragraphs to three predecessor editions: *Fortran IV* by Organick and Meissner (1974), *A Fortran IV Primer* by Organick (1966), and *A Fortran Primer* by Organick (1961). The 1961 book was among the first Fortran textbooks published. Elliott Organick's flair for pedagogy and style insured the early success of this text and of later versions as well. The present textbook would undoubtedly also have benefited from Elliott's collaboration, but for his death in 1985 (before this project got seriously under way). I want to express my appreciation for Elliott Organick's contribution to whatever success this textbook may achieve. I would also like to thank Elliott's wife, Betty Organick, who has consented to the use of material from previous editions in this text.

Prologue
Rudiments of Fortran 90

This prologue presents the rudiments of Fortran 90 in narrative form. The fictional format may seem unusual for a book of this kind, but it is intended to be instructive as well as entertaining. Here is the cast of characters:

- Sam Spade, Private Investigator, is a professional gentleman from the old school. He enjoys the benefits of "high tech," but he is content to entrust the details in such matters to his competent staff while he concentrates on applying his skill as a detective.
- María Flores, Sam's technical assistant, is a brilliant young engineering graduate. She is a competent programmer in three computer languages: Fortran, Pascal, and C++. She is also a friendly and helpful person and likes to work with other people.
- Catherine Spade, Sam's niece, is a high school senior. After studying about computers for just a few weeks, she is fascinated and wants to learn all about them. She has been doing a bit of programming in Pascal at school, and her older brother has shown her some C++ programs. Seeing an Apple Macintosh computer in María's office, she hopes to broaden her programming experience.

Let's watch as María and Catherine create some short programs, which will serve as our first Fortran 90 examples.

P.1 FORTRAN PROGRAM STATEMENTS

Apple Pi?

Sam Spade, who is still the most famous P.I. in San Francisco,[1] slams down the phone and turns to his technical assistant, María Flores.

"It's Casper Gutman again! If he wasn't the richest man in town, I'd refuse to take on any more of his problems! But his retainer pays most of my rent."

"What's his trouble this time?"

"Somebody is suing him over a fender bender. Claims Gutman's chauffeur didn't stop in time. He wants me to work out something about the circumference of his wheels divided by the radius. The radius or the diameter — I don't know. Some mathematical thing, María, something you would understand. Of course, I couldn't let on that I didn't know what he was talking about."

"Pi?"

"No thanks. I just had lunch."

"You said ' mathematical'. He wants you to come up with π."

"You could bake one for him, María."

"Not pie, Sam. Pi. *P* . . . *i*.! Anyway, I'll just do it with the Apple."

"Hmm. I suppose Gutman would go for apple pie just as much as any other kind."

"And I'll do it in Fortran."

"Is that what you call the microwave oven we bought last July?"

"Sam, get with it! I thought you studied geometry in high school."

"That was a long time ago. Besides, what has geometry got to do with Gutman?"

"Oh, Sam! You ought to know. The circumference of a circle is 2π times the radius. Pi is a Greek letter used in math."

"Oh, so you're going to do something with that computer of yours."

"Now you've got it. I'm going to write a Fortran program and run it on my Apple Macintosh computer. You can call Mr. Gutman back in about five minutes and tell him the value of π to eight digits of precision."

"You always were a whiz at math, María. I really should brush up a bit."

"I'll show you how simple it is. I'll bet I can do it in three lines, but you'll have to take my word for some of the technical parts. Just for fun, I think I'll compute e in the same program. Don't look so puzzled! It's just another mathematical constant that's almost as famous as π. Maybe Mr. Gutman will be impressed."

"I'm impressed already, María. You're a genius. But what about those technical parts?"

"Fortran has a library full of mathematical functions. We can get π from the arctangent and e from the exponential."

---

[1] With apologies to Dashiell Hammett, who invented Sam Spade (in *The Maltese Falcon*, 1930) even before John Backus and his crew invented Fortran. It goes without saying that nobody mentioned in this tale is anyone you know.

María types three lines on the screen:

```
PROGRAM PIE
PRINT *, ATAN2 (0.0, -1.0), EXP (1.0)
END
```

"The line in the middle does all the work. ATAN2 is Fortran's name for arctangent, and EXP stands for exponential."

María pushes a couple of buttons, and the answers appear on the screen:

```
3.1415927  2.7182818
```

Sam makes a quick phone call, and the Casper Gutman case is finished.

Programming Style

"María, in a few months my niece, Catherine, will be able to help you. Her advanced math class started working on computers a couple of weeks ago. Not Fortran — some Frenchman."

"If she's in high school, it's most likely Pascal."

"Sounds right. She's fascinated with programming, but she says she keeps forgetting the semicolons. I don't see any semicolons in your program."

"Pascal uses semicolons between statements. Fortran recognizes the end of each line as the end of a statement, so you can leave out the semicolons."

"It's too technical for me. Anyway, she saw your computer and said she was going to stop by and ask you about it sometime. Hey! Here she comes now. You two can stay here and talk about Fortran and — that Frenchman. I'm getting out of here — I've got to do some research. I have a new lead on the Maltese falcon case."

"Maybe Catherine would like to see what a Fortran program looks like. I don't want to show her *this* thing. It runs OK — Fortran doesn't complain — but it has no comments or indentation, and all those capital letters make it look like a fugitive from the 1960s! I'll pretty it up a bit, so I can show her what a Fortran 90 program *should* look like. I'll just add some comments, change most of the capital letters to lower case, and indent some of the lines. There, that didn't take long!

"Hi, Cathy! I was just working on a short Fortran program that I wrote today for one of your uncle's clients. Thought I'd clean it up before I save it permanently."

María directs Cathy's attention to the screen:

```
! Program to print the values of "pi" and "e."
!   María Flores, 1 October 1999
  program PI_E                        ! (specification statement)
! start program PI_E                           (comment line)
    print *, ATan2 (0.0, -1.0), Exp (1.0)      ! (instruction)
  end ! (instruction)
```

"It looks interesting, Miss Flores. But what are those exclamation points? In my advanced math class, we use them for *factorial*, but these aren't in the right place."

"They're not factorials. In a Fortran 90 program, an exclamation point anywhere on a line marks the beginning of a *comment* that continues to the end of the line.[2] If the exclamation point is the first nonblank character on the line, the whole line is a comment. Otherwise, the line is a *statement*. And a statement line can have a *trailing comment* at the end."

"I get it, Miss Flores. It's like the comments in the C++ program that my brother showed me. So your Fortran program has three comment lines and three statement lines, and the statement lines all have trailing comments. What a lot of comments!"

"Experienced programmers make good use of comments. They always put comment lines at the beginning of a program to explain its purpose, and they explain unusual program features with comment lines or with trailing comments. I'll admit that a comment on every line is a little heavy."

"At school, I keep forgetting the semicolons in my Pascal programs. I think I'm going to like Fortran because it doesn't use semicolons."

"Fortran recognizes the end of each line as the end of a statement, so it doesn't need semicolons."

"So Fortran expects one statement per line?"

"Usually. There are exceptions, however. Sometimes you have a statement that is too long to fit on a line and must be extended onto a *continuation line*. You can't just skip to the next line — you have to end the first line of the statement with an ampersand symbol, like this:.

```
print *, ATan2 (0.0, 1.0), ATan2 (1.0, 0.0), &
  ATan2 (0.0, -1.0), ATan2 (-1.0, 0.0)
```

A complete explanation of Fortran 90 source program form rules appears in Appendix C. This appendix explains the modern *free source form* (used consistently in this text) as well as the traditional *fixed source form* that is still accepted by Fortran 90.

It's not too strange. Think of a story or an essay, where you put in a hyphen when you have to break a word at the end of a line. The ampersand has somewhat the same purpose."

"I get it."

"There is another exception. Once in a while, you may have two or three statements that are short and closely related. You can write more than one statement on a line, separated by semicolons, like this:

```
read *, X, Y; print *, X + Y
```

So semicolons creep back into the picture, but only when you put more than one statement on a line."

"Why do you capitalize some of the words, and write others all in lower case?"

"It's just the style that I like to use for all of my programs — when I take my time and do it right. I use all lowercase letters for *keywords*, like `program`, `print`, and `end`. I always capitalize *names*, either those that I've invented, such as the program name `PI_E`,

---

[2] Miss Flores forgets to mention that an exclamation point does not mark the beginning of a comment when it is inside a character string.

or the names of Fortran library procedures, such as ATan2 or Exp. Sometimes I capitalize letters in the middle of a name."

"Why did you indent some of the lines, but not all of them, Miss Flores?"

"To show the structure of the program. The first statement is the program statement and the last statement is the end statement. I always put in a comment line, beginning with the word start, between the descriptive statements at the beginning and the action statements farther down. These three — the program statement line, the end statement line, and the start comment line — are the only lines I leave unindented. They stand out like brackets around all the other lines.

Summary of Fortran 90 Source Program Form Rules

Names and keywords

- Fortran 90 does not distinguish between uppercase (capital) and lowercase letters, except in character data. For readability, however, you should adopt some consistent rules. For example, capitalize all names, including the names of Fortran intrinsic library functions such as ATan2; write Fortran keywords such as program, print, and end entirely in lower case.
- A name may be composed of letters, digits, and underscore characters, but the first character must be a letter. For example, Energy, Kinetic_Energy, Potential_Energy, Time_1, TimeIn, R1234 are all valid names. Other characters, including blanks, must not appear within a name. There must not be more than 31 characters in a name.
- At least one blank character must appear between adjacent names or between names and keywords.

Lines and statements

- An exclamation point anywhere on a line (except in character data) marks the beginning of a comment, which continues to the end of the line.
- A line that is entirely blank or one whose first nonblank character is an exclamation point is a comment line.
- Fortran recognizes the end of each line as the end of a statement; no semicolon or other statement termination symbol is required. However, multiple statements, separated by semicolons, may be written on a line:

```
read *, X, Y; print *, X + Y          ! Read two numbers and print their sum
```

- If a statement is too long to fit on a line, it may be extended onto one or more continuation lines. Each line of a statement, except the last one, ends with an ampersand symbol (which may be followed by a comment):

```
print *, ATan2 (0.0, 1.0), ATan2 (1.0, 0.0), &          ! See next line.
      ATan2 (0.0, -1.0), ATan2 (-1.0, 0.0)
```

Classification of Statements

"The `start` line in your program reminds me of `begin` in Pascal, Miss Flores."

"Yes, Cathy, it is similar, but Fortran does not require a `start` line. Look, it's really just a comment. This line is one of my personal style preferences. I like to put some visual separation between the Fortran statements that are descriptive — the *specification* statements — and the executable statements — the *instructions* that tell Fortran what actions to perform."

More detailed rules for placement of program statements are listed in Appendix C.

"So you write the specification statements before `start` and the instructions after it."

"Right. In general, Fortran requires that all of the specifications precede all of the instructions. I like to put in this special comment line as a separator that I can recognize easily."

"Tell me some more about the statements in this program."

"The statement between the two comment lines is a specification that gives the program a name. The two statements that follow the `start` comment line are instructions — each one will cause some action when the program is executed. You can think of instructions as the verbs of the Fortran language."

"You said specifications are descriptive, so I guess they're like adjectives."

"Right again, Cathy. Specifications are descriptive, and they have no direct counterpart in the execution sequence."

Specification Statements

The `program` statement is discussed later in this section and in Section 7.2.

"The only specification statement in this example is the `program` statement. It means that this is a complete program, and it gives the program a name."

"I think I understand it, Miss Flores."

"You know, Cathy, while we've been talking, I've thought of two more changes that I want to make."

"My teacher says no program is ever really finished."

Appendix A contains a complete description of all procedures in the Fortran intrinsic procedure library.

"I want to add an `intrinsic` specification near the beginning of the program. It will tell Fortran that `ATan2` and `Exp` are functions in the Fortran intrinsic procedure library.

"This declaration is optional, but it will help anyone who sees the program to understand these names. And if I put it in, Fortran will verify that these procedures are actually present in the library. Then, if Fortran complains, the most likely reason would be that I spelled a procedure name wrong.

The `end` statement is discussed later in this section and in Section 7.3.

"I also want to expand the `end` statement. Actually, this statement has some of the flavor of a specification as well as an instruction. I'll change this last statement to `end program PI_E`. When I put extra information like this in an `end` statement, Fortran will verify that it matches the `program` statement. Another safety check. I usually write my `end` statements this way.

I'm going to name this version 'Example P.1.' After I give it a final test, I'll save it without changing it any more."

```
! Example P.1. (Maria Flores, 1 October, 1999)
!   Print the values of "pi" and "e."
  program PI_E                                  ! (specification statement)
    intrinsic ATan2, Exp                        ! (specification statement)
! start program PI_E
    print *, ATan2 (0.0, -1.0), Exp (1.0)                   ! (instruction)
  end program PI_E                                          ! (instruction)
```

"But, Miss Flores, I don't see any *type declaration* statements. My teacher says we always have to put in type declarations."

"This program doesn't need any — just because it's so simple. It doesn't have any variables, so it doesn't need any type declarations."

Type declarations are introduced later, in Section P.2, and are discussed further in Section 1.2.

"No variables? That's weird!"

"You're right — a program so short that it has no variables is really unusual. Type declarations are actually the most important kind of specification statements in most programs. We can talk about them later."

Instructions

"Miss Flores, we have been looking at specification statements, but you said there are other kinds of statements called instructions. What about them?"

"I'd better back up a bit and remind you that a *program* is just a sequence of *lines of text*. *Execution* of the program is a separate *process* that goes on inside the computer when the program is executed.

"The program is a text file that contains comment lines and statement lines. You can display it on a screen or print it on paper. It will not change unless you take steps to edit the text file.

"But the internal state of the computer will change continually while Fortran executes a program. For example, the values of variables will be changed as Fortran carries out the instructions.

"Sometimes we say that the program statements are *static*, or fixed, while the execution process is *dynamic*, or changing. The statements can be displayed in *space*, and the execution occurs in a *time* dimension. These two separate entities, the static program and its dynamic execution, are closely related.

"The space relationship among the instruction statements of the static program and the time relationship among the steps of the dynamic process are parallel up to a point. But the program can dictate a different sequence. A famous man named Edsger W. Dijkstra once wrote,[3]

> '... We should do ... our utmost to shorten the conceptual gap between the static program and the dynamic process, to make the corre-

[3] Edsger W. Dijkstra, "Go To Statement Considered Harmful," *Communications of the ACM* (11:3) March 1968, pp. 147–48.

spondence between the program (spread out in text space) and the process (spread out in time) as trivial as possible.'

This sketch (Figure P.1) might help you understand what Dijkstra meant. The left side represents the static program, spread out in text space, as it might appear on a computer screen or on paper. The right side is the dynamic execution process, spread out in time, as the instructions might be executed one after another."

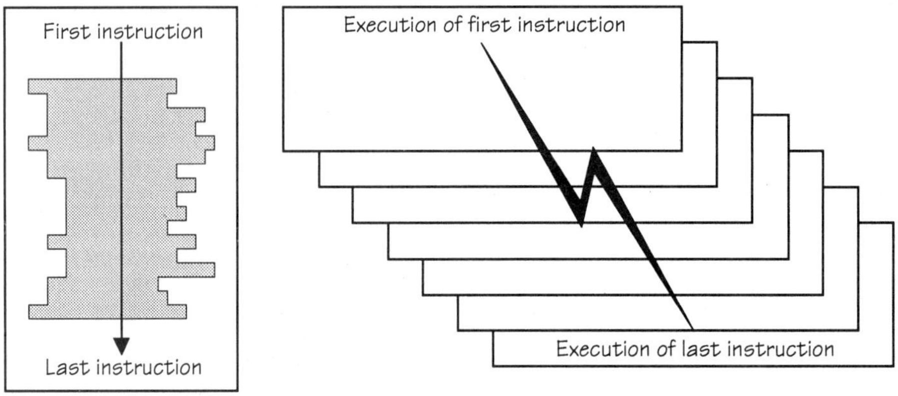

FIGURE P.1. Correspondence between the program and its execution process.

"Excuse me, Miss Flores, but isn't all of this just a complicated description of something that's really simple? The program is static, in space, on the screen. The execution process is dynamic, in time, inside the computer. I can understand that. It's just like a video tape. The action you see when you play the tape is stored magnetically on the tape, from one end to the other."

"It's simple enough, Cathy, but we can't really talk about instructions and their execution without some kind of framework."

"Fair enough, but I have another question. You said `start` is just an optional comment line that you put in to help you find the first instruction. Fortran ignores comments, so how does it know which instruction to execute first?"

"Well, you just 'start at the beginning and follow the yellow brick road.' Fortran starts with the *first instruction* in the statement sequence. The *normal execution sequence* in a Fortran program then follows the sequence of the statements, from top to bottom, the way they are written in the program.

"Look at this program again. It has only two instructions to be executed. The first instruction in the statement sequence is

```
print *, ATan2 (0.0, -1.0), Exp (1.0)
```

so the first step in the execution process will be to display the values that Fortran obtains from the two intrinsic procedures `ATan2` and `Exp`."

"But there isn't any printer connected to your Mac."

"That's true. Even though the keyword in this statement is `print`, it doesn't mean that Fortran has to print something on paper. The answers will be displayed right here on the terminal screen. I could use a slightly different setup if I had a printer attached to my Mac, or I could save the results in a file and print them later."

"So much for the `print` instruction. What about the other one?"

"There is only one more instruction in this program, so the next instruction for Fortran to execute is

```
end program PI_E                                    ! (instruction)
```

Executing the end statement is the last step in the program execution process."

Control Constructs and Procedures

"So Fortran always executes the statements from top to bottom, from the first instruction to the end statement?"

"No, Cathy. Remember, I only said that is the *normal execution sequence*. The actual sequence can change when Fortran comes to a *control construct* or a *procedure reference*. Look at this diagram (Figure P.2)."

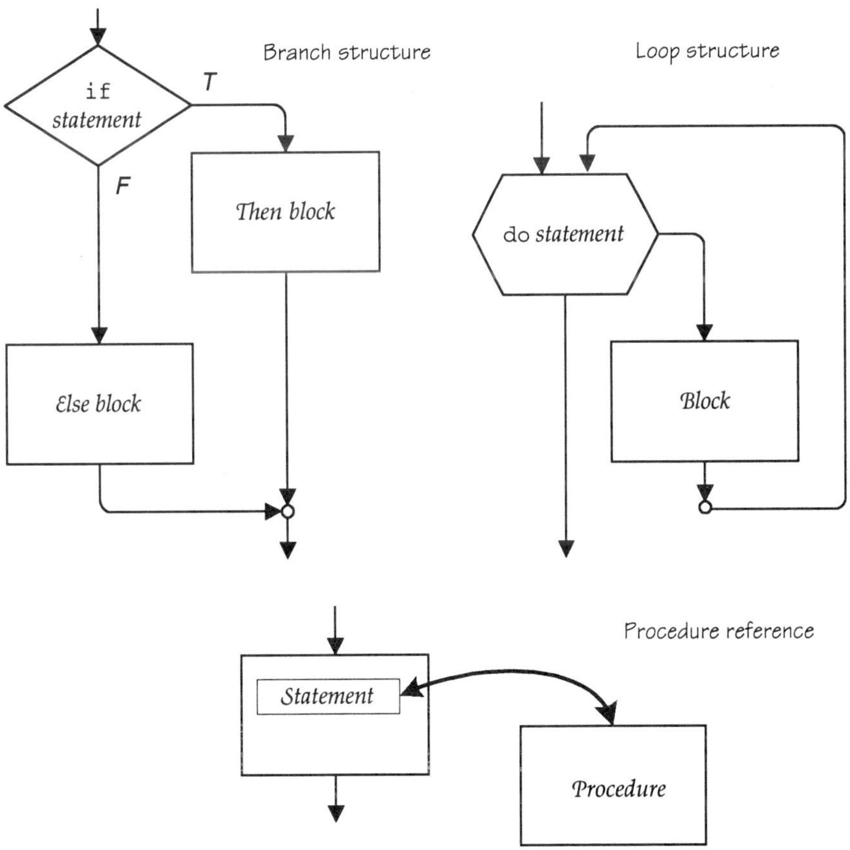

FIGURE P.2. Three ways to change the normal Fortran execution sequence.

The Fortran `if` control construct is introduced later, in Section P.4, and is covered more fully in Chapter 3 along with the `case` construct. The Fortran **do** construct is also introduced in Section P.4 and is explained further in Chapter 4.

"I remember. We had control statements in Pascal. They are `if` and `while`. An `if` statement controls two other statements. It makes a test to see which of these to execute, and it skips the other one. A `while` statement controls only one statement, and it makes a test to see whether to repeat it or not. They're just like skipping over part of a video tape with Fast Forward or rewinding part of it and playing it again."

"That's the general idea, Cathy, but Fortran uses **do** for repetition. I can show you the details later."

"Your diagram shows that, besides branching and looping, there is another way to change the sequence, Miss Flores."

"Yes, Cathy — the third way is *procedure reference.* In my program (Example P.1), the output list in the `print` statement consists of two expressions that refer to procedures, so execution is actually interrupted twice in the middle of this one statement. Fortran goes off and executes the arctangent procedure, and, as soon as that is finished, it goes away again and executes the exponential procedure. Here is another diagram (Figure P.3) to illustrate the idea. A procedure reference is a very small part of the static program, but it can correspond to a considerable amount of execution."

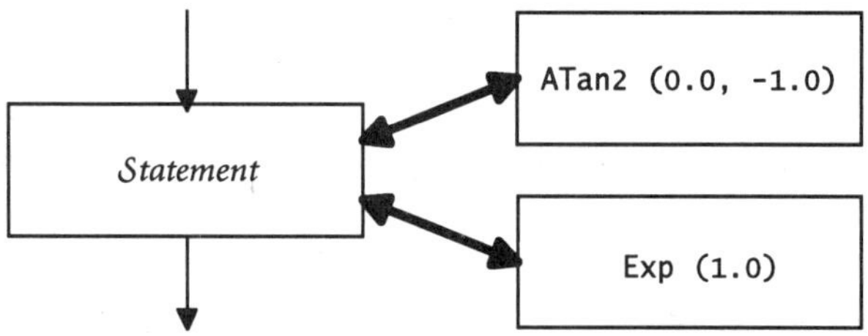

FIGURE P.3. Two procedure references made by the *print* statement.

"How does Fortran know what to execute when it comes to a procedure reference?"

"A good question. The arctangent and the exponential are *intrinsic* procedures. This means that they have been defined as part of the Fortran processor and are stored in the Fortran intrinsic procedure library, so they can be made available automatically whenever the program refers to them."

User-defined procedures are introduced in Sections P.2 and 1.4, and are discussed in detail in Chapters 7 and 8. See also Section 7.3 and Appendix C.

"My brother showed me how to bring in C++ library functions with `include`. Is that what you mean by automatic?"

"No, it's even more automatic than that. Fortran always recognizes intrinsic library functions by their names, even when there is no `intrinsic` specification in the program. Fortran does not require an `include` statement.[4]

You can also create your own procedures when you develop a Fortran program. You detach groups of statements from the program and make them independent. You can refer to a procedure that you have created in much the same way as you would refer to a procedure from the Fortran intrinsic library."

[4] Fortran provides an include facility, but for a different purpose. See Appendix D.11.

Internal and module subprograms, as well as main and module program units (also external program units and block data program units, Appendices D.6 and E.3), must have an **end** statement as the last line of program text.

"My teacher said procedures and functions are not the same thing, but I can't remember the difference."

"A Fortran *function* is one kind of procedure — the kind that returns a value. A *subroutine* is a procedure that does not return a value. Other programming languages use different terminology. For example, Pascal has *functions* that return a value and *procedures* that do not. And, in C++, everything is a *function*, but some functions return *void*."

"Thanks, Miss Flores. I've got to go now, but I'd like to come back again so that you can show me more."

"You're welcome, Cathy. I'll be happy to talk to you whenever you like."

The program *and* end *Statements*

The main program may begin with a `program` statement:

```
program Program name
```

Although the *Program name* is optional, its use is recommended as good program documentation. The last line of a program must be an `end` statement, which has one of the following forms:

```
end
end program
end program Program name
```

The optional *Program name* in the `end` statement is permitted only if it also appears in the `program` statement at the beginning. Inclusion of both the optional keyword and the optional program name in all `end` statements is recommended because it permits the programmer and the compiler to verify proper placement of statements.

Execution of the `end` statement causes program termination. In the source program text, the `end` statement also performs another role: it acts as a signal to Fortran (i.e., to the compiler) that the end of the program text has been reached.

P.1 Exercise

1. The following program has 6 lines. Which are comment lines, and which are statement lines? Identify each statement line as a specification or an instruction.

```
! Exercise P.1, Number 1. This program has six lines.
  program Ohms_Law
    real :: Current = 1.2, Resistance = 3.4
! start program Ohms_Law
    print *, Current, Resistance, Current * Resistance
  end program Ohms_Law
```

P.2 ASSIGNMENT STATEMENTS

Assignment and Expressions

A few days later, Cathy comes to visit María Flores again.

"I want to learn about some other Fortran instructions besides `print`, Miss Flores."

"Let's talk about *assignment,* Cathy. I think it is the most important kind of instruction. An example of a Fortran assignment statement is

```
Average = (X + Y) / 2.0
```

This assignment statement mentions three *variables,* `Average`, `X`, and `Y`, and one *numerical constant,* `2.0` .

"Two of the variables, `X` and `Y`, and the numerical constant `2.0`, appear in the *expression* on the right side of the assignment statement. Fortran uses the values of the variables and of the constant to calculate the expression `(X + Y) / 2.0` . If the value of `X` is `1.234` and the value of `Y` is `5.678`, for example, the expression value will be `3.456` . After calculating the value of this expression, Fortran *assigns* the value to the variable named `Average`. Here is an illustration of this process (Figure P.4)."

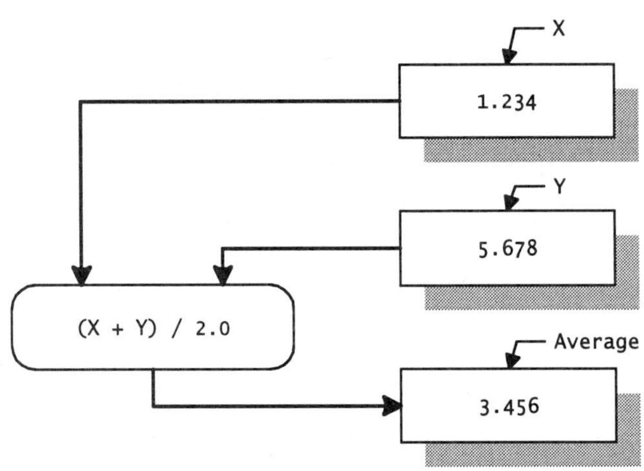

FIGURE P.4. How Fortran assigns the value of the expression *(X + Y) / 2.0* to *Average.*

"I think I understand, Miss Flores. An assignment statement has a variable name on the left and an expression on the right. In the expression, there can be variables and constants. Fortran finds the value of the expression on the right and gives that value to the variable whose name is on the left."

Variables and Constants

"My teacher told us about variables, constants, and expressions in Pascal. Variables and constants in a program represent *data objects* that can be manipulated when the program is executed. A constant has a *fixed* value, but a variable can change, or *vary*, during program execution."

"That's right, Cathy. Executing an assignment statement can change the value of a variable. Fortran reserves *storage* for each variable that is mentioned in the program. The value of each variable depends upon what has been stored in its particular space in the computer. Fortran changes a variable's value by replacing what is stored there.

"When a variable name appears in an expression, Fortran finds the stored value and uses it to compute the value of the expression. Using a variable in an expression does not have any effect on its value. Assignment gives the variable a new value. A variable can also get a new value as a result of an input operation, as you'll see later on."

Names

Fortran names are subject to a few other restrictions. See Section 1.2 for the details.

"Do you remember what I told you about the difference between the static program text and the dynamic execution process, Cathy? In the dynamic world, a variable is a stored object. But, in the program text — in specifications or instructions — a variable is referred to by its *name*. The names of Fortran 90 objects must be written in a certain way — with up to 31 characters, the first of which must be a letter. Names of variables have this form, and constants can have names of this form too. Later, you'll see that other Fortran names, including procedure names and type names, are also written this way."

Data Types

Structured types are discussed in Section 6.2. The old *implicit type specification* technique is described, in Appendix D.1, as one of the obsolete features that are no longer recommended.

"Does Fortran have *real* variables and *integer* variables, as Pascal does?"

"Yes, they are the principal *data types* for Fortran numerical data. Every Fortran variable or constant has a type. Fortran has five intrinsic, or built-in, types: *real*, *integer*, *complex*, *logical*, and *character*. There are also structured types defined by the user. For now, let's just concentrate on real and integer data types."

"Miss Flores, my brother told me that Fortran doesn't need type declarations."

"That's old-fashioned, Cathy. When Fortran was first invented, around 1956, it had some cute rules for establishing variable types without type declarations. But Fortran had only two types then — real and integer. We now understand that leaving out type declarations is an unsound programming practice, even though Fortran 90 still permits it."

"So how is it done now, Miss Flores?"

"In modern Fortran programs, we put type declarations near the beginning of the program to specify the data types of all variables. A `program` statement is the first statement, and it is directly followed by the specification statement `implicit none`, which instructs Fortran to verify that you have declared the type of each variable. Here is an example:

```
program Entropy
implicit none
  ⋮
end program Entropy
```

Type Declarations

"A type declaration, in its simplest form, consists of the name of the type, such as `integer` or `real`, a pair of colons, and a list of the variable names, as in these examples:

```
integer :: Amino_Acid, Quicksilver
real :: Average, X, Y
```

"I can figure these out, Miss Flores. This first type declaration means that `Amino_Acid` and `Quicksilver` are names of variables of integer type. The second one means that the names `Average`, `X`, and `Y` stand for variables of real type."

Some alternative type declaration forms are described in Section 1.2. See also Section 5.1.

"You're right. These type declaration statements have the form

Type name :: *List of names*

The *Type name* is a keyword such as `integer` or `real`. A *list* in a Fortran program is a sequence of one or more items, separated by commas if there is more than one."

Constants

"I think I understand about variables, Miss Flores. But what about constants? Why did you call 2.0 a *numerical* constant? Are there other kinds of constants?"

"There are constants of nonnumerical types. Character constants are written in a Fortran 90 program as quoted strings, such as `"Anemometer"`, and constants of logical type are written as truth values, either `.TRUE.` or `.FALSE.` . For every standard data type, there is a way to write *explicit* constants in the program — that is, to write constants in a conventional form whose value is obvious.[5]

"There are also *named constants* — constants that are represented in the program by a name. In fact, it's best to give names to almost all constants so that you can easily recognize a constant value that appears more than once in your program. You can write very simple constants, such as 0 and 1, in numerical form.

For more about the advantages of named constants, see Section 1.3.

"Fortran needs a declaration statement to define a named constant. A named constant definition is a type declaration that contains the keyword `parameter`. The name is followed by an equals sign, and then the value is written as an explicit constant:

Type , `parameter` :: *Name* = *Explicit constant*

I like to write the names of constants in all capital letters:

[5] Such a constant, written explicitly in a program in a conventional form whose value is obvious, may also be called a *literal* constant or a *manifest* constant.

```
real, parameter :: AVOGADRO = 6.0221367E23, &
  PLANCK = 6.6260755E-34
```

You can define several constants in the same declaration."

"Do numerical constants need data types, Miss Flores? Is there a difference between real constants and integer constants?"

"Yes, indeed. Fortran can determine the data types of numerical constants from the way they are written. If a numerical constant is written with a decimal point, such as `2.0`, its data type is *real*. If it is written as a string of digits without a decimal point, such as `2345609`, its data type is *integer*."[6]

Initialization

"When you declare the type of a variable, you can also give it *initial value*. In the type declaration, you just have to write an equals sign and a constant after the name of the variable. Here are some statements that declare the types of five variables and initialize four of them:

Named constants and initialized variables are discussed further in Sections 1.3 and 1.4.

```
real :: A, B = 1.234, C = 5.678
integer :: I = 9, J = 10
```

An initialized variable has a value when execution of the program begins."

Numerical Expressions

"What comes next?"

"After variables and constants, we can look at expressions. In fact, variable names and constants are expressions that have a very simple form."

"What about other expressions that are not quite so simple?"

"You can combine expressions with *arithmetic operators* such as +, -, *, or / to form more complicated numerical expressions. The asterisk denotes multiplication, and the slash is the division operator. Fortran also provides an exponentiation operator, written as two asterisks. You can also group expressions with parentheses. Here are some examples:

For more information about numerical expressions, see Section 2.2.

```
1.8 * Celsius + 32.0
(Fahrenheit - 32.0) / 1.8
Initial_Position + Distance
PI * (Radius ** 2)
Mass * (Vel_of_Light **2)
Current * Resistance
Minutes / 60
```

[6] The other standard numeric data type is *complex*. A complex numerical constant is written as a pair of real constants, enclosed in parentheses and separated by a comma — for example, `(1.0, 3.14)`.

Numeric Data Types

"If variables and constants have types, I suppose expressions must have types too."

"Right again, Cathy. In the simplest case, all of the variables and constants in an expression have the *same* type. When two operands of the same type are combined by an arithmetic operator, the resulting expression also has the same type."

"I think I see a problem, Miss Flores. What happens in integer division when the result is not an exact integer?"

"That's a problem, all right. Fortran's solution, when it divides two integer expressions, is to automatically *truncate* the result to the next smaller integer.[7] For example, when Fortran divides 3 by 2, it produces the integer result value 1, truncated from 1.5, and when Fortran divides 9 by 10 the result is 0, truncated from 0.9."

"Must all the operands in an expression have the same type?"

"No, *mixed* types are permitted. The rule is simple. When operands have different types, the integer operand is changed to real type before the operation is performed. In effect, the integer operand is replaced by an expression of real type with the same value. There is one exception: Raising a real expression to an integer power is just like repeated multiplication, so no type conversion is needed.

"Here are some examples. Suppose that R is a real variable and I is an integer:

```
I / 5                                 ! Expression of integer type
3.2 * R                                  ! Expression of real type
I * R                                    ! Expression of real type
(I / 5) * (3.2 * R)                      ! Expression of real type
R ** 2                      ! Real, to integer power - no conversion
```

In the third example, the value of I is converted to real type before the multiplication is performed. In the fourth example, (I / 5) is computed as an expression of integer type, with truncation, and this value is converted to real type before the multiplication is performed."

The Fortran Intrinsic Function Library

Appendix A describes all of the Fortran intrinsic library functions and shows the argument types that are permitted for each function and the types of the function results.

"So, Miss Flores, I think Fortran expressions look much like mathematical expressions, except for a few complications. But in advanced math we can do some operations besides addition, subtraction, multiplication, division, and exponentiation."

"That's a good point, Cathy. Fortran provides a lot of advanced mathematical operations. In a program, you can include *function references* along with the simple operations of arithmetic. Fortran's *intrinsic function library* has more than a hundred functions, including SqRt for square root, Abs for absolute value, and Exp for exponential. Three of the most useful categories of functions in this library are the data type conversion functions, the numerical utility functions, and the mathematical functions."

"You showed me some Fortran functions the other day. I remember that first program, where you computed π from the arctangent function and *e* from the exponential function. Are there some special rules for writing function references?"

---

[7] Negative quotients are truncated *toward zero*. Dividing -3 by 2 produces -1 .

"A function reference consists of the function name followed by a parenthesized list of argument expressions. For many library functions, the list consists of a single argument. If there are two or more arguments, they must be separated by commas. The data type of each argument must agree with the Fortran library specifications. The type of the function result may depend upon the types of the arguments."

"Did you say that some of the functions perform data type conversion?"

"Yes. A *conversion function* can produce a result with a data type that is different from the type of its argument. The most important conversion functions are these:

`Real` accepts an argument of integer type and delivers a result of real type.

`Int` accepts an argument of real type and delivers a result of integer type whose value is the next smaller integer (in absolute vaue).

`NInt` accepts an argument of real type and delivers a result of integer type whose value is the *nearest* integer.

The data type of the result, for any of the functions in this group, depends only on the function itself and is *independent* of the data type of the argument expression."

"What about utility functions?"

"Some especially useful numerical *utility functions* are `Abs`, `Sign`, and `Modulo`:

`Abs` is the absolute value function. The value of the result is obtained by ignoring the sign of the argument. The result is always positive or zero.

`Sign` has two arguments. The magnitude of the result is obtained from the first argument, and the sign of the result is obtained from the second argument.

`Modulo` has two arguments. The result is the remainder when the first argument is divided by the second.

The type of the argument expression for any of the functions in this group may be integer or real. If there are two or more arguments, all of them must have the same type. The result type is the *same* as the argument type."

"Let me guess. The mathematical functions include square root, exponential, logarithmic, and trigonometric functions."

"A good guess. Fortran *mathematical* functions do not accept arguments of integer type. The function values are defined as in mathematics. Arguments of the trigonometric functions are in radians. Results of the inverse trigonometric functions are between -π/2 and π/2 radians, except for `ATan2` whose result is between -π and π radians. The most important mathematical functions are these:

`SqRt (X)`, square root	`Sin (X)`, sine
`Exp (X)`, exponential (power of *e*)	`Cos (X)`, cosine
`Log (X)`. logarighm (base *e*)	`Tan (X)`, tangent
`Log10 (X)`, logarithm (base 10)	`ATan2 (Y, X)`, inverse tangent of `Y/X`

For more details, see Appendix A.

"Miss Flores, I made up this program (Example P.2) with all of the functions that you've been telling me about. I listed the function names in an `intrinsic` specification statements as you did in your first example program."

```
! Example P.2. (Catherine Spade, 4 October 1999)
!   Examples of Fortran intrinsic library functions.
  program Carnegie
    implicit none
    intrinsic Real, Int, NInt, Abs, Sign, Modulo, &
      ATan2, Cos, Exp, Log, Log10, Sin, SqRt, Tan
    real :: A, B = 1.234, C = 5.678
    integer :: I = 9, J = 10
! start program Carnegie
    A = SqRt (B) + Abs (C)
    print *, A, Int (A), NInt (A), Real(I), I
    print *, I / J, Modulo (I, J), Abs (I), Sign (I, 1), Sign (I, -1)
    print *, B, B / C, Modulo (B, C), Abs (B)
    print *, Sign (B, 1.0), Sign (B, -1.0)
    print *, ATan2 (0.0, -1.0), Exp (1.0)
    print *, Cos (1.0), Sin (1.0), Tan (1.0), Log (2.0), Log10 (2.0)
  end program Carnegie
```

"Yes, Cathy. The `intrinsic` specification statement is optional, but it helps a reader of the program to remember that the names do not represent variables. And Fortran can check for misspelled function names by verifying that each function named in the `intrinsic` specification is actually present in the Fortran intrinsic function library."

"Here are the answers from my program:"

```
6.6788554 6 7  9.0000000 9
0 9 9 9 -9
1.2340000  0.2173300  1.2340000  1.2340000
1.2340000  -1.2340000
3.1415927  2.7182818
0.5403022  0.8414709  1.5574077  0.6931471  0.3010300
```

Look, Miss Flores. The first line shows the difference between `Int` and `NInt`. On the second line, integer division gives zero because `I` is smaller than `J`. The fifth line is the same as the output from your program: It shows the value of π from the arctangent function and the value of e from the exponential function. The last line tests the other mathematical functions.

"This session has been fun, Miss Flores. I've learned a great deal about Fortran expressions, and I've summarized several items so that I can remember them."

Summary of Numerical Expressions

- Data objects are stored inside the computer.
- Every object has a data type. The main numeric types are integer and real.
- The type of a variable is specified in a type declaration for the variable's name.
- A name is a single letter or a letter followed by letters, digits, or underscores. A name cannot have more than 31 characters in all.
- An `implicit none` statement should follow the `program` statement in every program so that Fortran will check that all variables have been declared.
- A numerical constant doesn't need a type declaration because its type is obvious from the way it is written. An integer constant is a string of digits without a decimal point; a real constant has a decimal point or an exponent (or both).
- The value of a variable changes when an assignment statement replaces the stored value, but the value of a constant never changes.
- Numerical expressions can be created with operators for addition, subtraction, multiplication, and division. An asterisk denotes multiplication, and a slash is the division operator.
- Every expression has a type. If all of the operands in an expression have the same type, then the expression also has that type. You have to be careful about integer division because the result will be truncated to the next smaller integer.
- If an arithmetic operator has a real operand and an integer operand, Fortran automatically converts the integer operand to real type.
- There are many functions in the Fortran intrinsic function library: conversion functions, such as `Real`, `Int`, and `NInt`; utility functions, such as `Abs`, `Sign`, and `Modulo`, and mathematical functions, including square root, trigonometric, logarithmic, and exponential functions.

P.2 Exercises

1. Write type declarations for all variables mentioned in each of the following problem statements. Write named constant definitions (type declarations that specify the `parameter` attribute and define the named constant value) for all constants mentioned. All variables and constants should have real type.

   a. The area of a rectangle is determined by multiplying its length by its width.

   b. To find the average of three numbers, add them together and then divide by three.

   c. Voltage is current times resistance.

   d. Energy equals mass times the square of the speed of light.

2. For each of the computational tasks in Exercise 1, write an assignment statement that evaluates the given expression and assigns it as the value of a variable.

P.3 ON-LINE INPUT AND OUTPUT

Input and Output

Two days later, while María is working in her office at Sam Spade's detective agency, Sam's neice, Cathy, comes to the door. María remembers how much she enjoyed talking with Cathy and introducing her to Fortran. This time, she is going to show Cathy how to create a complete Fortran program.

"Miss Flores, my physics teacher gave me some homework — to convert temperatures from the Fahrenheit scale to Celsius. I'm going to build a Fortran program to do the calculations."

"That's fine, Cathy, but you should do some planning before you start writing program statements."

"I've been thinking about it, and I've written down some ideas. I want my program to read the Fahrenheit temperature, compute the Celsius temperature, and print the answer. I'll need two variables: one for the Fahrenheit temperature and one for the Celsius temperature. There are two real constants in the conversion formula — I'll call `1.8` the `SCALE` and `32.0` the `OFFSET`. I think I'll need three instructions: one to get the input data, one for the calculation, and one to display the answer."

"That sounds good. The Mac is already running. Just click the Fortran icon to get the edit window."

Cathy enters the program (Example P.3).

```
! Example P.3. (Catherine Spade, 6 October 1999)
!   Temperature Converter.
  program Con_Temp
    implicit none                                                   ! directive
    real, parameter :: SCALE = 1.8, OFFSET = 32.0             ! named constants
    real :: Fahr, Cels                                         ! type declaration
! start program Con_Temp
    read *, Fahr                                                        ! input
    Cels = (Fahr - OFFSET) / SCALE                                 ! assignment
    print *, Fahr, Cels                                                ! output
  end program Con_Temp
```

Cathy clicks the Run icon. The program is compiled and linked, and execution begins. But then nothing happens.

"Is something wrong?" Cathy asks.

"No, Cathy, it's just waiting for input from the keyboard. Fortran executes the statement

```
read *, Fahr
```

by reading a value from the terminal keyboard and assigning it to the variable named Fahr."

Cathy types a Fahrenheit temperature and presses the Enter key. Two numbers appear just below the input data:

```
98.6
98.6  37.0
```

"I see what's going on. Fortran has just executed the rest of the program. These last two numbers are the values of Fahr and Cels."

"You're right. When Fortran executes a statement of the form

read *, *Input list*

it waits for your input from the keyboard and assigns the values that you type to the *Input list* variables. When it comes to a statement of the form

print *, *Output list*

Fortran evaluates the expressions in the *Output list* and displays them on the terminal screen. The *Input list* in a read statement is a list of variable names. The *Output list* in a print statement is a list of expressions. In this statement, the expressions are just variable names. But it could also include constants or more complicated expressions."

"What if the program has a lot of input and output statements? I think it would be boring to type a hundred numbers on the keyboard, and mistakes would be hard to correct. And, if there were enough answers to fill up the terminal screen, some of them would scroll off the top and get lost."

Input from files and output to files are explained in Section 4.5 and in Chapter 9.

"What we've been doing is called *on-line* input and output — entering *input data* at the terminal keyboard and reading *output results* from the terminal screen. For larger amounts of data, you would use a text processor to prepare the input data and save it in a *file*. You would then instruct Fortran to read the input data file and to write the results on an output file where you could find them after execution is finished."

List-Directed Input and Output

For simple Fortran applications, the arrangement of the input and output data is of little concern. With *list-directed* formatting, the external arrangement of the data depends only upon the properties of the input or output list items. An asterisk immediately following the initial keyword read or print in an input or output statement indicates list-directed formatting:

For more information about the asterisk format specifier and about free-form input data, see Section 9.3.

```
read *, Fahr, Cels
read *, A, I, Current, Resistance
print *, Fahr, Cels
print *, ATan2 (0.0, -1.0), Exp (1.0)
print *, Current, Resistance, Current * Resistance
print *, A, Int (A), NInt (A), Real(I)
```

Input data values for on-line list-directed input are entered in *free form* on one or more lines. Blank characters must not be embedded within a single data value. Values may appear anywhere on a data line. Consecutive values must be separated by blanks. For example, data for the statement

```
read *, A, I, Current, Resistance
```

can be entered as

```
12.3 9
45.6

78.9
```

Execution of a `read` statement assigns input data values to the variables in the *Input list*. The sequence of data values entered at the keyboard will correspond exactly to the sequence of variables in the list. Several data values may be included in a single line of input data.

Execution of a `print` statement transmits values of the expressions in the *Output list*,, in sequence, to the terminal screen. The exact appearance of the output may vary from one device and Fortran processor to another. Depending upon the amount of output data, the values may occupy several lines. However, a new output line is initiated at the beginning of execution of each `print` statement.

On-line Output of Character Constants

The items in an output list are often variable names, but expressions of any form are permitted. In particular, an output list item may be a character constant. An explicit constant of character type is written as a string of characters between quotation marks. In this text, the symbol ⊥ in a character strings shows where a blank character would appear in the program:

More details concerning character output appear in Section 6.1.

```
print *, "⊥DIAMETER:⊥", Diameter, "⊥CIRCUMFERENCE:⊥", &
   3.1416 * Diameter
```

The quotation marks that enclose a character constant will not appear in the output. In most of the examples in this text, an extra blank character or some other separator has been inserted at the beginning and end of the constant string.

Prompting for On-line Input

A *prompting* message should be printed on the terminal screen to indicate that the program is waiting for input. The instruction for printing a prompting message may have the simple form

print *, *Message*

The *Message* may be a character constant — for example,

```
print *, "␣Please␣enter␣two␣numbers␣to␣be␣averaged.␣"
print *, "␣Please␣enter␣the␣diameter␣of␣a␣circle.␣"
print *, "␣Please␣enter␣the␣Fahrenheit␣temperature.␣"
```

Since input data entered at the keyboard is also displayed on the screen, it will remain visible when the results are printed (unless there is too much input and output data to fit on the screen at one time).

The following program (Example P.4) prints a prompting message just before each of the 3 `read` operations.

```
! Example P.4. Prompting for terminal keyboard input.
  program Run_Me
    implicit none
    real :: X, Y, Average, Diameter, Fahr, Cels
    real, parameter :: SCALE = 1.8, OFFSET = 32.0
! start program Run_Me
    print *, "␣Please␣enter␣two␣numbers␣to␣be␣averaged.␣"
    read *, X, Y
    Average = (X + Y) / 2.0
    print *, "␣The␣average␣of␣", X, "␣and␣", Y, "␣is:␣", Average
    print *, "␣Please␣enter␣the␣diameter␣of␣a␣circle.␣"
    read *, Diameter
    print *, "␣Circumference:␣", ATan2 (0.0, -1.0) * Diameter
    print *, "␣Please␣enter␣the␣Fahrenheit␣temperature.␣"
    read *, Fahr
    Cels = (Fahr - OFFSET) / SCALE
    print *, Fahr, "␣deg.␣F␣=␣", Cels, "␣deg.␣C␣"
  end program Run_Me
```

P.3 Exercises

1. Write a complete Fortran 90 program for one of the computational tasks in Exercise 1 of Section P.2. Include comments at the beginning of the program, `implicit none`, type declarations for all variables, prompting for input, a `read` statement, an assignment statement, and a `print` statement. If you prepare the program in computer-readable form, save it for Exercise 1 of Section P.4.

2. Prepare a text file containing the program in Example P.4. Save it for Exercise 2 of Section P.4 and for Exercise 3 of Section P.6.

P.4 CONTROL STRUCTURES

Repetition

"Miss Flores, it seems like extra trouble to rerun my program every time I want to convert another temperature. Can't I put it in a loop?"

"Of course, Cathy. Almost all useful programs contain groups of statements that are to be executed repeatedly. In practical applications, programs rarely read a single set of data values, perform a calculation, and print a single set of results. Much more commonly, a sequence of statements is repeated. For example, it may be that at each repetition a new set of data values is read, the calculation is performed, and results based on these data values are printed."

"We learned how to use the `while` statement to make Pascal repeat a calculation, Miss Flores. Are you going to show me `while`?"

"Maybe not. For many applications that are especially suitable for Fortran, the number of repetitions is known in advance, so a different loop construct, the indexed do, is more appropriate. It corresponds to Pascal's `for` statement."

"Well, here is my homework. I have 10 Fahrenheit temperatures to convert to Celsius. How should I do it?"

"First, you can copy the program that does the calculation once. Then you just put *loop control statements* around the part that will be repeated. You'll need a do statement before the repeated block and an end do statement after it:

do *statement*
  Block of statements to be repeated
end do

This diagram (Figure P.5) illustrates the idea. You'll probably want to indent the repeated *Block* of statements.

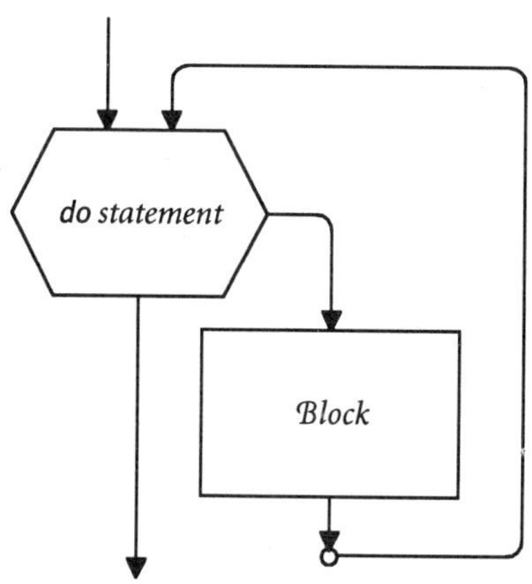

FIGURE P.5. Repetition with the *do* construct.

The do statement can have the form

do *Index variable* = 1, *Limit*

You should declare the *Index variable* as a variable of integer type. The *Limit* is the number of repetitions. You can write it as a named constant."

"OK, Miss Flores. This indexed do construct sounds pretty easy. I'll use the name Loop for the *Index variable* in my program (Example P.5).

```
! Example P.5. (Catherine Spade, 8 October 1999)
!   Temperature Converter with Repetition.
  program Con_Temp
    implicit none
    integer, parameter :: LIMIT = 10
    real, parameter :: SCALE = 1.8, OFFSET = 32.0
    real :: Fahr, Cels
    integer :: Loop
! start program Con_Temp
    do Loop = 1, LIMIT
      print *, "⊥Please⊥enter⊥the⊥Fahrenheit⊥temperature.⊥"
      read *, Fahr
      Cels = (Fahr - OFFSET) / SCALE
      print *, Fahr, Cels
    end do
  end program Con_Temp
```

There are four statements in the repeated *Block*:

```
print *, "⊥Please⊥enter⊥the⊥Fahrenheit⊥temperature.⊥"
read *, Fahr
Cels = (Fahr - OFFSET) / SCALE
print *, Fahr, Cels
```

Each time these statements are repeated, another Fahrenheit temperature will be converted to Celsius. I'll be done with my homework in no time!"

Designing a Loop Construct

"Cathy, this exercise illustrates the main point of loop design. You can create a loop in two stages: First you create the *Block* of statements that are to be repeated, and then you embed the *Block* in a loop construct. When you create the *Block*, you think only of the statements that you want Fortran to repeat. Separately, when you create the loop construct, you concentrate on how to control the repetition. For an indexed do construct, this means that you must decide how many times the *Block* will be executed.

"You can work on these two stages of loop design in either order. In your temperature conversion program, you already had the *Block* of statements for performing the conversion, and you just had to put loop control statements around them. That's

For more about program constructs for repetition, see Chapter 4.

called *bottom-up* program design: You work on the details first. Sometimes, when you're starting from scratch, *top-down* design is better: You work out the overall picture first — how you want the repetition to work — and you wait until later to think about what to put inside the *Block*."

Selection

"The next thing I should learn, after repetition, is `if-then-else`. How do I write *that* in Fortran?"

"Let's take a specific example, Cathy. Suppose you want your program to read the maximum temperatures for all 30 days in a certain month, which you're going to copy from reports in our local newspaper. You want to count how many days the temperature was at least 68 degrees Fahrenheit and how many days it was below 68. That is 20 Celsius, as you can find out from your temperature conversion program. The boundary between high and low temperatures should be a named constant."

"I think I have the general idea, Miss Flores. It's a loop with the test inside. I'll write the part of the program that contains the declarations and the loop (Example P.6). Then I'll go back and put in the test."

```
! Example P.6. (Catherine Spade, 8 October 1999)
!   Count high and low temperatures.
  program Loch_Lomond
    implicit none
    integer, parameter :: LIMIT = 30
    real, parameter :: BOUNDARY = 68.0
    real :: Temperature
    integer :: High_Count = 0, Low_Count = 0, Loop
! start program Loch_Lomond
    do Loop = 1, LIMIT
      print *, "␣Please␣enter␣the␣next␣temperature.␣"
      read *, Temperature
      ! PUT STATEMENTS HERE TO TEST AND COUNT
    end do
    print *, High_Count, "␣hot␣days,␣and␣", Low_count, "␣cold␣days␣this␣month."
  end program Loch_Lomond
```

I want the loop to repeat 30 times, so I'll declare 30 as a named constant. In the loop, I'll read a temperature and make a test. If the temperature is 68 or more, I'll add 1 to a counter. If it is below 68, I'll add 1 to a different counter. Of course, the counters have to be initialized to 0. At the end, I'll print the counter values.

"But you still have not told me how to write the test in Fortran. I know I'll need an `if-then-else`, as this diagram shows (Figure P.6). I'll test whether the `Temperature` is greater than or equal to 68. In the *Then block*, I'll add one to `High_Count`; in the *Else block*, I'll add one to `Low_Count`."

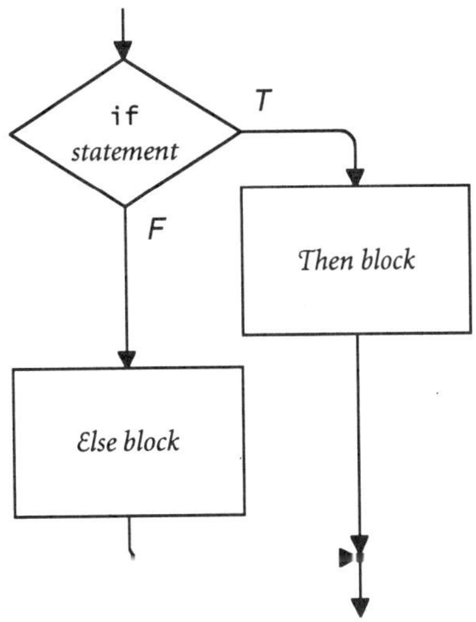

FIGURE P.6.
Selection with the *if* construct.

"That's right, Cathy. You write the test as an `if` statement consisting of the keyword `if` followed by the condition enclosed in parentheses, as `(Temperature >= BOUNDARY)`, followed by the keyword `then`."

"That's just like Pascal, except for the parentheses."

"It is quite similar: You use an `if` statement with a *Condition* in parentheses, a *Block* of statements to be executed if the condition is true, an `else` statement, and another *Block* of statements to be executed if the condition is false. The Fortran construct closes with an `end if` statement. The principal difference from other languages, besides the parentheses around the *Condition* and the `end if` statement, is the statement structure."

"What do you mean by that?"

"In Fortran, each `if`, `else`, or `end if` control statement has to be written as an individual statement. Normally, you would write each of these three statements on a line by itself."

"Is this how you write it?"

```
if (Temperature >= BOUNDARY) then
  High_Count = High_Count + 1
else
  Low_Count = Low_Count + 1
end if
```

"Looks good to me, Cathy, but I should mention that some comparison operations — especially, comparisons for equality and inequality — are written differently in Fortran 90 than in some other languages. Here is a handy reference table that shows the Fortran 90 operators:"

Notation	Meaning	Notation	Meaning
==	Is equal to	<=	Is less than or equal to
/=	Is not equal to	>	Is greater than
<	Is less than	>=	Is greater than or equal to

"I think I can remember all of them. Here is the final version of my program (Example P.7) with the control statements."

```
! Example P.7. (Catherine Spade, 8 October 1999)
!   Count high and low temperatures.
  program Loch_Lomond
    implicit none
    integer, parameter :: LIMIT = 30
    real, parameter :: BOUNDARY = 68.0
    real :: Temperature
    integer :: High_Count = 0, Low_Count = 0, Loop
! start program Loch_Lomond
    do Loop = 1, LIMIT
      print *, "␣Please␣enter␣the␣next␣temperature.␣"
      read *, Temperature
      if (Temperature >= BOUNDARY) then
        High_Count = High_Count + 1
      else
        Low_Count + 1
      end if
    end do
    print *, High_Count, "␣hot␣days,␣and␣", Low_count, "␣cold␣days␣this␣month."
  end program Loch_Lomond
```

P.4 Exercises

1. Modify the Fortran program that you wrote for Exercise 1 of Section P.3 to repeat the computation several times.
2. Modify the program in Example P.4 to repeat all of the instructions seven times.
3. Write a program to read one integer and test it. If its value is 1, change it to 2; otherwise, change it to 1. Print the value before and after changing it.

P.5 PROGRAMS WITH PROCEDURES

Procedural Refinement

Sam Spade has been working long and hard, trying to solve the Maltese falcon case. His desk is littered with ship arrival and departure lists, maps of exotic Oriental lands, and historical documents dating from the Crusades. "Can you make any sense of all this stuff, María?" he asks.

"Have you tried the 'divide and conquer' approach, Sam?"

"Of course. That's one of the techniques I use to get a handle on my big, complicated cases. But how should I divide this one up? Geographically? Chronologically? What do you think, María? If I can't figure out how to divide it, it is going to conquer *me!*"

"Give me until tomorrow. I'll try to come up with a 'divide and conquer' strategy that will help us start organizing all the facts we have collected about this legendary bird."

Cathy, who is visiting her uncle's agency again, has overheard their conversation. "What's a 'divide and conquer' strategy?" she asks.

"I'm sure you are familiar with the general idea," María replies as they walk down the hall from Sam's office to María's. "It's a technique that has long been known as a way of managing complex tasks. If you subdivide a large task into a few relatively independent chunks and then analyze each of the chunks without thinking too much about any of the others, you can keep the overall problem organization in mind surprisingly well."

"I would like to try my hand at a complex task — well, maybe not too complex. The little programs I have been working on are interesting, Miss Flores, but I can hardly wait to start writing some bigger programs — programs that really accomplish something significant."

"A big program is made of small programs, Cathy. You can divide a large project into parts and develop each part as a separate procedure. For example, you can subdivide a data processing task into three parts: input, computation, and output. You write a procedure for each of these parts and build a main program to connect the procedures together. Here is a sketch of the idea (Figure P.7).

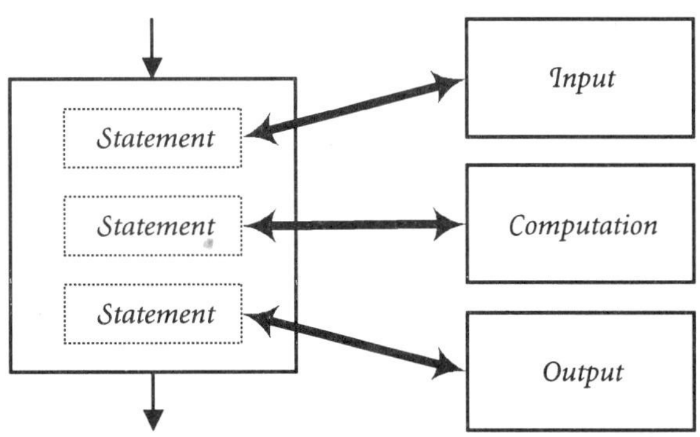

FIGURE P.7. Three procedures: one for input, one for computation, and one for output.

"Writing programs with procedures takes a bit of planning. You need to have an idea of what the main program will do and what information it expects to transmit to and from each procedure. Then, when you're developing any one of the separate procedures, you can concentrate on its internal details and on its relation to the main program. For the most part, you can forget about the other procedures during this phase.

"In programming terminology, the divide and conquer approach is called refinement. With *procedural refinement*, you divide a program into procedures and work on them independently. Why don't you try to apply procedural refinement to your temperature conversion program (Example P.8) ?"

```
! Example P.8. (Catherine Spade, 11 october 1999)
!   Temperature Converter.
  program Con_Temp
    implicit none
    real, parameter :: SCALE = 1.8, OFFSET = 32.0
    real :: Fahr, Cels
! start program Con_Temp
    print *, "⊥Please⊥enter⊥the⊥Fahrenheit⊥temperature.⊥"
    read *, Fahr
    Cels = (Fahr - OFFSET) / SCALE
    print *, Fahr, "⊥deg.⊥F⊥=⊥", Cels, "⊥deg.⊥C⊥"
  end program Con_Temp
```

"But the program is so short, Miss Flores. Even if I count the `end` statement and the `print` statement that prompts for input, it has only five instructions. If I divide it up, there won't be anything left."

"You have a point, Cathy. Procedural refinement works well for large programs, but for small ones it sometimes seems to be more trouble than it's worth. Traditionally, Fortran programs have been written in fairly large chunks.[8] Nowadays, we understand the importance of program readability. Even a small program, if it is subdivided into procedures, can be easier to understand, to construct correctly, and to modify later.

"Plus, you can learn a lot about the techniques of procedural refinement by practicing on a tiny example. Your program has only five instructions, but it performs a complete data processing task. You can identify the three parts — input, computation, and output — and make a procedure for each part."

"OK, I'll give it a try. Should the procedures be subroutines or functions?"

"Think about it, Cathy. The input procedure will get a value for the Fahrenheit temperature from the terminal keyboard. The computation procedure will accept the Fahrenheit temperature from the main program and will use it to find the Celsius temperature. These two procedures return values, so they should be functions.

[8] Internal procedures were not available in traditional versions of Fortran. External subroutines and functions (which were provided almost from the beginning) entail a bit more overhead, which motivates the tendency to package them in larger sizes.

"The output procedure can be a subroutine because it does not return a value to the main program. Its purpose is to take Fahrenheit and Celsius temperature values from the main program and send them to the terminal screen.

"You can start by making a copy of your temperature conversion program (Example P.3). Use the text editor to insert a `contains` statement just before the `end` statement. Then put the procedures between `contains` and `end`.

"You have to name the procedures so that you can refer to each procedure by name from the main program. You also need to name the *result variable* in each function. The function will assign its final result to this variable."[9]

"Miss Flores, I think I'll name the input function `Temp_F` because that is how I want to think of the result that it returns. In the main program, I'll assign the function result to the variable named `Fahr`. I'll name the computation function `Temp_C`. The main program will assign this function result to `Cels`. Inside the functions, I'll name the temperature variables `FT` and `CT`. Finally, I'll name the output subroutine `Output`."

"Sounds good, Cathy. You can put the heading for the input function on the line right after `contains`:

```
real function Temp_F () result (FT)
```

This specification statement gives the following information:

The result type is real.
The procedure is a function.
Its name is `Temp_F`.
Its argument list is empty.
The result variable is named `FT`.

Within the function, this heading statement serves as a type declaration for the result variable `FT`. It also serves, in the main program, as a `real` type declaration for the function reference `Temp_F()` when it appears in an expression. The main program needs no futher declaration for the name of an internal function."

"OK, I'll type this statement in.... It seems strange to have an empty argument list, but I see that there is no information to be sent from the main program to the function.

"Now I want the function to read the result variable, FT. How does this look, Miss Flores?

```
print *, "⊥Please⊥enter⊥the⊥Fahrenheit⊥temperature.⊥"
read *, FT
```

"You're doing fine, Cathy. Just add the `end function` statement:

```
end function Temp_F
```

9 Fortran 90 permits the result variable and the function to share the same name, but it is less confusing to use different names. (Traditional Fortran does not provide any way to declare a separate result variable.)

When your main program refers to this function, the function will read a value and return it as the function result."

"Do I need `implicit none` after the function heading statement?"

"No, you don't. An `implicit none` directive in the main program also applies to all of the internal procedures that it contains. Now go ahead and write the conversion function and the output subroutine.

The `intent` attribute is described in Sections 2.4 and 8.1.

"Don't forget to include type declarations for all of the argument variables. I forgot to tell you that it's a good idea to specify `intent (in)` for arguments that transmit values into the procedure and `intent (out)` for arguments that transmit values out from the procedure."

"I'll put in all of the declarations, Miss Flores. The conversion function needs one argument, the Fahrenheit temperature, which is the value that the main program sends to the function. The output subroutine needs two arguments, the Fahrenheit temperature and the Celsius temperature.

```
contains

  real function Temp_F () result (FT)
    print *, "⊥Please⊥enter⊥the⊥Fahrenheit⊥temperature.⊥"
    read *, FT
  end function Temp_F

  real function Temp_C (FT) result (CT)
    real, intent (in) :: FT
    CT = (FT - OFFSET) / SCALE
  end function Temp_C

  subroutine Output (FT, CT)
    real, intent (in) :: FT, CT
    print *, FT, "⊥deg.⊥F⊥=⊥", CT, "⊥deg.⊥C⊥"
  end subroutine Output
```

"Now I have to redo the main program so that it will use the functions. I can put the function names `Temp_F` and `Temp_C` in expressions, and I'll just use each function reference as the expression on the right side of an assignment statement. I'll assign the function result from `Temp_F` to a variable, and I'll use that variable as the argument to `Temp_C`. I'll refer to the subroutine with a `call` statement. I always have to make sure that the number of arguments and the types of the arguments are the same in each procedure reference as in its definition."

Here is my final version (Example P.9)— let's see what happens when I run it several times."

```
Please enter the Fahrenheit temperature.
  98.6
  98.6 deg. F = 37.0 deg. C
```

```
Please enter the Fahrenheit temperature.
  32.0
  32.0 deg. F = 0.0 deg. C
Please enter the Fahrenheit temperature.
  212.0
  212.0 deg. F = 100.0 deg. C
Please enter the Fahrenheit temperature.
  40.0
  40.0 deg. F = -40.0 deg. C
```

```
! Example P.9. (Catherine Spade, 11 October 1999)
!   Temperature Converter with Procedures.
  program Con_Temp
    implicit none
    real, parameter :: SCALE = 1.8, OFFSET = 32.0
    real :: Fahr, Cels
! start program Con_Temp
    Fahr = Temp_F ()                              ! Reference to function Temp_F
    Cels = Temp_C (Fahrenheit_Temp)                         ! Reference to Temp_C
    call Output (Fahr, Cels)                                ! Subroutine reference
  contains
    real function Temp_F () result (FT)
      print *, "␣Please␣enter␣the␣Fahrenheit␣temperature.␣"
      read *, FT
    end function Temp_F
    real function Temp_C (FT) result (CT)
      real, intent (in) :: FT
      CT = (FT - OFFSET) / SCALE
    end function Temp_C
    subroutine Output (FT, CT)
      real, intent (in) :: FT, CT
      print *, FT, "␣deg.␣F␣=␣", CT, "␣deg.␣C"
    end subroutine Output
  end program Con_Temp
```

Local and Global Names

"Cathy, I want to show you the difference between *local* names and *global* names. Let's make a list of all the names that appear in this program."

Names of constants declared in the main program:
`real, parameter :: SCALE, OFFSET`

Names of variables declared in the main program:

```
real :: Fahr, Cels
```

Names of internal procedures:

```
real function Temp_F
real function Temp_C
subroutine Output
```

Names of variables declared in `Temp_F`:

```
real :: result (FT)
```

Names of variables declared in `Temp_C`:

```
real :: result (CT)
real, intent (in) :: FT
```

Names of variables declared in `Output`:

```
real, intent (in) :: FT, CT
```

"Names that are declared in the main program and names of internal procedures contained in the main program can be used anywhere in the main program or in any of its internal procedures. In this program, it happens that the named constants `SCALE` and `OFFSET`, which are declared in the main program, are used in the function `Temp_C`. A reference to these constants from any internal procedure has the same effect as a reference appearing in the main program. Internal procedures can *inherit* names from the main program.

"Names that are declared in an internal procedure are known only within that procedure. Likewise, procedure argument names and the function result name have no meaning outside the procedure where they are declared."

P.5 Exercises

1. Rewrite the program of Example P.9 to remove the constant names `SCALE` and `OFFSET` from the main program and to make these names local to the procedure in which they are used. Can you see any situation in which it would be preferable for these constant names to be global?

2. Rewrite the program of Example P.9 to remove the arguments `FT` and `CT` from the internal procedure `Output`. Modify the internal procedure to inherit the global variables `Fahr` and `Cels` instead. (See Section 2.4 for a discussion of the advantages and disadvantages of inheritance.)

3. Besides making the modifications described in Exercise 2 here, also change the functions `Temp_F` and `Temp_C` to subroutines (with empty argument lists), replacing the function result variables by the global variables `Fahr` and `Cels`.

P.6 THE FORTRAN PROCESSOR

File processing is described in Section 4.5 and in Chapter 9.

When you begin preparing a program to be executed, you must consider the input data. The way you write the program and the steps you must take to cause its execution will depend upon how the input and output data is to be processed. If the amount of input data is very small, you can write the program so that data is to be entered at the terminal during execution. An alternative is to prepare the data in advance, in a file, perhaps with the aid of some automatic data collection device, such as a scientific instrument that produces digital output to a file.

Before Fortran can execute a program, it must first translate the statements into computer code consisting of more primitive steps that can be directly processed by the computer hardware. You do not need to know any of the details of this translation process or of the computer code, but it is useful to know that some kind of conversion is performed. Each computer that will accept Fortran programs is equipped with a system of supporting programs. The computer, operating under the control of this software, is a Fortran *processor*. This software includes both the compiler that translates Fortran statements into computer code and the intrinsic procedure library that is precompiled into computer code. It also includes a *linker* to gather various parts of the compiled code and the library procedures that are needed and a *loader* to position all of the code inside the high-speed memory of the computer and to prepare it for execution.

Fortran 90 source program form rules are explained in full detail in Appendix C.

You prepare your *source program,* in the form of a text file, by following the source program form rules in Section P.1.

Next, you instruct Fortran to process your program source file. During translation of the program to computer code, the compiler may detect statements that fail to conform to Fortran language rules. In this case, you must modify the program and compile it again. If you make the proper changes, the compiler will detect fewer errors. When the compiler detects no errors, it accepts the Fortran program and generates a complete computer code version.

Then, you instruct Fortran to load and execute the computer code that the compiler has generated. Other errors may become evident during execution of the program, such as mistakes in the program structure or control logic that the compiler did not find. Input data preparation errors may also be detected during program execution.

Debugging

Statements that do not conform to Fortran language rules and gross errors in the input data are relatively easy to detect and repair. Errors in program structure or control logic usually result when insufficient care is taken during the design of an algorithm and are often difficult to detect after the program statements have been written.

Many programmers find themselves looking for help when debugging their programs. The testing or debugging of a program is not unlike the checking of any other system or device. There is no substitute for careful work, the self-discipline that leads to complete analysis of a problem, and the faithful application of checklists. In short, good work habits are as necessary here as in any other endeavor.

You may find it beneficial to represent the program in more than one way:

1. In a *pseudocode* version, a sequence of English sentences is written to describe the steps of the problem solution. Each English sentence is then converted to one or more program statements. The original pseudocode may be retained as a preliminary *program specification*, which may be modified or checked against the final program after its development is complete.
2. If the program will have several loops or branches, a *flowchart* version may be advantageous. Symbols like those in Figure P.2 can clarify the relationship among the various statement blocks.

Another very helpful technique is a *walk-through* of the Fortran program as soon as it has reached the point of error-free compilation. You review ("walk through") the program, statement by statement, recalling the purpose of each statement, what it is intended to accomplish, and its effect upon the data involved. If the purpose of some statement is not completely obvious, you should rewrite it so that it can easily be understood.

If possible, you should conduct the walk-through orally — you should *verbalize* the intent of each statement and explain it to an interested observer. For best results, choose someone who is familiar with the problem specification. Verbalization can still be effective, however, even when you have a sympathetic listener who knows nothing about computers.

This point in the program development cycle offers a good opportunity to complete the initial documentation of the program. You should write comment lines near the beginning of the program to explain the general purpose and characteristics of the program, the significance of each variable, and procedures that the program references. You should add similar general comments at the beginning of each major section of the program.

At the walk-through, if not before, you should add comments liberally to document the purpose of individual statements or groups of statements. However, you should be sure to modify the initial documentation as program development proceeds. Comments that are out of date so that they no longer reflect the actual significance of the related program statements can seriously hinder the detection of errors.

The Operating System

Most computers that execute Fortran programs operate under the control of a sophisticated program known as an *operating system*, which processes tasks more efficiently than would be possible if a human operator handled each job individually. For example, many personal computers are controlled by MS-DOS, Windows, or the Macintosh operating system; a popular operating system for workstations is UNIX.

Typically, you use a text processor to prepare the program at a terminal, and you store it in a source program file. You then instruct the Fortran processor to read the source program text and generate computer code, to prepare the code for execution, and to begin executing the code that has been generated from your program.

Although the Fortran 90 standard specifies the form of a source program itself, the further steps that you must take are not so well standardized. Various Fortran processors have quite different conventions in this regard. At your first encounter with a particular computing system, you must learn what actions to take.

Two different processor environments, chosen as examples from among the many possibilities that you may encounter, are described next. For the first example, you enter a sequence of job control instructions on *command lines* to make the Fortran processor compile, link, load, and execute the source program. The second illustrates an *integrated programming environment* controlled by a graphical user interface (GUI) such as Windows.

Command Line Examples

Here are two examples that show typical job control instruction sequences based on UNIX operating system commands. These examples assume that you have prepared the Fortran source program and stored it on a text file named `myprog.f90`.[10]

If input data is to be typed on the terminal keyboard during program execution, and results will appear on the terminal screen, the following job control instruction sequence might be appropriate:

```
f90 myprog.f90
a.out
```

The first of these two job control instructions causes the Fortran compiler (known to the UNIX operating system as `f90`) to be executed, with `myprog.f90` as its input file. Some compilers assume that the file name extension indicates free or fixed source program text form, where `.f90` signifies free form and `.f`, `.for`, or `.ftn` signify fixed form.

After you enter the first command, you may have to wait a few seconds (or longer, depending on the size of your source program and on the speed of your computer) while the compiler analyzes the program. If it detects mistakes in the program, Fortran will send messages to the terminal screen, in which case you will have to take further steps to find the mistakes and to modify and recompile the source program file. When compilation is successful, the computer code will have been stored in a file named `a.out` (the default file for UNIX `f90` output in the absence of information to the contrary). You then enter the second command to execute the file `a.out`. The operating system assumes that input data comes from the terminal keyboard and that output goes to the terminal screen unless you give different directions.

In the UNIX tradition, the command `f90` can be followed by various *options* of the form `-xxx` . Consult your processor documentation.

For file processing, a slightly different instruction sequence is required. Consider the following example:

[10] UNIX file names are conventionally written entirely in lower case and are case sensitive. Therefore, in this description identifiers are not spelled with an initial capital letter.

```
f90 myprog.f90
a.out <myinput >myoutput
```

The first command causes compilation of the Fortran source program, just as it did before. However, the command to execute `a.out` *redirects* input and output, so that data will be read from the file `myinput` and results will be written on the file `myoutput`. (If a file named `myoutput` already exists, its contents will be destroyed before the new file is written.)

Programming Environment Example

An integrated programming environment, controlled by a graphical user interface, combines text processing, debugging, and execution functions.

You perform text processing with the *edit window*, which is displayed when you enter the programming environment. If your Fortran source program does not already exist as a text file, you create it in the edit window and save it. You may also use the edit window to create and save text files that your program will read during execution.

You may select various *options* from the menus of the programming environment, which may include compiler options (such as choice of free or fixed source program form) and specification of directory names and file names. For a large Fortran program that consists of several files, you can open a *project* that contains all parts of the program.

Menu items that are now available may have names such as `compile`, `run`, and `make` (or `build`). The latter is a general-purpose process that automatically compiles, links, loads, and executes your program.

One advantage of the integrated environment is its *error window*, which can be displayed in parallel with the edit window where your program text is shown. When you select a particular error message in the error window, the offending program line is highlighted in the edit window. Thus you can quickly correct simple errors and again attempt to compile the program.

An integrated *debugger* is also provided for analyzing execution problems after all compiler errors have been corrected. With the debugger, you can designate breakpoints at certain places in your program so that execution will pause there and the values of selected variables will be displayed.

P.6 Exercises

1. Copy the program from Example P.1. Be extremely careful to copy all punctuation symbols exactly as they are shown. Instruct your computer to compile, link, and execute the program. Some information concerning this process is given in Section P.6. You may need to obtain additional information.

2. Copy the program from Example P.4. Instruct your computer to compile, link, and execute it. If on-line input and output are not provided by your computer system, you

must prepare the data in advance, and you must direct the output to a file for later printing. (Information on this subject is given in Sections 4.5 and 9.4.)

a. When the message

```
Please enter two numbers to be averaged.
```

appears on your terminal screen, enter

```
1.234 5.678
```

Type a space between the numbers, but do not type a space within either of the numbers. Press the Enter or Return key after typing the numbers. The following message should appear on your screen:

```
The average of 1.234 and 5.678 is: 3.456
```

Perhaps a slightly different value such as `3.45599` will be printed at the end. If the result is significantly different, you have probably made an error in preparing your program, or in entering your data, or you may have given the wrong control instructions. Find and correct the errors, if any, and run the job again until correct results are obtained.

b. When the message

```
Please enter the diameter of a circle.
```

appears, enter

```
1.0
```

You should expect the following output:

```
Circumference: 3.141592
```

At the message

```
Please enter the Fahrenheit temperature.
```

enter

```
98.6
```

The output should be

```
37.0
```

3. Run one or more of the programs that you developed for Exercise 2 of Section P.3 on a computer, with data of your choice or with data provided by your instructor. Make changes and rerun the program, if necessary, until you obtain correct answers.

Part I
NUMERICAL COMPUTING

With all its modern features, Fortran 90 is still largely a language for "*for*mula *trans*lation." The basic building blocks in a Fortran program are numerical *variables* and numerical *constants,* which are discussed in Chapter 1. Each Fortran variable has a *data type*, which should be described in a *type declaration*. A type declaration for a variable can also specify its *initial value*. Giving each constant a *name* (except perhaps for very simple constants such as 0 and 1) makes the program easier to read and to maintain.

Although integer and real data types are the principal subject of Part I, other types are mentioned. Constant character strings may be printed to prompt for on-line input or to label output data. Fortran provides a complete set of declarations and operations for complex data type, which in this text is marked as an *advanced* feature that may be omitted at first reading. Study of the `kind` feature, whose primary application is control of real precision, is treated as *optional.*

The discussion of *expressions* in Chapter 2 begins with the four basic operations of arithmetic plus a fifth one, exponentiation. The *assignment* operation gives a variable the value of a specified expression. Fortran interprets arithmetic expressions with more than one operator according to *precedence rules*. Fortran permits a mixture of numeric data types in an expression, and it changes the types of subexpressions, when necessary, to the type of the resulting expression.

The basic Fortran arithmetic operators are augmented by a library of *intrinsic functions*, a sample of which is presented in Chapter 2. Included in this sample are type conversion functions, numerical utility functions, and elementary mathematical functions.

A Fortran 90 program may contain one or more *internal procedures*, which may include *subroutines* and *functions*; an internal procedure may also be *recursive*. Data may be shared between a main program and its internal procedures in either of two ways: by *argument passing* (argument association) or by *inheritance* (host association).

Chapter 1
Variables and Constants

1.1 FORTRAN DATA TYPES

Fortran 90 executes a program by manipulating information — reading input data, processing the data to obtain results, and displaying the results. Fortran manipulates information in three forms: as *numbers*, as *characters*, and as *bits*:

1. Numbers occur mainly in scientific and commercial applications. Most of these applications require *real* numbers. *Integers* are appropriate for counting and for indexing, and *complex* numbers are sometimes needed in electronics, optics, and other applications.
2. Character data — *strings* of text — may play a secondary role to numbers in a numerical application. For applications such as record keeping, the principal data consists of character strings.
3. Bits can represent data whose value is *true* or *false*, and they can be combined into *bit maps* for graphics and other applications.

Each item of information processed by Fortran has a *data type* (often referred to simply as its *type*), which affects the way the information is represented internally by the computer, the range of its possible values, and the kinds of operations that Fortran can perform upon it.

Numbers in Fortran have one of three data types: *integer*, *real*, or *complex*. Nonnumeric types are *character* and *logical* (Fortran's primary bit representation). Most of this chapter deals with numerical data; nonnumeric types are introduced later in this section. Character type is covered fully in Section 6.1. Logical data type and other forms of bit data are described further in Section 3.4.

Numeric Data Types

Real and Integer Types

As mentioned, information of *real* type is suitable for most numerical computing work, including scientific, engineering, and statistical applications, and *integers* are appropriate for purposes such as counting and indexing. Most computers have distinct data representations for numbers of these two types: They use a *fixed-point* representation for integer data and a *floating-point* representation for real data.

Many computers have more than one fixed-point representation or more than one floating-point representation. In effect, Fortran 90 recognizes these variant representations as *subtypes* of the real and integer data types. Each variant subtype is designated by a different `kind` *type parameter* value (see Section 1.6).

The floating-point representation provided by typical computers covers only a sample (some 10^{39}, for example) of the infinitely many real numbers. Some uncertainty is therefore introduced when real numbers are approximated in a computer. (Section 1.6 describes Fortran 90 models for number representation.) At a few points, the consequences of this uncertainty are noted; however, a full treatment of *numerical analysis* is beyond the scope of this text.

Is a separate data type for integers really needed? In principle, it would be possible to perform all numerical computing with real numbers. However, integers are convenient for some special purposes, such as for counting repetitions and for selecting an array element. Furthermore, fixed-point operations on most computers are faster, and sometimes more accurate, than the corresponding floating-point operations.

Complex Type (Advanced)

Fortran supports another standard numerical data type, *complex* (as defined in mathematics), that is appropriate for some specialized applications in fields such as electronics and optics (see Section 1.5). A complex number is represented as a pair of real (i.e., floating-point) numbers. The first component of the pair represents the *real part* of the complex data object, and the second represents the *imaginary part*.

Fortran provides arithmetic operations and intrinsic functions that apply directly to data of complex type and that considerably simplify program development for applications involving complex numbers. Built-in operations on complex numbers in Fortran include addition, subtraction, multiplication, division, and exponentiation. Many of the functions in the Fortran intrinsic procedure library also accept complex arguments.

Nonnumeric Data Types

Only a few features of character and logical data types are mentioned here. Character type is treated fully in Section 6.1; logical type, in Section 3.4.

Character Type

An object of *character* type is a *string* of one or more characters. A Fortran character variable or constant is a *fixed-length* string: Its length is established when the object is created, and it does not change.

Unlike some other languages, Fortran does not have a separate data type for representing single characters; a single character in Fortran is a string whose length happens to be 1. A character expression is one of the following:

A character constant or variable name

A pair of character expressions combined by the *concatenation* operator `//`

A reference to a function that produces a result of character type

A character expression enclosed in parentheses

Fortran deduces the length of a character expression from the lengths of its component parts.

Logical Type (Advanced)

An object of *logical* data type has the value *true* or *false*. A *logical expression* may have any of the following forms:

A logical constant or variable name

A pair of logical expressions combined either by one of the logical operators `.and.`, `.or.`, or `.not.` or by one of the logical relational operators `.eqv.` or `.neqv.`

A relational expression comparing numerical or character values

A function that produces a result of logical type

A logical expression enclosed in parentheses

1.2 NAMES AND DECLARATIONS

A *data object* is either a *variable* that can be changed or a *constant* that never changes. A data object may be an indivisible item of information, or it may be a composite object constructed from simpler components. Examples of composite objects are strings of characters (such as names, headings, and sentences) and arrays (such as vectors and matrices). You can create a table whose rows are *structures* made from components of different types. (See Chapter 5 for arrays and Chapter 6 for character strings and structures.)

A variable — a data object that can change during program execution — occupies *storage* inside the computer. For each variable that is declared in a program, Fortran reserves an area of storage whose amount and configuration depend upon the variable's type and its other properties. Whenever the *name* of the variable appears in the Fortran program, it refers to this storage area; the contents of this storage area determines the *value* of the variable. For example, Figure 1.1 indicates that a certain variable named X has `1.234` as its value. To change the value of a variable during program execution,

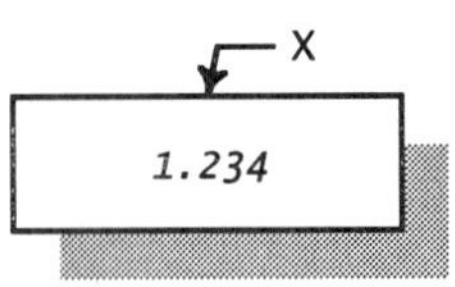

FIGURE 1.1. How Fortran stores the value of the variable named *X*.

Fortran changes the contents of the storage area that has been reserved for the variable. You can combine variables in an *expression*. During program execution, Fortran obtains the values of the variables from the storage areas that have been reserved for them and performs the indicated operations.

A constant in a program may have an *explicit* form, such as a numerical constant, a character constant, or a logical constant; or it may be represented by a *name*. As we shall see, named constants are usually preferable to explicit constants. An explicit constant has a conventional form, such as a numerical integer, whose value is obvious from the way it is written. The value of a named constant is established by a declaration in the program.

Names

Fortran data objects, including variables and constants, may have *names* — for example, `Average`, `X`, `Y`, `Einstein`, or `Kinetic_Energy`. Names in a Fortran program must conform to three rules:

1. A name may contain up to 31 letters, digits, and underscore characters.
2. The first character of a name must be a letter. Letters, including the initial letter, may be written either in upper case (as capital letters) or in lower case.
3. Imbedded blank characters are not permitted in a name.

As we shall see, other Fortran names, such as procedure names, must conform to these same rules. Fortran *keywords*, such as `program`, `print`, and `end`, are similar in form but are not actually names. Although a keyword has the same appearance as a name, Fortran recognizes that in certain contexts it has special significance. Fortran keywords are *not* reserved words. The characters that comprise a keyword (such as `program` or `read`) could also be used as a name (but this practice is *not* recommended). The following perfectly legal Fortran statement is confusing, to say the least:

```
print *, Read, End                                    ! ☹
```

In the example programs in this text, we write names with an `Initial` capital letter; keywords, entirely in `lower` case; and named constants, entirely in `UPPER` case (as capital letters). Fortran does not require this distinction and, in fact, ignores it, but a consistent style can make the text of a program more readable.

Type Declarations

A Fortran program may contain *type declarations*, which are specifications that describe the data type and other properties of data objects. Type declarations in Fortran establish the data type of each variable, as in these examples:

```
integer :: Atomic_Number, Quicksilver
real :: Average, X, Y, Atomic_Mass, Radius
```

```
complex :: Z, Impedance, Attenuation_Coefficient
logical :: Flag, Save, Done
```

The first example type declaration states that `Atomic_Number` and `Quicksilver` are names of variables of integer type. The second indicates that the names `Average`, `X`, `Y`, `Atomic_Mass`, and `Radius` denote variables of real type. In the third, we see that `Z`, `Impedance`, and `Attenuation_Coefficient` have complex type. The last declaration specifies logical type for the variables `Flag`, `Save`, and `Done`.

Your program should include type declarations for all variables and named constants. Type declarations collect the names of variables and constants in a group of statements near the beginning of the program so that you can easily find them.

The `implicit none` *Directive*

Suppose that your program stores a value for the variable `Resistance` and that you accidentally misspell the name as `Resistence` in an expression. Fortran cannot read your mind, so it has no way of knowing that you intended both names to denote the same object. However, if you have listed all program variables in type declarations, Fortran can detect that the misspelled name has not been declared. If your program contains an `implicit none` directive, Fortran 90 will refuse to accept undeclared variable or constant names.

Fortran does not enforce the use of type declarations. It permits an alternative system of *implicit* type specifications. According to this system (described in Appendix D.1), the type of an undeclared object depends upon the first letter of its name. The implicit type system may have been satisfactory for early Fortran versions that provided only integer and real types, but it is inadequate for the much richer type repertoire of Fortran 90.

It is strongly recommended that you write the specification statement

```
implicit none
```

near the beginning of every program, as a *directive* announcing your intention to declare all variables.[1] It instructs Fortran to check that a type declaration appears for each variable and to treat undeclared names as program errors. Here is an example:

```
program Research
implicit none
   :
end program Research
```

[1] Each module and each external procedure, as well as the main program, should include an `implicit none` directive. Internal procedures and module subprograms, which are contained inside another program unit or subprogram, do not need `implicit none` statements if there is one in the host program unit or subprogram. (See Sections 2.4 and 7.2.)

Type Declaration Form

A type declaration, in its simplest form, begins with a *keyword* that names the data type (such as `integer`, `real`, or `complex`). This keyword is followed by a pair of colons and then by a list of the variable names:[2]

> *Type name* :: *List of names*

Other type declaration forms are described later in this section (as well as in Appendix D.1).

Consider the following example. Three type declarations are preceded by an `implicit none` directive:

```
implicit none
integer :: Count, Loop_Index
real :: Current, Resistance, Voltage
complex :: Snell
```

The first type declaration begins with the keyword `integer` and indicates that the subprogram contains two variables of integer type named `Count` and `Loop_Index`. The second declares three variables of real type called `Current`, `Resistance`, and `Voltage`. The third describes a complex variable whose name is `Snell`.

The type names `integer`, `real`, and `complex` are keywords. Although data object names are invented for each variable or constant in a program, keywords are permanently defined as part of the Fortran language and each one has special significance. For example, renaming the variable `Count` to `Enumerate` would have very little effect on the program, but you could not arbitrarily change the keyword `real` to `zeal` in a type declaration.

Keywords (such as type names) in Fortran are *not* reserved words — in fact, Fortran has no reserved words. Although this practice is *not* recommended, Fortran permits the use of `real`, `complex`, `print`, `if`, `end`, and other keywords as names of variables or constants. Some keywords (such as `real`) are also intrinsic function names. The typographical conventions that are used in this text (such as upper and lower case) can help you to distinguish between various uses of these words. However, it is important to remember that Fortran makes no distinction between uppercase and lowercase letters. If your program contains the keyword `real`, the intrinsic function name `Real`, and the constant name `REAL`, the capitalization is useful to you when you look at the program text, but it is ignored by Fortran. If you use each of these three words correctly, the rules of Fortran permit the compiler to distinguish among them by analyzing the position of the words in type declarations, assignment instructions, or other statements — that is, by the *context* in which the words appear.

---

[2] A *list* in the text of a Fortran program is a sequence of one or more items, separated by commas if there is more than one: X, Y, Z is a list, and so is X. A *parenthesized list* is a list that is enclosed in parentheses: (X, Y).

Type Properties and Attributes (Advanced)

A data object has other characteristics besides its type. These include `kind` and string length, which are called *type properties*:

1. A variable of any intrinsic type has a `kind` type parameter, which designates a subtype or variant of the intrinsic type and thus determines the particular computer representation that Fortran will use for it.
2. A variable of character data type has a string length property (see Chapter 6).

Note that on a given Fortran processor, each intrinsic data type has a *default* computer representation. Besides the default, a processor may provide one or more variant representations (see Section 1.6). A Fortran processor must at least provide a higher-precision variant for the real and complex data types. Note also that, for each intrinsic data type, a set of integers is defined by the Fortran 90 processor to be used as kind type parameter values. On a particular processor, for real data type, for example, the number 4 may designate the default representation and the number 8 may designate a higher-precision variant.[3]

The `kind` and string length properties of an object are inseparable from its type. Independent from these type properties are the following *data attributes*:

`parameter` (see Named Constants, Section 1.3), `save` (Section 5.6), and `data` (Appendix D.3)
`dimension` (Section 5.1)
`allocatable`, `pointer`, and `target` (Section 6.3)
`public` and `private` items in a module (Section 7.2)
`intent` (Sections 2.4 and 8.1) and `optional` (Section 8.7) dummy arguments
`intrinsic` (Section 2.3) and `external` (Appendix D.6) procedures

In a type declaration, type property specifiers (a `kind` subtype selector, a character length specifier, or both) may appear in parentheses after the *Type name*. If no subtype is specified, Fortran 90 selects the default computer representation:

Type name (*Type properties*) :: *List of names*

(See also Section 6.1 and Appendix D.1 for alternative ways of specifying character length.) As we shall see, named constants are usually preferable to explicit numerical constants for specifying type properties.

Other data attributes may be specified between the type properties and the double colon. All of the type properties and attributes that are specified to the left of the double colon will apply to all of the data object names listed to the right of the double colon:

[3] Unfortunately, these kind value *constants* are not portable. Two different Fortran processors (even different Fortran compilers for the same hardware configuration) may designate the same representation with different integer values. As explained in Section 1.6, the intrinsic inquiry functions Kind, Selected_Int_Kind, and Selected_Real_Kind provide portable kind specification.

Type name (*Type properties*), *Attributes* :: *List of names*

For arrays, dimension attribute information may alternatively be specified in the *List of names* (see Section 5.1).

The following example type declarations specify that Element_Name has string length 20 and that the variables Chart and List are arrays of size 12:

```
integer, parameter :: ARRAY_SIZE = 12, SL = 20
character (len = SL) :: Element_Name
integer, dimension(ARRAY_SIZE) :: Chart, List
```

See Section 1.6 for kind subtype specification examples.

Fortran 90 provides two alternative type declaration forms: entity-oriented and attribute-oriented. The *entity-oriented* declaration form, previously described, can be recognized by the presence of a double colon, which separates the *Type name, Type properties,* and *Attributes* from the *List of names* to which the specifications apply.

Attribute-Oriented Declarations (Optional)

As an alternative (and traditional) form, an *attribute-oriented* specification statement can declare a single attribute for a list of names. This form can be recognized by the absence of the double colon.

The attribute-oriented form may be useful for declaring several variables that share most, but not all, of their attributes. The shared attributes may be listed in an entity-oriented type declaration for all of the variables, and then separate attribute-oriented declarations may be written to cover the exceptions. For example, attribute-oriented declarations in a separate dimension statement are sometimes preferable for arrays (see Section 5.1).

The attribute-oriented initialization statement data provides an additional feature. In a data statement, but not in an entity-oriented type declaration, integer constants that specify initial values may be written in binary, octal, or hexadecimal form. (See Nondecimal Representation of Integers in Appendix D.3.)

Attribute-Oriented Type Declarations

For declaring *only* type and type properties, attribute-oriented declarations should rarely be used because the entity-oriented form is simpler for this restricted purpose. The attribute-oriented form is

Type name (*Type properties*) *List of names*

Except for the double colon, this declaration has the same form as an entity-oriented type declaration that specifies no additional attributes. For example, compare these three type declarations to those given earlier in this section:

```
integer Count, Loop_Index
real Current, Resistance, Voltage
complex Snell
```

Type properties (`kind` subtype and character length) may be specified in the same way in an attribute-oriented type declaration as they are in an entity-oriented declaration; that is, they are given in parentheses following the *Type name.* Character length specification is illustrated in the following example (attribute-oriented `kind` subtype specification is illustrated in Section 1.6):

```
integer SL
parameter (SL = 20)
character (len = SL) Element_Name
```

Attributes other than type properties are not permitted in an attribute-oriented type declaration. Attributes such as `parameter` must be specified in separate declarations, as described next. Thus, attribute-oriented declaration of a named constant would require two separate statements:

```
integer SL
parameter (SL = 20)
```

Other Attribute-Oriented Specification Statements

Attributes such as `parameter` and `dimension` may be specified, separately from the type and type properties, in attribute-oriented specification statements. Each different attribute has its own attribute-oriented statement form:

```
integer ARRAY_SIZE, R_HIGH, SL
parameter (ARRAY_SIZE = 12, SL = 20)
character (len = SL) Element_Name
integer Chart, List
dimension Chart(ARRAY_SIZE), List(ARRAY_SIZE)
```

In the following example, five variables share most, but not all, of their attributes. Type properties and shared attributes are listed in an entity-oriented type declaration, and separate attribute-oriented declarations cover the exceptions:

```
real, dimension(3, 3) :: A, B, C, D, E
save C
target D, E
```

Type properties (`kind` subtype and character length) are part of the type and must be specified in a type declaration. There are no separate attribute-oriented specification statement forms for these type properties.

Transition Tips

Sections with this title give some hints for migrating from traditional Fortran to modern Fortran 90 programming style. The suggestions are principally intended as aids for converting a running Fortran program to Fortran 90.

- Convert all source program text to free source form (see Appendix C). A public domain converter that accepts Fortran 77 program text is available from John Reid at Rutherford Labs, UK (email: `jkr@cc.rl.ac.uk`).
  If you have already incorporated fixed-form Fortran 90 statements in your code, ask your Fortran 90 supplier whether your compiler has an option to generate a free-form version of your program.
- Insert an `implicit none` statement immediately after the heading statement of every program and external subprogram. Declare the type of every variable. Compile your program to find undeclared variables, and add type declarations as needed.
- (Optional) Write all type declarations in entity-oriented form (with the double colon). Specify attributes other than type (such as `dimension`) in the entity-oriented type declaration.

1.2 Exercises

1. Which of the following are not valid Fortran names? Why not?

```
Oscilloscope    oscilloscope    OscI11OscOpe    Oscillo_Scope
1234s           Nn              N/4             A15_aa
7g46h           G46$            1Z2             lZ2
O0o             0Oo             o0O             Ooo
I111            Il11            lI11            1Iii
```

2. Which of the following are not valid Fortran names? Why not?

```
Mary        2mary       Polar       ALBERT EINSTEIN
Ipool       I15z        I234        Planck's_Constant
N-5         2Z          M22         N3
I1234tt     OOOOOOOO    00000000    O0000000
A234567890B234567890C234567890D
This_31-Character_Variable_Name
This_Long_Name_Has_32_Characters
```

3. Which of the following are not valid Fortran names? Why not?

```
X$                  x123x           PI              E
X123A_              2EAx            _A              1.23E14
Xy                  xY              X&Y             X_Y
Two's_Complement                    Quick_Silver
Name_Of_An_Alligator                My_Dog's_Name
A_Very_Long_Variable_Name678901
An_Even_Longer_Variable_Name9012
A-Rather-Long-Variable-Name8901
```

4. Write four type declarations, preceded by an `implicit none` directive, to specify types for the following variables:

   a. Complex type — `Enigmatic`, `Multifarious`, and `Perplexing`

   b. Real type — `Tangible`, `Concrete`, and `Palpable`

   c. Integer type — `Entire`, `Whole`, and `Undivided`

   d. Logical type — `Truth` and `Consequences`

1.3 A CLOSER LOOK AT CONSTANTS

Recall that a *constant* is an object whose value is fixed and cannot change during program execution. A constant in a program may have an *explicit* form, or it may be represented by a *name*. An explicit constant has a conventional form whose value is obvious; the value of a named constant is established by a declaration in the program. At most points in a Fortran 90 program where you might want to write an explicit constant, it is recommended that you write a named constant with the same value instead.

Explicit Constants

An explicit constant may be a *numerical constant*, a *character constant* (see Section 6.1), or a *logical constant* (see Section 3.4). The form of an explicit constant depends upon its data type:

1. You can write a numerical constant of integer type in the usual way, as a string of decimal digits without a decimal point. (Alternative binary, octal, and hexadecimal forms are permitted for input values and in `data` specification statements; see Nondecimal Representation of Integers in Appendix D.3.)
2. You can write a numerical constant of real type with or without an exponent. (See the examples that follow.) Without an exponent, a real numerical constant is simply a string of decimal digits containing a decimal point. Or, after a string of digits with a decimal point, you can write the letter E and then an integer exponent denoting a power of ten.[4] You must not insert a blank, a comma, or any other extraneous character in a numerical constant.
3. A complex constant appears as a pair of integer or real numerical constants, separated by a comma and enclosed in parentheses. (For further information, see Section 1.5.)

---

[4] A real exponent may be denoted by any of the letters E, e, D, or d. (See Section. 1.6, for a preferred alternative to D or d.)

Fortran distinguishes explicit constants from names in a program on the basis of their appearance. In particular, the first character of a name must be a letter, but the first character of an explicit constant of real or integer type is a digit or a decimal point. Here are some examples.

Integer constants:

```
0    1    356    2    123456789
```

Real constants (without exponents):

```
0.0      1.0  14.37       .00547   3.14159265358979
```

Real constants (with exponents):

```
1.75E8    2.76E4    6.0221367E23    6.6260755E34
```

Complex constants:

```
(0.0,1.75e8)     (1, 0)
```

Integer Constants

You can write a constant of integer type as a string of digits *without* a decimal point. You may include extra nonsignificant zeros at the left without affecting the value of the constant. For example, all of the following are integer constants:

```
1776      1492      555      1234567890
3         0         007      000022
```

Real Constants

You can write real numbers as numerical constants in the ordinary way, *with* a decimal point. You must not omit the decimal point from a real constant, even if its value happens to be an exact whole number. All of the following are real constants (without exponents):

```
2.0          0.001293     39.37     14.37       2.71828182846
3280.84      0.0          1.0       .00547      3.14159265358979
```

Real numbers that are very large or very small may have several zeros to the right or left of the decimal point, as in 0.0008761 and 175000000. You may omit some or all of the nonsignificant zeros if you write an exponent to specify the position of the decimal point. For example, recognizing that 1,000,000 (one million) is the sixth power of 10, or 10^6, you can write $175 \cdot 10^6$ instead of 175000000. You could also write the same number in other ways, such as $1.75 \cdot 10^8$ or $0.175 \cdot 10^9$. In each case, the exponent indicates the number of places to move the decimal point to the right to restore the indicated decimal value.

Among alternative positions for the decimal point, the most common in applications is *scientific style*, with one significant digit to the left of the decimal point, as in

$1.75 \cdot 10^8$. An alternative *normalized style*, with the first significant digit immediately to the right of the decimal point, as in $0.175 \cdot 10^9$, often appears in computer documentation because of its relation to the floating-point internal representation of numbers by the computer hardware. Each of the following Fortran real constants is written in scientific style:

Constant	Meaning
`1.75E8`	The value 175,000,000
`2.76E-4`	The value 0.000276
`6.0221367E23`	Avogadro's Number (gm^{-1})
`6.6260755E-34`	Planck's constant (joule sec)
`2.299792458E8`	Speed of light (m/sec)

In Fortran, the exponent is written with the letter E replacing 10, and the exponent is not raised above the line. Thus, the value 175000000. is represented in scientific style and in normalized style, respectively, by the two following real constants:

```
1.75E8      0.175E9
```

You can write very small numbers in an analogous way, except that the exponent is negative, indicating that the decimal point must be moved left to obtain the proper interpretation of the number. For example, the value .0008761 is represented in scientific style and in normalized style, respectively, by the two following real constants:

```
8.761E-4    0.8761E-3
```

For readability, it is recommended that real constants be written with at least one digit on each side of the decimal point. Fortran ignores zeros at the right end of a real constant (to the right of the decimal point) and at the left end (to the left of the decimal point). Thus, on each of the following lines, all three constants represent the same value; on each line, the second form is preferred:

```
  1.         1.0        1.00
100.       100.0      100.00
   .1        0.1       00.1
   .01       0.01      00.01
   .0        0.0       00.0
  0.         0.0        0.00
```

Fortran requires at least one digit, either to the left or to the right of the decimal point; in other words, a decimal point by itself is not a valid real constant.

Named Constants

A constant in a program has a fixed value that does not change while the program is being executed. However, a value that is correct for one instance of program execution may need to be changed before the program is executed again. A program constant such as the size of an array or the length of a character string may need to be revised. Searching for all the appearances of a certain constant among the statements of a long program can be a tedious and an error-prone task.

Fortunately, an explicit constant anywhere in a Fortran subprogram can be replaced by a *named constant* with the same value. The name of a constant looks just like the name of a variable. (In this text, constant names are written entirely with uppercase letters, but this makes no difference to Fortran.) You must list this name in a type declaration that states the type and announces that the name denotes a constant. By a quirk of terminology, the Fortran keyword `parameter` designates a named constant. According to Fortran rules, any name that is declared with the `parameter` attribute is the name of a constant.

The Houdini Principle

According to one programming style suggestion, all constants except 0 and 1 should be written as named constants rather than as explicit constants. W. B. Jones has called this rule the Houdini principle, which says, *"Don't use magic numbers."* Translation: Zero and one are fundamental constants of mathematics; other constants in a program usually seem to materialize in a magical fashion.

So, before you write an explicit constant in your program, you should ask, "Why this value?" For example, does the size of this array have to be 12? Will it always be 12? If the value is not dictated by a law of nature (and perhaps even if it is), it should be written as a named constant rather than as an explicit constant. Then you can change the value of the named constant by simply changing a single declaration — a much easier task than locating and changing all instances of a particular explicit constant in the program text. If the same constant will be needed in more than one subprogram, you can define it in a *module* (see Chapter 7) as a *global* named constant.

A named constant is *not* just a variable whose value happens to be known at the time the program is written. The name that denotes a named constant is written as a substitute for the explicit constant. Such a name must not appear on the left-hand side of an assignment statement or in the *Input list* of a `read` statement because it is not the name of an object to which a value can be assigned. On the other hand, named constants as well as explicit constants may be used in initialization expressions (described later in this section) or in specification expressions (Section 8.4) to define attributes such as array size.

Declaration for a Named Constant

You start the declaration for a named constant with the type name, the keyword `parameter`, a pair of colons, and the name. After the name, you write an equals sign and give the actual value of the named constant. Consider these examples:

```
integer, parameter :: LENGTH = 12
real, parameter :: PLANCK = 6.6260755E-34
```

In a program that contains these two declarations, you can now write the name `LENGTH` instead of the numerical constant `12` and you can change all instances of the constant throughout your program merely by modifying this one type declaration. Similarly, you can now write the name PLANCK, which is easier to remember than the numerical form of Planck's constant.

If there are several named constants of the same type in your program, you can list them all in one declaration of the form

Type name , parameter :: *List of names*

where each list item has the form

Name = *Value definition*

Each of the following declarations contains more than one named constant of the same type:

```
integer, parameter :: ARRAY_LENGTH = 100, S = 2
real, parameter :: AVOGADRO = 6.0221367E23, PLANCK = 6.6260755E-
34
integer, parameter :: ONE = 1, TWO = 2, A = 9, B = 7, NEON = 20
```

Value of a Named Constant

A Fortran named constant is a name with the `parameter` attribute. In the type declaration for such a name, the value of the named constant is specified following the double colon. The value specification has the form of an assignment that includes the name, an equals sign, and an expression that defines a value for the name. This latter expression is often an explicit constant, but it may have a slightly more general form. (See the rules for initialization expressions given shortly.)

The `integer` type declaration statement in the following example defines four constants whose names are S_LEN, J, M, and NJM:

```
integer, parameter :: S_LEN = 5, J = 4. M = 7, NJM = 4 * M
```

Note that the value of the named constant NJM is defined by an expression that involves the named constant M, whose value is defined earlier in the program text.

Initialization Expressions (Advanced)

The value of a named constant, the initial value of a variable (see Section 1.4), or a `kind` subtype value (see Section 1.6) may be specified as an *initialization expression*. The detailed rules for initialization expressions are rather complicated, but they may be summarized essentially as follows.

1. The expression must not contain any variables (except in certain contexts such as arguments to inquiry functions) but may contain named constants declared in previous declarations or earlier in the same declaration.
2. Certain intrinsic function references (see Sections P.2 and 2.3 and Appendix A) with constant arguments are allowed, provided that they can be evaluated prior to pro-

gram execution and provided that they have arguments and return values of integer or character type. Inquiry functions such as `Len`, `Size`, `Kind`, and `UBound` are permitted, provided that their values can be determined prior to program execution. For example, array arguments in these function references must not be assumed-shape arrays (Section 8.2):

```
intrinsic Max                                    ! (Optional)
integer, parameter :: I = 6, J = 3, K = Max (I, J)
```

3. Exponentiation is restricted to exponent expressions of integer type.
4. If the expression contains an array subscript (Section 5.1), an array constructor (Section 5.5), or a character substring (Section 6.1), expressions in any of these must be (constants or) initialization expressions.

The data type (and type properties) of a numerical initialization expression may be different from that of the object whose value is being defined. The expression value is coerced (see also Sections 1.6 and 2.2) to the type and subtype of the object. Rules for character length coercion are explained in Section 6.1.

As we shall see in Section 1.6, the inquiry functions `Kind`, `Selected_Real_Kind`, and `Selected_Int_Kind` are especially useful for defining named constants that will be used to specify `kind` subtype values:

```
intrinsic Kind, Selected_Real_Kind, Selected_Int_Kind
integer, parameter :: SAME = Kind (X), &
  SHORT = Selected_Real_Kind (6)
```

A complete explanation of initialization expressions, as well as of the related class of specification expressions (see Section 8.4), appears in the *Fortran 90 Handbook.*[5]

The general principle is that initialization expressions are limited to those that the compiler can be expected to evaluate. Thus, the compiler must be able to deduce all necessary values from the program text, without executing the program. Furthermore, the compiler is supposed to be able to perform simple operations on numbers and character strings, but it cannot be expected to have access to a complete function library.

Specification expressions, on the other hand, are evaluated during program execution, at the time of a procedure reference. The necessary information must be accessible in static storage, in an active area of automatic storage, or in heap storage with an accessible descriptor or pointer. A slightly broader class of operations is permitted, but the intent is to avoid arbitrarily complicated operations that would unduly increase procedure reference overhead.

[5] J. C. Adams et al., *Fortran 90 Handbook* (New York: McGraw-Hill, 1992), sec 7.9 (pp. 247ff).

Summary of Simple Input and Output

List-directed input and output are employed in the exercises and in many of the examples that follow. This topic was introduced in Section P.3. Chapter 9 discusses Fortran input and output in full detail.

- Simple list-directed Fortran input or output is controlled by a `read` or `print` statement with an asterisk immediately following the keyword `read` or `print`:

  ```
  read *, Input list
  print *, Output list
  ```

  For example:

  ```
  read *, A, I, Current, Resistance
  print *, ATan2 (0.0, -1.0), Exp (1.0)
  ```

- Input data values for on-line list-directed input are entered (typically, at the computer terminal keyboard) in free form on one or more lines. Blank characters must not be embedded within a single data value. Values may appear anywhere on a data line. Consecutive values must be separated by blanks. For example, data for the statement

  ```
  read *, A, I, Current, Resistance
  ```

  can be entered as

  ```
  12.3      9      45.6
  78.9
  ```

- Execution of a `read` statement assigns input data values to the variables in the *Input list*. The sequence of data values entered at the keyboard will correspond exactly to the sequence of variables in the list. Several data values may be included in a single line of input data.
- Execution of a `print` statement transmits values of the expressions in the *Output list*, in sequence, to the terminal screen. The exact appearance of the output may vary from one device and Fortran processor to another. Depending upon the amount of output data, the values may occupy several lines. However, a new output line is initiated at the beginning of execution of each `print` statement.
- The items in an *Input list* must be variable names. The items in an *Output list* are often variable names, but arbitrary expressions are permitted.
- An output list item may be a character constant, written as a string of characters between the quotation marks. (The quotation marks will not appear in the output.) In this text, the symbol ⊥ is used in character strings where a blank character would appear in the program:

  ```
  print *, "⊥Please⊥enter⊥the⊥diameter⊥of⊥a⊥circle.⊥"
  read *, Diameter
  print *, "⊥DIAMETER:⊥", Diameter, "⊥CIRCUMFERENCE:⊥", 3.1416 * Diameter
  ```

Transition Tip

- Look through your program for "magic numbers" (usually, any constants other than 0 or 1) and declare them as named constants in `parameter` statements.

1.3 Exercises

1. Classify each of the following as ID, a valid Fortran name; RC, a valid Fortran real constant; IC, a valid Fortran integer constant; or N, none of these.

```
123       $1.98      Love         X            1234
Ijk       Hate       X3           123.4        I*J*K
3.        3X         Land_Scape   Police_Man   3.00000
3*X       Computer   0.00003      123,400.000
Kite      Biter      Miter        A1B2         1A2B
```

2. Which of the following are not valid Fortran names or numerical constants? Be especially careful to distinguish between O (letter *oh*) and 0 (digit *zero*) and between I (letter *eye*), l (letter *ell*), and 1 (digit *one*).

```
Opera     0pera      little      1ittle
l23.4     123.4      o.1234      0.1234
I.0       Illinois   I111n01s    1II1n01s
```

3. Write each of the following real constants without an exponent:

```
3.08E0    522.4E-2    3.E5    .291E-4
99.E-1    .001E+7
```

4. Write each of the following as a real constant with an exponent, in scientific style (with one significant digit to the left of the decimal point):

`.000276` `41900.` `10.0` `0.1` $0.1234 . 10^5$

5. Write each of the following as a real constant with an exponent, in scientific style (with one significant digit to the left of the decimal point):

```
1,000,000    .000008    432.1    0.314
```

6. Write declarations for the following named constants:

   a. Integer type – `Count` is 120; `Prime` is 17; `Fibonacci` is 34. Write only one declaration, combining the separate items in a single list.

   b. Real type — The first five significant digits of π. Think of an appropriate name to remind yourself that the value is not exact.

7. Write type declarations for all variables mentioned in each of the following problem statements. Write named constant definitions (type declarations that specify the `parameter` attribute and define the named constant value) for all constants mentioned. All variables and constants should have real type.

   a. The area of a triangle is one-half the product of its base and its altitude.

   b. The new volume of a gas is the old volume times (the old pressure divided by the new pressure) times (the new temperature divided by the old temperature).

   c. Fahrenheit temperature minus 32.0, divided by 1.8, is Celsius temperature.

   d. Celsius temperature times 1.8, plus 32.0, is Fahrenheit temperature.

1.4 INITIAL VALUES FOR VARIABLES

At any particular time, a variable may or may not have a *value*:

1. When a variable has no value, we say that it is *undefined*. (A constant, on the other hand, is never undefined.)
2. The type declaration for a variable can specify an initial value (as described shortly), in which case the variable has a defined value when execution of the program begins.
3. If no initial value is specified in the type declaration, the variable is undefined at the beginning of program execution.
4. During program execution, a variable becomes defined if it is named in the input list of a `read` statement or on the left side of an assignment statement.

Your program must be constructed so that each variable will be given a definite value (either initially or during program execution) before any statement is executed that uses its value. Some programmers make it a practice to declare initial values for all variables.

Declaring an Initial Value

An equals sign and the initial value, usually in the form of an explicit constant (see also Initialization Expressions in Section 1.3) may follow the variable name in the type declaration. In a type declaration for several variables, you can initialize some or all of them:

Type name :: *List of names*

where each list item has either the form

Name

or the form

Name = *Initial value*

The first of the following type declarations creates four integer variables and gives initial values to two of them; the second creates two real variables and initializes both of them:

```
integer :: Montague, Lariat = 12, Flag = 100, Loop_Index
real :: X = 1.234, Y = 5.678
```

EXAMPLE 1.1 A single type declaration can declare both initialized variables and uninitialized variables. In this example, the variables S, V, and Nobody remain undefined until the read statement is executed.

```
! Example 1.1. Initial value in type declaration.
  program Initial_3
    implicit none
    real :: R = -9.25, S, T = 5.9, U = 0.0, V, W = 0.0
    integer :: Mt = 14, Nobody
! start program Initial_3
    read *, S, V, Nobody
    print *, R, S, T, U, V, W
    print *, Mt, Nobody
  end program Initial_3
```

The data statement, an alternative facility for initialization, is described in Appendix D.3. In a data statement, but not in a type declaration, integer constants that define initial values may be written in binary, octal, or hexadecimal form; see Nondecimal Representation of Integers in Appendix D.3.

Initialized Variables Versus Named Constants

Some Fortran programmers find it difficult to distinguish between named constants and initialized variables. Some of this confusion stems from the close resemblance between a named constant specification and an initial value specification when either appears in a type declaration. In this case, they are identical in form, except that a type declaration for a named constant includes the additional keyword parameter before the double colon.

It should be noted that the keyword parameter in a named constant specification applies to all of the listed names; therefore, each name that follows the double colon in the specification denotes a constant and must be accompanied by an explicit constant (or other initialization expression) giving its value. On the other hand, a type declaration for variables may initialize some but not others (see Example 1.1).

There are some programming situations where either a named constant or an initialized variable would serve. For most purposes, however, only one of the two is appropriate.

It may happen that a particular variable is initially defined and that no other program statements change its value, although it appears in expressions. Such a variable would be used in much the same way as a constant. There is an essential difference, however. Remember, the value of a constant *cannot* and *must not* be changed — a program is invalid if it contains a statement that attempts to change the value of a constant. Even a named constant, which appears in the program as a name and looks very much like the name of a variable, must not be changed. So, keep the following in mind:

1. The value defined for a named constant is *permanently* attached to the name.
2. The initial value of a variable can be changed later — for example, by an assignment operation — during execution of the program.

An initially defined variable can, for example, appear on the left in an assignment statement or appear in the input list of a `read` statement. An initial value specification gives a value to the variable at one specific point in time — that is, just before execution of the program begins. Like any other variable, its value can be changed by an assignment or input operation as execution proceeds.

Named constants commonly appear in type declarations or other declarations. Variables, even if initialized, cannot be used in declarations (except in certain contexts, such as for arguments to inquiry functions and in specification expressions for dummy arguments; see Section 8.4) to provide attribute values such as a character string length or an array dimension. (See Initialization Expressions in Section 1.3.)

EXAMPLE 1.2 In this example, `P` and `R` are named constants because the keyword `parameter` is included in the type declarations for these names. On the other hand, `Mt` and `Nobody` are initialized variables.

```
! Example 1.2. Named constants and initialized variables.
  program Initial_4
    implicit none
    integer, parameter :: P = 3                              ! Named constants
    integer :: Mt = 14, Nobody = 0, J, X               ! Initialized variables
    real, parameter :: R = -9.25                             ! Named constant
! start program Initial_4
    read *, J, X
    print *, P, Mt, Nobody, J
    print *, R
  end program Initial_4
```

Transition Tips

- Initialize most variables in type declarations. (See Section 5.5 for initialization of arrays.)
- (Optional) Convert most `data` declarations to type declarations that specify the `parameter` attribute.

1.4 Exercises

1. Write type declarations for a real variable named `Total` and an integer variable named `Count`. In the type declarations, initialize each variable to zero. In each case, use a numerical constant of the same type as the variable.

2. Examine the following type declarations. Which names are the names of initialized variables, and which are the names of constants?

```
Exercises 1.4, Number 2.
  program Distinction
    implicit none
    integer, parameter :: ABLE = 1, BAKER = 2
    integer :: Charlie = 3, Delta = 4
    real, parameter :: EPOXY = -5.0
    real :: Total = 0.0
! start program Distinction
    print *, ABLE, BAKER, Charlie, Delta
    print *, EPOXY, Total
  end program Distinction
```

1.5 COMPLEX NUMBERS IN FORTRAN (Advanced)

Applications in fields such as optics and electronics often involve complex variables. Fortran 90 provides facilities for operating on complex numbers as a whole, without separating them into their component parts.

A complex number can be expressed in *rectangular* form with two components that represent the real part and the imaginary part, or it can be expressed in *polar* form with components for amplitude and phase. Fortran employs the rectangular representation. However, some of the following examples are described in terms of the polar form. Later (in Sections 7.2 and 7.5), we shall see how to implement procedures for converting between the two forms and for performing operations directly with the polar representation.

Applications

Described next are three example applications, for which Fortran programs are presented later (in Examples 1.3, 1.4, and 1.5).

Electronics — Impedance of a Circuit Element

A *phasor* is a complex number F that can represent the amplitude and phase of a sinusoidal waveform $F\exp(j\omega t)$. The frequency of the sinusoid is fixed and is supposed to be known by means that are not of concern here. The amplitude of the phasor is the amplitude of the waveform, and phase is measured relative to some fixed sinusoid of the same frequency. Operations on sinusoidal waveforms can be computed by applying analogous operations to the phasors as complex numbers. In particular, the following formulas can be shown to apply.[6]

1. A phasor representing the sum of two sinusoids of the same frequency is obtained by simply adding the two phasors:

   ```
   F_Sum = F1 + F2
   ```

2. To obtain a phasor that represents the time derivative of a sinusoid, the phasor for the original sinusoid is multiplied by a complex constant whose real part is zero and whose imaginary part is the angular frequency of the sinusoid (in an electronics application, this complex constant would, of course, be written as $j\omega$):

   ```
   complex, parameter :: JW = (0.0, Omega)
   DF = JW * F
   ```

   For example, in a simple circuit loop with a voltage source, resistance, and inductance (all in series), let the phasor V0 represent the voltage source and let the resistance and inductance be given by real numbers R and L. The phasor representing current is

   ```
   Current = V0 / (R + JW * L)
   ```

3. The average value of a product of two sinusoids of the same frequency is a real number equal to one-half the real part of the complex product of the first phasor with the conjugate of the second phasor. Thus, averge power (real) may be computed from the phasors representing current and source voltage:

   ```
   Average_Power = 0.5 * Real (Current * Conjg (V0))
   ```

[6] These formulas are adapted from W. G. Oldham and S. E. Schwarz, *An Introduction to Electronics* (New York: Holt, Rinehart and Winston, 1972), chap. 4.

4. Impedance is a complex number but is not a phasor because it does not represent a waveform. The impedance of a circuit element is obtained by dividing the phasor for the voltage across the element by the phasor for the current flowing through it:

```
Impedance = Voltage / Current
```

See the Fortran program in Example 1.3, which applies these formulas to calculate current, average power, and impedance.

Optics — Absorption and Reflection at the Surface of a Metal

When an electromagnetic wave (visible light, for example) encounters a planar surface, the resulting effects can be described in terms of a complex quantity, the *index of refraction,* which is specific to the material and depends upon wavelength.

The power density as a function of depth y is the *irradiance,* $I(y)$:

$$I(y) = I_0 \exp(-\alpha y)$$

Here, I_0 is the *incident power density*, and α is the *absorption coefficient,* which depends upon the *wavelength* λ of the incident wave and upon the imaginary part N_I of the index of refraction N:

$$\alpha = \frac{4\pi N_I}{\lambda}$$

The depth y at which $I(y) = (1/e)I_0$ is called the *absorption length* (for metals, the *skin depth*). This depth is given by $y = 1/\alpha$.

For normal incidence, the *reflectance* R of a metal in contact with vacuum also depends upon the index of refraction:

$$R = \left| \frac{N-1}{N+1} \right|^2$$

See the Fortran program in Example 1.4, which calculates absorption coefficient, absorption length (skin depth), and reflectance from a given wavelength and index of refraction.[7]

Mathematics — Multiple *n*th Roots of a Complex Number

A complex number has two square roots, three cube roots, and so on. In general, the number of nth roots is n. This may be understood by noting that, in polar form, a complex number with amplitude α and phase ϕ cannot be distinguished from complex numbers with phases $\phi + 2\pi$, $\phi + 4\pi$, and so on. The multiple roots all have the same amplitude but different phases, which are obtained by dividing the phases of these indistinguishable complex numbers by n. The *principal root* is the one whose phase is greater than $-\pi/n$ and is less than or equal to π/n, and the phase of each of the others is that of the principal root increased by $2\pi k/n$, for $k = 1, 2, \ldots, n-1$.

---

[7] See also E. Hecht, *Optics* (2nd ed.). (Reading, Mass.: Addison-Wesley, 1987), chap. 4.

The $1/n$ power of a complex number is, by definition, the same as the nth root. The m/n power is the nth root of the mth power, and it again has n values (if m and n have no common divisors). As before, the principal value is the one whose phase is greater than $-\pi/n$ and is less than or equal to π/n, and the phase of each of the others is that of the principal value increased by $2\pi k/n$, for $k = 1, 2, \ldots, n-1$. (Raising a complex number to an irrational power may be considered equivalent to applying a rational exponent whose denominator is infinite; therefore, all complex numbers on a circle with the correct amplitude may be considered correct results. Computer numbers are never truly irrational, but the practical effect is much the same.)

See the Fortran program in Example 1.5, which computes multiple roots or m/n powers of a complex number. The principal value is returned directly by the Fortran exponentiation operation.

Fortran Facilities

The Fortran language provides variables, constants, and expressions of complex type as defined in mathematics. A complex number Z consists of a pair of real numbers X and Y, called the *real part* and the *imaginary part*, respectively. Fortran represents a data object of complex type as a pair of real objects.

An explicit complex constant in a Fortran program is written as a pair of explicit real or integer constants (of any valid form) separated by a comma and enclosed in parentheses. Either of the two constants may be preceded by a plus or minus sign. The first constant is the real part of the complex constant, and the second constant is the imaginary part.

A type declaration for a complex variable is analogous to that for a real variable — for example,

```
complex :: Z1, Z2, Z3
```

Operations of addition, subtraction, multiplication, division, or exponentiation of a pair of expressions of complex type are automatically interpreted by Fortran according to the mathematical rules of complex arithmetic.

Complex Addition

The following statement assigns to Z1 the complex value whose real part is 6.94 + 3.941, or 10.881, and whose imaginary part is 5.8975:

```
Z1 = (6.94, -5.9) + (3.941, 2.5E-3)
```

Complex Multiplication and Exponentiation

Most Fortran processors implement exponentiation of a complex value to an integer power by repeated multiplication. Thus, the following two statements have the same effect: Each assigns to Z2 the square of the complex value whose real part is 6.94 and whose imaginary part is -5.9. According to the mathematical definition of complex multiplication, $6.94^2 - 5.9^2$ is the real part of the product and $2 \cdot 6.94 \cdot (5.9)$ is the imaginary part of the product:

```
Z2 = (6.94, -5.9) ** 2
Z2 = (6.94, -5.9) * (6.94, -5.9)
```

Exponentiation of a complex value to a real power or of any numerical value to a complex power is usually implemented with logarithms.

Complex Division

The following statement assigns to Z3 real and imaginary parts computed according to the mathematical rules for complex division:

```
Z3 = Z1 / Z2
```

Mixing Complex with Other Types in an Expression

Expressions of mixed real, integer, and complex types are permitted in Fortran. An operand of integer or real type will be coerced automatically to a complex value with a zero imaginary part, and then the operation will be performed in complex arithmetic.

Assignment of a complex expression to a real or an integer variable automatically includes any required coercion (see Section 2.2) of the real part of the complex expression value.

Variables of complex type may appear in an input or output list; constants and other expressions of complex type may also appear in an output list. For list-directed input, a data value corresponding to a complex list item is prepared as a pair of real constants of any valid form separated by a comma and enclosed in parentheses.

The intrinsic function Cmplx combines two real expression arguments to produce a result of complex type. For example, the complex quantity whose real part is zero and whose imaginary part is A + B, where A and B are real, can be constructed by means of the function Cmplx:

```
Z = Cmplx (0.0, A + B)
```

For the interpretation of other intrinsic functions with complex arguments, see Complex Arguments and Results in Section 2.3.

Program Examples

EXAMPLE 1.3 For the electronics application described earlier, this program creates a complex phasor in rectangular form from the amplitude and phase of the source voltage. It then reads the resistance and inductance values and calculates and prints current and average power. Finally, it reads the amplitude and phase of the voltage across a circuit element and calculates the impedance based on the current that was obtained previously.

```
! Example 1.3. Complex Impedance of a Circuit Element.
  program Circuit
    implicit none                                                 ! directive
    intrinsic Complex, Conjg, Cos, Sin, Real                      ! (Optional)

    real, parameter :: Omega = 98.7E6              ! Frequency is 98.7 megahertz
    complex, parameter :: JW = (0.0, Omega)                 ! complex constant
    real :: VA, VP, R, L, Average_Power                    ! type declarations
    complex :: Vo, Current, Voltage, Impedance

! start program Circuit
    print *, "⊥Please⊥enter⊥source⊥voltage⊥amplitude⊥and⊥phase.⊥"
    read *, VA, VP
    Vo = Complex (VA * Cos (VP), VA * Sin (VP))

    print *, "⊥Please⊥enter⊥resistance⊥and⊥inductance⊥values.⊥"
    read *, R, L
    Current = Vo / (R + JW * L)
    Average_Power = 0.5 * Real (Current * Conjg (Vo))
    print *, Current, Average_Power

    print *, "Please⊥enter⊥amplitude⊥and⊥phase⊥of⊥voltage⊥across⊥an⊥element. "
    read *, VA, VP
    Voltage = Complex (VA * Cos (VP), VA * Sin (VP))
    Impedance = Voltage / Current
    print *, Impedance

  end program Circuit
```

EXAMPLE 1.4 Based on the optics application presented earlier, this program calculates absorption coefficient, absorption length (skin depth), and reflectance from a given wavelength and (complex) index of refraction.

```
! Example 1.4. Absorption and Reflection at the Surface of a Metal.
  program Refractory
    implicit none                                           ! directive
    intrinsic Abs, AImag, ATan2                             ! (Optional)
    real :: Pi, Lambda = 598.3, Alpha, Y, R          ! type declarations
    complex, dimension(3) :: N
    integer :: I
! start program Refractory
    Pi = ATan2 (0.0, -1.0)
    print *, Lambda
    N(1) = (.04, 2.4)          ! Complex index of refraction for Sodium.
    N(2) = (1.5, 5.3)             ! Complex index of refraction for Tin.
    N(3) = (3.7, 5.4)         ! Complex index of refraction for Gallium.
    do I = 1, 3
      Alpha = 4.0 * Pi * AImag (N(I)) / Lambda   ! Absorption coefficient.
      Y = 1.0 / Alpha                                     ! Skin depth.
      R = Abs ((N(I) - 1.0) / (N(I) + 1.0)) ** 2          ! Reflectance.
      print *, N(I), Alpha, "⊥Depth:⊥", Y, "⊥Reflectance:⊥", R
    end do
  end program Refractory
```

The results obtained from execution of the program in Example 1.4. are as follows:

Metal	Absorption Coefficient	Skin Depth	Reflectance
Sodium	0.0504	19.8	0.977
Tin	0.111	8.98	0.825
Gallium	0.113	8.82	0.711

EXAMPLE 1.5 For the mathematics application described earlier, this program finds multiple nth roots or m/n powers of a complex number. The calculation of `Multiplier` is somewhat inaccurate if n is large. The program may be modified to minimize the increasing amounts of error introduced by consecutive multiplications of `Root` by `Multiplier`.

```
! Example 1.5. Rational Powers of a Complex Number.
  program Power_Trip
    implicit none                                                    ! directive
    intrinsic ATan2, Real, Cmplx                                    ! (Optional)
    complex :: Z, Root, Multiplier
    integer :: M, N, Loop
    real :: X, Y, Phase_Increment
! start program Power_Trip
    print *, "␣Please␣enter␣real␣and␣imaginary␣parts.␣"
    read *, X, Y
    Z = Cmplx (X, Y)
    print *, "␣Please␣enter␣numerator␣and␣denominator␣of␣exponent.␣"
    read *, M, N
    Root = Z ** (Real (M) / Real (N))
    Phase_Increment = 2.0 * ATan2 (0.0, -1.0) / Real (N)            ! 2 * PI / N
    Multiplier = Cmplx (Cos (Phase_Increment), Sin (Phase_Increment))
    do Loop = 0, N - 1
      print *, Loop, "␣␣", Root
      Root = Root * Multiplier
    end do
  end program Power_Trip
```

1.5 Exercises

1. What is the sum of the complex constants (1.2, 3.4) and (7.8, 5.6)?

2. Euler's formula gives $e^{ix} = \cos x + i \sin x$. Write a program that verifies Fortran's agreement with Euler's formula. Read a real value X and print values of the following expressions:

```
Exp (Cmplx (0.0, X))                    ! "e" to power "i x"
Cmplx (Cos (X), Sin(X))                 ! "cos x + i sin x"
```

1.6 NUMBER REPRESENTATION (Optional)

For nonnumeric data representations, see the Fortran 90 logical model in Section 3.4 and the Fortran 90 character model in Section 6.1.

Numerical Precision and Range

In recent years, transfer of Fortran programs among computers with widely varying hardware representations (e.g., from an early personal computer with 8- or 16-bit integer word length to a supercomputer with 64 or 80 bits) has become increasingly common.

Standard Fortran programs traditionally provided no means for selecting an integer representation. For real representation, they provided only two precision specifications, `real` and `double precision`, whose significance was processor-dependent and varied widely among various computers.

Careful Fortran users are often well aware of their precision requirements, but they may be less familiar with the diverse number representation systems employed by computer hardware. The user's requirement, for example, may be 9 decimal digits of numerical precision, which can be satisfied with single-precision arithmetic if the computer word length is 64 bits but requires double-precision arithmetic if the word length is 32 bits.

Fortran 90 provides `kind` selection for much more flexible control of integer and real (as well as complex) precision and range:

1. On a given Fortran processor, each intrinsic data type has a *default* computer representation, which corresponds to the traditional Fortran representation. A processor may provide one or more variant representations. A Fortran processor must at least provide a higher-precision variant for real data type. Fortran represents a complex value as a pair of real values; consequently, for each variant real representation there is a corresponding complex representation.
2. Each different representation is, in effect, a *subtype* of the basic data type. The `kind` type parameter of a data object determines the particular computer representation (subtype) that Fortran 90 will use for it. Integer objects of different `kind` subtypes may have different ranges of values (i.e., largest possible magnitude). The internal floating-point representations for real or complex objects of different `kind` subtypes may have different precisions and exponent ranges.
3. For each intrinsic data type, the Fortran 90 processor defines a set of integer `kind` subtype selector values. These integer values do not necessarily have any inherent meaning; Fortran 90 does not require `kind` values to be related in any particular way to properties of the numeric representation. A typical (but by no means universal) convention is that the `kind` selector value is the number of bytes (e.g., 1, 2, or 4) occupied by the computer representation and that the `kind` value is 801 for a representation that occupies a single bit.

4. Every data object of an intrinsic type — integer, real (including complex and double precision), logical, or character — has a `kind` subtype as well as a type. If no subtype is declared, a default `kind` value (specific to the type and to the processor) is assumed. Default `kind` values correspond to traditional Fortran representations.
5. The `kind` value for a variable or named constant may be specified in the type declaration. An explicit constant may contain a `kind` subtype selector: For numeric and logical types, the constant is followed by an underscore and the `kind` selector; for character type, the `kind` selector and an underscore precede the constant.

Traditional versions of Fortran include double precision as an intrinsic type similar to real type, except that arithmetic operations are performed with greater numerical precision. Fortran 90 views double precision as a particular subtype of real type, but it accepts `double precision` type declarations for compatibility with previous versions. Fortran processors are required to support at least two real subtypes that correspond to the traditional real and double-precision types. Single- and double-precision complex subtypes must therefore also be supported; a processor with more than two real subtypes requires further complex subtypes as well.

Portability Considerations with the `kind` *Type Parameter*

The most significant advantage of Fortran 90's subtype facility is that it is controlled by numeric values, which can be evaluated at the beginning of program execution or even later in the execution process. This feature contrasts with methods based on keywords, such as have been used with traditional Fortran (`real` and `double precision`) and with other languages (e.g., `short` and `long`). Keywords are embedded in the program text and are difficult to modify systematically. To implement this facility, Fortran 90 provides intrinsic inquiry functions so that the numeric `kind` value for a variable can be derived from that of another variable (for example, a local object in a procedure can be related to a dummy argument) or computed from a known decimal precision requirement.

As we have seen, each Fortran 90 processor defines integer `kind` values for each of its integer representations and for each of its real representations. However, it is recommended that these processor-dependent values *not* be used as `kind` selectors because of the problems that result when a program is moved to a different processor.

Instead of explicit integer constants, named constants should be used as `kind` selectors. Furthermore, the values of such named constants should be defined with one of the inquiry functions `Kind`, `Selected_Real_Kind`, or `Selected_Int_Kind` (see also Initialization Expressions in Section 1.3). Use of these functions permits precision specification in terms meaningful to the user; in this way, the Fortran 90 program can maintain a given precision requirement when it is transported from one processor to another:

1. The intrinsic function `Kind (X)` returns an integer value that is the `kind` selector value for objects with the same subtype as the expression `X`. This function makes it

possible to relate the subtype of a particular variable to that of some other variable or constant. In particular, X may be a constant of the traditional integer, real, or double-precision type. For example, `Kind (1)` returns the value chosen by the processor for the `kind` value corresponding to traditional integer type on that processor, `Kind (1.0)` returns the value for traditional real type on that processor, and `Kind (1.0D0)` returns the processor `kind` value that signifies double precision on that processor. (Numerical constants written with the letter D instead of E preceding the exponent are double-precision constants, just as in traditional versions of Fortran.) Only the data type and form of the argument are significant; the argument value is immaterial.

2. The intrinsic inquiry function `Selected_Int_Kind (N)` returns the `kind` value for a processor representation that will accommodate any integer less than 10^N in absolute value.
3. Fortran applications often require a given minimum number of decimal digits of real precision. The intrinsic inquiry function `Selected_Real_Kind (P)`, where P is an expression of integer type denoting the number of significant decimal digits required, returns the `kind` value for a processor representation that supplies at least P decimal digits of precision (according to the Fortran 90 real model defined in this section). If there is more than one such `kind` value, the value returned is that of the *least precise* representation that satisfies the precision requirement. For example, `Selected_Real_Kind (6)` returns a processor `kind` value that provides at least 6 decimal digits of precision. Of course, Fortran cannot guarantee that all digits represented are actually correct.

Specifying the `kind` *Type Parameter*

A numerical constant may be followed by an underscore and a `kind` selector:

```
678_SHORT
12_LONG
3.141592_HIGH
```

See also logical constants (Section 3.4) and character constants (Section 6.1).

A type declaration for a variable or a named constant of integer, real, or complex type may optionally specify the `kind` subtype parameter. The `kind` selector may be a named constant of integer type. Consider the following examples:

```
integer, parameter :: SHORT = Kind (1), &
  LONG = Selected_Int_Kind (7), HIGH = Selected_Real_Kind (9)
integer (kind = SHORT) :: First, Second
integer (kind = SHORT), parameter :: THIRD = 678_SHORT
integer (kind = LONG), parameter :: FOURTH = 12_LONG
real (kind = HIGH) :: Average, X = 1.234, Y = 5.678
complex (kind = HIGH) :: Impedance = (1.0_HIGH, 0.0_HIGH)
```

EXAMPLE 1.6 In this example, SHORT_INT is a named constant that designates traditional integer type, and SHORT_REAL designates a real representation that supplies at least four digits of precision.

```
! Example 1.6. Specifying the kind type parameter.
  program Gentleman
    intrinsic Kind
    integer, parameter :: SHORT_INT = Kind (1), &
      SHORT_REAL = Selected_Real_Kind (4)
    integer (kind = SHORT_INT) :: One, Two
    real (kind = SHORT_REAL) :: Actual
! start program Gentleman
    One = 1_SHORT_INT
    Two = 2_SHORT_INT
    Actual = 3.0_SHORT_REAL
    print *, One, Two, Actual
  end program Gentleman
```

If the declaration for a variable of integer or real type does not include a `kind` selector, Fortran assumes a *default kind* — that is, a default hardware representation — which is that of the traditional Fortran integer or real data type.

An integer type declaration may include a `kind` selector along with the type:

```
integer, parameter :: D5 = Selected_Int_Kind (5)
integer (kind = D5) :: Count
```

If no `kind` selector is given for a variable or constant of integer type, Fortran selects the *default integer* subtype, which is the traditional Fortran integer type on whatever processor happens to be executing the program.

EXAMPLE 1.7 In this example, the named constant `D5`, when used as a `kind` selector, will guarantee space for at least 5 decimal digits and a sign. The integer variable `Count` is then declared with this `kind` selector. The variable `National_Debt` is explicitly declared to have the default integer `kind` subtype. The assignment statement illustrates `kind` specification for an integer constant.

```
! Example 1.7. Subtype specification for integer type.
    program Kindliness
    implicit none
    intrinsic Selected_Int_Kind, Kind
    integer, parameter :: &
      D5 = Selected_Int_Kind (5), DEFAULT = Kind (1)
    integer (kind = D5) :: Count
    integer (kind = DEFAULT) :: National_Debt = 9                ! Trillions
! start program Kindliness
```

```
    Count = 12345_D5
    print *, Count, National_Debt
  end program Kindliness
```

The Fortran 90 `kind` type selector can designate the equivalent of real or double-precision type or some other representation provided by a particular processor. If no `kind` parameter is selected for a particular variable or constant of real type, Fortran selects the *default real* subtype, which is the traditional Fortran real type.

EXAMPLE 1.8 In this example, the named constants SINGLE and LONG designate traditional real type and double-precision type, respectively. The named constants permit easy adaptation for use on another processor.

```
! Example 1.8. Default real and double precision kinds
  program Kindergarten
    implicit none
    intrinsic Kind, ATan2
    integer, parameter :: SINGLE = Kind (1.0), LONG = Kind (1.0D0)
    real (kind = SINGLE) :: Actual = 5.0
    real (kind = LONG) :: Long_PI
! start program Kindergarten
    Long_PI = ATan2 (0.0_LONG, -1.0_LONG)
    print *, Actual, Long_PI
  end program Kindergarten
```

The `real` type declarations for RX and RY in the following example have the same effect, and the two variables have the same internal representation:

```
real (kind = Kind (1.0)) :: RX
real :: RY
```

Also the two constants in the following example have the same `kind` subtype value (i.e., default real) and the same internal representation:

```
integer, parameter :: SHORT = Kind (1.0)
real (kind = SHORT) :: RX
real :: RY
RX = 3.14159265358979_SHORT
RY = 3.14159265358979
```

Every standard Fortran processor is required to provide at least two different real subtypes that correspond to the real and double-precision data types of traditional Fortran. Fortran accepts double-precision constants, with their traditional form. They look just like real constants written with an exponent, except that the letter D appears in place of the E in the exponent. For example, the double-precision constant

```
12.543210009876D3
```

means $12.543210009876 \cdot 10^3$. The D, like the E in a real constant, indicates that the following integer constant is an exponent to be applied as a power of 10.

The keyword `double precision` is permitted in a type declaration. This keyword has the same effect as `real (kind = Kind (1.0D0))`. In other words, DX and DY in the following example are two variables of the same real subtype:

```
real (kind = Kind (1.0D0)) :: DX
double precision :: DY
```

Thus, Fortran 90 views the traditional double-precision data type as a particular real subtype, which is one of the two real subtypes that every Fortran processor must provide. Neither a type declaration specifying double-precision type nor a constant with the exponent letter D is permitted to contain a further subtype specification.

Fortran 90 views default real type and double-precision types as just two among many possible representations. However, these two traditional real subtypes are given special consideration with regard to *storage association*, as described in Appendix E.1.

The hardware representation for a complex value in Fortran is the same as for a pair of real numbers of the corresponding real subtype. The hardware representation for complex data of *default kind* (i.e., a pair of default real numbers) is the same as the traditional Fortran complex representation. Because every Fortran processor is required to support at least two real kind subtypes (default real and traditional double precision), it follows that at least two complex kind subtypes must also be supported.[8] Any object of complex type has a single kind parameter.

A program may construct a complex value from two real (or integer) values:

1. An explicit complex constant may be written as a pair of explicit *real constants* separated by a comma and enclosed in parentheses. If the two constants have different real subtypes, Fortran 90 applies `kind` coercion so that both parts will have the same `kind` subtype as the part with the higher precision.
2. Either or both of the parts of an explicit complex constant may be explicit *integer constants.* If one part is an integer, it is converted to real type with the same `kind` subtype as the real constant. If both parts are integers, they are converted to default real. In the construction of a complex constant, the subtype of any explicit integer constant part is ignored.
3. The intrinsic function `Cmplx` constructs a complex value from two real or integer argument *expressions.* The `kind` parameter of the result is independent of the subtypes of the arguments: It is the default subtype unless a third `Kind` argument is present to specify a subtype for the function result.

EXAMPLE 1.9 This example shows how to specify a kind selector in a type declaration for a complex variable (compare to Example 1.8):

---

[8] Appendix E.1 explains that the traditional double-precision representation and the traditional complex representation each occupy two numeric storage units, but that the complex double-precision representation does *not* occupy four numeric storage units.

```
! Example 1.9. Kind type parameter for complex variables.
  program Enigmatic
    implicit none
    intrinsic Kind, Selected_Real_Kind
    integer, parameter :: &
      TRAD = Kind (0.0), D6 = Selected_Real_Kind(6)
    complex (kind = TRAD) :: X
    complex (kind = D6) :: A = (1.0_D6, 10.0_D6), B
! start program Enigmatic
    B = (6.94_TRAD, 5.9_D6)              ! Both parts coerced to highest precision
    X = A + B
    print *, X, A, B
  end program Enigmatic
```

Conversion of `kind` Values

Coercion in Arithmetic Expressions and Assignment

The following rules apply:

1. If an arithmetic operator has one operand of integer type and one operand of real or complex type, the type and the `kind` parameter of the result are those of the real or complex operand. The `kind` parameter of the integer operand is ignored.
2. If an arithmetic operator has two integer operands with different `kind` parameters, the result has the `kind` parameter that represents the larger exponent range.
3. If an arithmetic operator has two real or complex operands with different `kind` parameters, the result has the `kind` parameter that represents the higher decimal precision.
4. The expression on the right of an assignment statement is coerced, if necessary, to the type and `kind` parameter of the variable on the left. (See also Section 2.2.)

Intrinsic Functions for Explicit `kind` Conversion

Several intrinsic functions for type conversion — namely `AInt`, `ANInt`, `Cmplx`, `Int`, `NInt`, and `Real` — have an optional argument for specifying the desired `kind` parameter of the function result. The function `Int` may be used with an integer argument (or `Real`, with a real argument) to perform `kind` conversion without type conversion or any other effect. When any of the foregoing functions is used without the optional `Kind` argument, the result has default `kind`. The function `Dble`, with an integer, a real, or a complex argument, is the same as `Real`, except that the result `kind` is always that of double-precision real type. (For further details, see Section 2.3 and Appendix A.)

Fortran 90 Numeric Models

Every standard Fortran processor must provide at least one integer number representation and at least two real number representations. (Each real representation provided by the processor also applies to complex type.) Many processors find it advantageous to provide more subtypes than Fortran requires. Shorter numbers require less storage space and permit faster arithmetic, while longer versions can satisfy more stringent real precision, real exponent range, or integer size requirements. Fortran numerical operations and intrinsic function values, for various subtypes, are defined on the basis of representation *models* that are idealizations of actual hardware fixed-point or floating-point numbers.

Integer Model

The Fortran 90 integer model is an idealized fixed-point representation consisting of a sign and a sequence of digits. Parameters of the model are the *radix* (the number base) for the sequence of digits and the number of digits in the sequence. The Fortran model does not concern itself with certain other hardware-related details, such as ones- versus twos-complement sign representation, or how bits are numbered within a byte or word.

As an example, an obvious model for 4-byte integers (32 bits) has radix 2 and sequence length 31. The 32nd bit is the sign. For 1-, 2-, or 8-byte integer representations, the model could be the same, except for different parameter values.

Real Model

The Fortran 90 real model is an idealized floating-point representation. Separate portions of the representation denote the sign, the exponent, and the fractional part of a real numerical value. The *radix* (the base to which the exponent applies) is a parameter of the model. The most common radix value is 2, but some computers use other values such as 16 or 10. Other parameters of the model are the exponent range (minimum and maximum) and the number of digits (based on the radix) in the fractional part.

For example, 4 bytes can hold one single-precision floating-point value that conforms to the IEEE standard for single-precision binary arithmetic. In the Fortran 90 real model for this representation, the radix is 2, the (base-2) exponent range is -126 to 127, and the fractional part contains 24 bits (base-2 digits). An 8-byte (double-precision) IEEE representation has radix 2, exponent range -1023 to 1024, and 53 bits in the fractional part. For other real representations, Fortran uses the same model, but with different parameter values.

Numerical Inquiry Functions

These functions are defined in terms of the number representation models for the processor (some functions return information based on the attributes of the argument, but they do not necessarily compute its value):

`Digits (X)`, the number of significant (radix) digits in the model
`Epsilon (X)`, the number that is almost negligible compared to 1.0

Huge (X), the value of the largest number in the model

Kind (X), the kind selector value for objects with the same real or integer subtype as X

MaxExponent (X), the maximum (radix) exponent in the model

MinExponent (X), the minimum (radix) exponent in the model

Precision (X), the decimal precision

Radix (X), the radix of the model

Range (X), the decimal exponent range

Selected_Real_Kind (P, R), the kind selector value for reals with specified decimal precision P and decimal exponent range R (note that argument P or R, but not both, may be omitted)

Tiny (X), the value of the smallest number in the model

Transition Tip

- Change double precision type declarations to real with a specified kind parameter. Use the intrinsic function Selected_Real_Kind to define a named integer constant denoting the kind parameter value for the decimal precision you want, and use this constant in type declarations for variables of high-precision real type.

1.6 Exercises

1. Obtain documentation from your computer center or from your instructor concerning the integer and real kind values supported by the processor (computer hardware and Fortran compiler software) that you will be using. Which real kind values correspond to default real and to double-precision real?

2. The following program (Explore) determines the parameters of the Fortran 90 models for integer (default kind) and real (default kind and double precision).

   a. Prepare the program and run it on your computer. Read the descriptions in Appendix A of the intrinsic functions that this program uses.

   b. If you have found (from Exercise 1 here) that your processor provides additional integer or real kinds, extend this program or write a different one to determine the model parameters for each available kind.

```
! Exercises 1.6, Number 2.
  program Explore
    implicit none
    intrinsic Kind, Digits, Radix, Range, Huge, Bit_Size
    intrinsic MaxExponent, MinExponent, Precision
    intrinsic Epsilon, Tiny, Spacing
```

```
    integer, parameter :: I = 1
    real, parameter :: R1 = 1.0
    double precision, parameter :: R2 = 1.0D0
! start program Explore
    print *, "DEFAULT␣INTEGER"
    print *, "KIND␣number␣=␣", Kind (I)
    print *, "Digits␣=␣", Digits (I)
    print *, "Radix␣=␣", Radix (I)
    print *, "Range␣=␣", Range (I)
    print *, "Huge␣=␣", Huge (I)
    print *, "Bit_Size␣=␣", Bit_Size (I)
    print *
    print *, "DEFAULT␣REAL"
    print *, "KIND␣number␣=␣", Kind (R1)
    print *, "Digits␣=␣", Digits (R1)
    print *, "MaxExponent␣=␣", MaxExponent (R1)
    print *, "MinExponent␣=␣", MinExponent (R1)
    print *, "Precision␣=␣", Precision (R1)
    print *, "Radix␣=␣", Radix (R1)
    print *, "Range␣=␣", Range (R1)
    print *, "Epsilon␣=␣", Epsilon (R1)
    print *, "Spacing␣=␣", Spacing (R1)
    print *, "Tiny␣=␣", Tiny (R1)
    print *, "Huge␣=␣", Huge (R1)
    print *
    print *, "DOUBLE␣PRECISION␣REAL"
    print *, "KIND␣number␣=␣", Kind (R2)
    print *, "Digits␣=␣", Digits (R2)
    print *, "MaxExponent␣=␣", MaxExponent (R2)
    print *, "MinExponent␣=␣", MinExponent (R2)
    print *, "Precision␣=␣", Precision (R2)
    print *, "Radix␣=␣", Radix (R2)
    print *, "Range␣=␣", Range (R2)
    print *, "Epsilon␣=␣", Epsilon (R2)
    print *, "Spacing␣=␣", Spacing (R2)
    print *, "Tiny␣=␣", Tiny (R2)
    print *, "Huge␣=␣", Huge (R2)
  end program Explore
```

Chapter 2
Expressions, Assignment, and Procedures

2.1 ASSIGNMENT STATEMENTS AND THEIR EXECUTION

A Fortran 90 program is composed of statements interspersed with *comments.* Comments are ignored by Fortran; they are intended as documentation for the benefit of the original programmer or for other persons who may read the program later. A Fortran statement is a specification or an instruction. The type declarations described in Section 1.2 are *specifications.* Assignment statements, the principal subject of this chapter, are *instructions.* For more information concerning comments, specifications, and instructions, see also Section P.1 and Appendix C.

An *assignment statement* has three parts: a variable name, an equals sign (the *assignment operator*), and an expression:

Variable name = *Expression*

Fortran executes an assignment statement by first finding the value of the expression, and then assigning that value to the variable (Figure 2.1).

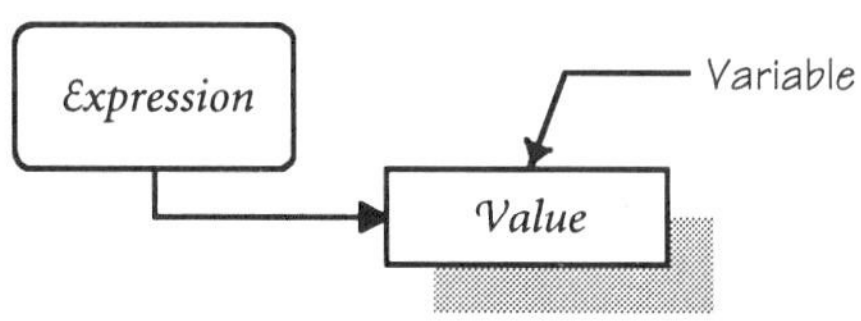

FIGURE 2.1. How Fortran executes an assignment statement of the form *Variable name = Expression.*

The expression may be quite simple; it may even consist of nothing but a numerical constant. The assignment statements in Example 2.1 have this simple form. Note that the constant expression in each of these assignment statements has the same data type as the variable. Where the type is character, the lengths also match. Mixed-type assignment is introduced in Section 2.2.

EXAMPLE 2.1

```
! Example 2.1. Assignment statements with constant expressions.
 program Assign_1
   implicit none
   integer, parameter :: Name_Length = 19
   real :: Avogadros_Number
   integer :: Many
   complex :: Z
   logical :: Flag
   character (len = Name_Length) :: Name
! start program Assign_1
   Many = 346021                                    ! Integer type
   Avogadros_Number = 6.0221367E23                     ! Real type
   Z = (0.0, 1.75E8)                                ! Complex type
   Name = "James␣Clerk␣Maxwell"               ! Character type, length 19
   print *, Many, Avogadros_Number, Z, Name
 end program Assign_1
```

When the expression on the right-hand side is a constant, its evaluation is trivial. Fortran merely assigns the constant value to the variable named on the left-hand side (Figure 2.2).

FIGURE 2.2. How Fortran assigns the value of a constant to a variable.

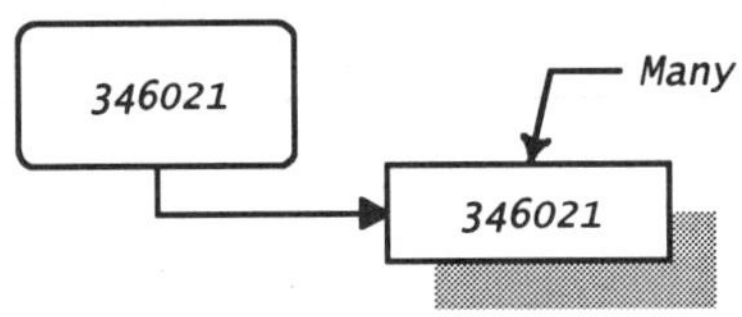

Example 2.2 illustrates the next simplest form that an assignment statement may have. The expression in each of these assignment statements is a single variable. Fortran evaluates the expression by simply copying the value of variable on the right, which then becomes the value of the variable on the left.

An assignment is not valid if the expression on the right is undefined (see Section 1.4). Where necessary in Example 2.2, variables are initialized with type declarations. Thus, when program execution begins, the variables `Y`, `Pi`, `Count`, `I`, and `Flag` will have defined values, but the values of `X`, `Theta`, `Many`, `K`, and `Done` will be initially undefined. In the assignment statements in Example 2.2, the data types (and character lengths) of the left and right sides are matched (not mixed).

EXAMPLE 2.2

```
! Example 2.2. Assignment statements with variable expressions.
 program Assign_2
   implicit none
   ! Type declarations with initialized variables:
   real :: Y = 1.23, Pi = 3.141592
   integer :: Count = 173
   character (len = 8) :: I = "␣Optics␣"
   logical :: Flag = .TRUE.
   ! Type declarations with uninitialized variables:
   real :: X, Theta
   integer :: Many
   character (len = 8) :: K
   logical :: Done
! start program Assign_2
   X = Y                                                    ! Real type
   Y = X
   Theta = Pi
   Many = Count                                          ! Integer type
   K = I                                     ! Character type, length 8
   Done = Flag                                           ! Logical type
   print *, Y, Pi, X, Theta, Count, Many, I, K, Flag, Done
 end program Assign_2
```

Dialogue: Sequence of events during assignment

If you have read the prologue, you have met María Flores and Cathy Spade. María is a brilliant young engineer, and her friend, Cathy, is a high school student. Cathy's advanced math class has been learning to write programs in Pascal, and María has been teaching her Fortran.

"I'm a bit confused, Miss Flores. The first two assignment statements in Example 2.2 look like they are just doing the same thing twice. My math teacher says that the commutative law means there is no difference between X = Y and Y = X."

"You're forgetting one thing, Cathy. You're thinking of the commutative law for the operation of equality. This is not equality — it is *assignment.* The confusing part is that the Fortran assignment operator is the same symbol that means equality in math. The Pascal assignment operator, := , is less confusing."

"I remember now. The difference between the two assignments in Example 2.2 is the execution sequence."

"Right. To execute the first assignment statement,

X = Y

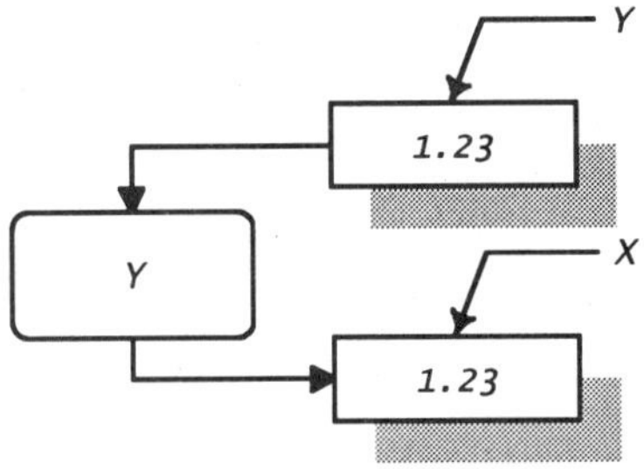

FIGURE 2.3. How Fortran executes the assignment statement $X = Y$.

Fortran copies the current value of the variable Y without changing the value of Y and assigns it as the new value of X. Here is a sketch that shows how it works (Figure 2.3).

"After this first assignment operation, the values of both variables, X and Y, will be 1.23. To execute the second assignment statement,

```
Y = X
```

Fortran now copies the current value of X that resulted from the first assignment and assigns this value to Y. After the second assignment, both variables end up with the value that Y originally had."

"But where does the original value of Y come from?"

"It's initialized in the type declaration, which means it has a value when execution of the program begins. X is not initialized because the assignment gives it a value before it's used for anything."

"I see now. The other variables that are used before they are assigned, Pi, Count, I, and Flag, are initialized in type declarations too. These other variables, Theta, Many, K, and Done, do not have to be initialized because they first appear on the left in assignment statements."

"Watch what happens to a variable if more than one statement refers to it. The value of the variable at any time will be the last number that has been assigned to it. Look at this sequence of assignment statements:

```
X = 1.2
Y = 3.4
X = Y
Y = 5.6
```

Executing the first two statements gives the value 1.2 to X and gives the value 3.4 to Y. Fortran executes the third statement by finding the value of Y, which is 3.4, and changing X to that value. After the fourth statement is executed, 5.6 will be the value of Y."

"I'm catching on, Miss Flores. The execution sequence of the statements proceeds from top to bottom, just like when you read a page. But there is something strange about the execution sequence in an assignment statement. On a page, you read each line from left to right. But, in assignment, you have to first look at the expression on the right and find its value. Then you look at the variable on the left to see where the value goes."

"You just have to get used to it, Cathy. Even in an expression, Fortran does not always compute the values from left to right. Later, you'll see several rules that can modify the left-to-right sequence."

"So the sequence is somewhat like reading a page, but not exactly."

"Can you see how to write statements to exchange the values of X and Y? You can't just write

```
X = Y
Y = X
```

These are the first two assignment statements that we just looked at in Example 2.2. The first statement destroys the original value of X, but we need to save this value so that we can assign it to Y."

"I suppose I could put it somewhere else. Maybe I'll invent a new variable:

```
New = X
X = Y
Y = New
```

The new variable will hold the value of X until I'm ready to use it. Of course, I have to add a type declaration for the new variable."

"Very good, Cathy. You can even extend the same method to *cyclically permute* values of three or more variables. You can save the original value of the first value until the end, like this:

```
New = X
X = Y
Y = Z
Z = New
```

2.1 Exercise

1. Write Fortran statements to cyclically permute four variables named W, X, Y, and Z.

2.2 ARITHMETIC EXPRESSIONS AND ASSIGNMENT

Fortran arithmetic expressions include the four basic operations of addition, subtraction, multiplication, and division. Fortran can apply these four operations, as well as exponentiation, to objects of any numerical data type (integer, real, or complex). Although integers are defined mathematically as a subset of the real numbers, Fortran operates on integers in some special ways. For example, dividing one integer by another always produces an integer result. Integers are especially suitable for choosing an element in an array and for counting repetitions. Some examples of arithmetic expressions follow.

Addition and subtraction:

```
X + 2.0
I - 5
Length - 1
X + Y - 2.53
```

Multiplication and division:

```
X * 2.0
I / 5
13 / 5
Old_Vol * (Old_Press / New_Press) * (New_Temp / Old_Temp)
```

Exponentiation:

```
X ** 2.0
I ** 55
(X ** 2 + Y ** 2) ** 0.5             ! See also SqRt in Section 2.3.
0.5 * Mass * Velocity ** 2
```

Numerical Expressions

A *numerical expression* of integer or real type may have any of the following forms:

The name of a variable of integer or real type

An explicit integer constant or real constant or the name of a named constant of integer or real type

A pair of simpler numerical expressions combined by any of the arithmetic operators, +, -, *, /, or **

A numerical expression preceded by the operator - (negation) or + (identity)

A numerical expression enclosed in parentheses

As we shall see, a numerical expression may also be a reference to a function that produces a numerical result.

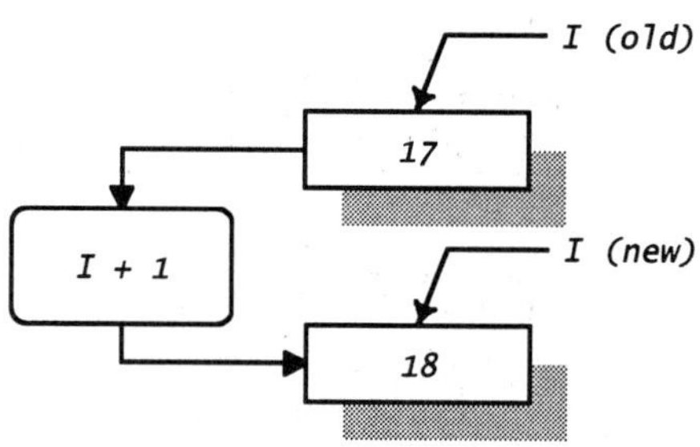

FIGURE 2.4. How Fortran executes the assignment statement *I = I + 1.*

Assignment Statements with Expressions

Some assignment statements with arithmetic expressions are shown in Example 2.3.

EXAMPLE 2.3

```
! Example 2.3. Assignment statements with arithmetic expressions.
 program Express
   implicit none
   real, parameter :: GRAVITY = 9.8
   real :: Old_Vol, Old_Press, Old_Temp, New_Vol, New_Press, New_Temp
   real :: Mass, Velocity

   real :: Pressure, Density, Height
   integer :: J = 6, I
! start program Express
   I = J + 1
   print *, I

   read *, Old_Vol, Old_Press, Old_Temp, New_Temp
   New_Vol = Old_Vol * (Old_Press / New_Press) * (New_Temp / Old_Temp)
   print *, Old_Vol, Old_Press, Old_Temp, New_Vol, New_Press, New_Temp

   read *, Mass, Velocity
   Kinetic_Energy = 0.5 * Mass * Velocity ** 2
   print *, Mass, Velocity, Kinetic_Energy

   read *, Pressure, Density, Velocity, Height
   Bernoulli = Pressure + Density * (0.5 * Velocity ** 2 + GRAVITY * Height)
   print *, Pressure, Density, Velocity, Height, Bernoulli

 end program Express
```

The left-hand side of an assignment statement *must* be the name of a variable. The expression on the right may also refer to this same variable. It is important to understand that the expression on the right will be completely evaluated before assignment to the variable on the left takes place. Consider the assignment statement

```
I = I + 1
```

The variable I must, of course, have a defined value before execution of this statement begins. Suppose, as in Figure 2.4, that the value of I is 17 before the assignment begins. The expression I + 1 is evaluated using this value of I, *after which* the new value, 18, is assigned to I.

More complicated expressions can be constructed in several ways, as Example 2.4 illustrates.

EXAMPLE 2.4

```
! Example 2.4. More assignment statements.
  program Accentuate
    implicit none
    real :: A = 1.234, B = 5.567, Average_1, Average_2
    integer :: I = 139, J = 245, K = 7, Mean, Negation, Identity
! start program Accentuate
    Average_1 = (A + B) / 2.0                              ! Assignment statements
    Average_2 = 0.5 * (A + B)
    Mean = (I + J) / 2
    Negation = -I * (-J / (-K))
    Identity = +I * (+J)
    print *, Average_1, Average_2, Mean, Negation, Identity
  end program Accentuate
```

When you are constructing a complicated expression, remember the following:

1. You can enclose an expression in parentheses and then combine the parenthesized expression with other expressions.
2. A minus sign at the beginning of an expression or parenthesized subexpression indicates *negation*. Negation differs from subtraction in that it has only one operand expression, whereas subtraction is denoted by a minus sign written between two operand expressions.
3. A plus sign may appear as an operator at the beginning of an expression or parenthesized subexpression. A plus sign with one operand is called the *identity* operator; it has no effect on the value of the expression.

You may write a plus or minus sign in front of an explicit constant of integer, real, or complex type. In an expression, the sign is not a part of the constant. A plus sign is interpreted as an identity operator, and a minus sign is a negation operator, with the constant as its operand. However, a *signed constant*, in which the sign is interpreted as an integral part of the constant, may appear in certain contexts:

As an input data value
As the exponent in a real constant such as `6.6260755E-34`
As the real part or the imaginary part of a complex constant (see Section 1.5)
As a scale factor in a `format` specification (see Appendix B.9)
In the *List of constants* in a `data` statement (see Appendix D.3)

A rule that must be followed in writing Fortran expressions is that two operators must not appear side by side in an expression. (Fortran treats the double asterisk that denotes exponentiation as one operator.) In practice, this restriction rarely presents any problem, except when a minus sign indicating negation appears in the middle of an expression. The difficulty can always be avoided by the insertion of extra parentheses:

```
A * (-B)                                                        ! ☺
A * - B                                                         ! ☹
```

The assignment statements in Example 2.5 illustrate exponentiation as well as some miscellaneous composite expressions.

EXAMPLE 2.5

```
! Example 2.5. Assignment statements with exponentiation.
 program Exponents
   implicit none                                     ! Type declarations
   real :: Base = 2.78, Exponent = 5.0, R_Power
   real :: Length = 12.0, Width = 3.0, Height = 4.0, Diagonal
   real :: A = 5.0, B = 8.0, C = 3.0, Discriminant, Root
   real :: X = 1.0
   integer :: I = 2, E = 10, I_Power
! start program Exponents
   R_Power = Base ** Exponent                      ! Assignment statements
   Diagonal = (Length ** 2 + Width ** 2 + Height ** 2) ** 0.5
   Discriminant = B ** 2 - 4.0 * A * C
   Root = (-B + Discriminant ** 0.5) / (2.0 * A)
   X = 0.5 * (X + (A / X))
   I_Power = I ** E
   print *, R_Power, Diagonal, Discriminant, Root, X, I_Power
 end program Exponents
```

Application: Loop Currents

As an example of expressions and assignment statements, let's consider the simple electrical circuit shown in Figure 2.5. For analysis, we choose one loop containing the resistors R_1 and R_3 and the voltage source V_0, and a second loop containing the resistors R_2 and R_3.

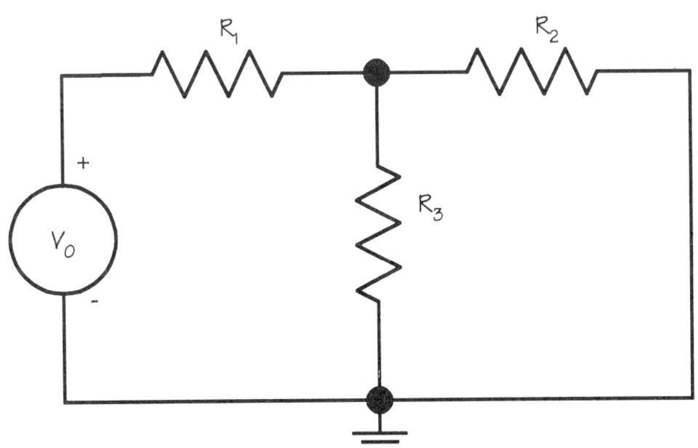

FIGURE 2.5. Electrical circuit application.

The following equations express the fact that the total voltage drop along each of these closed loops is zero:

$$I_1 R_1 + (I_1 - I_2) R_3 - V_0 = 0$$
$$I_2 R_2 + (I_2 - I_1) R_3 = 0$$

Suppose that the resistors and the voltage source have known values: $R_1 = 8.2$ ohms, $R_2 = 12.3$ ohms, $R_3 = 75$ ohms, and $V_0 = 120$ volts. Write the loop equations as two simultaneous algebraic equations in the unknown currents I_1 and I_2:

$$(R_1 + R_3) I_1 - R_3 I_2 = V_0$$
$$-R_3 I_1 + (R_2 + R_3) I_2 = 0$$

Recall that the solution of a system of two linear algebraic equations

$$A \cdot I_1 + B \cdot I_2 = E$$
$$C \cdot I_1 + D \cdot I_2 = F$$

can be computed directly by Cramer's rule:[1]

EXAMPLE 2.6

```
! Example 2.6. Two simultaneous equations by Cramer's rule.
  program Loop_Currents
    implicit none
    real :: R1, R2, R3, V0, A, B, C, D, E, F, I1, I2
! start program Loop_Currents
    read *, R1, R2, R3, V0
    A = R1 + R3; B = -R3
    C = -R3; D = R2 + R3
    E = V0, F = 0.0
    I1 = (D * E - B * F) / (A * D - B * C)
    I2 = (A * F - C * E) / (A * D - B * C)
    print *, "␣I1␣=␣", I1 ";␣I2␣=␣", I2
  end program Loop_Currents
```

Putting in the given resistance and voltage values, we obtain the following results:

`I1 = 6.3942; I2 = 5.4933`

[1] Cramer's rule is intolerably slow for more than a few simultaneous equations, but it is appropriate for two equations.

The Importance of Numerical Data Types

As explained in Section 1.6, the internal computer representation of integers (as described by Fortran 90 numeric models) is different from that of real numbers. Code generated by the compiler instructs Fortran to perform either fixed-point (integer) arithmetic or floating-point (real) arithmetic. An expression consisting entirely of integer variables and integer constants (with arithmetic operators, parentheses, etc.) will be evaluated with fixed-point arithmetic, whereas an expression consisting entirely of real variables and real constants (with arithmetic operators and so on) will be evaluated by means of floating-point arithmetic.

In effect, then, each arithmetic operator does double duty. (We say that the operators are *generic* or *overloaded.*) A plus sign indicates the operation of fixed-point addition when it appears between a pair of integer expressions; it indicates floating-point addition when it appears between real expressions. It is important to keep the following in mind:

1. When both operands in an addition, subtraction, multiplication, or division operation are real, the result type is real. When both operands are integers, the result type is integer.
2. Data type is especially crucial in the interpretation of integer division. The quotient of any two Fortran expressions of integer type is *truncated* to the next smaller integer (in absolute value); that is, the fractional part of the quotient is chopped off. For example, the result of evaluating the expression `9 / 5` is the integer value 1, and the result of evaluating `-9 / 5` is `-1`. No such truncation occurs during evaluation of the real quotient expression `9.0 / 5.0`, in spite of the fact that the real constants `9.0` and `5.0` happen to have values that are whole numbers; the result is the real value 1.8. (See also the special note on integer division given later in this section.)
3. When a real expression is raised to an *integer power,* the data type of the result is real. The integer exponent simply denotes repeated real multiplication. For example, `A ** 5` (mathematically, A^5) means that five copies of the value of `A` are to be multiplied together, as if it were written as `A * A * A * A * A`. This expression is real, even though the exponent is an integer constant. The exponent does not, of course, have to be a constant; it can be any integer expression, such as `A ** (I + 3)`. Most Fortran processors can evaluate the expression `A ** 5` more efficiently than `A ** 5.0`.

Interpreting Expressions

Summary of rules for evaluating expressions

- Rule 1.[2] Subexpressions enclosed in parentheses are computed first — that is, before the value is combined with other parts of the expression. If there are parentheses within parentheses, the innermost parenthesized subexpression is evaluated first.
- Rule 2. The arithmetic operations within any expression or parenthesized subexpression are performed in the following order of *precedence*:

  First — exponentiation operations
  Second — multiplication and division operations
  Third — addition, subtraction, negation, and identity operations

- Rule 3. When an expression (or parenthesized subexpression) involves two or more operations at the same precedence level, their position within the expression determines the order in which these operations are performed.
  Multiplication and division operations (or addition, subtraction, and negation operations) are performed in order from left to right. Thus, A / B * C means (A / B) C; that is, divide A by B and then multiply the result by C (see Example 2.8, given shortly).
  In accordance with mathematical convention, however, two or more consecutive exponentiation operations are performed in order from right to left. Thus, A ** B ** C means that A is to be raised to the power B^C.
- Rule 4. A fourth rule for determining precedence in the evaluation of expressions (see Section 2.3) applies to expressions that require evaluation of a function, such as `0.5 * (SqRt (X) + A / SqRt (X))` or `Abs (A) * B / C`. According to this fourth rule, function evaluation takes precedence over all other operations.

Dialogue: Interpretation of Fortran expressions

"Miss Flores, when I write `A / B * C` in Fortran, how can I tell whether it is `(A / B) * C` or as `A / (B * C)`? When I write a Fortran expression, how do I know it will be interpreted the way I mean it?"

"Basically, Cathy, you just use common sense and apply the standard conventions of mathematics. In case of doubt, you can add parentheses to force the interpretation you want. But Fortran has only one kind of parentheses, and sometimes too many parentheses are more confusing than helpful, so you fall back on the Fortran evaluation rules."

[2] The rules given here actually describe the *interpretation* of Fortran expressions. Fortran is permitted to actually *evaluate* any "mathematically equivalent" expression, except that parentheses (rule 1) must be respected.

"To analyze an expression, you can apply these rules to figure out which operation will be performed first. Then you assume that the first operation has been performed, and you replace the operator and its operands by a single numerical result that you can call R1. At this point, you go back to the rules to decide which operation is to be performed next, and you replace the next operator and its operands by a new result, R2. You continue in this way until you get a single result that is the value of the whole expression. After the expression has been reduced to a single value, assignment can take place."

EXAMPLE 2.7

Assignment statement	Rule	Replace		Result
`Q = A ** 2 + B ** 2`	2, 3	`A ** 2`	by	R1
`Q = R1 + B ** 2`	2	`B ** 2`	by	R2
`Q = R1 + R2`		`R1 + R2`	by	R3
`Q = R3`				

"Rule 3 is a tie-breaking rule. Note that multiplication and division are both on the second level in the precedence list. Addition, subtraction, negation, and identity are all on the third level. In the next example, you must apply the left-to-right rule to the evaluation of the expression because it contains two operations on the same level. The expression contains no parentheses, and both operations are at the second precedence level, so the operation on the left is performed first."

EXAMPLE 2.8

Expression	Rule	Replace		Result
`V2 = V1 / P2 * P1`	3	`V1 / P2`	by	R1
`V2 = R1 * P1`		`R1 * P1`	by	R2
`V2 = R2`				

"It is clear from this example that the Fortran expression V1 / P2 * P1 means the same as (V1 / P2) * P1, and not V1 / (P2 * P1), because of the tie-breaking rule.

However, the following example includes parentheses, so rule 1 applies. Within each subexpression enclosed in parentheses, you then proceed according to rules 2 and 3."

EXAMPLE 2.9

Expression	Rule	Replace		Result
`V2 = V1 * P1 * T2 / (P2 * T1)`	1	`(P2 * T1)`	by	`R1`
`V2 = V1 * P1 * T2 / R1`	3	`V1 * P1`	by	`R2`
`V2 = R2 * T2 / R1`	3	`R2 * T2`	by	`R3`
`V2 = R3 / R1`		`R3 / R1`	by	`R4`
`V2 = R4`				

Dialogue: Special note on integer division

"It is important to remember that integer division produces an integer result; any fractional part of the quotient is discarded. Thus, 3 / 4 yields the quotient 0, and 5 / 2 yields the quotient 2. An easy way to remember the effect of integer division is to write out the quotient as a (positive or negative) real number and then discard the decimal point and all digits to the right of it:

Fortran expression	Real value	Fortran result
`31/8`	3.875	3
`-825/16`	-51.5625	-51

"Because of this truncation, the order of computation is much more important for determining the meaning of an integer expression than it is for a real expression. In algebra, the two following expressions would have the same value, regardless of the values of the variables:

```
(L - M) / N * J
J * (L - M) / N
```

But, if the type of all of the variables is integer, you should not be surprised when Fortran obtains different numerical results for the two expressions. This truncation of the quotient occurs in any expression or subexpression where both operands in a division operation have integer type."

EXAMPLE 2.10

```
! Example 2.10. Integer division.
  program Divide
    implicit none
    integer :: J = 5, L = 7, M = 4, N = 5, Result_A, Result_B
! start program Divide
    Result_A = (L - M) / N * J                          ! (7 - 4) / 5 * 5 is zero
    Result_B = J * (L - M) / N                            ! 5 * (7 - 4) / 5 is 3
    print *, J, L, M, N, Result_A, Result_B
  end program Divide
```

Mixed-Type Assignment and Expressions

Mixed-Type Assignment

Fortran permits mixed-type assignment among the three numeric data types, integer, real and complex. That is, expressions of any numeric type may be assigned to variables of any other numeric type. Fortran applies *type coercion* (automatic conversion) to the expression result, after it has been completely evaluated, to obtain a value of the same data type as the variable to which it will be assigned.

If the assignment statement has the form

Real variable = *Integer expression*

Fortran computes the value of the expression with integer arithmetic. Then the representation of this result is changed (coerced) to that of a real number with the same value. In effect, you could say that Fortran inserts a decimal point. Actually, it generates a number that has the same value but is represented according to the real Fortran 90 model (see Section 1.6), complete with significant digits and exponent. This real value is then assigned to the variable on the left.

If the assignment statement has the form

Integer variable = *Real expression*

Fortran first evaluates the expression with real arithmetic. To represent this result as an integer value and assign it to the variable on the left, Fortran must truncate the real value. In effect, Fortran deletes the decimal point along with all digits that would have appeared to the right of it since a value of integer type cannot have a decimal point or a fractional part.

To assign a complex expression to a real variable, Fortran deletes the imaginary part. For assignment to an integer variable, Fortran also truncates the real part to obtain an integer value. When Fortran assigns an integer expression or a real expression to a complex variable, the expression value becomes the real part of the complex variable and the imaginary part is set to zero.

Mixed-type Expressions

In all of the assignment statements in the foregoing examples, each statement contained variables and constants of a single data type throughout (except for real expressions raised to an integer power). When all operands in an expression have the same data type, the expression result has this same type. In particular, when Fortran divides two integer expressions, the result is automatically truncated to the next smaller integer (in absolute value), as we have seen.

Numerical expressions with mixed integer and real types are also permitted. Fortran automatically replaces the integer operand by an expression of real type having the same value before it performs the operation. In the following examples, suppose that `A` is a real variable and `I` is an integer:

```
I /5                                    ! Expression of integer type
3.2 * A                                 ! Expression of real type
I * A                                   ! Expression of real type
(I / 5) * (3.2 * A)                     ! Expression of real type
```

In the third example, the value of I is coerced to real type before the multiplication is performed. In the fourth example, (I / 5) is computed as an expression of integer type, whose value is then coerced to real type before the multiplication is performed.

So, any operation having one operand of integer type and the other of real type produces a result of real type. Except for exponentiation of a real expression to an integer power (which is interpreted as repeated multiplication), Fortran coerces the integer operand to real type before performing the operation. As another example, an expression to compute the average of the real variables X and Y could be written as

```
(X + Y) / 2
```

The integer constant 2 will be coerced to real type, and the result will be computed correctly.

Fortran also permits mixed-type numerical expressions that include complex operands. That is, any operation having one operand of integer or real type and the other of complex type produces a result of complex type. Except for raising a complex expression to an integer power, which is interpreted as repeated multiplication, Fortran coerces the integer or real operand to complex type (with zero imaginary part) before performing the operation.

Type Conversion Functions

Many Fortran programmers find that mixed-type expressions or mixed-type assignment can introduce programming mistakes that are hard to locate. The coercion process is so automatic that they sometimes forget that Fortran performs this extra execution step. Fortran provides the type conversion functions Real, Int, and Cmplx, which make type changes obvious.

The remainder of this section introduces these functions to explain type conversion. Section 2.3 considers these functions in greater detail, along with other functions for converting from real to integer type. (See also Appendix A for a complete description of the Fortran library of intrinsic functions.)

A function reference whose argument has one type and whose result has a different type is not considered a mixed-type expression. The type conversion functions Real and Int therefore avoid some of the disadvantages of automatic type coercion:

```
implicit none
real :: X, Average, Total
integer :: I, J, Number
X = Real (I + 3) / 3.0
J = Int (X) + I
Average = Total / Real (Number)
```

In each of these three assignment statements, the variable on the left of the assignment operator has the same data type as the expression on the right. Furthermore, in each expression on the right, the two operands of each operator have the same data type.

The type conversion function `Real` may be applied to an expression of integer type to produce an expression of real type:

`Real (` *Integer expression* `)`

This function may also be applied to a complex argument:

`Real (` *Complex expression* `)`

The value of this result is the real part of the argument; the result type is real.

The type conversion function `Int`, when applied to an expression of real type, produces a result of integer type:

`Int (` *Real expression* `)`

Truncation to the next smaller integer in absolute value (as with integer division or mixed-type assignment) is applied to the value of the real expression so that the function value can be represented as an integer. (Other intrinsic functions, `Floor`, `Ceiling`, and `NInt`, which also convert a real argument to integer type, are described in Section 2.3.) The function `Int` may also be applied to a complex argument. The value of

`Int (` *Complex expression* `)`

is obtained by truncating the real part of the argument.

The type conversion function `Cmplx` may be applied to an expression of real type to produce an expression of complex type:

`Cmplx (` *Real expression* `)`

The real part of the complex result is the same as the argument value; the imaginary part of the result is zero. This function may also be applied to an integer argument: the argument is converted first to real type and then to complex type. The function `Cmplx` may have two arguments of integer or real type. The result of

`Cmplx (` *Real expression* `,` *Real expression* `)`

is a complex value whose real part is obtained from the first argument and whose imaginary part is obtained from the second argument. If either argument is an integer, it will be converted to real type.

Interpreting Statements with Mixed Types

It is especially important to observe the order of evaluation of subexpressions in a statement that involves mixing of data types. In particular, integer division may truncate the value of a subexpression before it is coerced to real type. Consider the two assignment statements in Example 2.11.

EXAMPLE 2.11

```
! Example 2.11. Two assignments with mixed types.
  program Mixed_Types
    implicit none
    real :: A = 3.0
    integer :: K = 3, M1, M2
! start program Mixed_Types
      M1 = (A / 4) * K                                      ! M = (3.0 / 4) * 3
      M2 = (K / 4) * A                                      ! M = (3 / 4) * 3.0
    print *, M1, M2
  end program Mixed_Types
```

These two statements might be expected to produce identical results, but analysis reveals that the first assignment statement is interpreted as if it were written as

`M1 = Int ((A / Real (4)) * Real (K))`

while the second assignment is interpreted as

`M2 = Int (Real (K / 4) * A)`

The final value of `M1` is 2, while the final value of `M2` is 0.

Truncation may occasionally produce unexpected results because many numbers cannot be represented exactly in a computer with finite numerical precision and range. For instance, the result of dividing `1.0` by `3.0` (with real arithmetic) is 0.33333 . . . , which is slightly less than 1/3. Multiplying this result by `3.0` will not produce `1.0` but rather 0.99999 . . . ; truncating this value, you obtain 0 rather than 1.

What are the values assigned when the program in Example 2.12 is executed?

EXAMPLE 2.12

```
! Example 2.12. Unexpected results due to truncation (thirds).
  program Thirds
    implicit none
    real :: R = 3.0, X
    integer :: L, M, N
! start program Thirds
    X = 1.0 / R1                                           ! Set X to 0.33333....
    L = 3.0 * X                         ! Truncate 0.99999... and assign 0.
    M = R * X                           ! Truncate 0.99999... and assign 0.
    N = X + X + X                       ! Truncate 0.99999... and assign 0.
    print *, R, X, L, M, N
  end program Thirds
```

The values of L, M, and N will all be set to zero because of the truncation that occurs along with the automatic data type coercion.

Particularly insidious is the fact that, because most computers employ a binary number representation, some simple decimal fractions (such as 0.1 and 0.02) are approximated in the computer by slightly smaller numbers (which you may think of as 0.0999 . . . , 0.0199 . . . , etc.). Thus, in binary arithmetic, the Fortran assignment statements in Example 2.13 will also give zero as the values of L, M, and N.

EXAMPLE 2.13

```
! Example 2.13. Unexpected results due to truncation (tenths).
  program Insidious
    implicit none
    real :: R = 10.0, X
    integer :: L, M, N
! start program Insidious
    X = 1.0 / R ! Set X to 0.09999···
    L = 10.0 * X
    M = R * X
    N = X + X + X + X + X + X + X + X + X + X
    print *, R, X, L, M, N
  end program Insidious
```

The same truncations are produced by explicit type conversion (with the functions Real and Int). Appearance of the explicit conversion functions in a statement calls attention to the fact that truncation may be taking place, however, so you may be able to avoid hidden errors that might have occurred with expressions of mixed type. It takes very few seconds longer to write

```
(A / 4.0) * Real (K)
Real (K / 4) * A
```

and these expressions are in a form that makes evident the difference between their values. The shorter mixed-type expressions

```
(A / 4) * K
(K / 4) * A
```

may seem more convenient at first, but if you misinterpret the expressions, the time you will spend locating the error may be substantially greater than the time it would have taken to put in the explicit conversion functions.

Mixed-type Exponentiation

Recall the special rules for mixed-type exponentiation: An expression for raising a real expression to an integer power, such as `R ** I`, is already a real expression, and Fortran interprets it merely as repeated multiplication. Fortran interprets a complex expression raised to an integer power, such as `C ** I`, in a similar way. On the other hand, in an expression of the form `I ** R` or `I ** C`, Fortran coerces the operand `I` to real or complex type before performing the exponentiation.

A problem may arise when integer division occurs in the exponent. If you try to compute the square root of `X` by writing, for example,

```
X ** (1 / 2)
```

the integer division will be performed first, with truncation, and the effect will be the same as if you had written

```
X ** 0
```

For correct results, the exponent could be written as the ratio of two real expressions

```
X ** (1.0 / 2.0)
```

or as a real constant,

```
X ** 0.5
```

In this particular case, an even better solution is the intrinsic function `SqRt (X)`.

Transition Tip

- (Optional) Where automatic type coercion occurs in expressions, insert type conversion intrinsic functions instead.

2.2 Exercises

1. Assume that `RP`, `RL`, `RW`, and `Pi` are real variables; that `I`, `J`, `K`, and `L` are integer variables; and that `SqRt` is the Fortran square root intrinsic function. Which of the following are valid Fortran assignment statements?

   a. `RP = 2.0 * (RL + RW)`

   b. `I = I + 1`

   c. `I + 1 = I`

   d. `L = I + J + K`

   e. `3.14159 = Pi`

   f. `SqRt (4.0) = 2.0`

2. Let J, K, KK, and L be declared as follows:

```
integer :: J = 2, K = 2, KK = 7, L = -3
```

What is the value of each of the following Fortran expressions?

a. `J * (K - KK) / (9 + L)`

b. `J * ((K - KK) / (9 + L))`

c. `(J * (K - KK) / 9 + L)`

d. `(J * (K - KK)) / (9 + L)`

3. Let A, B, C, and D be declared as follows:

```
real :: A = 2.0, B = 3.0, C = 2.0, D = 3.0
```

What is the value of each of the following Fortran expressions?

a. `A * B / C ** D`

b. `(A * B / C) ** D`

c. `A * (B / C) ** D`

4. Let the real variables A, B, Theta, and XYZ and the integer variables I, J, and K be declared as follows:

```
real :: A = 1.0, B = 3.5, Theta = 10.0, XYZ = 5.0
integer :: I = 5. J = 7, K = 3
```

What is the value of each of the following Fortran expressions?

a. `-(A + Theta)`

b. `(B + (XYZ / Theta)) / (4.0 * A)`

c. `(I * J) / K`

d. `I * (J / K)`

e. `(I / K) * J`

f. `-(K + 7) / J`

5. Let the real variables A, B, Theta, and XYZ and the integer variables I, J, and K be declared as follows:

```
real :: A = 1.0, B = 3.5, Theta = 10.0, XYZ = 5.0
integer :: I = 5. J = 7, K = 3
```

What is the data type and the value of each of the following Fortran expressions?

a. `-(A + Theta - 2) / 3`

b. `(B + (XYZ / Theta)) / (J - K)`

c. `(I * J) / K + 1.0`

d. `I * (J / K) + 1.0`

e. `(I / K) * J + 1.0`

f. `-(K + 7) / J + 1.0`

6. With the same variable values as in Exercise 1 here, what is the data type and the value of each of the following Fortran expressions?

a. `I / J`

b. `Real (I) / Real (J)`

c. `Real(I) / J`

d. `I / Real (J)`

e. `(I + 0.0) / (J + 0.0)`

f. `(I / J) + 0.0`

2.3 NUMERICAL INTRINSIC FUNCTIONS

A Selection of Intrinsic Functions

The Fortran 90 language provides an extensive library of *intrinsic functions* for performing a number of valuable operations that are more complicated than the simple arithmetic operations of addition, subtraction, multiplication, division, negation, and exponentiation. Fortran recognizes these functions by name and automatically makes them available to the program. Descriptions of all the functions in the standard Fortran intrinsic function library are listed in Appendix A.

The following sections summarize some of the more important functions that require numerical arguments and produce numerical results. These include *type conversion* functions, *numerical utility* functions, and *elementary mathematical* functions.

A reference to an intrinsic function consists of the function name followed by a list of arguments enclosed in parentheses. Most of these functions take a single argument. If there are two or more arguments, they must be separated by commas. The data type of the result from each function reference is defined by Fortran and may depend upon the types of the arguments. A function reference may appear in any expression, provided that the result type is acceptable.[3]

[3] There are some exceptions. For example, some functions are prohibited in initialization expressions.

Fortran restricts the types permitted for each argument when any of these functions is referenced. It is essential that the number and data type (and `kind` subtype) of arguments agree with the specifications in the definition of the functions (see Appendix A). A function argument of the wrong data type will *not* be coerced automatically to an acceptable type. Some Fortran processors do not even detect such errors and may produce unexpected results. For example, `SqRt(2)` and `SqRt(I)` are not valid Fortran expressions when `I` has integer type. Type conversion as in, for example, `SqRt(Real(I))`, will produce a valid result.

Expressions with function references are illustrated in Example 2.14.

EXAMPLE 2.14

```
! Example 2.14. Examples of Fortran intrinsic library functions.
  program Library
    implicit none
    intrinsic ATan2, Exp, SqRt, Abs
    real :: A, B, C, Term
! start program Library
    print *, ATan2 (0.0, -1.0), Exp (1.0)
    read *, A, B, C
    Term = SqRt (Abs (B ** 2 - 4.0 * A * C))
    print *, A
  end program Library
```

The statement on the fourth line of Example 2.14 is an `intrinsic` specification statement, which lists all of the intrinsic function names that appear in the program. (This statement is not required, but it helps a reader of the program to recall the meaning of the function names. Furthermore, Fortran can check for misspelled function names by verifying that each function named in the `intrinsic` specification is actually present in the Fortran intrinsic function library.) The result from `ATan2 (Y, X)` is the arctangent (between 0 and 2π radians) of `Y/X`, and `Exp` is the exponential function. The expression `Abs (B ** 2 - 4.0 * A * C)` gives the absolute value of the quadratic discriminant, and the intrinsic function `SqRt` computes its square root.

Further examples of expressions with function references are given in Example 2.15.

EXAMPLE 2.15

```
    Modulo (Minute, 60)
    Max (Abs (I - 5), I, 1)
    SqRt (SqRt (A))
    1 + NInt (SqRt (Real (Abs (J))))
```

Note that each argument may be any expression of an acceptable data type; it may include arithmetic operations, as well as references to other functions or even to the same function. However, some restrictions apply to the argument *values* for mathematical reasons. For example, the argument of `SqRt` must not be negative, the second argument of `Modulo` (remainder from integer division) must not be zero, and the argument of `Log` (natural logarithm) must be positive.

The function name, along with the arguments in parentheses, forms a *function reference* expression. This expression can be employed in the same way as any other expression. Thus, we may add a rule, similar to rule 1 of Section 2.2, to cover the evaluation of expressions that contain functions:

- Rule 4. Function evaluation always occurs *before* the value of the function reference expression is combined with other parts of the expression. Expressions that occur as function arguments will be completely evaluated as the first step in evaluating any subexpression. If an expression in the argument list includes a function, the inner function takes precedence.

Example 2.16 shows how rule 4 applies to a function reference expression.

EXAMPLE 2.16

Expression	Rule	Replace		Result
`SqRt (SqRt (A))`	4	`SqRt (A)`	by	`R1`
`SqRt (R1)`		`SqRt (R1)`	by	`R2`
`R2`				

Type Conversion Functions

Operation	Function name	Number of arguments	Type of arguments	Type of result
Type conversion	`Real`	1 or 2	Integer, real, or complex	Real
Type conversion with truncation toward 0	`Int`	1 or 2	Integer, real or complex	Integer
Type conversion with truncation toward -∞	`Floor`	1	Real	Integer
Type conversion with truncation toward ∞	`Ceiling`	1	Real	Integer
Type conversion with rounding	`NInt`	1 or 2	Real	Integer
Rounding	`ANInt`	1 or 2	Real	Real
Truncation	`AInt`	1 or 2	Real	Real

Note that Fortran 90 provides one function for converting from integer type to real, and four different functions for converting from real type to integer. (The data type of the result is specific to the function and is independent of the data type of the argument expression. The five functions `Real`, `Int`, `NInt`, `ANInt`, and `AInt` each have an optional second argument of integer type that specifies the subtype of the result; see Section 1.6.)

1. `Real` converts from integer type to real type. The result has the same numerical value as the argument, and its type is real.
2. `Int` truncates toward zero. The type of the result is integer, and its value is the nearest integer whose absolute value is less than or equal to the absolute value of the argument. `Int` gives the same result as `Floor` for positive arguments and the same result as `Ceiling` for negative arguments. This function performs the same kind of truncation that occurs during data type coercion in mixed-type assignment, in the evaluation of mixed-type expressions, and in integer division.
3. `Floor` truncates toward $-\infty$. The type of the result is integer, and its value is the nearest integer that is less than or equal to the argument.
4. `Ceiling` truncates toward ∞. The type of the result is integer, and its value is the nearest integer that is greater than or equal to the argument.
5. `NInt` rounds the argument expression. The type of the result is integer, and its value is the integer nearest to the argument. If the fractional part of `R` is exactly `0.5`, the value of `NInt(R)` is the next *larger* integer in absolute value. (See Example 2.17 or Appendix A.)

Each of the four real-to-integer conversion functions `Floor`, `Ceiling`, `NInt`, and `Int` accepts an argument of real type and returns an integer near the argument value. If the argument value is exactly a whole number, any of these functions returns a result whose value is the same as that of the argument. For argument values very close to a whole number, however, only `NInt` always gives a result whose value is very close to that of the argument.

Two other functions accept an argument of real type and round or truncate to produce a result that is a whole number near the argument value. However, the result type is real. The functions are as follows:

1. `ANInt` rounds to the nearest whole number. The result is the whole number nearest to the argument, and its type is real. An application for this function is rounding a real value to the nearest integer without changing the type.
2. `AInt` truncates to the next smaller whole number (absolute). The result is the nearest whole number whose absolute value is less than or equal to the argument, and its type is real.

The data type of the argument expression for `Real` or `Int` may be integer or real. Note that `Real` may be applied to a real argument, and `Int` may be applied to an integer argument. These type combinations are permitted for completeness or for changing the `kind` parameter as described shortly.

The type conversion functions are compared in Example 2.17.

EXAMPLE 2.17

Argument Value	Result Value AInt	Int	ANInt	NInt	Floor	Ceiling
-2.000	-2.0	-2	-2.0	-2	-2	-2
-1.999	-1.0	-1	-2.0	-2	-2	-1
-1.500	-1.0	-1	-2.0	-2	-2	-1
-1.499	-1.0	-1	-1.0	1	-2	-1
-1.000	-1.0	-1	-1.0	1	-1	-1
-0.999	0.0	0	-1.0	1	-1	0
-0.500	0.0	0	-1.0	1	-1	0
-0.499	0.0	0	0.0	0	1	0
0.000	0.0	0	0.0	0	0	0
0.499	0.0	0	0.0	0	0	1
0.500	0.0	0	1.0	1	0	1
0.999	0.0	0	1.0	1	0	1
1.000	1.0	1	1.0	1	1	1
1.499	1.0	1	1.0	1	1	2
1.500	1.0	1	2.0	2	1	2
1.999	1.0	1	2.0	2	1	2
2.000	2.0	2	2.0	2	2	2

Complex arguments and results (Advanced). The functions `Int` and `Real` also accept arguments of complex type. The type of the result is integer or real, is specific to each function, and is not affected by the type of the argument expression. The result value is based on the real part of the complex argument; the imaginary part is ignored.

The type conversion function `Cmplx` may be applied to an expression of real type to produce an expression of complex type:

`Cmplx (` *Real expression* `)`

The real part of the complex result is the same as the argument value; the imaginary part of the result is zero. This function may also be applied to an integer argument. The argument is converted first to real type and then to complex type. The function `Cmplx` may have two arguments of integer or real type. The result of

`Cmplx (` *Real expression* `,` *Real expression* `)`

is a complex value whose real part is obtained from the first argument and whose imaginary part is obtained from the second argument. If either argument is an integer, it will be converted to real type.

The `kind` parameter (Optional). The type conversion intrinsic functions accept arguments with any subtype (see Section 1.6). If any of these functions is referenced with one argument, the subtype of the result is the default and is not affected by the subtype of the argument.

Six of the type conversion functions — namely `Real`, `Int`, `NInt`, `ANInt`, `AInt`, and `Cmplx` — have an optional `Kind` argument (see Section 1.6), which, if present, selects a `kind` parameter for the result. The function `Real` applied to a real argument or `Int` applied to an integer argument or `Cmplx` applied to a complex argument, with the `Kind` argument present, changes the subtype of the argument expression without changing its type or its value.

Another function, traditionally classified as a type conversion function, is now viewed as performing `kind` conversion. The function `Dble` (see Section 1.6), with one argument of integer, real, or complex type with any subtype, produces the same result as `Real`, except that the subtype of the result is that of traditional double precision.

Numerical Utility Functions

Operation	Function name	Number of arguments	Type of arguments	Type of result
Absolute value	`Abs`	1	Integer, real, or complex	Integer or real
Maximum	`Max`	2 or more	Integer or real	Generic
Minimum	`Min`	2 or more	Integer or real	Generic
Sign transfer	`Sign`	2	Integer or real	Generic
Excess	`Dim`	2	Integer or real	Generic
Remainder with `Floor`	`Modulo`	2	Integer or real	Generic
Remainder with `Int`	`Mod`	2	Integer or real	Generic

Note that the intrinsic function `Abs` will produce a result of real type when its argument is a real or complex expression, but the result has integer type when its argument is an integer expression. Note also that the result type for several of these functions is generic. Such a function accepts arguments of more than one type and returns a result of the same type as that of the argument. When such a function has two or more arguments, all must have the same type at a given reference.

The type of the argument expression for any of the functions in this group may be integer or real; if there are two or more arguments, all must have the same type:

1. `Abs` produces the absolute value. If the type of the argument is integer or real, the value of the result is obtained by ignoring the sign of the argument. (The result is always positive or zero.)

2. `Max` produces the largest argument value (two or more arguments). The result takes the value of the (algebraically) largest of its arguments.
3. `Min` produces the smallest argument value (two or more arguments). The result takes the value of the (algebraically) smallest of its arguments.
4. `Sign` transfers the sign of the second argument to the first argument. The magnitude of the result is obtained from the first argument and the sign of the result is obtained from the second argument. (The sign of the first argument and the magnitude of the second argument are ignored.)
5. `Dim` gives a nonnegative difference after subtracting the second argument from the first. If the difference is positive or zero, it is taken as the value of the result; if the difference is negative, the result is zero.
6. `Modulo` gives the remainder from integer division based on `Floor`; that is, `Modulo (A, P)` is `A – P * Floor (Real (A) / Real (P))`.
7. `Mod` gives the remainder from integer division based on `Int`; that is, `Mod (A, P)` is `A – P * Int (A / P)`.

The two remainder functions, `Modulo` and `Mod`, are discussed in more detail later in this section.

In the following function reference expressions, assume that the types of `J` and `K` are integer, the types of `X` and `Z` are real, and the value of `J` is 3, `K` is 5, `X` is –2.5, and `Z` is 7.8.

EXAMPLE 2.18

Function reference	Value	Function reference	Value
`Real (J)`	3.0	`Sign (1.0, X)`	–1.0
`ANInt (X)`	–2.0	`Dim (Z, 8.0)`	0.0
`ANInt (Z)`	8.0	`Max (X, 0.0, Z)`	7.8
`Abs (X)`	2.5	`Min (J, K)`	–5
`Modulo (K, J)`	2	`SqRt (9.0)`	3.0
`Mod (K, J)`	2	`Log10 (10000.0)`	5.0

Complex arguments and results (Advanced). The function `Abs` may be applied to a complex argument to produce a real result (the absolute value of the complex number). None of the other functions in this group accepts arguments of complex type. Note that this function is the only one in this group whose result type can be different from the argument type.

The `kind` parameter (Optional). For the numerical utility functions, the argument expression may have any subtype. If there are two or more arguments, all must have the same subtype. For any of the functions in this group, the `kind` parameter of the result is the same as that of the argument expression. If `Abs` is applied to a complex argument, the result is real with the same `kind` parameter as the argument.

Elementary Mathematical Functions

Operation	Function name	Number of arguments	Type of arguments	Type of result
Inverse cosine	ACos	1	Real	Real
Inverse sine	ASin	1	Real	Real
Inverse tangent	ATan	1	Real	Real
Inverse tangent	ATan2	2	Real	Real
Cosine	Cos	1	Real or complex	Generic
Double precision product	DProd	2	Real or complex	Generic
Hyperbolic cosine	CosH	1	Real	Real
Exponential	Exp	1	Real or complex	Generic
Natural logarithm	Log	1	Real or complex	Generic
Common logarithm	Log10	1	Real or complex	Generic
Sine	Sin	1	Real or complex	Generic
Hyperbolic sine	SinH	1	Real or complex	Generic
Square root	SqRt	1	Real	Real
Tangent	Tan	1	Real or complex	Generic
Hyperbolic tangent	TanH	1	Real	Real

The result type for several of these funcions is *generic*. Such a function accepts arguments of more than one type and returns a result of the same type as that of the argument. When such a function has two or more arguments, all must have the same type at a given reference.

The function values are defined as in mathematics. Arguments of the trigonometric functions are in radians. Results of inverse trigonometric functions are between $-\pi/2$ and $\pi/2$, except for ATan2, whose result is between $-\pi$ and π. For more details, see Appendix A. Note the function DProd, which accepts two arguments of default real type and returns their double-precision product.

Complex arguments and results (Advanced). The intrinsic functions Cos, Exp, Log, Log10, Sin, SqRt, and Tan accept arguments of real or complex type. The data type of the result is the same as that of the argument. The other functions in this group (the inverse trigonometric functions, the hyperbolic functions, and `DProd`) require arguments of real type.

Fortran provides additional intrinsic functions for applications with complex type. The function `Conjg` computes the complex conjugate. The functions `Real` and `AImag` return the real and imaginary parts of a complex expression argument as results of real data type. (See Appendix A.)

The `kind` parameter (Optional). For the elementary mathematical functions, the argument expression may have any subtype. If there are two or more arguments, all must have the same type and subtype. The type and subtype of the result are the same as those of the argument expression. `AImag` or `Real` may be applied to a complex argument of any subtype to produce a result of real type with the same subtype as the argument. The function result for `Conjg` also has the same subtype as its argument.

Some Applications of Intrinsic Functions

Rounding

The "nearest integer" or rounding function `NInt` is usually preferable to `Int` for producing a value of integer type corresponding to a given real value, except where it is important to simulate the truncation that occurs automatically during implicit type coercion.

`NInt` requires an argument of real type and produces a result of integer type. The value of the result is the whole number nearest to the value of the argument; if the argument is exactly midway between two integer values, it is rounded up if positive and down to a more negative integer if negative.

This function avoids some of the more troublesome effects of truncation that were mentioned in Section 2.2.

EXAMPLE 2.19

```
! Example 2.19. Compare Example 2.12.
  program Vicinity
    implicit none
    intrinsic NInt
    real :: R = 3.0, X
    integer :: L, M, N
! start program Vicinity
    X = 1.0 / R                                            ! Set X to 0.33333···
    L = NInt (3.0 * X)                     ! Round 0.99999··· and assign 1
    M = NInt (R * X)                       ! Round 0.99999··· and assign 1
    N = NInt (X + X + X)                   ! Round 0.99999··· and assign 1
  end program Vicinity
```

The statements in Example 2.19 set the values of L, M, and N to 1, as expected. On the other hand, automatic type coercion (described in Section 2.2) or the function `Int` will produce zero values for L, M, and N.

As another example, the integer nearest the square root of N may be obtained as the value of the expression `NInt (SqRt (Real (N)))`.

Integer Division with Remainder

Some applications require the remainder from integer division. For instance, the easiest way to test whether one integer can be divided exactly by another is to perform the division and see if the remainder is zero. This idea suggests the possibility of breaking down an integer into its prime factors or of finding the greatest common divisor of two integers.

Another example is a cyclical number system, which repeats after a certain number is reached, such as the hours in the day. For example, to find the time five hours later than the hour of eleven o'clock, you may add 5 to 11 and then find the remainder after dividing by 12.

To find the lowest digit of a decimal number, you need the remainder upon division by 10. Similarly, the remainder from division by 100 or 1000 gives the lowest two digits or three digits, respectively.

The remainder from division of A by P is given by the Fortran expression `Modulo (A, P)`. For example, the value of `Modulo (11 + 5, 12)` is 4, corresponding to the fact that eleven o'clock plus five hours is four o'clock.

If the types of A and P are real and the value of P is not zero, then `Floor (Real (A) / Real (P))` and `Modulo (A, P)` form a matched pair, one giving the quotient (truncated algebraically to the next lower integer) and the other giving the remainder. The remainder produced by the function `Modulo` will correspond exactly to the quotient. That is, in the following sequence of assignment statements,

```
Q = Floor (Real (A) / Real (P))
R = Modulo (A, P)
X = P * Q + R
```

it will always be true (unless P is zero) that the final value of X will be identical to the original value of A.

To see precisely what result will be produced by the function `Modulo` for arguments of real type, you may imagine computing the remainder by hand, in the following way:

1. Divide the first argument by the second.
2. Truncate the quotient to the (algebraically) next lower integer — that is, to `Floor (Real (A) / Real (P))`.
3. Multiply the truncated quotient by the second argument, and subtract the product from the first argument.

This process may be recognized as analogous to the process of long division taught in elementary arithmetic. The truncated quotient corresponds to the successful trial divisor in the long division process.

The two arguments in any particular reference to the function must both have the same data type. If both arguments have integer type and are *positive*, the truncated quotient value is the same as that obtained from integer division according to the rules of Fortran.

Notice that there are two remainder functions. `Modulo` is the modulo or modulus function, as defined in mathematics and usually written *A modulo P*. The function `Mod` has a similar purpose and produces a result identical to `Modulo` if `A` and `P` have the same sign. The definition of `Mod` is based on `Int` rather than `Floor`. The function `Mod` is retained for compatibility with previous versions of Fortran that lacked the `Floor` function. The two remainder functions are compared in Example 2.20.

EXAMPLE 2.20

Function reference	Value	Function reference	Value
`Modulo (8.0, 5.0)`	3.0	`Mod (8.0, 5.0)`	3.0
`Modulo (8, 5)`	3	`Mod (8, 5)`	3
`Modulo (8, –5)`	–2	`Mod (8, –5)`	3
`Modulo (–8, 5)`	2	`Mod (–8, 5)`	–3
`Modulo (–8, –5)`	–3	`Mod (–8, –5)`	–3

Disconnecting the Sign of a Number

The function `Abs` produces the magnitude (absolute value) of a number of integer or real type, ignoring the algebraic sign of the argument. The function `Sign`, on the other hand, ignores the magnitude and produces a result that depends only on the algebraic sign of its argument.

Storing and processing a disembodied sign would be difficult and awkward, however. Accordingly, the function `Sign` transfers the sign of its second argument to another number specified as the first argument. For example, if the first argument is 1, then the function value is +1 if the second argument is positive or –1 if the second argument is negative. Both arguments must have the same data type, and the type of the result is defined to be the type of the arguments.

What is the sign of the result when the value of the second argument is zero? In some applications, either sign would be satisfactory, but you might like to know in advance what result will be produced in this case. Fortran decrees that the result of `Sign` is positive when the second argument is zero. Thus, the value of `Sign (X, 0.0)` is exactly the same as the value of `Abs (X)`.

In mathematical applications, there is sometimes a need for a *signum* function. As defined in mathematics, signum has one argument; the function value is –1 if the argument is negative, 0 if the argument is zero, or +1 if the argument is positive. Except for the zero case, the value of signum x is the same as the value of `Sign (1.0, X)`. A more complicated expression that will give the desired mathematical result for all real argument values, including zero, is

```
Sign (0.5, X) - Sign (0.5, -X)
```

Concerning Integer Versus Real Exponents

As noted, a real expression may be raised to an *integer* power. How does this operation differ from raising a real expression to a *real* power? What is the difference between the two expressions A ** 2 and A ** 2.0 ? If A were 5.0, the value of each of these expressions would be 25.0. However, most processors evaluate an exponent of integer type more efficiently than one of real type if the exponent value is small. In translating the expression A ** 2, most Fortran processors generate the same computer code as for A * A. Similarly, for A ** 3, the equivalent of A * A * A is generated. If the value of the exponent is any small integer, the compiler generates a repetitive multiplication operation.

By contrast, evaluation of an expression with an exponent of real type (even if the value of the real exponent is a whole number) involves the application of the logarithm and exponent functions. If R and P represent any real expressions, the operation R ** P is evaluated in the form Exp (P * Log (R)). Execution of the logarithm and exponential functions is usually less efficient than multiplication and may introduce greater computational error. For this reason, exponents of integer type are generally preferred when the actual value of the exponent is an integer.

Further restrictions are imposed on the values of operands for exponentiation to avoid inherent mathematical difficulties. For example, an expression whose value is zero must not be raised to a negative or zero power, and a negative expression must not be raised to any real power. These restrictions are necessary because the values of such expressions are not well-defined real numbers in the mathematical sense.

The value of SqRt (X) should be expected, on mathematical grounds, to be the same as the value of X ** 0.5. The square root function is probably more efficient, and perhaps more accurate, on most Fortran processors.

Transition Tip

- (Optional) Consider changing the intrinsic function Int to NInt or Floor and changing Mod to Modulo.

2.3 Exercises

1. In each of the following assignment statements, wherever automatic coercion between integer and real types would occur, insert the type conversion function Real or Int to produce the same result. Assume that I, J, and K are integer variables and all other variables mentioned are real.

   a. `R = A + I`

   b. `W = I - 1.3 + J`

   c. `K = 2 / 3 * 6.6`

   d. `I = 123456789 + B`

   e. `P = X ** 5`

2. Let Z be a variable of complex type. Write statements that use the intrinsic functions `Real`, `AImag`, `Abs`, and `ATan2` (see Appendix A.2 and A.3) to compute the components of a polar representation of Z. (See also Examples 6.25, 7.1, 7.2, and 7.14.)

3. What will be printed when the following program is executed?

```
! Exercise 2.3, Problem 3.
  program Absolute
    Intrinsic Abs
    complex :: Z = (3.0, 4.0)
! start program Absolute
    print *, Abs (Z)
  end program Absolute
```

4. The period *T* of a simple pendulum of length *L* is given by the formula $T = 2\pi\sqrt{L/g}$.

   a. Write Fortran statements to evaluate this formula.

   b. Write a complete program that will read the length of a pendulum and print its period.

5. Conversion between Cartesian and spherical coordinates: Given a position in three-dimensional Cartesian coordinates (X, Y, Z), the corresponding spherical coordinates `R`, `Theta`, `Phi` are given by

```
R = Sqrt (X ** 2 + Y ** 2 + Z ** 2)
Theta = ATan2 (Y, X)
Phi = ATan2 (X ** 2 + Y ** 2, Z)
```

   The inverse relations are

```
X = R * Cos (Theta) * Sin (Phi)
Y = R * Sin (Theta) * Sin (Phi)
Z = R * Cos (Phi)
```

   Write a program to read X, Y, and Z, print the corresponding spherical coordinates, and then convert back to Cartesian coordinates for comparison. Use test data in all eight solid octants, such as (1.0, 1.0, 1.0), (1.0, 1.0, −1.0), (1.0, −1.0, 1.0), (1.0, −1.0, −1.0), (−1.0, 1.0, 1.0), (−1.0, 1.0, −1.0), (−1.0, −1.0, 1.0), (−1.0, −1.0, −1.0).

6. In the following expressions, check for arguments whose data type is unacceptable. Write the expressions correctly by changing the data types of constants, by applying explicit type coercion, or in some other way. Assume that the data types of `I`, `J`, and `Leg` are integer and that the types of Y and Z are real.

   a. `Abs(I + 1)`

   b. `SqRt (J)`

   c. `SqRt (Real (NInt (Y) + 1.0))`

d. `Abs (NInt (J + 3))`

e. `Modulo (Y, NInt (Z))`

f. `Exp (Real (Leg + 3.0))`

7. Write a Fortran expression equivalent to each of the following mathematical expressions:

a. $A \sin (\theta - t)$

b. $\sin \frac{y}{\sqrt{x^2 + y^2}}$

c. $\tan \theta$

d. $\sin 2\pi L$

e. $\sin \left(\tan^{-1} \frac{\sqrt{a^2 + b^2}}{|c|} \right)$

8. What is the value of the variable Z after the following sequence of assignment statements is executed?

```
X = 3.0
Y = 4.0
Z = SqRt (X ** 2 + Y ** 2)
```

9. How many boxes, each 0.18 meter wide, will fit side by side on a shelf 1.57 meters long? How many meters of shelf space must remain unoccupied because the shelf is too short to hold another box? Write Fortran expressions giving the answer to each of these questions.

10. What results will be printed by the following program?

```
! Exercises 2.3, Number 10.
program Conversions
  implicit none
  intrinsic AInt, ANInt, Ceiling, Dim, Floor, &
   Min, Mod, Int, NInt, Sign
  real :: X = -9.99
! start program Conversions
  print *, AInt (X), ANInt (X), Ceiling (X), &
   Floor (X), Int (X), NInt (X)
  print *, Mod (5, -3), Dim (3, 5), Min (-123, -122, 56789, 0)
  print *, Sign (X, 0.0), Sign (X, -0.0), Sign (X, +0.0)
end program Conversions
```

11. What results will be printed by the following program?

```
! Exercises 2.3, Number 11.
program Utilities
  implicit none
  intrinsic Abs, SqRt, Real, Sign, Modulo, Max, NInt
  real :: A = 16.0, B = 4.0, C = 0.25, Theta = -0.5, X = 4.0
  integer :: I = 1, J = -256, L = 4, M = 17, N = 8, Minute = 61
! start program Utilities
  print *, Abs (A) * B / C
  print *, SqRt (Real (((M - 9) / L) * N))
  print *, A * Sign (Theta, 1.0)
  print *, 0.5 * (SqRt (X) + A / SqRt (X))
  print *, Abs (I - 5)
  print *, Modulo (Minute, 60)
  print *, Max (Abs (I - 5), I, 1)
  print *, SqRt (SqRt (A))
  print *, SqRt (B ** 2 - 4.0 * A * C) / (2.0 * A)
  print *, 1 + NInt (SqRt (Real (Abs (J))))
end program Utilities
```

12. What results will be printed by the following program?

```
! Exercises 2.3, Number 12.
program Math
  implicit none
  intrinsic ACos, ASin, ATan, ATan2, Cmplx, Cos, CosH, Exp
  intrinsic Log, Log10, Sin, SinH, Tan, TanH
  real :: Pi, E
! start program Math
  Pi = ATan2 (0.0, -1.0)
  E = Exp (1.0)
  print *, Pi, 4.0 * ATan (1.0)
  print *, Sin (-Pi / 2), Cos (Pi), Tan (Pi / 4.0)
  print *, Log (E ** 1.234), Log10 (10000.0)
  print *, ACos (-1.0), ASin (-1.0)
  print *, CosH (0.0), SinH (0.0), TanH (0.0)
  print *, Exp (Cmplx (0.0, Pi))
end program Math
```

13. Test the proposed signum function described in Section 2.3. How should you test this function? What test values should you use?

14. Write a group of statements to perform each of the following tasks.

a. Diagonal of a box: Read real values A, B, C and compute $D=\sqrt{A^2+B^2+C^2}$. Use the following data:

A	B	C
3.0	4.0	12.0
3.2	3.2	3.0

b. Read positive integer values I1 and I2; print I1 and I2 as well as the truncated quotient I1 / I2 and the remainder. (Hint: Use the function Modulo.) Use the following data:

I1	I2
17	4
5	6
18	3
5	4

15. The text asserts that time in hours can be reduced by means of the function Modulo, with 12 as the second argument value. However, closer scrutiny reveals that the result from this function is in the range (0, 11), whereas hours conventionally run from 1 to 12.

a. Show how to write an expression with Modulo that will do all of the following: convert 0, 12, 24, . . . , to 12; leave all values between 1 and 11 (inclusive) unchanged; and reduce any value in each of the ranges (13, 23), (25, 35), (37, 47), . . . , to the range (1, 11).

b. The position of the minute hand of the clock at a certain instant is First_Minute minutes after the hour, where First_Minute is an integer between 0 and 59 (inclusive). Write an assignment statement that will set the value of the variable Second_Minute to the position of the minute hand More minutes later. (Hint: Use the function Modulo.) Incorporate this assignment statement into a program, reading the values of First_Minute and More and printing Second_Minute. Use the following data:

First_Minute	More
7	12
56	8
45	15
16	59
23	60
18	120

16. Making change: Find the amount of change from a dollar for a purchase of 99 cents or less. Here are some hints on designing the program.

1. It is probably simpler to work with integer variables representing cents, rather than with real variables representing dollars.
2. First find the amount of change, in cents:
```
Change_100 = 100 - Purchase
```
3. Find the number of 50-cent pieces (the largest coin) by integer division:
```
Number_50 = Change_100 / 50
```
4. Find the remainder by using the function `Modulo`. The amount of change that remains after taking as many 50-cent pieces as possible out of `Change_100` is given by the expression `Modulo (Change_100, 50)`:
```
Change_50 = Modulo (Change_100, 50)
```
5. Continue with steps similar to steps 3 and 4 to find `Number_25` and `Change_25`; then find `Number_10` and `Change_10`; and finally find `Number_5` and `Change_5`. That is, find the number of pieces of each coin and the remaining change, in order of decreasing value.
6. The remainder, after as many 5-cent pieces as possible have been taken out, is the number of 1-cent pieces. Following the previous pattern, the number of 1-cent pieces would be found by integer division:
```
Number_1 = Change_5 / 1
```
However, dividing by 1 has no effect, so this step can be simplified.

a. Write the necessary statements to read `Purchase` and to compute and print `Number_50`, `Number_25`, `Number_10`, `Number_5`, and `Number_1`.

b. Rewrite the program for the case in which there are no 50-cent pieces available; that is, start with 25-cent pieces.

c. Modify the program to take care of amounts up to $19.99 when the customer presents a $20 bill; that is, also compute and print `Number_1000`, `Number_500`, and `Number_100`.

d. Rewrite the program to read both `Purchase` (the amount of the purchase) and `Amount_Tendered` (the amount of money presented), assuming that the amount presented is more than the amount of the purchase and that the change is less than $20.00 (see `Amount_Tendered` in data that follows).

e. Rewrite the program, keeping all calculations in integer cents, but doing all input with real numbers.

Data for a and b	Data for c	Data for d and e	
Purchase	Purchase	Purchase	Amount tendered
17	13.09	16.95	20.95
9	19.99	29.99	39.98
1	16.95	19.99	33.08
75			

2.4 INTERNAL PROCEDURES

It is often appropriate to subdivide a computational task — especially a large one — into subtasks that can be developed and analyzed independently. The overall task may be organized as a set of *procedures* that implement the subtasks. Each procedure is then defined as an independent block of statements.

This process of subdivision is called *procedural refinement*. For example, you can subdivide a data processing task into three parts: input, computation, and output. You write a procedure for each of these parts, and a main program to connect the procedures together, as illustrated by Figure 2.6.

The first step in procedural refinement is to plan what the main program will do and what information it should transmit to and from each procedure. Then, during the development of each of the separate procedures, you concentrate on its internal details and on its relation to the main program. For the most part, you forget about the other procedures during this phase.

This *divide and conquer* approach has long been known as a technique for managing complex tasks. If you subdivide a large task into a few relatively independent chunks and then analyze each of the chunks without thinking too much about any of the others, you can keep the overall problem organization in mind surprisingly well.

From the viewpoint of the internal procedure, the main program is considered the *host*. A main program may contain more than one internal procedure. You must group the internal subprograms at the end of the main program and separate them from the body of the main program by a `contains` statement:

```
program Program name
  :
contains
  Internal subprograms
    :
end program Program name
```

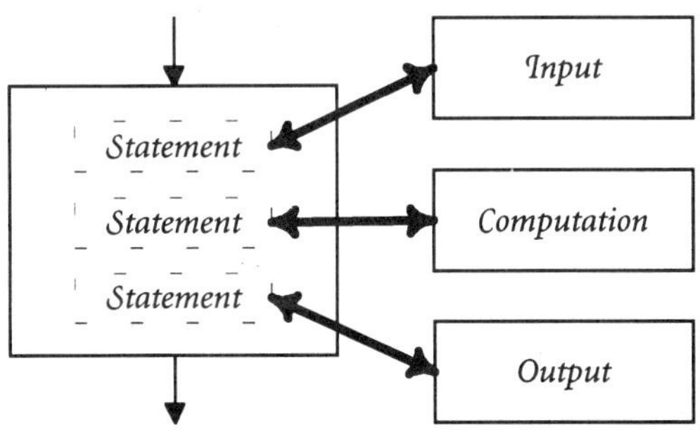

FIGURE 2.6. Internal procedures for input, computation, and output.

The `contains` statement declares that the following lines, to the end of the main program, contain definitions for internal subroutines or functions. Although several internal procedures may appear (following the `contains` statement) within the same main program, Fortran does not permit nesting of internal procedures within other internal procedures. (See also Figure 7.1.)

Defining an Internal Procedure

A Fortran procedure that returns a value is a *function*; one that does not return a value is a *subroutine*. A procedure begins with a `subroutine` or `function` statement that names the procedure and lists its *dummy arguments*.

If the procedure is a function, it must have a type. A function may have a *result variable* with a name that is different from the function name; inside the function, the value to be returned by the function will be assigned to the result variable. It is recommended that you use a separate result variable and that you specify the data type of the result in the `function` statement; alternatives are described in Section 7.3.

A `function` statement, according to these recommendations, has the following form:

Type `function` *Function name* `(` *Dummy arg list* `)` `result` `(` *Result name* `)`

The *Type* applies to the result name inside the procedure and to the function reference expression in the main program. The *Function name* is followed by a parenthesized list of dummy arguments. If the function requires no arguments (the list is empty), the parentheses must *not* be omitted:

```
real function Temp_C (FT) result (FT)
real function Temp_F () result (FT)
```

A `subroutine` statement has the following form:

`subroutine` *Subroutine name* `(` *Dummy arg list* `)`

The *Subroutine name* is followed by a parenthesized list of dummy arguments. If the subroutine requires no arguments (the list is empty), the parentheses may be omitted:

```
subroutine Output (FT, CT)
subroutine Calorimeter ()
subroutine Calorimeter
```

No `implicit none` statement is needed in an internal procedure if there is one in the main program because the requirement for explicit type declaration of all variables is "inherited" from the main program. (See also Appendix D.1.)

Dummy argument names and names whose type (or other attributes) are declared in the procedure are *local names* in the procedure. If the same name is declared in the main program or in another procedure, it refers to a different object.

On the other hand, some nonlocal names may be referenced within an internal procedure. (For example, a named constant declared in the main program might appear in the length specification for a character string in an internal procedure.) For data objects that are not dummy arguments of the procedure and are not declared within the procedure, the data type and other attributes are established in the main program. We say that such objects are *inherited* from the main program. (Standard Fortran 90 terminology for this concept is *host association*.)

Procedure Reference

A reference to an internal procedure may appear anywhere in the main program or in any internal procedure contained in the main program. Execution of a procedure reference interrupts the normal Fortran execution sequence, which then continues from the first instruction of the procedure. Thus, execution of a procedure reference implies execution of statements in the procedure. When the procedure terminates, the main program (or the internal procedure from which the procedure reference originated) resumes its execution sequence immediately following the procedure reference.

A reference to a procedure may have either of two forms:

1. A reference to a *function* produces a value, so a function reference appears as part of an expression.
2. A reference to a *subroutine* does not return a value. A subroutine reference appears as a separate `call` statement.

Either kind of procedure reference must mention the procedure name and may include a parenthesized list of *actual arguments*. The correspondence between actual arguments and dummy arguments is usually positional: The first actual argument is substituted for the first dummy argument, and so on. (See Section 8.7 for an exception to this positional correspondence rule.)

A `call` statement that refers to a subroutine consists of the keyword `call` followed by the subroutine name and the argument list. If there are no actual arguments, the parentheses may be omitted:

`call` *Subroutine name* `(` *Actual arg list* `)`

A reference to a function is an expression consisting of the function name with its argument list. The parentheses must appear even if the argument list is empty.

`...` *Function name* `(` *Actual arg list* `) ...`

A function reference is executed during evaluation of the expression in which it appears. The function returns a *result value* that becomes the value of the function reference expression.

A function has a type, which is specified as part of the function definition. The function result must be a single value, which may be a simple (scalar) value or a composite (array, string, or derived-type structure) value.[4] For a composite value, two or more scalar assignment operations in the function may be required to establish all parts of the result.

---

[4] A function result may also have the `pointer` attribute (see Section 6.3).

The program in Example 2.21 is duplicated from an example presented earlier (Example P.9). It consists of a main program and three procedures: one for input, one for computation, and one for output.

The input procedure is a function named Temp_F. This function has an empty argument list. It reads a Fahrenheit temperature value and returns it as the function result.

The computation procedure is a function named Temp_C, which accepts a Fahrenheit temperature value and uses it to compute the Celsius temperature. Note that the two named constants SCALE and OFFSET are used in the function Temp_C but are declared in the main program.

The output procedure is a subroutine with two arguments, which are the Fahrenheit and Celsius temperatures. This procedure displays the two argument values.

EXAMPLE 2.21

```
! Example 2.21. Temperature Conversion Program with Internal Procedures.
 program Con_Temp
   implicit none
   real, parameter :: SCALE = 1.8, OFFSET = 32.0
   real :: Fahr, Cels
! start program Con_Temp
   Fahr = Temp_F ()                               ! Reference to function Temp_F
   Cels = Temp_C (Fahrenheit_Temp)                         ! Reference to Temp_C
   call Output (Fahr, Cels)                               ! Subroutine reference
 contains
   real function Temp_F () result (FT)
     print *, "␣Please␣enter␣the␣Fahrenheit␣temperature.␣"
     read *, FT
   end function Temp_F
   real function Temp_C (FT) result (CT)
     real :: FT
     CT = (FT - OFFSET) / SCALE
   end function Temp_C
   subroutine Output (FT, CT)
     real :: FT, CT
     print *, FT, "␣deg.␣F␣=␣", CT, "␣deg.␣C␣"
   end subroutine Output
 end program Con_Temp
```

Several observations are in order:

1. Each procedure is defined in a sequence of statements that starts with a `function` statement or a `subroutine` statement and ends with an `end` statement.
2. A `contains` statement separates the internal procedures from the program body.

3. The names FT and CT in the procedure definitions are *dummy argument* names that correspond to the *actual argument* names `Fahr` and `Cels` in the procedure reference. In the subroutine `Output`, with two arguments, the correspondence between actual arguments and dummy arguments is positional: the first actual argument, `Fahr`, corresponds to the first dummy argument, FT, and the second actual argument, `Cels`, corresponds to the second dummy argument, CT. In this program, the procedures do not change the values of the dummy arguments; the arguments transmit values only from the main program to the procedure.
4. In this example there are no local names, except for the dummy arguments, in any of the procedures. The two named constants `SCALE` and `OFFSET` in the function `Temp_C` are inherited from the main program. These two constants are not used anywhere else in the program, so they could be declared inside the function `Temp_C` instead. On the other hand, we might contemplate expanding the program to include another procedure that converts temperatures from Celsius to Fahrenheit. This procedure would use the same two constants, `SCALE` and `OFFSET`. If the program were augmented in this way, we could keep the two named constant declarations in the main program to make them accessible (either by inheritance or as arguments) to more than one procedure.

Recursive Procedures (Optional)

Any Fortran 90 procedure (subroutine or function) may be *recursive*, which means that it may reference itself either directly or indirectly (through other procedures). If a subroutine or function is recursive, this fact must be declared in the `subroutine` or `function` header statement in the program unit:

> `recursive` *Type* `function` *Function name* `(` *Dummy arg list* `) &`
>   `result (` *Result name* `)`
> `recursive subroutine` *Subroutine name* `(` *Dummy arg list* `)`

The subroutine in Example 2.22 is recursive. (This subroutine is a part of Example 8.10.) Recursion is discussed further in Section 4.6.

EXAMPLE 2.22

```
! Example 2.22. Print the Tree or Subtree whose Root is Current_Ptr.
  recursive subroutine Print_Tree (Current_Ptr)
    type (Box_Type), pointer :: Current_Ptr    ! Derived type inherited from host
! start subroutine Print_Tree
    if (Associated (Current_Ptr)) then
      call Print_Tree (Current_Ptr % Left)  ! Recursive call to print Left subtree
      print *, Current_Ptr % Name
      call Print_Tree (Current_Ptr % Right)! Recursive call to print Right subtree
    end if
  end subroutine Print_Tree
```

Input Arguments and Output Arguments: The `intent` *Attribute (Advanced)*

It is recommended that an `intent` attribute be declared for each argument in a procedure (except for pointers; see Section 6.3). This attribute may appear in a type declaration between the type designator and the double colon. It has one of three forms:

```
intent (in)
intent (out)
intent (in out)
```

An example is

```
real, intent (in) :: FT, CT
```

If the `intent` attribute has the value `in`, the dummy argument must not be given a value within the procedure. The matching actual argument in the referencing procedure may be a variable, a constant, or an expression that contains one or more operators.

If the `intent` attribute is `out` or `in out`, the corresponding actual argument must be a variable; that is, it must not be a constant or an expression other than a variable. Note that the following are variables: arrays (see Chapter 5), array elements, structures and structure components (see Section 6.2), strings, and substrings (see Section 6.1).

If the `intent` attribute is `out`, the procedure must give the dummy argument a value before using it; that is, the procedure must be written as if the dummy argument value is undefined when execution of the procedure begins.

If the `intent` attribute is `in out`, the corresponding actual argument must have a defined value when execution of the procedure begins.

If no `intent` attribute is declared, the procedure may use the dummy argument value or may give it a value during execution of the procedure. If the procedure gives a value to the dummy argument, the corresponding actual argument must not be a constant or an expression other than a variable. If the procedure does not give the dummy argument a value before using it, the corresponding actual argument must have a defined value when execution of the procedure begins.

If a dummy argument (with no declared `intent` attribute or with `in out` or `out` as its `intent` attribute) is given a value during execution of the procedure, that value becomes the value of the actual argument when the procedure terminates.

Implementation of the `intent` attribute is described in Section 8.8.

EXAMPLE 2.23 The internal procedure Swap interchanges the values of two variables X and Y. This procedure is written as a subroutine rather than as a function because it does not generate a definite value that can be returned as a function result. The arguments X and Y are declared to have `intent (in out)` because they pass information both to and from the subroutine.

The procedure is to be referenced with the statement

call Swap (*Dummy arg list*)

In this example, the main program reads three numbers, swaps the first pair, and then swaps the second pair.

```
! Example 2.23. Program with internal subroutine Swap.
  program Swap_Test
    implicit none
    real :: A, B, C
! start program Swap_Test
    print *, "␣Please␣enter␣three␣numbers."
    read *, A, B, C
    print *, "␣Thank␣you.␣You␣have␣entered:␣", A, B, C
    call Swap (A, B)
    print *, "␣After␣the␣first␣swap:␣", A, B, C
    call Swap (B, C)
    print *, "␣After␣the␣second␣swap:␣", A, B, C
  contains
    subroutine Swap (X, Y)
      real, intent (in out) :: X, Y
      real :: Aux
!   start subroutine Swap
      Aux = X
      X = Y
      Y = Aux
    end subroutine Swap
  end program Swap_Test
```

Several observations are in order:

1. The procedure is defined by the sequence of statements beginning with `subroutine Swap` . . . and ending with `end subroutine Swap`.
2. The two dummy arguments in the procedure are declared to have `intent (in out)` so that they may transmit values from the procedure to the main program as well as from the main program to the procedure.
3. The variable named `Aux` is local to the internal procedure. This procedure does not inherit any objects from the main program.
4. In the first `call` statement, the actual argument names `A` and `B` correspond to the dummy argument names `X` and `Y` in the program unit. In the second `call` statement, the actual argument names `B` and `C` correspond to the same dummy argument names `X` and `Y`.

Subroutine Versus Function Procedures

As we have seen, the only real difference between a function and a subroutine is that a function returns a result value. However, we have also seen that a subroutine can return a value as an argument whose `intent` attribute value is `out` or `in out`. To illustrate the relation between subroutine and function procedures, let's rewrite the temperature conversion program so that all internal procedures are subroutines. In Example 2.24, the former function result variables become `intent (out)` dummy arguments.

EXAMPLE 2.24

```
! Example 2.24. Temperature Conversion with Subroutines.
  program Con_Temp
    implicit none
    real, parameter :: SCALE = 1.8, OFFSET = 32.0
    real :: Fahr, Cels
! start program Con_Temp
    call Input (Fahr)
    call Calculate (Fahrenheit_Temp, Cels)
    call Output (Fahr, Cels)
  contains
    subroutine Input (FT)
    real, intent (out) :: FT
      print *, "⊥Please⊥enter⊥the⊥Fahrenheit⊥temperature.⊥"
      read *, FT
    end subroutine Input
    subroutine Calculate (FT, CT)
      real, intent (in) :: FT
      real, intent (out) :: CT
      CT = (FT - OFFSET) / SCALE
    end subroutine Calculate
    subroutine Output (FT, CT)
      real, intent (in) :: FT, CT
      print *, FT, "⊥deg.⊥F⊥=⊥", CT, "⊥deg.⊥C"
    end subroutine Output
  end program Con_Temp
```

Note the following:

1. The names `Fahr` and `Cels` in the main program correspond to FT and CT in the procedures. The function names Temp_F and Temp_C no longer appear.
2. Assignment to the `intent (out)` dummy argument FT in the subroutine `Input`, or to CT in the subroutine `Calculate`, changes the value of the corresponding actual argument `Fahr` or `Cels` in the main program.

Data Sharing by Inheritance

A principal advantage of a procedure is that its local data is *separated* from the data of the main program and other procedures. Fortran guarantees that local data objects (other than dummy arguments and function results) are inaccessible outside the procedure.[5] Changes to these local objects cannot have causes or effects outside the procedure. It is this assurance that permits us to develop each procedure independently, more or less ignoring the rest of the program.

However, it is almost always necessary to share some data between the procedure and the main program. Data that is shared data through an argument list is accessible only in ways that are carefully controlled — especially if `intent` attributes are declared in the procedure for all dummy arguments.

Achieving this data independence and this control over data access increases the complexity of the procedure. We must take extra steps to define and declare the dummy arguments and to ensure that the correct positional correspondence is established between the actual and dummy argument lists.

In simple situations, we sometimes avoid the added complexity of argument passing by sacrificing some independence. An internal procedure can inherit the entire "data space" of its host program. Such a procedure has an independent statement sequence, but it has no independent data. As an illustration, Example 2.25 further modifies the temperature conversion program by changing from argument passing to inheritance:

EXAMPLE 2.25

```
! Example 2.25. Temperature Conversion with Inheritance.
  program Con_Temp
    implicit none
    real, parameter :: SCALE = 1.8, OFFSET = 32.0
    real :: Fahr, Cels
! start program Con_Temp
    call Input
    call Calculate
    call Output
  contains
    subroutine Input
      print *, "␣Please␣enter␣the␣Fahrenheit␣temperature.␣"
      read *, Fahr
    end subroutine Input
    subroutine Calculate
      Cels = (Fahr - OFFSET) / SCALE
    end subroutine Calculate
```

[5] This guarantee is valid only if the procedure contains no `use` statements (see Section 7.2) or `common` statements (see Appendix E.3).

```
    subroutine Output
      print *, Fahr, "␣deg.␣F␣=␣", Cels, "␣deg.␣C"
    end subroutine Output
  end program Con_Temp
```

Note the following:

1. The internal procedures `Input`, `Calculate`, and `Output` have no arguments. They each inherit the entire data space of the main program.
2. The variables `Fahr` and `Cels`, as well as the constants `OFFSET` and `SCALE`, which are declared in the main program, are assigned and referenced in the procedures as well as in the main program.

Data sharing by inheritance is possible only when a particular data object in the procedure always corresponds to the *same* main program object. An argument list is required for a procedure like `Swap` because the dummy arguments correspond to different actual arguments each time the procedure is called.

Combinations of inheritance and argument passing are also possible. Objects in a procedure that always correspond to the same main program object may be inherited, while those whose correspondence changes may be passed as arguments. For example, a subroutine to exchange two elements of an array might gain access to the array by inheritance, while receiving the subscript values as `intent (in)` arguments (see Example 5.5).

The choice between these two data sharing techniques is not always easy. Inheritance implies *rigidity* in the relationship between data in the procedure and data in the main program, while *flexibility* is achieved with argument passing. On the other hand, inheritance is often appealing in the short run because of its simplicity, and it is especially convenient for very small problems, for internal procedures that share larger amounts of data with the main program, and for programs that are not intended for reuse in a variety of applications. Inheritance may also improve efficiency by eliminating the overhead associated with argument passing.

Experience shows, however, that procedures are reused more frequently than might be expected. In a new situation, the relationship between main program data and pro-

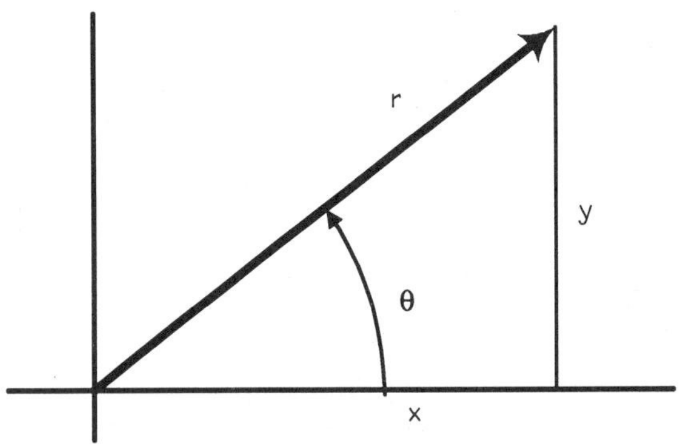

FIGURE 2.7. Relation between rectangular and polar coordinates.

cedure data is likely to change, and the rigidity of inheritance may have to be abandoned in spite of some increase in complexity.

Transition Tips

- Change all statement functions to internal function procedures.
- Where possible, delete statement label `assign` and assigned `go to` statements, and rewrite the program with internal procedures.

2.4 Exercises

1. Rewrite the program of Example 2.21 to remove the constant names `SCALE` and `OFFSET` from the host program, making these names local to the procedure in which they are used.

2. An actual argument may be an expression; it does not have to be a variable name. In the main program of Example 2.21, the result from the function `Temp_C` is assigned to the variable `Cels`, which is then used as an argument in the call to `Output`. Modify the main program to eliminate this variable: Replace the second argument in the call to `Output` by the reference to `Temp_C`, remove `Cels` from the type declaration, and delete the second assignment statement. (Test your modified program.) Why can't you eliminate the variable `Fahr` with a similar trick?

3. Refer to Figure 2.7. (See also Examples 6.25, 7.1, 7.2, and 7.14.)

   a. Write an internal subroutine with two `intent (in)` arguments `R` and `Theta` that represent a complex number in polar form and one `intent (out)` argument `Z` that gives the representation of the same complex number in standard Fortran style:

   ```
   X = R * Real (Cos (Theta))
   Y = R * Real (Sin (Theta))
   Z = Cmplx (X, Y)
   ```

   b. Write an internal subroutine with one `intent (in)` argument `Z` that is a complex number expressed in standard Fortran style and two `intent (out)` arguments `R` and `Theta` that give the representation of the same complex number in polar form:

   ```
   R = Abs (Z)
   Theta = ATan2 (AImag (Z), Real (Z))
   ```

4. Write a program that reads values of `X`, `Y`, `Z`, and `T` and prints the value of four-dimensional relativistic distance:

   ```
   X ** 2 + Y ** 2 + Z ** 2 - T ** 2
   ```

   Compute the distance with a function that obtains `X`, `Y`, and `Z` from the host as arguments, but that obtains `T` from the host by inheritance.

Part II
CONTROL

The three basic forms of control in any programming language are *sequence*, *selection*, and *repetition*. Part I discussed sequential control — the normal execution sequence. Part II describes Fortran 90 statements and constructs for selection and repetition.

Chapter 3 describes the Fortran *selection constructs* `if` and `case`. The `if` construct is normally a *two-way* selection construct, but it can be expanded to *multi-way* selection with `else if`; it can also be abbreviated by omitting either of the alternatives. The `case` construct is appropriate for selection based on an integer or a character expression. Fortran also provides *simplified* selection with the simple `if` statement and the intrinsic function `Merge`. Selection in an `if` construct depends on a designated expression that may be either true or false. Such an expression has *logical* data type. Chapter 3 also describes variables and constants of logical data type, as well as logical operations.

Chapter 4 deals with the three basic Fortran 90 *loop constructs*: the indexed `do`, `do` forever, and `do while`. The indexed `do` construct, with its *count-controlled* loops, is still the main workhorse. An `exit` statement may appear in a `do` construct (of any of the three forms) to cause premature termination. If no increment is specified for the loop index, the default increment value is 1. The *simple* `do` (or `do` forever) is listed in second place because of its great flexibility. This loop construct has no natural termination condition; termination is often achieved with an `exit` statement. The simple `do` construct is especially useful for file input. The `do while` construct, which handles *conditional* loops, is perhaps less important in Fortran than in some other languages, although it is appropriate for some applications. Chapter 4 also deals with loop *nesting* as well as with *recursion* (a completely different approach to repetition).

Chapter 3 Program Patterns for Selection

The normal execution sequence for program statements is sequential, from top to bottom, as the statements would appear on a terminal screen or on a printed page. There are three principal exceptions to this normal sequence. A selection structure, a repetition structure, or a procedure reference can modify the normal top-to-bottom sequence. Chapter 2 introduced procedure reference, which will be discussed further in Chapters 7 and 8. Repetition is covered in detail in Chapter 4. Selection, or *branching*, is the subject of this chapter.

Selection constructs provide two or more alternative courses of action, one of which is to be selected when the program is executed. The first two sections of this chapter cover Fortran's principal selection patterns, the `if` construct and the `case` construct. The third section describes two simpler Fortran selection patterns, the simple `if` statement and the intrinsic function `Merge`. The fourth section is devoted to logical data type, a subject closely related to selection.

3.1 TWO-WAY SELECTION

The `if` Construct

The program in Example 3.1 reads a data value and prints its square root. The square root is to be computed by the intrinsic function `SqRt`. However, `SqRt` requires a nonnegative argument. To avoid difficulty, this program checks for invalid data values. The function reference is executed if the data is valid, but an error message is printed if the data is invalid. Thus, there are two blocks of statements; one block or the other will be executed, depending upon whether or not the input data value is nonnegative.

EXAMPLE 3.1 The following program includes the `if` construct with its two blocks, along with specifications and input and output statements.

```
! Example 3.1. Square root with test for negative argument.
  program Limb
    implicit none
    intrinsic SqRt
    real :: Next_Datum, Root
! start program Limb
    print *, "␣Please␣enter␣a␣number␣whose␣square␣root␣is␣wanted.␣"
    read *, Next_Datum
    if (Next_Datum >= 0.0) then             ! Choose "then" block or "else" block.
      print *, SqRt (Next_Datum)
    else
      print *, "␣Can't␣find␣the␣square␣root␣of␣a␣negative␣number␣"
    end if
  end program Limb
```

The most important statement in the program of Example 3.1 is

```
if (Next_Datum >= 0.0) then
```

This statement contains the expression `Next_Datum >= 0.0` enclosed in parentheses and surrounded by the keywords `if` and `then`. The symbol `>=` is a *relational operator* that means "is greater than or equal to." During program execution, Fortran tests whether the expression `Next_Datum >= 0.0` is true or false, and modifies the execution sequence accordingly. The flowchart in Figure 3.1 corresponds to Example 3.1 and illustrates the use of an `if` construct to avoid negative arguments.

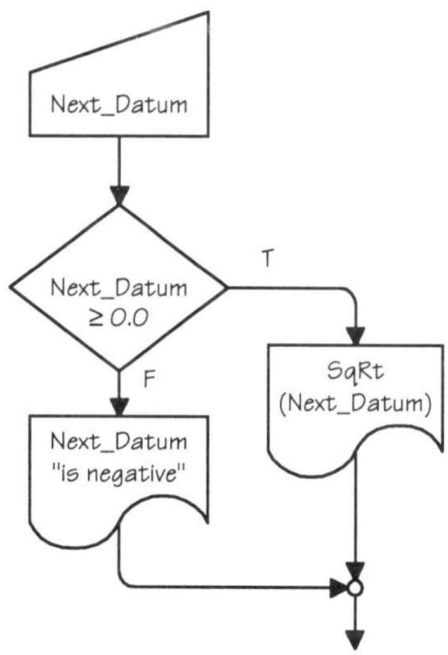

FIGURE 3.1. Flowchart corresponding to Example 3.1.

The *Condition* that controls the execution is an expression (`Next_Datum >= 0.0` in this example) that can be either true or false. This *Condition must* be enclosed in parentheses:

```
if ( Condition ) then
```

As we shall see (Section 3.4), a branch control *Condition* may be any expression of logical data type.

Between the `if-then` statement and the `end if` statement, there are two blocks of statements separated by an `else` statement. If the *Condition* is true, the first of these blocks (called the *Then block*) will be executed (in Example 3.1, the square root will be calculated and printed). If the *Condition* is false, the second block (the *Else block*) will be executed instead (in Example 3.1, the message

```
Can't find the square root of a negative number
```

will be printed). In either case, the execution sequence will continue with the statement that follows `end if`. Thus, it is evident that an `if` construct for two-way selection has the following general form (see also Figure 3.2):[1]

```
if ( Condition ) then

   Then block

else

   Else block

end if
```

Points discussed so far concerning the `if` construct and its use for two-way selection may be summarized as follows:

1. An `if` construct begins with the statement `if ( Condition ) then`, and terminates with the statement `end if`. Note that `end if` may be written with or without a blank between `end` and `if`; see Appendix C.1. In the middle of the `if` construct, there is an `else` statement that separates the first block from the second.
2. The first block, the *Then block*, consists of all the statements following the `if-then` statement and preceding the `else` statement. The second block, the *Else block*, consists of all the statements following the `else` statement and preceding the `end if` statement. The `if-then` statement, the `else` statement, and the `end if` statement belong to the `if` construct as a whole but are not considered part of either block.
3. If the *Condition* is true, the *Then block* will be executed and the *Else block* will be skipped. If the *Condition* is false, the *Then block* will be skipped and the *Else block*

[1] As we shall see (Section 3.2), the `else` statement and the *Else block* may be omitted if no special action is to be performed when the *Condition* is false.

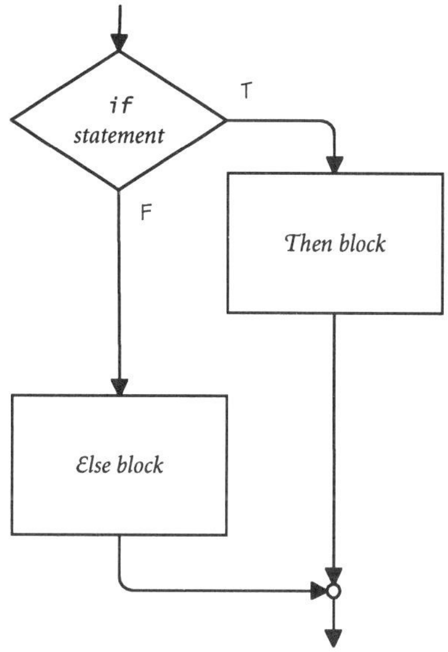

FIGURE 3.2. Two-way selection with the *if* construct.

will be executed. In either case, execution resumes with the statement immediately following the `end if` statement.

Blocks of statements in the control construct examples in this text are indented for emphasis, to make it easy for you to see which statements are part of each block. Fortran does not require this style convention. However, you should observe that

```
if ( Condition ) then
```

must be written as a *single statement*, all on one line, in accordance with the rules for Fortran statements.[2] Similarly, the `else` statement and the `end if` statement must each be written as a single statement on a separate line.

Summary of Repetition Constructs

Program constructs for repetition are treated at length in Chapter 4. The simplest form of the indexed do construct is explained here, because it appears in several examples in this chapter.

A *Block of statements* may be repeated a fixed number of times. The value of a named constant, `LIMIT`, determines the number of repetitions. The *Block of statements* to be repeated is enclosed by the two repetition control statements do and end do:

```
do Loop = 1, LIMIT
   Block of statements
end do
```

[2] As we have seen, each Fortran statement normally occupies a single line. For exceptions to this rule, see Appendix C.

```
! Example 3.2. Count and total weights of male and female cats.
 program Heavy_Cat_1
   implicit none
   integer, parameter :: MALE = 1, FEMALE = 2, LIMIT = 24
   integer :: Male_Count = 0, Female_Count = 0, Loop, Sex
   real :: NextWeight, Male_Total = 0.0, Female_Total = 0.0
! start program Heavy_Cat_1
   do Loop = 1, LIMIT
     print *, "␣Please␣enter␣the␣weight␣of␣the␣next␣cat,␣in␣kilograms.␣"
     read *, NextWeight
     print *, "␣Please␣enter␣the␣sex␣of␣the␣cat␣(1␣for␣male,␣2␣for␣female).␣"
     read *, Sex
     if (Sex == MALE) then
       Male_Count = Male_Count + 1                        ! This cat is male.
       Male_Total = Male_Total + NextWeight
     else
       Female_Count = Female_Count + 1                  ! This cat is female.
       Female_Total = Female_Total + NextWeight
     end if
   end do
     print *, Male_Count, Male_Total, Female_Count, Female_Total
   end program Heavy_Cat_1
```

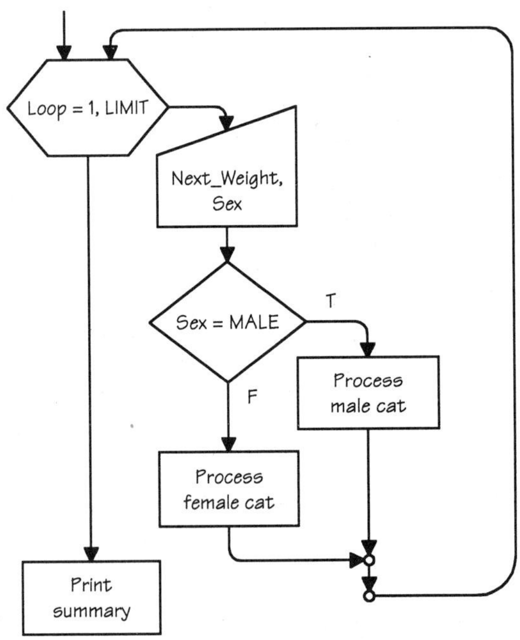

FIGURE 3.3.
Flowchart for
Example 3.2.

EXAMPLE 3.2 As part of a research project, Professor Katzenzähler separately counts male and female cats and totals their weights. The weight of each cat and the sex (coded as 1 for male and 2 for female) will be entered as input data.

In this program, the *Condition* that controls the `if` construct is `Sex == Male`. For male cats, this *Condition* is true, so the *Then block* is executed and the *Else block* is skipped. For female cats, the *Condition* is false, so the *Then block* is skipped and the *Else block* is executed. The flowchart in Figure 3.3 corresponds to Example 3.2.

EXAMPLE 3.3 Professor Katzenzähler's research grant has been extended. He must now calculate the average weight of all male cats after all of the data in Example 3.2 has been read and processed. However, he realizes that in some of his experiments there may be no male cats. To avoid dividing by the `Male_Count` when its value is zero, he provides a separate statement sequence to be executed in this circumstance.

```
! Example 3.3. Average weight of all male cats.
 program Heavy_Cat_2
   implicit none
   intrinsic Real
   integer, parameter :: MALE = 1, FEMALE = 2, LIMIT = 24
   integer :: Male_Count = 0, Female_Count = 0, Loop, Sex
   real :: NextWeight, Male_Total = 0.0, Female_Total = 0.0
! start program Heavy_Cat_2
   do Loop = 1, LIMIT
     print *, "␣Please␣enter␣the␣weight␣of␣the␣next␣cat,␣in␣kilograms.␣"
     read *, NextWeight
     print *, "␣Please␣enter␣the␣sex␣of␣the␣cat␣(1␣for␣male,␣2␣for␣female).␣"
     read *, Sex
     if (Sex == MALE) then
       Male_Count = Male_Count + 1                            ! This cat is male.
       Male_Total = Male_Total + NextWeight
     else
       Female_Count = Female_Count + 1                      ! This cat is female.
       Female_Total = Female_Total + NextWeight
     end if
   end do
   if (Male_Count > 0) then
     print *, "␣Average␣weight:␣", Male_Total / Real (Male_Count)
   else
     print *, "␣There␣are␣no␣male␣cats␣in␣this␣sample.␣"
   end if
 end program Heavy_Cat_2
```

In the output list of the first `print` statement of Example 3.3, the expression to be printed contains the explicit type conversion function `Real`. This explicit type conversion is not strictly necessary; the mixed-type expression `Male_Total / Male_Count` would induce automatic type coercion and would produce the same result. However, explicit type conversion is regarded as good programming practice, and its use is therefore encouraged.

EXAMPLE 3.4 Two real data values, X and Y, are given. The following program sets the values of corresponding integer variables X_Rank and Y_Rank to indicate the relative sizes of the X and Y values (assuming for the moment that the values of X and Y are not equal).

```
! Example 3.4. Rank two numbers.
 program Seniority
   implicit none
   real :: X, Y
   character (len = 7) :: X_Rank, Y_Rank
! start program Seniority
   print *, "␣Please␣enter␣a␣pair␣of␣real␣numbers␣to␣be␣ranked.␣"
   read *, X, Y
   print *, "␣You␣have␣entered:␣", X, Y
   if (X > Y) then
     X_Rank = "larger␣"; Y_Rank = "smaller"
   else
     X_Rank = "smaller"; Y_Rank = "larger␣"
   end if
   print *, X, "␣is␣", X_Rank, "␣and␣", Y, "␣is␣", Y_Rank
 end program Seniority
```

EXAMPLE 3.5 The following rather trivial problem appears in several examples in this chapter that illustrate a variety of approaches to programming with selection constructs:

> Assume that the value of I is either 1 or 2. If I is 1, change it to 2; if it is 2, change it to 1.

Notice that the desired result is actually the value of a very simple expression. The value of the expression $3 - I$ is 2 when I is 1; also, $3 - I$ is 1 when I is 2. Therefore, the assignment

```
I = 3 - I
```

will accomplish the specified result without a control construct. Nevertheless, as an illustration of the if construct, the following program for calculating the required value is presented.

```
! Example 3.5. Trade the values 1 and 2.
  program Trade_1
    implicit none
    integer :: I
! start program Trade_1
    print *, "⊥Please⊥enter⊥1⊥or⊥2.⊥"
    read *, I
    print *, "⊥Thank⊥you.⊥⊥You⊥have⊥entered:⊥", I
    if (I == 1) then                                      ! if construct
      I = 2                                               ! if construct
    else                                                  ! if construct
      I = 1                                               ! if construct
    end if                                                ! if construct
    print *, "⊥Your⊥value⊥was⊥changed⊥to:⊥", I
  end program Trade_1
```

A very short if construct like the one in Example 3.5 could be written on a single line. This style might be preferred especially when it is desirable to deemphasize the details of the if construct:

```
if (I == 1) then; I = 2; else; I = 1; end if
```

Note that the semicolon separators must not be omitted when more than one statement is written on a line.[3]

EXAMPLE 3.6 James Clerk Maxwell (1831–1879) hypothesized a daemon (a sort of perverse supernatural being) who could arrange the molecules in a beaker of water so that one side is boiling while the other side is freezing. Conceptually, the daemon examines each molecule as it moves within the beaker and steers the fast molecules to the hot side and the slow molecules to the cold side. The following program performs part of this task by separately counting the fast and slow molecules. The program first reads a boundary value and then reads the velocity of a molecule. If the velocity is above the boundary, a tally is added to the count of fast molecules; otherwise, the count of slow molecules is tallied.

[3] Other programming languages have constructs somewhat similar in appearance. Pascal, for example, provides a compound `if` *statement* of the form `if` *Predicate* `then` *Statement* `else` *Statement*; no punctuation is required (or permitted) between parts of the `if` *statement*. In Fortran, on the other hand, `if–then`, `else`, and `end if` are three distinct statements and must be separated by semicolons if they are not written on different lines.

```
! Example 3.6. Count fast and slow molecules.
  program Maxwells_Imp
    implicit none
    integer, parameter :: LIMIT = 100
    integer :: Fast_Molecule_Count = 0, Slow_Molecule_Count = 0, Loop
    real :: Boundary, Velocity
! start program Maxwells_Imp
    print *, "␣Please␣enter␣the␣velocity␣boundary␣for␣Maxwell's␣Daemon.␣"
    read *, Boundary
    do Loop = 1, LIMIT
      print *, "␣Please␣enter␣the␣velocity␣of␣the␣next␣molecule.␣"
      read *, Velocity
      if (Velocity > Boundary) then
        Fast_Molecule_Count = Fast_Molecule_Count + 1
      else
        Slow_Molecule_Count = Slow_Molecule_Count + 1
      end if
    end do
    print *, Fast_Molecule_Count, Slow_Molecule_Count
  end program Maxwells_Imp
```

The Branch Control Condition

Let's return to reconsider one component of an `if` construct in greater detail. This component is the *Condition* in the `if-then` statement, which is an assertion, or alleged statement of fact, that may be either true or false.

Relational Expressions

A *relational expression* consists of a pair of expressions separated by a relational operator:

Expression$_1$ *Relational operator* *Expression*$_2$

Each of the *Expressions* may be any valid expression of integer, real, or character type. The *Relational operator* is one of the following:[4]

Notation	Meaning	Notation	Meaning
==	Is equal to	<=	Is less than or equal to
/=	Is not equal to	>	Is greater than
<	Is less than	>=	Is greater than or equal to

[4] The six traditional relational operator forms, `.eq.`, `.ne.`, `.le.`, `.lt.`, `.ge.`, and `.gt.`, which may be considered obsolete, are described in Appendix D.2.

Two additional relational operators for comparing expressions of logical type are presented in Section 3.4.

Note the difference between the relational operator for equality, ==, and the assignment operator, =. Note also the Fortran 90 inequality operator, /=, which is written as <>, !=, or # in some other programming languages.

The data types of the expressions to be compared must both be numeric (integer, real, or complex), or they must both be character:

```
Tony == Alpha
X > Y + SqRt (3.0)
I >= X
Sex == "Male"
```

If the expressions have different numeric types, the value of the relational expression is computed by subtracting the second expression from the first, interpreting the subtraction operation as a mixed-type expression (Section 2.2), and comparing the result with zero. Thus, if the type of `I` is integer and the type of `X` is real, the relational expression

```
I >= X
```

is equivalent to the following, with mixed-type evaluation of `I - X`:

```
I - X >= 0.0
```

Character strings can be compared in a relational expression. Some of the examples of this chapter illustrate matching between strings of the same length. Rules for comparing strings of different lengths are covered in Section 6.1.

Matching and Ranking

There are a few differences between the two relational operators that perform *matching* — namely,

==	Is equal to
/=	Is not equal to

and the four *ranking* operators, which are

<	Is less than
<=	Is less than or equal to
>	Is greater than
>=	Is greater than or equal to

One difference is that expressions of complex type can be matched, but they cannot be ranked. The only complex relational operators permitted are == and /= because complex numbers are unordered.

Matching Real Expressions — A Pitfall to Avoid

Caution is required when the matching operators are applied to expressions of real (or complex) type. Because of the limited precision of computer number representations, the computed value of a real expression may deviate slightly from its expected value. Thus, two expressions that are expected to have the same value may differ by a small amount. (In fact, we should consider it unusual when any two real expressions have exactly the same computed value.) A test for the exact equality of such a pair of expressions may therefore produce unexpected results. Consequently, any matching operator applied to a pair of real expressions, such as

```
X == 2.7                                              ! ☹
A /= B                                                ! ☹
```

should be viewed with suspicion. The real expressions will often be unequal, when, on mathematical grounds, we would have expected them to be equal.

In particular, the values of simple decimal fractions (such as 0.1 and 0.02) are not represented exactly on computers with a binary (base 2) number representation. They are often represented by slightly smaller values, just as the constant 1/3 is represented by a slightly smaller value when carried out to any finite number of decimal places as 0.33333 .... Therefore, the result of adding 10 copies of the constant 0.1, for instance, will not be equal to the value of the constant 1.0 but will be slightly smaller on any binary computer.

Instead of asking whether two expressions are exactly equal or whether an expression is exactly equal to zero, we should usually test for approximate equality by using some small tolerance, such as 1.0×10^{-6}. The tolerance value must be chosen carefully in each specific instance to avoid an unacceptable broad definition of approximate equality. The intrinsic function Spacing (see Appendix A) may be of assistance in determining a portable value for the tolerance. In the examples in this text, a tolerance value usually appears as a named constant. We could write a relational expression, such as

```
Abs (A - X) < 10 * Spacing (A)                        ! ☺
```

that will be true whenever the two expressions are approximately equal to within the stated tolerance.

Compound Relations

Two or more relational expressions can be combined to express a more complicated condition:

Relation	Fortran relational expression
I is either 1 or 2.	`(I == 1) .or. (I == 2)`
A is zero and B is not zero.	`(A == 0.0) .and. (B /= 0.0)`
X is between 0.0 and 1.0.	`(X > 0.0) .and. (X < 1.0)`
X is between 0.0 and 1.0.	`(0.0 < X) .and. (X < 1.0)`
X is between 0.0 and 1.0, inclusive.	`(0.0 <= X) .and. (X <= 1.0)`

The connectives *or*, *and*, and *not* form compound relations. In Fortran, these connectives are written as .or., .and., and .not., respectively. These connectives combine entire relations (complete relational expressions or compound relations). They must not be applied to the arithmetic expressions or other parts of a relation. Thus, in the foregoing list of examples, it would be unacceptable to write relations in forms such as the following:

```
I == 1 .or. 2                                         ! ☹
(A .and. B) /= 0.0                                    ! ☹
X > 0.0 .and. < 1.0                                   ! ☹
```

Also unacceptable is the following mathematical form:

```
0.0 < X < 1.0                                         ! ☹
```

Each of the following is a valid relational expression (assuming that the variable names are declared appropriately):

```
(X > 3.0) .and. (X + 2.0 > Y)                         ! ☺
((A <= X) .and. (B >= Y)) .or. (C > Z)                ! ☺
((I > 3) .or. (J <= 2)) .and. (.not. (Gamma < Eps))   ! ☺
(Abs (X1 - X2) / X1 <= Eps) .and. (Log (X1) > Eps)    ! ☺
.not. ((X < Y) .or. (G > GG) .or. (P ** 2 < Rmax))    ! ☺
```

Nested `if` *Constructs*

A block of statements within an `if` construct may, in turn, contain another `if` construct.

EXAMPLE 3.7 Professor Katzenzähler's research grant has been still further extended. His sponsor now wants separate counts of small male cats and large male cats, separated on the basis of a boundary value to be supplied as data. The following program separates cats first by sex, then by weight. Female cats are not separated by weight.

```
! Example 3.7. Count large males, small males, and females.
 program Cats_1
   implicit none
   integer, parameter :: LIMIT = 24
   integer :: Hi_Male_Count = 0, Low_Male_Count = 0, Female_Count = 0, Loop
   real, parameter :: BOUNDARY = 4.3                ! Boundary for small vs. large
   real :: Male_Total = 0.0, Female_Total = 0.0, Next_Weight = 0.0
   character (len = 1) :: Sex

! start program Cats_1

   do Loop = 1, LIMIT
     print *, "␣Please␣enter␣sex␣of␣cat:␣M␣or␣F.␣"
     read *, Sex
     if ((Sex == "M") .or. (Sex == "m")) then                    ! Cat is male.
       print *, "␣Please␣enter␣the␣weight␣of␣the␣male␣cat.␣"
       read *, Next_Weight
       Male_Total = Male_Total + Next_Weight
       if (Next_Weight > BOUNDARY) then
         Hi_Male_Count = Hi_Male_Count + 1
       else
         Low_Male_Count = Low_Male_Count + 1
       end if
     else    ! Cat is female if Sex is not "M" or "m"
       print *, "␣Please␣enter␣the␣weight␣of␣the␣female␣cat.␣"
       read *, Next_Weight
       Female_Total = Female_Total + Next_Weight
       Female_Count = Female_Count + 1
     end if
   end do
   print *, Hi_Male_Count, Low_Male_Count, Male_Total
   print *, Female_Count, Female_Total
 end program Cats_1
```

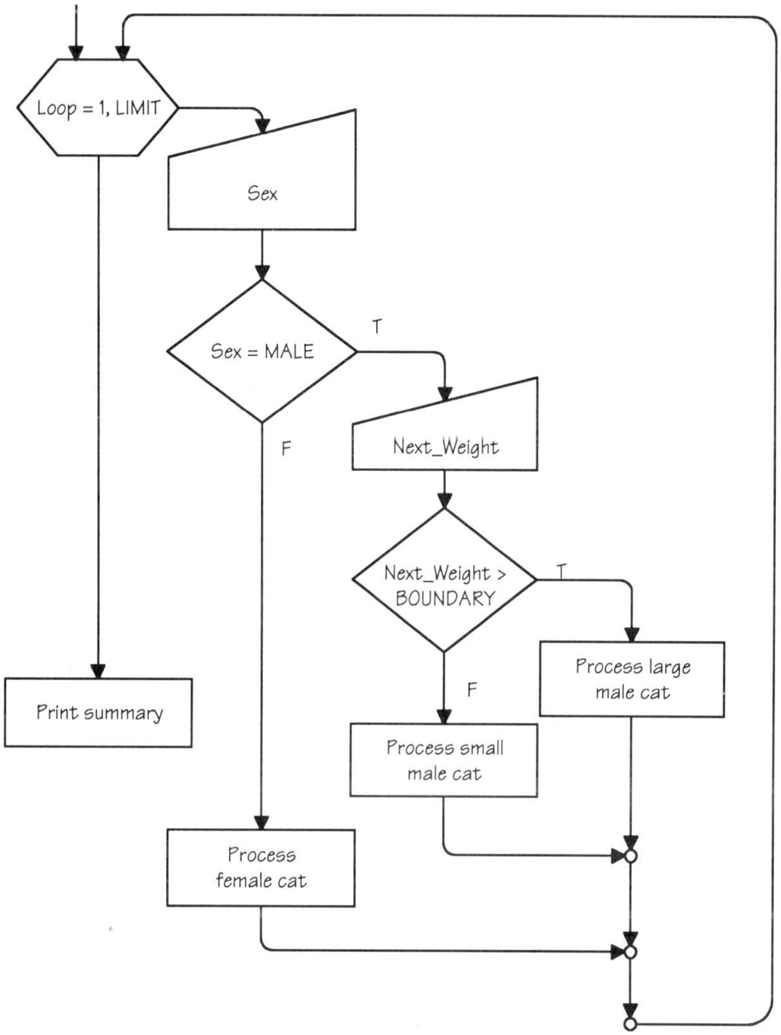

FIGURE 3.4. Flowchart for Example 3.7.

The flowchart in Figure 3.4 corresponds to Example 3.7 and illustrates the use of nested `if` constructs. One of the blocks of the outer `if` construct, controlled by the statement

```
if (Sex == "M") then
```

is to be chosen according to the sex of the cat. The *Then block* contains an inner `if` construct, controlled by the statement

```
if (Next_Weight > BOUNDARY) then
```

which adds 1 to `Hi_Male_Count` or to `Low_Male_Count`.

EXAMPLE 3.8 Professor Katzenzähler now wants to count large, medium, and small cats, without regard to sex. In the following program, large cats are processed by the *Then block* of the outer `if` construct; in the outer *Else block*, a further test is made to separate medium cats from small cats.

```
! Example 3.8. Count large, medium, and small cats.
 program Cats_2
   implicit none
   integer, parameter :: LIMIT = 24
   integer :: Hi_Count = 0, Mid_Count = 0, Low_Count = 0, Loop
   real, parameter :: MID_BOUNDARY = 2.7                    ! Small vs. medium cats
   real, parameter :: HI_BOUNDARY = 4.3                     ! Medium vs. large cats
   real :: Next_Weight
! start program Cats_2
   do Loop = 1, LIMIT
     print *, "⊥Please⊥enter⊥weight⊥of⊥next⊥cat.⊥"
     read *, Next_Weight
     if (Next_Weight > HI_BOUNDARY) then
       Hi_Count = Hi_Count + 1
     else
       if (Next_Weight > MID_BOUNDARY) then
         Mid_Count = Mid_Count + 1
       else
         Low_Count = Low_Count + 1
       end if
     end if
   end do
   print *, Hi_Count, Mid_Count, Low_Count
 end program Cats_2
```

EXAMPLE 3.9 (Compare Example 3.5.) If the value of I is 1, change it to 2; if it is 2, change it to 1. However, if the value of I is neither 1 nor 2, print an error message.

```
! Example 3.9. Trade the values 1 and 2.
 program Trade_2
   implicit none
   integer :: I
! start program Trade_2
   print *, "⊥Please⊥enter⊥1⊥or⊥2.⊥"
   read *, I
   print *, "⊥Thank⊥you.⊥⊥You⊥have⊥entered:⊥", I
```

```
if ((I == 1) .or. (I == 2)) then
  if (I == 1) then
    I = 2
  else
    I = 1
  end if
  print *, "⊥Your⊥value⊥was⊥changed⊥to:⊥", I
else
  print *, "⊥Your⊥value⊥was⊥not⊥1⊥or⊥2;⊥it⊥was:⊥", I
end if
end program Trade_2
```

Construct Names (Optional)

Deep or complicated nests of control constructs should be avoided where possible. Indenting the statements of the program in some consistent manner according to the level of nesting is an aid to the management of such complicated nests. However, compilers do not check for consistency of indentation; furthermore, indentation is no longer effective after perhaps five or six levels.

More practical is the use of *construct names* that can be appended to the control constructs. Incorrect nesting of named constructs can be detected by the compiler. Therefore, construct naming, although optional, is recommended as an aid to detection of incorrect nesting of constructs. This recommendation especially applies when deep or complicated construct nesting is unavoidable.

A construct name has the same form as a variable name. An `if` construct, a `case` construct (see Section 3.2), or a do construct (see Chapter 4) may have a construct name. A construct name must not be the same as the name of any variable, constant, procedure, or derived type (see Section 6.2) that can be referenced from the part of the program where the construct appears. Construct naming requires the following steps:

1. The construct name followed by a colon is written on the left, just preceding the keyword `if`, `case`, or `do` in the opening statement of the construct.
2. The same name without a colon must then be written on the right, following the keyword `end if`, `end select`, or `end do` in the closing statement of the construct.
3. As a further option, the same name without a colon may be written on the right, following the keyword in an `else` statement, following the keyword `then` in an `else if-then` statement (see Section 3.2), or following the case selector list or the keyword `default` in a `case` statement (see Section 3.2).

EXAMPLE 3.10 The following program illustrates an application of `if` constructs in a slightly longer program. This program finds all the roots of the quadratic equation $Ax^2 + Bx + C = 0$, given the coefficients A, B, and C. Several tests are required to handle special situations that arise when one or more of the coefficients are zero.

```
! Example 3.10. Find all roots of a quadratic equation,
!   given the coefficients A, B, and C.
  program Quadratic_Formula
    implicit none
    intrinsic SqRt, Abs
    real :: A, B, C, Part_1, Part_2, Discriminant, First_Root
! start program Quadratic_Formula
    read *, A, B, C
    print *, "␣Coefficients␣are:␣", A, B, C
    If_1: if (A /= 0) then If_1
      ! .. A is not zero. Find discriminant.
      Part_1 = -B / (2.0 * A)
      Discriminant = B ** 2 - 4.0 * A * C
      Part_2 = SqRt (Abs (Discriminant)) / (2.0 * A)
      If_2: if (Discriminant >= 0.0) then If_2
        ! .. Discriminant is nonnegative. Roots are real.
        ! .. For maximum accuracy, change sign of Part_2, if necessary,
        !    to agree with sign of Part_1.
        Part_2 = Sign (Part_2, Part_1)
        First_Root = Part_1 + Part_2
        ! .. For maximum accuracy, compute second root as
        !    C / (A * First_Root) rather than as Part_1 - Part_2,
        !    unless First_Root is zero.
        If_3: if (First_Root /= 0.0) then If_3
          print *, "␣Real␣roots:␣", First_Root, C / (A * First_Root)
        else If_3
          print *, "␣Real␣roots:␣", First_Root, Part_1 - Part_2
        end if If_3
      else If_2
        ! .. Discriminant is negative. Roots are complex.
        print *, "␣Complex␣roots:␣", Part_1, "␣+␣or␣-␣i␣", Part_2
      end if If_2
    else If_1
      ! .. A is zero. Equation is not a full quadratic.
      If_4: if (B /= 0) then If_4
        print *, "␣Not␣a␣quadratic.␣␣Root␣is:␣", -C / B
      else If_4
        print *, "␣Equation␣has␣the␣form␣C␣=␣0; C␣is:␣", C
      end if If_4
    end if If_1
  end program Quadratic_Formula
```

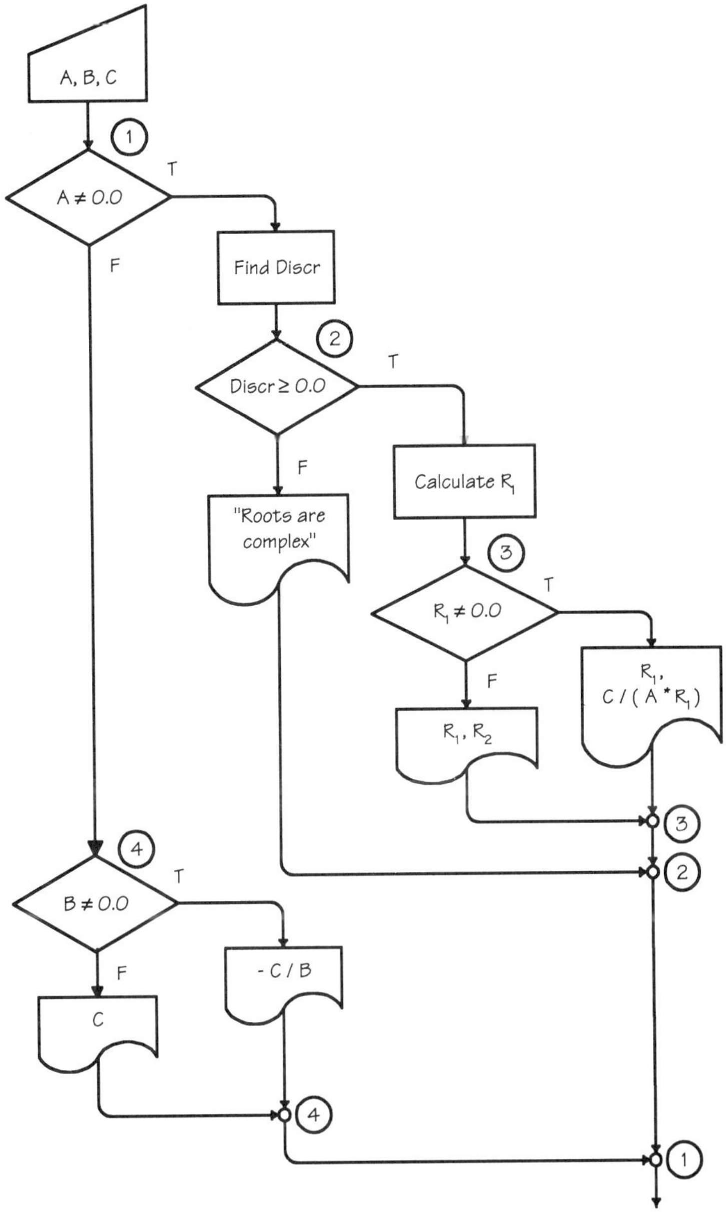

FIGURE 3.5.
Flowchart for
Example 3.10.

The flowchart in Figure 3.5 corresponds to Example 3.10. Circled numbers in this flowchart indicate the beginnings and ends of named `if` constructs.

Transition Tip

- Change all arithmetic `if` statements (see Appendix D.4) to `if` constructs. See also the remaining sections of this chapter.

3.1 Exercises

1. Consider Example 3.4.

   a. What will be printed if the values of X and Y happen to be equal?

   b. Modify the program to set both X_Rank and Y_Rank to "equal␣␣" in this case.

2. Write a program that contains an ifconstruct and that will read the lengths of two objects and will print the longer of the two lengths. Use the following data:

	Length_1	Length_2
Set 1:	123.4	14.3
Set 2:	−0.930	−0.931
Set 3:	0.0	111.1

3. Write a program to read two values, Voltage and Resistance. If Resistance is not zero, print the quotient Voltage / Resistance. If Resistance is zero, print an appropriate message.

4. The area of a triangle is given by

   ```
   SqRt (S * (S - A) * (S - B) * (S - C))
   ```

   where A, B, and C are the lengths of the three sides, and S is one-half the sum of the lengths of the sides. However, the quantity whose square root is to be computed will be negative if the values of A, B, and C are incorrect and do not represent the sides of a real triangle — for example, 1, 2, 4. Write a program that will read values for A, B, and C and will print the area of the triangle. However, if the values are incorrect, print an error message instead. Use the following data:

	A	B	C
Set 1:	7.0	8.0	9.0
Set 2:	3.0	4.0	5.0
Set 3:	123.4	432.1	399.9
Set 4:	1.0	2.0	4.0

5. Write an if construct to set the integer variable Sign_Of_X to −1 if the real variable X is negative, to 0 if X is zero, or to 1 if X is positive.

6. Correct any errors you can find in the following relational expressions:

   a. `I = N`

   b. `X and Y > 3.4`

   c. `(G = 3) .or. (A != 3.6)`

   d. `X <> Y`

e. `X != Y`

f. `1.0 > X > 0.0`

7. Correct any errors you can find in the following relational expressions:

a. `(C > D) .or. (.not. (A + B < D)`

b. `A .or. B < 99.0`

c. `(A < B) .and. (B < A)`

d. `A = B`

e. `A == 1 .or. 2`

f. `X => J`

8. Write conditions corresponding to the following:

a. `Acceleration` is greater than 3 and not greater than 6, and `Velocity` is between 5 and 20 (inclusive).

b. X lies between 0 and 1 (inclusive), or it lies between 3 and 4 (inclusive).

9. Write a compound relation corresponding to each of the following conditions:

a. X exceeds Y, and F is less than 2 or G equals 4 (or both).

b. X lies between 0 and 3 times `A`. (Hint: X is greater than 0 and X is less than 3 times A.)

c. P exceeds X, or it exceeds Y, or it exceeds `Z`.

d. A is not equal to `B`; and C is not equal to G nor to H nor to `J`.

e. The absolute value of F is less than or equal to 3 times `G`.

f. A and B both lie between 1 and 8 (inclusive).

g. A lies between 1 and 8 (inclusive), but B lies outside these limits.

h. X exceeds 4 while Y is less than 5; or X is less than 5 while Y is greater than 4.

i. The distance between the points in the plane having coordinates (`X1, Y1`) and (`X2, Y2`) is greater than the distance between (`X1, Y1`) and (`X3, Y3`).

j. A and B are both negative or both nonnegative.

k. Either A is 0 or B is 0, but not both.

10. Write Fortran `if` constructs to find the largest of three real variable values. Your program should work properly even if two or three of the values are identical.

11. Read three integers and compare them. If no two are alike, print `0`. If there is a pair, identify the pair; for instance, if the first and third are equal, print `1` and `3`. If all three are identical, print `3`. Use the following data:

Set 1:	7	8	7
Set 2:	99	89	79
Set 3:	1	3	3
Set 4:	6	6	6

12. Write a program to read three integers and print them on one line in descending order. (Compare Example 3.16.)

    a. Use the following data:

Set 1:	7	8	9
Set 2:	7	9	8
Set 3:	8	7	9
Set 4:	8	9	7
Set 5:	9	7	8
Set 6:	9	8	7

    b. Create your own data, but include sets designed to test the operation of the program when two or three of the data values are equal.

13. Some of these exercises can be programmed without `if` constructs by taking advantage of the power of intrinsic functions such as `Max` and `Min`. Write a single statement, without using `if`, corresponding to each of the following.

    a. Exercise 2 in this section

    b. Exercise 5 in this section (Hint: See Section 2.3.)

    c. Print the value of `A` if it is positive, `0` if `A` is zero, and `-A` if `A` is negative. (Thus, if `A` is negative, a positive number with the same magnitude as `A` is to be printed.)

14. Write a program that uses complex arithmetic to compute all roots of a quadratic equation. (Compare Example 3.10.) Use the quadratic formula except when `A` is zero. Do not test the sign of the discriminant.

3.2 MULTI-WAY SELECTION

We have seen how to create a program construct for two-way selection — that is, for selecting either of two alternative sequences of statements. We shall now focus on ways of selecting among three or more alternatives.

Any multiple-selection problem can, in principle, be recast as a combination of two-way selections. However, such a transformation introduces an apparent hierarchy among the alternatives, which is usually artificial and is often distracting and detrimental to program comprehension. The following two Fortran 90 constructs permit multi-way selection with no artificial hierarchy:

1. A generalized form of the `if` construct with `else if`
2. The `case` construct

The `if` Construct with `else if`

In its most general form, an `if` construct begins with an `if-then` statement and ends with an `end if` statement. Between these statements, there may be any number of `else if-then` statements followed by at most one `else` statement. Thus, an `if` construct of the following general form, which includes a sequence of three or more alternative statement sequences, is permitted:

```
if ( Condition ) then
   Then block
else if ( Condition ) then
   Block
   :
[ Optional additional else if-then statements and Blocks ]
   :
else
   Else block
end if
```

The `if-then` statement, each of the `else if-then` statements, and the `else` statement all appear as heading statements for *Blocks* (alternative statement sequences), only one of which is to be executed.

The `else if-then` statement appears only in multi-way selection constructs. This statement has the form

```
else if ( Condition ) then
```

Note that `else if` may be written with or without a blank between `else` and `if`; see Appendix C.1.

Execution of the alternative statement sequences, or *Blocks,* is controlled by the *Conditions* in the `if-then` and `else if-then` statements. These conditions are tested (in order of their appearance) until a true one is found, at which time execution of the corresponding *Block* begins. Execution of the selected block is followed by an automatic transfer to the end of the entire multiple-selection construct. If none of the conditions is found to be true, the *Else block* is executed. Compare Example 3.11 to Example 3.8. See also the flowchart in Figure 3.6.

EXAMPLE 3.11

```
! Example 3.11. Count large, medium, and small cats.
  program Cats_3
    implicit none
    integer, parameter :: LIMIT = 24
    integer :: Hi_Count = 0, Mid_Count = 0, Low_Count = 0, Loop
    real, parameter :: MID_BOUNDARY = 2.7, HI_BOUNDARY = 4.3
    real :: Next_Weight
! start program Cats_3
    do Loop = 1, LIMIT
      print *, "⊥Please⊥enter⊥weight⊥of⊥next⊥cat.⊥"
      read *, Next_Weight
      if (Next_Weight > HI_BOUNDARY) then
        Hi_Count = Hi_Count + 1
      else if (Next_Weight > MID_BOUNDARY) then
        Mid_Count = Mid_Count + 1
      else
        Low_Count = Low_Count + 1
      end if
    end do
    print *, Hi_Count, Mid_Count, Low_Count
  end program Cats_3
```

Although the effects of the programs in Example 3.11 and Example 3.8 are similar, there is an essential difference in viewpoint between the two. In Example 3.8, the cats are first divided into two categories, and then one of these is further subdivided. In Example 3.11, the basic selection construct treats the three categories as being equally important, which is emphasized by parallel indentation of the blocks.[5]

[5] This point may be confusing to readers familiar with some other programming languages (such as Pascal) which require that multi-way selection with if constructs be organized as nested two-way selection constructs. Note especially that the `else if-then` statements in Fortran are not matched by `end if` statements. Blocks preceded by `else if-then` are considered *parallel* to the *Then block* and the *Else block* in a Fortran `if` construct.

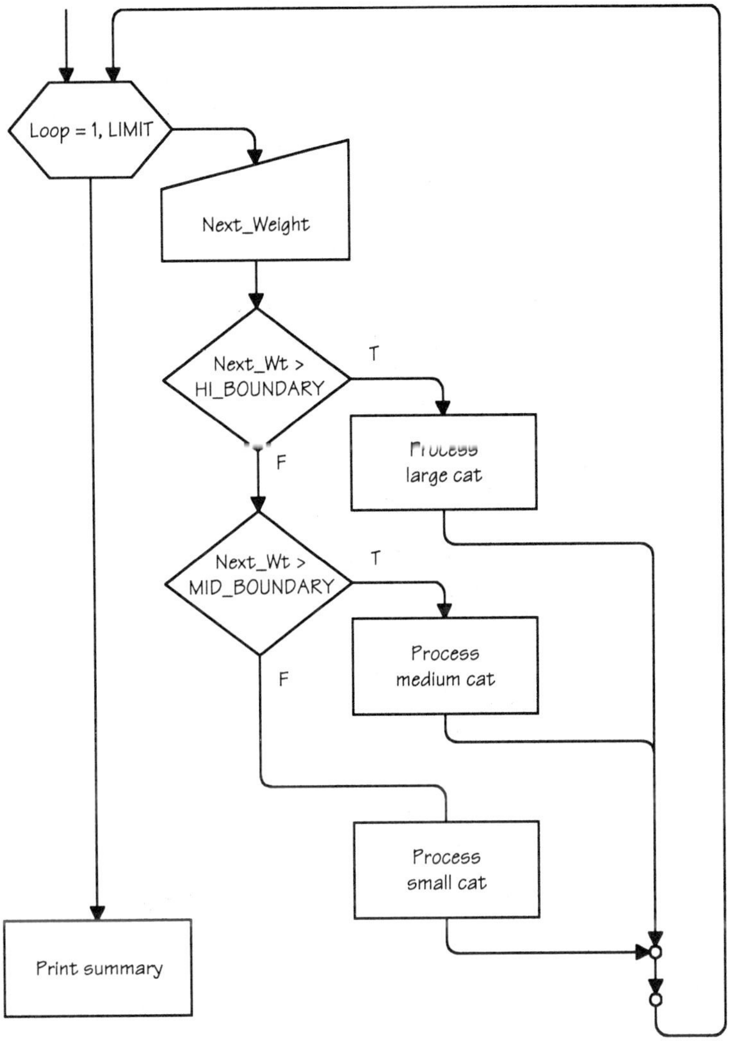

FIGURE 3.6. Flowchart for Example 3.11.

EXAMPLE 3.12 The value of Y is omputed by one of three formulas, depending on the value of X. If X is negative, Y has the constant value 1. If X is between 0 and 1 (inclusive), the value of Y is obtained from the expression 4.0 * X + 1.0 . If X is greater than 1, Y is -10.0 * X + 15.0.

```
! Example 3.12. Compute Y by one of three formulas, depending on X.
  program Three_Formulas
    implicit none
    real :: X, Y
! start program Three_Formulas
    print *, "⊥Please⊥enter⊥the⊥value⊥of⊥X.⊥"
    read *, X
    if (X < 0.0) then
      Y = 1.0
    else if (X <= 1.0) then
      Y = 4.0 * X + 1.0
    else
      Y = -10.0 * X + 15.0
    end if
    print *, "⊥The⊥values⊥of⊥X⊥and⊥Y⊥are:⊥", X, Y
  end program Three_Formulas
```

In the program of Example 3.12, the first condition (X < 0.0) is tested and, if it is found to be true, the value of Y is set to 1; execution then proceeds from the `end if` statement. If the first condition is false, however, the next condition is tested, in turn, to determine whether X is less than or equal to 1; if so, the value of Y is computed according to the second formula. If neither of these conditions is found to be true, it may be concluded that X is greater than 1. The *Else block* will be executed in this instance, and Y will be computed by the third formula.

It is important to note that exactly one of the *Blocks* in this example will be executed. When a true condition is found, the corresponding block is executed, followed by a transfer to the end of the `if` construct. The *Else block* covers the situation in which none of the conditions is found to be true.

In Examples 3.11 and 3.12, the *Conditions* in the `if-then` block and in all of the `else if-then` blocks are related; that is, the various conditions consist of different tests applied to the same variable or expression. Although this relationship among the conditions in a multi-way `if` construct is typical, it is not required by Fortran language rules, as may be observed from Example 3.13.

EXAMPLE 3.13 In mathematics, the (X, Y) plane is divided into four quadrants. In this program, the value of Z is to be computed by one of three different formulas, depending upon the (X, Y) quadrant. The first formula applies in the two quadrants where the value of Y is positive. If the Y value is not positive, then X is tested to determine whether to apply the second or third formula. See also Figure 3.7.

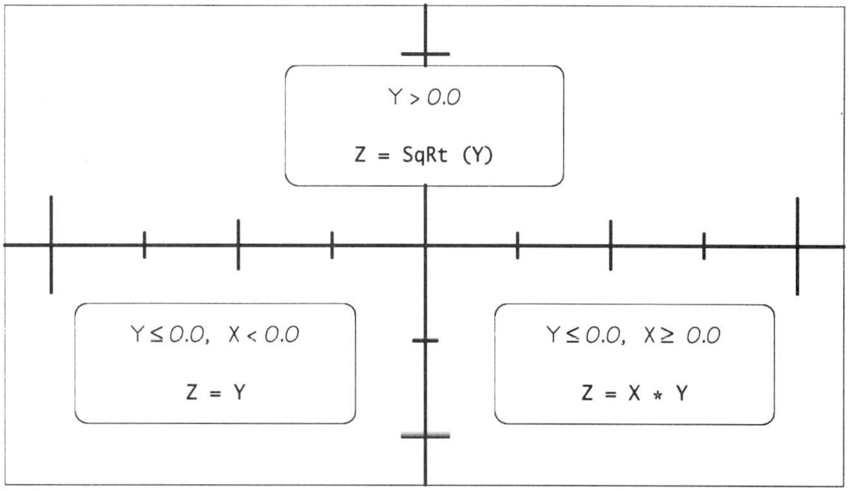

FIGURE 3.7. Choice of *Z* formula in Example 3.13.

```
! Example 3.13. Choose formula for Z according to (X, Y) quadrant.
  program Quadrant
    implicit none
    real :: X, Y, Z
! start program Quadrant
    print *, "⊥Please⊥enter⊥values⊥of⊥X⊥and⊥Y.⊥"
    read *, X, Y
    if (Y > 0.0) then                     ! Northeast and northwest quadrants
      Z = SqRt (Y)
    else if (X < 0.0) then                               ! Southwest quadrant
      Z = Y
    else                                                 ! Southeast quadrant
      Z = X * Y
    end if
    print *, "⊥Values⊥of⊥X,⊥Y,⊥and⊥Z⊥are:⊥", X, Y, Z
  end program Quadrant
```

In the program of Example 3.13, the condition in the `if-then` statement is based on the value of Y, but the condition in the `else if-then` statement is based on the value of X. Note carefully that (because of the sequential evaluation of the conditions in an `if` construct) this condition in the `else if-then` statement includes the *implied negation* of the condition in the `if-then` statement. Without the first condition, true values of X < 0.0 occur in both the northwest and southwest quadrants. However, the fact that the execution sequence has reached the `else if-then` statement rules out the northwest quadrant: If Y were positive, the *Then block* would have been executed and the `else if-then` statement would never have been reached.

Let's summarize what we have learned about the generalied form of the `if` construct with `else if` and about the use of this construct for multi-way branching:

1. The most general Fortran `if` construct opens with a control statement of the form `if (` *Condition* `) then` and ends with the statement `end if`.
2. Between these two statements, there may be at most one `else` statement and any number of statements of the form `else if (` *Condition* `) then`, all of which must precede the `else` statement (if there is one).
3. The `if-then`, `else if-then`, and `else` statements are followed by *Blocks* of statements to be executed conditionally, depending upon the truth of the *Conditions* in the `if-then` and `else if-then` statements.
4. Every `if-then` statement must be matched by an `end if` statement. The `else if-then` statements are not matched. The `end if` statement marks the end of the entire `if` construct that begins with the `if-then` statement. The `else if-then` and `else` statements isolate intermediate blocks within the construct.
5. The block of statements following `else` acts as a catchall to handle situations not covered by any of the conditions. An `if` construct without an `else` statement (and the *Else block* that follows it) is perfectly valid under Fortran language rules. But, in a complete `if` construct, where the `else` statement is not omitted, we can be sure that exactly one of the alternative blocks will be executed.

Empty Statement Sequences

It may happen that no action is to be taken (no statements are to be executed) under certain of the conditions specified in an `if` construct. In such an eventuality, it is permissible to have an *empty block* (with no statements) following an `if-then`, `else if-then`, or `else` statement.

EXAMPLE 3.14 (Compare Examples 3.5 and 3.9.) If the value of I is 1, change it to 2; if it is 2, change it to 1. However, if the value of I is neither 1 nor 2, leave it unchanged.

```
! Example 3.14. Trade the values 1 and 2.
  program Trade_3
    implicit none
    integer :: I

! start program Trade_3
    print *, "⊥Please⊥enter⊥1⊥or⊥2.⊥"
    read *, I
```

```
    if (I == 1) then
      I = 2
    else if (I == 2) then
      I = 1
    else                                              ! Leave I value unchanged.
    end if
    print *, I, "␣was␣computed␣from␣the␣value␣you␣entered.␣"
  end program Trade_3
```

In the program of Example 3.14, the empty *Else block* will be executed if I is neither 1 nor 2; thus, no change will be made in the value of I in this instance.

EXAMPLE 3.15 Professor Katzenzähler's (ever fickle) grant sponsor is no longer interested in small cats. The professor (always agreeable ☺) changes the *Else block* in the program of Example 3.11 to an empty block.

```
! Example 3.15. Count large and medium cats.
  program Cats_4
    implicit none
    integer :: Hi_Count = 0, Mid_Count = 0
    real, parameter :: MID_BOUNDARY = 2.7, HI_BOUNDARY = 4.3
    real :: Next_Weight
! start program Cats_4
    print *, "␣Please␣enter␣weight␣of␣next␣cat.␣"
    read *, Next_Weight
    if (Next_Weight > HI_BOUNDARY) then
      Hi_Count = Hi_Count + 1
    else if (Next_Weight > MID_BOUNDARY) then
      Mid_Count = Mid_Count + 1
    else                                                      ! Do nothing.
    end if
    print *, Hi_Count, Mid_Count
  end program Cats_4
```

The *Then block* or the *Else block* in a two-way `if` construct, or any one or more blocks in a multiple `if` construct, may be empty. A nested `if` construct may also include empty statement sequences, as illustrated by the following example.

EXAMPLE 3.16 Given three values, A, B, and C, sort them into ascending order. In other words, rearrange them as necessary so that A is less than or equal to B, which, in turn, is less than equal to C. You can refine the statement of this problem into two main steps:

1. Determine which of the values, A, B, or C, is larger; swap this larger value with the value of C.
2. Determine which of the values, A or B, is larger; swap this larger value with the value of B.

Note that the swap operations can be omitted when it is known that the larger value is already in its correct position. Thus, by further refining step 1, you obtain the following:

> If A is greater than B, then (either A or C is largest):
> > If A is greater than C, then swap A and C;
> > Else do nothing;
>
> Else (either B or C is largest):
> > If B is greater than C, then swap B and C;
> > Else do nothing.

Refinement of step 2 is somewhat simpler:

> If A is greater than B, then swap A and B;
> > Else do nothing.

This analysis can be implemented with the following program. The internal procedure Swap was presented in Example 2.23. Refinement steps that require no action correspond to empty *Then blocks* or *Else blocks* in the program.

```
! Example 3.16. Sort three values into increasing order.
  program Trivial_Sort_1
    implicit none
    real :: A, B, C

! start program Trivial_Sort_1

    print *, "␣Please␣enter␣three␣numbers␣to␣be␣sorted.␣"
    read *, A, B, C
    if (A > B) then
      if (A > C) then
        call Swap (A, C)
      else                                                  ! Do nothing.
      end if
    else
      if (B > C) then
        call Swap (B, C)
      else                                                  ! Do nothing.
      end if
    end if
```

```
  ! C now contains the largest of the three values.
  if (A > B) then
    call Swap (A, B)
    else                                                         ! Do nothing.
  end if
  print *, "␣The␣sorted␣values␣are:␣", A, B, C
contains
  subroutine Swap (X, Y)
    real, intent (in out) :: X, Y
    real :: Aux
    Aux = X
    X = Y
    Y = Aux
  end subroutine Swap
end program Trivial_Sort_1
```

Omitting the `else` Statement

The `else` statement and the *Else block* may be omitted. Such an abbreviated `if` construct has the form

```
if ( Condition ) then
  Then block
end if
```

or the form

```
if ( Condition ) then
  Then block
else if ( Condition ) then
  Block
end if
```

If the *Else block* is empty, execution of the `if` construct is the same whether the *Else block* is retained or deleted.

Nevertheless, there is a good reason for including an empty *Else block* in a program. As mentioned earlier, when there is an *Else block* in the `if` construct, we can be sure that exactly one of the alternatives will be selected (even though the selected alternative *Block* may be empty). This assurance can contribute significantly to program reliability and readability.

The case *Construct*

For selecting among multiple alternatives on the basis of a single expression value, a `case` construct can illuminate the structure of a program. The *Selector expression* is written once, followed by a listing of the various values that the expression can be expected to take on and the corresponding *Block* of statements to be executed in each case. Figure 3.8 shows the skeleton flowchart for a typical `case` construct.

A `case` construct often provides better program comprehensibility and reliability than the equivalent `if` construct written with a sequence of `else if–then` statements. Furthermore, some computer architectures provide computer instructions that make the execution of `case` constructs especially efficient. However, the `case` construct is subject to two restrictions that do not apply to `else if–then`:

1. The type of the *Selector expression* must be integer, logical, or character — in other words, a type whose values (unlike those of real type) form a *discrete* set. Character type is illustrated in Chapter 6; integer type appears in the following examples. (A `case` construct with a *Selector expression* of logical type has little practical value.) The expressions that control an `if` construct may contain values of real type or other types.
2. The `case` values that determine which block is to be executed must be specified by *initialization expressions* (see Section 1.3), which are simple expressions that may contain constants but not variables. The expressions that control an `if` construct may contain variables.

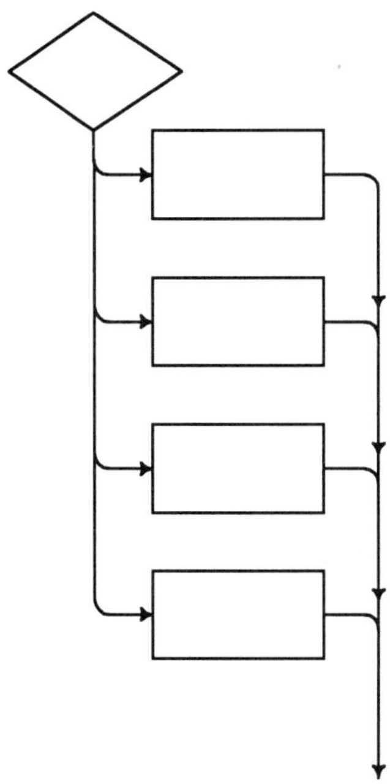

FIGURE 3.8. Skeleton flowchart for a typical *case* construct.

The case construct may be viewed as a specialization or restriction of the `if` construct. The `case` construct does not fit every situation, but, when it can be applied, it usually leads to cleaner program style and increased efficiency of execution.

EXAMPLE 3.17 The following program reads integers representing a year and a month and prints the number of days in the month. Depending upon the month, one of four different statement sequences (`case` blocks) is executed. The first of these blocks contains an assignment statement that covers 30-day months (September, April, June, and November). The second `case` block, to be executed when `Month` is 2 (February), contains an `if` construct that sets the number of days to 29 or 28 depending upon `Year`. (Note that the leap year test is incomplete.) The final `case` block is a `case default` block, which performs much the same role as the *Else block* in an `if` construct. Presence of the `case default` block guarantees that exactly one of the `case` blocks will be executed. This block will be executed for months that have 31 days, as well as for illegitimate input `Month` values.

```
! Example 3.17. Thirty days hath September...
  program Autumn_Daze
    implicit none
    intrinsic Modulo
    integer :: Month, Year, NDays
! start program Autumn_Daze
    print *, "⊥Please⊥enter⊥the⊥year⊥(4⊥digits).⊥"
    read *, Year
    print *, "⊥Please⊥enter⊥the⊥month⊥number⊥(1⊥to⊥12).⊥"
    read *, Month
    select case (Month)
      case (9, 4, 6, 11)                                   ! Sep, Apr, Jun, Nov
        NDays = 30
      case (2)                                                     ! February
        if (Modulo (Year, 4) == 0) then
          NDays = 29                                              !Leap year
        else
          NDays = 28
        end if
      case default                         ! Jan, Mar, May, Jul, Aug, Oct, Dec
        NDays = 31
    end select
    print *, "⊥The⊥number⊥of⊥days⊥in⊥month:⊥", Month, "⊥is:⊥", NDays
  end program Autumn_Daze
```

Form of the case *Construct*

A `case` construct begins with a `select case` statement and ends with an `end select` statement. Between these two statements, there may be any number of `case` statements, at most one of which may be a `case default` statement. Although Fortran 90 permits the `case default` statement (when present) to appear in any order among the sequence of `case` statements in a `case` construct, good programming style suggests that it should appear last.

The anatomy of the case construct is as follows:

1. A `select case` statement has the form

   `select case (` *Selector expression* `)`

   where *Selector expression* is an expression of integer, character, or logical type.
2. A `case` statement has the form

   `case (` *List* `)`

   or

   `case default`

   In the first of these forms, each *List* item designates a value or a range of values to be matched against the *Selector expression* in the `select case` statement.
3. A *Case block* consists of all statements *following* a `case` statement and *preceding* the next `case` statement or `end select` statement of the same `case` construct.
4. An `end select` statement has the form:

   `end select`

Thus, the general form of a `case` consıruct is the following:

```
select case ( Selector expression )
   Case statement
      Case block
   Case statement
      Case block
      ⋮
end select
```

In a `case` statement other than `case default`, the *List* must not be empty. Each *List* item has one of four forms:

Expression
Expression $\mathcal{A}$: *Expression* $\mathcal{B}$
Expression $\mathcal{A}$:
: *Expression* $\mathcal{B}$

(If the type of the *Selector expression* is logical, however, only the first of these forms is permitted.)

The type of *Expression*, *Expression* $\mathcal{A}$, and *Expression* $\mathcal{B}$ in each *List* item must be the same as the type of *Selector expression* in the `select case` statement. In the form *Expression* $\mathcal{A}$: *Expression* $\mathcal{B}$, the value of *Expression* $\mathcal{A}$ must be less than or equal to the value of *Expression* $\mathcal{B}$.

Each *List* item defines a *range*, which may be described in one of the following ways (depending upon the form of the *List* item):

1. If the *List* item has the form *Expression*, the range consists of the value of *Expression*.
2. If the *List* item has the form *Expression* $\mathcal{A}$: *Expression* $\mathcal{B}$, the range consists of all values between *Expression* $\mathcal{A}$ and *Expression* $\mathcal{B}$ (inclusive).
3. If the *List* item has the form *Expression* $\mathcal{A}$:, the range consists of all values greater than or equal to the value of *Expression* $\mathcal{A}$.
4. If the *List* item has the form : *Expression* $\mathcal{B}$, the range consists of all values less than or equal to the value of *Expression* $\mathcal{B}$.

The ranges of all of the *List* items in all of the `case` statements in a given `case` construct must be *disjoint*. That is, there must be no value that is in the range of more than one *List* item (among all of the `case` statements in the construct).

A *Case block* may be *empty*. That is, there need not be any instructions between the `case` statement and the next `case` statement or `end select` statement of the same `case` construct.

A `case` construct may have a construct name. Naming a `case` construct requires the following steps:

1. The construct name followed by a colon is written on the left, just preceding the keyword `select case` in the opening statement of the construct.
2. The same name without a colon must then be written on the right, following the keyword `end select` in the closing statement of the construct.
3. The construct name without a colon may also appear at the end of a `case` or `case default` statement.

Execution of the case *Construct*

Execution of a `case` construct begins with evaluation of the *Selector expression* in the `select case` statement. The `case` statements of the `case` construct (except the `case default` statement, if any) are then executed in the order of their appearance; that is, in each `case` statement, the value of *Selector expression* is compared with each *List* item (in order):

1. If the value of *Selector expression* is in the range of the *List* item, a *match* occurs; remaining items (if any) in the *List* currently being examined are ignored, and the *Block* headed by the `case` statement where the match was found is selected for immediate execution.
2. If no match occurs during examination of the *Lists* in all `case` statements, and the construct contains a `case default` statement, the *Case block* headed by the `case default` statement is selected for execution.

3. If there is no match and no `case default`, execution of the `case` construct terminates without any *Case block* being executed. If a *Case block* is selected, its execution proceeds normally, beginning with the first statement in the block. If the execution sequence reaches the end of the last statement in the *Case block*, it transfers directly from that point to the end of the entire `case` construct.[6]

It is recommended that a `case default` block — even if it is empty — be included as the last *Case block* of every `case` construct, to ensure that exactly one alternative *Case block* in the construct will be executed. If there is no `case default` statement and no match occurs, the `case` construct terminates without execution of any *Case block*.

EXAMPLE 3.18 Version 6 of the MS-DOS operating system for Intel 80486-based computers reserves memory in four separate areas. The following program reads a memory address (expressed in kilobytes) and prints the name of the memory area that contains the given address. In the `case` construct, the first Case block is selected when `Address` is –1 or less and the last Case block is selected when `Address` is 1088 or greater.

```
! Example 3.18. MS-DOS PC memory allocation.
  program Elephant
    implicit none
    integer :: Address
! start program Elephant
    print *, "␣Please␣enter␣a␣memory␣address,␣expressed␣in␣kilobytes.␣"
    read *, Address
    select case (Address)
      case (: -1)
        print *, "The␣address␣", Address, "␣does␣not␣exist␣in␣memory.␣"
      case (0: 639)
        print *, "The␣address␣", Address, "␣is␣in␣Conventional␣Memory.␣"
      case (640: 1023)
        print *, "␣The␣address␣", Address, "␣is␣in␣the␣Upper␣Memory␣Area.␣"
        print *, "␣(This␣is␣a␣part␣of␣Extended␣Memory.)␣"
      case (1024: 1087)
        print *, "␣The␣address␣", Address, "␣is␣in␣the␣High␣Memory␣Area.␣"
        print *, "␣(This␣is␣a␣part␣of␣Extended␣Memory.)␣"
      case (1088: )
        print *, "The␣address␣", Address, "␣is␣in␣Extended␣Memory.␣"
    end select
  end program Elephant
```

6 Unlike the case constructs in some programming languages (notably `switch` in C and C++, which requires `break` to avoid control flow into the next block), Fortran's `case` construct does not require an explicit control statement to cause transfer to the end of the construct.

EXAMPLE 3.19 At some schools, the fall semester lasts from September through January, and the spring semester lasts from February through June. In this program, notice that there are two *List* items in the first `case` statement, the range `9: 12` and the separate item `1`. Also notice the `case default` *Case* block.

```
! Example 3.19. Fall and spring semesters, by months.
  program Academy
    implicit none
    integer :: M
! start program Academy
    print *, "␣Please␣enter␣a␣month␣number␣between␣1␣and␣12.␣"
    read *, M
    select case (M)
      case (9: 12, 1)
        print *, "␣Month␣", M, "␣is␣in␣the␣fall␣semester.␣"
      case (2: 6)
        print *, "␣Month␣", M, "␣is␣in␣the␣spring␣semester.␣"
      case default
        print *, "␣School␣is␣not␣in␣session␣during␣month␣", M
    end select
  end program Academy
```

EXAMPLE 3.20 In this `case` construct, selection is based on the value of a real variable that is converted to an integer. The program tabulates the number of survey respondents in each of several salary ranges. Open-ended ranges select very low or very high values.

```
! Example 3.20. Salary survey.
  program Tycoon
    implicit none
    intrinsic Floor
    real :: Salary
    integer, parameter :: LIMIT = 100
    integer :: S2 = 0. S3 = 0, S4 = 0, S5 = 0, S6 = 0, S7 = 0, S8 = 0, Loop
! start program Tycoon
    do Loop = 1, LIMIT
      print *, "␣Please␣enter␣the␣next␣salary.␣"
      read *, Salary
```

```
    select case (Floor (Salary))
      case (: 29999)
        S2 = S2 + 1
      case (30000: 39999)
        S3 = S3 + 1
      case (40000 : 49999)
        S4 = S4 + 1
      case (50000 : 59999)
        S5 = S5 + 1
      case (60000 : 69999)
        S6 = S6 + 1
      case (70000 : 79999)
        S7 = S7 + 1
      case (80000: )
        S8 = S8 + 1
    end select
  end do
  print *, S2, S3, S4, S5, S6, S7, S8
end program Tycoon
```

EXAMPLE 3.21 (Compare Examples 3.5, 3.9, and 3.14.) If the value of I is 1, change it to 2; if it is 2, change it to 1. However, if the value of I is neither 1 nor 2, leave it unchanged.

```
! Example 3.21. Trade the values 1 and 2.
 program Trade_4
   implicit none
   integer :: I
! start program Trade_4
   print *, "⊥Please⊥enter⊥1⊥or⊥2.⊥"
   read *, I
   print *, "⊥Thank⊥you.⊥⊥You⊥have⊥entered:⊥", I
   select case (I)
     case (1)
       I = 2
     case (2)
       I = 1
     case default                              ! Leave I value unchanged.
   end select
   print *, I, "⊥was⊥computed⊥from⊥the⊥value⊥you⊥entered.⊥"
 end program Trade_4
```

In the program of Example 3.21, either the first *Case block*, the second *Case block*, or the case default *Case block* is executed, depending on the value of `I`. The empty `case default` *Case block* will be executed if `I` is neither 1 nor 2; thus, no change will be made in the value of `I` in this situation.

EXAMPLE 3.22

```
! Example 3.22. Nested case constructs.
 program Eagle
   implicit none
   integer :: First_Int, Second_Int, Num = -2
   real :: A = -2.0

! start program Eagle
   read *, First_Int, Second_Int
   L1: select case (First_Int)                ! select case statement at level 1
     case (: -1)                                         ! case block at level 1
       Num = -1
       L2: select case (Second_Int)           ! select case statement at level 2
         case (-5)                                       ! case block at level 2
           A = 1.0
         case default                              ! case default block at level 2
           A = 0.0
       end select L2                             ! end select statement at level 2
     case (0)                                            ! case block at level 1
       Num = 0
     case default                                        ! case block at level 1
       Num = 1
   end select L1                                 ! end select statement at level 1
   print *, Num, A
 end program Eagle
```

Transition Tip

- Change three-branch arithmetic `if` statements (see Appendix D.4) to `case` constructs or to `if` constructs with `else if`. Change all computed `go to` statements to `case` constructs.

3.2 Exercises

1. Write a program that reads a pH value between 1.0 and 14.0 and prints a message giving the color of a certain chemical indicator for that pH value. The program should print an intermediate color (orange, green, purple, or pink) if the pH is in the critical range. Use a `case` statement based on one of the following indicators:

Indicator	Color in Acid	pH Range of Color Change	Color in Base
Methyl orange	Red	3.1–4.4	Yellow
Bromthymol blue	Yellow	6.0–7.6	Blue
Litmus	Red	4.5–8.3	Blue
Phenolphthalein	Colorless	8.3–10.0	Red

2. If all of the `if` constructs in a program are two-branch constructs — that is, if there are no `else if-then` statements — there should be as many `end if` statements as there are statements ending with the keyword `then`. (This rule applies even in a program with nested `if` constructs.) State a similar rule that applies in the more general case in which `else if-then` statements are permitted.

3. Fill in the following values:

	Value of I: 0	1	2	3
a) Value of `3 - I`				
b) Result from Example 3.5.				
c) Result from Example 3.9.				
d) Result from Example 3.14				
e) Result from Example 3.21.				

4. Rewrite the program in Example 3.17, using a nested `case` construct instead of an `if` construct in the test for leap year.

5. Exactly what will be printed by the program in Example 3.17 if the `Month` value entered is not between 1 and 12 (inclusive)?

6. Modify the program in Example 3.18, replacing the last `case` block (which detects negative `Address` values) by a `case default` block.

7. Write a `case` construct to set the real variable `Sign_Of_X` to –1.0 if the real variable `X` is negative, to 0.0 if `X` is zero, or to 1.0 if `X` is positive.

3.3 SIMPLIFIED SELECTION PATTERNS

Two simple Fortran selection mechanisms that do not require control constructs, the simple `if` statement and the intrinsic function `Merge`, are described next.

The Simple `if` Statement

It sometimes happens that a single statement is to be executed or skipped, depending on the truth of some *Condition*. Fortran's simple `if` statement simplifies this form of selection:

```
if ( Condition ) Dependent statement
```

Here are some examples:

```
if (A >= 0.0) X = SqRt (A)
if (B /= 0.0) Quotient = A / B
if (My_Luv_4_U) print *, "␣I␣love␣you.␣"
if (String_1 >= String_2) String_Max = String_1
if (EoF < 0) stop "␣End␣of␣data.␣"
if (I == 1) Sum = 0.0
if (I <= N) read *, A, B
if (A >= 0.0) print *, SqRt (A)
if ((I == 1) .or. (I == 2)) I = 3 - I
```

It is important to note the following:

1. The *Dependent statement* may be any statement except another simple `if` statement or an `end` statement.
2. The only effect of the *Condition* in a simple `if` statement of the form just shown is to determine whether or not the *Dependent statement* will be executed. The statement following the simple `if` statement will be executed in either case.
3. If the *Dependent statement* is not a control statement, the statement that follows the simple `if` statement will always be executed. If the *Condition* in the simple `if` statement is true, execution of the *Dependent statement* will take place, followed by execution of the statement that follows. If the *Condition* is false, the *Dependent statement* will be skipped and the statement that follows `if` will be executed without further ado.
4. If the *Dependent statement* is a control statement — for example, an `exit` statement (see Sections 4.1 and 4.4) — executing the *Dependent statement* when the *Condition* is true will generally cause one or more of the statements following `if` to be skipped. A simple `if` statement, with an `exit`, `cycle`, `stop`, `return`, or `call` statement as the *Dependent statement* may be used to control termination of a loop, procedure, or program.

Note the difference in form between a simple `if` statement and an `if-then` statement. The simple `if` statement has a *Dependent statement* following the *Condition*, rather than the keyword `then`, and is not matched by an `end if` statement.

A simple `if` statement is precisely equivalent in its effect to an `if` construct in which the *Then block* consists only of the *Dependent statement* — that is, to an `if` construct with only four statements, of the form

```
if ( Condition ) then
  Dependent statement
  else
end if
```

(The construct would be reduced to three statements if we chose to omit the `else` statement.) The single-statement form may therefore be regarded simply as a convenient shorthand notation for the longer form. Where it is important to emphasize the precise structure of the algorithm, however, writing out the full `if` construct may be preferable.

EXAMPLE 3.23 The following program has the same effect as Example 3.16, but it is shorter because several `if` constructs with empty *Else blocks* have been replaced by simple `if` statements. (The internal procedure Swap in this example is the same as in Examples 2.23 and 3.16.)

```
! Example 3.23. Sort three values into increasing order.
  program Trivial_Sort_2
    implicit none
    real :: A, B, C
! start program Trivial_Sort_2
    print *, "␣Please␣enter␣three␣numbers␣to␣be␣sorted.␣"
    read *, A, B, C
    print *, "␣You␣have␣entered:␣", A, B, C
    if (A > B) then
      if (A > C) call Swap (A, C)
    else
      if (B > C) call Swap (B, C)
    end if
    ! C now contains the largest of the three values.
    if (A > B) call Swap (A, B)
    print *, "␣The␣sorted␣values␣are:␣", A, B, C
  contains
    subroutine Swap (X, Y)                         ! See Example 3.16
      ⋮
    end subroutine Swap
  end program Trivial_Sort_2
```

The Intrinsic Function Merge *(Advanced)*

The Fortran 90 intrinsic function Merge provides a sort of conditional expression:[7]

Merge (*Expression*$_1$, *Expression*$_2$, *Condition*)

The function result is the value of *Expression*$_1$ if the *Condition* is true or the value of *Expression*$_2$ if the *Condition* is false. The two expressions may have any type, but both must have the same type and subtype, and they must have the same length if they are character strings. The *Condition* may be any expression of logical type (see Section 3.4).

Some examples are as follows:

```
X = SqRt (Merge (A, -A, A >= 0.0))
Quotient = A / Merge (B, 1.0, B /= 0.0)
print *, Merge ("␣I␣love␣you.␣", "␣I␣hate␣you.␣", My_Luv_4_U)
String_Max = Merge (String_1, String_2, String_1 >= String_2)
```

In the first of these examples, the result from Merge is A if A is greater than or equal to zero and is -A otherwise. In the second example, A will be divided by B, unless B is zero, in which case A will be divided by 1.0. In the third example, My_Luv_4_U is a *variable* of logical type that is either true or false. The function value that will be printed is one or the other of the two messages. Note that the two messages are equal in length. In the fourth example, String_1 and String_2 must have the same length. The function value will be the larger string (based on string comparison as described in Section 6.1). For example, if the two strings are "AIRCRAFT" and "AIRPLANE", the second string will be assigned to String_Max.

Note that the first two examples are not quite equivalent to

```
X = Merge (SqRt (A), SqRt (-A), A >= 0.0)
Quotient = Merge (A / B, A, B /= 0.0)
```

because of the Fortran rule that all function arguments are evaluated before the function is called. In these latter statements, SqRt (A) will be evaluated before Merge is called even if A < 0.0, and A / B will be evaluated before Merge is called even if B = 0.0. These erroneous values will be computed, with potentially disastrous results, even though they would be discarded immediately by Merge.

The lesson is this: When using Merge to avoid a possible error condition, check that the actual arguments to Merge will be properly defined even in the error case.

[7] The Fortran intrinsic function Merge does not have the power of the true conditional expressions provided by such languages as C, C++, and Lisp. The comparative weakness of the Fortran version lies in the assumption that all actual argument expressions are evaluated before the function is applied. With a true conditional expression, the predicate would be evaluated first, followed by exactly one of the alternative expressions.

3.3 Exercises

1. Write an expression involving Merge with the value specified in each case:

   a. The result is "AM" if Time is greater than 0.0 but less than or equal to 12.0; otherwise, the result is "PM".

   b. The result is the smaller of the values of the real variables X and Y.

   c. The result is 366 if Year is a multiple of 4; otherwise, the result is 365. (Hint: Use Modulo; see Section 2.3.)

   d. The result is 1 if I is 2; the result is 2 if I has any other value.

2. In the first set of examples at the beginning of Section 3.3, rewrite each of the nine simple if statements as a complete two-branch if construct.

3. What is the disadvantage of the following program as compared to those of Examples 3.5, 3.9, 3.14, and 3.21?

```
! Exercises 3.3, Number 3. Trade the values 1 and 2.
 program Trade_5
  implicit none
  integer :: I
! start program Trade_5
  print *, "␣Please␣enter␣1␣or␣2.␣"
  read *, I
  print *, "␣Thank␣you.␣␣You␣have␣entered:␣", I
  if (I == 1) I = 2
  if (I == 2) I = 1
  print *, "␣Your␣value␣was␣changed␣to:␣", I
 end program Trade_5
```

   (Hint: If the original value of I is 1, what will its value be after the first simple if statement is executed? In this case, will the condition in the second simple if statement be true or false?)

4. In Exercise 3 of Section 3.1, explain why it would *not* be advisable to replace the if construct with a reference to Merge.

3.4 LOGICAL DATA TYPE (Advanced)

At this point, let's interrupt the discussion of selection and consider *logical* data type. Logical expressions appear primarily as *Conditions* in the statements

```
if ( Condition ) then
```

and

```
do while ( Condition )
```

though these are by no means their only applications. Data of logical type is appropriate for any purpose that requires a value that is either true or false. (Examples 5.38 and 5.39 in Section 5.4 show an application of logical data type to the analysis of a directed graph.)

The examples in Section 3.1 illustrate relational expressions that compare numeric or character values. A relational expression is one form of logical expression. Fortran also provides variables, constants, and expressions of logical type.

We have noted that the type of an item of information affects the set of its possible values, the kinds of operations that can be performed upon it, and the way it is stored or represented in the computer. Note the following points concerning logical type:

1. For logical type, the range of possible values is especially simple; it consists of only two values, true and false.
2. The logical operators `.and.`, `.or.`, and `.not.` (as well as the less common logical relational operators `.eqv.` and `.neqv.`, described later in this section) may combine expressions of logical type. Assignment of a logical expression to a logical variable is also permitted.
3. Simple (list-directed) output of a logical expression produces `T` or `F`. Input data values may be written either as `T` and `F` or as `.TRUE.` and `.FALSE.` (see also Section 9.3).

Logical Variables and Constants

A type declaration may list one or more names that denote variables of logical type — for example,

```
logical :: G, H, Data_Is_Exhausted, Flag
```

A logical variable may be assigned the value true or false at some point in the program and tested at some other point. For such simple uses, a logical variable has little advantage over an integer variable whose value is set at one point and tested somewhere else. However, when the test involves combinations of logical values (as in Example 3.27 given later in this section), operations with logical variables are more appropriate.

The forms `.TRUE.` and `.FALSE.` represent the two explicit logical constants. These logical constants may be written in either upper or lower case; this text uses upper case because they are similar to named constants. An initialized variable or a named constant may be declared to have one of these values:

```
logical :: Data_Is_Exhausted = .FALSE. ! initialized variable
logical, parameter :: NIL = .FALSE.           ! named constant
```

EXAMPLE 3.24 As the following program shows, a named logical constant can be employed in the same way as other logical expressions, for example, on the right side of an assignment statement.

```
! Example 3.24.
  program Reason
    implicit none
    logical :: Data_Is_Exhausted = .FALSE., Flag          ! initialized variable
    logical, parameter :: NIL = .FALSE.                      ! named constant
! start program Reason
    if (Data_Is_Exhausted) Flag = NIL
    print *, Flag
  end program Reason
```

The simplest logical expressions are explicit logical constants, named logical constants, and variables of logical type. A relational expression is an expression of logical type (since its value is either true or false) even though the operands of the relational operator are not logical expressions.

More complicated logical expressions can be formed with the logical operators .and., .or., and .not. joining simpler subexpressions. Any logical expression may appear on the right side of an assignment statement with a logical variable on the left.

A logical variable, like any other expression of logical type, may be used as the *Condition* in a selection context. Consider Examples 3.25 and 3.26.

EXAMPLE 3.25 Suppose that a certain logical variable is to be set to true if X is greater than Y and to false otherwise. The following program will print T if X is greater than Y; otherwise, it will print F.

```
! Example 3.25.
  program X_Or_Y_1
    implicit none
    real :: X, Y
    logical :: Big_X
! start program X_Or_Y_1
```

```
  print *, "␣Please␣enter␣values␣for␣X␣and␣Y.␣"
  read *, X, Y
  if (X > Y) then
    Big_X = .TRUE.
  else
    Big_X = .FALSE.
  end if
  print *, "␣The␣proposition␣'X␣exceeds␣Y'␣is:␣", Big_X
end program X_Or_Y_1
```

EXAMPLE 3.26 The following simpler program achieves the same result as in Example 3.25. Here, the relational expression X > Y will be evaluated, and its value (true or false) will be assigned as the value of the logical variable Big_X. Thus, if X is 6.0 and Y is 7.0 when the assignment is executed, the value false will be assigned to Big_X.

```
! Example 3.26.
 program X_Or_Y_2
   implicit none
   real :: X, Y; logical Big_X
! start program X_Or_Y_2
   print *, "␣Please␣enter␣values␣for␣X␣and␣Y.␣"
   read *, X, Y
   Big_X = X > Y
   print *, "␣The␣proposition␣'X␣exceeds␣Y'␣is:␣", Big_X
 end program X_or_Y_2
```

Expressions of Logical Type

Expressions of logical data type may be composed of the following elements:

- Relational expressions, such as P < 7.0, consisting of a pair of arithmetic expressions (or character expressions; see Chapter 6) connected by a relational operator
- Explicit logical constants, .TRUE. or .FALSE., and named constants
- Logical variables
- Combinations of the above, produced with the logical operators .and., .or., and .not. or with the logical relational operators .eqv. and .neqv.

EXAMPLE 3.27

```
! Example 3.27.
  program Logical_Express
    implicit none
    real :: X = 1.0, G = 4.99
    logical :: Flag, Logical_Variable, Goal_Test = .FALSE.
! start program Logical_Express
    Flag = (X == 0.0)                          ! Use of parentheses is optional.
    Logical_Variable = Flag
    Goal_Test = (Goal_Test .or. Logical_Variable)
    Goal_Test = (G >= 0) .and. (G <= 5.0) .and. (.not. Flag)
    Logical_Variable = Logical_Variable .and. (G > 1.0)
    if (Flag) X = 0.0
    print *, Flag, Goal_Test, Logical_Variable, X
  end program Logical_Express
```

Several of the expressions in Example 3.27 contain parentheses, which can be omitted, provided that the precedence rules stated later in this section are carefully observed. However, it is often advisable to insert extra parentheses in a logical expression so that its meaning can be more easily understood.

When the first assignment statement in the program of Example 3.27 is executed, `Flag` will be assigned the value true if the value of `X` is zero; otherwise, `Flag` will be given the value false. The second assignment statement will assign to `Logical_Variable` the current value (true or false) of `Flag`.

After execution of the third assignment statement, the new value of `Goal_Test` is true if its old value is true or if `Logical_Variable` is true (or both); otherwise, the new value of `Goal_Test` is false.

The fourth and fifth assignment statements combine relational expressions with logical variables. The fourth assignment sets `Goal_Test` to true only if the value of the real variable `G` is between 0.0 and 5.0 (inclusive) and `Flag` is false. The fifth assignment combines `Logical_Variable` with a relational expression.

The simple `if` statement

```
if (Flag) X = 0.0
```

sets `X` to zero if `Flag` is true. If `Flag` is false, nothing happens to `X`.

Note that the simple condition `Flag` is sufficient for this purpose. It should be unnecessary to point out that this condition is true if the value of `Flag` is true and is false if the value of `Flag` is false. A statement of the form

```
if (Flag == .TRUE.)
```

not only is unnecessarily complicated, but also is invalid because the operands of the relational operator == are required to have numeric or character (not logical) type.

Logical Operators

The logical expression

$\mathcal{E}xpression_1$ `.and.` $\mathcal{E}xpression_2$

is true if both of the subexpressions $\mathcal{E}xpression_1$ and $\mathcal{E}xpression_2$ are true. If either subexpression is false, the entire expression is also false.

The expression

$\mathcal{E}xpression_1$ `.or.` $\mathcal{E}xpression_2$

is true if either of the subexpressions $\mathcal{E}xpression_1$ or $\mathcal{E}xpression_2$ is true or if both are true. If both subexpressions are false, the entire expression is also false.

The expression

`.not.` *Expression*

is true when *Expression* is false, and it is false when *Expression* is true.

Operands for the logical operators `.and.`, `.or.`, and `.not.` must be expressions of logical type; operands of any other type are invalid. Note that the expression

Expression `.and. .FALSE.`

is always false, whereas the expression

Expression `.or. .TRUE.`

is always true, regardless of the truth value of the logical expression *Expression*. The truth value of either of the expressions

Expression `.and. .TRUE.`
Expression `.or. .FALSE.`

is the same as the truth value of *Expression*.

Comparing Logical Expressions

Section 3.1 presented relational operators whose operands must be a pair of numerical expressions or a pair of character expressions. Those operators and, in particular, the matching operators == and /= cannot have operands of logical type. However, there are two additional relational operators, written as `.eqv.` and `.neqv.`, that test a pair of logical expressions for equality or inequality.

A relational expression of the form

Logical expression `.eqv.` *Logical expression*

is true if and only if the two *Logical expressions* are both true or both false. A relational expression of the form

Logical expression `.neqv.` *Logical expression*

is true if and only if one of the *Logical expressions* is true and the other is false. The .neqv. operator is also known as *exclusive or.*

Let's consider some examples. Assume that A, B, X, and Y are real variables and that Flag, Flag_1, and Flag_2 are logical variables:

```
(A > B) .eqv. Flag
Flag_1 .neqv. Flag_2
(X >= 0.0) .neqv. (Y >= 0.0)          ! X and Y have opposite signs.
Flag .eqv. .TRUE.                                ! Not recommended.
```

If an operand of .eqv. or .neqv. is the constant .TRUE. or .FALSE., as in the fourth example, it is likely that the relational expression is unnecessarily complicated and can be simplified. That is,

```
if (Flag .eqv. .TRUE.)
if (Flag .neqv. .FALSE.)
```

are just complicated ways of writing

```
if (Flag)
```

Operator Precedence

A logical expression may involve logical operators, relational operators, and (within the arithmetic expressions in a relational expression) arithmetic operators. Rules of precedence may be taken into account to establish the meaning of an expression such as

```
Logical_Variable .or. A > B + C
```

(assuming that Logical_Variable has logical type and that A, B, and C are real). Questions of precedence may, of course, be avoided by inserting parentheses.

In the absence of parentheses (or within a given pair of parentheses), the following precedence rules apply:

1. Arithmetic expressions are evaluated first, according to the rules set forth in Chapter 1.
2. Relational expressions are evaluated next.
3. The logical operators are applied last. Among the logical operators, .not. has highest precedence, .and. is intermediate, and .or. is lowest. Thus,

   $\mathcal{E}xpression_1$ .or. $\mathcal{E}xpression_2$ .and. $\mathcal{E}xpression_3$

   means

   $\mathcal{E}xpression_1$ .or. ($\mathcal{E}xpression_2$ .and. $\mathcal{E}xpression_3$)

   rather than

   ($\mathcal{E}xpression_1$ .or. $\mathcal{E}xpression_2$) .and. $\mathcal{E}xpression_3$

Applications of Logical Data

As we have seen, a logical expression may appear as the *Condition* in a selection construct. The *Conditions* in the examples of Sections 3.1 to 3.3 are simple relational expressions or compound relations consisting of two or more relational expressions connected by logical operators. We now see that a logical expression of any form can appear as a *Condition*, for example (assuming that `Flag` and `Logical_Variable` are declared to have logical type),

```
if (Flag) then
if (Logical_Variable .and. X > Y) then
if (Logical_Variable .and. .not. Flag) then
if (Logical_Variable .neqv. Flag) then
```

In Section 4.3, we shall see how to use a logical expression as the *Condition* that controls a repetition construct.

Logical data may also be applied in other ways. Names of logical variables may appear in an input or output list. Constants and other expressions of logical type (including relational expressions) may also appear in an output list. For list-directed input, a data value corresponding to a logical list item may consist simply of the letter `T` for true or the letter `F` for false.

Digital Logic Circuits

With variables and expressions of logical type, we can simulate input digital circuit elements such as AND gates, OR gates, and inverters or NOT elements. For example, a two-input adder, or *half-adder*, whose inputs are the logical variables `X` and `Y`, has `Half_Sum` and `Half_Carry` outputs that are defined by the following logical expressions:

```
Half_Carry (X, Y) = X .and. Y
Half_Sum (X, Y) = (X .neqv. Y)
```

Two integers, in binary notation with each digit represented as `.TRUE.` for 1 and `.FALSE.` for 0, can be added in parallel with a set of *three-input adders*, one for each binary digit position of the numbers to be added. The three inputs to each adder are the corresponding digits of the operands and the carry from the next lower digit position. The lowest digit position requires only a two-input adder since it has no carry input. The output is a binary sum digit for each position and a carry from each digit position including the highest. A three-input adder may be constructed as follows:

```
Sum (X, Y, Z) = X .neqv. (Y .neqv. Z)
Carry (X, Y, Z) = (X .and. Y) .or. (X .and. Z) .or. (Y .and. Z)
```

Arrays of Logical Data

The whole-array facilities described in Section 5.3 include the extension of logical operators to logical arrays. Certain intrinsic functions, such as `MatMul` and `Dot_Product`, have a special interpretation for logical arguments (see Example 5.37 and Appendix A). When the arguments to these intrinsic functions are logical arrays, the operator `.and.` replaces multiplication and the operator `.or.` replaces addition.

Later in this section we discuss a *packed* representation whereby storage space may be conserved by representing logical values as single bytes or even as single bits. The logical operators `.and.`, `.or.`, `.not.`, `.eqv.`, and `.neqv.` applied to whole arrays and array sections provide a powerful mechanism for bit processing applications.

Many operations with logical data are analogous to those that apply to data of other types. As we have seen, there are logical constants and variables, logical expressions, and input or output list items of logical type.

However, there are some restrictions with regard to the mixing of types. Although expressions of integer, real, complex, or character types are permitted in relational expressions that are components of a logical expression, a mixed-type expression must not include one operand of logical type and the other of numeric (real, integer, or complex) or character type. Such mixed expressions make no sense. Mixed-type assignment between logical and numeric types is also prohibited.

Logical Data Representation and `kind` *Parameters (Optional)*

As noted in Section 1.6, numerical data — variables and constants of real and integer types — may have a `kind` subtype, which designates a particular Fortran 90 numeric (fixed-point or floating-point) representation model. Logical type may also have variant subtypes. For example, logical subtypes are employed by some processors for a *packed* computer representation.

A `kind` parameter value may be written at the end of a logical constant, separated by an underscore (compare Section 1.6):

```
.TRUE._1
.FALSE._PACKED
```

The `kind` subtype for a logical variable may be specified in a type declaration in the usual way.

A Fortran processor is required to support, as the default `kind` for logical data, a representation wherein a (scalar) object of logical type occupies the same amount of storage as an integer or a real (scalar) object of default `kind`. This requirement is imposed by the need to maintain compatibility with programs that depend on storage association (see Appendix E). A variable of default logical subtype occupies one *numeric storage unit* (Appendix E.1), which, because of the precision requirements of real data, occupies 32 or more bits (4 or more bytes) on most computers.

Packed Logical Data

A large array of logical data may be required for a bit map in a graphics application or as a mask such as might be used either with masked assignment (as described in Section 5.7) or as the `Mask` argument to an intrinsic function (see Appendix A, especially Section A.5). In such applications, the amount of storage required by the default logical `kind` might well be intolerable.

Maximum packing would be achieved if each logical variable occupied only a single bit. With some computer architectures, however, access to single bits is awkward and inefficient while access to a *byte* (a sequence of 8 bits) is easy and efficient. Fortran 90 processors that provide a packed logical subtype (which may occupy 1 bit or 1 byte, depending upon the processor) can save a significant amount of storage.

Manipulating Bit Sequences

Fortran 90 can process bit data in either of two quite different ways:

1. For maximum flexibility, bits can be manipulated as values of logical type.
2. For compatibility with traditional Fortran versions, an integer value can be interpreted as a sequence of binary digits that express the integer in radix 2 notation. However, this method of manipulating bit sequences becomes unwieldy when the length of the sequence exceeds the number of bits that the processor can handle as a single integer value. Furthermore, such operations are heavily processor dependent.

Bit Sequences as Logical Arrays

The array features of Fortran 90 facilitate logical operations on sequences of bits represented as logical vectors or as logical arrays of higher dimension. For example, the logical operators `.and.`, `.or.`, `.not.`, `.eqv.`, and `.neqv.` can be applied *elementwise* to arrays of logical data type (see Section 5.2).

An array can, of course, have a `kind` parameter that corresponds to a packed subtype.

Integers as Bit Strings: The Fortran 90 Bit Model

The Fortran 90 bit model applies to bit sequences represented as integers in radix 2 notation. Note that the Fortran 90 bit model applies to data of integer type and is unrelated to the logical data type of Fortran. Bits are "numbered from right to left beginning with 0": The bit in the low-order (units) position is number 0. The model may have variants corresponding to different integer subtypes provided by the processor.

Twelve standard intrinsic procedures are provided for manipulating strings of bits according to the Fortran 90 bit model. Bit strings are stored as integers; these may have any integer subtype, but if a procedure reference includes more than one integer actual argument, their subtypes must agree.

Eleven of the twelve procedures (including those defined in U.S. MIL-STD 1753) are functions; the twelfth, `MvBits`, is a subroutine. (See Appendix A for complete definitions of these intrinsic functions.) The twelve procedures may be classified as follows:

1. For logical *or*, *and*, *exclusive or*, and *not* bit string operations —

   `IOr (I, J)`, bitwise *or* of `I` and `J`
   `IAnd (I, J)`, bitwise *and* of `I` and `J`
   `IEOr (I, J)`, bitwise *exclusive or* of `I` and `J`
   `Not (I)`, bitwise *not* of `I`

2. For determining the number of bits in the Fortran 90 bit model —

   `Bit_Size (I)`, number of bits for integers in the model

3. For shifting the bits within an integer —

   `Ishft (I, Shift [, Size])`, end-off left shift [`Size` rightmost] bits of `I` by `Shift` positions (right if `Shift` is negative)
   `IshftC (I, Shift [, Size])`, circular left shift [`Size` rightmost] bits of `I` by `Shift` positions (right if `Shift` is negative)

4. For referencing a substring of bits within an integer —

   `IBits (I, Pos, Len)`, extract `Len` bits from `I` beginning at `Pos`

5. For manipulating a single bit —

   `BTest (I, Pos)`, true if specified bit position of `I` contains "1"
   `IBSet (I, Pos)`, set specified bit position of `I` to "1"
   `IBClr (I, Pos)`, set specified bit position of `I` to "0"

6. For copying a substring of bits from one integer to another —

   `MvBits (From, FromPos, Len, To, ToPos)`, copy `Len` bits from `From` to `To` (note that `From` and `To` are variables; `FromPos` and `ToPos` are integers that designate bit positions within the variables)

Binary, Octal, and Hexadecimal Integers

Fortran 90 permits nondecimal integers for explicitly formatted input or output with format codes `B`, `O`, and `Z` (see Appendix B.2). The corresponding field of the input or output record consists of binary, octal, or hexadecimal digits, respectively.

Constants in a `data` initialization statement (see Appendix D.3) may be written with the letter `B`, `O`, or `Z` followed by a character string (delimited by quotation marks or by apostrophes) containing binary, octal, or hexadecimal digits, respectively.

Transition Tip

- Where possible, change bit manipulation operations to logical array operations. Find out what logical `kind` parameter value represents packed (single bit or byte) bit representation. Declare this `kind` value as a named constant, and use it in type declarations for packed bit arrays.

3.4 Exercises

1. Write a reference to the intrinsic function `Merge` (see Section 3.3) that returns "X" if the logical variable `Big_X` is true and "Y" otherwise.

2. If A and B are logical variables, show that `(A .or. .FALSE.)` always has the same value as A, and that `(B .and. .TRUE.)` always has the same value as B.

3. Write a fully parenthesized expression that is equivalent to the following (taking into account the rules of operator precedence):

```
A + B > C .or. X + Y == Z
```

4. Write a main program with internal procedures that calculate results of logical type for the operations `Sum` and `Carry` that are described under Digital logic circuits in Section 3.4. The main program should test the procedures by reading three logical variables and printing the results from `Sum` and `Carry`. Test the program with all eight possible combinations of three logical input values. You should interpret the result as a two-digit binary number, with `Carry` in the high-order position and `Sum` in the low-order position. The value of this binary number is between 0 and 3 (inclusive) and is the number of logical input values that are .TRUE.. (Note: This exercise is extended, in the exercises for Section 5.4, to logical vectors representing multidigit binary integers.)

5. Is the compound logical expression, printed by each of the five internal subroutines in the following program, true or false?

```
! Exercises 3.4, Number 5.
  program Logic_Tests
    implicit none
! start program Logic_Tests
    call Test_1
    call Test_2
    call Test_3
    call Test_4
    call Test_5
  contains
    subroutine Test_1
      real :: G = 5.0, P = 9.0, Q = 10.0
      integer :: A = 32, B = 41
```

```
! start subroutine Test_1
    print *, (G * P / Q > 4.0) .or. (.not. (A > B))
  end subroutine Test_1
  subroutine Test_2
    real :: B = 1.0, C = 15.0
    integer :: I = 3, J = 5, K = 2
! start subroutine Test_2
    print *, (I ** 2 /= J + K) .and. (3.0 >= B + Abs (C - 20.0))
  end subroutine Test_2
  subroutine Test_3
    real :: A = 0.0, B = 21.0, C = 0.042
    integer :: J = 17, K = 44, M = 8
! start subroutine Test_3
    print *, .not. ((A + C * B < 5.0E1) .and. (J < (4 + K) / M))
  end subroutine Test_3
  subroutine Test_4
    logical :: L = .TRUE.
    real :: A = 5.0, B = 1.0, C = 2.0
! start subroutine Test_4
    print *, L .or. .not. A > B + C
  end subroutine Test_4
  subroutine Test_5
    logical :: L1 = .TRUE., L2 = .TRUE.
! start subroutine Test_5
    print *, L1 .and. .not. L2
  end subroutine Test_5
end program Logic_Tests
```

6. What will be printed by the following program?

```
! Exercises 3.4, Number 6.
program More_Logical
  implicit none
  logical :: L1 = .TRUE., L2 = .FALSE., L3 = .TRUE., L4 = .FALSE.
! start program More_Logical
  print *, L1 .eqv. L3, L1 .eqv. L4, L2 .eqv. L3, L2 .eqv. L4
  print *, L1 .neqv. L3, L1 .neqv. L4, L2 .neqv. L3, L2 .neqv. L4
end program More_Logical
```

7. Rewrite the program in Example 3.25, eliminating the logical variable `Big_X` and the assignment statement that gives this variable a value obtained from a relational expression. Instead of printing the logical variable, print the value of the relational expression.

Chapter 4 Program Patterns for Repetition

It is hardly possible to do any serious programming without encountering groups of statements that are to be executed repeatedly. Few practical programs merely read a single set of data values, perform a calculation, and print a single set of results. Much more common are programs in which a sequence of statements is repeatedly executed. For example, it may be that at each repetition a new set of data values is read, the calculation is performed, and results based on these data values are printed. The interesting problem, as it turns out, is not how to repeat a block of statements but how to stop the repetition at the proper time. (Some intriguing tales for children have been woven around this question: Did you know that the ocean is salty because nobody knows how to stop the magic salt machine that is grinding away forever at the bottom of the ocean? And did you hear about the little boy who said he knew how to spell BANANA, except that he could never remember when to stop?)

The block of program statements to be repeated may be incorporated into a repetition construct, or *loop*. Execution of a loop is illustrated by the flowchart in Figure 4.1.

The distinctive Fortran keyword for repetition is do. A Fortran 90 do construct consists of a block of statements preceded by a do statement and followed by an end do statement:

> do *statement*
>   *Block of statements to be repeated*
> end do

where the do *statement* consists of the keyword do (followed by an optional comma, which is consistently omitted in this text) and a loop control clause:

> do *Loop control*

Note that the keyword end do may be written with or without a blank between end and do; see Appendix C.1.

The do construct has three variants, depending on the form of *Loop control* in the do *statement*:

1. The traditional Fortran indexed do (Section 4.1), whose do *statement* has the form[1]
   do *Index variable* = *Initial value* , *Limit* , *Increment*
2. The simple do, or do forever (Section 4.2), whose do *statement* is simply
   do
3. The conditional do or do `while` (Section 4.3), whose do *statement* is
   do `while` (*Condition*)

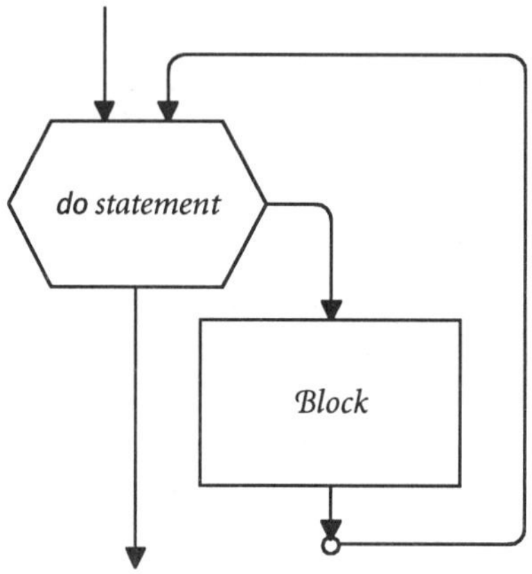

FIGURE 4.1. General loop flowchart.

When a do construct is executed, the *Loop control* is evaluated to determine how many times, if any, the *Block of statements* should be repeated.

An `exit` statement (see Sections 4.1 and 4.4) or a `cycle` statement (see Section 4.4) may appear in the *Block of statements* in any of the three do construct forms. When an `exit` statement is encountered during execution of a do construct, execution of the construct terminates immediately and the execution sequence continues with the statement following end do. When a `cycle` statement is encountered, any remaining statements in the block are skipped and execution returns to the *Loop control*.

4.1 COUNT-CONTROLLED LOOPS

An indexed do is the appropriate repetition construct for an application where the number of repetitions of a block of statements is known in advance. It is controlled by a *counter* (or *index variable*).

[1] Section 4.1 introduces the less general indexed do form: do *Index variable* = 1, *Limit*.

In traditional versions of Fortran, the indexed do was the only language construct for repetition. Simple repetition and conditional repetition were not provided, although similar effects could be synthesized from other statements of the language. The indexed do was originally invented for array processing, which has always been considered an extremely important Fortran application. In a typical one-dimensional array processing example, the block of repeated statements describes an operation that is to be performed on each array element, the number of repetitions is the same as the number of elements in the array, and the index variable appears as a subscript within the block to select each array element in turn. Matrices and other arrays of two or more dimensions are often processed in *nested* loops, with one level of nesting for each dimension of the array. Further discussion of array applications is deferred until arrays have been introduced in Chapter 5; the indexed do examples in this chapter illustrate applications that do not pertain to arrays.

The simplest indexed do examples merely repeat a *Block* of statements a predetermined number of times. For such applications, the index variable is a counter that takes on integer values in sequence, beginning with 1 and increasing by 1 at each iteration until a predetermined limit value is reached. A do *statement* that is appropriate for these simple applications has the form

do *Index variable* = 1, *Limit*

where *Limit* is an an integer constant (preferably a named constant). The *Index variable* will take on each of the integer values from 1 to *Limit* as the *Block* of statements is repeatedly executed. In this pattern, the value of *Limit* indicates the number of times the *Block* of statements is to be executed.

In Example 4.1, the number of iterations is 10 (the value of LIMIT); in Example 4.2, the number of iterations is 50 (the value of MANY). These two examples illustrate the fact that the *Index variable* value is not required to appear anywhere in the body of the *Block* of statements, although it must, of course, appear in the do *statement* that controls the repetition. (Examples 4.4, 4.5, 4.6, and 4.7 also illustrate this possibility.)

EXAMPLE 4.1 The following program averages 10 pairs of input data values.

```
! Example 4.1. Average 10 pairs of input data values.
  program Many_Pairs
    implicit none
    integer, parameter :: LIMIT = 10
    integer :: Loop
    real :: Average, X, Y
! start program Many_Pairs
    do Loop = 1, LIMIT
      print *, "⊥Please⊥enter⊥two⊥numbers⊥to⊥be⊥averaged.⊥"
      read *, X, Y
      Average = (X + Y) / 2.0
      print *, X, Y, Average
    end do
  end program Many_Pairs
```

In Example 4.1 the *Block* of statements to be repeated consists of the three instructions

```
read *, X, Y
Average = (X + Y) / 2.0
print *, X, Y, Average
```

Each time these statements are repeated, another pair of data values is read and processed, and their average is printed.

EXAMPLE 4.2 The following program prints a table of values of a quadratic polynomial, $AX^2 + BX + C$, for 50 equally spaced values of X at intervals of 0.1 beginning with 0.0.

```
! Example 4.2. Tabulate values of a quadratic polynomial.
  program Polynomial
    implicit none
    integer :: J
    real, parameter :: DELTA_X = 0.1
    real :: A, B, C, X = 0.0
    integer, parameter :: MANY = 50
! start program Polynomial
    print *, "⊥Please⊥enter⊥three⊥coefficients⊥for⊥a⊥quadratic⊥polynomial.⊥"
    read *, A, B, C
    do J = 1, MANY
      print *, X, A * X ** 2 + B * X + C
      X = X + DELTA_X
    end do
  end program Polynomial
```

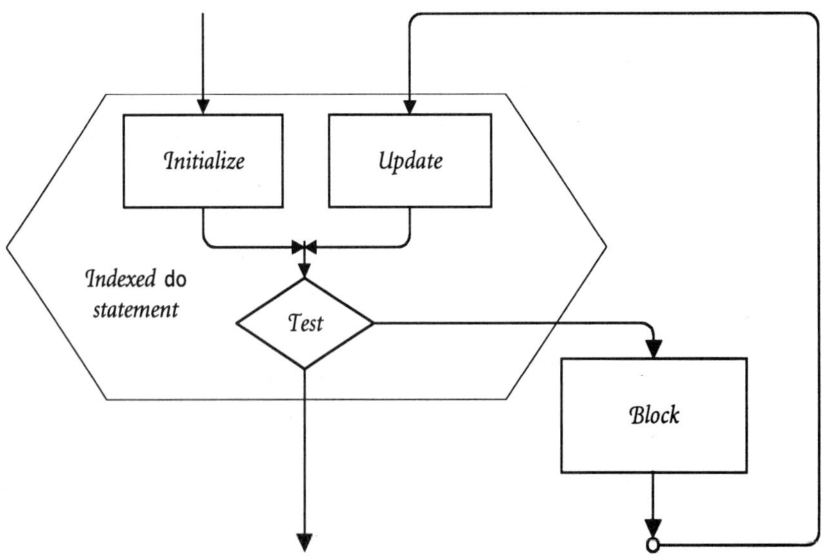

FIGURE 4.2. Execution details of the indexed *do* statement.

Generalizations of the Indexed do

The simple indexed do illustrated by Examples 4.1 and 4.2 may be generalized in the following ways:

1. The *Index variable* may have an *Initial value* different from 1.
2. The *Limit* may be an arbitrary expression of integer type.
3. The do *statement* form may be extended to include an explicit *Increment* value.

These generalizations are discussed in the remainder of Section 4.1. The do *statement* form for the first two of these generalizations is

do *Index variable* = *Initial value* , *Limit*

and the form for the third generalization is

do *Index variable* = *Initial value* , *Limit* , *Increment*

The *Index variable* is a scalar variable of integer type; the *Initial value*, the *Limit*, and the *Increment* are arbitrary expressions of integer type.[2]

Initial Value and Limit Expression for the Index Variable

Many mathematical applications begin counting at zero; in other applications, the count begins at a point determined by the value of some variable. Fortran 90 accommodates such applications by permitting an *Initial value* expression that is a constant, a variable, or an expression with any integer value. The counter *Limit* may be determined from an input variable or some other nonconstant expression. Some examples are as follows:

```
do Loop = I_Min, 3 * I_Min
do Loop = 0, 7
do I = 1, Floor (SqRt (Real (N)))
do I2 = 1, I1 - 1
do I = 0, Maximum
do Loop = -21, I_Spy
```

Execution of an indexed do construct takes place in several stages. As the flowchart in Figure 4.2 indicates, the *Initialize*, *Test*, and *Update* steps all take place during execution of the do statement itself. During a given execution of the do construct, the do statement will usually be executed several times. When the do statement is encountered at the initial entry to the do construct, the *Initialize* step is performed, followed by the *Test* step. Following execution of the *Block*, the do statement is encountered again, but at this point the *Update* step is performed, followed by the *Test* step.

---

[2] Some other variant loop control forms are described in Appendix D.5. The types of the *Index variable*, the *Initial value*, and the *Limit* may be real. All forms of the Fortran do statement have an optional comma after the keyword do. This comma is consistently omitted throughout this text, except in Appendix D.5.

The stages involved in the execution of a do construct may be summarized as follows (see also Figure 4.2).

1. *Initialize*: Set the *Index variable* to its *Initial value*, and then repeat steps 2–4 until termination occurs.
2. *Test*: Compare the current value of the *Index variable* with the value of the *Limit* expression. If the *Index variable* value is greater than the *Limit* value, terminate execution of the construct. Note that this can happen the first time the test is made, in which case the *Block* of statements is never executed (see Example 4.3).
3. *Execute* the *Block* of statements, beginning with the statement that directly follows the do *statement*, in the usual manner.
4. *Update*: If the execution sequence reaches the end do statement, increase the value of the *Index variable* by 1 and continue execution from step 2. (The value of the *Index variable* during the *i*th repetition of the *Block* of statements will be equal to the *Initial value* plus $(i - 1)$. If the *Initial value* is 1, the value of the *Index variable* during the *i*th repetition of the *Block* of statements will be i.)

The *Index variable* of an indexed do construct must not be redefined (given a value) during execution of the *Block* by an assignment statement, by a read statement, or by any means other the normal *Update* step that is a part of execution of the indexed do statement.

As we have seen, when the *Initial value* is 1 the total number of repetitions will be equal to the *Limit* value. More generally, the number of repetitions, referred to as the *trip count*, will be equal to

1 + (*Limit* – *Initial value*)

If the *Limit* value is less than the *Initial value*, the trip count will be zero.

EXAMPLE 4.3 The following program calculates the factorial of Limit — that is, the product of all positive integers not exceeding Limit.

```
! Example 4.3. Calculate factorial of Limit.
  program FOL_1
    implicit none
    integer :: Factorial = 1, Limit, Loop

! start program FOL_1

    print *, "␣Please␣enter␣the␣number␣whose␣factorial␣is␣wanted.␣"
    read *, Limit

    do Loop = 1, Limit
      Factorial = Factorial * Loop
    end do

    print *, "␣Factorial␣of:␣", Limit, "␣is:␣", Factorial
  end program FOL_1
```

Example 4.3 illustrates the fact that the *Block* is never executed if the initial value of the *Index variable* is greater than the *Limit* value. In this example, if the value of `Limit` is 0, termination occurs with no repetitions of the *Block*, and none of the effects of executing the *Block* will be produced. In this case, `Factorial` (correctly) retains its initial value, 1.

Note that the program in Example 4.3 works correctly only for fairly small values of `Limit` because factorial values grow rapidly and soon overflow the maximum integer size provided by typical computers. The factorial of 8 is larger than 2^{15}, the factorial of 13 exceeds 2^{31}, and 21 factorial is more than 2^{63}. Approximate factorials may be computed with real arithmetic. See also Example 4.21.

EXAMPLE 4.4 By carefully examining the sequence of steps in the execution of the do construct illustrated in Figure 4.2, we see that the *Index variable* is always set to a new value (by either the *Initialize* step or the *Update* step) just before a *Test* for termination occurs. Thus, when *normal termination* (as a result of the *Test*) occurs, the *Index variable* value will have the value we should have expected if the loop had been traversed one more time. Consider the following program.

```
! Example 4.4. Print index value at normal termination.
  program Normal
    implicit none
    integer :: I
    real :: Datum, Total = 0.0
    integer, parameter :: LIMIT = 40
! start program Normal
    do I = 1, LIMIT
      read *, Datum
      Total = Total + Datum
    end do
    print *, I, Total
  end program Normal
```

In the program of Example 4.4, the `print` statement is executed immediately after normal termination occurs. The value of `I` will have been set to 41 (1 more than `LIMIT`) by the *Update* step just before the *Test* that resulted in termination.

EXAMPLE 4.5 Recall that the *Limit* in an indexed do statement may be an expression and need not be a constant. In particular, the *Limit* may be a variable. Thus, it is not necessary to know the number of repetitions at the time a program is written. In the following program, the `Total` of a number of data items is to be computed. A separate input item precedes the values to be totaled and indicates the number of items that follow.

```
! Example 4.5. Compute the total of Limit data values,
!   where the value of Limit is provided as the first data item.
  program Repeat
    implicit none
    real :: Total = 0.0, Datum
    integer :: Limit, Loop
! start program Repeat
    read *, Limit
    print *, Limit, "␣items␣will␣be␣read.␣"
    do Loop = 1, Limit
      read *, Datum
      Total = Total + Datum
      print *, Datum, "␣added␣to␣give␣current␣total:␣", Total
    end do
  end program Repeat
```

EXAMPLE 4.6 The average of an arbitrary number of data items is computed by the following program. The steps that read input data and accumulate the sum are the same as in the previous example. Further steps for computing the Average have been appended after the loop.

```
! Example 4.6. Compute the average of some data values, where
!   the number of values is provided as the first data item.
  program Arithmetic_Mean
    implicit none
    intrinsic Real

    real :: Total = 0.0, Datum
    integer :: Limit, Loop
! start program Arithmetic_Mean
    read *, Limit
    print *, Limit, "␣items␣will␣be␣averaged.␣"
    do Loop = 1, Limit
      read *, Datum
      Total = Total + Datum
      print *, Datum, "␣added␣to␣give␣current␣total:␣", Total
    end do
    if (Limit > 0) then
      Average = Total / Real (Limit)
      print *, "␣Summary:␣", Total, Limit, Average
    else
      print*, "␣Number␣of␣items␣is␣zero.␣"
    end if
  end program Arithmetic_Mean
```

Indexed do *with Explicit Increment*

An indexed do statement may have the following form, which includes an *Increment* expression whose value indicates the amount by which the *Index variable* is to be increased each time the loop is traversed:

do *Index variable* = *Initial value* , *Limit* , *Increment*

An indexed do construct with an explicit *Increment* is executed in the following manner, as the flowchart in Figure 4.3 indicates.

1. *Initialize*: Set the *Index variable* to its *Initial value,* and then repeat steps 2–4 until termination occurs (as a result of the *Test* at step 2, or prematurely as a result of executing an `exit` statement or other control statement in step 3).
2. *Test*: Compare the current value of the *Index variable* with the value of the *Limit* expression (the second expression after the = operator in the do statement). If the *Index variable* value has gone beyond the *Limit* — that is, if the *Index variable* value is greater than the *Limit* value and the value of the *Increment* (the third expression after the = operator in the do statement) is positive, or if the *Index variable* is less than the *Limit* and the *Increment* value is negative — terminate execution of the construct. Note that this can happen the first time the test is made, in which case the *Block* of statements is never executed. If the *Index variable* value has not gone beyond the *Limit,* continue with step 3.
3. *Execute* the *Block* of statements, beginning with the statement that directly follows the do statement, in the usual manner.
4. *Update*: If the execution sequence reaches the end do statement, add the value of the *Increment* to the *Index variable* and continue execution from step 2. (The value of the *Index variable* during the *i*th repetition of the *Block* of statements will be equal to the *Initial value* plus (*i* 1) times the *Increment.*)

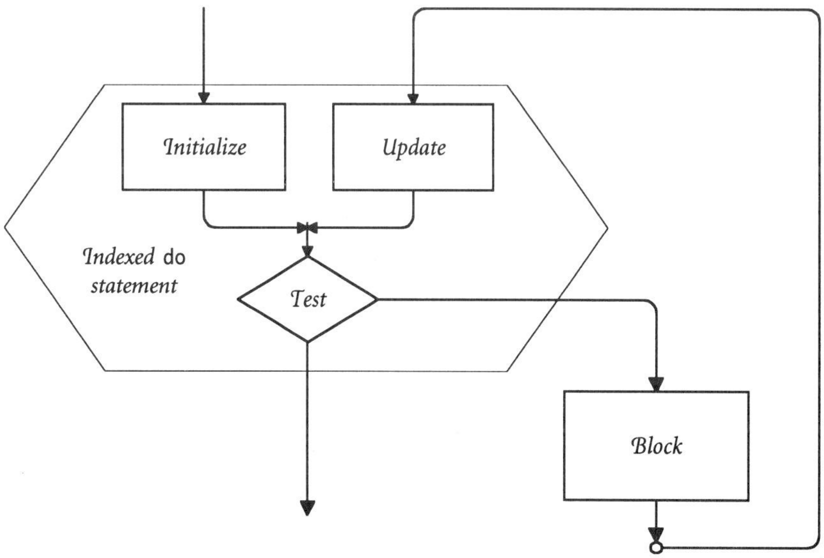

FIGURE 4.3. Execution details of the indexed *do* statement.

The execution details for an indexed do without an explicit increment were listed earlier and are illustrated by the flowchart in Figure 4.2. The list of steps given here for an indexed do with an explicit increment is a direct generalization of the previous list, and the flowchart in Figure 4.3 is identical to the one in Figure 4.2. It may be seen that omitting the increment has the same effect as specifying an explicit increment with the value 1.

Note that the normal Fortran statement sequence is interrupted at two points during execution of an indexed do construct:

1. In the *Test* step, the do statement has two possible successors in the execution sequence (the first statement in the *Block* of statements or the statement that follows end do). A choice between these two alternatives is made by comparing the do variable with the *Limit*.
2. After the *Update* step (when the end do statement is reached), the execution sequence returns to the *Test* step.

Here are some examples:

```
do Many = 1, 5
do I = 2, 9, 4
do Loop_Down = 10, 1, -1
do IJK = 2, 1
```

In the first of these examples, the *Block* of statements will be executed 5 times, as Many takes on the sequence of values 1, 2, 3, 4, 5. In the second example, the *Initial value* is 2, the *Limit* is 9, and the *Increment* is 4. The *Block* of statements will be executed 2 times, as I assumes the values 2, 6. At the second *Update* step, I is increased from 6 to 10. Since 10 is beyond the limit value, at the following *Test* step the construct terminates.

In the third example, the *Increment* is –1. The *Block* of statements will be executed 10 times, as Loop_Down assumes the values 10, 9, 8, . . . , 1. In the fourth example, the *Initial value* is 2, the *Limit* is 1, and the *Increment* has the default value 1. The *Block* of statements will not be executed. At the first *Test* step, IJK is 2, which is beyond the *Limit* value.

The "trip count," or number of repetitions of the *Block* of statements, is given by the following formula:

1 + Floor ((*Limit* – *Initial value*) / (*Increment*))

However, the trip count is zero if the value of this expression is negative.

The following examples illustrate this formula.

```
do I = 1, 10, 4
do J = 10, 9, 2
do I = 10, 1, -1
```

In the first example, 2.25 is the value of the quotient (10 – 1) / (4). Floor truncates this value to the integer 2. Adding 1, we find that the trip count is 3. The *Block* will be repeated 3 times, with 1, 5, and 9 as the values of I during these 3 repetitions of the *Block*. In the second example, the quotient is –0.5, which Floor truncates to –1, so the *Block* will be "repeated zero times" (it will not be executed). In the third example, the value of the quotient (1 – 10) / (–1) is 9.0, so the result from `Floor` is 9. Adding 1, we find that the *Block* will be repeated 10 times, with 10, 9, 8, . . . , 1 as the values of `I` during these 10 repetitions of the *Block*.

Note that when the *Initial value* is the same as the *Limit*, the quotient is 0 and the trip count is 1. For example, the *Block* in an indexed do construct headed by the statement

```
do K = 2, 2
```

will be executed just once.

Premature Termination with the `exit` *Statement*

An `exit` statement (see also Section 4.4) will cause termination of an indexed `do` construct before the `do` variable value goes beyond the *Limit*, as the following example illustrates. A careful study of the steps of loop execution reveals that the value of the *Index variable* is preserved when an exit occurs.

EXAMPLE 4.7 The following program is expected to read a value of `X` from each of `N` records of an input file and to compute and print the square root of each input value. However, the process terminates if a negative `X` value is encountered.

```
! Example 4.7. Compute square roots of input values.
  program Rutabaga
    implicit none
    intrinsic SqRt
    integer, parameter :: N = 20
    integer :: I
    real :: X
! start program Rutabaga
    do I = 1, N
      read *, X
      if (X <= 0) exit
      print *, SqRt (X)
    end do
    print *, "⊥Number⊥of⊥valid⊥input⊥values:⊥", I - 1
  end program Rutabaga
```

In Example 4.7, the `exit` statement causes premature termination of the repetition when a negative data value is read. The value of `I` is preserved when this premature termination occurs and is therefore equal to 1 more than the number of *valid* data values that have been read. The `exit` statement causes the execution sequence to skip to the `print` statement that follows `end do`.

Transition Tips

- Change all do loops to do-end do constructs. Remove labels from do statements and insert matching end do statements. If the statement label is referenced inside the block, leave the labeled terminal statement in place and insert end do after it.
- If several do loops terminate on the same labeled statement, insert end do statements to match each of the do statements, following the labeled terminal statement. If a do loop terminates on an assignment statement or other action statement, insert an `end do` statement following the terminal statement. (See Appendix D.5 for further details.)
- Change `go to` statements that transfer to a point just beyond the end of the loop to `exit` statements.

4.1 Exercises

1. Correct any Fortran language errors you find in the following indexed do statements:

   a. `do I = 1. N`

   b. `do for I = 1 to N - 1`

   c. `do Jolly == 12, 62`

   d. `do 1 = (I: N)`

   e. `do (1 = I, N)`

2. In Example 4.4, the variable `Total` is initialized to zero in the type declaration. Test the given program. Then delete the initialization from the type declaration and substitute each of the following. Test each modified program.

   a. Insert an assignment statement that sets `Total` to zero, prior to the first instruction of the program.

   b. Insert a `read` statement to obtain a value for `Total`. During execution, enter the value zero.

   c. Specify `Total` as a named constant with the value zero. What happens when you try to run this version of the program? Explain what you observe.

3. Divisors of an integer: Write a program to read an integer N (larger than 1) and print all of its divisors. A first approach is to test each integer, I, between 1 and N, to see whether it divides N:

   ```
   if (Modulo (N, I) == 0) . . .
   ```

   A little thought suggests that if I divides N, then (N / I) also divides N. Therefore, the divisors can be found and printed two at a time, and only those integers that do not exceed the square root of N need to be tested. Use a loop whose *Limit* expression is `Floor (SqRt (Real (N)))`.

4. Evaluate the intrinsic functions Sin and Cos for large multiples of π. Try multiples from 100 to 1000 with increment 100. Try the computation with decimal precision 6 and then with 12 (or more, depending on your processor). You may use the following statements as part of your program:

```
program Sinus
  implicit none
  intrinsic ATan2, Sin, Cos, Selected_Real_Kind, Real
  integer, parameter :: P = 6, K = Selected_Real_Kind (P)
  integer :: Loop
  real (kind = K) :: Pi, RL
! start program Sinus
  Pi = ATan2 (0.0_K, -1.0_K)
   :
end program Sinus
```

5. Quadrature (numerical integration): The integral of a function may be estimated numerically by dividing the range of integration into small intervals and applying the composite trapezoidal rule (which approximates the integrand function by a straight line over each interval) or by the composite Simpson's rule (which approximates the integrand function by a parabolic arc over each pair of intervals).[3] Let the limits of integration be A and B. For some *even integer* value of N, set Delta_X = (B - A) / Real (N). The integrand function will be evaluated at X = A + *i* Delta_X, for *i* = 0 to N. Separately sum values of the integrand function for odd and even values of *i*, excluding the limit values 0 and N. (You may employ a single loop in which the index I goes from 1 to N - 1 and test whether or not Modulo (I, 2) is 0.)

   The approximate integral calculated by the composite trapezoidal rule is then

```
Delta_X * (F(A) + F(B)) / 2.0 + Odd_Sum + Even_Sum
```

   and the composite Simpson's rule gives

```
Delta_X * (F(A) + F(B) + 4.0 * Odd_Sum + 2.0 * Even_Sum) / 3.0
```

   Write a program to compute the integral by both methods, and print them for comparison. You may write the function F as an internal procedure (but see also Section 8.6). Test your program first with a simple function that always returns 1.0 on the interval [0.0, 1.0] with various values of N; then, with Exp (-X ** 2) on [-10.0, 10.0] with N = 100 or more (the computed integral should approximate the square root of π, 1.77245385 ...); then, with 1 / X on $[10^{-6}, 1.0]$ with N = 100 and 200. (Do not be surprised if the latter function exhibits strange behavior.)

[3] See any numerical analysis text—for example, R. L. Burden and J. D. Faires, *Numerical Analysis*, 5th ed. (Boston: PWS Publishing, 1993), pp. 184ff.

4.2 SIMPLE LOOPS

The simple do statement consists merely of the keyword do. The do statement itself does not control termination of the repetition; some other means of termination must be incorporated among the statements of a block. Consequently, this form of do statement is sometimes called do *forever*.

In comparison to the execution steps for an indexed do construct, execution of the simple do construct consists of repeating the following single step until termination occurs (see Figure 4.4):

1. *Execute* the *Block* of statements.

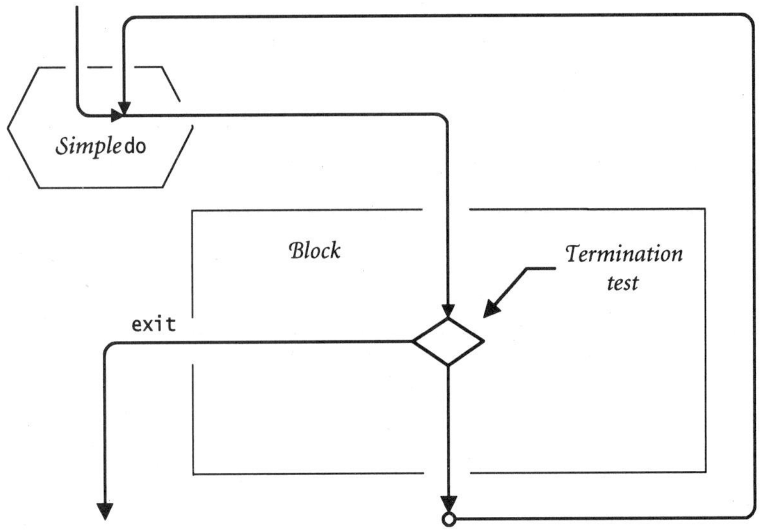

FIGURE 4.4. Execution details of simple *do* statement.

Termination with the `exit` Statement

The most common means of termination is an `exit` statement. This statement may consist simply of the keyword `exit` (see also Section 4.4). An `exit` statement often appears as the *Dependent statement* of a simple `if` statement, such as

```
if (EoF < 0) exit
```

When an `exit` statement is encountered within a do construct, execution of the construct terminates immediately. The execution sequence continues with the statement following end do. Consider Example 4.8.

EXAMPLE 4.8 The following program calculates the sum of the alternating harmonic series (1 - 1/2 + 1/3 − 1/4 + 1/5 − 1/6 + · · ·) until the next term is smaller than .0001. (Note that this series converges very slowly to ln(2.0) = 0.69315 . . . ; the computed sum after 10,000 terms is 0.69309 . Compare Example 4.11.)

```
! Example 4.8. Sum alternating harmonic series until term is small enough.
  program Harmonica
    implicit none
    intrinsic Real, Abs
    real :: Sum = 0.0, Sign = 1.0, Next_term
    integer :: N = 1
    real, parameter :: TOLERANCE = 1.0E-4
! start program Harmonica
    do ! forever
      Next_term = Sign / Real (N)
      Sum = Sum + Next_term
      if (Abs (Next_term) <= TOLERANCE) exit
      N = N + 1
      Sign = - Sign
    end do
    print *, "␣The␣sum␣after:␣", Abs (N), "␣terms␣is:␣", Sum
  end program Harmonica
```

Now consider the following problem, originally posed by Leonardo of Pisa, surnamed Fibonacci (c. 1170–1230):

> A certain man put a pair of rabbits in a place surrounded by a wall. How many pairs of rabbits can be produced from that pair in a year, if it is supposed that every month each pair begets a new pair which from the second month on becomes productive?[4]

The solution is obtained by observing that the number of pairs, from the third month on, is obtained by adding together the number of pairs for the previous two months. Assuming that the original pair was newborn when placed in the cage so that no offspring are produced until the second month, we obtain the classical Fibonacci sequence

1, 1, 2, 3, 5, 8, 13, 21, 34, 55, 89, 144, . . .

The Fibonacci sequence is of interest in modern mathematics because of several remarkable properties, including the fact that the *ratio* of two consecutive numbers in the sequence approaches the "golden ratio" 1.61803399 . . . . This number was considered mystically significant by the Pythagoreans in ancient Greece because it is the ratio between two lengths, a and b, such that $a / b = (a + b) / a$. This ratio equals $(1+\sqrt{5})/2$ or

[4] J. Gies and F. Gies, *Leonardo of Pisa and the New Mathematics of the Middle Ages* (New York: Crowell, 1969).

1.61803399 . . . , as some algebraic manipulation will show. (Hint: Let the ratio be r; then $r = 1 + 1 / r$ or $r^2 - r - 1 = 0$.) The golden ratio is illustrated geometrically in Figure 4.5.

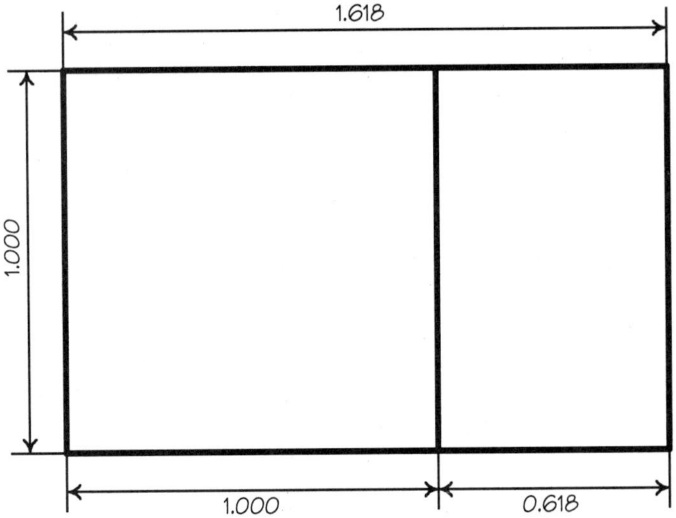

FIGURE 4.5. Geometric representation of the golden ratio 1.618 . . . .

EXAMPLE 4.9 The numbers in the Fibonacci sequence grow rather rapidly. In the following program, an `exit` statement causes the loop to terminate if the next sum to be calculated would exceed `Huge (1)`, which is the largest number in the Fortran 90 integer model (for application to integers of default `kind`, see Section 1.6 and Appendix A).

```
! Example 4.9. Compute Fibonacci sequence; exit to avoid overflow.
 program Rabbits
   implicit none
   intrinsic Huge
   integer :: FI = 1, FJ = 1, Next
! start program Rabbits
   print *, 1, FI
   print *, 2, FJ
   do
     if (FJ > Huge (1) - FI) exit
     Next = FI + FJ
     FI = FJ
     FJ = Next
     print *, FJ
   end do
 end program Rabbits
```

EXAMPLE 4.10 The motion of a particle moving without resistance along the x axis, under the influence of a force proportional to x, is described by the initial value problem, $dx / dt = v$, $dv / dt = -\omega^2 x$, $x(0) = 0$, $v(0) = 1$. The motion can be simulated by a very simple, but rather inaccurate method, which is implemented in the following program.

```
! Example 4.10. Simple harmonic motion
!   (coupled first-order differential equations).
  program Motion
  implicit none

! start program Motion

    do
      print *, "␣Please␣enter␣Time␣step␣(or␣0␣to␣quit).␣"
      read *, H
      if (H <= 0) stop
      print *, "␣Please␣enter␣initial␣values␣for␣T,␣X,␣and␣V.␣"
      read *, T0, X0, V0
      do
        print *, "␣How␣many␣more␣steps?␣"
        print *, "␣Enter␣zero␣to␣exit.␣"
        read *, Steps
        if (Steps <= 0) exit

        do Loop = 1, Steps
          T = T + H
          X = X + H * V
          V = V - H * W ** 2 * X
          print *, T, X, V
        end do

      end do

    end do

  end program Motion
```

Position of the `exit` *Statement*

In a simple do construct, the event that defines the termination condition may appear anywhere in the *Block*. There may be more than one condition that should cause termination, in which case there may be more than one `exit` statement in the *Block*.

The termination test may be the first statement in the *Block* (as it is in Example 4.9), in which case the construct is equivalent to `do while` (see Section 4.3). However, there is a difference in the way the termination test is written: A simple do construct is terminated when the *Condition* in the termination test is true, whereas a `do while` construct is terminated when the *Condition* in the `do while` statement is false.

A simple do construct with the termination test at the end of the *Block*, as in Example 4.11, is equivalent to another construct that is provided by some languages — for example, Pascal's `repeat-until`. It is a property of this class of repetition constructs that the termination test is not made until the end of the first execution of the *Block*. This form is especially appropriate when the termination test refers to some variable that is undefined when the do statement is executed.

EXAMPLE 4.11 The following program calculates the sum of the power series $(1 + 1/2 + 1/4 + 1/8 + 1/16 + \cdots)$ until the next term is smaller than `1.0E-6`.

```
! Example 4.11. Sum a power series until next term is small enough.
  program Tail
    implicit none
    real :: Sum = 0.0, Next_term = 1.0
    real, parameter :: TOLERANCE = 1.0E-6
! start program Tail
    do
      Sum = Sum + Next_term
      Next_term = 0.5 * Next_term
      if (Next_term < TOLERANCE) exit
    end do
    print *, "␣Sum␣of␣terms␣greater␣than:␣", TOLERANCE, "␣is:␣", Sum
  end program Tail
```

Bounding an Indexed do *Loop*

The simple do construct is very elegant and general, easy to understand, and easy to use. It is the construct of choice when the number of repetitions is not fixed in advance.

Nevertheless, the simple do has one major weakness. In case of a mistake in the program or in the preparation of data, it may happen that the condition for terminating the repetition is never satisfied. For example, in an approximation process, the tolerance may have been set too tight.

In practice, the programmer or the problem originator almost always has some idea of an ultimate *maximum* number of times a block should be repeated. The exact number of steps required by an approximation process may be impossible to determine in advance, but it may be known that, if the process goes beyond 100 steps (pick a "magic number"), there is something wrong and further repetition is of no interest. Therefore, the programmer may wish to take into account the possibility that something may go wrong.

What is needed is a *bounded* repetition construct — one that will terminate either when a given exit condition is satisfied or when the specified maximum number of repetitions is reached. Such a construct is, of course, just an indexed do that contains an `exit` statement. However, we now view execution of the `exit` statement as normal termination and completion of the trip count as abnormal termination.

This technique is appropriate for a wide range of applications. The principal exceptions are file processing applications that process each input data item separately, where the file size does not need to be known in advance and a maximum size for the file cannot always be predicted.

Consider the following problem: Professor Hasenzähler (a colleague of Professor Katzenzähler) goes to Critter Island to study population dynamics among the rabbits and foxes that live there. The rabbits eat skunk cabbages, of which there are plenty on the island, and the foxes eat rabbits. The professor's observations confirm that the birthrate of rabbits, RB, depends directly on the number of rabbits, R, and that the death rate of rabbits, RD, depends on the number of rabbits, R, and on the number of foxes, F:

```
Delta_R = (RB - RD * F) * R * Delta_T
```

He also finds that the birthrate of foxes, FB, depends on both the number of rabbits, R, and the number of foxes, F, while the death rate of foxes, FD, depends directly on the number of foxes, F:

```
Delta_F = (FB * F - FD) * F * Delta_T
```

Professor Hasenzähler finds that the birthrate and death rate proportionality constants (with time measured in years) are

```
RB = 3.0        FB = 0.0006
RD = 0.002      FD = 0.5
```

EXAMPLE 4.12 Professor Hasenzähler counts 1000 rabbits and 200 foxes when he arrives on Critter Island.[5] Thereafter, he tabulates the population of rabbits and of foxes four times a year. His grant will continue for four years, unless one of the populations becomes extinct before that time. His research assistant writes the following program to simulate the population dynamics on the island. (To reduce error, the simulation program computes the populations at a much smaller interval, `Delta_T`, but it prints the results only at the wider interval `T_Out`.)

```
! Example 4.12. Predator-prey population dynamics.
 program Critters
   implicit none
   intrinsic NInt

   real, parameter :: RB = 3.0, RD = 0.002, FB = 0.0006, FD = 0.5
   real :: R = 1000, F = 200, T, Delta_R, Delta_F, Delta_T = 0.001, &
     T_Out = 0.25, T_Max = 4.0
   integer :: N, Loop, N_Out

! start program Critters
   N = NInt (T_Max / Delta_T)
   N_Out = NInt (T_Out / Delta_T)

   do Loop = 0, N
     T = Loop * Delta_T
     Delta_R = (RB - RD * F) * R * Delta_T
     Delta_F = (FB * R - FD) * F * Delta_T
     if (Modulo (Loop, N_Out) == 0) print *, T, R, F, Delta_R, Delta_F
     R = R + Delta_R
     F = F + Delta_F
     if (R <= 0.0) stop "␣No␣more␣rabbits.␣"
     if (F <= 0.0) stop "␣No␣more␣foxes.␣"
   end do
 end program Critters
```

The simulation shows wide fluctuations in both populations during the four-year study. Starting with 1000 rabbits and 200 foxes, the rabbit and fox populations both increase at first. After 1 year, there are 8541 rabbits and 1436 foxes, and the rabbit population begins to decrease. After 1.5 years, there are only 1050 rabbits and 5050 foxes, so the foxes begin to starve to death. At the end of the study, there are 0.3 rabbit (!) and 1588 foxes. However, if we continue the simulation, we see that the rabbit population will recover, while the fox population continues a slow decline. At about 8.6 years, both

[5] The numerical values in this problem are from an exercise in R. L. Burden and J. D. Faires, *Numerical Analysis, 5th ed.* (Boston: PWS Publishing, 1993), pp. 303. Note that accuracy of the simulation can be improved by applying a more sophisticated solution method, such as Adams' predictor-corrector (op. cit., p. 279).

populations return to approximately their original levels, and the fox population begins to increase again.

EXAMPLE 4.13 John wants to evaluate the exponential power series in the obvious way, based on the Taylor series expansion. William has read that it may be better to compute the negative exponential and take its reciprocal. They decide to write a Fortran program to compute the exponential by the two different power series methods and to compare the results with the intrinsic exponential function. Note that all real variables and constants have `kind` subtype parameters (see Section 1.6) based on the named constant `P`. The intrinsic function `Spacing` (see Appendix A) returns a value that is suitable as a tolerance for deciding when the next term is small enough to ignore.

```
! Example 4.13. Compare positive and negative exponential power series.
 program Power_Trip
   implicit none
   intrinsic Exp, Abs, Selected_Real_Kind, Real, Spacing
   integer, parameter :: P = 4, K = Selected_Real_Kind (P)
   integer :: N
   real (kind = K) :: Term, Sum_1, Sum_2, X, Sign
! start program Power_Trip
   do
     print *, "␣Please␣enter␣X␣"
     read *, X
     if (Abs (X) <= 4.0 * Spacing (1.0_K)) exit        ! Stop if X is close to 0.
     !  Initialize power series for new value of X:
     Sum_1 = 0.0_K; Sum_2 = 0.0_K; Term = 1.0_K; Sign = 1.0_K
     do N = 0, 100                   ! Exit when Term is small or after Term is 100.
       Sum_1 = Sum_1 + Term                                        ! E^X power series
       Sum_2 = Sum_2 + Term * Sign                              ! E^(-X) power series
       print *, N, Real (Term), Real (Sum_1), Real (Sum_2), Real (1.0_K / Sum_2)
       if (Abs (Term) < Spacing (1.0_K)) exit
       Term = Term * X / Real (N + 1, K)
       Sign = - Sign
     end do
     print *, "␣X:␣␣␣␣␣␣␣␣␣␣␣␣␣␣␣␣", X
     print *, "␣Exp␣Intrinsic:␣␣␣␣", Exp (X)
     print *, "␣E^X␣power␣series:␣", Sum_1
     print *, "␣1␣/␣E^(-X):␣␣␣␣␣␣␣", 1.0_K / Sum_2
   end do
 end program Power_Trip
```

4.2 Exercises

1. Modify the Fibonacci program of Example 4.9 as follows: Just before the end of the *Block* of statements, insert a statement to print the value of the ratio `FJ / FI`. After the loop, print the "theoretical" value of this ratio, $(1+\sqrt{5})/2$, which may be computed as `0.5 + SqRt (1.25)`.

2. Perform some further experiments with the predator-prey problem of Example 4.12.

   a. Extend `T_Max` to 12 years. Start with 1000 rabbits and 200 foxes, as before.

   b. Make rough plots of the result of part a, with the number of rabbits on one axis and the number of foxes on the other. Note that the graph is approximately elliptical. One of the populations will become extinct if the ellipse crosses an axis.

   c. Show that both populations are stable when the number of rabbits is 833 and the number of foxes is 1500. (Hint: `Delta_R` and `Delta_F` are both zero for these values of `R` and `F`.)

3. Make some runs with the program of Example 4.13. Use both positive and negative values for `X`, with magnitudes 0.5, 1.0, 4.0, and 8.0. For which values does each method give results closer to the intrinsic function value? Repeat the runs with the precision parameter `P` set to a higher value, such as 12.

4. Modify the program in Example 4.13 to evaluate complex exponentials with the intrinsic function Exp and with the power series expansion. Compare the results for e^{x+iy} with `Exp (X) * Cmplx (Cos (Y), Sin (Y))`.

4.3 CONDITIONAL LOOPS (Optional)

Many applications require conditional looping, or repetition of a block of statements an indefinite number of times, so long as some condition holds. This condition presumably involves some of the variables in the program. It has been found that, for appropriate applications, a program with loops controlled in this way can be especially easy to comprehend. Fortran 90 provides the `do while` construct for conditional repetition.

For example, many mathematical algorithms consist of a loop in which some variable is modified by a process of successive approximations and becomes closer at each step to an ideal value. The approximation process continues until the difference from the ideal becomes insignificant in comparison to a predetermined tolerance. The number of repetitions is not known in advance since the rate of progress toward the ideal value may involve some parameters whose values have not been established when the program is designed.

Let's write a program to find the square root of a positive real number by Newton's method. (It would be much more sensible, of course, to obtain the square root from the intrinsic function SqRt. Nevertheless, the Newton algorithm is instructive.) We start with a rather arbitrary first guess and then compute a closer approximation to the square root at each repetition of the *Block* of statements in a do while construct. Repetition terminates when the current approximation is close to the square root of the given number.

EXAMPLE 4.14 In the following program, we always use 1.0 as our first approximation. To obtain a closer approximation, we note that if the current approximate Root is larger than the square root of X, then X / Root is smaller than the square root of X. So, for a better approximation, we take the average of Root and X / Root. For example, if X is 2.0 and the first approximation is 1.0, then the second approximation is the average of 1.0 and 2.0 / 1.0, or 1.5, which we see is already fairly close to the true value 1.41421356 . . . . The third approximation is the average of 1.5 and 2.0 / 1.5, which is about 1.4167. The fourth approximation is correct to six significant decimal digits. As in most problems of this kind, we do not test for termination by directly comparing the current approximate value with the ideal value. After all, if the ideal value were available, the computation would be pointless. (Remember that we are pretending not to know about the SqRt intrinsic function.) Instead, we compare the *square* of the approximate root with the given number. Actually, we compare the ratio Root ** 2 / X with 1.0. This ratio would equal 1.0 if the root were exact.

```
! Example 4.14. Square root by Newton's method.
  program Newt_Root
    implicit none
    intrinsic Abs
    real :: X, Root = 1.0                        ! Use 1.0 as first guess for Root.
    real, parameter :: TOLERANCE = 1.0E-5
! start program Newt_Root
    print *, "␣Please␣enter␣the␣number␣whose␣square␣root␣is␣wanted.␣"
    read *, X
    X = Abs (X)                   ! This algorithm requires that X be nonnegative.
    do while (Abs (Root ** 2 / X - 1.0) > TOLERANCE)
      Root = 0.5 * (Root + X / Root)
      print *, Root
    end do
    print *, "␣Square␣root␣of:␣", X, "␣is:␣", Root
  end program Newt_Root
```

The following output is generated by the program in Example 4.14:

```
Please enter the number whose square root is wanted.
2.0
1.5000000
1.4166666
1.4142157
Square root of: 2.000000 is: 1.4142157
```

Form of the do while *Construct*

A `do while` construct consists of a `do while` statement, a *Block* of statements to be repeated, and an `end do` statement. The `do while` statement consists of the keyword `do while`, followed by a parenthesized *Condition*:

`do while (` *Condition* `)`

Execution of a `do while` construct consists of repeating the following two steps until termination occurs (see Figure 4.6):

1. *Test*: Evaluate the *Condition* in the `do while` statement. If it is found to be false, terminate execution of the construct.
2. *Execute* the *Block* of statements.

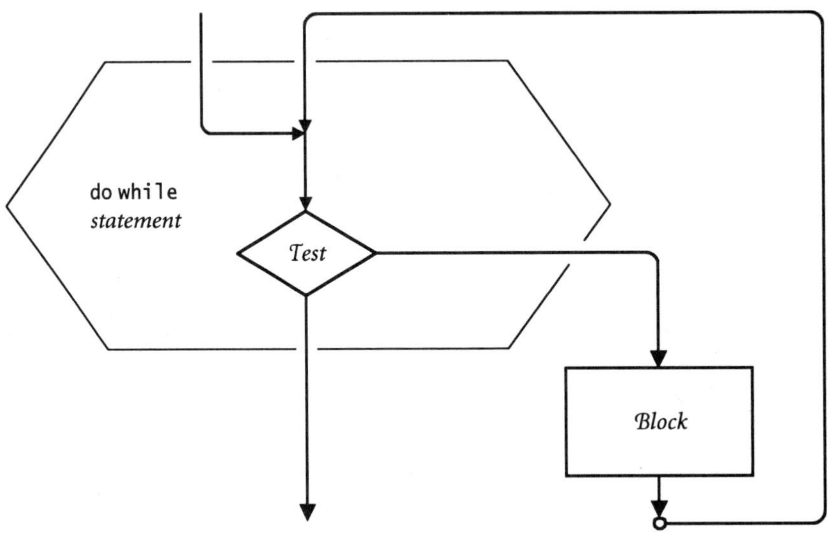

FIGURE 4.6. Execution details of the *do while* statement.

Several observations about the do while construct are in order:

1. The *Condition* may become false during execution of some statement in the *Block*. Nevertheless, execution of statements in the *Block* continues. Termination of the construct, due to the *Condition* becoming false, does not occur until the next execution of the do while statement. (However, termination may occur during execution of the *Block* for other reasons; for example, there may be an exit statement in the *Block*.)
2. If the *Condition* is false the first time it is tested, the *Block* is never executed. (If X is 1.0 in Example 4.14, the first guess already happens to be the correct Root and no repetition is needed.)
3. Variables that appear in the *Condition* must have defined values at the beginning of execution of the do while construct. The *Condition* is meaningless if it contains undefined variables. Thus, a do while construct should not be employed in an application where the *Condition* does not become defined until the *Block* is executed. Various means of circumventing this difficulty are inferior to replacing do while by the simple do construct described in Section 4.2.
4. An incorrectly programmed *Condition* or unexpected data values may create a situation in which repetition never terminates. (A very small TOLERANCE value in Example 4.14 may never be achieved, or too many negative data values in Example 4.15 may prevent the Total from ever reaching the desired level.) A way to guarantee termination is to ensure that each repetition carries the loop toward its goal by some minimum amount. However, many applications are not amenable to this technique.[6] Except in simple situations, it may be difficult to guarantee termination of a do while construct.
5. If the *Block* does not contain any exit statements or other means of premature termination, the *Condition* is known to be false when execution of the do while construct terminates. Formal program verification methods take advantage of this principle.

With these observations in mind, let's consider a data gathering experiment — for example, in particle physics — that is to continue until a given total amount of experimental material has been processed.

[6] The fact that each step moves toward a goal does not guarantee that the goal will be reached in a finite number of steps, as may be seen by consideration of the sum $(1 + 1/2 + 1/4 + 1/8 + \cdots)$. On the other hand, a goal may be reached by an erratic or circuitous route that includes some backward steps, so a test for constant forward progress would fail.

EXAMPLE 4.15 The following program continues to read data items and add them to a total until the total reaches (or exceeds) the predetermined value. It is not always possible to predict in advance how many data items will be needed.

```
! Example 4.15. Accumulation of experimental material.
  program Gather
    implicit none
    real :: Total = 0.0, Next_Point
    real, parameter :: AMOUNT = 1.0E3
! start program Gather
    do while (Total < AMOUNT)
      read *, Next_Point
      Total = Total + Next_Point
    end do
    print *, Total
  end program Gather
```

EXAMPLE 4.16 (See also Example 8.12.) The following program finds a zero of $\sqrt{x} - e^{-x}$ between 0 and 1 by the bisection (midpoint) method.

```
! Example 4.16. Bisection procedure for finding an approximate zero of a function.
  program Zero
    implicit none
    intrinsic Spacing, Abs
    integer, parameter :: Max_Div = 20
    real :: A = 0.0, B = 1.0
  ! start program Zero
      FA = Fun (A); FB = Fun (B)
      !.. Check for error in initial values of A and B.
      if (FA * FB > 0.0) then
        print *, "␣Improper␣starting␣values.␣"
      else
        ! Subdivide the (A, B).
        do while (Abs (A - B) > 100.0 * Spacing (A))
          C = 0.5 * (A + B); FC = Fun (C)
          if (Abs (FC) < 100.0 * Spacing (FC)) then
            exit
          else if (FC * FA > 0.0) then
            A = C
          else
            B = C
          end if
```

```
      end do
    end if
contains
  function Fun (T) result (R)
    intrinsic SqRt, Exp
    real :: R
    real, intent (in) :: T
! start function Fun
    R = SqRt (T) - Exp (-T)
  end function Fun
end program Zero
```

Termination with the `exit` Statement

An `exit` statement (see also Section 4.4) will cause premature termination of a `do while` construct (before the *Test* step encounters a false *Condition*).

Dialogue: Using an `exit` statement in a `while` loop

"Miss Flores, my teacher said that, when she learned Pascal, they told her never to jump out of a loop."

"Well, Cathy, during the heyday of 'structured programming' in the late 1970s, some experts insisted that the only 'good' repetition constructs were `while` loops without abnormal exits. One reason was that they hoped to develop practical techniques for proving program correctness, which would be more difficult if exits were permitted.

"But other equally well-respected experts pointed out that some loops should *not* be carried to their natural conclusion. For example, a loop for searching may achieve *premature success*, or a data processing loop may encounter a condition that causes *premature failure*. In either case, it would be foolish to continue with useless iterations.

"A sort of truce was reached. Even though there are ways to exit from the middle of a Pascal loop, most Pascal textbooks recommend a `while` loop with an extra `Flag` variable in its *Condition*. The variable `Flag` is set true before the loop is entered and is set false inside the loop to cause premature termination. The next time loop control is processed, the loop will end if `Flag` is found to be false. Of course, you can use the same method to get out of a Fortran `while` loop."

"I know about that method, Miss Flores. That is the way my teacher taught us to write loop exits in Pascal. But I think the extra variable is more confusing than a simple jump out of the loop."

"That can sometimes be true, Cathy. And the method doesn't work very well when you need to exit from an indexed loop. The `Flag` method has just one real difference: It sets a *data value* that will be tested *later* to determine control flow, but the `exit` statement modifies the *control sequence immediately*. Most Fortran experts agree that there is nothing wrong with using an `exit` statement for abnormal exit from a `while` loop."

4.3 Exercises

1. Modify the program in Example 4.14 to compute the Nth root of X, where N and X are input values. The principal modification is to change the iteration step to

```
Root = ((N - 1) * Root + X / (Root ** (N - 1))) / N
```

You may wish to include a bound on the number of repetitions (as in Example 4.12). Test your program with appropriate data.

2. In agricultural science, ripening of crops is related to the total number of degree-days. For each day on which the temperature exceeds some minimum value, such as 80 degrees Fahrenheit, the excess number of degrees is added to a total. Write a program to read daily maximum temperatures and accumulate the excess over 80 (consider using the intrinsic function `Dim`), continuing until the sum exceeds 240. Assume that the total will reach this value within the first 50 data items. Print the number of days and the total. Use the following data:

89	83	75	97	71	96	101	86	79	69
81	91	69	71	74	100	76	75	68	77
80	69	89	83	68	97	100	84	77	86
87	76	94	82	88	82	78	77	101	86
81	103	93	103	93	100	106	85	87	99

3. The derivative of log x is $1 / x$. Write a program to estimate the numerical derivative of the logarithm from the difference quotient

```
(Log (X + Delta_X) - Log (X)) / Delta_X
```

For X, use `1.0` or an input value. Starting with `Delta_X = 0.25`, decrease `Delta_X` until it is not greater than `2.0 * Spacing (X)`. Print the analytical derivative for X, and, for each `Delta_X` value, print the numerical derivative. (Option: Repeat the calculation with different real precision values; see Section 1.6.)

4.4 NESTING OF LOOPS AND BRANCHES

As we have seen, Fortran 90 provides the `if` construct and the `case` construct for selection (Chapter 3), and the do construct in three flavors (indexed do, simple do, and do `while`) for repetition (Sections 4.1, 4.2, and 4.3). Examples have included `if` constructs nested within each of these constructs. Each `if-then`, `else`, `else if-then`, `case`, do `while`, simple do, or indexed do statement in these control constructs is followed by a *Block* of statements whose execution it controls. (A *Block* of statements may be empty.) A *Block* of statements in any of the control constructs may contain any other control construct or another instance of the same control construct. The only restriction is that the inner control construct must be entirely within one *Block* of the outer construct. It must not be partly inside the *Block* and partly outside, and it must not overlap from one *Block* to another.

Thus, an entire control construct may appear in a program in any position where a single instruction (such as an assignment statement or a read statement) is permitted.[7] Two or more control constructs of any form may appear in the same *Block* of an outer construct, for example, and nesting may extend to more than two levels. An inner construct may have further constructs nested within any of its *Blocks*. Fortran does not limit the nesting level of control constructs. Each construct, at any level of nesting, must, of course, have all of the components required for a construct of its form, including an end if, end select, or end do statement.

One point concerning nested do constructs is worth emphasizing: When an inner do construct is encountered during repetition of the outer construct, the inner loop will continue to completion before any other part of the outer construct is executed. In particular, if the outer construct is an indexed do, the value of the *Index variable* of this outer do remains fixed while the execution of the inner construct is proceeding.

EXAMPLE 4.17 The following program contains an outer simple do construct and an inner indexed do construct. It continues calculating factorials until a negative Limit value is entered.

```
! Example 4.17. Calculate factorial of Limit.
 program FOL_2
   implicit none
   integer :: Factorial, Limit, Loop
! start program FOL_2
   do
     Factorial = 1
     print *, "⊥Please⊥enter⊥the⊥number⊥whose⊥factorial⊥is⊥wanted.⊥"
     read *, Limit
     if (Limit < 0) exit
     do Loop = 1, Limit
       Factorial = Factorial * Loop
     end do
     print *, "⊥Factorial⊥of:⊥", Limit, "⊥is:⊥", Factorial
   end do
 end program FOL_2
```

A *sentinel* data value — one that can never occur as a valid input value — terminates execution of the outer do construct. This tactic is often appropriate where input data is entered at a terminal. An alternative is an end-of-file test, as described in Sec-

[7] There are some exceptions. For example, in a simple if statement, the *Dependent statement* may be a single instruction, but it cannot be a selection or repetition construct.

tion 4.5. Some processors recognize a particular character on the terminal keyboard, such as Control-D or BREAK, as a manual end-of-file signal.

EXAMPLE 4.18 The following program reads groups of real numbers and prints the average of each group. It assumes that actual data values are never zero. A zero entry acts as a sentinel to indicate the end of the group. The program terminates if a zero is entered as the first item in a group.

```
! Example 4.18. Average groups of real Numbers.
  program Assembly
  implicit none
  intrinsic Real
  real :: Next, Total, Average
  integer :: Count
! start program Assembly
    print *, "⊥Please⊥enter⊥a⊥group⊥of⊥numbers⊥to⊥be⊥averaged.⊥"
    print *, "⊥Enter⊥zero⊥to⊥end⊥the⊥group.⊥"
    print *, "⊥To⊥quit,⊥enter⊥zero⊥as⊥the⊥first⊥number⊥in⊥a⊥group.⊥"
    do
      Count = 0
      Total = 0.0
      do
        print *, "⊥Next⊥number:⊥"
        read *, Next
        if (Next == 0.0) exit                             ! Exit from inner loop.
        Count = Count + 1
        Total = Total + Next
      end do
      if (Count == 0) exit                                ! Exit from outer loop.
      Average = Total / Real (Count)
      print *, "⊥The⊥average⊥of⊥", Count, "⊥Numbers⊥is:⊥", Average
    end do
  end program Assembly
```

EXAMPLE 4.19 Monte Carlo simulation can be used to approximate the area of a plane figure. For a rough version of the method, the figure is enclosed in a rectangle and random points are generated to cover the rectangle uniformly. The fraction of points that lie inside the figure, multiplied by the area of the rectangle, gives an estimate for the area of the figure. As a simple example, the following program estimates the area of a quadrant of a circle. It shows one (not very efficient) way to calculate the value of /4.

```
! Example 4.19. Estimate the area of a quadrant of a circle.
  program Casino
  implicit none
  intrinsic Random_Number, Real
  real :: Total = 0.0, Hits = 0.0, X(2)
  integer :: Count = 0, Loop, Tries
! start program Casino
    do
      print *, "⊥How⊥many⊥more⊥tries?⊥"
      print *, "⊥Enter⊥zero⊥to⊥quit.⊥"
      read *, Tries
      if (Tries <= 0) exit
      do Loop = 1, Tries
        Count = Count + 1
        Total = Total + 1
        call Random_Number (Harvest = X)
        if (X(1) ** 2 + X(2) ** 2 < 1.0) Hits = Hits + 1.0
      end do
    print *, "⊥Estimated⊥area⊥is⊥now:⊥", Hits / Total
    end do
  end program Casino
```

Construct Names (Optional)

A `do` construct of any of the three forms may have a construct name. Recall (from Sections 3.1 and 3.2) that an `if` construct or a `case` construct may also have a construct name. A construct name has the same form as a variable name. It must not be the same as the name of any variable, constant, procedure, or derived type (see Section 6.2) that can be referenced from the part of the program where the construct appears. Construct naming requires the following steps:

1. The construct name followed by a colon is written on the left, just preceding the keyword `do`, `if`, or `select case` in the opening statement of the construct.
2. The same name without a colon must then be written on the right, following the keyword `end do`, `end if`, or `end select` in the closing statement of the construct.
3. The construct name without a colon may also appear in other statements within the construct. In an `if` construct, the name may appear at the end of an `if-then`, `else if-then`, or `else` statement (Section 3.1). In a `case` construct, the name may appear at the end of a `case` or `case default` statement (Section 3.2). In a `do` construct, the name may appear in an `exit` or a `cycle` statement, as described later in this section.

EXAMPLE 4.20 The following program contains four named control constructs. The constructs named A and B are do constructs, while C and D are `if` constructs. The Fortran compiler will verify that the named end do and end `if` statements correspond correctly to the named do and `if` statements.

```
! Example 4.20. Print divisors of all integers from 1 to Limit.
  program Continental
    implicit none
    intrinsic Floor, SqRt, Real, Modulo
    integer :: N, Limit, I
! start program Continental
    print *, "␣Please␣enter␣limit␣for␣table␣of␣divisors.␣"
    read *, Limit
      A: do N = 1, Limit
      print *, "␣Divisors␣of:␣", N
      B: do I = 1, Floor (SqRt (Real (N)))
        C: if (Modulo (N, I) == 0) then
          D: if (I ** 2 == N) then
            print *, I
          else
            print *, I, N / I
          end if D
        end if C
      end do B
    end do A
  end program Continental
```

An `exit` statement may appear anywhere among the statements in the *Block* of a do construct of any of the three forms. As we have seen, the `exit` statement is often employed to cause termination of a simple do construct or premature termination of a do construct of one of the other forms. When an exit statement appears in a *named* do construct, the `exit` statement may mention this name:

`exit` *Do construct name*

Execution of the `exit` statement terminates the do construct designated by the *Do construct name*. Execution of an `exit` statement that does not reference a *Do construct name* terminates the *innermost* do construct that encloses that `exit` statement.

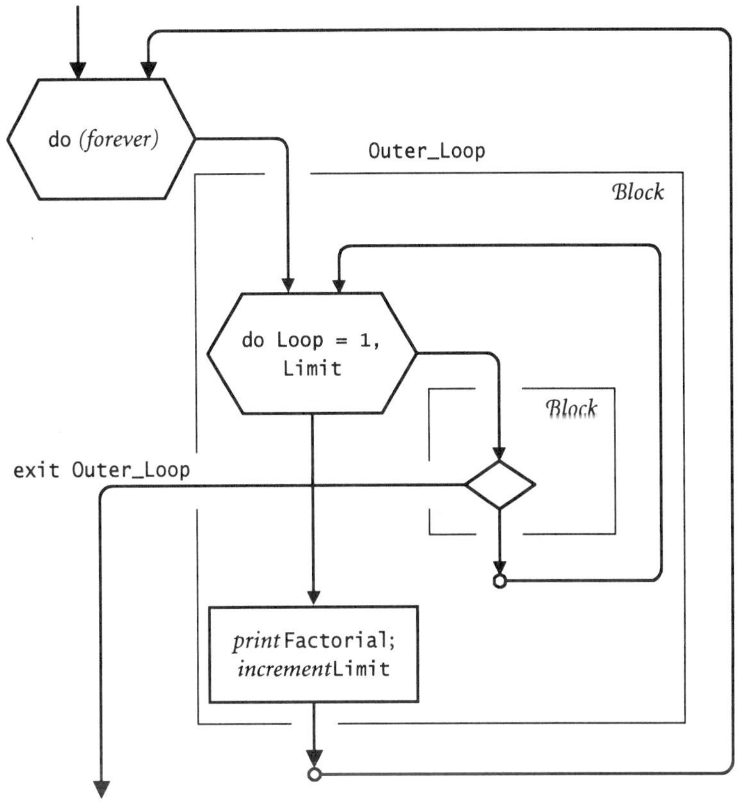

FIGURE 4.7. An *exit* statement with a construct name can cause termination of an outer loop.

An `exit` statement in an inner loop may reference the construct name of an outer loop. Such an `exit` statement terminates the inner loop as well as the outer loop. See Figure 4.7 and Example 4.21.

EXAMPLE 4.21 The following program computes the factorials of integers, beginning with zero. For each iteration of the outer loop, it calculates the factorial of the next integer. The inner loop is the same as in Example 4.17, except that a test is made to see whether the result of the next multiplication step would be too large. An `exit` statement in the inner loop causes both the inner and the outer loops to terminate if the factorial currently being calculated would exceed `Huge (1)`, which is the largest number in the Fortran 90 integer model for default integers (see Section 1.6 and Appendix A).

```
! Example 4.21. Compute factorials of all nonnegative integers.
  program Factory
    implicit none
    intrinsic Huge
    integer :: Limit = 0, Factorial, Loop
! start program Factory
    Outer_Loop: do
      Factorial = 1
      do Loop = 1, Limit
        if (Factorial > Huge (1) / Loop) then
          print *, "␣The␣factorial␣of␣", Limit, "␣is␣a␣very␣large␣integer.␣"
        exit Outer_Loop
        else
          Factorial = Factorial * Loop
        end if
      end do
      print *, "␣The␣factorial␣of␣", Limit, "␣is:␣", Factorial
      Limit = Limit + 1
    end do Outer_Loop
  end program Factory
```

The program in Example 4.21 was tested on a processor for which the value of Huge (1) is $2^{31} - 1$, or approximately $2.15 \cdot 10^9$ (the factorial of 13 is about $6.23 \cdot 10^9$). The following results were obtained:

```
The factorial of 0 is: 1
The factorial of 1 is: 1
The factorial of 2 is: 2
The factorial of 3 is: 6
The factorial of 4 is: 24
The factorial of 5 is: 120
The factorial of 6 is: 720
The factorial of 7 is: 5040
The factorial of 8 is: 40320
The factorial of 9 is: 362880
The factorial of 10 is: 3628800
The factorial of 11 is: 39916800
The factorial of 12 is: 479001600
The factorial of 13 is a very large integer.
```

The cycle *Statement (Optional)*

A cycle statement may appear anywhere among the statements in the *Block* of a do construct of any of the three forms. If the construct has a name, the cycle statement may mention this name:

cycle *Do construct name*

Execution of the cycle statement discontinues execution of the *Block* of the do construct designated by the *Do construct name* (or of the innermost *Block* that contains the cycle statement if there is no *Do construct name*), causing the execution sequence to continue immediately with the *Update* step. For do constructs other than the indexed do, there is nothing to update, so execution proceeds to the *Test* step.

Often, the cycle statement appears in an inner loop and references the name of an outer loop. When such a cycle statement is executed, the inner loop terminates and any portions of the designated loop *Block* that follow the inner loop are skipped; execution continues with the *Update* and *Test* steps for the designated loop.

The following difference should be kept in mind:

1. A *named* cycle statement transfers control to the *Update* step of the loop with the *corresponding construct name.*
2. An *unnamed* cycle statement transfers control to the *Update* step of the *innermost* loop that contains the cycle statement.

EXAMPLE 4.22 The following program contains an indexed do construct with a cycle statement. It reads numbers and computes their square roots; negative input data values are ignored.

```
! Example 4.22. Compute square roots of input data values.
  program Rutile
    implicit none
    intrinsic SqRt
    integer, parameter :: LIMIT = 20
    integer :: Loop
    real :: X
! start program Rutile
    do Loop = 1, LIMIT
      print *, "⊥Please⊥enter⊥a⊥number⊥whose⊥square⊥root⊥is⊥wanted.⊥"
      read *, X
      if (X < 0) cycle
      print *, "⊥Square⊥root⊥of:⊥", X, "⊥is:⊥", SqRt (X)
    end do
  end program Rutile
```

A single-level cycle operation merely skips the statements in the loop between the cycle statement and the end do. The same effect can be achieved with an if construct that encloses this same set of statements:

```
do Loop = 1, LIMIT
  print *, "⊥Please⊥enter⊥a⊥number.⊥"
  read *, X
  if (X <= 0) then
    print *, "⊥Square⊥root⊥of:⊥", X, "⊥is:⊥", SqRt (X)
  end if
end do
```

Exit Alternatives

Charles Zahn has pointed out that some loops have two or more natural exits.[8] For example, a search loop usually leads to one sequence of actions if the search is successful and to a quite different sequence of actions if unsuccessful. The `exit` statement provides a convenient branch to a point just beyond the loop, but this point is the same one that is reached at normal loop termination. There is still no provision for making a choice during execution of the loop between two blocks of statements to be executed when the repetition ends.

Consider the following fragment from a program to search for a key in an ordered list stored as an array. If there is an item in the list that matches the key, we wish to *Update* the existing item; if there is no matching item, we wish to *Insert* it as a new item in the list (presumably both *Update* and *Insert* are nontrivial operations requiring extensive blocks of statements).

```
do I = 1, List_Length
  if (List(I) == Search_Key) then
      ! Update
    else if (List(I) > Search_Key) then
      ! Insert
  else
      ! Continue searching
  end if
end do
  ! Insert (List is exhausted; Search_Key not found)
```

There are two ways of detecting an unsuccessful search in an ordered array. If the search encounters a list item larger than the search key, it has gone beyond the point where a matching item would be if it were in the list. The search also fails if it reaches the end of the list without matching the search key. We could position the *Insert* statements after the loop and put an `exit` statement in the *Else* block. But if we put the *Update* statements in the *Then block*, what happens at the end of the *Update* operation? An `exit` from that point would jump to the *Insert* statements.

---

[8] Charles T. Zahn, "A Control Statement for Natural Top-Down Structured Programming," Proc. Colloque sur la Programmation, Paris, April 1974. See also Donald E. Knuth, "Structured Programming with GO TO Statements," *Computing Surveys* (6: 4), December 1974, pp. 261–301.

A solution in traditional Fortran style might retain the *Update* statements in the *Then block* of the `if` construct in the search loop, with the *Insert* statements following the loop. A `go to` statement (see Appendix D.4) at the end of the *Update* operation would be employed to jump to a point just beyond the *Insert* statements. The *Else* block would contain a second `go to` or (better) an `exit` statement to jump to *Insert*.

An alternative, close to the spirit of Zahn's original proposal, is a `case` construct whose *Selector expression* references an internal function procedure (of integer or character type). Separate *Case blocks,* to be selected by the function result value, contain the *Update* statements and the *Insert* statements. The internal function procedure performs the actual search; when the result of the search is determined, it sets the function result to indicate "update" or "insert" and returns. Thus there are `return` statements in the *Then block* and in the *Else block* of the `if` construct in the search loop, besides the automatic `return` at the end of the function.

Transition Tips

- Change `go to` statements that transfer to the loop terminal statement to `cycle` statements.
- (Optional) If nesting is deep or complicated, use construct names.

4.4 Exercises

1. Consider the following program

```
! Exercise 4.4, Number 1.
  program Loops
    implicit none
    intrinsic Real
    integer :: I, J, K, L
    real :: Test, Total = 0.0
! start program Loops
    read *, K, L
    do I = L, K
      do J = 1, I
        Test = Real (I + J - 8)
        if (Test > 0.0) Total = Total + Test
      end do
    end do
    print *, Total
  end program Loops
```

For each of the following sets of data,

Set 1: K = 6 L = 3
Set 2: K = 4 L = 5

a. How many times will the `if` statement in the inner loop will be executed?

b. What will be the final value of `Total`?

4.5 LOOPS IN FILE PROCESSING

Input from the on-line terminal keyboard and output to the terminal screen (as described in Section P.3) are often suitable when the amount of data is not large. For processing larger quantities of data, it may be desirable to transmit the input data and results to and from separate *files*.

Many Fortran processors provide means for *redirection* of the data stream so that input and output files are accessed by the same simple Fortran on-line input and output instructions that can refer to the terminal keyboard and screen (see Section P.6). This method offers great flexibility and should be adopted when it is available unless portability is a primary concern.

A more general method for file input and output is supported by all Fortran processors. (See also Section 9.4.) The input and output statements for this file processing method have the slightly longer forms

read (*Unit* , *) *Input list*
write (*Unit* , *) *Output list*

Note that the keyword in a file output statement is `write` rather than `print`.

The *Unit* number is an integer that is associated with a file name. The asterisk that follows the *Unit* number designates list-directed formatting. (An explicit format specification can appear at this point: see Chapter 9.) The form of the *Input list* or *Output list* is the same as for on-line input or output (see Sections P.3 and 9.2).

Additional specifiers, besides the *Unit* number and the asterisk, may appear in this longer statement form in the parentheses between the `read` or `write` keyword and the *Input list* or *Output list*. In general, these parentheses enclose a *Control list* that may contain several specifiers:

read (*Control list*) *Input list*
write (*Control list*) *Output list*

Later in this section, we shall encounter the *Exception* specifier, which permits detection of the end of an input file. (Other possible *Control list* specifiers are described in Section 9.1.)

For compatibility with on-line input and output, another asterisk is permitted in place of the *Unit* number in a *Control list*. Most processors interpret an asterisk in the *Unit* number position as designating on-line input and output. In effect, Fortran treats the terminal keyboard as a special "file" connected to the asterisk input unit and the terminal screen as a special "file" connected to the asterisk output unit. This alternative permits additional *Control list* specifiers in conjunction with on-line processing. (See, for example, `advance=` in Sections 9.1 and 9.2.)

The Input or Output Unit

A *Unit* specifier in a file input or output statement is an integer that designates a named file. A Fortran `open` statement establishes a connection between the *Unit* number and a *File name*:

open (*Unit* , file = *File name*)

(Additional information that may appear in an `open` statement is described in Section 9.4.)

The *Unit* number is an integer expression — most often, an integer constant. The value may be chosen arbitrarily by the programmer. Once the `open` statement has been executed, this integer value in an input or output statement anywhere in the Fortran program will refer to the file that is connected to this *Unit*.

The *File name* is a character expression — usually, a character constant. The *File name* must have a form that is acceptable to the particular processor that will execute the program. File names such as the following are accepted by some typical processors:

```
open (9, file = "data.txt")
open (2, file = "My_File")
open (11, file = "c:\docs\results.txt")
```

File Input

Input Records

A `read` statement normally transmits one or more complete *records* from the input device. (See also nonadvancing input in Sections 9.1 and 9.2.) If the input data is prepared ahead of time on a file, each `read` statement transmits as many records (lines of text) as are needed to contain the data elements listed in the statement. A file processing application often reads sets of data, one from each record of an input file, and applies the same computational steps to each data set.

Echo Printing

If input data is not entered at the terminal, it should be "echo printed" along with the results. Here is an example.

EXAMPLE 4.23 The following program prints the values of X and Y along with Average, and it prints the value of Diameter along with the circumference.

```
! Example 4.23. Echo printing.
  program Run_Me
    implicit none
    real :: Average, X, Y, Diameter
! start program Run_Me
    open (11, file = "data.txt")
    open (12, file = "results.txt")
    read (11, *) X, Y
    Average = (X + Y) / 2.0
    write (12, *) "⊥The⊥average⊥of⊥", X, "⊥and⊥", Y, "⊥is⊥", Average
    read (11, *) Diameter
    write (12, *) "⊥DIAMETER:⊥", Diameter
    write (12, *) "⊥CIRCUMFERENCE:⊥", 3.1416 * Diameter
  end program Run_Me
```

Input data:

```
1.234   5.678
1.0
```

Results:

```
The average of 1.2340000 and 5.6780000 is 3.4559999
DIAMETER: 1.0000000
CIRCUMFERENCE: 3.1415999
```

Loop Construct for File Processing

Typically, each record of an input file is to be read and processed in approximately the same way. A loop construct is obviously appropriate for this pattern of instructions. The instructions in the *Block* usually include branching constructs for handling various situations that are detected as the records are read. Processing continues until the end of the data is reached.

Often, the last data record is immediately followed by an *end-of-file* mark, which, in Fortran, is called an "endfile record" because it is processed in much the same way as a data record. (The file save operation in most text editors puts such a mark at the end of text files.) A program that is intended to read all the data from the file may continue to process records until this end-of-file indication is detected.

Because of the hardware characteristics of files, Fortran must perform an ordinary input operation in order to detect the end-of-file mark. A `read` instruction somewhere in the *Block*, which would normally read the next record, instead encounters the special end-of-file indication and recognizes that the current `read` instruction did not transmit any new data. The steps in the loop that process new data should be skipped, possibly by execution of a conditional `exit`, when the end-of-file mark is encountered.

This processing pattern is sometimes called *loop and a half*. The entire *Block* is repeated as many times as needed, and then the first part (down to the `read` instruction that detects the termination condition) is executed during the last repetition.

Note that the loop-and-a-half pattern can be much more appropriately programmed with the simple `do` than with either the indexed `do` construct or the `do while` construct. An indexed loop requires a fixed upper bound (set by the program) that may be difficult to establish in advance, and a `do while` construct requires that the condition for termination be defined prior to loop entry.

End of File

To permit detection of the end-of-file mark, an *Exception* specifier of the form `iostat` = *Integer variable* may be included in the *Control list* of the `read` statement:

`read (` *Unit* `, *, iostat =` *Integer variable* `)` *Input list*

Fortran will set the designated *Integer variable* to zero after a normal read operation or to a negative value when an end-of-file mark is read. The variable will later be tested to determine whether data processing is to be continued or terminated. The two statements that set and test the *Integer variable*, here named `EoF`, might appear in an input loop as follows:

```
do
  read (*, *, iostat = EoF) Next_Datum                 ! Set EoF.
  if (EoF < 0) exit                                    ! Test EoF.
    :                                          ! Process Next_Datum
end do
```

The program in Example 4.24 uses a similar pattern. (Compare Examples 3.2 and 3.3.)

EXAMPLE 4.24

```
! Example 4.24. Weights of male and female cats.
  program Cats_6
    implicit none
    integer :: Male_Count = 0, Female_Count = 0, EoF
    real :: Next_Weight, Male_Total = 0.0, Female_Total = 0.0
    character (len = 1) Sex
! start program Cats_6
    open (unit = 2, file = "myfile.txt")
    do
      read (2, *, iostat = EoF) Sex, Next_Weight
      if (EoF < 0) exit
      if ((Sex == "M") .or. (Sex == "m")) then                    ! Cat is male.
        Male_Count = Male_Count + 1
        Male_Total = Male_Total + Next_Weight
      else                                                       ! Cat is female
        Female_Count = Female_Count + 1
        Female_Total = Female_Total + Next_Weight
      end if
    end do
    print *, Male_Count, Male_Total, Female_Count, Female_Total
    if (Male_Count > 0) then
      print *, "⊥Average⊥weight:⊥", Male_Total / Real (Male_Count)
    else
      print *, "⊥There⊥are⊥no⊥male⊥cats⊥in⊥this⊥sample.⊥"
    end if
  end program Cats_6
```

In some applications, particularly those involving a *search*, there may be more than one `exit` statement in the *Block* of a do construct. Consider Example 4.25.

EXAMPLE 4.25 The following program searches for negative data in a file. When a negative data item is found, the location of this item in the file is printed. However, if none of the items in the file is negative, the end of the data file will be reached before a negative item is reached. In the former case, we say that the search *succeeds*; in the latter case, that it *fails*.

```
! Example 4.25. Exit when a negative data item is found
!   or when the end of file is encountered.
  program File_Search
    implicit none
    integer :: Record_Number = 1, EoF
    real :: Next_item
! start program File_Search
    open (2, file = "zahlen.txt")
    do
      read (2, *, iostat = EoF) Next_item
      if (EoF < 0) then
        print *, "␣No␣negative␣items␣in␣file␣"
        exit
      else if (Next_item < 0.0) then
        print *, "␣Negative␣item␣found␣at␣record␣number:␣", Record_Number
        exit
      else
        Record_Number = Record_Number + 1
      end if
    end do
  end program File_Search
```

A variant of this program is applicable when data input is to be terminated at a particular point, but before the end of the data file is reached. A special artificial data item, or *sentinel*, is created and is placed on the file following the normal data. The input loop terminates when the sentinel item is encountered. For this method to work, the sentinel item must have a value that can never appear as a normal data item.

Application: Simple Statistics

The following examples demonstrate the possibility of computing simple statistics (mean, variance, correlation, and linear regression) from data that is read from a file, without storing it in an array.

EXAMPLE 4.26 The average, or *arithmetic mean,* of a set of n numbers is defined as the sum of the numbers divided by n. The following program reads a data value from each record of an input file and computes the arithmetic mean, X_Mean, of the data values.

```
! Example 4.26. Arithmetic mean of values from an input file.
  program Statistics_1
    implicit none
    real :: Count = 0.0, X, X_Sum = 0.0, X_Mean
    integer :: EoF
! start program Statistics_1
    open (2, file = "numeroso.txt")
    do
      read (2, *, iostat = EoF) X
      if (EoF < 0) exit
      Count = Count + 1.0
      X_Sum = X_Sum + X
    end do
    if (Count > 0.0) then
      X_Mean = X_Sum / Count
      print *, "␣Arithmetic␣mean:␣", X_Mean
    else
      print *, "␣There␣is␣no␣data␣in␣this␣file.␣"
    end if
  end program Statistics_1
```

EXAMPLE 4.27 The *variance* and the *standard deviation* can be computed similarly:

1. During input, we accumulate the `Count`, the sum of the data values, `X_Sum`, and the sum of the squares, `XX_Sum`. (We add the square of each input data value to `XX_Sum`.)
2. When the end of the file is reached, we compute the arithmetic mean, `X_Mean`, as in the preceding program.
3. We find the variance, `X_Var`, according to the formula

   `X_Var = (XX_Sum / Count) - X_Mean ** 2.`

4. The standard deviation, `X_Dev`, is the square root of `X_Var`.

```
! Example 4.27. Mean, variance, and standard deviation.
  program Statistics_2
    implicit none
    intrinsic SqRt
    real :: Count = 0.0, X, X_Sum = 0.0, XX_Sum = 0.0, X_Mean, X_Var, X_Dev
    integer :: EoF
```

```
! start program Statistics_2
   open (2, file = "numeroso.txt")
   do
     read (2, *, iostat = EoF) X
     if (EoF < 0) exit
     Count = Count + 1.0
     X_Sum = X_Sum + X
     XX_Sum = XX_Sum + X ** 2
   end do
   if (Count > 1.0) then
     X_Mean = X_Sum / Count
     X_Var = (XX_Sum / Count) - X_Mean ** 2
     X_Dev = SqRt (X_Var)
     print *, Mean, X_Var, X_Dev
   else
     print *, "␣There␣is␣no␣data␣in␣this␣file.␣"
   end if
 end program Statistics_2
```

EXAMPLE 4.28 When we have a sequence of (X, Y) number pairs, we can compute not only the separate arithmetic means, X_Mean and Y_Mean, and the separate standard deviations, X_Dev and Y_Dev, but also the *covariance*, Covar, and the *correlation* between the sequence of X values and the sequence of Y values, Correlation. Assuming that each record of a file contains an X value and a Y value, we write a program to perform this calculation as follows:

1. During input, we accumulate the Count, and we accumulate separately the sum of the X values and of the Y values, X_Sum and Y_Sum, the sum of the squares of the X values and of the Y values, XX_Sum and YY_Sum, and the sum of the products of corresponding values, XY_Sum.
2. When the end of the file is reached, we compute X_Mean, Y_Mean, X_Dev, and Y_Dev.
3. The covariance is given by

   `Covar = (XY_Sum / Count) - X_Mean * Y_Mean`

4. The correlation is

   `Correlation = Covar / (X_Dev * Y_Dev)`

Note that the correlation is undefined unless there are at least two items, because the deviations for one item are 0.

```
! Example 4.28. Statistics with covariance and correlation.
  program Statistics_3
    implicit none
    intrinsic SqRt
    real :: Count = 0.0, X, Y, X_Sum = 0.0, Y_Sum = 0.0, &
      XX_Sum = 0.0, YY_Sum = 0.0, XY_Sum = 0.0, &
      X_Mean, Y_Mean, X_Dev, Y_Dev, Covar, Correlation
    integer :: EoF
! start program Statistics_3
    open (2, file = "numeroso.txt")
    do
      read (2, *, iostat = EoF) X, Y
      if (EoF < 0) exit
      Count = Count + 1.0
      X_Sum = X_Sum + X
      Y_Sum = Y_Sum + Y
      XX_Sum = XX_Sum + X ** 2
      YY_Sum = YY_Sum + Y ** 2
      XY_Sum = XY_Sum + X * Y
    end do
    if (Count > 1.0) then
      X_Mean = X_Sum / Count
      Y_Mean = Y_Sum / Count
      X_Dev = SqRt ((XX_Sum / Count) - X_Mean ** 2)
      Y_Dev = SqRt ((YY_Sum / Count) - Y_Mean ** 2)
      Covar = (XY_Sum / Count) - X_Mean * Y_Mean
      Correlation = Covar / (X_Dev * Y_Dev)
      print *, X_Mean, Y_Mean, X_Dev, Y_Dev, Covar, Correlation
    else
      print *, "␣Insufficient␣data␣in␣this␣file.␣"
    end if
  end program Statistics_3
```

EXAMPLE 4.29 Statistics problems are notorious for numerical difficulties, some of which can be alleviated by use of an updating method for variance and standard deviation, as described here.[9]

[9] My thanks to Mark Durst of Lawrence Livermore National Laboratory for bringing to my attention the following references: T. T. Chan, G. H. Golub, and R. J. LeVeque, "Algorithms for Computing the Sample Variance: Analysis and Recommendations," *The American Statistician* 37 (1983): 242–47. E. A. Youngs and E. M. Cramer, "Some Results Relevant to Choice of Sum and Sum of Product Algorithms," *Technometrics* 13 (1971): 657–65.

The variance formula,

```
X_Var = (XX_Sum / Count) - X_Mean ** 2
```

is sometimes difficult to compute accurately because the two terms to be subtracted may be large and the variance may be small. (This difficulty is sometimes called *catastrophic cancellation.*) Better results may be obtained by accumulating the Count and the X_Sum and updating the *residual*, XX_Res, which is Count times X_Var, as each X value is read, by the formula

```
XX_Res = XX_Res + &
  (Count * X - X_Sum) ** 2 / (Count * (Count - 1))
```

We update YY_Res, which is Count times Y_Var, by a similar formula, and XY_Res, which is Count times Covar, by the formula

```
XY_Res = XY_Res + &
  (Count * X - X_Sum) * (Count * Y - Y_Sum) &
    / (Count * (Count - 1))
```

We apply these residual formulas beginning with the second set of data values. (For the first, we set all three residuals to zero.) At the end, we compute the variances and covariances from the residuals.

```
! Example 4.29. Statistics by updating method.
  program Statistics_4
    implicit none
    intrinsic SqRt
    real :: Count = 0.0, X, Y, X_Sum = 0.0, Y_Sum = 0.0, &
      XX_Res = 0.0, YY_Res = 0.0, XY_Res = 0.0, &
      X_Dev, Y_Dev, Covar, Correlation
    integer :: EoF
! start program Statistics_4
    open (2, file = "numeroso.txt")
    do
      read (2, *, iostat = EoF) X, Y
      if (EoF < 0) exit
      Count = Count + 1.0
      X_Sum = X_Sum + X
      Y_Sum = Y_Sum + Y
      if (Count > 1.0) then
        XX_Res = XX_Res + (Count * X - X_Sum) ** 2 / (Count * (Count - 1.0))
        YY_Res = YY_Res + (Count * Y - Y_Sum) ** 2 / (Count * (Count - 1.0))
        XY_Res = XY_Res + (Count * X - X_Sum) * (Count * Y - Y_Sum) &
          / (Count * (Count - 1.0))
      end if
    end do
```

```
  if (Count > 1.0) then
    X_Dev = SqRt (XX_Res / Count)
    Y_Dev = SqRt (YY_Res / Count)
    Covar = XY_Res / Count
    Correlation = Covar / (X_Dev * Y_Dev)
    print *, X_Dev, Y_Dev, Covar, Correlation
  else
    print *, "␣Insufficient␣data␣in␣this␣file.␣"
  end if
end program Statistics_4
```

Note that additional declarations are required. In Example 4.28, additional steps are required to explicitly calculate `X_Var` as well as `A` and `B`. In Example 4.29, it is necessary to explicitly calculate `X_Mean` and `Y_Mean` from `X_Sum` and `Y_Sum` and to calculate `X_Var` from `XX_Res` and `Count`.

EXAMPLE 4.30 We may suspect a linear relation between two measured variables — for example, the thickness of tree rings during a sequence of years as compared with the amount of rainfall. If there were such a linear relation, it could be expressed in the form $y = a + bx$. The problem of determining the "best" values of a and b for a relation of this form (the *coefficients of linear regression*) is closely related to the foregoing statistical problems. We can obtain the regression coefficients a and b by inserting the following Fortran statements near the end of Example 4.28 or 4.29.

```
! Example 4.30. Linear regression coefficients
    ⋮
  B = Covar / X_Var
  A = Y_Mean - B * X_Mean
    ⋮
```

Transition Tip

- (Optional) Change straightforward file processing loops to use the simple do construct with `exit` when the end of the file is encountered.

4.5 Exercises

1. Prepare a file containing a sequence of records. Each record contains a single number of real type. (It is likely that your text editor automatically puts an end-of-file mark immediately after the last record when you save your file. You may wish to verify this by reading the text editor documentation or by asking your instructor or computer center staff.) Write a Fortran program that does the following:

Sets the initial value of a total to zero.

Reads a real data value from each record of the file and adds it to the total.

After the entire file has been read, prints the total.

Test your program with a file containing several records, with a file containing just one record, and with a file containing no records (only the end-of-file mark).

2. Write a program (compare Example 4.25) to read and accumulate data until any one of the following events occurs: The total exceeds a predetermined amount, or more than 50 items have been processed, or a negative (sentinel) data value is found, or the end of the file is reached. For each termination condition, print a message that indicates the reason for termination. (If you wish, you may use a `stop` statement with the message in a *Stop code,* as explained in Section 7.3.)

3. You are working as a laboratory assistant for Professor Smythe-Heppelwaite, and you are helping him prepare data to be processed at the campus computer center. The professor gives you a file of records, each containing the measured thickness of the wing of one of the butterflies in his rare butterfly collection. The professor states that he has arranged the data so that the variable values are in ascending order, but from past experience you have reason to be skeptical.

   Write a program to read the records one at a time and, for each record after the first, test for a stepdown error in the sequence of data values — that is, for a data value that is smaller than the previous one. When a stepdown error occurs, print the current record number and the two data values involved. Also count the stepdown errors. After the entire file has been read, print the total number of stepdown errors that were found. Use the following data:

1393	1394	1418	1429	1437	1465	1445	1455	1463	1497
1565	1578	1584	1585	1591	1597	1610	1657	1658	1673
1685	1707	1711	1717	1723	1730	1733	1738	1757	1765
1811	1842	1853	1879	1881	1887	1903	1905	1906	1909
1913	1920	1931	1946	1961	1976	1977	1986	1994	1987
2009	2024	2025	2026	2040	2041	2048	2049	2050	2072
2073	2074	2075	2088	2096	2089	2099	2101	2105	2120
2129	2135	2141	2142	2144	2145	2162	2167	2169	2170
2173	2176	2181	2189	2183	2221	2229	2233	2258	2264
2269	2272	2277	2288	2296	2309	2310	2352	2368	2377

4. Test the programs in Examples 4.28 and 4.29 with a data file containing the "clustered" large numbers $x = 1001, 1002, \ldots, 1009$; $y = 3009, 3008, \ldots, 3001$. Which of the two programs gives more accurate results? (On a perfect calculator, the large constant offsets would have no effect on any of the statistics except the mean and the regression coefficients. For the given data, `X_Var` and `Y_Var` should both be 60/9, and `Covar` should be the negative of this value.) If there is no noticeable difference on your computer, add another zero in the middle of each data value.

5. Run the program in Example 4.29 to calculate correlations from one or more of the following sets of data. Or make the modifications suggested in Example 4.30 and obtain the regression coefficients as well.

a. Set 1: Thickness of tree rings versus amount of rainfall

Year	1	2	3	4	5	6	7	8
Rainfall (cm)	18.1	15.1	11.4	35.6	33.2	15.0	33.1	35.3
Thickness (mm)	7.0	3.5	2.0	7.3	6.9	3.5	5.7	5.1

b. Set 5: Population of world (logarithm) versus time

Year	1	2	3	4	5	6	7	8
Population	9.465	9.471	9.472	9.479	9.484	9.488	9.490	9.491

c. Set 6: Inflation versus increase in money supply

Year	1	2	3	4	5	6
Increase in money supply (%)	5	8	10	6	8	15
Inflation (%)	5	6	8	5	7	10

d. Set 7: Deaths from lung cancer (thousands) versus U.S. tobacco production ($ million)

Year	1	2	3	4	5	6	7	8
U.S. tobacco production	1319	1326	1387	1406	1390	1354	1293	1228
Deaths from lung cancer	26.7	27.4	28.4	28.7	28.6	27.5	26.1	24.7

e. Set 8: Motor vehicle fatalities versus number of vehicles registered (millions)

Year	1	2	3	4	5	6	7	8
Vehicles	44.7	49.2	51.9	53.3	56.3	58.6	62.7	65.2
Fatalities	31,701	34,763	36,996	37,955	35,586	38,426	38,426	39,628

	9	10	11	12	13	14	15
	67.6	68.8	72.1	74.5	76.4	79.9	83.5
	38,702	36,981	37,910	38,137	38,091	40,804	43,564

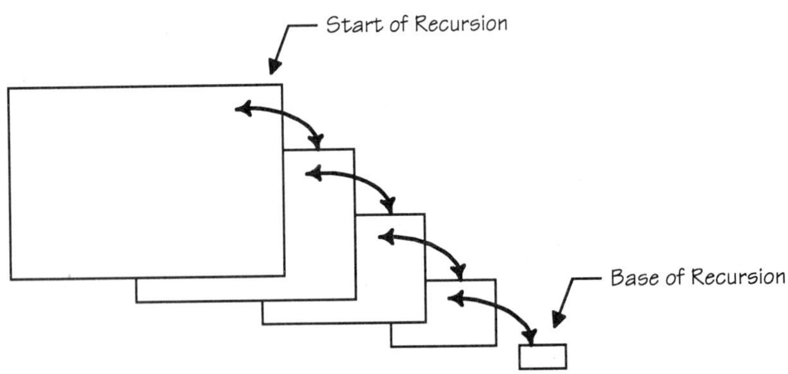

FIGURE 4.8.
Recursion.

4.6 RECURSION (Optional)

A completely different approach to repetition, in contrast to the method of *iteration* that we have been studying so far, is *recursion*, as illustrated in Figure 4.8. This form of repetition starts with a call to a procedure that performs the set of steps that are to be repeated. The procedure continues the repetition by calling itself, unless no further repetitions are needed. In that case (called the *base* of the recursion), the recursion begins to unwind by terminating execution of all the recursive procedure calls (beginning with the last one called).

Recursive procedures should be created with some care. It is especially necessary to be sure that the recursion will eventually reach the base. For a very common class of recursive procedures, with an integer argument that decreases with each recursive call and a small integer base such as 1 or 0, termination is assured. It has been shown that iteration is equivalent to a special form of recursion called *tail recursion.*[10] With this form of recursion, the recursive call is executed as the last step, just before the recursive procedure ends.

Many problems can be described more naturally as recursive processes than as iterative processes. If you normally think of a factorial as an integer times a smaller factorial, you can translate that problem description directly into a recursive program. On the other hand, recursion usually entails some loss in efficiency, including extra procedure-call overhead and "hidden" storage requirements. However, some modern optimizing compilers detect tail recursion and translate it, when possible, to iteration. You can design the program in more natural terms, and the compiler makes it efficient.

For example, factorials can be computed either iteratively or recursively. An iterative factorial function can be built with an indexed `do` construct (see Example 4.3) according to a definition of the factorial as a product of consecutive integers. The recursive version follows a different definition. That is, to find the factorial of `N` recursively,

1. If `N` is 0 (the base case), the result is 1.
2. Otherwise, find the factorial of `N - 1` (by a recursive call) and multiply it by `N`.

This definition may seem rather mysterious, but in fact it can easily be translated directly into a recursive procedure for finding the factorial (see Example 4.31). The recursive procedure is called for the first time from the main program and then continues to call itself until the base is reached.

---

[10] For an excellent discussion of iteration versus (linear) recursion, see H. Abelson and G. J. Sussman, *Structure and Interpretation of Computer Programs* (Cambridge, Mass.: MIT Press, 1985), pp. 30–34.

EXAMPLE 4.31 The recursive function `Factorial` in the following program, when called with actual argument `N`, calls itself recursively with actual argument `N - 1`. If the argument value is 0, the procedure does not call itself but immediately returns the result value 1; it is this base case that terminates the repetition after the desired number of recursive calls.

```
! Example 4.31. Recursive factorial.
 program Dervish
   implicit none
   integer :: Factorial = 1, Limit
! start program Dervish
   print *, "␣Please␣enter␣the␣number␣whose␣factorial␣is␣wanted.␣"
   read *, Limit
   print *, "␣Factorial␣of:␣", Limit, "␣is:␣", Factorial (Limit)
 contains
   recursive integer function Factorial (N) result (Fac)
     integer N
 ! start function Factorial
     if (N == 0) then
       Fac = 1
     else
       Fac = N * Factorial (N - 1)                ! Recursive call to Factorial
     end if
   end function Factorial
 end program Dervish
```

EXAMPLE 4.32 This recursive program reads a list of integers from a file and prints them. The method may be described, in terms of an operation called "recursive-print," as follows:

To recursive-print a list of integers:

If the list is empty, do nothing.

Otherwise, print the first integer, and then recursive-print a list that consists of all except the first integer.

```
! Example 4.32. Recursive-print a list of integers.
 program Babe
   implicit none
! start program Babe
   open (2, file = "zahlen.txt")
   call Recursive_Print                             ! Recursive print a list.
 contains
```

```
  recursive subroutine Recursive_Print
    integer :: A, EoF
! start subroutine Recursive_Print
    read (2, *, iostat = EoF) A         ! Read first integer in remainder of list.
    if (EoF = 0) then
      print *, A                                          ! Print first integer.
      call Recursive_Print                    ! Recursive print remainder of list.
    else                                                ! Do nothing if EoF /= 0.
    end if
  end subroutine Recursive_Print
end program Babe
```

A few features of this problem description are common to many recursive problem definitions:

1. The method for performing a *sequence of tasks* ("recursive-print a list of integers") is described quite differently from the method for performing a *component task* ("print an integer").
2. The way to perform a *component task* ("print an integer") is supposed to be already known or to be directly defined somewhere else.
3. The way to perform a *sequence of tasks* ("recursive-print a list") is not described explicitly, but is described only in terms of performing of a *component task* ("print an integer") and a *smaller sequence of tasks* ("recursive-print all except the first").
4. However, the performance of a certain *base sequence* ("recursive-print an empty list") is described directly.

Section 7.4 contains further examples of recursive subroutines and functions.

4.6 Exercises

1. Prepare a text file consisting of several records, with one integer in each record. Prepare and execute the program in Example 4.32 using this text file as input.
2. Modify the program in Example 4.32 by interchanging the two lines

```
print *, A
call Recursive_Print
```

and run it again with the same input file. What do you observe? (Note that the modified subroutine is not tail-recursive. See Example 7.10.)

Part III
DATA OBJECTS

Chapter 5 is devoted to *array processing*, which has always been a strong feature of Fortran. There are several ways to declare an array; it may be desirable to group array declarations in one or another of these ways depending upon which attributes appear together. Fortran 90 permits operations on *whole arrays* and *array sections*. An array section may consist of contiguous elements, of elements separated by a fixed *stride*, or of an array "slice" of lower *rank* (dimensionality). For most purposes, the components of a whole-array expression must all be arrays of the same shape or scalars. Most scalar intrinsic functions apply *elementwise* to array objects, and additional intrinsics are provided for whole-array operations. A user-defined function may return a whole-array result. *Array constructors* permit description of an array as a list of expressions, which may be constants. *Allocatable arrays* may be created in heap storage during program execution in response to needs that develop as the computation proceeds. Temporary or working storage in a procedure, for example, can be created as required and does not need to be passed in the argument list.

Chapter 6 deals with *strings* (character data type), *structures* (of user-defined types), and *pointers*. String features include *substrings* and *concatenation*, *zero-length* strings, and variant character *subtypes* that can be specified with `kind` type parameters. A *structure* is an object of a user-defined type, which may have scalar or array components of intrinsic types or of user-defined types. A *pointer* has a *target* that may be either a newly allocated object (in heap storage) or a preexisting declared object. Simple linked list and binary tree implementations use pointers to generate flexible lists or trees by linking structures together.

Chapter 5
Arrays

A Fortran *array* is a variable that is composed of *array elements*. All elements of a particular array must have the same data type, type properties, and all other attributes. One consequence of this uniformity is that computer hardware can quickly and efficiently locate any particular element on the basis of its sequential position within the array.

A Fortran array name has the same form as other variable names: It must consist of from 1 to 31 letters, digits, or underscore characters, and the first character must be a letter. In the example programs in this text, we write array names in the same way as other variable names, with an initial uppercase (capital) letter.

An array element is designated by the name of the array along with a parenthesized list of *subscript expressions*. Only one subscript is required to designate a particular element of a *one-dimensional array* (also called a *vector*); two are required for a *two-dimensional array* (or *matrix*). Other Fortran arrays may require as many as seven subscripts:

```
List(17)
Vector(I + 1)
Matrix(I, J)
Cube(3, 3, 3)
Hyper_Cube(S1, S2, S3, S4, S5, S6, S7)
```

The number of subscripts in an array element name is called the *rank*, or *dimensionality*, of the array. The rank of each array is one of its declared attributes and cannot change during program execution. For some purposes, a *scalar* (a data object that is not an array) may be considered to be an array of rank 0.

Two simple matrix applications are described next. Programs for these two applications, presented later in the chapter, illustrate some of the array features that Fortran 90 provides:

1. A horizontal beam supports a system of n vertical forces at positions $x_1, x_2, \ldots, x_n$, as illustrated in Figure 5.1. Each force f_i produces a deflection $y_i = y(x_i)$ at each position x_i. We may represent the forces by a vector f of length n and the deflections by a vector y of length n. Assuming that the beam is elastic and satisfies a generalized Hooke's law, the deflections are related to the forces by the matrix equation y = A·f, where A is an n by n matrix of coefficients of influence or of flexibility; its inverse is called the *stiffness* matrix. The stiffness matrix of a conservative system is symmetric. A related Fortran program is shown in Example 5.23 (see Section 5.3).

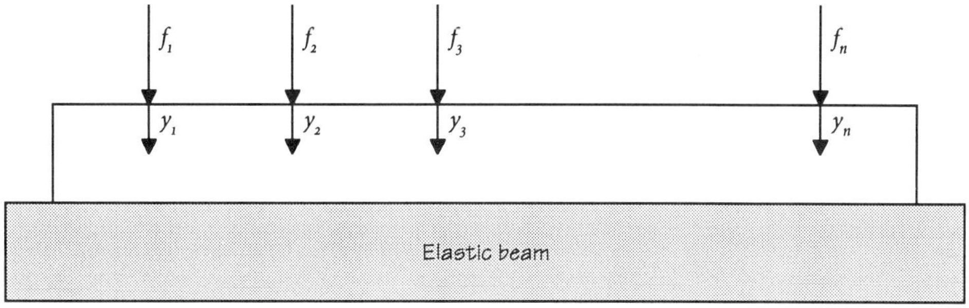

FIGURE 5.1. Elastic beam with forces and deflections.

2. Consider a general n-mesh alternating current in the steady state. Let the various complex mesh currents have the values $i_1, i_2, \ldots, i_n$, and let the complex voltages impressed on the contours of the meshes be $e_1, e_2, \ldots, e_n$. The voltages and currents are related by the matrix equation $\mathbf{e} = Z \cdot \mathbf{i}$, where Z is a complex n by n matrix of *impedances*. In a static network, the impedance matrix is symmetric. In a Fortran program for applications of this kind, it is not necessary to separate the real and imaginary parts of the complex variables. A related Fortran program is shown in Example 5.24 (Section 5.3).

5.1 ARRAY SHAPE

Declaration for an Array

An array variable may be declared in the usual way — that is, in a type declaration that specifies the type, type properties, and other attributes to the left of the double colon, and the array name to the right. All elements of the array have exactly the same properties and attributes as the array, except for dimension.

The dimension attribute for an array is specified in parentheses after the array name:

```
Stiffness(20, 20)
Impedance(17, 17)
Able(17)
Array(3)
Chessboard(8, 8)
Ising(5, 5, 5), Ones(5, 5, 5), Count(5, 5, 5), Threshold(5, 5, 5)
```

The dimension attribute is specified by a list of *Subscript bounds*, one for each dimension. In the simplest case, the *Subscript bound* for each dimension is given as an integer constant, designating the maximum array subscript value permitted for that dimension. As we shall see, a minimum subscript bound may also be specified; if none is given, Fortran assumes that the lower bound is 1.

It is recommended that named constants, rather than numerical constants, be used in *Subscript bound* specifications. With the named constant declaration

```
integer, parameter :: BIG = 20, SIZE = 17, BOARD = 8, FEW = 3
```

we might write the following specifications:

```
Matrix(BIG, BIG)
Able(SIZE)
Array(FEW)
Chessboard(BOARD, BOARD)
Cube(FEW, FEW, FEW)
```

Research problems often begin with a simple model involving only a few data points. As more details of the problem come to light, the model expands. In a matrix application, the matrix size may be a parameter that grows as the model develops. This parameter may appear as a subscript bound in several related array declarations, as well as in limit expressions of indexed do loops, and possibly at other places in the program. If this parameter value is designated by a named constant, only one program change is required when the size of the model increases.

Fortran 90 provides several ways of specifying the dimension attribute, three of which are presented here. The first two methods incorporate dimension information in the type declaration, to the left or right side of the double colon; the third method uses a `dimension` statement that is separate from the type declaration (see the discussion of entity-oriented and attribute-oriented declarations in Section 1.2).

It will be evident from a review of the following examples that the choice among these methods depends upon how similar the various arrays are with regard to dimension and other attributes. Of course, mixtures of the three methods are also possible.

First Entity-Oriented Form — Left Side of Type Declaration

A type declaration may include names of array variables to the right of the double colon. To the left, between the *Type name* and the double colon, a `dimension` attribute specifier of the form

`dimension(` *Subscript bounds* `)`

may appear — for example:

```
real, dimension(20, 20) :: Matrix_1, Matrix_2
```

This form requires that all arrays listed on the right have the same shape and all other attributes. It is often preferable for simple examples, because it corresponds most closely to the standard type declaration form introduced in Section 1.2:

Type name `(` *Type properties* `),` *Attributes* `::` *List of names*

The following example illustrates this entity-oriented form. For each different combination of dimension and other attributes, we must write a separate type declaration statement. Note that, in a program such as this one, with a large variety of different array shapes, this form requires many separate declarations.

```
implicit none
integer, parameter :: Low = Selected_Real_Kind(6)
integer, parameter :: BIG = 20, SIZE = 17, BOARD = 8, FEW = 4, &
  SHORT = 20, LONG = 144, GAP = 5, M = 3
integer, dimension(FEW) :: Array
integer, dimension(BOARD, BOARD) :: Chessboard
real, dimension(BIG, BIG) :: Matrix
real :: Look, J
real, dimension(SIZE) :: Able
real, dimension(LONG) :: John, Baker, Delta
real, dimension(SHORT) :: Sponsor, A
real, dimension(M): Doe
real (kind = Low), dimension(BIG) :: X
real (kind = Low), dimension(FEW) :: Y
real (kind = Low) :: Z
real (kind = Low), dimension(SHORT) :: Drum, Xylophone, Tuba
real, intent (in out), dimension(3, 3, 3) :: Cube
character (len = GAP), dimension(SHORT) :: Sponsor, A
character (len = BIG) :: Word
character (len = BIG), dimension(FEW) :: Hamlet
```

Second Entity-Oriented Form — Right Side of Type Declaration

Arrays of different shapes, as well as scalars, may be combined in a type declaration. The name of each array variable to the right of the double colon is immediately followed by its dimension attribute specification, which has the form

(*Subscript bounds*)

Names of scalar variables (without a dimension specification) may be interspersed — for example,

```
real :: Matrix_1(20, 20), Look, Able(17)
```

All variables in a single declaration must have the same type properties and all other attributes except dimension. Note that the keyword `dimension` never appears in this declaration form.

The following example contains a separate declaration for each different combination of type properties and other attributes except dimension. A declaration may combine scalars and arrays of various shapes because dimension information is specified separately for each variable.

```
implicit none
integer, parameter :: Low = Selected_Real_Kind(6)
integer, parameter :: BIG = 20, SIZE = 17, BOARD = 8, FEW = 4, &
  SHORT = 20, LONG = 144, GAP = 5, M = 3
real :: Matrix(BIG, BIG), Look, J, Able(SIZE), John(LONG),
Baker(LONG), &
  Delta(LONG), Sponsor(SHORT), A(SHORT), Doe(M)
real (kind = Low) :: X(BIG), Y(FEW), Z, Drum(SHORT), &
  Xylophone(SHORT), Tuba(SHORT)
real, intent (in out) :: Cube(3, 3, 3)
integer :: Array(FEW), Chessboard(BOARD, BOARD)
character (len = BIG) :: Word, Hamlet(FEW)
character (len = GAP) :: Sponsor(SHORT), A(SHORT)
```

Attribute-Oriented Form — Dimension Statement (Advanced)

A `dimension` statement specifies the dimension attribute for one or more arrays. Data type and other attributes are specified in a type declaration (which may precede or follow the `dimension` statement) — for example,

```
real :: Matrix
dimension Matrix(20, 20)
```

A single `dimension` statement may combine arrays that have different data types and other attributes. The form is

`dimension` *List*

where each *List* item has the form

Array name (*Subscript bounds*)

In the following example, we declare the types and other attributes except dimension, in type declarations for all array variables and for the scalar variables `Look`, `J`, `Z`, and `Word`. Separately, we declare the shapes of all the arrays in `dimension` statements. The grouping and the ordering of array names in the `dimension` statements are arbitrary:

```
implicit none
integer, parameter :: Low = Selected_Real_Kind(6)
integer, parameter :: BIG = 20, SIZE = 17, BOARD = 8, FEW = 4
integer, parameter :: SHORT = 20, LONG = 144, GAP = 5, M = 3
real :: Matrix, Look, J, Able, John, Baker, Delta, Doe
real (kind = Low) :: X, Y, Z, Drum, Xylophone, Tuba
real, intent (in out) :: Cube
```

```
integer :: Array, Chessboard
character (len = BIG) :: Word, Hamlet
character (len = GAP) :: Sponsor, A
dimension Matrix(BIG, BIG), Able(SIZE), X(BIG), Y(FEW)
dimension Array(FEW), Chessboard(BOARD, BOARD), Hamlet(FEW)
dimension Cube(3, 3, 3), John(LONG), Baker(LONG), &
  Delta(LONG), Drum(SHORT), Xylophone(SHORT), Tuba(SHORT), &
  Sponsor(SHORT), A(SHORT), Doe(M)
```

Upper and Lower Subscript Bounds (Advanced)

A subscript range for any of the dimensions may include a *Lower bound* as well as an *Upper bound* for subscript values — for example,

```
real :: W(0: 4), X(-3: 9), M(1: 4), Title(6: 9)
```

Here, the vector `W` has 5 elements, numbered from 0 to 4; `X` has 13 elements, numbered from –3 to 9; `M` has 4 elements, numbered from 1 to 4, just as if the declaration had been `M(4)`; and `Title` has 4 elements, numbered from 6 to 9 (inclusive).

If no *Lower bound* is declared, the default lower subscript bound is 1. If a *Lower bound* is present, it is followed by a colon and the *Upper bound*. Thus, the following two forms are allowed:

Upper bound
Lower bound : *Upper bound*

The *extent* (number of elements) along this dimension of the array is *Upper bound* - *Lower bound* + 1. If no *Lower bound* is specified, the extent is equal to the *Upper bound* value.

The following examples include arrays with ranks 1, 2, and 3:

```
integer :: Threes (0: 4, -1: 3, 6: 9)
real :: A(0: 6), B(0: 6, 0: 6), C(7, 2: 8)
```

Here, `Threes` has rank 3; the first subscript ranges from 0 to 4, the second from –1 to 3, and the third from 6 to 9. `A` has rank 1; its single subscript ranges from 0 to 6. `B` has rank 2; each subscript range extends from 0 to 6. `C` has rank 2; the first subscript must be between 1 and 7 and the second between 2 and 8.

As we have seen, the extent of an array along a particular dimension is the number of elements (*Upper bound* – *Lower bound* + 1). The *shape* of an array is a sequence of integers giving the extent along each dimension. Thus, two arrays may have the same shape but different *Subscript bounds*. For example, each of the following arrays has shape (5, 5):

```
real :: A(5, 0: 4), B(0: 4, 5), C(11: 15, 11: 15)
```

The *size* of an array is the total number of elements, which may be calculated by multiplying together the extents along all of the dimensions. In the following example,

```
real :: Vector(4), Matrix(20, 20), Fives(3, 4, 5, 6, 2)
```

the total number of elements in `Vector` is 4, `Matrix` has 400 elements, and `Fives` contains 720 elements.

Constants and variables in array bound expressions . The *Lower bound* and *Upper bound* values are usually written as constants of integer type. Named constants are especially suitable for this purpose. Constant *expressions* of integer type are permitted. They may contain arithmetic operators as well as references to computational intrinsic functions (or to certain inquiry functions) with constant arguments.

An array that is not a dummy argument in a procedure is an *explicit-shape* array or a *deferred-shape* array; see Example 5.1:

1. An explicit-shape array that is not a dummy argument is a *fixed-size* array or an *automatic* array. A fixed-size array must have constant dimension bounds. An automatic array may be declared in a procedure with bounds that are specification expressions to be evaluated at the time of procedure entry.[1] Note that a function result may be an automatic array.
2. A deferred-shape array is an allocatable array (see Section 5.6) or an allocatable pointer target (see Section 6.3). The dimension bounds are not declared; they are specified at the time the array is allocated.

An array that is a dummy argument in a procedure is an *assumed-shape* array, an *explicit-shape* array, or an *assumed-size* array; see Example 5.1. In this text, the last two of these are considered obsolete (see Appendix D.6):

1. An assumed-shape array is a dummy argument array for which the rank is specified but the dimension bounds are not. At procedure entry, such an array assumes the shape of the corresponding actual argument. It is recommended that all dummy argument arrays be declared with assumed shape (see Section 8.2).
2. An explicit-shape dummy argument array (obsolete) is a *fixed-size* array or an *adjustable* array. A fixed-size array must have constant dimension bounds. An adjustable dummy argument array may be declared with bounds that are specification expressions to be evaluated at the time of procedure entry (see Appendix D.6).
3. An assumed-size dummy argument array (obsolete) is like a fixed-size array or an adjustable dummy argument array, except that the upper bound for the last dimension is not specified (see Appendix D.6).

[1] Specification expressions (see Section 8.4) may refer to variables that are dummy arguments, are inherited from a host subprogram, are imported from a module, or are in a common block (see Appendix E.3).

EXAMPLE 5.1

```
! Example 5.1. Constants and variables in array bound expressions.
 function A (N, B, C, D, E, F) result (G)
   implicit none
   intrinsic Size
   integer, parameter :: K = 17
   integer, intent (in) :: N                                        ! Argument
   real, intent (in), dimension(:) :: B          ! Assumed-shape argument array
     ! The next two lines are obsolete (see Appendix D.6).
   real, intent (in) :: C(K), D(N)    ! Fixed-size and adjustable argument arrays
   real, intent (in) :: E(K, *), F(N, *)         ! Assumed-size argument arrays
   real, dimension(Size (B)) :: G, Y         ! Automatic result and local arrays
   real :: X(K)                                        ! Fixed-size local array
   real, allocatable, dimension(:) :: Z               ! Allocatable local array
   integer :: SB

! start function A
   SB = Size (B)
   allocate (Z(SB))
   G = B
     :
 end function A
```

In Example 5.1, the function A has a scalar dummy argument named N and four array dummy arguments named B, C, D, E, and F. B is an assumed-shape array because its dimension bounds are unspecified. C is a fixed-size array because its dimension bound is a constant. D is an adjustable array because its dimension bound is a dummy argument. E and F are assumed-size arrays because the last dimension bound is an asterisk. (The first bound for E is fixed and for F is adjustable.)

G and Y are automatic local arrays because their lengths are specification expressions that can be evaluated at procedure entry; G is the function result variable. X is an ordinary fixed-size array. Z is allocatable because it is a local array declared with unspecified dimension bounds.

Dialogue: Zero Array Size

"How can the size of an array be zero, Miss Flores?"

"It's easy, Cathy. The number of elements along any of the dimensions of an array can be zero."

"But the total number of elements is the *product* of the number of elements for all of the dimensions, so the array wouldn't have any elements at all. That seems like a pretty stupid array. Who would declare an array like that?"

"Well, Cathy, it is probably true that nobody would write the integer constant 0 in an array declaration. But there can be a named constant in the array bounds that sometimes happens to be zero.

There is also another possibility. The shapes of array sections, array procedure arguments, and some other array objects can depend on the value of a variable, so those arrays could have zero size for certain values of the variable. Fortran 90 array operations are carefully designed to give well-defined and mathematically correct results for arrays of zero size."

Array Element Names

An array is a variable composed of other variables that are its *elements*. A particular array element is designated by the name of the array along with a parenthesized list of *subscript expressions*, one for each dimension of the array. The values of the subscript expressions collectively specify an array element by giving the position of that element relative to other elements of the array. The following array element names might appear in a program as designators for particular elements of the rank-1 array (vector) A:

```
A(3)
A(K)
A(John + 2)
A(Lover - 1)
A(2 * Mary)
A(73 * I + 4961)
A(3 * Jim - 1)
A(50 * Line + Letter)
A(NInt (SqRt (0.5 * X) + A(K) + 7.5))
```

Subscript Expressions

Each subscript in an array element designator is an expression of integer type. It need not be a constant. The value of each subscript expression must be within the declared subscript range for the corresponding dimension:

1. Each subscript value must be less than or equal to the *Upper bound* specified for the corresponding array dimension.
2. Each subscript value must be greater than or equal to the specified *Lower bound*; or, if no *Lower bound* is explicitly specified, it must be greater than or equal to 1 (the default *Lower bound*).

EXAMPLE 5.2 The following program contains some array element designators.

```
! Example 5.2. Array element names.
  program Fingers
    implicit none
    integer, parameter :: EXTENT = 20
    integer :: K1 = 1, K0 = 0, L3 = 3, M1 = 1, I2 = 2, &
      J1 = 1, L0 = 0, L16 = 16, I4 = 4, M2 = 2
    real :: X0, X1(EXTENT), X2(EXTENT, EXTENT), X3(EXTENT, EXTENT, EXTENT)
! start program Fingers
    read *, X1(6)
    print *, X1(I4 + 2), X1(3 * M2)
    read *, X3(L3 - 1, 2 * M1, 13 * I2 - 7)
    print *, X3(2, 2, 19)
    read *, X2(3 * J1 - 1, 3 * L0 + L16)
    print *, X2(2, 16)
    read *, X1(3)
    read *, X2(K, J0 + 2)
    X1(1) = X1(3) + L16
    X1(I4) = 17.42
    X0 = X1(6) + X2(1, 2)
    print *, X1(K), X1(4), X0
  end program Fingers
```

It is important to recognize that a particular array element is indicated by the *name* of the array along with the *values* of the subscript expressions. The form of the subscript expressions is of no consequence. For example, in the preceding program we see that X1(6), X1(I4 + 2), and X1(3 * M2) all denote the same array element, since the value of I4 is 4 and M2 is 2.

Array Elements in Expressions

An array element is a variable. Thus, an array element designator can appear in most expressions where the name of a scalar variable of the same type would be permitted. For example, an array element name is permitted on the right or left side of an assignment, in an input or output list, or as an operand in any expression that is appropriate for the data type of the array.

EXAMPLE 5.3 The following program performs some operations on elements of a one-dimensional array (vector).

```
! Example 5.3. Vector element operations.
  program Dementia
    implicit none
    integer, parameter :: L = 3
    real :: Height(L)
! start program Dementia
    Height(1) = 123.45
    print *, "␣Please␣enter␣a␣real␣number.␣"
    read *, Height(2)
    Height(3) = 2.0 * Height(1) + Height(2)
    print *, Height(1), Height(2), Height(3)
  end program Dementia
```

EXAMPLE 5.4 The following program illustrates similar operations with arrays of higher rank.

```
! Example 5.4. Operations with arrays of higher rank.
  program Watson
    implicit none
    integer, parameter :: I = 3, J = 1
    real :: Vector(14), Matrix(20, 20), Fives(3, 4, 5, 6, 2)
! start program Watson
    print *, "␣Please␣enter␣two␣real␣numbers.␣"
    read *, Matrix(16, 3), Fives(3, 4, 2, 6, 2)
    Vector(I) = Matrix(J + 15, I) + Fives(I, J, 4, 2, J + 1)
    print *, Vector(I + 3)
  end program Watson
```

Note that the type of a subscript expression must be integer. It may involve a type conversion intrinsic function applied to a real expression, as in the following statements:

```
real, parameter :: A = 25.0, X = 0.01
  :
print *, Vector(NInt (SqRt (A + X)))
```

In this case, the fifth element of `Vector` will be printed. The rounding function `NInt` is preferable to `Int` for this conversion because small errors in the representation of the real expression might cause its value to be just less than the expected integer.

EXAMPLE 5.5 Suppose that we want to interchange the Ith and Jth elements of an array. The following program first reads array element values from a file. (The `stop` statement in the input loop terminates the program, as explained in Section 7.3, if the file does not contain enough data.) The program then reads two integers and swaps the array elements designated by these integers as subscripts. The procedure Swap gains access to the array by inheritance while receiving the subscript values as `intent (in)` arguments. (Compare Example 2.22 in Section 2.4)

```
! Example 5.5. Program with internal subroutine Swap.
  program Swap_Elements_1
    implicit none
    integer, parameter :: ARRAY_SIZE = 10
    real, dimension(ARRAY_SIZE) :: Data_Array
    integer :: I, J, Loop
! start program Swap_Elements_1
    open (1, file = "array.txt")
  do Loop = 1, ARRAY_SIZE                                 ! See Example 5.7.
      read (1, *, iostat = EoF) Data_Array(Loop)
      if (EoF < 0) stop
    end do
    print *, "␣Please␣enter␣subscripts␣of␣elements␣to␣be␣swapped.␣"
    read *, I, J
    call Swap (I, J)
    print *, Data_Array
  contains
    subroutine Swap (I, J)
      integer, intent (in) :: I, J
      real :: Aux
!   start subroutine Swap
      Aux = Data_Array(I)
      Data_Array(I) = Data_Array(J)
      Data_Array(J) = Aux
    end subroutine Swap
  end program Swap_Elements_1
```

In Example 5.5, what happens if I and J are equal? It would seem inefficient to swap an array element with itself. The three assignment operations could be avoided at the expense of a preliminary step to compare the values of I and J. In a situation like the present one, the assignments probably take hardly any more time than the preliminary comparison, and the program is simpler without the comparison. However, if the array elements were long character strings or structures (see Chapter 6), the preliminary comparison would be worthwhile.

EXAMPLE 5.6 Professor Rättenlehrer uses 10 identical mazes to train rats. On a certain day he places a rat in each of the 10 mazes. Each time a rat successfully reaches the end of its maze, it is automatically rewarded with food and transported back to the beginning of the maze. An integer identifying the rat, along with the elapsed time, is recorded on a file that is later processed by a computer to analyze the progress of each rat. The analysis program, as shown next, uses two arrays — one to count the number of successful runs for each rat and one to accumulate the total elapsed time for each rat.

```
! Example 5.6. Rodent evaluation.
  program Amazement
    implicit none
    integer, parameter :: N_Rats = 10
    real :: Time, Total(N_Rats) = 0.0
    integer :: Rat_ID, Runs(N_Rats) = 0
! start program Amazement
    open (1, file = "rat_data.txt")
    do
      read (1, *, iostat = EoF) Rat_ID, Time
      select case (Rat_ID)
        case (1: N_Rats)
          Runs(Rat_ID) = Runs(Rat_ID) + 1                 ! Choose an array element.
          Total(Rat_ID) = Total(Rat_ID) + Time
        case default
          print *, "␣Rat␣ID␣number␣is␣not␣between␣1␣and␣", N_Rats
      end select
    end do
    do Rat_ID = 1, N_Rats
      if (Runs(Rat_ID) > 0) then
        print *, Rat_ID, "␣Runs:␣", Runs(Rat_ID), &
          "␣Average␣time:␣", Total(Rat_ID) / Runs(Rat_ID)
      else
        print *, Rat_ID, "␣No␣runs.␣"
      end if
    end do
  end program Amazement
```

Vectors, Matrices, and Other Arrays

An array of rank 1 is often called a *vector;* an array of rank 2, a *matrix.* These one-dimensional and two-dimensional arrays may be interpreted in special ways according to the rules of linear algebra. Some of the functions in the Fortran intrinsic procedure library, such as `MatMul`, `Dot_Product`, and `Transpose`, perform operations that are useful in this context.

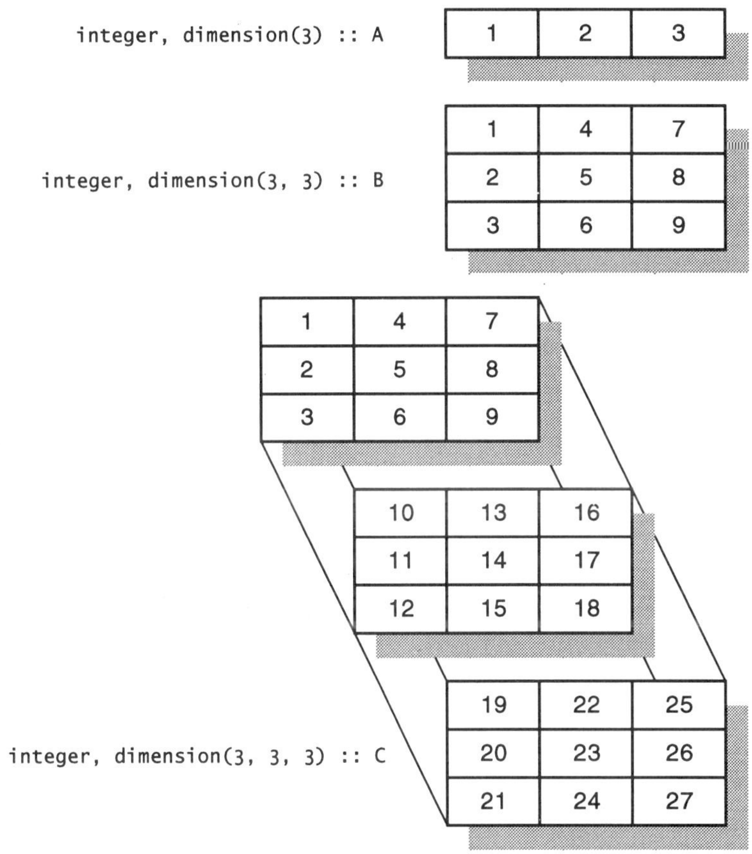

FIGURE 5.2. Arrays of ranks 1, 2, and 3 (in standard Fortran array element sequence).

An array of rank 3 may be viewed as a stack of cubes forming a large block (parallelepiped), as illustrated in Figure 5.2. The array name applies to the entire stack of cubes, and an individual element (cube) is indicated by the values of three subscripts appended to the array name. In a finite approximation of a certain region of space, such an array might represent "cells," each of which corresponds to an interval of X, Y, and Z coordinate values. The following arrays are three-dimensional:

```
Space(I, J, K)
Space(NInt (X), NInt (Y), NInt (Z))
A(2, 5, 3)
B(3, 2, 2)
Table(I, J, K)
Alpha(K, 3, 4 * I - 2)
```

Economic analysis or statistics of quantities that depend on three or more variables may require a subscript for each variable. An array whose rank is greater than 3 cannot, of course, be visualized geometrically in three dimensions. The rank of a Fortran array cannot exceed 7.

The numbering of the array elements in Figure 5.2 reflects a *standard Fortran array element sequence* (see Section 5.2) that is applied during whole-array input or output and in some other contexts.

5.1 Exercises

1. Write array declarations corresponding to each of the following array descriptions (all lower bounds are 1 unless specified):

   a. The chessboard named `Chess` has 8 rows and 8 columns, and its type is integer.

   b. The complex matrix `D` has 7 rows and 10 columns.

   c. `X`, `Y`, and `Z` are real vectors that have 13 elements each; `J` is an integer vector that has 39 elements.

   d. `Newton` is a vector whose subscript values may range from 0 to 49 (inclusive).

2. Correct any errors that you find in the following declarations (the purpose of each declaration is described above it; supply any declarations that appear to have been omitted):

   a. Arrays `C` and `D` are each real arrays with 16 elements.

   ```
   dimension, real(16) :: C, D
   ```

   b. The real array `Del` has 50 rows and 50 columns.

   ```
   real, Del :: (2500)
   ```

   c. The real array `Pel` has 50 columns and 50 rows.

   ```
   real, Rel(50, 50)
   ```

d. The real array `Kel` has 40 columns and 30 rows.

```
real :: dimension(40, 30), Kel
```

e. The real array `Kel` has 30 columns and 10 rows. `Rel` is the same size.

```
real :: Kel(10, 30), Rel
```

3. Each of the following describes a sequence of five array elements Write a subscript expression involving the variable `J` that will designate each of the five elements in turn as `J` takes on the sequence of values 1, 2, 3, 4, 5:

   a. Each of the five elements of the vector `Beta` in turn

   b. The third through seventh elements of the vector `Alpha`

   c. The odd-numbered, first through ninth, elements of the vector `Gamma`

4. Write an array declaration for an array `Carton` arranged according to three index values, where the value of the first subscript ranges from 1 to 5, the value of the second subscript ranges from 1 to 4, and the value of the third subscript ranges from 1 to 17.

5. Referring to Figure 5.3, give the value of each of the following array elements:

   a. `B(1)` b. `J(3)` c. `B(62)` d. `J(K)` e. `B(K - 2)`
   f. `J(11)` g. `B(K + 56)` h. `J(9)` i. `J(K + 6)` j. `J(10)`

6. Referring to Figure 5.3, give the value of each of the following array elements:

   a. `J(K)` b. `J(J(K))` c. `B(K)` d. `B(J(K))`
   e. `B(J(J(K)))` f. `J(NInt (SqRt (B(K))))`

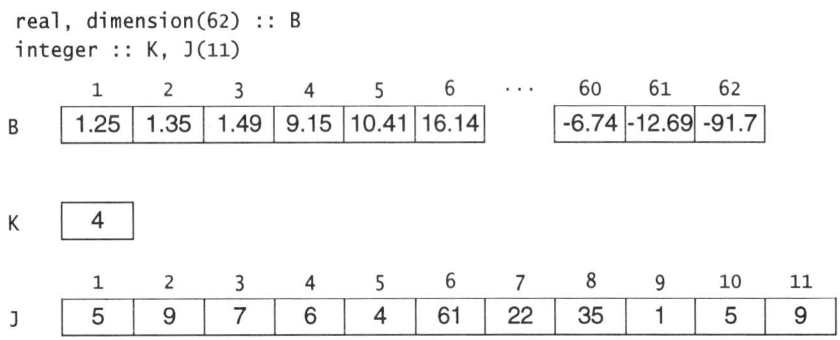

FIGURE 5.3. Arrays for exercises 5 and 6.

5.2 WHOLE ARRAYS AND ARRAY SECTIONS

A Fortran array is a variable; thus, the array name (without a subscript) represents all elements of the array. For example, an array name in an input or output list causes input or output of all the array elements. For a vector, the elements are read or written in the obvious sequence. The array element sequence for arrays of higher rank is described at the end of this section.

Fortran 90 permits a very rich set of operations on whole arrays and extends most scalar operations to whole-array operands. A whole-array operation is applied to all elements of the array. For example, if B and C are arrays that have the same shape, the expression B + C means that each element of B is to be added to the corresponding element of C. The operations of arithmetic and the elementary mathematical intrinsic functions (see Section 2.3) apply *elementwise* to whole arrays.

Furthermore, Fortran 90 provides a large set of intrinsic functions (see Section 5.3) for performing a variety of operations that would require indexed do loops in a traditional Fortran program. Whole-array constants (as a form of array constructors; see Section 5.5) are also provided.

Whole-Array Input and Output

EXAMPLE 5.7 The following program treats a whole array as an input or output list item, replacing the input loop in Example 5.5 by a single statement.

```
! Example 5.7. Program with internal subroutine Swap.
  program Swap_Elements_2
    implicit none
    integer, parameter :: ARRAY_SIZE = 10
    real, dimension(ARRAY_SIZE) :: Data_Array
    integer :: I1, I2
! start program Swap_Elements_2
    open (1, file = "array.txt")
    read (1, *, iostat = EoF) Data_Array                    ! Read the whole array.
    if (EoF < 0) stop
    print *, "␣Please␣enter␣subscripts␣of␣elements␣to␣be␣swapped.␣"
    read *, I1, I2
    call Swap (I1, I2)
    print *, Data_Array
  contains
    subroutine Swap (I, J)                                      ! See Example 5.5.
      :
  end program Swap_Elements_2
```

Whole-Array Expressions and Assignment

A whole array, denoted by the array name without a subscript, is an *array variable*. Fortran 90 permits an array variable in most contexts where a scalar variable is permitted.

Assignment is permitted between whole arrays of the same shape:

1. The shape of an array is determined by its rank (number of dimensions) and by its extent (number of elements) along each dimension.
2. Two arrays have the same shape if they have the same rank and if their extents agree along each dimension.
3. The subscript ranges (upper and lower subscript bounds) are not required to agree.

The left and right sides of a whole-array assignment statement may have different types and other type properties, if the type, `kind`, and character length coercion rules that apply to assignment of scalars are observed.

EXAMPLE 5.8

```
! Example 5.8. Whole-array assignment.
  program Doughnut_Set
    implicit none
    real :: A(5, 7), B(5, 7), C(0: 4, 0: 6)
    integer :: I(5, 7)
! start program Doughnut_Set
    open (1, file = "f35.in")
    open (2, file = "f35.out")
    read (1, *) B
    C = B
    I = C                                  ! Type coercion, with truncation, occurs.
    A = I
    write (2, *) A
  end program Doughnut_Set
```

Whole arrays may be combined in *array expressions* by any operator that can be applied to variables whose type is that of the array elements. All arrays in such an expression must have the same shape. Each operator in an array expression denotes an elementwise operation upon corresponding elements of each array in the expression.

EXAMPLE 5.9

```
! Example 5.9. Arithmetic and relational operations on whole arrays.
  program Doughnut_Ops
    implicit none
    real, dimension(5, 7) :: A, B, C
    logical :: T(5, 7)
    real, dimension(20) :: V, V_Squared
! start program Doughnut_Ops
    open (7, file = "myinput.txt")
    open (2,  file = "myoutput.txt")
    read (7, *) B, C, V
    A = B + C
    T = B > C
    C = A * B
    V_Squared = V * V
    write (2, *) T, C, V
  end program Doughnut_Ops
```

In the program of Example 5.9, the first assignment statement sets each element of A to the sum of the corresponding elements of B and C. This operation is illustrated in Figure 5.4. The second assignment statement sets each element of the logical array T to true or false, depending upon the relation between the corresponding elements of B and C.

The expression on the right side of the third assignment statement forms the product of corresponding elements of A and B. Note that A * B denotes elementwise whole-array multiplication, *not* matrix multiplication as defined in linear algebra. The fourth assignment stores in V_Squared the squares of corresponding elements of V.

The Whole-Array Assignment Model

Of great importance for supercomputers that perform operations in *parallel* is the fact that Fortran 90 does not artificially impose any particular element sequence upon whole-array assignment. Although conceptually all of the elements are processed in parallel, the actual sequence is arbitrary. The essential point is that assignment to the array variable named on the left side must not affect the evaluation of the right-hand side in any way:

```
real, dimension(L) :: First, Second
  :
First = First + Second
```

A possible model for whole-array assignment assumes a temporary "array-sized register," or *shadow* of the left-hand side, whose elements are assigned as they are calculated. As a final step, the shadow register is copied into the designated left-hand side array. It is important to note that an implementation of whole-array assignment need not actually incur the extra space or time penalties that this model implies.

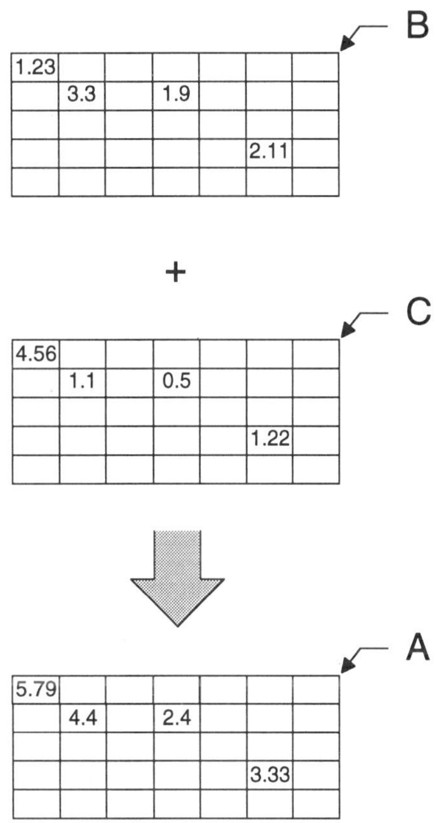

FIGURE 5.4. Whole-array addition: $A = B + C$.

Scalars in Whole-Array Expressions

An array expression may include *scalar* subexpressions along with whole arrays. When an operator has a scalar operand and a whole-array operand, the result is an array of the same shape as the whole-array operand. Each element of the result is obtained by combining the scalar with the corresponding element of the whole array. For example, the whole-array operation

```
A = 2.0 * B
```

combines the scalar `2.0` with each element of `B` and assigns the result to the corresponding element of `A`. This operation is illustrated in Figure 5.5.

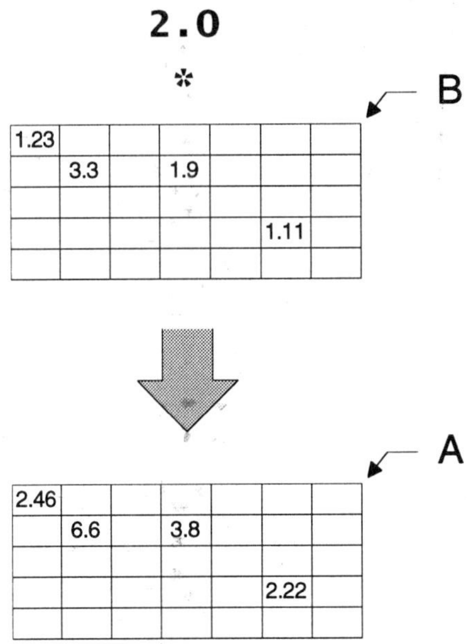

FIGURE 5.5. Whole-array multiplication: *A = 2.0 * B.*

EXAMPLE 5.10

```
! Example 5.10. Mixed scalar and whole-array expressions.
  program Broadcast
    implicit none
    real, dimension(5, 7) :: A, B, E, D = 0.0
    logical, dimension(5, 7) :: T
! start program Broadcast
    open (1, file = "myinput.txt")
    open (2, file = "myoutput.txt")
    read (1, *) B
    A = 2.0 * B
    T = (B /= 0.0) .and. (A > 2.0)
    E = 1.0
    write (2, *) D, A, T, E
  end program Broadcast
```

In the program of Example 5.10, the value assigned to each element of A is obtained by multiplying the corresponding element of B by the scalar 2.0. Similarly, the relational expression in the second assignment statement is evaluated elementwise and assigned to corresponding elements of the logical array T. In the type declaration for D, all elements of this array are given the initial value zero. Note that a scalar is interpreted in much the same way in whole-array initialization as in whole-array assignment.

Application: Strain Tensor

Some formulas in elasticity can be expressed with whole-array operations. For example, suppose that an elastic solid is deformed, with each point (x, y, z) undergoing a small displacement (u, v, w). The nine elements of the strain tensor, which may be represented as a 3 by 3 matrix called `Strain`, depend on the partial derivatives of u, v, and w with respect to x, y, and z, as follows:

$$\begin{matrix} u_x & (u_y + v_x) & (u_z + w_x) \\ (v_x + u_y) & v_y & (v_z + w_y) \\ (w_x + u_z) & (w_y + v_z) & w_z \end{matrix}$$

The dilation, T, is defined as the *trace* of the strain matrix:

```
T = Strain(1, 1) + Strain(2, 2) + Strain(3, 3)
```

The elastic forces produced by the deformation are given by the stress tensor, `Stress`, which is represented as another 3 by 3 matrix related to `Strain` by Hooke's law:

```
Stress = A * Strain + B * T * Delta_IJ
```

where `A` and `B` are positive scalar constants that depend upon the material, and `Delta_IJ` is represented as a 3 by 3 identity matrix.

A related tensor, of importance to plasticity, is the *deviatoric strain tensor*:

```
Deviator = Strain - (T / 3) * Delta_IJ
```

It is easy to show that the trace of `Deviator` is zero.

Shape Conformance

In whole-array expressions (and in some other contexts as well, such as actual arguments to certain intrinsic functions), shape conformance rules are extended to permit mixing of scalars with arrays of the same shape. The shapes of two expressions are *conformable* if they are both whole arrays and have the same shape, or if either of the expressions is a scalar. This same extended definition of shape conformance also applies to assignment when the object on the left is a whole array and the expression on the right is scalar valued. As we shall see, array sections are also conformable with whole arrays of the same shape and with scalars.

Elemental Intrinsic Functions

Many functions in the Fortran intrinsic procedure library (see Appendix A), notably including the mathematical functions, are classified as *elemental*. An elemental intrinsic function accepts either a scalar or an array as its argument. When the argument is an array, the function performs its operation elementwise, applying the scalar operation to every array element and producing a result array of the same shape. The following statements apply the intrinsic functions `Max` and `Sin` elementwise to whole-array arguments:

```
implicit none
intrinsic Max, Sin
real, dimension(5, 7) :: A, B, C
logical :: T (5, 7)
  :
A = Max (B, C)
T = Sin (A) > B
```

The following Fortran intrinsic library procedures are elemental.

Numerical manipulation functions:
`Exponent, Fraction, Nearest, RRSpacing,`
`Scale, Set_Exponent, Spacing`

Conversion functions:
`AChar, AImag, AInt, ANInt, Char, Cmplx, Conjg, Dble,`
`IAChar, IBits, IChar, Int, Logical, NInt, Real`

Numerical computation functions:
`Abs, ACos, ASin, ATan, ATan2, Ceiling, Cos, CosH,`
`Dim, DProd, Exp, Floor, Log, Log10, Max, Min,`
`Mod, Modulo, Sign, Sin, SinH, SqRt, Tan, TanH`

Character computation functions:
`AdjustL, AdjustR, Index, Len_Trim, LGE, LGT, LLE, LLT, Scan, Verify`

Bit computation functions:
`BTest, IAnd, IBClr, IBSet, IEOr,.IOr, Ishft, IshftC, Not`

Bit copy subroutine:
`MvBits`

The intrinsic function `Merge` (introduced in Section 3.3) is also elemental. It has three arguments:

```
Merge (Expression_1, Expression_2, Mask)
```

Any or all of the arguments may be scalars. All arguments that are arrays must have the same shape. The first two arguments must have the same type and type parameters; the type of `Mask` must be logical. The result has the same type and type parameters as the first two arguments; unless all arguments are scalars, it is an array with the same shape as the array arguments. The result is `Expression_1` in positions where `Mask` is true, and it is `Expression_2` in positions where `Mask` is false.

Array Sections

An especially useful Fortran 90 feature permits operations on all the elements in a designated portion of an array. An *array section* is permitted in most situations that accept a whole array. Most operations that are valid for scalars of the same type may be applied (elementwise) to array sections as well as to whole arrays. An array section may be an actual argument to an elemental intrinsic function.

The simplest form of array section is a sequence of consecutive elements of a vector. Such an array section is designated by the array name followed by a *pair* of subscript expressions that are separated by a colon and represent the subscript limits of the array section. Either expression (but not the colon) may be omitted; the default limits are the declared array bounds:

```
real :: Baker(40), John(5: 17), Able(144)
Baker(1: 29)
Baker(: 29)                        ! Default lower limit is 1.
John(5: 11)
John(: 11)                    ! Default is declared lower bound.
Able(134: 144)
Able(134: )                   ! Default is declared upper bound.
```

The *array length* of any of these one-dimensional array sections is the upper subscript limit minus the lower subscript limit (declared or default) plus one.

An array section may be combined in an expression with whole arrays or other array expressions (of the same shape) and with scalars, and it may appear on the left side in an assignment statement. Note that Fortran 90 does not prescribe a time ordering for the individual element assignments, except that assignment is not permitted to affect the value of the right-hand side expression.

EXAMPLE 5.11

```
! Example 5.11. Array sections.
  program Scotty
    implicit none
    integer, parameter :: SMALL_ARRAY = 20, LARGE_ARRAY = 144
    real, dimension(SMALL_ARRAY) :: John
    real, dimension(LARGE_ARRAY) :: Baker = 0.0
! start program Scotty
    read *, John
    Baker(10: 20) = 2.0 * John(1: 11)                  ! Array sections
    print *, Baker
  end program Scotty
```

Each of the following assignment statements moves a consecutive subset of the elements of a vector.

```
real :: X(100), Y(5), Z(5)
X(1: 50) = X(51: 100)
Y(2: 5) = Y(1: 4)
Z(1: 4) = Z(2: 5)
```

Array Sections with Increment (Stride) Designator (Advanced)

An array section designator may include a third expression, analogous to the third control parameter of an indexed do construct. This *Increment* (in this context, often called the *stride*) gives the spacing between those elements of the underlying parent array that are to be selected for the array section:

```
real :: A(2), B(4)
A = B(1: 3: 2)
```

By analogy to an indexed do with explicit increment, we see that the values assigned to A are those of B(1) and B(3). A negative *Increment* value reverses the normal array element sequence:

```
A = B(4: 1: -1)
```

Here, elements of the reversed array section — the elements B(4), B(3), B(2), and B(1), in that order — are assigned to the consecutive elements of A.

Array Section Examples

Figure 5.6 shows some simple examples of sections formed from arrays of rank 1 and 2. The arrays are declared as

```
real :: V(18), M(5, 7)
```

A more complicated example is the following:

```
real :: E(3, 5), F(2, 3)
F = E(1: 3: 2, 1: 5: 2)
```

Here, on the second line, the first subscript of E takes on values 1, 3 and the second subscript of E takes on values 1, 3, 5. The array section is a two-dimensional array object whose shape matches that of F.

Any of the three components of an array section designator may be omitted. The final colon must be omitted if the third component is omitted:

```
real :: A(100)
A(: 50)                      ! Same as A(1: 50) or A(1: 50: 1)
A(: 14: 2)                               ! Same as A(1: 14: 2)
A(2: )                     ! Same as A(2: 100) or A(2: 100: 1)
A(2: : 3)                               ! Same as A(2: 100: 3)
A(: : 2)                                ! Same as A(1: 100: 2)
A(:)                  ! Same as A(1: 100) or A(1: 100: 1) or A
A(: : -1)   ! Same as A(1: 100: -1); array section of zero size
A(1: 100: )                                       ! Prohibited
```

The default *Initial value* is the lower subscript bound for the array dimension, the default *Limit* value is the upper subscript bound for the array dimension, and the default *Increment* value is 1.

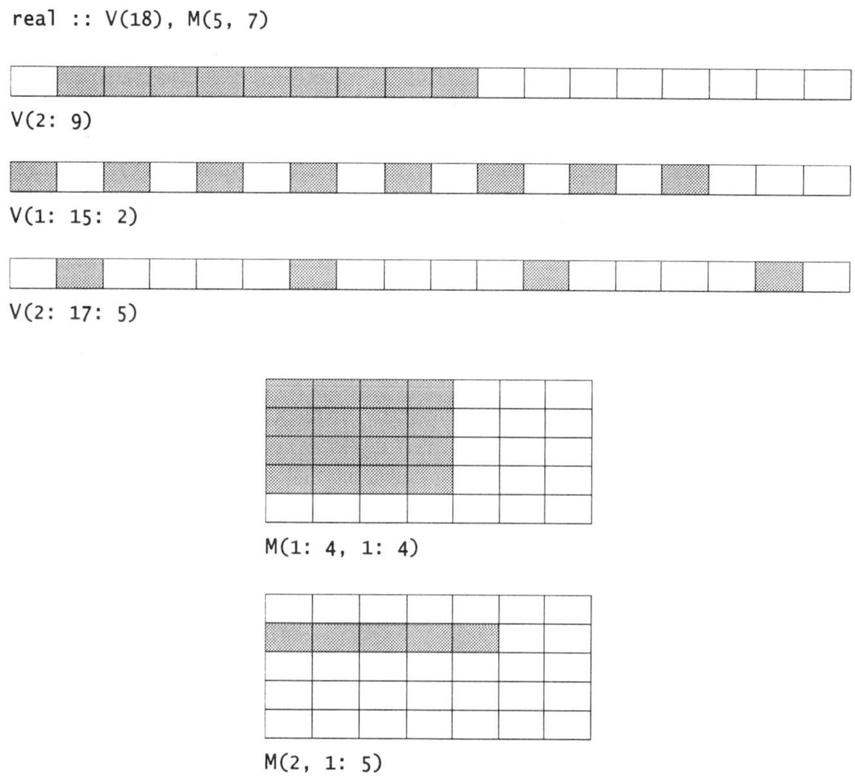

FIGURE 5.6. Array sections, from arrays declared as *real :: V(18), M(5, 7)*.

EXAMPLE 5.12 In the following program, the `print` statement causes four elements of a vector to be printed on each line.

```
! Example 5.12. Print four array element values per line.
  program Four_in_line
    implicit none
    real :: X(100) = 1.0
! start program Four_in_line
    do L = 1, 100, 4
      print *, X(L: L + 3)
    end do
  end program Four_in_line
```

Note that, in Example 5.12, the print statement is first executed with 1 as the value of L and X_1, X_2, X_3, and X_4 are printed. The second time it is executed, the value of L is 5 and X_5, X_6, X_7, and X_8 are printed. The value of L during the 25th and last traversal is 97, and X_{97}, X_{98}, X_{99}, and X_{100} are printed.

EXAMPLE 5.13 The following statements provide a flexible way to accomplish the input or output of a matrix, or of a major section of a matrix, by using an array section to transmit the elements in a single row of the vector, and then enclosing the `read` or `print` statement with this list in an indexed do construct so that it is executed once for each row.

```
! Example 5.13. Matrix input by rows.
  program Simply
    implicit none
    integer, parameter :: N_ROWS = 5, N_COLS = 8
    integer :: Row
real :: Vector(N_ROWS, N_COLS)
! start program Simply
    do Row = 1, N_ROWS
      read *, Vector(Row, 1: N_COLS)
    end do
      :
  end program Simply
```

In Example 5.13, we see that the `read` statement will cause input of row Row of `Vector`, while the do statement permits Row to vary from 1 to N_Rows. The values of the named constants N_Rows and N_Cols are 5 and 8, so five complete rows of eight elements each will be transmitted. It is important to note that a new input record will be read for each row since each execution of the do block causes a new `read` statement to be executed.

EXAMPLE 5.14 Similarly, for output of an M by N matrix, we can write the following completely general sequence of statements that will cause printing of each row of the matrix to start on a new line.

```
! Example 5.14. Matrix output by rows.
   :
  implicit none
  integer, parameter :: M = 5, N = 8
  integer :: Row
  real :: Vector(M, N)
! start
   :
  do Row = 1, M
    print *, Vector(Row, 1: N)
  end do
   :
```

Compare the statement sequences in Examples 5.13 and 5.14 with the whole-array forms

```
read *, Vector(1: M, 1: N)
print *, Vector(1: M, 1: N)
```

which will transmit the identical sequence of vector elements but will not advance to a new record of the output file for each row.

Array Sections of Reduced Rank

Array section designators may be combined with single subscripts to designate an array object of lower rank (see Figure 5.6):

```
V(: 6) = M(2, 1: 5)
```

Here, the elements `M(2, 1)` through `M(2, 5)` form a one-dimensional array section that is assigned to the first six elements of `V`.

As another example, `A(3, :)` designates the third row of the matrix `A` (all elements whose first subscript is 3), and `A(:, 5)` designates the fifth column of the matrix `A` (all elements whose second subscript is 5).

The *rank* of an array section is the number of subscript positions in which at least one colon appears. A colon in a subscript position (or two colons in the same subscript position if the increment component is present) signals that there is a *range* of subscript values for that dimension.

In the absence of a colon, a fixed subscript value must appear; fixing one subscript value reduces the rank by 1. If `Fours` is an array of rank 4, then `Fours(:, :, :, 1)` is the rank-3 array that consists of all elements of `Fours` whose fourth subscript is 1. `Fours(:, :, 1, 1)` is the matrix (rank-2 array) that consists of all elements of `Fours` whose third and fourth subscripts are both 1. `Fours(:, 1, 1, 1)` is the vector (rank-1 array) that consists of all elements of `Fours` whose second, third, and fourth subscripts are all 1. Finally, `Fours(1, 1, 1, 1)` is a scalar, which, for most purposes, may be considered a rank-0 array. Note that `Fours(1: 1, 1: 1, 1: 1, 1: 1)` is not a scalar but an array whose rank is 4 and whose size is 1. This latter array may also be denoted as `Fours(: 1, : 1, : 1, : 1)`.

EXAMPLE 5.15

```
! Example 5.15. Rank of array sections.
  program Ranks
    implicit none
    real, dimension(3, 3) :: A = 1.0, B =  3.0
! start program Ranks
    A(2, :) = 0.0                               ! Put zeros in second row of A.
    B(:, 2) = A(2, :)                       ! A row of A goes into a column of B.
    B(:, 2: 2) = A(:, 1: 1)                                  ! 3 by 1 matrices
    print *, B(1: 2, :)                                      ! Rows 1 and 2 of B
    A(:, :) = B;    A(1:3, 1:3) = B(:, :)              ! Two equivalent statements
    print *, A, B
  end program Ranks
```

Application: Parallel Evaluation of Polynomials

Several polynomials of the same degree may be evaluated at the same point if their coefficients are arranged as the rows of a matrix. Horner's method for polynomial evaluation is applied to the columns of the matrix. For example, we may have three cubic polynomials

$$1 + 2t - 3t^2 + 4t^3$$
$$2 - 3t + 4t^2 - 5t^3$$
$$3 + 4t - 5t^2 + 6t^3$$

represented by the matrix `M`:

$$\begin{bmatrix} 1 & 2 & -3 & 4 \\ 2 & -3 & 4 & -5 \\ 3 & 4 & -5 & 6 \end{bmatrix}$$

The following Fortran 90 expression evaluates any number of cubic polynomials in parallel for a given (scalar) value of `T`:

```
M (:, 1) + T * (M (:, 2) + T * (M(:, 3) + T * M (:, 4)))
```

The result is a vector with one element for each polynomial; that is, the vector length equals the number of rows of the matrix.

EXAMPLE 5.16 More generally, we have the following function. The intrinsic function `Size` is permitted in a specification expression (see Section 8.4). The loop applies Horner's method, using the columns of `M` from right to left.

```
! Example 5.16. Parallel evaluation of polynomials.
  function Quetzal (M, T) result (P)
    implicit none
    intrinsic Size
    real, intent (in) :: M(:, :), T                          ! Assumed-shape array
    real, intent (out), dimension(Size (M, Dim = 1)) :: P ! Automatic result array
    integer :: Degree, Loop
! start function Quetzal
    Degree = Size (M, Dim = 1) - 1
    P = 0.0
    do Loop = Degree, 1, -1
      P = P * T + M(:, Loop)                       ! Vector * scalar + column of matrix
    end do
  end function Quetzal
```

Vector Subscripts (Optional)

The name of a vector of integer type may appear as a subscript in an array section designator, along with any of the other allowed forms. The designated array section is formed by applying the elements of the vector subscript in sequence as subscripts to the parent array. Thus, the value of each element of the vector subscript must be within the array bounds for the parent array.

For example, suppose that Z is a 5 by 7 matrix and that U and V are vectors of lengths 3 and 4, respectively. Assume that the elements of U and V have the following values:

```
U   1, 3, 2
V   2, 1, 4, 3
```

Then, `Z(3, V)` consists of elements from the third row of Z in the following order:

```
Z(3, 2), Z(3, 1), Z(3, 4), Z(3, 3)
```

Also, `Z(U, 2)` consists of elements from the second column:

```
Z(1, 2), Z(3, 2), Z(2, 2)
```

And, `Z(U, V)` consists of the following elements:

```
Z(1, 2), Z(1, 1), Z(1, 4), Z(1, 3),
Z(3, 2), Z(3, 1), Z(3, 4), Z(3, 3),
Z(2, 2), Z(2, 1), Z(2, 4), Z(2, 3)
```

In the most useful applications, the elements of the subscript vector consist of a permutation of consecutive integers, as in these examples.

Fortran 90 permits the same integer to appear more than once in a subscript vector, but this practice is error-prone and should therefore be done only with great care. An array section designated by a vector subscript with a repeated value must not appear on the left side of an assignment statement nor as an input list item.

Vector subscripts are prohibited in certain situations. In particular, an actual argument to a procedure must not be an array section with a vector subscript if the corresponding dummy argument array is given a value in the procedure.

EXAMPLE 5.17 Methods for solving systems of linear algebraic equations with *pivoting* require that some of the equations be interchanged. However, instead of actually exchanging rows of the stored coefficient matrix LU, we may record the desired exchanges by permuting the elements of a vector P (of integer type). We then use a section of this permutation vector as a vector subscript, in the row subscript position, in every reference to LU, as illustrated in the following two examples. Example 5.25 uses the same method except that it omits the pivoting step and so has no need for a vector subscript; the array reference `LU(P(M: N), M)` in this example is replaced there by `LU(M: N, M)`. (The matrix intrinsic functions `Dot_Product`, `MatMul`, and `MaxLoc` are described in Section 5.3 and in Appendix A.)

```
! Example 5.17a. Solving triangular systems with permuted rows.
   program For_Back
     implicit none
     intrinsic Dot_Product, MatMul, MaxLoc
       :
     do M = 1, N                                             ! Forward substitution
       W(M) = B(M) - Dot_Product (LU(P(M), 1: M - 1), W(1: M - 1)) / LU(P(M), M)
     end do
     do M = N, 1, -1                     ! Backward substitution with unit diagonal
       X(M) = W(M) - Dot_Product (LU(P(M), M + 1: N), X(M + 1: N))
     end do
       :
```

```
! Example 5.17b. Crout factorization A = L * U with scaled partial pivoting.
   :
  do M = 1, N
    ! Reduce column M and choose Pivot.
    LU(P(M: N), M) = LU(P(M: N), M) &
      - MatMul (LU(P(M: N), 1: M - 1), LU(P(1: M - 1), M))
    if (All (Abs (LU(P(M: N), M)) <= 0.0)) stop
    I_Temp = M - 1 + MaxLoc (Abs (LU(P(M: N), M)) / W(P(M: N)))
      ! I_Temp is a rank-1 array.
```

```
   call Permute (M, I_Temp(1))
     ! Internal procedure to exchange elements M and I_Temp(1) of P.
   ! Reduce row M.
   LU(P(M), M + 1: N) = (LU(P(M), M + 1: N) &
     - MatMul (LU(P(M), 1: M - 1), LU(P(1: M - 1), M + 1: N))) / LU(P(M), M)
 end do
   :
```

Shape of an Array Section

The rank of an array section is the number of subscript positions that contain either a colon or the name of an integer vector (vector subscript). The extent of an array section along each dimension is simply the number of elements specified by the section designator for that dimension. For a vector subscript, the extent is determined by the number of elements in the vector.

Array Input and Output

An array variable reference in the *Input list* of a `read` statement or an array-valued expression in the *Output list* of a `print` or `write` statement designates a set of array elements. The elements are ordered according to the standard Fortran array element sequence, which is described after Example 5.18. For an array of rank 1, the elements are transmitted in increasing subscript order.

EXAMPLE 5.18 In the following program, the read statement causes input of Data_Array$_1$, Data_Array$_2$, . . . , Data_Array$_5$, and the print statement results in output of the first four of these array elements in the same order.

```
! Example 5.18. Input and output of whole arrays and array sections.
 program Emphasis
   implicit none
   integer, parameter :: ARRAY_SIZE = 5
   integer, dimension(ARRAY_SIZE) :: Data_Array
! start program Emphasis
   read *, Data_Array                                              ! Whole array
   print *, "The␣first␣four␣values␣are:␣", Data_Array(: 4)        ! Array section
 end program Emphasis
```

Standard Fortran Array Element Sequence

Some operations and intrinsic functions on whole arrays require that a standard element sequence be defined. For a vector, the obvious sequence is that of increasing subscript value. For an array of two or more dimensions, the standard Fortran sequence depends on the subscript values as follows: The leftmost subscript is varied first, then the next subscript, and so on. The array elements in Figure 5.7 are numbered to indicate the standard Fortran array element sequence.

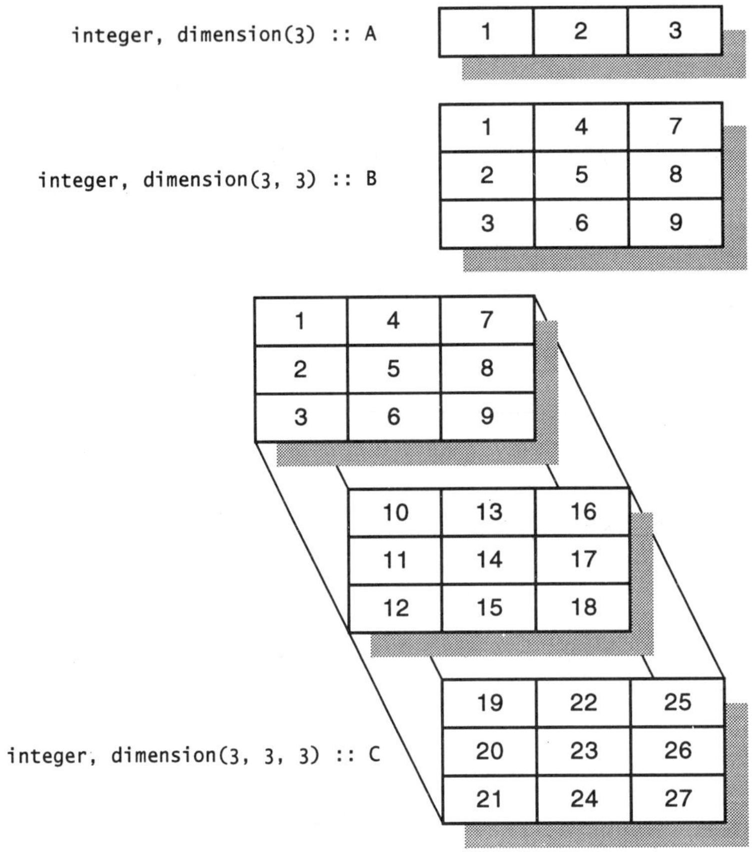

FIGURE 5.7. Array elements are numbered in standard Fortran array element sequence.

Array Element Sequence Formula (Optional)

Suppose that the declaration for an array is

Type , `dimension(` $UBound_1$, $UBound_2$, $UBound_3$ `) ::` *Array name*

Then, a reference to

Array name($Subscript_1$, $Subscript_2$, $Subscript_3$)

will designate the element whose sequential position is

$$S_1 + U_1 \cdot (S_2 - 1) + U_1 \cdot U_2 \cdot (S_3 - 1)$$

where U represents an upper bound value in the declaration and S represents a subscript in the reference.

For arrays with explicit lower subscript bounds as well as upper bounds, the formula of course involves the bound values. Suppose that an array is declared with lower bounds L_1, L_2, L_3 and upper bounds U_1, U_2, U_3. An element is referenced with subscript values S_1, S_2, S_3. The sequential position of this element is given by the following formula:

$$1 + (S_1 - L_1) + (U_1 - L_1 + 1) \cdot (S_2 - L_2) + (U_1 - L_1 + 1) \cdot (U_2 - L_2 + 1) \cdot (S_3 - L_3)$$

This formula can easily be extended to more than three dimensions.

Fortunately, a programmer rarely needs to refer to this formula; it is most often applied by the Fortran compiler during analysis of an expression. Nevertheless, the formula can be helpful as a reference in examples such as the following:

1. The first element in the sequence is designated by setting each subscript S_i to the value of the corresponding lower subscript range bound Li_I (or to 1 if no lower bounds are declared). This first array element is called the *base element.*
2. The last element in the sequence, whose sequential position value is equal to the number of elements, is obtained when each subscript S_i in the formula is equal in value to the corresponding upper subscript range bound U_i.

Note that U_3, the upper subscript range bound for the last dimension, does not appear in this formula. This last upper bound value has a role in determining the total size of the array, but it has no effect on the array element sequence.

Transition Tip

- Wherever possible, use whole-array and array section notation to eliminate looping or to reduce the depth of loop nesting.

5.2 Exercises

1. Assume the following declaration:

```
real :: A(12), B(3, 6), C(3, 6, 9), D(4, 4, 4, 4, 4, 4, 4)
```

Give the rank (number of dimensions), the shape (extent along each dimension), and the size (total number of elements) of each of the following array sections:

a. `A(1: 3)`
b. `A(: 5)`
c. `A(:)`
d. `B(:, 3)`
e. `B(3, :)`
f. `B(:, 1:5:2)`
g. `C(3, :, 8)`
h. `C(:, :, 1:9:4)`
i. `C(:, :, :)`
j. `D(:2, :2, 2, 2, 2, :2, :2)`
k. `D(1: 0, :, :, : :, :, :)`

2. Write a program involving an array of three dimensions for use in a biological analysis problem concerning genetic factors — four different hair colors, four different eye colors, and four different skin color tones. The program should read a line of data for each individual. The data consists of an integer (1, 2, 3, or 4) identifying hair color, an integer (1, 2, 3, or 4) identifying eye color, and an integer (1, 2, 3, or 4) identifying skin color tone. As each set of data is read, the program should add 1 to the appropriate element of the array. After all the data has been read, the program should print, for each element in the array, the number of individuals found to have the corresponding set of genetic factors. (Note: Initialize the entire array to zero.)

3. A musical melody has been coded as a sequence of integers representing the notes (ignoring time values); each integer in this sequence occupies one record of an input file. Write a program to count, for each different possible pair of notes, how often the first note of the pair is followed by the second note of the pair. Assume that all the notes are within one octave of middle C. Thus, there are 25 different notes, including sharps and flats. (Hint: Store the result in a 25 by 25 matrix.)

4. Use of subscripts for tallying: A class of 40 students takes a test consisting of 100 true–false questions. After grading the test papers, the instructor assigns letter grades according to the number of questions answered correctly, as follows:

50 or below	F	66–70	C+	86–90	A–
51–55	D	71–75	B–	91–95	A
56–60	C–	76–80	B	96–100	A+
61–65	C	81–85	B+		

Write a program to read each student's name and score and to print name, score, and letter grade. The program should also count the number of students achieving each of the 11 different letter grades and print a summary of the counts at the end.

5. Let Tax be a vector having 22 elements. Assume that the first 20 elements have been assigned values but the last 2 are undefined. Move each element down two places, and set Tax_1 and Tax_2 to zero. (Hint: Use array sections.)

6. Write programs for each of the following:

   a. Move the N elements of the vector Pig to the vector Poke, storing them in reverse order. (Hint: Use array sections.)

   b. Reverse the elements of the vector A.

7. Write a program to copy all the elements of the vector A into the corresponding positions in the vector B. (Hint: Use whole-array assignment.)

5.3 PROCEDURES FOR ARRAY PROCESSING

Intrinsic Functions for Array Operations

Fortran 90 provides intrinsic functions that perform many operations that would otherwise have to be programmed with loops. A selection of these functions is listed in the following summary. (For a complete list with full details, see Appendix A, Sections A.1, A.4, and A.5.) Note the absence of any "matrix divide" operation, such as a matrix inverse or a way to solve `AX = B` for `X`. Many of these intrinsic functions have optional arguments, which are indicated here in brackets.

1. `Reshape (Source, Shape [, Pad] [, Order])` takes all elements from `Source` in standard Fortran array element order, combines them into an array expression of specified `Shape` [in subscript order permuted by `Order`] [, and appends elements from `Pad` if necessary]. `Shape` is an integer vector whose length is between 1 and 7 (inclusive), and `Order` is a vector containing a permutation of the integers from 1 to `N`, where `N` is the size of the vector `Shape`. (See Section 5.5.)
2. `Sum (Array [, Dim] [, Mask])`computes the sum of all [selected] elements of `Array` [along the specified dimension].
3. `Product (Array [, Dim] [, Mask])`computes the product of all [selected] elements of `Array` [along the specified dimension].
4. `Any (Mask [, Dim])` evaluates to true if any element of `Mask` is true.
5. `All (Mask [, Dim])` evaluates to true if all elements of `Mask` are true.
6. `Count (Mask [, Dim])` counts the true elements of `Mask`.
7. `MaxLoc (Array [, Mask])` finds the location of a maximum element in `Array`. The type of `Array` must be integer or real, and its size (after applying the `Mask`, if any) must not be zero. The result is an array of rank 1 whose length is the rank of `Array`.
8. `MaxVal (Array [, Dim] [, Mask])` returns the maximum element value in `Array`. The type of `Array` must be integer or real.
9. `MinLoc (Array [, Mask])` finds the location of a minimum element in `Array`. The type of `Array` must be integer or real, and its size (after applying the `Mask`, if any) must not be zero. The result is an array of rank 1 whose length is the rank of `Array`.
10. `MinVal (Array [, Dim] [, Mask])` returns the minimum element value in `Array`. The type of `Array` must be integer or real.
11. `Transpose (Matrix)` forms the transpose of a matrix (rank-2 array) of any type.
12. `Dot_Product (Vector_A, Vector_B)` computes the numerical or logical dot product (scalar product) of rank-1 arrays.
13. `MatMul (Matrix_A, Matrix_B)` forms the product of matrices (rank-2 arrays) of any numerical type, as defined in linear algebra, or the analogous product of logical

matrices. It also forms matrix–vector products: Either Matrix_A or Matrix_B, but not both, may have rank 1.

14. CShift (Array, Shift [,Dim]) performs a circular left shift of complete rank-1 sections of Array [along specified dimension] (right if Shift is negative).
15. EOShift (Array, Shift [, Boundary] [, Dim]) performs an end-off left shift of complete rank-1 sections of Array [along specified dimension] [and fills with copies of a boundary value] (right if Shift is negative).
16. Pack (Array, Mask [, Vector]) creates a vector from elements of Array selected by Mask. [If Vector is present and is longer than the number of true positions in Mask, it appends the remaining elements from Vector.]
17. Unpack (Vector, Mask, Field) forms an array expression by placing consecutive elements from Vector into positions where Mask is true, in standard Fortran array element sequence (see Section 5.2), and copying Field where Mask is false. Field may be a scalar, or it may be an array whose shape is the same as that of Mask.

The Mask argument in Sum, Product, Any, All, Count, MaxLoc, and MinLoc is a logical array, and the function is applied to elements where Mask is true. Mask may also be a logical scalar (see Section 5.2). If it is an array, it must have the same shape as the principal Array argument.

The optional Dim argument in Any, All, and Count is an integer that designates one of the dimensions of Mask along which the function is to be applied.

The Shift argument of CShift and EOShift may be a scalar, or it may be an integer vector whose length is one less than the rank of Array and whose positive or negative element values specify the Shift separately for each dimension of Array.

These intrinsic functions appear in the examples in this chapter, as follows: Sum, 5.19; Product, 5.19; Any, 5.22; MaxLoc, 5.17, 5.20; MinLoc, 5.20, 5.21, 5.22; MinVal, 5.21; Dot_Product, 5.17, 5.25; MatMul, 5.17, 5.23, 5.24, 5.25, 5.37, 5.47; CShift, 5.45.

Array Inquiry Functions

Fortran 90 provides the following array inquiry functions. (For details, see Appendix A.1.)

Allocated (Array) evaluates to true if Array is an allocatable array that is currently allocated (see Section 5.6).

Lbound (Array [, Dim]) returns the lower bound [in the specified dimension], or a vector of lower bounds.

Shape (Source) returns a vector containing the extents in each dimension.

`Size (Array [, Dim])` returns the extent [in the specified dimension], or the total size.

`Ubound (Array [, Dim])` returns the upper bound [in the specified dimension], or a vector of upper bounds.

Application: Logical Queries with Array Intrinsics

The intrinsic functions allow quite complicated questions about tabular data to be answered without branching or repetition constructs. Consider a simple tabulation of student test scores. Let the array `T` contain test scores for `M` students who have taken `N` different tests. The elements of `T` are integers between 0 and 100 (inclusive). For example, let `T` hold the following scores for four tests made by three students:

$$T = \begin{bmatrix} 85 & 76 & 90 & 60 \\ 71 & 45 & 50 & 80 \\ 66 & 45 & 21 & 55 \end{bmatrix}$$

Question: What is each student's top score?
Answer: `MaxVal (T, Dim = 2)`; in the example, (90, 80, 66)

Question: What is the average of all the scores on all tests?
Answer: `Sum (T) / Size (T)`; in the example, 62

Question: How many of the scores in the table are above average?
Answer:

```
Above = T > (Sum (T) / Size (T))
N = Count (Above)
```

In the example, `Above` is the logical array

$$\text{Above} = \begin{bmatrix} \textit{true} & \textit{true} & \textit{true} & \textit{false} \\ \textit{true} & \textit{false} & \textit{false} & \textit{true} \\ \textit{true} & \textit{false} & \textit{false} & \textit{false} \end{bmatrix}$$

and `Count (Above)` is 6.

Question: What is the lowest score in the above-average group of scores?
Answer: `MinVal (T, Mask = Above)`; in the example, 66

Question: Is there a student whose scores were all above average?
Answer: `Any (All (Above, Dim = 2))`; in the example, false

Sum *and* Product

The intrinsic functions Sum and Product compute the sum or product of all elements of an array or array section of any numerical type.

EXAMPLE 5.19

```
! Example 5.19. Sum and Product intrinsic functions.
  program Array_Ops
    implicit none
    intrinsic Sum, Product
    integer, parameter :: N = 10
    real :: Z(N, N)
    real ZSum, ZProduct
! start program Array_Ops
    read *, Z
    ZSum = Sum (Z)
    ZProduct = Product (Z)
    print *, ZSum, ZProduct
  end program Array_Ops
```

Here are two additional examples:

1. The *variance* of a set of data values can easily be computed with the intrinsic function Sum. If x is a vector of length *n*, the expression

$$\sum_{i=1}^{n}(x_i - x_{mean})^2$$

is generated by the Fortran statements

```
X_Mean = Sum (X) / Size (X)
Variance = Sum ((X - X_Mean) ** 2)
```

2. The *Frobenius norm* of a matrix is simply the square root of the sum of the squares of all the matrix elements:

```
SqRt (Sum (A ** 2))
```

Sum of selected elements — the optional argument Mask. When the optional Mask argument is present, Sum and Product operate only on the array elements selected by the mask. Mask is an array of the same shape as the first argument array or it is a scalar, and its type is logical.

1. In the following assignment, ZMSum is set to the sum of all elements of Z that are larger than 100:

```
ZMSum = Sum (Z, Mask = (Z > 100))
```

2. The *conditional sum* $\sum_{x_i > 0.0} x_i$ is denoted by the Fortran 90 expression

```
Sum (X, Mask = (X > 0.0))
```

The mask locates the positive elements of the vector X. If X has the value (0.0, -0.1, 0.2, 0.3, 0.2, -0.1, 0.0), the result of this expression is 0.7.

3. Suppose that we wish to compute the *Fourier sum* $F = \sum_{i=1}^{n} a_i \cdot \cos x_i$ but to include only those terms $a_i \cdot \cos x_i$ for which $a_i < 0.01$. We can use the intrinsic function Sum with a Mask argument that restricts the summation of elements of the array A * Cos (X) to those that correspond to true elements of Mask. Here, the mask required is the array-valued logical expression Abs (A) < 0.01. Thus, we can write the following conditional whole-array expression:

```
Conditional_Fourier = Sum (A * Cos (X), Mask = Abs (A) < 0.01)
```

If the mask is false for all elements, the value of Conditional_Fourier is zero.

The optional argument Dim. The optional Dim (dimension) argument simplifies computation of the sums or products of all rows or columns of a matrix or along any one dimension of an array of higher rank. The result array has one less dimension than Matrix; the dimension designated by Dim is deleted, or rather it is reduced to a scalar. If the rank of Matrix is 2, Sum (Matrix, Dim = 1) produces a vector containing the column sums, and Sum (Matrix, Dim = 2) produces a vector containing the row sums.

Let A be an M by N matrix declared as follows:

```
real, dimension(M, N) :: A
```

As an example, let M and N each have the value 3, and let the value of A be

$$\begin{bmatrix} 1 & 2 & 3 \\ 4 & 5 & 6 \\ 2 & 1 & 1 \end{bmatrix}$$

The function Sum with two different Dim argument values returns the vector of column sums (7, 8, 10) and the vector of row sums (6, 15, 4).

1. The *sum of products* $\sum_{j=1}^{n}\prod_{i=1}^{m} a_{ij}$ is denoted by the Fortran 90 expression

```
Sum (Product (A, Dim = 1))
```

The argument `Dim = 1` means that the product is to be computed down each column of `A`. In the example, the result of `Product` is the vector `(8, 10, 18)`, whose `Sum` is 36.

2. The *product of sums* $\prod_{i=1}^{m}\sum_{j=1}^{n} a_{ij}$ is denoted by the Fortran 90 expression

```
Product (Sum (A, Dim = 2))
```

The argument `Dim = 2` means that the sum is to be computed along each row of `A`. In the example, the result of `Sum` is the vector `(6, 15, 4)`, whose `Product` is 360.

For a higher-dimensional array, the argument `Dim` similarly reduces the rank of the result by 1. For example, with an array declared as `X(3, 4, 5, 6)`, the shape of the result from `Sum (X, Dim = 1)` is (4, 5, 6) and each element of the result is the sum of three array elements. Similarly, the shape of the result from `Sum (X, Dim = 3)` is (3, 4, 6) and each element of the result is the sum of five array elements.

Any, All, *and* Count

The intrinsic functions `Any`, `All`, and `Count` operate on a logical array which, for many applications, is the value of a relational expression with array operands. For example, it might be useful to determine whether there is an element in the array section `D(1: I - 1)` that has a larger value than `T`:

```
if (Any (D(1: I - 1) > T)) ...
```

Here, the argument of `Any` is a logical array produced by a relational operator with an array section as one operand and a scalar as the other operand.

Note that `Any` can be viewed as a logical *sum* (.or.) operator. Similarly, `All` can be viewed as a logical *product* (.and.) operator.

In a sense, `Any` and `All` are merely special cases of `Count`. `Any` is true when `Count` is not zero, and `All` is true when `Count` is equal to the size of the argument array.

For a higher-dimensional array, the argument `Dim` reduces the rank of the result by 1, as before. For example, with an array declared as `Mask(3, 4, 5, 6)`, the shape of the result from `Any (Mask, Dim = 1)` or `All (Mask, Dim = 1)` is (4, 5, 6) and each element of the result is the logical sum or product of three elements of `Mask`. Similarly, the shape of the result from `Any (Mask, Dim = 3)` or `All (Mask, Dim = 3)` is (3, 4, 6) and each element of the result is the logical sum or product of five elements of `Mask`.

MaxLoc, MinLoc, MaxVal, *and* MinVal

The intrinsic functions `MaxLoc` and `MinLoc` find subscript values for the largest or smallest element of an argument array. These functions return an integer vector whose *length* is equal to the *rank* of a given integer or real array. Each element of the result vector is set to one of the subscript valucs dcsignating the largest (smallest) element of the argument array. If more than one array element has this maximum (minimum) value, the *first* such element in standard Fortran array element sequence (see Section 5.2) is selected. These functions may be applied to a reverse section such as `A(U_Bound, L_Bound,-1)` to find the last such element in A.

EXAMPLE 5.20

```
! Example 5.20. Location of an array element.
  program Find_1
    implicit none
    intrinsic MaxLoc, MinLoc
    integer, parameter :: N = 10
    real :: Z(N, N)
    integer, dimension(2) :: ZMax, ZMin
! start program Find_1
    read *, Z
    ZMax = MaxLoc (Z)                                  ! Array assignment
    ZMin = MinLoc (Z)
    print *, ZMax, Z(ZMax(1), ZMax(2)), ZMin, Z(ZMin(1), ZMin(2))
  end program Find_1
```

The vector of subscripts returned by `MaxLoc` or `MinLoc` cannot be applied directly to the same array. For example, the designated largest or smallest value cannot be referenced directly as `Z(ZLoc)`. However, a reference of the form `Z(ZLoc(1), ZLoc(2))` is permitted.

With a `Mask` argument, these functions operate only on the array elements selected by the mask. `Mask` is an array of the same shape as the array or it is a scalar, and its type is logical. In the following assignment, `ZMMin` is set to the location of the smallest element of `Z` that is larger than 100.

```
ZMMin = MinLoc (Z, Mask = (Z > 100))
```

When these functions are applied to an array object whose lower bound value is not 1 or to an array expression (such as an array section) that does not have a declared lower bound value, the subscript values returned as the function result are *relative* values, as if the argument were an independent array with lower bound value 1 in all dimensions. This fact introduces a slight complication in applications such as Example 5.17b. In the following statement, `MaxLoc` returns a subscript value relative to the array section `P(M: N)`. If the first element of this section is the largest, the value of `MaxLoc(1)` will be 1 rather than `M`. To recover the designated element subscript value with relation to the original array `P`, it is necessary to add `M - 1` to the function result:

```
I_Temp = M - 1 + MaxLoc (P(M: N))
```

There is no intrinsic function to directly locate an element whose value is *equal to* that of a given scalar. Either of the functions MaxLoc or MinLoc, applied to Z with the mask (Z == X), will locate the first such element, if any exists. However, the result is unpredictable if the mask is empty: Any or Count should first be applied with the same mask:

```
if (Any (Z == X)) X_Loc = MinLoc (Z, Mask = (Z == X))
```

The intrinsic functions MaxVal and MinVal are also provided, which return the *value* of the largest or smallest array element. For example, the function reference MinVal (Abs (Z – X)) will return the value of an element of Z that is closest to X in absolute value, and MinLoc will return the location of an element with this value. Thus, there is an alternative way to find an exact match when one exists. If X exactly matches any element of Z, the minimum absolute value will, of course, be zero.

EXAMPLE 5.21

```
! Example 5.21. Find element of array Z closest to scalar value X.
  program Find_2
    implicit none
    intrinsic Abs, MinLoc, MinVal
    integer, parameter :: N = 10
    real :: Z(N, N), X, ZVal
    integer :: ZLoc(2)
! start program Find_2
    read *, Z                                                ! Read an array.
    read *, X                                                ! Read a scalar.
    ZVal = MinVal (Abs (Z - X))
    ZLoc = MinLoc (Abs (Z - X))
    print *, ZLoc, Z(ZLoc(1), ZLoc(2)), ZVal
  end program Find_2
```

For a higher-dimensional array, the argument Dim again reduces the rank of the result by 1. For example, with an array declared as X(3, 4, 5, 6), the shape of the result from MaxVal (X, Dim = 1) is (4, 5, 6) and each element of the result is the largest of three array elements. Similarly, the shape of the result from MinVal (X, Dim = 3) is (3, 4, 6) and each element of the result is the smallest of five array elements.

Some useful vector and matrix norms can be computed with `MaxVal`. The *vector* norms are members of the family of p-norms defined by the formula

$$\|\mathbf{x}\|_p = \left\{ \sum_{i=1}^{n} |x_i|^p \right\}^{1/p}$$

The two most interesting cases are $p = 1$ and $p = \infty$. (The case $\pi = 2$ is also interesting, but it is much more difficult to calculate.) For $p = 1$, this formula reduces to the sum of the absolute values of the vector elements, which is given by the Fortran 90 function reference `Sum (Abs (X))`. In the limit, for $p = \infty$, large terms in the sum become dominant and the norm is the maximum of the absolute values of the vector elements, which is given by the Fortran 90 function reference `MaxVal (Abs (X))`.

Corresponding *matrix* p-norms for $A = \{A_{ij}\}$ are obtained from the following Fortran 90 expressions:[2] For $p = 1$, the matrix norm is the largest column sum, given by `MaxVal (Sum (Abs (A), Dim = 1))`. For $p = \infty$, the matrix norm is the largest row sum, given by `MaxVal (Sum (Abs (A), Dim = 2))`. In the 3 by 3 matrix example shown earlier, the matrix 1-norm (largest column sum) is 10, and the matrix -norm (largest row sum) is 15. The Frobenius norm is about 9.849, and the p-norm for $p = 2$ (computed by other means, for comparison) is 9.747.

Limitations of *MaxLoc* and *MinLoc*. The functions `MaxLoc` and `MinLoc` are not as convenient as they might be for argument arrays of rank 1, because the result is an array of rank 1 and not a scalar. (Note that several other similar functions, such as `All` and `Count`, return a scalar result when the argument is a vector.) Furthermore, these two functions as well as `MaxVal` and `MinVal` are not applicable to argument arrays of character type. Also, when a `Mask` argument is given or if there is a possibility that the array size is zero, `Any` or `Count` should first be applied with the same mask, as described earlier. (Section 7.6 presents user-defined generic procedures that transcend some of these limitations.)

Application: List Insertion with `MinLoc`

EXAMPLE 5.22 The following program adds items to a list of integers, maintaining the list in numerical order and keeping only one copy of each different element value in the list. The intrinsic function `MinLoc` finds the insertion point; that is, it finds the *smallest* array element that *exceeds* the new item. To insert an item at the right place in the list, the program must move all items between the insertion point and the end of the list; it performs this move operation by array section assignment.

[2] See, for example, G. W. Stewart, *Introduction to Matrix Computations* (New York: Academic Press, 1973), chap. 4.

```
! Example 5.22. Find and insert with MinLoc.
  subroutine Find (Vec, V_Size, E, L_Size)
    intrinsic Any, MinLoc
    integer, intent (in) :: V_Size                          ! Maximum list size
    real, intent (in out) :: Vec (1: V_Size)                             ! List
    real, intent (in) :: E                  ! Element to find or insert in list
    integer, intent (in out) :: L_Size                      ! Current list size
    integer, dimension(1) :: Loc                    ! To hold result from MinLoc
!   start subroutine Find
    if (Any (Vec == E)) then
      Loc = MinLoc (Vec, Vec == E)               ! Find an element that matches E.
      print *, "␣Found:␣", E, "␣at␣", Loc(1), "␣of␣", L_Size
    else                                          ! No matching element; insert E.
      if (L_Size >= V_Size) stop "␣Array␣is␣full␣"
      L_Size = L_Size + 1                                  ! Adjust current size.
      if (Any (Vec > E)) then                             ! If any elements > E...
        Loc = MinLoc (Vec, Vec > E)                          ! find the smallest.
      else
        Loc(1) = L_Size                                   ! Append at end of list.
      end if
      ! Move all elements beyond Loc(1) to make space.
      Vec(Loc(1) + 1 : L_Size) =  Vec(Loc(1) : L_Size - 1)
      Vec(Loc(1)) = E                                        ! Insert at Loc(1).
      print *, "␣Inserted:␣", E, "␣at␣", Loc(1), "␣of␣", L_Size
    end if
  end subroutine Find
```

In Example 5.22, the procedure Find first applies Any to check whether the element is already present. If so, it merely reports that the element has been found.

Otherwise, the item is to be inserted into the list, so the next step is to find out whether there is room in the vector for another list item. If so, MinLoc finds the insertion point, which is the smallest item that exceeds E. If there are several equal items with this smallest value, MinLoc will locate the first such item. Note that Any is used to avoid difficulty if there is no list item larger than E.

All items between the insertion point and the end of the list must be moved up by one position to make room for the new item. This operation is accomplished with array section assignment: The lower limit of the array section is the insertion point, and the upper limit is the last item in the current list. Note that this array section has zero size (there are no items to be moved) if the insertion point is at the end of the list.

A version of the insertion sort algorithm can be implemented with the subroutine in Example 5.22. Input items are read and inserted in turn into an expanding list, as illustrated in Figure 5.8. This version of insertion sort does not insert duplicates that may occur among the input items.

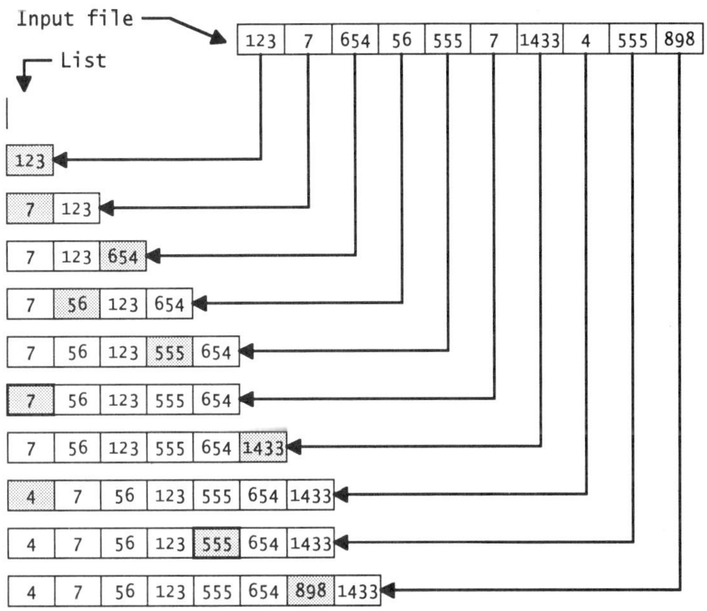

FIGURE 5.8. Insertion sort (eliminating duplicates).

Array Intrinsics for Linear Algebra Applications

The intrinsic functions `Transpose`, `Dot_Product`, and `MatMul` perform essential operations of linear algebra. `Transpose` forms the transpose of a matrix of any type:

```
real :: A(3, 5), B(5, 3)
  :
B = Transpose (A)
```

`Dot_Product` forms the sum of products of corresponding elements of two vectors, which must have the same length. The following assignment statement finds the cosine of the angle between two vectors:

```
real :: X(5), Y(5), Cos_X_Y
  :
Cos_X_Y = Dot_Product (X, Y) &
  / SqRt (Dot_Product(X, X) * Dot_Product(Y, Y))
```

`MatMul` forms the product of a p by r matrix (or a vector of length r) and an r by s matrix (or a vector of length r); the result is a p by s matrix. The arguments must not both be vectors. Note that r may be zero. If the first argument is a vector of length r, the result is a vector of length s; if the second argument is a vector of length r, the result is a vector of length p. Thus, we have, for example,

```
real :: A(5), X(5, 3), B(3), C(5), D(3)
  :
C = MatMul (A, X)
D = MatMul (X, B)
```

The types of the arguments to `Dot_Product` and `MatMul` must both be integer, real, or complex; or else they must both be logical. If the first argument of `Dot_Product` is complex, it will be conjugated. If the arguments are logical, logical sum (.or.) operations replace addition and logical product (.and.) operations replace multiplication.

Matrix–vector products. The following two examples illustrate the two matrix applications that were mentioned at the beginning of this chapter.

EXAMPLE 5.23

```
! Example 5.23. Stiffness matrix.
  program Deflect
    implicit none
    intrinsic MatMul
    integer, parameter :: N = 10
    real :: Stiffness (N, N), Loads (N), Deflections (N)
! start program Deflect
    open (1, file = "stiffness.txt")
    read (1, *, iostat = EoF) Stiffness
    if (EoF < 0) stop
    read (1, *, iostat = EoF) Loads
    if (EoF < 0) stop
    Deflections = MatMul (Stiffness, Loads)                  ! Intrinsic function
    print *, Deflections
  end program Deflect
```

EXAMPLE 5.24

```
! Example 5.24. Impedance matrix.
  program Voltaire
    implicit none
    intrinsic MatMul
    integer, parameter :: N = 13
    real :: Impedance (N, N), Currents (N), Voltages (N)
! start program Voltaire
    open (1, file = "impedance.txt")
    read (1, *, iostat = EoF) Impedance
    if (EoF < 0) stop
```

```
  read (1, *, iostat = EoF) Currents
  if (EoF < 0) stop
  Voltages = MatMul (Impedance, Currents)                    ! Intrinsic function
  print *, Voltages
end program Voltaire
```

Crout method for linear systems. The procedure in the following example solves a system of linear algebraic equations by the Crout method, a variant of Gauss elimination.[3] As explained in Section 8.2, the procedure is implemented as a module subprogram, and the dummy arguments A, B, and X are declared as *assumed-shape* arrays whose actual shape will be determined at the time of procedure entry. The local arrays LU and W are allocated (see Section 5.6) during execution of the procedure. A main program to invoke this procedure appears in Section 5.6.

The principal steps of the Crout algorithm are column and row reduction with MatMul, pivoting (omitted from this example; see Example 5.17b), and forward and backward substitution with Dot_Product (see also Example 5.17a). At some stages of this process, the array operands have zero size, but the intrinsic functions give the correct results nevertheless.

1. Column reduction: A section of column M from the main diagonal downward, LU(M: N, M), is reduced by a matrix product. The first operand in this matrix product is the array block to the left of the column section, LU(M: N, 1: M - 1). The second operand is the portion of column M above the main diagonal, LU(1: M - 1, M).
2. Pivoting: This program omits the pivoting step, which should appear at this point. Pivoting can be performed by any of several strategies, such as selection of a row that does not have a zero element in column M (*simple pivoting*) or selection of the row that has the largest element (in absolute value) in column M (unscaled *partial pivoting*; see Example 5.17b). The selected row (or a pointer to it) is interchanged with row M.
3. Row reduction: A section of row M to the right of the main diagonal, LU(M, M + 1: N), is reduced by a matrix product. The first operand in this matrix product is the portion of the row M to the left of the main diagonal, LU(M, 1: M - 1). The second operand is the array block above the row section, LU(1: M - 1, M + 1: N). The reduced row section is divided by the diagonal element LU(M, M).
4. Forward substitution: The intermediate result vector W is calculated, one element at a time. The corresponding element of B is reduced by the dot product of a portion of a row, LU(M, 1: M - 1), times the previously calculated portion of the result vector, W(1: M - 1).

[3] See M. J. Maron and R. J. Lopez, *Numerical Analysis,* 3rd ed. (Belmont, Calif.: Wadsworth, 1991), algorithm 4.4B, p. 220. The simplified version presented here does not include pivoting. Example 5.17b shows how pivoting can be implemented with vector subscripts.

5. Backward substitution: The solution vector X is calculated, one element at a time. The corresponding element of W is reduced by the dot product of a portion of a row, LU(M, M + 1: N), times the previously calculated portion of the solution vector, X(M + 1: N).

EXAMPLE 5.25

```
! Example 5.25. Solve linear system by Crout method
!   without pivoting. See Example 5.17.
  module Crout_Elimination
    implicit none
  contains
    subroutine Solve (A, B, X)
      intrinsic Dot_Product, MatMul, Size
      ! A and B are assumed-shape array arguments (see Section 8.2).
      real, intent (in) :: A(:, :), B(:)
      real, intent (out) :: X(:)
      real, allocatable :: LU(:, :), W(:)     ! Allocatable local arrays (Sec. 5.6)
      integer :: N, M
    ! start subroutine Solve
      ! Determine problem size; allocate work space and copy A.
      N = Size (A, Dim = 1)                    ! Extent of A along first dimension
      allocate (LU(N, N), W(N))                                ! See Section 5.6.
      LU = A
      ! Perform factorization A = L * U with no pivoting.
      do M = 1, N
        ! Reduce column M and row M.
        LU(M: N, M) = LU(M: N, M) - MatMul (LU(M: N, 1: M - 1), LU(1: M - 1, M))
        LU(M, M + 1: N) = (LU(M, M + 1: N) &
          - MatMul (LU(M, 1: M - 1), LU(1: M - 1, M + 1: N))) / LU(M, M)
      end do
      ! Perform forward substitution to solve L * W = B.
      do M = 1, N
        W(M) = B(M) - Dot_Product (LU(M, 1: M - 1), W(1: M - 1)) / LU(M, M)
      end do
      ! Perform backward substitution to solve U * X = W.
      do M = N, 1, -1
        X(M) = W(M) - Dot_Product (LU(M, M + 1: N), X(M + 1: N))
      end do
      deallocate (LU, W)
    end subroutine Solve
  end module Crout_Elimination
```

User-Defined Array-Valued Functions

A function can return a result of any type (and subtype). The function result will affect the value of expressions from which it is referenced; therefore, it can have any properties and attributes that are appropriate to that expression. In particular, a function can return a character string, an array of any rank (up to 7), or a user-defined structure (see Section 6.2).

If `dimension` or `pointer` attributes need to be declared for the function result, it is usually most convenient to omit the type specification from the function header and declare all attributes in a separate type declaration for the result variable inside the procedure (see also Section 7.3).

Again it is recommended that the result variable name be distinct from the function name. An advantage of this practice is that references to elements of the result array cannot be misinterpreted as recursive calls to the function. Note that attributes are declared for the result name, not the function name. These same attributes apply to the function result in the expression that invokes the function, even though it is the function name (with actual argument list) that appears there.

EXAMPLE 5.26 For some purposes, it is convenient to select the diagonal elements of a matrix as an array expression of rank 1. Although array section notation is very flexible, it can select only portions of an array whose borders are parallel to the array axes. In particular, there is no straightforward array section notation for a rank-1 array composed of the diagonal elements of a given matrix. The following internal procedure is called with a matrix argument and returns the diagonal of the matrix as a vector-valued result.

```
! Example 5.26. Diagonal of a matrix.
 program Oblique
   implicit none
   integer, parameter :: IMax = 3, JMax = 4
   real :: A(IMax, JMax)
   integer I, J
! start program Oblique
   do I = 1, IMax
     do J = 1, JMax
       A(I, J) = (I - 1) * JMax + J
     end do
   print *, I, A(I, :)
   end do
   print *, Diagonal(A)
 contains
```

```
  function Diagonal (Matrix) result (Vector)
    intrinsic Min, Size
    real, intent (in), dimension(:, :) :: Matrix
    real, dimension(MinVal (Shape (Matrix))) :: Vector
    integer :: Limit, Loop
! start function Diagonal
    Limit = Min (Size (Matrix, 1), Size (Matrix, 2))
    do Loop = 1, Limit
      Vector (Loop) = Matrix (Loop, Loop)
    end do
  end function Diagonal
end program Oblique
```

Notice the specification expression `MinVal (Shape (Matrix))` in the `dimension` declaration for `Vector`. Notice also that the expression assigned to `Limit` at the beginning of execution of `Diagonal` is not a valid Fortran 90 initialization expression (because `Matrix` is an assumed-shape array; see Section 8.2), so `Limit` is declared as a variable rather than as a named constant. (See Sections 1.3 and 8.4 for further discussion of initialization expressions and specification expressions.) The program in Example 5.26 produces the following output:

```
1 1.0000000 2.0000000 3.0000000 4.0000000
2 5.0000000 6.0000000 7.0000000 8.0000000
3 9.0000000 10.0000000 11.0000000 12.0000000
 1.0000000 6.0000000 11.0000000
```

Transition Tips

- Study the array functions in the Fortran intrinsic function library (Appendix A, Sections A.1, A.4, and A.5). Replace loops by calls to intrinsic functions where possible.
- Where possible, write a user-defined array-valued function to replace a user-defined function that is called for each array element.

5.3 Exercises

1. Write a program that will examine a real vector `A` having 40 elements, and locate the last *i* such that `A(`*i*`)` is negative.
2. Write a program to find the product of all the `N` elements of the vector `Factor`. (Hint: Use the intrinsic function `Product`.) What result should you expect when `N` is zero?
3. Use the intrinsic function `Sum` to compute the row sums, column sums, and grand total of the elements of a square array of 5 rows and 5 columns.

4. Given a vector of N integers, $K_1, K_2, \ldots, K_n$, some of which may be zero, count those that are positive and even and those that are negative and even, producing the separate tallies `NPos` and `NNeg`. Zeros and odd numbers are to be ignored. (Hint: Use the intrinsic function `Count`. Use `Modulo(Array, 2) == 0` as part of the mask expression.)

5. Review the mathematical definition of matrix multiplication (from linear algebra). Describe the product of a 5 by 0 matrix and a 0 by 7 matrix, noting that an "empty" sum has the value 0.

5.4 ARRAY APPLICATIONS WITH LOOPS

There are many applications for which whole-array operations are suitable, but some cases require individual mention of the separate array elements. The most natural program structure for these applications is an indexed do construct.

Indexed do Loops

EXAMPLE 5.27 The following program sets A to the Hilbert matrix, a critical test matrix for numerical linear algebra algorithms.

```
! Example 5.27. Generate Hilbert matrix
  program David
    implicit none
    intrinsic Real
    real, allocatable :: A(:, :)            ! Allocatable array (see Section 5.6)
    integer :: N, I, J
! start program David
    read *, N
    allocate (A (N, N))
    do I = 1, N
      do J = 1, N
        A(I, J) = 1.0 / Real (I + J - 1)
      end do
      print *, I, A(I, :)
    end do
    deallocate (A)
  end program David
```

EXAMPLE 5.28 A two-dimensional pattern may often be generated and printed one line at a time, so it is not necessary to create a two-dimensional array. The following program calculates all the elements of Pascal's triangle up to row M. Pascal's triangle may be viewed as an infinite lower-triangular matrix $C_{n,r}$. In row n, the value of the second subscript r ranges from 0 to n. An element of this array represents the number of ways to choose r different objects from among n objects; this same number is the coefficient of x^r in the binomial expansion of $(1 + x)^n$. (For an alternative, but numerically inferior, method for calculating these numbers from factorials, see Example 8.16.) Note the following:

1. The first row ($n = 0$) contains one entry. Each succeeding row contains one more entry than the preceding row.
2. In each row, the first entry (at $r = 0$) and the last entry (at $r = n$) are 1.
3. Each of the other entries in a row is obtained from the formula

   $$C_{n,r} = C_{n-1,r} + C_{n-1,r-1}$$

   Thus the elements of row n can be stored in the same place as the elements of row $n - 1$ if they are calculated in order of *decreasing* values of r.

```
! Example 5.28. Pascal's triangle (binomial coefficients).
  program Blaise
    implicit none
    integer, parameter :: M = 20
    integer :: N, R, Pascal(0: M)
! start program Blaise
    do N = 0, M
      Pascal(0) = 1
      Pascal(N) = 1
      do R = N - 1, 1, -1
        Pascal(R) = Pascal(R) + Pascal(R - 1)
      end do
      print *, Pascal(0: N)
    end do
  end program Blaise
```

Implied do Loops

The *Input list* or *Output list* in a `read`, `write`, or `print` statement may incorporate notation that is called an *implied* do *loop* because of its resemblance to the control statement of an indexed do construct:

(*Sublist* , *Index* = *Initial value* , *Limit* [, *Increment*])

The *Sublist* consists of a sequence of items of any form that is permitted in the input or output list. The *Index*, the *Initial value*, and the optional *Increment* are subject to the same rules that apply to indexed do constructs (see Section 4.1). The increment, if not specified, is given the default value 1. (An implied do loop is also permitted in the list of variables in a data statement. See Appendix D.3.)

EXAMPLE 5.29 The following two lists are equivalent.

```
print *, (A(I), B(I), I = 1, 5)
print *, A(1), B(1), A(2), B(2), A(3), B(3), A(4), B(4), A(5), B(5)
```

EXAMPLE 5.30 An implied do loop may appear along with other items in a list. The sequence specified by a list is based on a left-to-right scan of the entire list. When an implied do loop is reached during the scan, all the elements it specifies are included in the sequence before the scan continues with the next item beyond the group. The following two lists are equivalent.

```
A, B, (P(K, K), K= 1, 3), D, E, F
A, B, P(1, 1), P(2, 2), P(3, 3), D, E, F
```

EXAMPLE 5.31 The following two lists are equivalent.

```
K, L, M, (A(I), B(I), I = 1, 3)
K, L, M, A(1), B(1), A(2), B(2), A(3), B(3)
```

EXAMPLE 5.32 The index variable does not have to appear as a subscript with any or all of the items of the sublist. Sublist items not involving the index variable will simply be repeated in the list sequence. The following are equivalent.

```
(C, A(4), T(I), D, I = 1, 3)
C, A(4), T(1), D, C, A(4), T(2), D, C, A(4), T(3), D
```

The major difference between an indexed do construct and an implied do loop is that the former consists of a group of *statements* to be repeated, while the latter consists of a *sublist* (a group of *list items* within a single statement) to be repeated. The beginning and end of an implied do loop are indicated by a pair of matching parentheses. The beginning and end of a do construct are established by the pair of statements do and end do. The successive values of the index variable are established identically in the two cases. A negative increment value for an implied do loop, for example, will cause the index value to decrease.

Certain values of the initial value, limit, and increment may result in a trip count less than 1, so that the sublist is scanned 0 times — for example,

```
J = 5
read *, (A(I), I = J, 4), X
```

Since the trip count for the implied do loop is 0, the first value read will be assigned to X.

A Restriction for Input Lists

We noted in Section 4.1 that the index variable of an indexed do construct must not be assigned a new value during execution of the loop. By analogy, the index variable of an implied do loop must not appear as a sublist item in an input list. Thus, the implied do loop

```
(I, A(I), B(I), I = 1, 3)                ! ☹ Not valid for input.
```

would not be valid in an input list. It could appear in an output list, however, and would be equivalent to the list

```
1, A(1), B(1), 2, A(2), B(2), 3, A(3), B(3)
```

A form that is valid in an input list is the following:

```
N, (A(I), I = 1, N)
```

For example, if the first data value read is the integer 4, this list is equivalent to the following.

```
N, A(1), A(2), A(3), A(4)
```

A list of this form should be used only with extreme caution, however, since a small error in data preparation could have a rather dramatic effect. Unless it is absolutely necessary to include N in the same list, it would be better to read N with a separate statement, make a check to ensure the validity of the data value just read, and then read (A(I), I = 1 , N) with another statement.

Nested Implied do Loops

An implied do loop may be included in a statement inside an indexed do construct or in a sublist within an outer implied do loop. An important form for a doubly nested implied do loop is as follows:

((*Sublist*$_1$, *Index*$_1$ = *Initial value*$_1$, *Limit*$_1$ [, *Increment*$_1$]) ,
Index$_2$ = *Initial value*$_2$, *Limit*$_2$ [, *Increment*$_2$])

The following are specific examples of this form:

```
((B(I, J), J = 1, 7), I = 1, 5)
((B(I, J), J = 1, 7), I = 2, 10, 2)
((D(L, M), L = 1, 5), M = 7, 1, -1)
((C(I, J), I = 1, J), J = 1, 3)
```

The last of these examples illustrates the fact that the index variable of the outer implied do loop can appear in any of the expressions for the parameters of the inner implied do loop. The number of nesting levels is not limited to 2.

The sequence of items specified by nested implied do loops may be inferred by analogy to ordinary do loops. However, a minor annoyance in the interpretation of such a nest is that the control for the outer loop, which must be established first, appears at the end of the nested loop description. Each time the outer loop index value is established, the entire sublist including the inner implied do loop is scanned. For example,

```
(A, B(J), (C(J, I), I = 2, 3), D, J = 1, 2)
```

is equivalent to the list

```
A, B(1), C(1, 2), C(1, 3), D, A, B(2), C(2, 2), C(2, 3), D
```

That is, the value of J is set to 1 and the list is scanned as though it were written

```
A, B(1), (C(1, I), I = 2, 3), D
```

Then, the value of J is set to 2 and the list is scanned as though it were written

```
A, B(2), (C(2, I), I = 2, 3), D
```

Alternatives to Implied do

Simple implied do loops, including nested examples, can often be replaced by array sections. The last two of the following statements are equivalent to the first two, but are simpler:

```
read *, (A(I), I = J, 4), X
print *, ((B(I, J), I = 1, 5), J = 1, 7)
read *, A(J: 4), X
print *, B(1: 4, 1: 7)
```

However, the implied do loop notation gives some control over the output sequence, while array sections are transmitted in standard Fortran array element sequence.

When a sublist includes elements of several arrays with the same subscript, further consideration is in order. Older Fortran applications often process a table as a group of parallel arrays; the more modern representation would be an array of structures, as described in Section 6.2.

Indexed do *Loop Application: Linear Search in an Array*

Finding the Largest Element

EXAMPLE 5.33 The intrinsic function MaxLoc (or the function Max_Loc that will be presented in Example 7.16) could be used to find the largest element in a vector (an array of rank 1). For illustrative purposes, however, we can create a function to accomplish this task. A linear search with an indexed do loop can find the largest element. The following procedure, Linear_Max, performs a linear search in an array to find the largest element. It does not assume that the array is ordered.

```
! Example 5.33. Linear max procedure.
  function Linear_Max (Vector) result (Loc)
    intrinsic Huge, Size
    real, dimension(:) :: Vector              ! Assumed-shape array (see Section 8.2)
    real :: Big = -Huge (Vector)
    integer :: Loc = 0, Loop, Limit
! start function Linear_Max
    Limit = Size (Vector)
    do Loop = 1, Limit
      if (Vector(Loop) > Big) then
        Big = Vector(Loop)
        Loc = Loop
      end if
    end do
  end function Linear_Max
```

In Example 5.33, the dummy argument is a vector of real data type. For a vector of integer or character type, the type declarations for `Vector` and `Big` would be changed.

The vector is declared as an assumed-shape array (see Section 8.2); a dummy argument array for which the declared bounds are omitted *assumes* (takes on) the shape of the actual argument array. The declared rank of the array must match that of the actual argument.

The first step in the procedure is to apply the intrinsic function `Size` to find the extent of the actual argument vector. At any point in the search, the variable `Big` contains the largest element found so far, and `Loc` records its location within the vector. Before entering the loop, the procedure sets `Big` to a very large negative value and `Loc` to 0. The loop then examines all elements and replaces `Big` and `Loc` when a larger element is found. If `Vector` has zero size, `Big` and `Loc` will retain their initial values.

The procedure must examine every element of the array to make sure it finds the desired element. If the array is large, examining each element separately can be very time-consuming.

Finding the Insertion Point

EXAMPLE 5.34 For insertion sorting, as illustrated in Example 5.22, the problem is to find the position where the new item belongs. If the new item matches an array element, the result should be the location of the matching element. Otherwise, the result should be the location at which to insert the new item — this could be the subscript of the *largest* array element that is *smaller* than the new item or of the *smallest* array element that is *larger* than the new item. Again, a linear search with an indexed do loop is possible. The following function, Search, accepts a real vector and a search key and returns a two-element result vector. The first element of the result vector will be set to the location of the largest array element that is at least as small as the key, and the second element of the result vector will be set to the location of the smallest array element that is at least as large as the key. These two locations will be the same if an element equal to the key is found in the vector.

```
! Example 5.34. Search for insertion point in unordered array.
  function Search (List, Key) result (Location)
    intrinsic Size, Huge
    integer :: Location(2) = 0, Loop
    real, dimension(:) :: List            ! Assumed-shape array (see Section 8.2)
    real :: Key, Big = -Huge(List), Small = Huge(List)
! start function Search
    do Loop = 1, Size(List)
      if ((List(Loop) <= Key) .and. (List(Loop) > Big)) then
        Big = List(Loop)
        Location(1) = Loop
      end if
      if ((List(Loop) >= Key) .and. (List(Loop) < Small) then
        Small = List(Loop)
        Location(2) = Loop
      end if
    end do
    end function Search
```

Searching in an Ordered Array

EXAMPLE 5.35 If the array is known to be in order, the linear search procedure can be considerably simplified. There is no need to save the largest item found so far because the *last* item selected will be larger than any selected previously. Furthermore, the loop can be terminated as soon as a value larger than the key is found.

```
! Example 5.35. Linear search in ordered array.
  function Search (List, Key) result (Location)
    intrinsic Size
    integer :: Location(2), Loop, L_Size
    real :: List(:), Key                        ! Assumed-shape array (see Section 8.2)
! start function Search
    L_Size = Size (List)
    Location(1) = 0
    Location(2) = L_Size
    read *, Key
    do Loop = 1, L_Size - 1
      if (List(Loop) <= Key) Location(1) = Loop
      if (List(Loop) >= Key) then
        Location(2) = Loop
        exit
      end if
    end do
    if (Location(1) < Location(2)) then
      List(Location(2) + 1 : L_Size) = List(Location(2) : L_Size -1)
      List(Location(2) = Key
    end if
  end function Search
```

The function in Example 5.35 must still examine all array elements until it finds one that is at least as large as the key. In a sorted array of random values, with a random key, the expected number of array elements to be examined is half the list size. This search can require considerable time if the array is a large one. The intrinsic array functions `MaxLoc`, `MinLoc`, and `Any` can improve the efficiency of this process, but these functions are unable to take advantage of the fact that the array is already in order.

At the end of the loop, `Location(1)` and `Location(2)` will have the same value if `Key` is found in the array. However, if `Key` is not found, `Location(1)` will be the index of the largest array element that is less than `Key`, and `Location(2)` will be the index of the smallest array element that is greater than `Key`. (What will be the values of `Location(1)` and `Location(2)` if all array elements are larger or if all are smaller than `Key`?) The portion of the array that contains elements larger than `Key` is moved by one element position, and `Key` is inserted. Note that the array section to be moved may have zero size.

A `while` *Loop Application: Binary Search in an Array*

A special method — *binary searching* — is possible for finding the insertion point (a specific key value) in an array that is known to be in order. A binary search can be much faster than a linear search, especially for large arrays.

The idea is to find out whether the key value is in the left half or the right half of the array. Since the array elements are in order, this determination can be made by examining just one element in the middle of the array. The selected half is again bisected, and the process continues until the search narrows down to a single element that matches the key or to two elements between which the key value lies.

Each time the array is cut in half, only one comparison of the key with an array element is required. Therefore, the total number of comparisons (and the total number of repetitions of the loop) is proportional to the (base 2) logarithm of the list size. A linear search in an ordered array of 10,000 list elements requires some 5,000 comparisons, but a binary search requires fewer than 60.

EXAMPLE 5.36 Examining the binary search procedure in this example, we see that, at each repetition of the loop, the following assertion is true:

```
List(Location(1)) Key List(Location(2))
```

For purposes of this assertion, we pretend that the array is extended by one more element at each end and that the imaginary element `List(0)` contains a very large negative value while the imaginary element `List(Last + 1)` contains a very large positive value. When the current middle element is examined, it may happen that this element matches the search key. In this case, there is no further need to continue bisecting the array, so the `while` loop is terminated.

```
! Example 5.36. Binary search in ordered array.
  function Search (List, Key) result (Location)
    intrinsic Size
    integer :: Location(2), Middle, Last
    character (len = NAME_LENGTH) :: List(:), Key

! start function Search

    Last = Size(List)
    Location(1) = 0
    Location(2) = Last + 1

    do while (Location(2) - Location(1) > 1)
      Middle = (Location(1) + Location(2)) / 2

      if (List(Middle) == Key) then
        Location = Middle                       ! Assign scalar to both vector elements.
        exit

      else if (List(Middle) > Key) then
        Location(2) = Middle

      else
        Location(1) = Middle
      end if

    end do

  end function Search
```

In some applications, there may be a sequence of identical matching items, and a specific one of these (such as the rightmost) may be wanted. For this situation, the `if` construct in Example 5.36 may be replaced as follows:

```
   :
if (List(Middle) == Key) then
   ! Move to the rightmost of a sequence of matching keys.
   do while ((Middle + 1 <= Last) .and. (List(Middle + 1) == Key))
      Middle = Middle + 1
   end do
   Location = Middle          ! Assign scalar to both vector elements.
   exit
end if
   :
```

Logical Matrix Application: Directed Graph

Connection Matrix by Sum Formula

The *adjacency relation* on a directed graph can be represented by a logical matrix A. The matrix is square, and its size is n by n, where n is the number of nodes in the graph. The matrix element A_{ij} is true if there is an arc from node i to node j. The *connection relation* on a directed graph may be computed from the adjacency relation. The connection relation is the transitive closure of the adjacency relation; in the closure matrix C, the element C_{ij} is true if there is a path (of any length) from node i to node j. One method is based on the formula

$$C = A + A^2 + A^3 + \cdots$$

The matrix powers in this formula can be evaluated with the intrinsic function `MatMul`. To multiply logical matrices, this intrinsic function replaces multiplication by the operator .and., and it replaces addition by the operator .or.. More efficient is Horner's method, which is commonly used for polynomial evaluation:

$$C = A + A \cdot (A + A \cdot (\cdots + A \cdot (A)))$$

EXAMPLE 5.37

```
! Example 5.37. Connection matrix by sum formula.
  program Connect
    implicit none
    intrinsic MatMul
    integer, parameter :: Nodes = 6
    logical, dimension(Nodes, Nodes) :: A, C
    integer :: Loop
! start program Connect
```

```
    do Loop = 1, Nodes
      read *, A(Loop, :)
    end do
    C = A
    do Loop = 2, Nodes
      C = A .or. MatMul (C, A)
    end do
    do Loop = 1, Nodes
      print *, C(Loop, :)
    end do
  end program Connect
```

Connection Matrix by Warshall's Algorithm

In 1962, S. Warshall published an especially efficient algorithm for computing the closure of a relation represented by a logical matrix. No auxiliary space is required, and considerably fewer logical operations are performed. This method can be even more efficient with a packed logical representation (see Section 3.4). The idea is as follows: If there is a path from *j* to *i*, then, for every path from *i* to *x*, there is also a path from *j* to *x*, so row *i* may be merged into row *j*.

EXAMPLE 5.38

```
! Example 5.38. Connection matrix by Warshall's algorithm.
  program Warshall
    implicit none
    integer, parameter :: Nodes = 6
    logical, dimension(Nodes, Nodes) :: A
    integer :: I, J
! start program Warshall
    do I = 1, Nodes
      read *, A(I, :)
    end do
    do I = 1, Nodes
      do J = 1, Nodes
        if (A(J, I)) A(J, :) = A(J, :) .or. A(I, :)      ! Merge row I into row J.
      end do
    end do
    do I = 1, Nodes
      print *, A(I, :)
    end do
  end program Warshall
```

	Data							Result				
T	F	T	F	T	F		T	F	T	F	T	F
F	T	F	F	T	F		F	T	F	F	T	F
T	F	F	F	F	F		T	F	T	F	T	F
T	F	F	T	T	T		T	T	T	T	T	T
F	F	F	F	F	F		F	F	F	F	F	F
F	T	T	F	F	F		T	T	T	F	T	F

Exponential of a Matrix

The exponential of a matrix, which is important in quantum mechanics and in the theory of linear differential equations, can be defined by analogy to the exponential power series (see Example 4.14). Horner's method is not suitable for this application because it must be computed from the highest power down. The dummy argument `M` is an assumed-shape array (see Section 8.2) that takes it shape from the actual argument, and the function result `E` is an automatic array (see Section 8.4) whose shape depends on that of `M`. We estimate the magnitude of `M` with the Frobenius norm (sum of squares of all elements); this number must be small to ensure convergence.

EXAMPLE 5.39

```
! Example 5.39. Compute exponential of a matrix.
  function Mat_Exp (M) result (E)
    implicit none
    intrinsic Selected_Real_Kind, Real, Size, Spacing, Sum
    integer, parameter :: P = 4, K = Selected_Real_Kind (P)
    real (kind = K), dimension(:, :), intent (in) :: M
    real (kind = K), dimension(Size(M, Dim = 1), Size(M, Dim = 2)) :: E
    integer :: I, N, M_Size(2)
    real (kind = K) :: Sign = 1.0
    real (kind = K), allocatable, dimension(:, :) :: Term, E
! start function Mat_Exp
    M_Size = Size (M)
    if (Sum (M ** 2) > 0.5_K) return   ! M will probably not converge fast enough.
    if (M_Size(1) /= M_Size(2)) return                ! M must be a square matrix.
    allocate (Term(M_Size(1), M_Size(2)), E(M_Size(1), M_Size(2)))
    E = 0.0_K                                          ! Initialize power series.
    Term = 0.0_K                                ! Initialize Term to identity matrix.
    do I = 1, M_Size(1)
      Term(I, I) = 1.0_K
    end do
```

```
  do N = 0, 100                      ! Exit when Term is small or after Term is 100.
    E = E + Term                                                ! Exp (M) power series
    if (Sum(Term ** 2) < 2.0_K * Spacing (1.0_K)) return             ! Converged OK.
    Term = MatMul (Term, M) / Real (N + 1, Kind = K)         ! Calculate next Term.
  end do
end function Mat_Exp
```

5.4 Exercises

1. Modify Example 1.4 (in Chapter 1), replacing the loop construct by whole-array operations. Use an implied do loop for output.

2. Apply Warshall's algorithm to the following adjacency matrix:

$$\begin{bmatrix} F & T & F & F & F & F \\ F & F & T & F & F & F \\ T & F & F & T & F & F \\ F & F & F & F & T & F \\ F & F & F & F & F & T \\ F & F & F & T & F & F \end{bmatrix}$$

3. Digital logic circuit for binary adder: Extend the main program of Exercise 4 of Section 3.4 to find the sum of two vectors of logical type that represent binary integers, using the same four internal logical function procedures as before. Beginning with the lowest-order binary digit, generate the corresponding digit of the output (sum) vector and generate the carry digit for input to the next higher binary digit. For the lowest digit, use a three-input adder with `.FALSE.` as its carry input. The output vector is one element longer than the input vectors. The final carry is stored in this extra position.

4. Linear interpolation: You are given a pair of vectors named `Height` and `Weight`.The array `Height` contains numbers representing possible heights of persons. For each subscript value j, the array element $\texttt{Weight}_j$ has a value representing the average weight of individuals whose height is $\texttt{Height}_j$. Assume that the heights are arranged in ascending order. Given the height of a particular individual, which might or might not coincide with one of the tabulated values, estimate the corresponding weight. Search the array of heights for a value near the specified height, `H`.That is, find a value of j such that `H` is greater than or equal to $\texttt{Height}_j$ and is less than $\texttt{Height}_{j+1}$. Then estimate the corresponding weight according to the following formula:

$$\texttt{W} = \texttt{Weight}_j + \frac{(\texttt{H} - \texttt{Height}_j)}{(\texttt{Height}_{j+1} - \texttt{Height}_j)} \cdot (\texttt{Weight}_{j+1} - \texttt{Weight}_j)$$

5. Write a program involving two vectors of integers, one containing 15 elements and the other containing 20 elements. After reading data to obtain values for all the items in

each array, your program should print the values of only those integers that appear in both arrays.

6. Polynomial arithmetic. Read the coefficients of two polynomials.

   a. Compute and print the coefficients of their sum and difference.

   b. Compute and print the coefficients of their product.

   c. "Divide" the first polynomial by the second; that is, calculate the coefficients of the quotient polynomial and of the remainder polynomial. The degree of the quotient polynomial should equal the difference between the degrees of the two given polynomials, and the degree of the remainder polynomial should be one less than the degree of the second given polynomial, except when the degree of the second given polynomial exceeds that of the first. In this case, the quotient polynomial consists simply of the "zero polynomial" (having nothing but a constant term, with value zero), and the remainder polynomial is the same as the first given polynomial. Note that in any case some or all of the coefficients of the remainder polynomial may be zero.[4] Make up your own data, or use data given by your instructor. Check that your program will work in special cases — for example, if the second polynomial consists simply of a nonzero constant term.

5.5 ARRAY CONSTRUCTORS AND ARRAY-VALUED CONSTANTS (Advanced)

An *array constructor* consists of a *List* of expressions and implied do loops, enclosed by the symbols (/ and /):

(/ *List* /)

The expressions, including those in the *Sublists* of the implied do loops, may be scalar expressions or array expressions, and all must have the same type and subtype.

One major application of array constructors is for expressing *array-valued constants,* as illustrated by the following examples:

EXAMPLE 5.40 The first two of the following array constructors form constant vectors of real type, while the third is a constant vector of integer type.

```
(/ 3.2, 4.01, 6.4 /)
(/ 4.5, 4.5 /)
(/ 3, 2 /)
```

[4] See also D. E. Knuth, *Seminumerical Algorithms,* vol. 2 of *The Art of Computer Programming* (Reading, Mass.: Addison-Wesley, 1969), p. 364.

A *List* item in an array constructor may be an implied do loop (or nested implied do loops) of the form described in Section 5.4:

```
(/ (I, I = 1, N) /)
(/ ((0.0, J = 1, I - 1), 1.0, (0.0, J = I + 1, N), I = 1, N) /)
```

However, it must be kept in mind that the rank of an array constructor is always 1.

An array constructor on the right side of an assignment statement must agree in shape with the array on the left. Fortran does not automatically truncate or pad to make the shapes agree. However, the left side may be an array section:

```
A(1: 7: 2) = (/ 11, 6, 14, 5 /)
```

An array constructor always creates an array of rank 1, but the intrinsic function `Reshape`, which changes the shape of an array, can be applied to an array constructor to create an array of higher rank. The first argument of `Reshape` must be an array of rank 1 — for example, an array constructor — with the correct total number of elements, and the second argument is a *shape* vector, as described in the following paragraph. The result from the intrinsic function is an array whose rank is the number of elements in the shape vector and whose extent along each dimension is given by the value of one of the elements of the shape vector.

`Reshape` has two required arguments, `Source` and `Shape`, and two optional arguments, `Pad` and `Order`. (See Section 8.7 for a discussion of optional arguments.) `Source` is an array of any type. `Shape` is a vector with one to seven positive integer elements. Each element of `Shape` gives the size along one dimension of the array produced by `Reshape`; thus, the product of the element values of `Shape` gives the total number of elements in the result array. If the number of elements in `Source` is less than the number of elements in the result, the optional argument `Pad` must be present to designate the values of the remaining elements of the result array. `Order` defines a permutation of the subscripts of the result array. (See also Appendix A.)

EXAMPLE 5.41

```
! Example 5.41.
  program Shaping
    implicit none
    integer, parameter :: N = 10
    integer :: I, J, YShape(2) = (/ 3, 2 /), ZShape(2) = (/ N, N /)
    real :: X(2), Y(3, 2), Q(N * N), Z(N, N)
! start program Shaping
    X = (/ 4.5, 4.5 /)
    Y = Reshape ((/ (I + 0.2, I = 1, 3), X, 2.0 /), YShape)
    Q = (/ ((0.0, J = 1, I - 1), 1.0, (0.0, J = I + 1, N), I = 1, N) /)
    Z = Reshape (Q, ZShape)
      :
  end program Shaping
```

In the program of Example 5.41, YShape and ZShape are initialized with array constants. Another array constant is assigned to X. The Source argument to the Reshape function is an array constructor with six components: The first three are given by an implied do loop, the next two come from the vector X, and the sixth is the constant 2.0, as shown in Figure 5.9. An array constructor is assigned to the vector Q, which is then reshaped to form Z and becomes an N by N identity matrix.

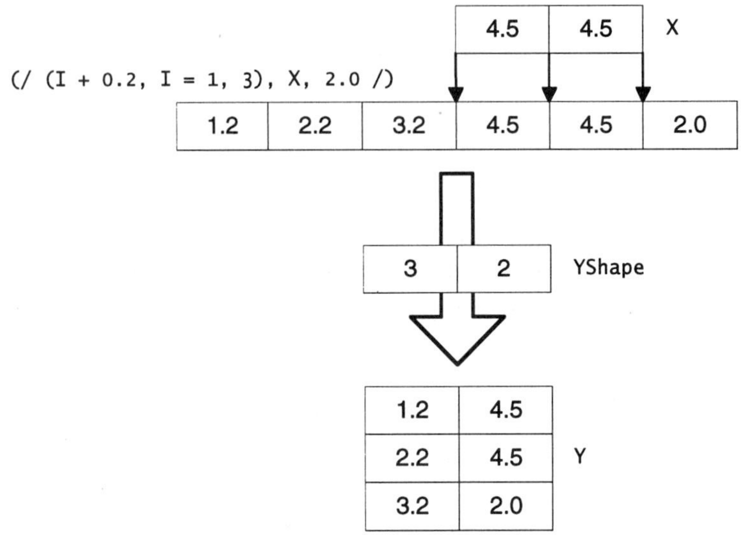

FIGURE 5.9. How the intrinsic function *Reshape* can create an array of higher rank.

A whole-array variable may be initialized in a type declaration, giving the initial value of the array by means of a scalar or an array constructor:

```
implicit none
real, dimension(100) :: Array = 0.0
integer :: Initial_Primes(5) = (/ 2, 3, 5, 7, 11 /)
integer, dimension(6) :: Zahlen = (/ 18, 0, (I, I = 3, 9, 2) /)
```

A named constant may be a whole array:

```
implicit none
intrinsic Reshape
integer, parameter :: CONST_PRIMES(5) = (/ 2, 3, 5, 7, 11 /)
real, parameter :: IDENTITY_MATRIX(3, 3) = &
  Reshape ((/ 1, 0, 0, 0, 1, 0, 0, 0, 1 /), (/ 3, 3 /))
```

Transition Tip

- For data statements that store constants in arrays, substitute array constructors where possible. Use Reshape to generate arrays of higher rank.

5.6 ALLOCATABLE ARRAYS (Advanced)

Storage Classes

The modern program environment, as it is implemented for Fortran 90 (and other languages) on most hardware systems, supports three classes of storage.

Static Storage

Static storage is set aside for data objects with the `save` attribute; this space is maintained independently of the procedural hierarchy of the program. For example, an external subroutine (see Appendix D.6) might be called to insert one item into a table. This table must continue to exist unchanged between calls to the procedure. Traditional Fortran programs may also declare some data objects in `common` statements (see Section 8.4); static storage is reserved for such objects as well. However, Fortran 90 *modules* provide superior facilities for achieving those purposes that have traditionally been served by the `common` feature.

Management of static storage during program execution is trivially simple. All static storage requirements are detected by the compiler, and the necessary space is created at the beginning of program execution.

Automatic Storage

Automatic storage holds objects that belong to a specific procedure.[5] These objects are the dummy arguments that are listed in the procedure heading statement and most of the local variables that are mentioned in type declarations within the program unit (including the *Result name* if the procedure is a function). Exceptions are local objects with the save attribute, which are stored statically along with global common data, and *heap-allocated* local data including allocatable arrays and pointer targets.

The automatic storage required for each procedure is organized into an *activation record*. It includes space for values of (or references to) the dummy arguments and for values of local variables except those with the `save` attribute and those that are allocated. The compiler generates references to any of these objects in terms of its location within the activation record for the procedure. Actual space for the objects in the activation record is not reserved until program execution begins, but the location of each object, *relative to* the activation record, is established by the compiler. For assumed-shape arrays (Section 8.2) and allocatable arrays, the location of the array descriptor (Section 8.8) is established by the compiler.

Execution-time management of automatic storage is straightforward, although not as simple as static storage management. As each procedure is called, an activation record

[5] For procedures that are not declared recursive, some Fortran processors adopt a simpler model, much like that employed by traditional Fortran processors, with all nonheap data stored *statically*.

for the procedure is created; upon exit from the procedure, the activation record is deleted; that is, the storage reserved for it is released so that it can be allocated to other procedures. Variables whose values will be needed later must be given the `save` attribute. Such objects will be located in static storage, and not in the activation record, so that their values will be preserved when the activation record is deleted upon exit from the procedure.

Most modern processors manage storage for the main program in the same way as for a procedure. An activation record for the main program, containing automatic objects belonging to the main program, is created at the beginning of execution of the main program. This activation record is not deleted until program execution terminates. Main program objects may have the `save` attribute, in which case they are located in static storage.

The activation record for a module is created at the beginning of execution of the first procedure that imports the module, and it is not destroyed so long as any such procedure is active.

Because procedure calls and exits always occur in a last-in-first-out (LIFO) sequence, the storage management system for automatic storage uses a *stack* called the *central stack* or the *activation record stack*. For this reason, automatic storage is often called *stack* storage.

Dynamic Storage

The third storage class is *dynamic storage,* or heap storage. Management of heap storage is somewhat more complicated than stack storage management because objects can enter or leave the heap in an arbitrary sequence. An object may be deleted between two other objects that remain on the heap, leaving a "hole" that may be too small for the next object that needs space. Sophisticated *garbage collection* techniques are required to reclaim such space — for example, to combine many small areas of available heap space into fewer large areas.

Fortran 90 communicates with the heap storage management system when it executes explicit `allocate` and `deallocate` instructions in the program. Fortran 90 objects in heap storage are allocatable arrays and allocated pointer targets (see Section 6.3). Allocatable arrays are not essentially different from allocated pointer target arrays, except that the facilities for allocatable arrays are slightly simpler. Allocating a pointer creates a descriptor as well as a target, and an allocated pointer target can be a scalar or array of any type.

Syntax for Array Allocation

Allocatable arrays and allocated pointer target arrays are *deferred-shape* arrays. Allocatable arrays are declared in the usual way, except that the keyword `allocatable` appears in the list of attributes and that the dimension attribute is only partly specified. Colons in the array shape specification determine the *rank* (number of dimensions) of the allocatable array, but the *Subscript bounds* are omitted from the declaration. The *Subscript bounds* remain to be established at the time the array is actually allocated:

```
real, allocatable :: Alimony(:, :), Alpenglow(:), Alabaster(:, :, :)
character (len = 6), allocatable, dimension(:) :: Aloysius
```

The first of these two statements describes three allocatable arrays of real type, each with a different rank. The second declares a one-dimensional array consisting of an unspecified number of strings.

At various points in the program, `allocate` statements can then be executed to create the arrays:

```
allocate (Alimony(5, 1000))
allocate (Alpenglow(0: Range), Alabaster(5, 1000, -17: -6))
```

The *Subscript bounds* in an `allocate` statement have the same form and the same significance as in an array shape declaration (Section 5.1).

Storage space that has been provided for the array can be released by execution of a `deallocate` statement:

```
deallocate (Alimony, Alabaster)
```

An array that has been deallocated may be reallocated with different *Subscript bounds*, but the rank cannot be changed.

An allocatable array that is local to a procedure, if it does not have the `save` attribute, must be explicitly deallocated before exit from the procedure occurs. Otherwise, the array value becomes undefined and its allocation status becomes undefined, so the array can no longer be referenced, defined, allocated, or deallocated. Note, however, that an allocated pointer target (see Section 6.3) may be returned as a function result.

It is an error to allocate an array that is currently allocated or to deallocate an array that is not currently allocated. The intrinsic function `Allocated` may be used to determine whether or not an array is currently allocated. If program control flow is relatively simple, the allocation status at a particular point in the program may be obvious. If not, it may be wise to make a test at the point of allocation or deallocation:

```
if (.not. Allocated (Alabaster)) &
  allocate (Alabaster(17, 5, 0: 3))
if (Allocated (Aloysius)) deallocate Aloysius
```

The `allocate` statement has an optional *Exception* specifier of the form `stat =` *Integer variable*:

```
allocate (Alimony(5, 1000), stat = Allocate_Error)
if (Allocate_Error != 0) stop
```

At the end of execution of the `allocate` statement, the designated *Integer variable* will be set to zero if the allocation is successful and to a positive value otherwise — for example, if one of the arrays is already allocated or if no heap storage space is available.

Application: Allocatable Arrays

A simple but important class of applications for allocatable arrays is for storage of input data when the amount of data is not fixed by the program but is provided as part of the input.

EXAMPLE 5.42 In the following program, data is to be read from a file and stored in an array. The amount of data is given as an integer in the first record of the file. The type declaration for the array includes the `dimension` attribute with unspecified bounds. The program reads the first record and allocates the array with the necessary amount of space, then reads the remainder of the file.

```
! Example 5.42. Allocatable array size given as input.
  program Emporium
    implicit none
    integer :: How_Many, EoF
    real, allocatable, dimension(:) :: Tank
! start program Emporium
    open (1, file = "datain.txt")
    read (1, *, iostat = EoF) How_Many
      if (EoF < 0) stop
    allocate (Tank(How_Many))
    read (1, *, iostat = EoF) Tank
      if (EoF < 0) stop
    print *, Tank
  end program Emporium
```

EXAMPLE 5.43 The following program extends that of Example 5.38. The number of nodes is the first input data item in each group. If zero is entered as the number of nodes, the outer loop (and the program) terminates; otherwise, the matrix A is allocated with the proper size and is deallocated after the result has been printed.

```
!  Example 5.43. Warshall's algorithm with array allocation.
 program Warshall
   implicit none
   logical, allocatable, dimension(:, :) :: A
   integer :: Nodes, I, J
!  start program Warshall
   do
     print *, "⊥How⊥many⊥nodes?⊥"
     read *, Nodes
     if (Nodes <= 0) exit
     allocate (A(Nodes, Nodes))
     do I = 1, Nodes
       print *, "⊥Please⊥enter⊥next⊥row⊥of⊥adjacency⊥matrix.⊥"
       read *, A(I, :)
     end do
     do I = 1, Nodes
       do J = 1, Nodes
         if (A(J, I)) A(J, :) = A(J, :) .or. A(I, :)    ! Merge row I into row J.
       end do
     end do
     print *, "⊥CONNECTION⊥MATRIX⊥by⊥Warshall's⊥Algorithm:⊥"
     do I = 1, Nodes
       print *, A(I, :)
     end do
     deallocate (A)
   end do
 end program Warshall
```

EXAMPLE 5.44 The following program would be suitable as a driver for the Crout elimination module in Example 5.25. The arrays A, B, and X are allocated after the problem size has been determined and deallocated at the end of the program. The module procedure Solve in Example 5.25 also allocates working arrays LU and W and deallocates them at the end of the subprogram.

```
! Example 5.44. Driver program for Example 5.25
  program Driver
    use Crout_Elimination
    implicit none
    integer :: EoF, N, I
    real, allocatable :: A(:, :), B(:), X(:), E(:)
    real :: X_Norm, E_Norm
! start program Driver
    open (11, file = "testdata.txt")
    read (11, *, iostat = EoF) N
    if (EoF < 0) stop "␣End␣of␣data␣file␣reached.␣"
    allocate (A(N, N), B(N), X(N))                          ! Allocatable arrays
    do I = 1, N                    ! Read input matrix A by rows and echo print it.
      read (11, *) A(I, :)
      print *, "␣Matrix␣A,␣Row␣", I, A(I, :)
    end do
    read (11, *) B
    print *, "␣B:␣", B
    call Solve (A, B, X)
    print *, "␣X:␣", X
    deallocate (A, B, X)
  end program Driver
```

Transition Tip

- Change local arrays, if declared with larger bounds than necessary, to allocatable arrays that can be created with precisely the shape needed.

C

1.23	0.11	3.14	1.97	0.0	-3.5	-1.0
0.0	-2.6	1.01	-0.7	9.18	0.0	0.0
0.0	0.0	-5.1	0.0	1.05	0.0	3.88
0.0	0.0	0.0	1.00	-3.19	-2.87	0.0
0.0	0.0	0.0	-9.8	-1.5	6.78	0.0

C /= 0.0 C > 0.0

FIGURE 5.10. A mask is a logical array expression used to select elements of other arrays.

5.7 MASKED ASSIGNMENT (Advanced)

We have seen that many of the array intrinsic functions have an optional `Mask` argument. The mask is a logical array whose shape conforms to that of the principal array argument of the function. The intrinsic function is applied only to those elements of the principal argument array that correspond to true positions of the mask. See Figure 5.10.

The `where` Statement

A mask such as `C /= 0.0` or `C > 0.0` may similarly be applied to a whole-array assignment operation in a `where` statement:

```
real, dimension(5, 7) :: A, B, C
where (C /= 0.0) A = B / C
```

Here, `A`, `B`, and `C` are all arrays of the same shape. Assignment takes place only for those elements of `A` corresponding to nonzero elements of `C`.

Application: The Ising Model

The Ising model arises in quantum mechanics and statistical mechanics.[6] This model simulates a ferromagnetic domain and partially explains how the spins of atoms become polarized in the same direction, giving rise to a macroscopic magnetic field. In two dimensions, the Ising model can be analyzed mathematically.

In three dimensions, we simulate the Ising model with a probabilistic cellular automaton stored as a logical array of shape `(N, N, N)`. The neighbors of cells on the boundary faces of the model cube are defined by assuming cubic periodicity. The effect is to extend the grid periodically by replicating it in all directions throughout space.

Each cell (array element) is be interpreted as either an up-spin (true) or a down-spin (false). The model operates by passing through many successive states. The transition from one state to the next is governed by a local probabilistic process. At each transition, all cells change state simultaneously. Every cell either complements its spin state or not, based on the current states of its six nearest neighbors in the surrounding three-dimensional grid. The probability of complementing a given cell depends on the number of neighbors whose current state agrees with that of the given cell. A different probability is assigned for each possible number of "like-minded" neighbors from 0 to 6. A preferred version of the model assigns probability 1 when the number of agreeable neighbors is 3 or fewer; this rule seems to promote neighborhood alignments and to lead to equilibrium in the long run.

Fortran 90 Implementation of the Ising Model

Let us implement the Ising model in Fortran 90 with a subroutine named `Transition` that is called at each transition step. In this subroutine, the dummy argument `Ising` is an assumed-shape array (see Section 8.2) that takes on the shape of the corresponding actual argument. The vector `P_In` contains the transition probabilities for various numbers of like-minded neighbors from 0 to 6 (for the preferred version of the model, elements 0 through 3 have the probability value 1.0):

```
subroutine Transition (Ising, P_In)
logical, intent (in out), dimension(:, :, :) :: Ising
real, intent (in), dimension(0: 6) :: P_In
```

The local arrays `Ones`, `Count`, and `P` are declared as allocatable arrays:

```
dimension(:, :, :) Ones, Count, P
integer :: Ones, Count
real :: P
integer :: N
  :
N = Size (Ising, Dim = 1)
allocate (Ones(N, N, N), Count(N, N, N), P(N, N, N), R(N, N, N))
```

The variable `N` cannot be initialized in the type declaration because the size of an assumed-shape array is not a valid initialization expression (see Section 1.3).

The first task for the subroutine `Transition` is to count the like-minded nearest neighbors — those that have the same state as the current cell. To obtain the integer values that determine the transitions, we use the logical array `Ising` to generate a corresponding integer array, `Ones`:

```
Ones = Merge (1, 0, Mask = Ising)
```

This statement employs the intrinsic function Merge as an elemental intrinsic function (see Section 5.2). The intrinsic function result takes on the shape of the Mask argument. Elements of Ones are assigned the value 1 or 0, corresponding to true and false elements of Ising.

We construct the next array, Count, by combining the six neighbors of each cell. The Fortran 90 expression generates a separate array expression for each of the six neighbor positions, circularly shifting Ones forward or backward by one subscript position along each of its dimensions. (This circular shifting reflects the cubic periodicity.) Whole-array addition of these six shifted copies of Ones sets Count to the number of neighboring up-spins (recall that true positions of the given logical array Ising represent up-spins):

```
Count = CShift (Ones, Shift = -1, Dim = 1) &
  + CShift (Ones, Shift = 1, Dim = 1) &
  + CShift (Ones, Shift = -1, Dim = 2) &
  + CShift (Ones, Shift = 1, Dim = 2) &
  + CShift (Ones, Shift = -1, Dim = 3) &
  + CShift (Ones, Shift = 1, Dim = 3)
```

At cells where the Ising model has an up-spin, Count now has the desired value. However, where the Ising model has a down-spin, we must reverse the count:

```
where (.not. Ising) Count = 6 - Count
```

Count now holds the number of like-minded neighbors of each cell. We use these numbers to decide which cells are to be complemented. The transition probability vector P_In along with Count creates transition probabilities for each of the cells. For each I, we copy P_In(I) to all positions of P that correspond to Count == I:

```
do I = 0, 6
  where (Count == I) P = P_In(I)
end do
```

Next, we call the intrinsic subroutine Random_Number to fill the local allocated array Random with random numbers (uniform, between 0 and 1). Then, we complement the logical array Ising at each cell where the generated random number is less than the transition probability stored in the corresponding element of P. Note that positions of Ising whose Count values correspond to transition probability 1.0 are guaranteed to change since the random numbers are always less than 1.0:

```
call Random_Number (Harvest = R)
where (R < P) Ising = .not. Ising
```

The complete subroutine listing is given in Example 5.45.

EXAMPLE 5.45

```
! Example 5.45. Ising transition model.
  subroutine Transition (Ising, P_In)
    intrinsic CShift, Merge, Random_Number, Size
    logical, intent (in out), dimension(:, :, :) :: Ising    ! Assumed-shape array
    real, intent (in), dimension(0: 6) :: P_In                 ! Fixed-shape array
    dimension(:, :, :) Ones, Count, P                      ! Allocatable local arrays
    integer :: Ones, Count
    real :: P, Random
    integer :: N
! start subroutine Transition
    N = Size (Ising, Dim = 1)                      ! Get size of allocatable array.
    allocate (Ones(N, N, N), Count(N, N, N), P(N, N, N), R(N, N, N))
    Ones = Merge (1, 0, Mask = Ising)        ! Merge elementwise according to Mask.
    Count = CShift (Ones, Shift = -1, Dim = 1) &                     ! Circular shift
      + CShift (Ones, Shift = 1, Dim = 1) &
      + CShift (Ones, Shift = -1, Dim = 2) &
      + CShift (Ones, Shift = 1, Dim = 2) &
      + CShift (Ones, Shift = -1, Dim = 3) &
      + CShift (Ones, Shift = 1, Dim = 3)
    where (.not. Ising) Count = 6 - Count                   ! Assignment with "where"
    do I = 0, 6
      where (Count == I) P = P_In(I)                        ! Assignment with "where"
    end do
    call Random_Number (Harvest = Random)
    where (Random < P) Ising = .not. Ising                  ! Assignment with "where"
  end subroutine Transition
```

The where *Construct (Optional)*

EXAMPLE 5.46 A block of assignment statements, in which all left-hand sides are arrays of the same shape, may be controlled by the same mask in a `where` construct. The construct may be extended to permit two blocks of assignment statements; the first, or *Where block,* is controlled by the specified mask, and the second, or *Elsewhere block,* is controlled by the complementary mask.

```
! Example 5.46. The where construct.
    implicit none
    real, dimension(5, 7) :: A, B, C, D
      ⋮
```

```
where (C > 0.0)
  A = B / C
  D = SqRt (C)
elsewhere
  A = 0.0
  C = 0.0
  D = -1.0
end where
  ⋮
```

Note the following points:

1. The mask must be a logical array expression.
2. The statements controlled by the mask must all be assignment statements, and the left side of each must be an array whose shape is the same as that of the mask array. Other statements (such as input statements, output statements, or control statements) are not permitted. *Where blocks* cannot be nested.
3. Branching into a *Where block* or an *Elsewhere block* is not permitted.
4. The mask is evaluated before execution of any of the assignments that it controls, and masking is not affected by any operation upon the mask that may be performed during execution of the controlled blocks.

EXAMPLE 5.47 A `where` construct with no *Elsewhere block* and with only one assignment in the *Where block* is exactly equivalent to a `where` statement. The `where` construct in Example 5.47 has the same effect as the following `where` statement:

```
where (C /= 0) C = MatMul (A, B) + 2.0 / C        ! Where statement
```

```
! Example 5.47. Where construct equivalent to a where statement.
  program Jack
    implicit none
    real :: A(5, 2) = 5.0, B(2, 3) = 3.0, C(5, 3) = 1.0
! start program Jack
    C(3, :) = 0.0
    C(:, 2) = 0.0
    where (C /= 0)                                          ! Where construct
      C = MatMul (A, B) + 2.0 / C
    end where
    print *, C
  end program Jack
```

In the `where` construct of Example 5.47, as in the `where` statement that precedes this example, only nonzero elements of C will be changed by the assignment. This example illustrates the fact that masking does not affect array arguments of functions that are not applied elementwise, such as `MatMul`. However, elementwise portions of the expression, as well as the assignment operation, are controlled by the mask.

An implementation model that may be kept in mind is the following: The entire expression on the right of each assignment statement is evaluated, but the assignment operation itself is controlled by the mask. This model is unrealistic, however, because Fortran 90 does not necessarily generate errors or other side effects that would result from full evaluation of the right-hand side expression. The Fortran 90 rule is that nonelementwise operations are evaluated in full (with side effects), but elementwise operations are performed under control of the mask.

EXAMPLE 5.48 The following program illustrates an important difference between execution of an `if` construct with an `else` block and of a `where` construct with an `elsewhere` block. In an `if` construct, *exactly one* of the two blocks is selected for execution; in a `where` construct, *both* blocks are executed in sequence, with complementary masks.

```
! Example 5.48. Interaction between where and elsewhere blocks.
  program Seeking
    implicit none
    logical :: MASK(4) = (/ .TRUE., .FALSE., .TRUE, .TRUE. /)
    real :: X(5) = 0.0
! start program Seeking
    where (MASK)
      X(2: 5) = 1.0
    elsewhere
      X(1: 4) = 2.0
    end where
    print *, X
  end program Seeking
```

In Example 5.48, the elements of `X(2: 5)` that correspond to true elements of `MASK` are `X(2)`, `X(4)`, and `X(5)`. These elements will be given the value 1.0 when the *Where block* is executed. The only element of `X(1: 4)` that corresponds to a false element of `MASK` is `X(2)`, so this element will be given the value 2.0 when the *Elsewhere block* is executed. Note that `X(2)` is changed both in the *Where block* and in the *Elsewhere block*.

Because of possible interactions between the assignments in the *Where block* and those in the *Elsewhere block*, as illustrated in Example 5.48, considerable care should be taken in all but the simplest and most straightforward cases. In simple applications, a similar effect can be achieved more directly with the intrinsic function `Merge`. The following statements have the same effect as the `where` construct in Example 5.46:

```
A = Merge (B / C, 0.0, C > 0.0)
D = Merge (SqRt (C), -1.0, C > 0.0)
```

Chapter 6
Strings, Structures, and Pointers

6.1 STRINGS (CHARACTER DATA TYPE)

Computers store and process information in three principal forms: as numerical information, logical information, and character (textual or verbal) information. Historically, Fortran programs were designed for numerical calculations; text was viewed as a tool for making printed numerical output data more readable. But Fortran's character manipulation features have evolved so that they are superior to those of many other programming languages.

As we have seen, the unit of numerical information is a single number of real or integer type, and a primitive data object of logical type is a single true or false value. In contrast, Fortran always processes character data in *composite* form, as groups, or *strings*, of characters. Operations provided by the Fortran language apply to strings rather than to the individual characters (letters, digits, or punctuation symbols) in a string. Fortran can manipulate a single character only as a one-character string — that is, as a string of characters whose length happens to be 1.

Character Constants

A Fortran character constant is a sequence of characters enclosed between quotation marks, as in the following examples:[1]

```
"Do⊥it⊥with⊥Fortran⊥90."
"123"
"Energy⊥cannot⊥be⊥created⊥or⊥destroyed."
"To⊥every⊥action⊥there⊥is⊥always⊥opposed⊥an⊥equal⊥reaction."
```

[1] In this book, the symbol ⊥ is used in character constants to show explicitly that there are blank characters at certain positions in the string. When the string appears on a terminal or printer, there will, of course, be blank spaces in these positions.

The information represented by a character constant does not include the enclosing quotation marks. In character data, blanks are just as significant as other characters. Character constants are not restricted to the 84 "Fortran characters" (uppercase and lowercase alphabets, digits, blank, and 21 symbols; see Appendix C); any characters supported by the processor may be included. For example,

```
"Didn't␣you␣see␣Mary's␣book?"
"Banks␣&␣CO.;␣#6␣Marlboro␣St."
"%␣&␣;␣<␣>␣?"
"UNIX␣[TM]"
```

The character constant "123" represents the three-character sequence 1, 2, 3. The enclosing quotation marks guarantee that this character constant will not be confused with the integer constant 123. Even if all of the characters represented by a character constant are numerical digits, it is still not an integer constant because of the enclosing quotation marks. A character string composed of digits is not permitted as an arithmetic operand, for example.

Apostrophes as string delimiters (Advanced). Apostrophes (single quotes) are permitted as alternative string delimiters, and are especially appropriate for delimiting strings that contain quotation marks:

```
'␣He␣said,␣"Hello."␣'
```

When a character constant contains both quotation marks and apostrophes, neither symbol is available for delimiting the string. We must resort to a special convention: In a string delimited by quotation marks, a pair of consecutive quotation marks represents a single quotation mark; in a string delimited by apostrophes, a pair of consecutive apostrophes represents a single apostrophe:

```
"Don't␣say,␣""ain't"",␣Billy!"
"Tell␣Billy,␣'Don't␣say,␣""ain't""!'␣"
'Don''t␣say,␣"ain''t",␣Billy!'
'Tell␣Billy,␣"Don''t␣say,␣''ain''t''!"␣'
'He␣said,␣"I␣will␣be␣there␣at␣four␣o''clock."␣'
'Didn''t'
```

Note carefully that the doubled character is the same as the outermost string delimiter — that is, the symbol (quotation mark or apostrophe) that delimits the entire character constant. In the first two character constants in this list of examples, the outermost delimiters are *quotation marks*, so internal *quotation marks* are doubled; in the last four cases, the outermost delimiters are *apostrophes*, so internal *apostrophes* must be doubled.

The length of a character constant is the number of individual characters between the enclosing quotation marks, with one exception. A doubled quotation mark or a doubled apostrophe (in a string delimited by the same character) is counted only once, for the character actually represented. Remember that blank characters are counted. Thus, the lengths of the four constants

```
"Do⊥it⊥with⊥Fortran⊥90."   "123"   "Hello⊥there."   'Didn''t'
```

are 22, 3, 12, and 6, respectively. The character counts for the first and third strings include the blanks. The constant `'Didn''t'` consists of the six characters `D`, `i`, `d`, `n`, `'`, and `t`, so its length is 6 in spite of the fact that there are actually seven characters in the constant between the outer delimiting apostrophes.

Character Variables and Named Constants

Each character variable in Fortran has a fixed *length*, which is a type property that must be specified when the variable is declared. The length specifier follows the keyword `character` in the type declaration and consists of the keyword `len`, an equals sign, and an integer constant (or, preferably, the name of a constant), all enclosed in parentheses. If the length specification is omitted, the default length value 1 is assumed.

Here are some examples:

```
character (len = 10) :: Print_Buffer, String, Text
character (len = 120) :: Line
integer, paremeter :: NAMED_CONSTANT = 64
character (len = NAMED_CONSTANT) :: Conservation_Law
```

The first declaration specifies that each of the three names `Print_Buffer`, `String`, and `Text` refers to a character variable of length 10, and the second declaration specifies a single character variable `Line` of length 120. The last two lines illustrate the point that the length specifier for a character string may be a named constant. (Other ways of declaring string length are described in Appendix D.1.)

Named constants of character type are also permitted. The length specifier for a named constant of character type may be declared as usual. As an alternative (which is recommended in most cases), the length may be determined *implicitly* from the defining constant string — for example,

```
character (len = *), parameter :: WORD = "Praseodymium"
```

An asterisk replaces the usual length constant in the type declaration. The actual length of the named constant `WORD` (12, in this example) is taken from the length of the literal constant string. With this notation, two or more named string constants of different lengths can be defined in the same declaration.

Constants and variables in string length specifications. A character variable that is not a dummy argument in a procedure is a *fixed-length* character variable or an *automatic* character variable:

1. A fixed-length character variable has constant declared length.
2. An automatic character variable in a procedure is declared with a length that is a specification expression (see Section 8.4) to be evaluated at the time of procedure entry. Note that a function result may be an automatic character variable.

A character variable that is a dummy argument in a procedure is a *fixed-length* character variable, an *adjustable* character variable, or an *assumed-length* character variable. The first two of these may be considered obsolete.

1. A fixed-length character variable has constant declared length.
2. An adjustable character variable is declared with a length that is a specification expression to be evaluated at the time of procedure entry.
3. An assumed-length character variable is a dummy argument character variable for which the length is not specified. At procedure entry, such a character variable assumes the length of the corresponding actual argument.

EXAMPLE 6.1

```
! Example 6.1. Constants and variables in string length specifications.
  function A (B, C, D, N) result (G)
    implicit none
    intrinsic Len
    integer, parameter :: K = 17
    character (len = *), intent (in) :: B                   ! Assumed-length
      ! The next two lines are obsolete (see Appendix D.6).
    character (len = K), intent (in) :: C                    ! Fixed-length
    character (len = N), intent (in) :: D                      ! Adjustable
    integer, intent (in) :: N
    character (len = Len (B)) :: G, Y                           ! Automatic
    character (len = K) :: X                                 ! Fixed-length
! start function A
    G = B
     :
  end function A
```

In Example 6.1, the function A has dummy arguments B, C, and D of character type and N of integer type. B is an assumed-length dummy argument because its length specifier is an asterisk. C is a fixed-length dummy argument because its length specifier is a constant. D is an adjustable dummy argument because its length specifier is a dummy argument. (We consider fixed-length and adjustable dummy arguments to be obsolete: see

Appendix D.6.) The function result G and the local variable Y are automatic because their length specifications are expressions that can be evaluated at procedure entry. X is an ordinary fixed-length local variable of character type.

Dialogue: Empty strings

"Can the length of a string be zero, Miss Flores?"

"Yes, Cathy. A string whose length is zero is called an *empty string* or a *null string*. Fortran 90 character operations are carefully designed to give valid results for empty strings."

"How can I write a character constant with zero length? I suppose I could write two quotation marks in a row with nothing between them."

"That's right, Cathy. And a character *variable* can also have zero length — you just have to declare it with zero as the value of the length specifier. You might not write the integer constant 0 as the length specification; more likely, the specification would be an expression whose value happens to be zero in a specific case. A zero-length string might be a procedure dummy argument of character type whose length depends on some values in the host program or in a referencing subprogram."

EXAMPLE 6.2 For making a rough plot of a function, we print a series of lines, each containing a symbol preceded by a certain number of blanks, determined by the function value. When the function takes on its minimum value, there are no blanks to print.

```
! Example 6.2. Empty strings.
  subroutine Sandpaper (Fun_Val)
    integer :: Fun_Val
    character (len = Fun_Val) :: Blanks = ""
! start subroutine Sandpaper
    print *, Blanks, "*"
  end subroutine Sandpaper
```

For each line to be printed, we call the subroutine with an integer argument whose value is between 0 and, say, 100, representing the function value. When the argument value is 0, the first list item in the print list is a zero-length string, so the asterisk symbol is the first character to be actually printed on the line.

Character Assignment

The value of a character constant or variable may be assigned to another variable of character type and of the same length, in the usual way. Mixed-length assignment is also possible. Length coercion rules are described later in this chapter.

EXAMPLE 6.3

```
! Example 6.3. Character assignment.
  program Assignment
    implicit none
    integer, parameter :: S_LEN = 9
    character (len = S_LEN) :: First, Second
! start program Assignment
    First = "⊥summary⊥"
    Second = First
  end program Assignment
```

A character variable may be initialized in the type declaration, in the usual way:

```
character (len = 3) :: First = "ABC", Second = "XYZ"
```

Character Arrays

Arrays of character strings are frequently required in applications. All the elements of a character array have the same length; there is no way to create a Fortran array containing some character strings of one length and others of a different length. (This rule conforms to the general principle that all the elements of a given array must have the same type, type properties, and other attributes.)

Character arrays in the following example store the names of certain amino acids and other alphabetic or symbolic information concerning a set of chemical compounds.

EXAMPLE 6.4

```
! Example 6.4. Arrays of character strings.
  program String_Arrays
    implicit none
    integer, parameter :: LN = 10, ARRAY_SIZE = 5
    character (len = LN), dimension(ARRAY_SIZE) :: Amino_Acids, Compounds
! start program String_Arrays
    Amino_Acids(1) = "Glycine⊥⊥⊥"
    Amino_Acids(2) = "Alanine⊥⊥⊥"
    Amino_Acids(3) = "Valine⊥⊥⊥⊥"
    Amino_Acids(4) = "Leucine⊥⊥⊥"
    Amino_Acids(5) = "Tyrosine⊥⊥"
    Compounds(1) = "Phenol⊥⊥⊥⊥"
    print *, Amino_Acids, Compounds(1)
  end program String_Arrays
```

Example 6.4 contains declarations for two 5-element arrays. Each array element is a character string of length 10 that holds the name of a chemical. The assignments store character information in each of the first five elements of the array named `Amino_Acids` and in the first element of the array named `Compounds`. As usual, an array element name consists of the array name followed by a subscript expression in parentheses.

Input and Output of Character Data

List-Directed Character Input and Output

We have already seen some examples using list-directed output to print a short message along with numerical results. The form of a list-directed input or output statement does not change when character data is included in the list.

EXAMPLE 6.5.

```
! Example 6.5. List-directed character input and output.
  program Chario
    implicit none
    integer, parameter :: S = 7
    character (len = S) :: First, Second
! start program Chario
    print *, "⊥Please⊥enter⊥two⊥words.⊥"
    read *, First, Second
    if (First == Second) then
      print *, First, "⊥and⊥", Second, "⊥are⊥equal.⊥"
    else
      print *, First, "⊥and⊥", Second, "⊥are⊥different.⊥"
    end if
  end program Chario
```

As with other data types, constants are permitted in the *Output list* of a `print` statement but not in the *Input list* of a `read` statement.

Input data for a list item of character type may be delimited with quotation marks or with apostrophes. Blank characters between the delimiters are, of course, permitted and become part of the character data value; blanks anywhere else among list-directed input data items are treated as separators.

Internal quotation marks and apostrophes in the input data items follow the same rules as for character constants: Apostrophes are permitted within a string delimited by quotation marks, and vice versa. Apostrophes or quotation marks must be doubled within a string whose outer delimiter is the same character.

If the declared length of an input list item of character type is different from the delimited string length on the input device, truncation from the right or padding on the right is applied, in the same way as for mixed-length string assignment (as described later). The input list item may be a zero-length string, or the input data item may consist of a pair of consecutive quotation marks or apostrophes denoting a zero-length string.

Undelimited Input

It is often inconvenient to delimit character input data with quotation marks or apostrophes, especially when data is entered at the terminal keyboard. In simple cases, where no ambiguity can occur, input data for a list item of character type may be *undelimited;* that is, it may be written without enclosing quotation marks or apostrophes. The input data must not contain any blank, comma, or slash characters.[2] (In particular, an input string consisting entirely of one or more blanks must be *delimited.* Also, an input data item representing an empty string cannot be expressed in undelimited form.) In the following example, input data for the read statement can consist simply of the letter `M` or `F`, without delimiting quotation marks:

```
print *, "⊥Please⊥enter⊥sex⊥of⊥cat:⊥M⊥or⊥F.⊥"
read *, Sex
if (Sex == "M") then                              ! Cat is male.
```

Note that a Fortran program does not need any special indication as to whether delimited or undelimited input is expected. In fact, a `read` statement will accept a mixture of delimited and undelimited input. If input data is to be entered from a terminal, it could be undelimited in simple cases and delimited when the data contains blanks or when it violates other restrictions on undelimited input. Consider Example 6.6.

EXAMPLE 6.6

```
! Example 6.6. List-directed input of (possibly undelimited) character data.
 program Deli
   implicit none
   integer, parameter :: S_LEN = 20
   character (len = S_LEN) :: Nutrient

! start program Deli
   do
     print *, "⊥Please⊥enter⊥the⊥name⊥of⊥a⊥nutrient.⊥"
     read *, Nutrient
     if (Nutrient == "⊥") exit
     print *, "⊥Your⊥diet⊥should⊥include⊥", Nutrient
   end do
 end program Deli
```

[2] Furthermore, the item must not begin with a quotation mark, an apostrophe, or an integer constant and an asterisk; and it must not cross a record boundary. Items that violate these rules might be confused with other list-directed input forms.

Data for Example 6.6 could be entered at the terminal as follows:

```
Carbohydrate
Protein
Iron
"Vitamin⊥A"
"Fiber,⊥soluble"
Manganese
"⊥"
```

The input strings that do not contain any blanks or commas are undelimited, but those containing blanks or commas are enclosed in quotation marks. The final item, which consists of a single blank character to terminate the input process, is also delimited. Note that strings with *internal* quotation marks or apostrophes, such as `Einstein's`, may be undelimited.

When character values are printed by list-directed `print` statements, enclosing quotation marks do not appear in the output. Also, quotation marks or apostrophes within the item that are doubled to match the enclosing delimiter appear singly in the output. For example, output from the statement

```
print *, "⊥Tell⊥Billy,⊥'Don't⊥say,⊥""ain't""!'⊥"
```

would appear as follows:

```
Tell Billy, 'Don't say, "ain't"!'
```

Explicitly Formatted Character Output

Sometimes, it is important to write character data in a carefully controlled format — for example, for generating a text file that is to be read later by another program. Each record of the output file may be prepared as an internal "line image," in one or more strings of characters inside the computer, and then written to the file.

However, because list-directed output may introduce some processor-dependent spacing, it may be desirable to write the records with explicit formatting. (An extensive discussion of explicitly formatted input and output appears in Chapter 9.)

If the output list consists of a single character string, the format specification may be written simply as `"(A)"`, as in the following examples:

```
print "(A)", Line_of_Text
write (Unit = 3, "(A)") Line_of_Text
```

Fortran will transmit all of the characters from the string named `Line_of_Text`, without inserting any extra spacing or other extraneous characters.

If several strings are to be written to the same output record, the number of strings is inserted just before the `A` format code. In the following example, there are three strings in the output list, so the format specification is `"(3A)"`:

```
print "(3A)", First_Part, Second_Part, Third_Part
write (Unit = 3, "(3A)") First_Part, Second_Part, Third_Part
```

Fortran will transmit the strings consecutively and will not insert any extraneous characters between the strings. (See also Section 9.2 and Appendix D.10.)

Combining Character Data with Other Types

An input or output list may include references to character data intermixed with references to data of other types, as illustrated in Example 6.7.

EXAMPLE 6.7

```
! Example 6.7. Input and output including character data.
 program Combine
   implicit none
   intrinsic Exp
   integer, parameter :: S_LEN = 14
   integer :: Atomic_Number
   real :: Atomic_Mass
   character (len = S_LEN) :: El_Name, Author = "␣María␣Flores␣"
   double precision :: Big_One = 1.0D9
   complex :: Pi_Eye = (0.0, 3.14159)
! start program Combine
   read *, El_Name, Atomic_Number, Atomic_Mass
   print *, Big_One, El_Name, Atomic_Number
   print *, X, Atomic_Number + 2, Author, Exp (Pi_Eye)
 end program Combine
```

Notice that the character variable `Author`, the double-precision variable `Big_One`, and the complex variable `Pi_Eye` are initialized in the program of Example 6.7. `El_Name`, `Atomic_Number`, and `Atomic_Mass` are not.

Data for input with the `read` statement in this program must, of course, be prepared with care. The *Input list* contains three variables whose types are a mixture of integer, real, and character. The data items in this example must be prepared in the proper input forms for the type sequence (character, integer, real), corresponding to the sequence of types in the *Input list*. The data items must be separated — for example, by one or more blanks.

Character data for `El_Name` will be a sequence of up to 14 characters, integer data for `Atomic_Number` will consist of a string of digits without a decimal point, and real data for `Atomic_Mass` may contain a decimal point or an exponent (or both). The character data item may be enclosed in quotation marks or apostrophes, or it may be undelimited if the restrictions that apply to this form are carefully observed. For example, the following input data would be suitable:

```
"␣Molybdenum␣␣␣" 42 95.99
```

Summary of Facts about Character Processing

- Fortran character data is always processed in composite form, as strings. Fortran treats a single character as a string whose length is 1. Strings of length 0 are permitted.
- A character constant is a sequence of characters enclosed between quotation marks or apostrophes.
- A variable of character type has a fixed length, which may be defined by a length specifier in the type declaration.
- The value of a character constant or variable can be assigned to a character variable of the same length. Mixed-length assignment is also permitted.
- Character data may be referenced in an input or output list. A character input item that does not contain any blank, comma, or slash characters may be an undelimited input string.
- Character data may be interspersed with data of other types in an input or output list.

Substrings and Character Expressions

Substrings

It is often necessary to refer to a portion of a string in a character expression. Fortran provides a facility to permit such a reference: A parenthesized *substring* specification may follow the name of a character variable or constant. The substring specification gives the first and last character positions of the designated substring. Character positions in a string are always numbered from 1. For example, the first four character positions of a string named `Compound` would be designated as `Compound(1: 4)`, and the second through ninth character positions of `El_Name` would be `El_Name(2: 9)`.

EXAMPLE 6.8

```
! Example 6.8. Substring notation.
  program Substrings
    implicit none
    integer, parameter :: S_LEN = 18
    character (len = S_LEN) :: &
      El_Name, Compound = "Zinc␣Hydroxide"
! start program Substrings
    El_Name = "Praseodymium␣␣␣␣␣␣␣"
    print *, Compound(1: 4)
    print *, El_Name(2: 9)
  end program Substrings
```

Execution of the program in Example 6.8 produces the following output:

```
Zinc
raseodym
```

A substring name consists of a name (the name of a character variable or constant), followed by a parenthesized substring designator that must include a colon. The integer expression to the left of the colon indicates the first character position of the desired substring, and the integer expression to the right of the colon indicates the final character position. See Figure 6.1.

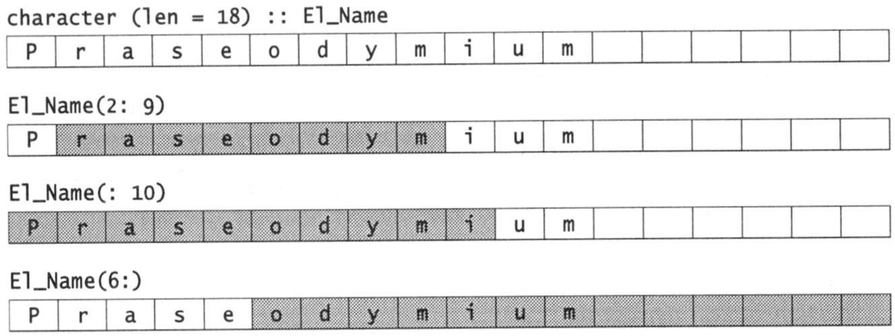

FIGURE 6.1. Substring examples.

A special meaning is attached to a substring designator in which one or both of the expressions (but not the colon) are omitted. Such a substring designator names a substring consisting of all character positions from 1 up to a certain point or from a certain point to the end of the string. In Figure 6.1, `El_Name(: 10)` is the same substring as `El_Name(1: 10)` — namely,

```
Praseodymi
```

while `El_Name(6: )` is the same substring as `El_Name(6: 18)` — namely,

```
odymium⊥⊥⊥⊥⊥⊥
```

Thus, a substring designator consists of parentheses enclosing a colon that separates two optional integer expressions; that is, it may have any of the following forms:

(*First position* : *Last position*)
(*First position* :)
(: *Last position*)
(:)

The *First position* and the *Last position* are integer expressions. If the *First position* is omitted, the default first character position is 1; that is, the substring begins with the first character of the string. If the *Last position* is omitted, the substring ends with the last character of the string. If both expressions are omitted, the entire string is denoted, just as if the character variable name were written without a substring designator. The colon must not be omitted.

In a substring specification, designator expressions that are not omitted must have valid values. Unless the substring specifier denotes an empty string, the first character position must be at least 1 and the last character position must not be beyond the length of the string.

Remember that the characters in a string are *always* numbered from 1. Although a lower subscript bound for an *array* may be declared to have a value other than 1, this option is not available for numbering character positions within a string.

Substring length. The length of a substring is the number of characters it contains, which may be calculated from the formula *Last position First position* `1`. The default *First position* or *Last position* is substituted in this formula if the designator is omitted. In particular, when *First position* is omitted, the substring length value is the same as *Last position*.

If the *First position* value is larger than the *Last position*, the substring is an empty string; more precisely, the length formula is `Max (0,` *Last position First position* `1)`.

A single character position may be referenced as a substring by giving the same value to both substring designator expressions; the only way to refer to a single character within a string is to treat it as a substring whose length is 1.

EXAMPLE 6.9 The following program reads a list of names from a file and prints the first letter of each.

```
! Example 6.9. Substring notation for a single character.
  program Print_Initials
    implicit none
    integer, parameter :: SL = 12
    integer :: I, EoF
    character (len = SL) :: Name
! start program Print_Initials
    open (11, file = "roster⊥txt")
    do
      read (11, *, iostat = EoF) Name
      if (EoF < 0) stop
      print *, Name(1: 1), "⊥", Name
    end do
  end program Print_Initials
```

Assignment to a substring. Assignment may replace a substring of a character string without altering the remaining characters. When a substring name appears on the left side of an assignment statement, only the designated character positions are assigned new values. Note that assignment to a zero-length substring has no effect.

EXAMPLE 6.10 The following program replaces the fifth through ninth characters of Praseodymium with XXXXX.

```
! Example 6.10. Replacement of a substring.
  program Replace
    implicit none
    integer, paremeter :: SL = 12
    character (len = SL) :: El_59 = "Praseodymium"
! start program Replace
    El_59(5: 9) = "XXXXX"
    print *, El_59                                  ! Prints: PrasXXXXXium
  end program Replace
```

In a character assignment statement, the same character variable can be referenced on both the right and left sides:

```
El_59(1: 3) = El_59(10: 12)
```

Character positions to which new values are to be assigned may also be referenced in the character expression on the right side. In the following assignment statement, for example, character positions 2 and 3 are referenced on both sides:

```
El_59(1: 3) = El_59(2: 4)
```

The usual rule applies: Fortran completely evaluates the expression on the right before assignment to the variable on the left takes place.

Substring input and output. When any variable name appears in the *Input list* of a read statement, execution of the statement is analogous to assignment with the variable name on the left. As with assignment, input to a substring variable affects only the designated character positions; the remaining characters of the string retain their previous values. Substrings are permitted in output lists, in the same way as other expressions.

EXAMPLE 6.11 The following program reads 5 characters into a designated substring, El_59(5: 9), and then prints the entire string, El_59, and a different substring, El_59(3: 6).

```
! Example 6.11. Substring input and output.
  program Sub_I_O
    implicit none
    integer, paremeter :: SL = 12
    character (len = SL) :: El_59 = "Praseodymium"
! start program Sub_I_O
    read *, El_59(5: 9)                    ! Input record contains "XXXXX".
    print *, El_59                                   ! Prints: PrasXXXXXium
    print *, El_59(3: 6)                                     ! Prints: asXX
  end program Sub_I_O
```

Substring of a constant. We have seen that a substring designator may be applied to a named character constant. A literal character constant may also be qualified by a substring designator. This feature might be useful for selecting a variable portion of a fixed string.[3]

EXAMPLE 6.12 The following program converts uppercase letters to lowercase letters. (Compare Example 6.17.) The intrinsic function `Index` is explained later in this chapter. Note that the variable `Next` selects a particular letter of the lowercase alphabet to be assigned to `Text(S: S)`.

```
! Example 6.12. Substring of a constant.
  program Sub_Con
    implicit none
    intrinsic Index
    integer, parameter :: STRING_LENGTH = 120
    character (len = STRING_LENGTH) :: Text
    integer S, Next
! start program Sub_Con
    read *, Text
    do S = 1, STRING_LENGTH
      Next = Index ("ABCDEFGHIJKLMNOPQRSTUVWXYZ", Text(S: S))
      if (Next /= 0) Text(S: S) = "abcdefghijklmnopqrstuvwxyz" (Next: Next)
    end do
    print *, Text
  end program Sub_Con
```

Substring of a character array. A substring of a *whole array* of strings is not permitted because of ambiguous notation. If `String_Array` is an array of strings, for example, is `String_Array(1: 5)` a substring or an array section? Fortran's answer is that it is an array section.

Substrings of *array sections* are permitted, however. The array section is designated first, and then the substring. As we have seen, an entire array can be designated with section notation. Here are two examples.

```
String_Array (1: 5)(1: 5)
String_Array (:)(1: 5)
```

The first of these examples is an array of five strings, each of length 5, obtained by selecting the designated substring from each array element in the section. The second is an array of strings consisting of the substring `(1: 5)` from each element of `String_Array`.

[3] Curiously, Fortran 90 considers such a string to be neither a variable nor a constant.

Concatenation of Character Expressions

A pair of strings may be joined into a single longer string. This operation is known as *concatenation*. It is specified by an operator that consists of two slashes written between a pair of character expressions. For example, "ABC" // "DEFG" represents the concatenation of the three-character string ABC with the four-character string DEFG to form the seven-character string ABCDEFG.

The character expressions that we have encountered so far have been character constants, character variable names, and substring names. We now see that a character expression can be formed by concatenation of character expressions. Later on, we shall encounter functions that produce values of character type; a reference to such a function is also a character expression.

Still another way to form a character expression is by enclosing a character expression in parentheses. However, there is little need to do this because there is only one operator; thus, there are no precedence problems with character expressions.

EXAMPLE 6.13

```
! Example 6.13. Concatenation of character expressions.
  program Joint
    implicit none
    integer, parameter :: LFS = 6, LL = 9, LS = 2, LAX = 14
    character (len = LFS) :: First, Second
    character (len = LL) :: Longer
    character (len = LS) :: Small
    character (len = LAX) :: A, X
! start program Joint
    First = "Hello."
    Longer = First // "␣z␣"                           ! Longer = "Hello.␣z␣"
    A = Longer(1: 7) // Longer(1: 7)                ! Longer(1: 7) = "Hello.␣"
    print *, Longer, A, ":"
    Small = "␣␣"
    Second = "there."
    X = Small // First(: 5) // "␣" // Second          ! X = "␣␣Hello␣there."
    print *, X
  end program Joint
```

Execution of the program in Example 6.13 produces the following result:

```
Hello.␣z
Hello.␣Hello.␣
␣␣Hello␣there.
```

Note that concatenation of more than two strings in a single expression is permitted. The strings are all joined from left to right, just as they appear in the expression.

In a character assignment statement, it is permissible for character positions mentioned in the expression on the right side to be included in the string named on the left side as well. As usual, the expression on the right is fully evaluated before any assignment takes place (compare the whole-array assignment model described in Section 5.2). For example:

```
X = "ZZ" // X(3: 14)
A = A(1: 8) // First
X = X(: 7) // "⊥" // X(9: )
X(1: 5) = "ABC" // X(2: 3)
```

Character expressions involving concatenation may appear in a `print` statement. Adding the following statement to the program in Example 6.13,

```
print *, "Because⊥it's⊥" // Second
```

would produce the printed result

```
Because⊥it's⊥there.
```

Mixed-Length String Assignment

Character assignment statements in the preceding examples have consistently been constructed with an expression on the left of precisely the same length as the variable or substring on the right. However, Fortran permits assignments in which the two sides have different lengths and provides rules that define the result of such an assignment:

1. In a character assignment, if the expression on the right is longer than the string (designated on the left) to which it is assigned, the expression is *truncated from the right* before assignment takes place. That is, characters are deleted from the end of the string if necessary.
2. If the expression is shorter than the string to which it is assigned, the expression is *extended with blanks on the right* before assignment takes place. That is, blank characters are appended to the end of the string if necessary.

   In the following examples, assume that `Datum` is a string of length 6.

Assignment statement	Result
`Datum = "ABCDEFGHI"`	ABCDEF
`Datum = "ABCD"`	ABCD⊥⊥

The length of the character constant `"ABCDEFGHI"` is 9, so the three rightmost characters are dropped and the first six characters are assigned to `Datum`. The length of the character constant `"ABCD"` is only 4, so two blanks are appended at the right.

Assignment to the character variable of length 6 always results in all six characters of `Datum` being replaced, regardless of whether the expression on the right is longer or shorter than six characters. If the expression is longer, the excess characters are, in effect, ignored. If it is shorter, extra blanks are inserted to complete the assignment so that characters of `Datum` for which no specific characters are provided in the expression are replaced by blank characters.

If it is desired to leave some characters of Datum unchanged during the assignment operation, then only a substring of Datum should be specified on the left. Suppose that Datum contains the characters ABCDEF before the following sequence of three assignments statements is executed:

Assignment statement	Result
`Datum(3: 4) = "XY"`	ABXYEF
`Datum(1: 1) = "LMN"`	LBXYEF
`Datum(3: 5) = "H"`	LBH⊥⊥F

The last two of these examples illustrate the fact that the rules of truncating or extending with blanks apply to a substring as well as to a character variable. When the substring on the left has length 1, for example, and the expression on the right is "LMN", only the first character, L, is assigned, while the remaining characters of Datum remain unchanged. Also, assignment of "H" to a substring of length 3 results in replacement of the entire substring after extending the one-character expression with two added blanks; again, the characters of Datum that are not part of the specified substring remain unchanged.

The same rules also apply, of course, when the character expression on the right-hand side of an assignment statement includes variables, substrings, or concatenation. The rules apply during input as well: The input data value is truncated or extended on the right before being assigned to the character data item specified in the *Input list*. The rules are not needed for list-directed character output because the number of characters transmitted is determined by the length of the character expression in the *Output list*.

EXAMPLE 6.14

```
! Example 6.14. Concatenation with mixed-length assignment.
  program Mix_Con
    implicit none
    integer, parameter :: LL = 10
    character (len = LL) :: Prefix
! start program Mix_Con
    Prefix = "The"
    print *, Prefix // "⊥impedance"
  end program Mix_Con
```

In the program of Example 6.14, the assignment statement places "The" in the first three character positions of Prefix and fills the remaining seven positions with blanks. Fortran does not "remember" that these seven blanks were merely inserted to fulfill the requirements of mixed-length assignment. Thus, the concatenation operation joins the second string to the end of the 10-character variable `Prefix` and the printed output will appear as follows:

```
The␣␣␣␣␣␣␣␣impedance
```

A more satisfactory result would be obtained by concatenating only a substring of `Prefix` with the constant string:[4]

```
print *, Prefix(: 3) // "␣impedance"
```

Mixed-length assignment rules apply to character assignments with length incompatibilities. Assignment must not mix character data with numerical data or with data of other noncharacter types. If either side of an assignment involves character data, then the other side must also have character type. However, relational expressions and functions applied to character strings may produce expressions of other types, as we shall see.

Comparison of Character Expressions

A pair of character expressions may be compared in a relational expression. The value of a character relational expression is either true or false. Here are some examples:

```
implicit none
integer :: J
integer, parameter :: LS = 6
character (len = LS) :: First, Hat, Good, H, F8
if (First >= Hat) J = 1
if (Good /= "pretty") stop
if (H == F8(1: 3) // "xyz") then
```

A character relational expression is a logical expression, and it can be assigned as the value of a logical variable or used in the same way as any other logical expression. The expressions to be compared in a character relational expression must both have character type.

Evaluation of character relational expressions depends upon a *collating sequence* defined by the particular processor for individual Fortran and non-Fortran characters. Character comparison operations for processors whose collating sequence is the ISO standard ASCII sequence are described next. Alternatives are described later in this chapter.

---

[4] Or, more generally, `Trim (Prefix) // ....` The Fortran intrinsic function `Trim` removes trailing blanks from its argument string. Note that assigning `Trim (Prefix)` to a (fixed-length) character variable has little value, but the function is valuable in concatenation and in other character expressions. Another intrinsic function, `Len_Trim`, returns the length of its argument string, ignoring trailing blanks. Some character intrinsic functions are described later in this chapter, and a complete list appears in Appendix A.

In the ISO standard ASCII sequence, the blank (space) character is ranked lowest, followed by

! " # $ % & ' ( ) * + , - . /
digits (0 through 9)
: ; < = > ? @
UPPERCASE ALPHABET (A through Z)
[\ ] ^ _ '
lowercase alphabet (a through z)
{ | } ~

Ranking of *strings* of characters is *lexicographic*. It is implied in the customary way by the ranking of individual characters: Given a pair of strings that are the *same* length, the initial characters of the two strings are first compared. Unless these characters are identical, the "larger" string is the one with the higher-ranked initial character. If the initial character is the same in both strings, the comparison proceeds with the second character of each string. Thus, lexicographic ranking of strings is determined solely by the first character position at which the two strings differ. If there is no such position, then the two strings are equal.

For example, the condition

```
"Douglas␣Stephen␣␣␣" < "Douglass␣Frederick"
```

is true. For purposes of the comparison, Fortran ignores the first seven character positions in these strings because they contain the identical characters `Douglas`. The comparison depends upon the remaining portion of each string — namely, `␣Stephen␣␣␣` on the left and `s␣Frederick` on the right. The key characters to be compared are a blank on the left and `s` on the right; therefore, the string on the left is considered "smaller" than the string on the right. Also true are the conditions

```
"April␣A" < "April␣B"
"April␣␣" < "April␣1"
"April␣1999" < "April␣2000"
"April␣␣␣␣␣" < "April␣morn"
```

Character strings of *different* lengths can also be compared. Fortran treats the shorter string as if it were extended with blanks to the length of the longer string. For example, the following conditions are considered true:

```
"as" < "aster"
"there" > "the"
"a␣book" < "a␣bookie"
"xyz" == "xyz␣␣"
```

The actual comparison is made as if the shorter strings were extended to `"as␣␣␣"`, `"the␣␣"`, `"a␣book␣␣"`, and `"xyz␣␣"`.

Intrinsic Functions for Character Processing

Len *(String Length)*

The intrinsic function Len, with a character string as its argument, returns a result of integer type that is the length of the character string. There is little benefit in applying this function to a string that has been declared with constant length since the result value will simply be the declared length. However, the function may be applied to a character expression or used in other situations where the length is less obvious. Some examples follow.

A string that is a named constant may have an asterisk as its length specifier. The length is then determined by the character expression (often a literal constant string) that gives a value to the named constant.

```
character (len = *), parameter :: STRING_A = &
  "⊥Matter⊥is⊥a⊥form⊥of⊥energy.⊥"
intrinsic Len
integer :: I = Len (STRING_A)
```

Here, the length of the named character constant STRING_A is 29, so the variable I is initialized to the value 29.

A dummy argument string may have an asterisk as its length specifier (see Section 8.3). The length is then "assumed" from the actual argument:

```
subroutine Holy (String_B)
intrinsic Len
character (len = *) :: String_B
character (len = Len (String_B)) :: String_C
```

In the subroutine, the local character variable String_C will have the same length as the dummy argument String_B. The length of a local variable in a procedure can be similarly derived from the length of another string variable that is inherited from the host or one that is imported from a module (see Sections 2.4 and 7.2).

As a variant of the previous example, the *function result length* may be derived from the length of a dummy argument or from the length of an imported or inherited variable:

```
character (len = *) function Moley (String_B) result (String_C)
intrinsic Len
character (len = *) :: String_B
character (len = Len (String_B)) :: String_C
```

The function result variable String_C will have the same length as the dummy argument String_B.

The intrinsic function Len may be applied to a character expression that has been formed by concatenation:

```
I = Len (String_D // String_E)
```

Here, the value assigned to `I` is the sum of the lengths of the two operand strings.

Note that the spelling of the intrinsic function `Len` is the same as the keyword `len`. For readability, in this text intrinsic function names are capitalized and keywords are written entirely in lowercase. However, Fortran ignores case and distinguishes between the intrinsic function and the keyword on the basis of context.

Index *(Pattern Matching)*

Applications involving lines or paragraphs of text frequently require that a certain (usually short) pattern be located within a (longer) string. For example, we might wish to search the string `Matter␣cannot␣be␣destroyed.` to find the location of the pattern `can`. The Fortran intrinsic function `Index` provides a simple way to perform such a search or pattern matching operation.

The function has two arguments of character type. The first identifies the longer string to be searched, while the second indicates the pattern to be located within the longer string. The function value is an integer giving the beginning character position of the pattern as a substring of the longer string. If the pattern is not found, the result from `Index` will be 0. For example, the value of

```
Index ("Matter␣cannot␣be␣destroyed.", "can")
```

is 8, since `can` is found as a substring beginning at the eighth character position in the longer string.

To extend this example, let's consider the following program:

EXAMPLE 6.15

```
! Example 6.15. Pattern matching with the intrinsic function Index.
 program One_Pattern
   implicit none
   intrinsic Index
   integer, parameter :: Lines = 5, L_S = 50
   character (len = *), parameter :: Pattern = "meter"
   integer :: Loc(Lines), Loop
   character (len = L_S) :: Scale(Lines)
! start program One_Pattern
   Scale(1) = "␣One␣centimeter␣equals␣ten␣millimeters.␣"
   Scale(2) = "␣One␣decimeter␣equals␣ten␣centimeters.␣"
   Scale(3) = "␣One␣meter␣equals␣ten␣decimeters.␣"
   Scale(4) = "␣Ten␣thermometers␣equals␣one␣meter.␣"                    ! ☺☺
   Scale(5) = "␣This␣is␣the␣key␣to␣the␣metric␣system.␣"
   do Loop = 1, Lines
     Loc(Loop) = Index (String = Scale(Loop), Substring = Pattern)
   end do
   print *, Loc
 end program One_Pattern
```

In Example 6.15, the first occurrence of the pattern `meter` in `Scale(1)` is at positions 11 to 15 in the word `centimeter`, so the first printed result will be `11`. The remaining results will be `10`, `6`, `12`, and `0`.

We note the following points concerning the function `Index` :

1. The function value is 0 if the pattern being searched for is not present anywhere in the given string. `Loc(5)` will be 0 because the pattern `meter` does not occur in `Scale(5)`.
2. The function value is also 0 in case the length of the second argument string exceeds that of the first argument, as in the expression

```
Index (String = "met", Substring = "meter")
```

3. If the second argument is a null string, the function value is always 1.

Of course the result from `Index` does not depend upon whether the string and the pattern are written in the program as variables or as constants. If the pattern is a variable, remember that all characters including any trailing blanks will be included in the search. It may be appropriate to express the pattern as a substring.

Note that the pattern may be found in the middle of a word. To find `the` only when it stands alone as a separate word, as in `Scale(5)`, we would have to look for the pattern consisting of the five characters `⊥the⊥`. The value of the expression

```
Index (Scale(5), "⊥the⊥")
```

is 9, indicating the occurrence of the five-character pattern `⊥the⊥` beginning at the ninth character of the longer string.

As a variant, we may wish to find *all* occurrences of a given pattern in a longer string, such as all appearances of `the`, either as a separate word or as part of another word, within `Scale(5)`. The expression

```
Index (Scale(5), "the")
```

(without blanks in the search pattern) has the integer value 10, indicating the location of the first occurrence. The next appearance of the same string can be found by searching a string that does not contain the case already located. A satisfactory technique is to search the substring beginning just beyond the location at which the pattern was already found:[5]

```
Min = 0
Loc = Index (Scale(5)(Min + 1), "the")
Min = Min + Loc
Loc = Index (Scale(5)(Min + 1: ), "the")
```

[5] The suggested method works, but, for searching very long strings, much more efficient methods are known, including the Knuth-Morris-Pratt, Boyer-Moore, and Rabin-Karp algorithms. See Robert Sedgewick, *Algorithms,* 2nd ed. (Reading, Mass.: Addison-Wesley, 1988), chap. 19.

The second value of Loc will be the location of the pattern within the substring beginning at the eleventh character of Scale(5) — that is, within the substring

```
he␣key␣to␣the␣metric␣system.
```

The second value of Loc is therefore 11, since the pattern the appears as characters 11 to 13 of this substring. The expression Min + Loc then gives the location of the second occurrence of the pattern in the original string — that is, position 21.

EXAMPLE 6.16 The following program uses this technique to examine each string in the array and find all occurrences of the pattern within each string. Note that the inner loop could have been written as a simple do, but, for safety, the loop is bounded with the string length L_S (as explained in Section 4.2).

```
! Example 6.16. Locate all occurrences of a pattern.
  program All_Patterns
    implicit none
    intrinsic Index
    integer, parameter :: Lines = 5, L_S = 50
    character (len = *), parameter :: Pattern = "the"
    integer :: Loop, Loc, I, Min
    character (len = L_S) :: Scale(Lines)
! start program All_Patterns
    Scale(1) = "␣One␣centimeter␣equals␣ten␣millimeters.␣"
    Scale(2) = "␣One␣decimeter␣equals␣ten␣centimeters.␣"
    Scale(3) = "␣One␣meter␣equals␣ten␣decimeters.␣"
    Scale(4) = "␣Ten␣thermometers␣equals␣one␣meter.␣"
    Scale(5) = "␣This␣is␣the␣key␣to␣the␣metric␣system.␣"
    do Loop = 1, Lines
      Min = 0
      do I = 1, L_S
        Loc = Index (Scale(Loop)(Min + 1: ), Pattern)
        if (Loc == 0) exit
        Min = Min + Loc
        print *, Loop, Loc, Min
      end do
    end do
  end program All_Patterns
```

The program in Example 6.16 prints the following results, indicating that the pattern is found in the fourth string at position 6, and in the fifth string at position 10 and again at position 21:

```
4 6 6
5 10 10
5 11 21
```

EXAMPLE 6.17 The function Index can also be applied to the task of character substitution — that is, changing all occurrences of a particular character to some other specific character. The following program provides a practical example: conversion of uppercase letters in a string to the corresponding lowercase letters.

```
! Example 6.17. Convert uppercase letters to lowercase letters.
 program Decapitation
   implicit none
   intrinsic Index
   integer, parameter :: STRING_LENGTH = 40
   character (len = STRING_LENGTH) :: Text_1, Text_2

! start program Decapitation
   read *, Text_1
   print *, Text_1
   Text_2 = Decap (Text_1)
   print *, Text_2

 contains

   function Decap (String) result (New_String)
     intrinsic Len
     character (len = *) :: String              ! Assumed length (see Section 8.3)
     character (len = Len (String)) :: New_String
     integer, parameter :: ALPHABET = 26
     character (len = ALPHABET) :: &
       UCAlph = "ABCDEFGHIJKLMNOPQRSTUVWXYZ", &
         LCAlph = "abcdefghijklmnopqrstuvwxyz"
     integer :: Next, S

  ! start function Decap
     New_String = String

     do S = 1, Len (String)
       Next = Index (UCAlph, String(S: S))
       if (Next /= 0) New_String(S: S) = LCAlph (Next: Next)
     end do

   end function Decap

 end program Decapitation
```

In the program of Example 6.17, each character of `String` in its turn becomes the second argument to `Index`, with the entire uppercase alphabet string `UCAlph` as the first argument. If the `String` character is an uppercase letter, the value of `Index` will be nonzero. Furthermore, this same value will indicate the particular character from the lowercase alphabet `LCAlph` that is to be assigned to `New_String` in place of the uppercase letter.

`AChar` *and* `IAChar` *(Integer Value of a Character)*

It is often useful to be able to obtain an integer "code number" from a single character of text. The Fortran intrinsic function `IAChar` has an argument consisting of a single character — that is, a character string of length 1 — and produces an integer value giving a unique code value for each different character.

The set of specific integer values produced by `IAChar` is related to the ASCII collating sequence as defined by the ISO standard. (For processors that do not support this character set, see `IChar` and `Char`, described shortly.) If the argument character is not among ASCII positions 0 to 127, the function result is processor-dependent.

The inverse function `AChar` produces a single character from an integer between 0 and 127. That is, if `J` is an integer in this range and if `X` is any character string of length 1, then `AChar (IAChar (X))` has the same value as `X` and `IAChar (AChar (J))` has the same value as `J`.

It is possible to determine whether a character is a letter or not by testing whether it lies between `A` and `Z` (inclusive):

```
if ((IAChar(Next) >= IAChar("A")) &
  .and. (IAChar(Next) <= IAChar("Z"))) ...
```

Other applications include transformations of the alphabet.

EXAMPLE 6.18. A simple cryptographic application illustrates this technique. The problem is to move each character down the alphabet by one position, changing `a` to `b`, changing `b` to `c`, and so on, finally changing `y` to `z`. Special provision is needed for changing `z` back to `a`.

```
Code = IAChar (Next)
Code = Code + 1
if (Code > IAChar ("z")) Code = Code - 26
New = AChar (Code)
```

Additional character computation functions. The Fortran intrinsic function library includes several other character manipulation functions, including the following. (For details, see Appendix A.3.)

`AdjustL (String)` moves leading blanks to the right end.

`AdjustR (String)` moves trailing blanks to the left end.

`Len_Trim (String)` returns the length of `String`, ignoring trailing blanks.

`Repeat (String, NCopies)` concatenates `String` with itself `NCopies` times.

Scan (String, Set [, Back]) returns the position of the leftmost character of String that is in Set (or the rightmost if Back is true), zero if none of the characters are in Set.

Trim (String) returns the initial substring of String, omitting trailing blanks.

Verify (String, Set [, Back]) returns the position of the leftmost character of String that is not in Set (or the rightmost if Back is true, zero if all of the characters are in Set.

Character Set and Collating Sequence (Optional)

Some operations on character strings will not give the same result on all processors because of differences in the way characters are represented by different Fortran processors. Up to this point, character operations have been described as they would be performed on a processor whose primary character set is 7-bit ASCII. The principal effects that would appear on a processor with a different primary character set, such as EBCDIC, are described next.

Character Comparison

Evaluation of character relational expressions assumes the existence of a collating sequence among all Fortran and non-Fortran characters. The precise sequence will vary from one processor to another, and it is usually based on interpreting the representation of each individual character as a binary integer.

To achieve a degree of consistency, the Fortran language imposes six rules to which all Fortran processors must conform:

1. All of the uppercase (capital) letters are in order from A to Z; that is, A is considered less than B, which is less than C, and so on.
2. If the processor supports lowercase letters, they are in order from a to z; that is, a is considered less than b, which is less than c, and so on.
3. The digits are in order from 0 to 9.
4. The digits do not overlap with the uppercase letters; that is, the digits either precede all of the uppercase letters or follow all of the uppercase letters.
5. If the processor supports lowercase letters, the digits do not overlap with the lowercase letters.
6. The blank character is less than any letter or digit.

Ordering of punctuation and other symbols, and of non-Fortran characters, is left unspecified; thus, it may vary among Fortran processors. The positions of the lowercase letters in relation to the uppercase letters is also unspecified.

Rules 1 and 6 guarantee that all processors will agree on the ranking of character strings consisting entirely of uppercase letters and blanks. Ranking of more complicated strings, including those with lowercase letters, punctuation, or a mixture of letters and digits, will depend on the particular processor. For example, the result of a comparison between April␣1999 and April␣morn is processor-dependent because Fortran does not specify a standard comparison between the letters and the digits.

Char *and* IChar

Fortran specifies that the values produced by IChar range from 0 up to $n - 1$, where n is the number of Fortran and non-Fortran characters recognized by the processor. The integer value corresponding to a given character is the position of that character in the collating sequence for the particular processor.

The collating sequence is governed by the six rules just listed, but these rules are not sufficiently restrictive to require IChar to produce the same integer result for a given character on different processors. The rules do not even force the uppercase alphabet to occupy 26 consecutive positions in the collating sequence. Other symbols, though not digits, may be interspersed among the letters.

Portable Collating Sequence for Characters

Character comparisons are based on a "native" collating sequence provided by each processor. Fortran provides intrinsic functions for character comparisons, which use the standard ASCII collating sequence even on processors whose native collating sequence is not ASCII.

The intrinsic functions LGE, LGT, LLE, and LLT have two arguments, each of which may be a character expression of any length. These functions return the logical value true or false, depending on a comparison of the two argument strings on the basis of the ASCII collating sequence. If the two argument strings have unequal length, the effect is to extend the shorter string on the right with blanks for purposes of the comparison. These intrinsic functions produce logical expressions that can be applied in exactly the same way as a character relational expression.

Also, for guaranteed portability, the intrinsic functions AChar and IAChar should replace Char and IChar. The former pair makes conversions between a character and an integer based on 7-bit ASCII coding, while the latter pair follows a processor-dependent representation of characters.

Character kind *Parameters*

As we saw in Sections 1.6 and 3.4, numerical and logical data may have a kind parameter, reflecting a choice among several representation methods provided by the processor.

Character type may also have variant subtypes corresponding to different processor representations. Character data of *default kind* is represented in the same way as the traditional Fortran representation. Other variant character subtypes might represent an entirely different character font interpretation such as Postscript or Adobe Symbol font, or a non-Roman alphabet such as Cyrillic (Russian) or Kanji (Japanese). A processor may support variant character subtypes whose individual characters occupy more or less than 1 byte.

The left and right sides of a character assignment statement or the two operands of a character relational operator must have the same subtype. Padding with blanks is also processor-dependent.

For a literal character constant, the `kind` parameter specification and an underscore precedes the constant (compare Section 1.6):

```
Spanish_"María␣Muñoz"
37_"Γρεεκ"
```

The `kind` subtype property for a character variable may be specified in a type declaration, along with the length property.

6.1 Exercises

1. Write a program to read employee name, pay rate, and hours worked and to print employee name and gross pay. (Optional: Include provision for overtime pay.) Assume that 20 characters are sufficient to contain the longest employee name. Process the following data with your program:

```
"Christopher␣Winters␣"      14.85     40.0
"Vernon␣Q.␣Demerest␣␣"      13.86     40.0
"Tanya␣Livingston␣␣␣␣"      13.62     32.0
"Carol␣Logan-Forbes␣␣"      14.15     41.0
"Roger␣Chillingworth␣"      14.19     40.0
```

2. Write a program to read and print the following character data, using list-directed input and output. In part d, process the digits as characters; do not treat them as numbers.

   a. `The␣quick␣brown␣fox␣jumps␣over␣the␣lazy␣dog.`
   b. `To␣be,␣or␣not␣to␣be,␣-␣that␣is␣the␣question:␣-`
   c. `The␣moving␣finger␣writes␣-␣and,␣having␣writ,␣moves␣on.`
   d. `Please␣remit: ␣$19.25␣(cash).`

3. What is the length of each of the following character constants?

   a. `"No,␣I'm␣not␣Armstrong-Jones."`
   b. `"␣'Twas␣brillig."`
   c. `"It's␣too␣late␣-␣I␣can't␣go."`
   d. `.""""`
   e. `"''"`

4. Write a substring name that designates the following:

   a. The characters ver in the string

      `The␣quick␣brown␣fox␣jumps␣over␣the␣lazy␣dog.`

b. The characters rk in the character constant

```
"It⊥won't⊥work."
```

5. A program contains the following character type declaration with initialization:

```
character (len = *) :: Jumping_Fox = &
"The⊥quick⊥brown⊥fox⊥jumps⊥over⊥the⊥lazy⊥dog."
```

Tell which characters are designated by the following substring specifications:

a. `Jumping_Fox(5: 19)`

b. `Jumping_Fox(: 25)`

c. `Jumping_Fox(27: )`

d. `Jumping_Fox(13: 18)`

6. A program contains the following character type declaration with initialization:

```
character (len = *) :: Month = "September"
```

Tell which characters are designated by the following substring specifications:

a. Month(3: 5)

b. Month(:)

7. Given the declarations

```
character (len = 4) :: List_1, List_2, List_3
character (len = 12) :: Longer
```

Write assignment statements to do the following:

a. Assign to `Longer` a string of 12 characters obtained by concatenating together `List_1`, `List_2`, and `List_3`.

b. Replace the eighth character of `Longer` by the letter `A`, leaving the remaining character positions unchanged.

c. Assign the sixth through ninth characters of `Longer` to `List_2`.

8. Write a loop to move one character at a time from string `A` to string `B`, reversing the order of the characters in the string. That is, the characters from the first position in `A` should go to the last position in `B`, and so on. Each string is 25 characters long. (Hint: Move `A(Loop: Loop)` to `B(26 - Loop: 26 - Loop)`.)

9. Removing leading blanks. Write a program to find the first nonblank character in string `A`, and then assign the substring consisting of all of `A` except the blanks that precede the first nonblank character to string `B`. The program might begin as follows:

```
implicit none
integer, parameter :: LS = 50
```

```
character (len = LS) :: A, B
do NBC = 1, LS
if (A(NBC: NBC) /= "␣") exit
```

If the `exit` statement is not executed by the time the loop terminates, what can you conclude about the string A? (Note: Fortran 90 provides the intrinsic function `AdjustL` to perform this same task. There are also intrinsic functions `AdjustR` and `Len_Trim`.)

10. Write a program to read a string of up to 500 characters, and then count the number of words, the number of characters, and the number of occurrences of `character`. Use the following text as input data:

```
A character string consists of zero or more characters. Even
though it is made up of individual characters, a character string
is considered to be a scalar. As with any data type, it is possible
to declare an array of character strings, all the same length. A
substring is a contiguous portion of a character string that has a
starting point and an ending point within the character string.
It is possible to reference a substring of a character scalar
variable or constant.
```

Variation: Count occurrences of `Character` or `character` for which the preceding and following characters are not letters.

11. Write a program to print text in lines of 50 characters or less, ending each line between words — that is, at a blank space. Put as many words as possible on each line. Apply this program to the text given in Exercise 10.

12. Modify the program in Exercise 11 to justify the lines of text. That is, whenever a line will contain fewer than 50 characters, change blanks early in the line to pairs of blanks so that each line will fill out the 50 character spaces (with a nonblank character in the last position). Do not justify the last line of text.

13. Cryptogram: As an extension of the cryptographic application in Example 6.18, each character might be moved down the alphabet by a fixed amount other than 1. For example, moving the characters by five positions would change `a` through `u` into `f` through `z`, and `v` through `z` into `a` through `e`. Given a coded message, you suspect that it has been transformed in this manner, but you do not know the distance by which each letter was moved in the encoding transformation. You attempt to decode the message by printing each of the 25 possibilities, and you try to recognize English words among the printed results.

    Write a program to read the following cryptogram and print all 25 possible decoded messages. Tell which one you consider most likely to have been the original message. (Note: Spaces have been deleted from the original message. Ignore the spaces that appear in the cryptogram.)

```
jural bhuni rryva vangr qgurv zcbff voyrj ungri
reerz nvafu bjrir evzce bonoy rzhfg orgur gehgu
```

14. Write a program containing three `print` statements, each of which will print a character string containing your name. In the first `print` statement, include your name as a character constant in the output list. In the second, print your name as a named constant. In the third, initialize a character variable with your name in a type declaration and print the variable.

15. Given a character array whose elements are strings that have been arranged in alphabetical order, write a program to find an array element string that matches a given input string.

16. The sentence "`the quick brown fox jumps over the lazy dog`" contains each of the letters of the alphabet at least once. Write a program to print the number of occurrences of each of the 26 letters; use lowercase letters only. (Hint: Store the result in a vector of size 26.)

17. A checkerboard is represented by a matrix of type `character (len = 2)` with eight rows and eight columns; the array elements are denoted by `Checker(I, J)`. If the value of `Checker(I, J)` is "`XX`", there is a checker in row `I` and column `J` of the checkerboard; "`00`" denotes the absence of a checker. Scan the checkerboard to determine the number of checkers on it. (Hint: Use the intrinsic function `Count`.)

18. As in Exercise 17, the value "`00`" denotes an empty square. However, the value "`XX`" denotes an ordinary checker and the value "`KK`" denotes a king. Scan the board to determine the number of ordinary checkers and the number of kings.

19. Expand Exercise 18 to make the values "`RM`", "`RK`", "`BM`", and "`BK`" denote, respectively, a red man, a red king, a black man, and a black king. Scan the board to determine the number of checkers of each type.

20. Write declarations for the following strings, using named constants for the lengths: `First` is a vector of 17 character strings, each of length 8; `Second` is a vector of 7 character strings, each of length 12.

21. Write a program to print the first character of a string, and then, for each blank in the string, print the character that follows the blank; compare Example 6.16. (For names written in a conventional way, this would print the initials.) As a further extension, when a blank is found, apply the intrinsic function `Verify` (see Appendix A) to find the next nonblank character: The first argument of `Verify` is the substring that begins at the blank, and the second argument is the constant string "`␣`". Print each nonblank character in the string that is immediately preceded by a blank.

6.2 STRUCTURES AND DERIVED TYPES

In Chapter 1, we saw that Fortran supports the five *intrinsic* (built-in) data types integer, real, complex, logical, and character. In this section, we shall see how to augment these intrinsic types with user-defined types that are *derived* from the intrinsic types.

To create a named type, the user defines a *structure*, which is a collection of *components*, or *fields*. Fortran 90 views a structure as a single variable whose data type is a *derived type* defined in the Fortran program. (In some other programming languages, user-defined types are called *record types* and structures are called *records*; Fortran reserves the term *record* for input and output.) In contrast to the components (elements) of an array, structure components do not necessarily all have the same type. They may be scalars or arrays, and their types may be any mixture of intrinsic types and derived types.

Each of the intrinsic data types possesses a set of *operations*. In Chapter 7, we shall see how to define operations on a derived type and package them in a module along with the derived type definition. Here, however, we focus on those aspects of structures that do not depend on user-defined operations: derived type definitions and structure declarations, component selection, whole-structure assignment, and structure "constructors" (including structure constants).

Derived Type Definition

A *derived type* is a particular way of arranging the components of a structure. Each derived type is defined in a *derived type definition* that names the new type and states the data type of each component. A derived type definition describes the shape or "template" for the derived type, but, unlike a type *declaration*, it does not create any objects of the new type.

A derived type definition is written as a sequence of statements, beginning with a `type` statement that specifies a name for the new type. The `type` statement is simply

```
type :: Type name
```

The `type` statement is followed by a list of component declarations that have the same form as data type declarations. The derived type definition ends with an `end type` statement.

An example of a derived type definition is the following:

```
type :: Chem_El_Type
  character (len = 18) :: Element_Name
  character (len = 3) :: Symbol
  integer :: Atomic_Number
  real :: Atomic_Mass
end type Chem_El_Type
```

According to the derived type definition in this example, a structure of `Chem_El_Type` consists of

a component `Element_Name` of character type, whose length is 18
a component `Symbol` of character type, whose length is 3
a component `Atomic_Number` of integer type
a component `Atomic_Mass` of real type

The component types may be any mixture of intrinsic types and derived types. If the type of a component is a derived type, the definition for that derived type must have appeared earlier in the program (except for components that have the `pointer` attribute; see Section 6.3). Thus, we say that the new type is *derived* from the (intrinsic and existing derived) types of its components.

Application of Structures: Tables

Many scientific applications require data stored as a *table*, with several columns that may have different types. Fortran 90 permits convenient representation of such a table as an array of structures, as will be described later in this section. An example is the periodic table of chemical elements (see Example 6.26). The table contains one structure for each of 109 chemical elements. For each element, the name, symbol, atomic number, and perhaps other data values are stored in the structure.

Chemists, physicists, or biologists may record data in a table while an experiment is under way. For each experimental case or sample, an automatic instrument may produce a record that becomes a row of the table. Likewise, surveyors tabulate distances and angles at each station along a traversed route.

For tables with rows of differing data types, an array of structures is superior to the traditional Fortran program technique that employs separate "parallel arrays," one for each different type of data in the table. The separate arrays are accessed with the same subscript value to locate all parts of a row. An alternative traditional technique is to declare a single two-dimensional array, with `equivalence` statements (see Appendix E.2) to change the data types of some of the columns.

Structures

An object of a derived type is a *structure*. A type *declaration* for a structure does not begin with an intrinsic type name. Instead, it begins with the keyword `type` followed by the derived type name in parentheses:

`type (` *Type name* `) ::` *List of names*

As in a declaration for objects of an intrinsic type, the type name is followed by a double colon and a list of names of variables and constants.

The following type declaration creates three variables named Neon_20, Argon_40, and Krypton_84, which are structures of the type C_E_Type:

```
type (C_E_Type) :: Neon_20, Argon_40, Krypton_84
```

In the following example, a new type named Station is created. An array named Traverse and a variable named Bench_mark are declared, with elements that are structures of this new type.

EXAMPLE 6.19

```
!Example 6.19. Structures.
  program Surveyor
    implicit none
    integer, parameter :: SEVERAL = 40, LENGTH = 5
    type :: Station                                     ! Derived type definition
      character (len = SEVERAL) :: Name
      real, dimension(LENGTH) :: Data
      integer :: Station_Number
    end type Station
    type (Station), allocatable, dimension(:) :: Traverse   ! Table of structures
    Type (Station) :: Bench_Mark
    integer :: Loop, N_Stations
! start program Surveyor
    read *, N_Stations
    allocate (Traverse(N_Stations))
    do Loop = 1, N_Stations
      read *, Traverse(Loop)                  ! Read all components of one structure.
    end do
    Bench_Mark = Traverse(1)                        ! Whole-structure assignment
      :
  end program Surveyor
```

Both derived type definitions and structure declarations begin with the keyword type. In spite of this similarity in form, the two serve quite different purposes. The following summary should be studied carefuly.

Summary of Derived Type Definition and Structure Declaration

Derived Type Definition

- A derived type definition describes a shape or "template" for structures, which are objects of the derived type. A derived type definition does *not* create a structure.
- The first line of a derived type definition consists of the keyword `type`, a double colon, and the name of the derived type. The derived type name is *not* enclosed in parentheses. Nothing (except perhaps a comment) follows the type name.
- Additional lines, which look exactly like type declarations, list the components.
- The last line of the definition consists an `end type` statement. The derived type name in this statement is optional, but we include it in our examples.

Structure Declaration

- A type declaration creates one or more objects.
- A type declaration for structures of a designated derived type has the same form as other type declarations, except that it begins with `type (` *Type name* `)` rather than with an intrinsic type name such as `integer`.
- The type name of the derived type is enclosed in parentheses.
- The parenthesized derived type name is followed by a double colon and a list of variable names.

Reference to a Structure Component

An individual component of a structure variable is designated by the structure name, with the component name as a *qualifier*. The component name is separated from the structure name by the component selection symbol %. In the following examples, the structure names `Carbon_12` and `Temp` are qualified by component names such as `Element_Name`, `Symbol`, `Atomic_Number`, and `Atomic_Mass`:

```
Temp % Element_Name
Temp % Atomic_Number
Carbon_12 % Symbol
Carbon_12 % Atomic_Mass
Temp % Atomic_Mass
```

Whereas some other programming languages use a period for component selection, Fortran uses that symbol so extensively for other purposes that the % has been adopted to avoid ambiguity.

You can use a structure component in the same way as any other variable of the same type — in an expression or in assignment, for example:

```
Bench_Mark % Name = "␣Intersection␣of␣SR5␣and␣US980.␣"
Bench_Mark % Data(3) = 456.7
print *, Bench_Mark % Name, Bench_Mark % Data(3)
Traverse(3) % Station_Number = 14
Traverse(5) % Data(3) = Bench_Mark % Data(3) + 1
```

Example 6.20 declares a derived type suitable for storing certain information concerning a chemical element. It then declares three structures of the new type, reads some data into one of them, and performs some arithmetic and assignment operations with this data.

EXAMPLE 6.20

```
! Example 6.20. Expressions with Structure Components.
  program Edifice
    implicit none
    integer, parameter :: NAME_LENGTH = 18
    type :: Chem_El_Type                              ! Derived type definition
      character (len = NAME_LENGTH) :: Element_Name
      character (len = 3) :: Symbol
      integer :: Atomic_Number
      real :: Atomic_Mass
    end type Chem_El_Type
    type (Chem_El_Type) :: &
      Carbon_12, Temp, Linoleum                             ! Type declaration
! start program Edifice
    read *, Carbon_12 % Atomic_Mass                       ! Structure component
    Temp % Atomic_Mass = Carbon_12 % Atomic_Mass + 0.532
    print *, Temp % Atomic_Mass
  end program Edifice
```

Nested Structures

In a derived type definition, the data type of any component may be a previously defined derived type that may, in turn, have derived type components to any level of nesting. In any case, at the deepest nesting level every structure has *ultimate components* whose types are intrinsic types.

EXAMPLE 6.21 In the following program, the derived type `Isotope_Type` is first defined and then used for the fifth component in the definition of `Chem_El_Type`.

```
! Example 6.21. Nested structures.
  program Cuckoo
    implicit none
    integer, parameter :: NAME_LENGTH = 18
    type :: Isotope_Type                              ! Derived type definition
      integer :: Nucleon_Count
      real :: Abundance
    end type Isotope_Type
    type :: Chem_El_Type                              ! Derived type definition
      character (len = NAME_LENGTH) :: Element_Name
      character (len = 3) :: Symbol
      integer :: Atomic_Number
      real :: Atomic_Mass
      type (Isotope_Type) :: Principal_Isotope            ! Previously defined
    end type Chem_El_Type
      :
  end program Cuckoo
```

Structure Constructors (Advanced)

A *structure constructor* consists of the type name followed by a parenthesized list of expressions, one for each component, in the order of their appearance in the derived type definition:

Type name (*List*)

The type of each expression in the *List* must match the declared type of the corresponding component. If a component is a structure, it may be specified by an embedded structure constructor. If a component is an array, it may be specified by an array constructor. All the components of a structure must be included: a constructor can not correspond to *part* of a structure. If a component of the derived type has the `pointer` attribute, the corresponding constructor item will be assigned to the pointer by pointer assignment.

A structure constructor whose components are constants (or initialization expressions: see Section 1.3) may be used to initialize a named constant of derived type or used in any other position where a constant is permitted. Constant structure constructors are illustrated in Example 6.22.

EXAMPLE 6.22

```
! Example 6.22. Constant structure constructors.
  program Con_Struct
    implicit none
    integer, parameter :: NAME_LENGTH = 10
```

```
  type :: Chem_El_Type_2                                  ! Derived type definition
    character (len = 12) :: Element_Name
    character (len = 3) :: Symbol
    integer :: Atomic_Number
    real :: Atomic_Mass
  end type Chem_El_Type_2

  type (Chem_El_Type_2) :: &                                    ! Type declaration
    Carbon_12 = Chem_El_Type_2("Carbon␣␣␣␣", "C␣␣", 6, 12.01), &
    Linoleum  = Chem_El_Type_2("Linoleum␣␣", "Lm␣", 200, 499.9)

! start program Con_Struct
  print *, Carbon_12 % Symbol, Linoleum % Atomic_Mass
 end program Con_Struct
```

EXAMPLE 6.23 In this more complicated example, the structure A of type Big contains an array component named Data, whose elements are structures of type Small. The structure A is initialized in a type declaration with a structure constructor of type Big that contains an integer and an array constructor. The array constructor, in turn, contains two structure constructors of type Small. The print statement illustrates reference to a component of a nested structure and to a substring of an array element in the inner structure.

```
! Example 6.23. Nested structure constructor and component reference.
 program Hologram
   implicit none

   type :: Small
     integer :: I, J
     character (len = 5), dimension(2) :: Word
   end type Small

   type :: Big
     integer :: Count
     type (Small), dimension(2) :: Data
   end type Big

   type (Big) :: A = &
     Big ( 123, (/ &
       Small (1, 1, (/ "ABCDE", "FGHIJ" /) ), &
       Small (2, 2, (/ "KLMNO", "PQRST" /) ) &
         /) )

! start program Hologram
   print *, A % Count, A % Data(1) % J, A % Data(2) % Word(2)(3: 5)
 end program Hologram
```

Operations with Whole Structures

As mentioned earlier, one of the properties of a type is a set of operations that can be performed upon objects of that type. Fortran 90 permits assignment and input or output of whole structures. In Section 7.5, we shall see how to create a module that *encapsulates* a user-defined type along with user-defined operations on objects of that type. Here, we consider some examples of whole-structure input, output, and assignment, and we further examine operations on structure components.

EXAMPLE 6.24

```
! Example 6.24. Whole-structure assignment.
 program Assign
   implicit none
   integer, parameter :: NAME_LENGTH = 18
   type :: Isotope_Type                              ! Derived type definition
     integer :: Nucleon_Count
     real :: Abundance
   end type Isotope_Type
   type :: Chem_El_Type_3                            ! Derived type definition
     character (len = NAME_LENGTH) :: Element_Name
     character (len = 3) :: Symbol
     integer :: Atomic_Number
     real :: Atomic_Mass
     type (Isotope_Type) :: Principal_Isotope           ! Previously defined
   end type Chem_El_Type_3
   type (Chem_El_Type_3) :: Carbon_12, Temp_E            ! Type declaration
   type (Isotope_Type) :: Temp_I
! start program Assign
   read *, Temp_E, Temp_I
   Carbon_12 = Temp_E
   Carbon_12 % Principal_Isotope = Temp_I
   print *, Temp_E, Carbon_12
 end program Assign
```

In Example 6.24, the two variables named `Temp_E` and `Carbon_12` are objects of the derived type called `Chem_El_Type_3`. The structure component `Carbon_12 % Principal_Isotope` and the separate variable `Temp_I` are objects of the derived type called `Isotope_Type`. Accordingly, both assignment statements in this example are valid (if the variables named on the right have been given values).

Assignment between whole structures of the *same derived type* is permitted (see also Section 7.2). Assignment between whole structures of two difierent derived types is not permitted, even if the two types have exactly the same components. Other operations between whole structures, such as comparison for equality or inequality, are not permitted.

List-directed input and output of whole structures is permitted. During list-directed input to a structure, Fortran 90 expects an input value for each ultimate component, in the order of their appearance in the derived type definition (or nest of definitions). In Example 6.24, input data for `Temp_E` consists of the following:

Two character strings for `Temp_E % Element_Name` and `Temp_E % Symbol`
An integer for `Temp_E % Atomic_Number`
A real number for `Temp_E % Atomic_Mass`
An integer for `Temp_E % Principal_Isotope % Nucleon_Count`
A real number for `Temp_E % Principal_Isotope % Abundance`

Input data for `Temp_I` is the following:

An integer for `Temp_I % Nucleon_Count`
A real number for `Temp_I % Abundance`

Application: Complex Numbers in Polar Form

Fortran's complex data type is, in a sense, a built-in derived type with two real components. However, this type antedates the systematic derived type feature that Fortran 90 now provides. Example 6.25 introduces a separate derived type with two real components that represent a complex number in polar form. The derived type named `Polar` is defined in the main program.

Two internal functions perform conversions of complex numbers between standard Fortran style and polar form. `P_Complex` is an internal function whose `intent (in)` argument is a complex number expressed in standard Fortran style and whose result is a variable of type `Polar` giving the representation of the same complex number in polar form. `F_Complex` has an `intent (in)` argument of type `Polar` and returns a result of Fortran complex type.

EXAMPLE 6.25 The main program reads two complex numbers, converts them to polar form, computes their product (which is very easy to do in polar form), and converts the product to Fortran style.

```
! Example 6.25. Complex numbers in Fortran style and in polar form.
 program Driver
   implicit none
   type :: Polar
     real :: R
     real :: Theta
   end type Polar
   complex :: Z1, Z2, Z3
   type (Polar) :: P1, P2, P3
! start program Driver
   read *, Z1, Z2
   print *, "␣Complex␣numbers␣in␣Fortran␣style:␣"
   print *, Z1, Z2
   P1 = P_Complex (Z1); P2 = P_Complex (Z2)
   print *, "␣Same␣complex␣numbers␣in␣polar␣form:␣"
   print *, P1, P2
   P3 % R = P1 % R * P2 % R
   P3 % Theta = P1 % Theta + P2 % Theta
   print *, "␣Complex␣product␣in␣polar␣form:␣"
   print *, P3
   Z3 = F_Complex (P3)
   print *, "␣Complex␣product␣in␣Fortran␣style:␣"
   print *, Z3
 contains
   type (Polar) function P_Complex (Z) result (S)
     intrinsic Abs, AImag, ATan2, Real
     complex, intent (in) :: Z
 ! start function P_Complex
     S % R = Abs (Z)
     S % Theta = ATan2 (AImag (Z), Real (Z))
   end function P_Complex
   complex function F_Complex (P) result (Ursa)
     intrinsic Real, Sin, Cos, Cmplx
     type (Polar), intent (in) :: P
     real :: X, Y
 ! start function F_Complex
     X = P % R * Real (Cos (P % Theta))
     Y = P % R * Real (Sin (P % Theta))
     Ursa = Cmplx (X, Y)
   end function F_Complex
 end program Driver
```

Input data:

```
(0.8660254, 0.5) (0.5, 0.8660254)
```

Output:

```
Complex numbers in Fortran style:
 ( 0.8660254, 0.5000000) ( 0.5000000, 0.8660254)
Same complex numbers in polar form:
 1.0000000 0.5235988 1.0000000 1.0471976
Complex product in polar form:
 1.0000000 1.5707964
Complex product in Fortran style:
 ( -4.3711388E-08, 1.0000000)
```

Combining Arrays with Structures

Array in a Structure

A component of a derived type may be an array. In the following example, the sixth component of `Chem_El_Type_4` is an array of 10 integers, which might be the nucleon counts for up to 10 stable isotopes.

EXAMPLE 6.26

```
! Example 6.26. Array in a structure.
  program Lump
    implicit none
    integer, parameter :: NAME_LENGTH = 18, MAX_ISO = 10
    type :: Chem_El_Type_4                              ! Element with isotopes
      character (len = NAME_LENGTH) :: Element_Name
      character (len = 3) :: Symbol
      integer :: Atomic_Number
      real :: Atomic_Mass
      integer :: N_Iso, Nucleon_Count(MAX_ISO)                 ! Isotopes
    end type Chem_El_Type_4
      :
  end program Lump
```

Arrays of Structures: Tables

All elements of an array must have the same type; this may be an intrinsic type or a derived type. In the following example, `Periodic_Table` is a one-dimensional array (vector) containing 109 elements that are structures of type `Chem_El_Type_5`.

EXAMPLE 6.27

```
! Example 6.27. Array of structures.
 program Mend
   implicit none
   integer, parameter :: NAME_LENGTH = 18, VECTOR_LENGTH = 109
   type :: Chem_El_Type_5
     character (len = NAME_LENGTH) :: Element_Name
     character (len = 3) :: Symbol
     integer :: Atomic_Number
     real :: Atomic_Mass
   end type Chem_El_Type_5
   type (Chem_El_Type_5), dimension(VECTOR_LENGTH) :: Periodic_Table
     :
 end program Mend
```

A *table* is often implemented as an array (usually a vector) of structures. In a table, the rows usually represent similar items, while the columns represent difierent aspects of a particular item. Each row of the table may be implemented as a structure whose components correspond to the columns of the table.

Application: Temperature Records

Suppose that a computer stores temperature data once hourly for a year, as in Example 6.28. It saves the data for each day in a 24-element vector, determines the maximum and minimum, and copies the vector and the two extreme temperatures to one of the structures in an array of 365 (or 366) structures.

EXAMPLE 6.28 The following program calls a function to determine the temperature at each hour. The program simulates the temperature input with a periodic function of time modified by a random number.

```
! Example 6.28. Temperature records.
 program Edison
   implicit none
   intrinsic ANInt, Random_Number, Real, Sin
   type :: Day
     integer :: Temperature (24), Max_Temp, Min_Temp
   end type Day
   type (Day) :: Today
   type (Day), allocatable, dimension(:) :: Year
   integer :: N_Days, I, J
```

```
! start program Edison
    open (unit = 9, file = "temperat.txt", position = "rewind")
    print *, "␣Please␣enter␣the␣year.␣"
    read *, Year
    write (unit = 9, format = *) Year                          ! Write header record.
    N_Days = Merge (366, 365, Modulo (Year, 4) == 0)             ! Is it leap year?
    allocate (Year(N_Days))
    do I = 1, N_Days
      do J = 1, 24
        Today % Temperature(J) = Input (I, J)
      end do
      Today % Max_Temp = MaxVal (Today % Temperature)
      Today % Min_Temp = MinVal (Today % Temperature)
      Year(I) = Today
      print *, Today
      write (unit = 9, format = *) Today
    end do
  contains
    function Temp_In (Day, Hour) result (Temperature)
      integer, intent (in) :: Day, Hour
      integer :: Temperature
      real :: Random_Term
  ! start function Temp_In
      call Random_Number (Harvest = Random_Term)          ! Uniform between 0 and 1
      Temperature = ANInt (68.0                           ! Mean annual temperature
        + 30.0 * Sin (6.2832 * (Real (Day) + 250.0) / 365.0) &      ! Annual cycle
        + 10.0 * Sin (6.2832 * (Real (Hour) + 15.0) / 24.0) &        ! Daily cycle
        + 5.0 * Random_Term)
    end function Temp_In
  end program Edison
```

Application: Expanding List

When an expanding list is stored in an array, as in Example 5.22, it is often desirable to create a single data structure that contains both the array and an integer whose value is the current list size. This single structure can then be passed as an argument to procedures that process the data.

EXAMPLE 6.29 The following program is an embellishment of Example 5.22. The list is now stored in an array of structures, which is combined with an integer variable in a structure named `C_Table`. Thus, `C_Table % Data` is the array of structures, and `C_Table % L_Size` is the current list size. In the list processing procedure, these are known as `C_Tbl % Data` and `C_Tbl % L_Size`, respectively.

```
! Example 6.29. Expanding list as an array of structures.
 program Array_List
   implicit none
   integer, parameter ::  NAME_LENGTH = 12, TBL_SIZE = 20
   type :: Compound
     integer :: Count
     character (len = NAME_LENGTH) :: Name
   end type Compound
   type :: Table                    ! Structure to hold list and current list size
     type (Compound) :: Data (TBL_SIZE)                      ! Array of compounds
     integer :: L_Size                                        ! Current list size
   end type Table
   type (Compound) :: Element = Compound (0, "␣")        ! Structure constructor
   type (Table) :: C_Table
   integer :: EoF = 0
! start program Array_List
   C_Table % L_Size = 0
   open (unit = 1, file = "compounds.txt")
   do
     read (1, *, iostat = EoF) Element % Name
       if (EoF < 0) exit
     if (.not. Find (C_Table, TBL_SIZE, Element)) exit
   end do
   ! At this point EoF < 0 or attempted to insert in full list.
   call Print_List
  contains
   logical function Find (C_Tbl, T_Size, Element) result (Fit)
     ! Result is .FALSE. on attempt to insert when Tbl is full.
     integer, intent (in):: T_Size                           ! Maximum list size
     type (Table), intent (in out) :: C_Tbl                              ! List
     type (Compound), intent (in) :: Element  ! Element to find or insert in list
     integer, dimension(2) :: Loc                    ! To hold result from Search
!    start function Find
     Loc = Search &
       (C_Tbl % Data(: C_Tbl % L_Size) % Name, Element % Name)
```

```
      if (Loc(1) == Loc(2)) then
        print *, "␣Found␣at␣", Loc(2), "␣of␣", C_Tbl % L_Size ": ", Element
        C_Tbl % Data(Loc(2)) % Count = C_Tbl % Data(Loc(2)) % Count + 1
        Fit = .TRUE.                          ! Current list size has not changed.
      else                                          ! No matching element; insert.
        if (C_Tbl % L_Size < T_Size) then
          Fit = .TRUE.                          ! There is room to insert element.
          C_Tbl % Data(Loc(2) + 1 : C_Tbl % L_Size + 1) = &
            C_Tbl % Data(Loc(2) : C_Tbl % L_Size)
                 ! Move elements up to make space at insertion point.
          C_Tbl % Data(Loc(2)) = Element                              ! Insert.
            ! Adjust current size.
          C_Tbl % L_Size = C_Tbl % L_Size + 1
          print *, "␣Inserted␣at␣", Loc(2), "␣of␣", C_Tbl % L_Size ", Element
        else
          Fit = .FALSE.                        ! There is no room to insert element.
          print *, "␣List␣full.␣", Loc(2), "␣of␣", C_Tbl % L_Size : ", Element
        end if
      end if
    end function Find
    subroutine Print_List
      ⋮
    end subroutine Print_List
    function Search (List, Key) result (Location)
      ⋮
    end function Search
  end program Array_List
```

In Example 6.29, the procedure `Find` first calls for a search of the column of the `Data` table that contains the element keys. This is component `Name` of an array section (from the beginning to the element whose subscript value is `C_Tbl % L_Size`) in the array `C_Tbl % Data`. The column is therefore denoted by

```
C_Tbl % Data(: C_Tbl % L_Size) % Name
```

The corresponding dummy argument in the procedure `Search` is an array of strings. The procedure does not need to know that the strings are components of an array of structures. In fact, the same procedure could be called on some other occasion with an array of strings that are not structure components.

The search function returns a two-element vector of integer type. The first element is the subscript of the last array element whose value is less than or equal to the search key (or 0 if there is no such element), and the second is the subscript of the first array element whose value is greater than or equal to the search key (or `Size (List) + 1` if there is no such element). If the two integers are equal, there is an element in the list with a matching key; the Count component of the list item is increased by 1. Otherwise, the input element is to be inserted at the position indicated by the second integer returned from the search function.

A Search procedure such as the linear search function in Example 5.35 or the binary search function in Example 5.36 may be inserted into this program. The following subroutine Print_List may also be inserted.

```
 subroutine Print_List
  integer Loop
! start subroutine Print_List
  print *, "␣Final␣size:␣", C_Table % L_Size
  do Loop = 1, C_Table % L_Size
   print *, C_Table % Data(Loop)
  end do
 end subroutine Print_List
```

Execution of the program with the input

```
C C
```

produces the following output:

```
 Inserted at 2 of 2: 1 C
 Found at 2 of 3: 2 C
Final size: 1
2 C
```

Arrays of Structure Components (Advanced)

It is possible to designate a component of a whole array of structures or of a section from such an array. If a particular component is selected from all of the structures in an array, the selected components form an array that has the same rank and shape (but not the same type) as the host array. If the host array is viewed as a table, the array of components is a column of the table.

In Figure 6.2, New_Type is a derived type with components A, B, C, D, and E. Suppose that we declare Voltmeter to be a variable of this type, and Instruments as a vector containing five elements of this type. Component D of element 5 of this vector is designated as Instruments(5) % D. We may select component D from the whole array; Instruments % D is a vector consisting of component D of each element of the array of structures.

In Example 6.27, Periodic_Table is an array of 109 structures of type Chem_El_Type_5. Therefore, Periodic_Table % Symbol is an array of 109 character strings, and Periodic_Table % Atomic_Mass is an array of 109 real numbers.

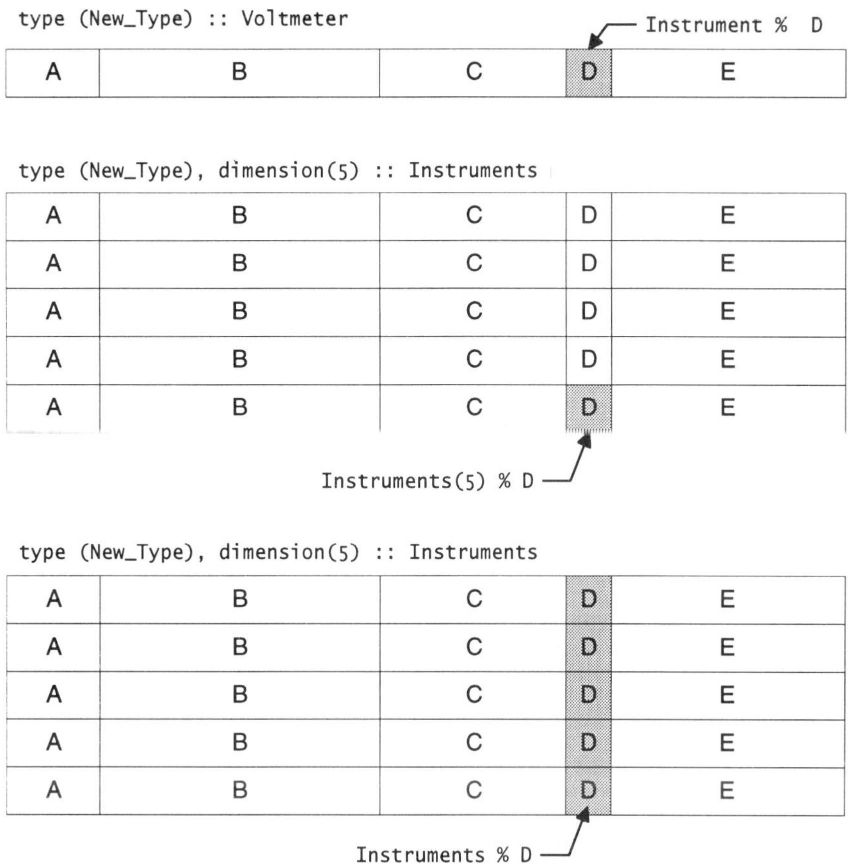

FIGURE 6.2. Array of structure components.

EXAMPLE 6.30 In the following program, `Some_Isotopes` is an array of 10 structures of type `Isotope_Type`. Thus, each array element has an integer component named `Nucleon_Count` and a real component named `Relative_Abundance`.

```
! Example 6.30. Array of structure components.
 program Column_1
   implicit none
   type :: Isotope_Type                              ! Data for a single isotope
     integer :: Nucleon_Count
     real :: Relative_Abundance
   end type Isotope_Type
   type (Isotope_Type), dimension(10) :: Some_Isotopes
     :
 end program Column_1
```

In Example 6.30, the 10 real variables, consisting of the `Relative_Abundance` component of each array element, form an array of 10 structure components. For example, these elements could be copied to a vector:

```
real, dimension(10) :: Abundances
  :
Abundances = Some_Isotopes % Relative_Abundance
  ! Array of components
```

An array of components is permitted as a whole-array expression, but it must not be referenced with a subscript. To choose a component of one element of the primary array, the array element must be selected before the component is designated:

```
Some_Isotopes % Relative_Abundance (2)          ! ☹ Illegal
Some_Isotopes (2) % Relative_Abundance         ! ☺ Permitted
```

When an array of structures is to be sorted, one component of each structure is usually selected as a *sort key*. (It is also possible to designate additional components as secondary sort keys.) The key components of the whole array of structures form an array that can be passed to a comparison procedure. (See Example 6.29.)

Transition Tip

- Traditional Fortran programs often create a "table," whose rows consist of data of mixed types, as a set of parallel arrays (one for each different type) that are referenced with a common subscript value (row number). Change such tables to arrays of structures.

6.3 POINTERS (Advanced)

Typical Fortran programs make heavy use of arrays, and the Fortran language provides excellent facilities for array processing. Nevertheless, arrays have one principal drawback — namely, fixed size and shape. Although the shapes of some arrays can be established during program execution (see Section 5.6 for allocatable arrays, Section 8.2 for assumed-shape arrays, and Section 8.4 for automatic arrays), the shape of an array cannot be changed after data has been stored in it. If the amount of data to be processed is not known in advance, the user is in a dilemma: Make the array too large and waste storage space, or make it too small and run out of space during program execution.

Flexible data structures linked with *pointers* provide an escape from this dilemma. Linked lists and trees permit separate allocation of space, during program execution, for each individual item of data. As each new data item is added, additional space for it is created in heap storage. As we shall see, linked lists incur a time penalty in that they do not permit direct access to an arbitrary item of data. This penalty is largely alleviated with tree data structures.

The `pointer` *Attribute*

A variable of any data type may be declared to have the `pointer` attribute. The value of such a variable is stored in the form of a *pointer* to a *target object* of the specified type:

```
real, pointer :: Root, Temp                    ! type declaration
```

The type declaration creates (reserves space for) pointers as local objects in automatic or static storage, but it does not create (does not reserve space for) the target objects and it does not give the pointers any defined values. (See Figure 6.3.)

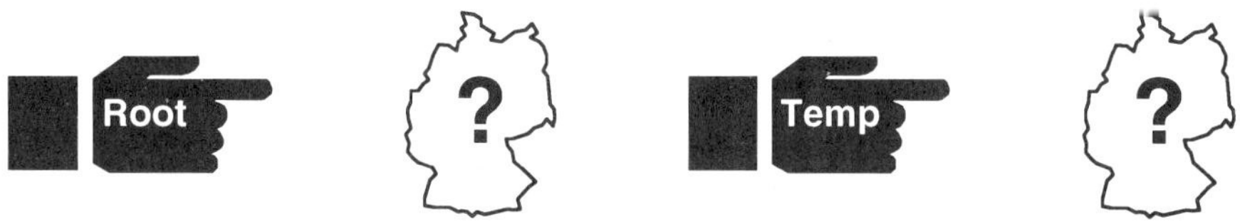

FIGURE 6.3. Type declarations for pointers do not give the pointers any defined values.

The *contents* of the storage area reserved for a pointer is the *value* of the pointer. When a pointer has a target, the pointer value is a mark that indicates the specific target. This mark (actually, the address of an area of heap storage) is not accessible to the Fortran program except by means of the operations described in this section. In particular, the mark that represents the pointer value cannot be printed or be used as an arithmetic operand. As we shall see, Fortran 90 applies *automatic dereferencing*, which means that most references to pointer names designate the target rather than the pointer.

A pointer that is currently associated with a target has a defined value that indicates the particular target. When a pointer has no target, its value is undefined. Because there is no way to initialize a pointer — that is, to associate it with a target in a type declaration — all pointer values are initially undefined.

Association Status

The *association status* of a pointer is "associated" if the pointer is currently associated with a target, and it is "disassociated" if the pointer is not currently associated with a target. The association status is undefined if Fortran 90 cannot tell whether or not the pointer is currently associated with a target. The association status of all pointers is initially undefined:[6] Until a pointer has been nullified, allocated, or assigned (as de-

[6] This feature is currently under review by the technical committees responsible for Fortran standards. Pending further standardization action, the safe assumption is that the association status of pointers is initially undefined — pointers are neither initially associated with a target nor initially nullified. A pending proposal, which some processors may implement as a compatible extension, is that all pointers shall be initially nullified by the Fortran processor. An alternative proposal provides a way to initially nullify a pointer in the type declaration.

scribed shortly), there is no way to tell whether or not it is associated with a target. The question marks in Figure 6.3 denote undefined association status.

There are three ways to give a pointer a defined association status. Since pointers cannot be initialized, most pointer application programs begin by applying one of these operations to each declared pointer:

1. Executing a `nullify` statement sets the association status of a pointer to disassociated, indicating that the pointer does not currently have a target.[7]
2. Executing an `allocate` statement creates (reserves space for) a new target object in heap storage, sets the pointer value to indicate that the pointer is associated with the newly created object, and sets the association status to associated.
3. Executing a pointer assignment statement can associate the pointer with an existing target object.

Automatic Dereferencing

Fortran 90 does not give a separate name to the target of a pointer. The target has the same name as its pointer. When a variable has the `pointer` attribute, Fortran 90 is able to determine from the context whether an occurrence of the name is intended to designate the target or the pointer itself. A name designates the *target* when it appears in an expression, when it appears on the left side of an assignment statement, or when it appears in an `allocate` or `deallocate` statement. It designates the *pointer* when it appears in a `nullify` statement or when it appears in a pointer assignment statement.

If you are unfamiliar with pointer operations or if you have written programs in another language that employs a special "target of" dereferencing symbol, you may find the Fortran 90 notation confusing at first.[8] Accordingly, in this text, the special symbol ⊙ is sometimes appended to indicate reference to a target. For example, `Root`⊙ designates the *target* of the pointer whose name is `Root`. This target symbol cannot actually be written as a Fortran program character — it is used here only for further clarification.

Ways to Define the Status of a Pointer

As we have seen, a pointer is created with an initially undefined association status and with an initially undefined value. We now examine the three statements that can define the association status of a pointer. The last two of these can also give the pointer a target and thus define its value.

[7] Other programming languages achieve this effect by means of a special "null pointer" value or `NIL` constant.

[8] For example, the target of `Temp` is written as `Temp^` in Pascal or Modula 2, and as `*Temp` in C or C++. Like Fortran 90, Ada provides automatic dereferencing.

The `nullify` *Statement*

Executing the statement

```
nullify (Temp)
```

gives the pointer `Temp` a special disassociated status, indicating that `Temp` does not currently have a target. (See Figure 6.4.)

FIGURE 6.4. A *nullify* statement sets the pointer's association status to disassociated.

After the `nullify` statement has been executed, the association status of the pointer becomes defined as disassociated. The pointer value remains undefined because the pointer still has no target. In Figure 6.4, the symbol ∅ indicates that the association status is disassociated.

The only way to detect that a pointer has been nullified is by means of the intrinsic function reference `Associated (Temp)`, which examines the association status of the pointer.

```
Associated (Temp)                    ! intrinsic function reference
```

The result value is true if `Temp` is currently associated with a target so that its association status is associated. The function result is false if `Temp` has been nullified so that its association status is disassociated. The function reference is prohibited if the pointer association status is undefined.

The `allocate` *Statement*

An `allocate` statement creates a new target (in heap storage) for a pointer. For example, executing the statement

```
allocate (Root)                                ! Allocate Root⊙.
```

creates (reserves space for) a new target object of the type specified in the declaration for `Root`, associates the pointer `Root` with the new target, and sets the pointer's allocation status to associated. (See Figure 6.5.)

FIGURE 6.5. An *allocate* statement creates a new target for the pointer.

The `allocate` statement may be used with allocatable arrays (see Section 5.6) or with pointers. Thus, the designated name must have either the `allocatable` attribute or the `pointer` attribute. If the name designates a pointer, the association status of that pointer becomes defined as associated and the pointer value becomes defined; that is, the pointer now has a value that indicates or "points to" the new target. In Figure 6.5, the symbol ⊙ indicates that the association status is associated.

Allocated objects. As we saw in Section 5.6, typical Fortran 90 processors provide three classes of storage. A local data object in a main program or procedure normally occupies *automatic* (or central stack) storage. If such an object has the `save` attribute, it occupies *static* storage. Arrays and pointer targets that are allocated during program execution occupy dynamic *heap* storage.

The `allocate` statement can be used in either of two related ways: to create an allocated array (see Section 5.6) or to create a target for an existing pointer. The Fortran 90 allocated array facility is, in effect, a subset of the pointer feature, with two restrictions. First, an allocated array is created in heap storage but no pointer is made accessible to the program. And second, a pointer can be declared to have a target that is not an array. It is an error to allocate an allocatable array that is currently allocated, but it is not an error to allocate a pointer that is currently associated with a target. In the latter case, a new target object is created and the previous association of the pointer is terminated. If there was no other way to access the previous target, it becomes inaccessible.

The `allocate` statement has an optional *Exception* specifier of the form `stat =` *Integer variable*:

```
allocate (Root, stat = Allocate_Error)

if (Allocate_Error != 0) stop
```

At the end of execution of the `allocate` statement, the designated *Integer variable* will be set to zero if the allocation is successful and to a positive value otherwise — for example, if no heap storage space is available.

If an allocated pointer target is an array, it must be declared with *deferred shape*. (Allocatable arrays must also be declared with deferred shape; see Section 5.6.) This means that the `dimension` specifier must contain one or more colons to specify the rank, but no upper or lower dimension bounds. The `allocate` statement contains the actual subscript bounds:

```
real, pointer, dimension(:) :: Alabaster
  :
allocate (Alabaster(25))
```

Deallocating an allocated pointer target. Executing the statement

```
deallocate (Root)                         ! Deallocate Root⊙.
```

where Root is a pointer that is currently associated with a target object, destroys the association between the pointer and the target. It nullifies the pointer and releases the heap space occupied by the target object. (See Figure 6.6.) If the target had a defined value prior to deallocation, that value is lost.

FIGURE 6.6. Executing the statement *deallocate (Root¤)* releases the space occupied by the target object and nullifies the pointer.

Deallocation is permited only if the current association status of the pointer is associated, that is, if the pointer is currently associated with a target. After the deallocate statement has been executed, the association status of the designated pointer becomes defined as disassociated. The pointer value becomes undefined because the pointer no longer has a target.

The deallocate statement has an optional *Exception* specifier of the form stat = *Integer variable*:

```
deallocate (Alimony, stat = Deallocate_Error)
if (Deallocate_Error != 0) stop
```

At the end of execution of the deallocate statement, the designated *Integer variable* will be set to zero if the deallocation is successful and to a positive value otherwise — for example, if the pointer has no current target or if its target is a declared object in static or automatic storage.

Pointer Assignment

Pointer to a declared target object (Optional). A declared object (in static or automatic storage) may become the target of a pointer if its type declaration includes the target attribute:

```
real, target :: Bulls_Eye
```

The pointer name then refers directly to the target object and becomes an *alias* for the target object name. A target object may be a portion of a larger object that has been declared with the target atribute; for example, it may be an array element, an array section, a character substring, or a structure component. Use of the simple pointer name as an alias may be especially desirable if the target object is an embedded object, such as a component of a deeply nested structure, whose complete designator is quite long.

Both the pointer and the target must already exist, as a result of their respective type declarations, at the time the association between them is established. Note the following:

1. The target object must have been declared with the `target` attribute.
2. The target object must have the same declared type as the pointer.

Every Fortran 90 pointer must be declared with a specific type. Any target that becomes associated with a given pointer must then have the specified type. For allocated targets, there is no problem because the `allocate` statement automatically creates a target of the specified type. However, in a program to associate a pointer with a preexisting target object, care must be taken to ensure that the declared type of the target object agrees with the declared type of the pointer.

The Fortran 90 *pointer assignment* operator, with the name of an existing declared object on the right, associates the pointer with the designated object:

Pointer => *Declared object name*

As mentioned, the declared object must have the `target` attribute and must have the same data type as the pointer. Execution of the pointer assignment statement sets the association status of the pointer to associated and sets the pointer value to indicate the new target object. For example,

```
real, target :: Bulls_Eye
real, pointer :: Node
Node => Bulls_Eye
```

An array declared with the `target` attribute may be a deferred-shape array. This means that the dimension attribute specifier must contain one or more colons to specify the rank, but no upper or lower dimension bounds. The `allocate` statement contains the actual subscript bounds:

```
real, target, dimension(:) :: Alabama
real, pointer :: Space
  :
Space => Alabama(25)
```

The space occupied by an allocatable array target object such as `Alabama` may later be released by deallocating the *target*:

```
deallocate (Alabama)
```

In this case, the `deallocate` statement must not refer to the pointer. However, the association status of `Space` (or of any pointer currently associated with `Alabama`) will become undefined when the target is deallocated. Good programming practice would therefore suggest that `Space` be nullified (or redefined in some way) as soon as its target has been deallocated.

Assigning an associated pointer. The Fortran 90 pointer assignment operator may be used in another way, with the name of a pointer on the right:

$\mathit{Pointer}_1$ => $\mathit{Pointer}_2$

The assignment sequence is from right to left, as usual, even though the direction of the arrow might seem to indicate otherwise. The effect of such a pointer assignment is to "copy" $\mathcal{P}ointer_2$ to $\mathcal{P}ointer_1$. That is, the existing association status and target (if any) of $\mathcal{P}ointer_2$ now also become the association status and the target, respectively, of $\mathcal{P}ointer_1$. If the association status of $\mathcal{P}ointer_2$ is undefined or if $\mathcal{P}ointer_2$ has been nullified, the same will be true of $\mathcal{P}ointer_1$ after the pointer assignment has been executed.

For example, executing the following statement will set `Temp` to point to the same target (if any) as `Root`:

```
Temp => Root                                 ! Pointer assignment
```

The current target (if any) of the pointer named `Root` is now also the target of the pointer named `Temp`. The pointer assignment may be read as follows: "Assign the target of `Root` as the (new) target of `Temp`." Executing a later statement that changes `Root` (by means of a `nullify` statement, an `allocate` statement, or a pointer assignment statement) will not change the association status or the target of `Temp`. (See Figure 6.7.)

FIGURE 6.7. Executing the pointer assignment statement gives *Temp* the same target as *Root*.

Remember that, after a pointer assignment with a pointer on the right has been executed, the same target object is the target of two separate pointers. Care must be taken to avoid deallocating one of these pointers while the other still points to the same target.

In a pointer assignment statement, names of variables with the `pointer` attribute appear on each side of the pointer assignment operator. Note that an ordinary assignment statement may also have names of variables with the `pointer` attribute on each side of the assignment operator. However, the names in the pointer assignment statement designate the pointers, while the names in the ordinary assignment statement designate the targets. Instead of copying the pointer values, ordinary assignment copies *target* values (which must have compatible types and other attributes). For example, according to the declaration

```
real, pointer :: Root, Temp                  ! Type declaration
```

`Root` and `Temp` are the (indirect) names of objects of real data type, so the assignment

```
Temp = Root                                  ! Temp⊙ = Root⊙
```

will copy `Root⊙` to `Temp⊙`. The object named `Root⊙`, which is the current target of a pointer, will be copied to the object named `Temp⊙` which is the current target of another pointer.

Storage for Pointers and Allocated Targets

Recall that a type declaration creates (reserves space for) an object of the declared type in automatic storage (or in static storage if the `save` attribute is specified) at the beginning of execution of the main program or procedure in which the declaration appears. The same is true when the declared object is a structure (of a derived type). If a declared object has the `pointer` attribute, the pointer is created (space is reserved for it) in static or automatic storage, but initially no target is created.

Also recall that executing the statement `allocate (Root)` (where `Root` is an existing pointer that may or may not have been previously allocated or nullified) has two effects:

1. It creates (reserves space for) a new target object of the type specified in the declaration for `Root`.
2. It associates the pointer `Root` with the new target.

Storage for allocated pointer targets is obtained from a "heap" of free space that is administered by a sophisticated storage management system. Storage for allocatable arrays is allocated from this same heap.

Summary of Storage Management

It is important to remember that type declarations create objects in automatic or static storage, while `allocate` statements create objects in heap storage.

- Static objects are created at the beginning of execution of the main program, and they are never destroyed until the program terminates.
- Automatic objects are created at the beginning of execution of the program or procedure where they are declared, and they are destroyed (the storage reserved for them is released for possible reuse) when that program or procedure terminates.
- Allocatable arrays and pointer targets are created in heap storage when an `allocate` statement is executed, and they are destroyed when a `deallocate` statement is executed or when the main program terminates.[9]
- Allocatable arrays and pointer targets that are local to a procedure must be explicitly deallocated prior to procedure exit.

[9] Fortran 90 does not guarantee that any remaining allocated objects in heap storage will be deallocated when the main program terminates, but all known implementations support this assumption.

Management of Allocated Targets

Executing an `allocate` statement for a pointer causes space from the heap to be reserved for the target, and gives the pointer a value that permits Fortran to gain access to the target via the pointer. At this point, Fortran has no other way of obtaining access to the target — that is, to the area of heap space that has just been allocated.

Some care is required here to avoid storage management problems. If the pointer value is destroyed (by nullification, reallocation, or pointer assignment) but the target is not deallocated, the heap space becomes "garbage" — that is, it is still reserved by the storage management system but it is inaccessible to the program for which it was reserved. To ensure that the target space will be returned to the heap for possible further use when the pointer is nullified, a `deallocate` statement should be employed.

After a pointer assignment with a pointer on the right is executed, on the other hand, there is more than one pointer with the same target. So long as at least one of these pointers remains associated with the target, the others may be nullified.

But another problem can arise in this case. When two or more pointers have the same target, deallocating one of the pointers destroys the target object (and releases heap storage space) without afiecting the other pointers. The other pointers are now said to be "dangling references" — pointers to heap space that is no longer reserved.

Programs that manipulate pointers should strictly observe the following important rules:

1. If there is *only one* pointer currently pointing to a particular target object, do not change the value of (`nullify`, reallocate, or assign to) the pointer without first deallocating it.
2. If there is *more than one* pointer currently pointing to a particular target object, do not deallocate any of these pointers.

Unfortunately, many processors provide little assistance in enforcing these rules. The twin evils, garbage and dangling pointers, are the bane of heap storage management. Some modern storage management systems are able to cope with these issues, but they entail some cost in efficiency.

Pointers as Derived Type Components

A component of a derived type may have the `pointer` attribute. The type specified for each component in a derived type definition, *except* for components that have the `pointer` attribute, must be an intrinsic type or a previously defined derived type (a type declared earlier in the same program or subprogram or a type whose definition is inherited from the host or imported from a module; see Sections 2.4 and 7.2).

If a component that has the `pointer` attribute also has the `dimension` attribute, it must be a deferred-shape array. Thus, the subscript bounds are not specified in the derived type definition but must be given in the `allocate` statements for the pointer target array.[10]

A derived type may have a component that is a pointer to the same type. Such components occur most frequently in derived types that are intended for linked list applications.

EXAMPLE 6.31 Compare Example 6.21.

```
! Example 6.31. Pointer as a derived type component.
 program Finger
   implicit none
   type :: I_Type                                    ! Derived type definition
     integer :: Nuc_Count
     real :: Abundance
   end type I_Type
   type :: Chem_El_Type                              ! Derived type definition
     character (len = 16) :: El_Name
     character (len = 2) :: Symbol
     real :: Atomic_Num, Atomic_Mass
     type (I_Type) :: Prin                       ! Previously defined derived type
     type (Chem_El_Type), pointer :: Next      ! Pointer to structure of same type
   end type Chem_El_Type
   type (Chem_El_Type) :: Carbon_12                          ! Type declarations
   type (Chem_El_Type), pointer :: Root
! start program Finger
   Carbon_12 % Prin % Nuc_Count = 5                ! Component of substructure Prin
   allocate (Carbon_12 % Next)                      ! Allocate Carbon_12 % Next⊙.
   nullify (Carbon_12 % Next % Next)         ! Nullify Carbon_12 % Next⊙ % Next.
   Carbon_12 % Next % Symbol = "He"     ! Assign to Carbon_12 % Next⊙ % Symbol.
     :
   allocate (Root)
   nullify (Root % Next)                                ! Nullify Root⊙ % Next.
 end program Finger
```

In Example 6.31, as in Example 6.21, the derived type named `Chem_El_Type` has a component that is a structure of a previously defined derived type (here, `I_Type`). An additional component of `Chem_El_Type` in Example 6.31 is a pointer to another (potential) structure of the same type. Recall that derived type definitions do not create

[10] Fortran 90 does not permit an *array of pointers*. However, an array of structures, each having a single component that is a pointer, is permitted.

objects of the type being defined. Figure 6.8 shows the type definitions; the dotted lines indicate that no storage is reserved.

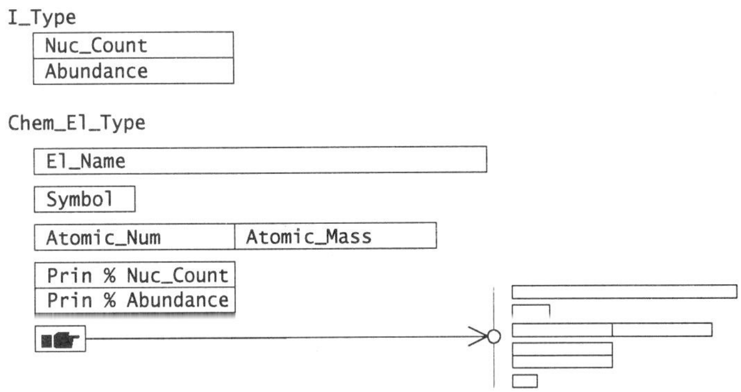

FIGURE 6.8
Components of the derived type *Chem_El_Type*.

`Carbon_12` is declared to be a structure of type `Chem_El_Type`. The type declaration creates a structure of this type in automatic storage, with six components named `El_Name`, `Symbol`, `Atomic_Num`, `Atomic_Mass`, `Prin`, and `Next`. (See Figure 6.9.) The first four of these are ordinary scalars, `Prin` is a substructure of type `I_Type`, and `Next` is a pointer. All of the ultimate components (see Section 6.2) of `Carbon_12`, which include the two components of the substructure `Prin`, are undefined. The association status of `Carbon_12 % Next` is undefined; the pointer is neither allocated nor nullified when the structure is created (prior to execution) by the type declaration.

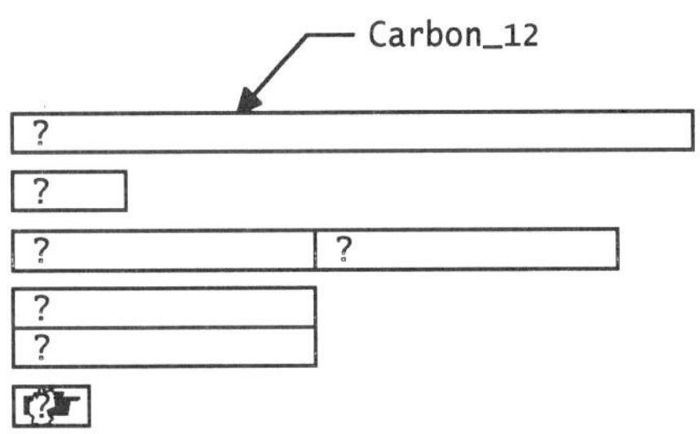

FIGURE 6.9.
Components of the declared structure *Carbon_12* are initially undefined.

Execution of the assignment statement

```
Carbon_12 % Prin % Nuc_Count = 5
```

sets the component `Nuc_Count` of the substructure `Carbon_12 % Prin` to the value 5 (see Figure 6.10).

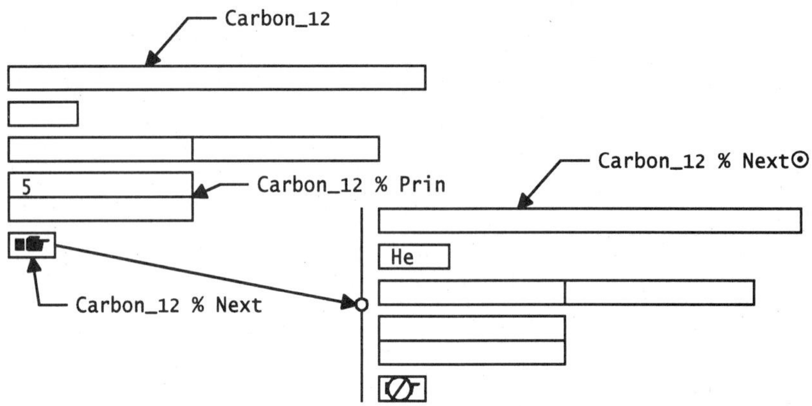

FIGURE 6.10. An assignment statement and a *nullify* statement give values to parts of the structure *Carbon_12 % Next⊙*.

Now execution of the statement

```
allocate (Carbon_12 % Next)
```

creates a target structure named `Carbon_12 % Next` in heap storage. At the time this structure is created by the `allocate` statement, all of its ultimate components are undefined. The next two statements give defined values to parts of this target structure (as indicated by Figure 6.10).

1. The `nullify` statement

   ```
   nullify (Carbon_12 % Next % Next)
   ```

   defines (as disassociated) the association status of the component **`Next`** in the structure `Carbon_12 % Next⊙`.
2. The assignment statement

   ```
   Carbon_12 % Next % Symbol = "He"
   ```

   assigns the string `"He"` to the component `Symbol` in the structure **`Carbon_12 % Next⊙`**.

Note carefully the difference between the assignment statement just mentioned and the deceptively similar assignment statement three lines above it in the program of Example 6.31. The variable name `Carbon_12 % Prin % Nuc_Count` consists of the name of a declared (automatic storage) structure, the name of a substructure, and the name of a component of the substructure. On the other hand, in the reference to the variable `Carbon_12 % Next⊙ % Symbol`, the component named `Next` has the **`pointer`** attribute, so `Carbon_12 % Next⊙` refers to the structure (in heap storage) that is the target of the pointer, and `Symbol` is a component of that target structure.

The last two statements in Example 6.31 illustrate that a pointer variable can be created in automatic storage as an independent object that is not part of a structure. The type declaration creates `Root` as a pointer to type `Chem_El_Type` but leaves its association status undefined. Executing the `allocate` statement creates a structure that is indirectly named `Root⊙` (which would be written in Fortran 90 as `Root`) but leaves all of its components undefined. Executing the `nullify` statement at the end of the example defines (as disassociated) the association status of `Root⊙ % Next`. (See Figure 6.11.)

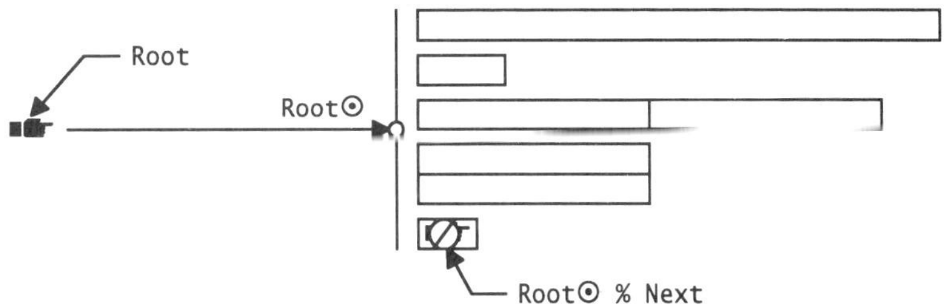

FIGURE 6.11. The *nullify* statement defines (as disassociated) the association status of the pointer *Root⊙ % Next.*

Application: Linked List

Techniques for organizing data into *linked lists*, which permit progressive allocation of heap storage as execution proceeds, avoid the inflexibility of fixed array size. Another advantage of linked lists, as compared to arrays, is that it is possible to insert a new list item in the middle without moving the existing items.

One disadvantage of linked structures is that the pointer components occupy extra storage space. If the linked items are small, the pointers may occupy a significant fraction of the total space for the structure. In practical applications, however, each list item is often a structure of considerable size. And in the modern computing environment, small amounts of storage space are rarely crucial, especially in applications where the advantages of linked structures are important.

A typical linked list is a sequence of structures. Each structure in the sequence has a pointer component, whose target is the next structure in the sequence. The linked list begins with a declared pointer in automatic (or static) storage that is called the *root* of the list.

EXAMPLE 6.32 The following program allocates three structures (a "magic number") and connects them together into a linked list. Figures 6.12, 6.13, and 6.14 illustrate the process. (In each figure, the dotted lines show the previous target of `Root`.) The internal procedure `Print_List`, which is called after the loop terminates, is described in Example 6.33.

```
! Example 6.32 Linked list: Read and Insert at Root.
  program Lynx
    implicit none
    intrinsic Associated
    integer, parameter :: S_LEN = 20, LIMIT = 3
    type :: Box_Type
      character (len = S_LEN) :: Name
      type (Box_Type), pointer :: Next
    end type Box_Type
    type (Box_Type), pointer :: Root, New_Item
    integer :: Loop
! start program Lynx
    nullify (Root)
    do, Loop = 1, LIMIT
      allocate (New_Item)
        ! Read next input item to Name component of new structure.
      read *, New_Item % Name                              ! New_Item⊙ % Name
        ! Copy Root to pointer component of new structure
      New_Item % Next => Root                              ! New_Item⊙ % Next
      Root => New_Item                                 ! Copy new pointer to Root
    end do
    nullify (New_Item)                                               ! Optional
    call Print_List (Root)
  contains
    subroutine Print_List (Point)
      :
    end subroutine Print_List
  end program Lynx
```

At the beginning of execution of the program in Example 6.32, a type declaration creates the pointer Root in automatic storage (in the activation record for the main program), but the pointer has been neither allocated nor nullified. The first program statement nullifies the pointer Root.

The loop consists of four steps. The first allocates a new structure (from the heap) as the target of the pointer New_Item, and the second reads a data item into the Name component of the new structure.

The two remaining statements are pointer assignments that rearrange the pointers so that the new structure is at the head of the list. These statements link the new structure into the list as the target of the pointer Root, as illustrated in the last part of Figure 6.12. The first of these two statements sets the Next component of the newly allocated structure to point to the previous list head so that the previous target of Root is now also the target of the Next component of the new structure. The final step resets

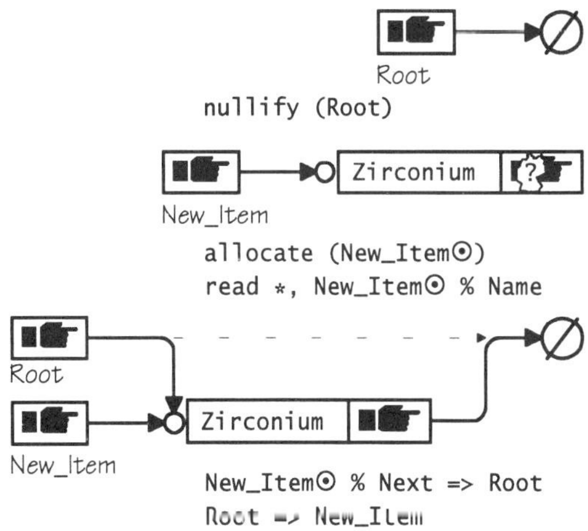

FIGURE 6.12. First structure created in heap storage and linked to the pointer *Root*.

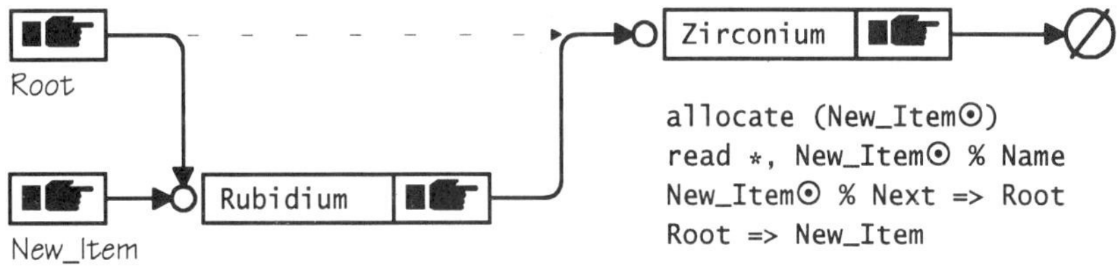

FIGURE 6.13. Second structure created and linked into list from *Root*.

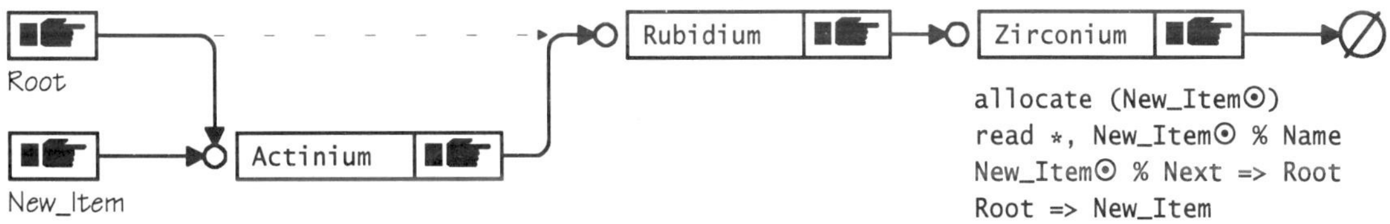

FIGURE 6.14. Third structure createand linked into list from *Root*.

`Root` to point to the new structure (instead of the previous list head) so that the new structure is now the head of the linked list. It is important that these two steps be executed in the order indicated here. (Why?)

After the loop terminates, the contents of the list is printed by a procedure that we shall examine next.

EXAMPLE 6.33 The following procedure inherits the type definition for Box_Type from the main program. (An intent attribute declaration is not permitted for pointer arguments; see Section 8.1). Note that the program in Example 6.32 links the structures together in such a way that newest structure is at the head of the linked list, so the Name components will be printed in last-in-first-out order.

```
! Example 6.33. Print procedure for linked list.
  subroutine Print_List (Point)  ! Print linked list, from Point to end of list.
    type (Box_Type), pointer :: Point, Trav
    Trav => Point        ! Copy to avoid destroying dummy argument pointer value.
    do while (Associated (Trav))                        ! Stop at nullified pointer.
      print *, Trav % Name
      Trav => Trav % Next
    end if
  end subroutine Print_List
```

Application: Binary Search Tree

Linked lists are *sequential* structures. Their organization is somewhat analogous to that of sequential files. Locating an item in a linked list requires a sequential search. Average search time is cut approximately in half if the list items are kept in order, but it is still significant (and perhaps intolerable) for a large list.

Tree structures can decrease search time significantly for large amounts of data. In a properly organized tree, the average time to locate an item is proportional to the logarithm of the number of items. In a linked list, on the other hand, the time is directly proportional to the number of items. For a million items, a linked list search requires perhaps a half million comparisons, while a tree may require fewer than 50.

Tree structures are naturally well suited to recursion because, at each node, a tree branches into *subtrees* of the same general structure as the parent tree. A tree has a *root* node that can serve as the base for recursion. Trees are generally implemented with a structure of some appropriate derived type at each node, containing some data and two or more pointer components.

A *binary tree* is one in which each node has exactly two subtrees, called the left and right subtrees, either or both of which may be empty. In a *binary search tree*, the nodes are ordered according to a *key* component: All keys in the left subtree of any node are less than the key at the node, which is in turn less than all keys in the right subtree. A recursive Fortran 90 program for inserting items in a binary search tree is presented in Section . (see Example 8.10).

A search in a binary search tree commences at the root. At each node, the search key is compared with the node key, and the search is directed to the left or right depending on the comparison. An unsuccessful search will end at an empty subtree or *leaf*, after which a new node may be inserted to replace the empty subtree.

The binary search tree has problems of its own, however. First, deletions from a tree may involve considerable extra processing to maintain the tree ordering. And second, the shape of a binary search tree depends entirely upon the sequence in which the keys were inserted. For example, inserting a sequence of keys that are already in order results in a tree with all left subtrees empty; such a tree is essentially a simple linear linked list. Modifications of the binary search tree algorithm to surmount these difficulties are well known, but they are beyond the scope of this text.

6.3 Exercise

1. In Example 6.32, what would be the effect of interchanging the two pointer assignment statements in the main program loop?

Part IV
PROGRAMS AND SUBPROGRAMS

Chapter 7 describes *programs*, *internal procedures*, and *modules*. An internal procedure is contained in a *host* main program or subprogram, and it may directly *inherit* portions of the data space of the host or may communicate with the host by argument passing. Nesting of internal procedures beyond the first level is not permitted. *Interface information* for internal procedures is accessible at the host program level (to the host program or subprogram as well as to other internal procedures at the same level).

Modules are useful for many purposes, including *global constant definition*, *global type definition*, and *data type encapsulation*. Module information is accessible to any program unit that includes a `use` statement for the module. A module has a three-level structure. The first level is the module itself, which has a *specification part* followed by a *subprogram part*. The subprogram part consists of definitions for *module procedures* — the second level — and they may contain internal procedures at the third level. Interface information for the module procedures is accessible at the outer module level, and interface information for the internal procedures is accessible at the module subprogram level. Data, type definitions, and module subprograms may be declared *private* (inaccessible outside the module).

The chapter also explains that a procedure may be classified as a *function* (which returns a value) or as a *subroutine* (which does not) and that it may be declared to be *recursive*. The chapter concludes by explaining how user-defined types can be *encapsulated* along with their operations and how user-defined *generic procedures* can be applied.

Chapter 8 covers issues related to *procedure arguments*. *Assumed-shape arrays* and *assumed-length strings* are especially recommended. A function result may be an *automatic* array or character string. Dummy arguments may be *pointers* or *procedure names*. *Keyword arguments* and *optional arguments* are permitted; the `Present` intrinsic function provides a test for the presence of an optional dummy argument.

Chapter 7
Procedures and Modules

7.1 OVERVIEW

There are two principal reasons for subdividing a program:

1. *Modularity* means dividing a project into pieces so that each piece can be studied independently, with minimal concern for the other pieces or for how they fit together. Thus, a problem that is too complicated to be comprehended as a whole may become manageable when it is subdivided into nearly independent parts.
2. *Data hiding* means protecting information in each part of the program from access — especially from being changed — by other parts of the program.

Fortran 90 provides *modules,* which are independent program units that can be *imported* in whole or in part by the main program, by external subprograms, or by other modules. Especially important is accessibility control: Certain data objects, procedures, or derived types can be declared private so that they will remain inaccessible when the module is imported.

One important application of modules is to provide a home for *global* data objects that need to be referred to from several different program units. Another is *data type encapsulation,* which can create a true data type that provides user-defined operations along with a user-defined structure.

This section covers program structure in general. Fortran 90 modules are discussed in detail in Section 7.2.

Program Units and Subprograms

Every Fortran program must include exactly one main program and may include additional program units. A Fortran program unit is a *main program,* a *module,* an *external subprogram* (see Appendix D.6), or a *block data program unit* (see Appendix E.3). Program units cannot be nested inside other program units. (See Figure 7.1.)

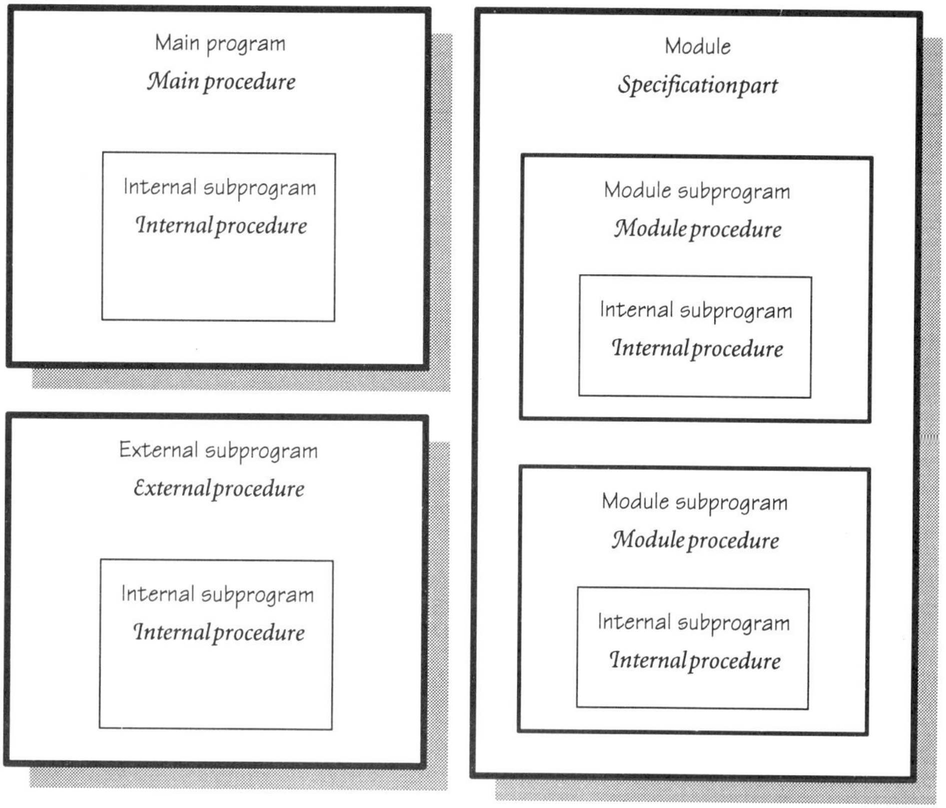

FIGURE 7.1. Structure of typical main program, external subprogram, and module.

A module has one more level of program structure than other program units. It can have a *subprogram part* with one or more module subprograms,[1] and it can have a *specification part*. As we shall see, either of these parts may be omitted. The containing module is called the *host* of the module subprograms (if any) in the subprogram part. Module subprograms cannot be nested inside each other. A module subprogram must be contained in a module.

A main program, a module subprogram, or an external subprogram may contain one or more *internal subprograms*. The containing program or subprogram is called the *host* of the internal procedure. Internal subprograms cannot be nested inside each other. An internal subprogram must be contained in a main program, a module subprogram, or an external subprogram.

[1] Note the difference between a *module*, which is a self-contained program unit, and a *module subprogram*, which is contained in the subprogram part of a module.

A procedure that is defined as part of a Fortran program is a *main procedure,* an *internal procedure,* a *module procedure,* an *external procedure,* or a *statement function*[2] (external procedures are described in Appendix D.6; statement functions, in Appendix D.9).

1. A main procedure is defined in the main program.
2. An internal procedure is defined by an internal subprogram.
3. A module procedure is defined in a module subprogram.
4. An external procedure is defined in an external subprogram.

A complete Fortran program consists of one main program along with the other program units (if any) to which it refers. If these program units contain references to other program units, those other units must be included as well. Most Fortran processors use a *linker* (as described in Section P.6) to combine all of the program units that are needed into an *executable Fortran program.* Intrinsic procedures are automatically made available by the processor; no action is needed to supply them.

Procedure Reference

An internal procedure, a module procedure, or an external procedure is classified as a *subroutine* or a *function,* depending on how it is referenced. Both subroutine references and function references include the *procedure name* (which has the same form as a variable name) and may include a parenthesized list of *actual arguments.*

1. A reference to a subroutine appears in a call statement, which consists of the keyword call followed by the subroutine name and the argument list:

   `call` *Subroutine name* `(` *Actual argument list* `)`

2. A reference to a function appears within an expression, and consists of the function name with its argument list:

   `. . .` *Function name* `(` *Actual argument list* `) . . .`

A function or a subroutine may be referenced more than once from the same procedure, just as intrinsic procedures such as `SqRt` and `Abs` may be used more than once.

Whenever the Fortran execution sequence reaches a procedure reference, execution of the statement containing the reference is discontinued. Execution jumps to the first statement of the designated procedure[3] and continues from there in the usual way

[2] Two kinds of procedures are defined outside the Fortran program. Intrinsic procedures are defined by the Fortran standard as part of the Fortran language and are automatically made available by the Fortran processor on demand. External procedures may be defined either in Fortran or "by means other than Fortran" — for example, by statements written in assembly language or in some other programming language.

[3] Fortran also permits an entry statement, which defines an entry point in a procedure other than the first executable statement (see Appendix D.7).

until the last statement of the procedure is reached or until a return statement in the procedure is executed. At that point, the procedure is terminated and execution resumes at a point immediately following the procedure reference.

Subroutine Reference

A subroutine must be referenced by means of a call statement, which has the form

call *Subroutine name* (*Actual argument list*)

For example, the statement

```
call Swap_It (A, B)
```

calls for execution of the procedure named Swap_It, which requires two arguments.

Subroutine calls may require no arguments, one argument, or many arguments. If there is more than one, the arguments inside the parentheses are separated by commas. If there are no arguments, the parentheses may be omitted and the following simpler form may be used:

call *Subroutine name*

Function Reference

A function is referenced by the appearance of the function name, with an actual argument list, in an expression:

. . . *Function name* (*Actual argument list*) . . .

Execution of a function reference results in the calculation of a single function value or result that is substituted in the expression at the point where the function name appears. For example, in the assignment statement

```
Y = A + B * Temp_C (F)
```

a numerical value is to replace `Temp_C (F)`, thus permitting calculation of the expression value that is to be assigned to `Y`. The function reference, `Temp_C (F)`, may therefore be said to "have a value" that is returned to the expression at the point where the reference appears. (A subroutine reference does not have a value in this sense.) A function result may be a structure, an array, or a character string.

A function reference may require no arguments, one argument, or many arguments. If there are two or more arguments inside the parentheses in a function reference, they are separated by commas. In the statement

```
Y = A + Area (L, W) * C
```

the value of the function `Area`, whose arguments are `L` and `W`, is returned. This value is multiplied by the value of `C`, and the value of `A` is added to obtain the expression value that will be assigned to `Y`.

If there are no arguments, the function name must be followed by an empty pair of parentheses:

```
Y = A + Fun () * C
```

Unlike the subroutine reference in a call statement, a function reference without the parentheses is prohibited. (Without the parentheses, Fortran might assume that Fun is a variable.)

Type, type properties, and attributes of a function reference. Since a function reference returns a *value*, a specific type (as well as type properties and perhaps other attributes) must be considered to apply to the reference, as part of the expression where it appears. The function definition specifies the type, type properties, and attributes of the function result, which become those of the function reference. (See Section 7.3 for details.) Note that a function result may be a structure, an array, or a character string.

Procedure Interface

Certain *interface information* relating to an internal procedure or to a module procedure is, in effect, a part of the specification information in the host program or subprogram. Appearance of the procedure definition within the host "declares" (specifies) this interface information and makes it available to the host, just as if it appeared in type declarations or other statements in the specification part of the host program or subprogram. For some purposes, it may be helpful to pretend that interface information for internal procedures or module procedures appears in declarations at the beginning of the host.

Interface information for an internal procedure or module procedure consists of the following:

The procedure name

The type and other properties and attributes of the dummy arguments

For functions, the type and other properties and attributes of the function result

As we shall see in Section 8.7, for procedure references with optional and keyword arguments the *names* and the *order* of dummy arguments, as well as their type properties and other attributes, are included in the interface.

When an internal procedure is contained in a module subprogram, it is only at the immediate host level (the module subprogram level) that interface information regarding the internal procedure is available. The interface is not accessible from the point of view of the outer module level because it is hidden by the intermediate module subprogram level.

Procedure interface information, like other information specified in the host program or subprogram, can be inherited by a module procedure or by an internal procedure from its host. Thus, an internal procedure can invoke (call or reference) any internal procedure in the *same host* program or subprogram, and a module procedure can invoke any module procedure in the *same host* module. An internal procedure contained in a module procedure can also invoke any *module procedure* in the same module because procedure interfaces, like other specifications, are inherited by the module procedure from the host module. However, an internal procedure cannot invoke internal procedures contained in module procedures other than its host.

Any program unit that imports a module (as described in Section 7.2) thereby gains access to information specified for the module, including interface information relating to the module procedures (but not their internal procedures) as well as names of objects that are declared in the specification part of the module and derived types that are defined there. (However, an exception is information declared by the module to be `private`, which is not made accessible outside the module.)

Name Inheritance

When the name of an object appears in an internal procedure, there are two possibilities:

1. The name may refer to a *local* object (one whose type or other attributes are specified in the internal procedure).
2. The name may refer to an object that the internal procedure *inherits* from its host (the main program, external subprogram, or module subprogram that contains the internal procedure).

A local object "belongs to" the internal procedure; an inherited object "belongs to" the host. Data object names, derived type names, and procedure interface information may all be inherited from a host program or subprogram.

A module subprogram can also inherit information from its host module. An internal procedure contained in a module subprogram can also inherit information from the host module subprogram, in the usual way. Some of this information may be inherited, in turn, by the module subprogram from the host module. Information that can be inherited from a host module subprogram or module includes objects declared in the host, derived types defined in the host, and interface information concerning procedures contained in the host. The `private` attribute does not restrict inheritance within a module; it only inhibits access from outside the module.

When an object is inherited, all attributes must be inherited along with the name. If the type or any attributes are declared in the inner procedure, the object is *local* and is not inherited from the host. Unspecified attributes of local objects or of dummy arguments assume default values in the usual way and have no connection with attributes that may be declared for similar names in the host. Specifying any other attribute without declaring the type would require implicit type specification (see Appendix D.1), which is an error when an `implicit none` directive is in effect.

A name may be used at more than one nesting level to denote the same object or different objects. A general rule applies in all cases: When a name appears in an inner subprogram, the *innermost* enclosing program or subprogram that *contains a definition or declaration* for the name determines its significance.

Note that a module subprogram or internal subprogram defines its procedure interface at the level of the *containing* program unit or subprogram. Thus, interfaces for all module procedures, but not their internal procedures, are accessible at the module level; in effect, these interfaces belong to the specification part of the module. A module procedure can be referenced from other module procedures or from their internal procedures, since those procedures can inherit the interface information from the module level.

Here is an example:

```
   module Mod_A
 ! Specification part
     implicit none
     type :: New
       integer :: J, K
     end type New
     ! Initialize X with constructor:
     type (New) :: X = New (1234, 5678)
 ! Subprogram part
   contains
     subroutine M_Sub_1
   ! start subroutine M_Sub_1
       call I_Sub
     contains
       subroutine I_Sub
     ! start subroutine I_Sub
       call M_Sub_2 (X % J, X % K)
       end subroutine I_Sub
     end subroutine M_Sub_1
     subroutine M_Sub_2 (I1, I2)
       integer, intent (in out) :: I1, I2
       integer :: X
   ! start subroutine M_Sub_2
       X = I1
       I1 = I2
       I2 = X
     end subroutine M_Sub_2
   end module Mod_A
```

A program or subprogram that imports this module may call the module subroutine M_Sub_1, which calls its internal subroutine I_Sub. The subroutine M_Sub_1 inherits interface information for M_Sub_2 from the module level, and I_Sub inherits this same interface information from M_Sub_1. Since I_Sub has access to the interface for M_Sub_2, the call to M_Sub_2 from the internal procedure is valid.

As described in Section 7.2, a main program, an external subprogram, or a module can contain a use statement whose effect is to import a designated module. Names defined or declared in the specification part of the designated module, including interface information for its module subprograms, are treated as belonging to the program unit or subprogram in which the use statement appears. This information can be inherited by internal procedures or module procedures that are contained in the host where the use statement appears.

7.2 PROGRAM ORGANIZATION

Main Program

The main program may begin with a `program` statement:

```
program Program name
```

Although the `program` header statement is optional, its use is considered good program documentation practice. If the `program` statement is omitted, Fortran recognizes the main program by the fact that its first statement is *not* one of the other statements (such as a `module` statement) that can appear as a header statement.

If the main program contains internal subprograms, they must be grouped at the end of the program unit, and a `contains` statement must be placed between the end of the main procedure definition and the first internal subprogram. Thus, we have the following pattern:

```
program Program name
   :
contains
   Internal subprograms
end program Program name
```

The `contains` statement declares that the following lines contain internal subprograms.

The main program must end with an `end` or `end program` statement. This statement follows the `end` statement of the last internal subprogram (if any) that it contains. An `end program` statement may include the *Program name* if the `program` header statement is present. The full form

```
end program Program name
```

is recommended and is shown in all of the examples in this text.

Internal Procedures

An internal procedure is a subroutine or function defined by an internal subprogram (Sections P.5 and 2.4). An internal subprogram is a block of statements within a main program, a module subprogram, or an external subprogram. The containing program or subprogram is the *host* of the internal procedure. Only one level of nesting is permitted. An internal subprogram cannot contain further internal subprograms, and it must not include a `contains` statement.

An internal subprogram begins with a `subroutine` or `function` statement and ends with an `end`, `end subroutine`, or `end function` statement. (See Section 7.3 for the form of a subroutine or function subprogram.) An `entry` statement (see Appendix D.7) is not permitted in an internal subprogram.

If an `implicit none` directive appears in the host, the explicit type declaration requirement applies to the internal procedure also. In effect, the directive is inherited from the host (see also Appendix D.1).

Modules

A module is a container for specifications and procedure definitions that can be "imported" into other programs or subprograms by means of a `use` statement. A module begins with a `module` statement and ends with an `end` or `end module` statement. The `module` statement includes the module name, which may also appear in an `end module` statement.

A module has a three-level structure, as shown in Figure 7.2:

1. The outer level consists of a *specification part* followed by a *subprogram part*. Either of these parts may be omitted.
2. The subprogram part, if present, consists of a `contains` statement followed by one or more module subprograms at the second level. Each module subprogram defines one module procedure.
3. A module subprogram may also contain one or more internal subprograms at the third level. No further nesting beyond this third level is permitted.

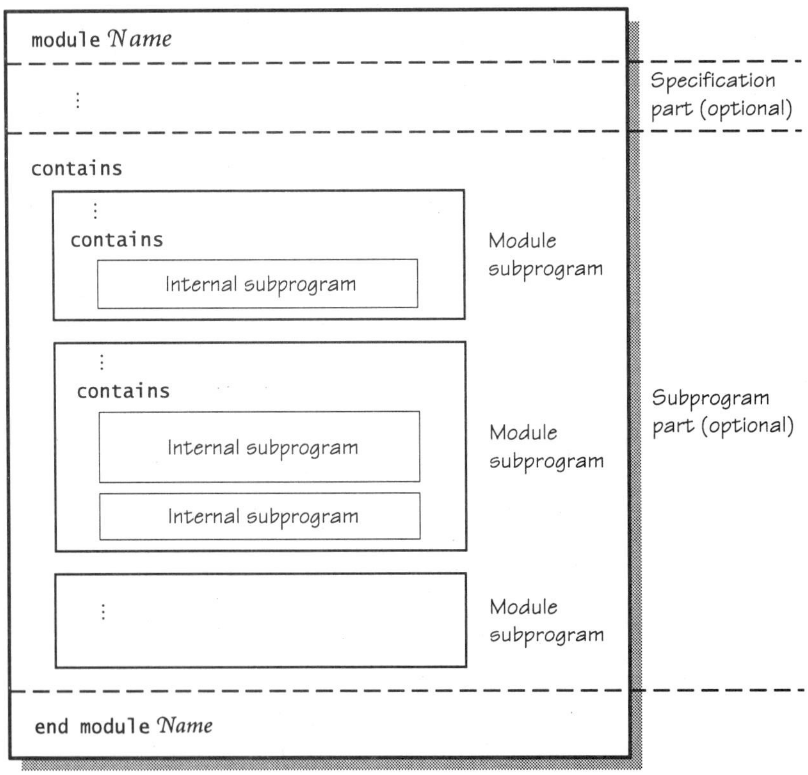

FIGURE 7.2. Three-level module structure.

The Specification Part

Data specifications at the beginning of a module may include any declarations that are permitted in other programs or subprograms (with some minor exceptions). In particular, there may be variable declarations, named constant declarations, and derived type definitions.

Object declarations and type definitions in the specification part of a module, as well as procedures defined by module subprograms, are accessible to all module subprograms and internal subprograms in the same module. This includes variable declarations, named constant declarations, and derived type definitions that appear in the specification part, as well as interface information for module procedures that are defined in the subprogram part (but not for their internal procedures).

Such declarations and definitions, except those that are given the `private` attribute, may also be imported into any program or subprogram that has a `use` statement referring to the module. A module that is imported in this way may be employed just as if the module text (except for `private` parts) were incorporated into the program or subprogram in which the `use` statement appears.

The Subprogram Part

Each module subprogram begins with a `subroutine` statement or a `function` statement and ends with an `end`, `end subroutine`, or `end function` statement. (See Section 7.3 for the form of a subroutine or function subprogram.) If any internal subprograms are present, the first one is preceded by a `contains` statement. The `end` statement of the module subprogram follows the `end` statement of the last internal subprogram.

If an `implicit none` directive appears in the host, the explicit type declaration requirement applies to the module procedure also. In effect, the directive is inherited from the host module (see also Appendix D.1).

An internal procedure contained in a module subprogram can inherit information from its host module subprogram, including information that the module subprogram inherits from the host module.

Applications of Modules

Some important module applications have been suggested:

Global constants. Named constants may be declared once in a module and imported into other program units. These constants could be universal constants or values specific to a given program run, such as the following:

```
module Global_Constants
real, parameter :: PI = 3.14159265355979323546264 3, &
  SPEED_OF_LIGHT = 2.99792458E8, AVOGADRO = 6.0221367E23
end module Global_Constants
```

```
module Today
  integer, parameter :: Patient_Load = 143, Staff = 17 &
    Stock_On_Hand = 1472
  character (len = *) :: Supervisor = "Charles␣Dickens"
end module Today
```

Global structure definitions. A derived type may be defined in a module and accessed from programs or subprograms that import the module. This is the only way to access the same derived type from more than one program unit. (As noted in Section 6.2, whole-structure assignment is permitted only between structures of the *same* derived type.) In the following example, the main program declares a structure named X whose type is defined in the module:

```
  module Linked_List_Node
    type :: Information_Part
      character (len = 20) Identification
      integer Sequence, Count
    end type Information_Part
    type :: Node
      type (Information_Part) Information
      type (Node), pointer :: Next
    end type Node
  end module Linked_List_Node
  program Caller
    use Linked_List_Node
    type (Node) :: X
! start program Caller
    read *, X % Information % Identification
    nullify (X % Next)
    :
  end program Caller
```

Global allocatable arrays. A program may need a large array whose size is determined — for example, by the value of an input variable — after execution begins. An allocatable array may be declared in a module and imported by all of the subprograms that need it. Soon after program execution begins, the size is determined — from input, for example — and the array is allocated. Allocation can take place in any subprogram that imports the module where the allocatable array is declared.

Imported common blocks. A common block (see Appendix E.3) and all of its associated declarations may be imported from a module into all of the subprograms where it is needed. With this programming technique, the Fortran compiler needs to process the specifications for the common block only once, which may result in some efficiency advantage over `include` (see Appendix D.11).

Data type encapsulation. A module may contain subprograms that define special operations applicable to structures of a derived type defined in the same module. The details of the operations may be declared `private` to guarantee proper "information hiding" and *encapsulation* of the derived type along with its operations. (See also Section 7.5.)

EXAMPLE 7.1 The module in this example defines a data type suitable for representing complex numbers in polar form.

```
! Example 7.1. Complex numbers in polar form.
  module Ursa
    implicit none
    type :: Polar
      real :: R
      real :: Theta
    end type Polar
  contains
    type (Polar) function P_Complex (Z) result (S)
      intrinsic Abs, AImag, ATan2, Real
      complex, intent (in) :: Z
  ! start function P_Complex
      S % R = Abs (Z)
      S % Theta = ATan2 (AImag (Z), Real (Z))
    end function P_Complex
    complex function F_Complex (P) result (Bear)
      intrinsic Real, Sin, Cos, Cmplx
      type (Polar), intent (in) :: P
      real :: X, Y
  ! start function F_Complex
      X = Polar % R * Cos (Polar % Theta)
      Y = Polar % R * Sin (Polar % Theta)
      Bear = Cmplx (X, Y)
    end function F_Complex
    type (Polar) function Mult_Polar (P1, P2) result (P)
      type (Polar), intent (in) :: P1, P2
  ! start function Mult_Polar
      P % R = P1 % R * P2 % R
      P % Theta = P1 % Theta + P2 % Theta
    end function Mult_Polar
  end module Ursa
```

The subprogram part contains three function definitions: P_Complex converts a Fortran-style complex number to polar form, F_Complex converts from polar form to Fortran style, and Mult_Polar forms the product of two complex numbers that are represented in polar form. The module could very easily be extended to divide and exponentiate complex numbers in polar form. (The program in Example 7.2 imports this module.)

Private Names

The names of data objects (including constants), derived type definitions, and module procedures may be declared to be `private`. That is, subprograms outside the module are not permitted to import them. This feature contributes to data protection by "hiding" (and thus protecting) unneeded information from the user of a module.[4]

Names declared `private` are typically those of objects and definitions that are to be shared by procedures within the module, but that should not be visible outside the module.

For a variable, named constant, or function result name, the keyword `private` may appear as an attribute specifier in a type declaration — for example,

```
integer, private, parameter :: Password = 7730, S_Length = 23
real, private :: Salary_of_CEO = 1000000.00
character (len = S_Length), private :: Secret_Word = "Groucho"
```

As we shall see, attributes of a function result *other than* type, type properties, and `recursive` must be declared inside the function definition and not in the header.

For a derived type definition, the keyword `private` may follow the keyword `type` on the first line of the definition:

```
type, private :: List_Item
  character (len = 20) :: Word
  integer :: Sequence, Count
end type List_Item
```

It is also possible to make the derived type accessible, without revealing its internal structure, by placing the keyword `private` alone on the second line:

```
type :: List_Item
  private
  character (len = 20) :: Word
  integer :: Sequence, Count
end type List_Item
```

This latter feature would be useful in a module that encapsulates a derived type along with a complete set of operations upon it. Consider that a Fortran program can ma-

---

[4] Names declared in a module have an "accessibility attribute" which is either *public* or *private*. The *public* attribute declaration is used much less frequently than *private*, for two reasons. First, the default accessibility attribute value is *public*, so explicit *public* declarations are rarely needed. Second, a *public* entity may have *private* components, but not vice versa.

nipulate floating-point numbers without access to any details concerning their sign, exponent, and significand parts. Similarly, the user of an encapsulated type could declare variables and manipulate them with module procedures, without separate access to the derived type components.

The `private` attribute for module procedures is specified in a separate `private` declaration (see the discussion of attribute-oriented declarations in Section 1.2) in the specification part of the module:

`private` *List*

Variables, named constants, and derived types may also be included in the *List*.

The `use` *Statement*

A `use` statement of the form

`use` *Module name*

may appear in a program or subprogram. The effect of this statement is to *import* interface information concerning variables, derived types, and procedures from the designated module (except those with the `private` accessibility attribute) into the program or subprogram where the `use` statement appears. There may be any number of `use` statements in a program or subprogram, and they must *immediately follow* the `program`, `subroutine`, or `function` header statement. Note that `use` statements are the only statements that may precede `implicit none`.

Because of the way the `use` operation behaves, an imported module may be employed just as if the declarations, type definitions, and procedure definitions in the module text (except those declared `private`) were incorporated into the program unit in which the `use` statement appears.

If a name imported from the module is the same as another name in the subprogram to which it is imported, the `use` statement may include a *rename clause* designating local names different from the names that appear in the module, for example:

```
use Math_Lib
use Stats_Lib, SProd => Prod
```

The second `use` statement includes a rename clause of the form

Local name => *Module name*

It is also possible to import only a selected list of names from a module:

`use` *Module name*, `only :` *List of names*

Here is an example:

```
use Global_Constants, only : PI, SPEED_OF_LIGHT
```

When a name is imported from a module via a `use` statement, the type and other attributes must *not* be specified in the procedure to which it is imported. The attributes are those specified in the module. If an imported name is changed by a rename clause in the use statement, the original attributes apply to the new name in the procedure to which it is imported.

EXAMPLE 7.2 The following program uses the derived type definition and the conversion and multiplication operations from the module Ursa that appears in Example 7.1. (Compare Example 6.25.)

```
! Example 7.2. Complex numbers in Fortran style and in polar form.
  program Driver
    use Ursa                             ! Import type and operations from module.
    implicit none
    complex :: Z1, Z2, Z3
    type (Polar) :: P1, P2, P3                 ! Derived type imported from module
! start program Driver
    read *, Z1, Z2
    print *, "␣Complex␣numbers␣in␣Fortran␣style:␣"
    print *, Z1, Z2
    P1 = P_Complex (Z1); P2 = P_Complex (Z2)
    print *, "␣Same␣complex␣numbers␣in␣polar␣form:␣"
    print *, P1, P2
    P3 = Mult_Polar (P1, P2)
    print *, "␣Complex␣product␣in␣polar␣form:␣"
    print, P3
    Z3 = F_Complex (P3)
    print *, "␣Complex␣product␣in␣Fortran␣style:␣"
    print *, Z3
  end program Driver
```

Input data:

```
(0.8660254, 0.5) (0.5, 0.8660254)
```

Output:

```
Complex numbers in Fortran style:
( 0.8660254, 0.5000000) ( 0.5000000, 0.8660254)
Same complex numbers in polar form:
1.0000000  0.5235988  1.0000000  1.0471976
Complex product in polar form:
1.0000000  1.5707964
Complex product in Fortran style:
( -4.3711388E-08, 1.0000000)
```

Transition Tip

- Change all external procedures to internal procedures or to module subprograms. An easy way to change external procedure subprograms (singly or in groups) to module subprograms is to enclose them between a `module` statement and an `end module` statement.

7.3 DEFINING A SUBROUTINE OR FUNCTION

A subroutine or function procedure definition consists of a collection of Fortran statement lines and comment lines, beginning with a `subroutine` or `function` statement and terminating with an `end`, `end subroutine`, or `end function` statement. The `subroutine` or `function` statement gives the name of the procedure that is being defined and lists its dummy arguments (if any).

A procedure is *recursive* if any statement in the procedure definition makes reference to the procedure being defined, either directly or indirectly (via other procedures). The keyword `recursive` must appear in the header statement for a recursive procedure. (Recursion is described in detail in Section 7.4.)

Procedure Definition Patterns

The `subroutine` and `function` Statements

A subroutine procedure definition begins with a `subroutine` statement and terminates with an `end` or `end subroutine` statement. The `subroutine` statement names the procedure that is being defined and lists its dummy arguments (if any):

```
subroutine Subroutine name ( Dummy argument list )
  ⋮
end subroutine Subroutine name
```

A function procedure definition begins with a `function` statement and terminates with an `end` or `end function` statement. The `function` statement names the procedure that is being defined and lists its dummy arguments (if any). Some variation is permitted in the form of a function header. The following function procedure definition pattern is recommended:

```
Type function Function name ( Dummy argument list ) &
  result ( Result name )
    ⋮
end function Function name
```

Although Fortran 90 does not require the separate *Result name* except when the function is directly recursive, it is recommended that a separate *Result name* be specified in all cases. The *Result name* is the name of a local variable (within the function definition) that must be given a value during execution of the function procedure. The final value of this variable, when execution of the procedure terminates, is the value returned by the function and becomes the function value in the expression where the function reference occurs. If there is no separate *Result name*, the *Function name* performs a double role, externally as the name of the function and internally as the name of the result variable.

For a recursive subroutine or function, the keyword `recursive` must precede the procedure name in the header statement. Note that in a function header the keyword `recursive` may precede the *Type* (if any), which is recommended, or it may appear between the *Type* and the keyword `function`.

EXAMPLE 7.3 Examples of `subroutine` and `function` statements are given next.

```
subroutine Swap_It (X, Y)
subroutine Find (A, N, X, Loc)
subroutine Reverse (A, N)
subroutine Swap_It (Int_1, Str_1, Int_2, Str_2)
recursive subroutine Find (A, N, X, Loc)

logical function Signal (X) result (Flag)
real (kind = DBL) function Sca_Pr (X, Y, N) result (Sum)
character (len = 10) function String (A, B) result (S)
function String (A, B) result (S)
integer function Factorial (K) result (Prod)
recursive function String (A, B) result (S)
recursive integer function Factorial (K) result (Prod)
integer recursive function Factorial (K) result (Prod)
```

Since the function *Result name* will acquire a value, the proper type (and other attributes) must be declared for the name.[5] The *Type* is omitted from the header statement if the *Type* (with other attributes, if any) is declared for the *Result name* elsewhere within the procedure definition. Note that a function result may be a structure, an array, or a character string.

It is recommended that the end statement in a procedure definition have one of the following forms:

`end subroutine` *Subroutine name*
`end function` *Function name*

Fortran requires the keyword `subroutine` or `function` in the end statement for internal subprograms and module subprograms. (This keyword is optional for external sub-

[5] Implicit type specification is also permitted, but is not recommended. See Appendix D.1.

programs; see Appendix D.6.) The name in the `end` statement is optional, and is not permitted unless the keyword `subroutine` or `function` appears. Consistently including *both* the keyword and the name makes it possible for the programmer and the compiler to verify proper placement of program units.

The `return`*,* `stop`*, and* end *Statements*

Every procedure presumably has a way of terminating normally so that the execution sequence can be resumed from the point of procedure reference. In the simplest case, normal termination is achieved when execution of the procedure reaches the `end` statement. However, it may be desirable to terminate procedure execution at some other point. The `return` statement causes resumption of the program or subprogram from which the procedure was referenced; the `stop` statement causes execution of the entire program to terminate.

The issue of program *robustness* is relevant at this point. This term relates to the ability of the program to produce reasonable output even when unexpected data values or other error situations are encountered. Insofar as possible, a program should make checks ahead of time and circumvent situations that would result in unacceptable program behavior. Three increasing levels of robustness may be identified.

1. Not robust: The program merely assumes that all data values will be within expected bounds, that input files will contain sufficient data, and the like. If these assumptions prove to be unjustified, totally unexpected (and potentially disastrous) program behavior may result. This level may be acceptable for short experimental runs that can be closely monitored by the problem originator, but it is entirely unacceptable in most programming situations. A difficulty is that experimental programs often migrate beyond the control of the originator without sufficient attention to enhancing robustness.
2. Somewhat robust: Checks are made for most conditions that could cause the program to abort. The current procedure may return a result that can be recognized as an indication of error, or the program may print an error message and terminate. Program examples in many textbooks, including this one, often aim for this level of robustness. The `stop` and `return` statements are useful at this level.
3. Robust: Software released for distribution outside the originating organization requires an ability to recover from error conditions of all kinds. Typically, execution is suspended and means are provided for interacting with operating personnel, after which execution is resumed if possible. In this environment, it is rarely useful to simply terminate a procedure, even with an error indication. Terminating a procedure in this way would usually require that the program be rerun from the beginning, which may be impossible if files have been updated or other permanent changes have been made.

The `return` statement. When a procedure is referenced, the first step to be executed will be the first executable statement of the procedure definition.[6] If the execution sequence reaches a `return` statement, execution of the procedure terminates. The sequence of execution reverts to the program unit where the procedure reference occurred and resumes at a point immediately following the procedure reference.

There may be several `return` statements in a program or subprogram. A `return` statement often appears as the dependent statement of a simple `if` statement (Section 3.3).

The *stop* statement. As we saw in Section P.6, most computers operate under control of an operating system, which deals with a queue of jobs and attempts to schedule the available computing resources in an efficient manner. The effect of the `stop` statement is to return control to the operating system so that the resources that were assigned to this job during its execution can be reallocated.

A `stop` statement may be encountered during execution of the main program or any other procedure. The effect of a `stop` statement is the same in a procedure as in the main program.

The `stop` statement has either of the following forms:

```
stop
stop Stop code
```

The *Stop code* is a digit string or a character constant, as in the following examples:

```
stop 1234
stop "⊥Execution⊥completed⊥successfully.⊥"
```

The Fortran standard requires that the *Stop code* be "available" when execution terminates, in a processor-dependent manner.

Executing an *end* statement. If execution of the *main program* reaches the end of the last statement, the `end` statement causes program termination — that is, executing an `end` statement in the main program has the same effect as executing a `stop` statement. If a `contains` statement and one or more internal subprograms appear in the main program, the execution sequence skips over them to the `end` statement of the main program.

If the execution sequence in a *procedure* reaches the `end` statement, execution of the procedure is terminated — that is, executing an `end` statement in a procedure has the same effect as executing a `return` statement. Execution resumes and proceeds from the point immediately following the procedure reference, in the program unit where the procedure reference occurred. If a `contains` statement and one or more internal sub-

[6] Fortran also permits an entry statement, which defines an entry point in a procedure other than the first executable statement (see Appendix D.7).

programs appear in the program unit, the execution sequence skips over them to the end statement.

EXAMPLE 7.4 (Compare Example 4.21.) When a loop exit leads directly to program termination, a `stop` statement may be preferable to an `exit` statement, and the *Stop code* may be employed as an indication of the reason for termination. The following program computes the factorials of consecutive integers until a potential overflow condition is encountered. A `stop` statement terminates the program if the factorial currently being calculated would exceed `Huge (1)`.

```
! Example 7.4. Compute factorials of all integers.
  program Factory
    implicit none
    intrinsic Huge
    integer :: Limit = 0, Factorial, Loop
! start program Factory
    Outer_Loop: do
      Factorial = 1
      print *, "␣Now␣finding␣the␣factorial␣of␣", Limit
      do Loop = 1, Limit
        if (Factorial > Huge (1) / Loop) &
          stop "␣The␣factorial␣is␣too␣large.␣"      ! Terminate program execution.
        Factorial = Factorial * Loop
      end do
      print *, "␣The␣factorial␣is:␣", Factorial
      Limit = Limit + 1
    end do Outer_Loop
  end program Factory
```

EXAMPLE 7.5 (Compare Example 4.19.) Executing a `return` statement within a procedure has much the same effect as executing an `exit` statement in a loop. The following program reads groups of real numbers and prints the average of each group. It assumes that actual data values are never zero. The main program and the internal subroutine each consist almost entirely of a simple do loop. The subroutine interprets a zero entry as the end of a group and executes a return statement that terminates both the loop and the subroutine. The main program interprets an empty group — one that *begins* with a zero entry — as the end of data and executes a stop statement that terminates both the loop and the program.

```
! Example 7.5. Averages of groups of real numbers.
  program Assembly
  implicit none
  intrinsic Real
  real :: Next, Total, Average
  integer :: Count
! start program Assembly
    print *, "␣Please␣enter␣a␣group␣of␣numbers␣to␣be␣averaged.␣"
    print *, "␣Enter␣zero␣to␣end␣the␣group.␣"
    print *, "␣To␣quit,␣enter␣zero␣as␣the␣first␣number␣in␣a␣group.␣"
    do
      Count = 0
      Total = 0.0
      call Group
      if (Count == 0) stop                        ! Terminate program execution.
        Average = Total / Real (Count)
        print *, "␣The␣average␣of␣", Count, "␣numbers␣is:␣", Average
    end do
  contains
    subroutine Group
      do
        print *, "␣Next␣number:␣"
        read *, Next
        if (Next == 0.0) return                 ! Terminate procedure execution.
        Count = Count + 1
        Total = Total + Next
      end do
    end subroutine Group
  end program Assembly
```

Defining a Subroutine

Examples of subroutine procedure definitions, along with simple main programs that might be used to reference them, are given next.

EXAMPLE 7.6 Suppose that most of the elements of a given array are zeros. We wish to locate the nonzero elements and move them to a smaller array. We also wish to keep a record of the position at which each of the nonzero elements was found within the original array. (Compare the intrinsic function `Pack` described in Appendix A.)

We use the subroutine `Find` to locate the next nonzero element in the array `A` beyond a designated beginning search position. This subroutine has three dummy arguments:

The array, A, to be searched

The beginning search position, N

A structure, R, that contains both the resulting nonzero element value, X, and the location, Loc, where the nonzero element was found in A

We define the subroutine Find in a module subprogram. Thus, the necessary interface information concerning the types, type properties, and other attributes of the dummy arguments is automatically available to the program from which the subroutine is called. (See Appendix D.6.) The dummy argument array A is an assumed-shape array because its declaration specifies only its rank and not its full shape (it will take on the shape of the actual argument array as explained in Section 8.2).

```
! Example 7.6a. (Module)
 module Find_M
   implicit none                              ! Specification part of module
   intrinsic Size, MaxLoc
   type :: Item
     integer :: Loc
     real :: X
   end type Item
 contains                                      ! Subprogram part of module
   subroutine Find (A, N, R)                          ! Module subprogram
       ! Subroutine to locate the next nonzero element, at position N
       ! or beyond, in an assumed-shape array A. X will be set to the
       ! value of the element found, and Loc will be set to the
       ! position in A at which it was found. If there are no nonzero
       ! elements in A(N: ), X will be set to zero and Loc will be
       ! set to Size (A) + 1.
     real, dimension(:), intent (in) :: A              ! Assumed shape array
     integer, intent (in) :: N
     type (Item), intent (out) :: R
     integer, dimension(1) :: Big
 ! start subroutine Find
     if (Any (A(N: ) /= 0.0)) then
       Big = MaxLoc (A(N: ), Mask = (A(N: ) /= 0.0))
       R % Loc = Big(1)
       R % X = A(R % Loc + N - 1)
     else
       R % Loc = Size (A) + 1
       R % X = 0.0
     end if
   end subroutine Find
 end module Find_M
```

The following main program uses `Find` to construct the condensed array. The main program specifies that the array named `Data` is to be searched, beginning at position `J`. The third actual argument in the `call` statement names the array element in which the nonzero element value and its location are to be stored.

```
! Example 7.6b. (Main program)
! Main program using Find to condense an array of 100 elements, most
! of which are zero.
  program Condense
    use Find_M
    implicit none
    integer, parameter :: BIG = 100, SMALL = 10
    real, dimension(BIG) :: Data
    type (Item), dimension(SMALL) :: Item_Array, R
    integer :: EoF, Dummy, I, J, K

! start program Condense
    open (1, file = "zahlen.txt")
    read (1, *, iostat = EoF) Data
    if (EoF < 0) stop

    J = 1
    do I = 1, SMALL
      call Find (Data, J, Item_Array(I))

      if (Item_Array(I) % Loc /= 0) then
        J = Item_Array(I) % Loc + 1

      else
        print *, (Item_Array(K), K = 1, I - 1)
        stop
      end if

    end do

    call Find (Data, J, R)            ! Small array is full. Is there another item?
    if (R % Loc > BIG) print *, "␣More␣than␣", BIG, "␣nonzero␣elements.␣"
    print *, (Item_Array(K), K = 1, I - 1)
  end program Condense
```

Note the following points:

1. In the main program, actual arguments in each reference to the subroutine agree in number, order, and type with the corresponding dummy arguments in the module subprogram.
2. Separate array declarations appear in the main program for the actual argument array `Data` and in the module subprogram for the dummy argument array `A`. The dummy argument array is declared as an *assumed-shape* array: The rank (number of dimensions) is specified, but the extent will be determined from the actual argument array.
3. Two `call` statements appear in the main program. The first is inside a loop, so it will be executed as many as 10 times. Each time a `call` statement is executed, control passes to the subroutine. Execution of the `return` statement in the procedure returns control to the main program, continuing with the statement following the `call`.
4. The subroutine name `Find` is not associated with any value, and it is not meaningful to regard this name as having any specifc type.
5. The names of the actual arguments do not have to agree with the names of the corresponding dummy arguments. At each reference, the specified actual argument value is substituted for the dummy argument name. The actual arguments may be array element names, in which case the subscript value may change at each reference.
6. The procedure `Find` is not recursive. Its definition is given by a module subprogram with no internal subprograms and corresponds to the subroutine pattern shown earlier.

EXAMPLE 7.7 The subroutine `Reverse` reverses the first `N` elements of the assumed-shape array. The actual argument list in a call to `Reverse` must specify an array and the value to be associated with `N`.

The module procedure `Reverse` contains a reference to the internal procedure named `Swap_It`, which is defined in an internal subprogram. `Swap_It` has dummy arguments `J` and `K` and the local variable `Temp`, whose types are declared in `Swap_It`. The array name `A` is referenced but not declared in `Swap_It`, so it is *inherited* from the host subprogram `Reverse`.

```
! Example 7.7a. (Module)
  module Reverse_M
    implicit none                              ! Specification part of module
    intrinsic Size
  contains                                       ! Subprogram part of module
  ! Subroutine to reverse the first N elements of an array A.
  ! N must not exceed Size (A).
    subroutine Reverse (A, N)                          ! Module subprogram
      real, dimension(:), intent (in out) :: A             ! Assumed shape
      integer, intent (in) :: N
      integer :: Loop
  ! start subroutine Reverse
      if (N > Size (A)) then
        print *, "⊥N⊥is⊥too⊥large.⊥"
        stop
      else
        do Loop = 1, N / 2
          call Swap_It (Loop, N + 1 - Loop)
        end do
      end if
    contains
      subroutine Swap_It (J, K)              ! Internal subprogram inherits A.
        integer, intent (in) :: J, K
        real :: Temp
    ! start subroutine Swap_It
        Temp = A(J); A(J) = A(K); A(K) = Temp
      end subroutine Swap_It
    end subroutine Reverse
  end module Reverse_M
```

The following simple main program illustrates how Reverse might be referenced. The integer variable L in this main program corresponds to the dummy argument N in the subroutine. (Of course, the value of L must not exceed the size of the array.)

```
! Example 7.7b. (Main program)
! Main program to test Reverse.
  program Test_3
    use Reverse_M
    implicit none
    intrinsic Min
```

```
    integer, parameter :: S = 200
    real, dimension(S) :: B
    integer :: L, I, EoF
! start program Test_3
    open (1, file = "zahlen.txt")
    do
      read (1, *, iostat = EoF) L, (B(1: Min (L, S)))
      if (EoF < 0) stop "␣End␣of␣data␣file.␣"
      if (L > S) stop "␣Too␣much␣input␣data.␣"
      print *, "␣Input:␣", L, B(1: L)
      call Reverse (B, L)
      print *, "␣Output:␣", B(1: L)
    end do
  end program Test_3
```

Defining a Function

The definition for an internal function, a module function, or an external function (see Appendix D.6) is similar to a subroutine definition, except that additional consideration must be given to the function result. (Note that a function result may be a structure, an array, or a character string.)

First, the procedure from which the function is referenced requires interface information concerning the type, type properties, and other attributes of the function result so that this value can be properly combined with other parts of the expression where the reference appears. This information is provided automatically if the function is defined in an internal subprogram or a module subprogram (but not if it is defined in an external subprogram; see Appendix D.6).

Second, the function result must be given a defined value. In the program or subprogram that defines the function, there is a local variable that is designated by a *Result name*. It is recommended that a separate `result` clause be included in the header statement; otherwise, the name of this local variable is the same as the *Function name*. The value returned by the function is the current value of this variable when function execution terminates. Its type, type properties, and other attributes are those specified for the *Result name*.

Within the procedure, it is necessary to give a value to the result variable. This can be achieved in any valid manner; the usual way is with an assignment statement of the form

Result name = *Expression*

where the *Expression* can have any legitimate form. There are other ways to give a value to the *Result name*, such as including the name in an *Input list*.

EXAMPLE 7.8 Given a value of X, the function `Clip` returns a value equal to the value of X, except that the value 0.0 will be returned by `Clip` if X is less than 0 and 1.0 will be returned if X is greater than 1. Note that there are three statements in the procedure that assign values to the name `Clip`; just one of these will be executed each time the function is referenced.

```
! Example 7.8a. (Function)
  real function Clip (X) result (Almost)
      ! This function returns the value of its argument, except that
      ! it returns 0.0 if the argument is less than 0, and it
      ! returns 1.0 if the argument is greater than 1.
    real, intent (in) :: X
! start function Clip
    if (X < 0.0) then
      Almost = 0.0
    else if (X > 1.0) then
      Almost = 1.0
    else
      Almost = X
    end if
  end function Clip
```

The following main program illustrates how such a function might be used as an internal procedure. The main program reads values of A, B, and C and uses the larger of A and B / C as the argument for `Clip`. The result is multiplied by C to obtain Z. Finally, the values of A, B, C, and Z are printed.

```
! Example 7.8b. (Main program)
! Main program to test Clip.
  program Clip_Test
    implicit none
    real :: A, B, C, Z
! start program Clip_Test
    read *, A, B, C
    if (A > B / C) then
      Z = C * Clip (A)
    else
      Z = C * Clip (B / C)
    end if
    print *, A, B, C, Z
  contains
    real function (Clip) result (Almost)
      ⋮
    end function Clip
  end program Clip_Test
```

Note the following points:

1. The function *Result name*, `Almost`, is declared in the `result` clause at the end of the `function` header statement. The data type of the result is real, as declared in the type declaration for `Almost`. In the function subprogram, a real value is assigned to the *Result name* in each of the three assignment statements.
2. In the main program, the function name `Clip` appears in two different assignment statements. In each, the function name `Clip` (with an argument list) appears in an expression. The value assigned to the *Result name* during execution of the function definition will be returned to the referencing procedure, where it will be combined with other parts of the expression in which the function name appears.
3. The actual argument list in each reference to `Clip` consists of one actual argument expression, such as `A` or `B / C`, which must agree in type with the corresponding dummy argument, `X`, in the function definition.
4. The main program obtains interface information — types, type properties, and other attributes of the arguments and of the function result — automatically from the internal procedure where the function is defined.
5. The result value from a function is the last value assigned to the variable identified by the *Result name* before the execution of the procedure is terminated. In Example 7.8a, there are three assignment statements that can give a value to the *Result name*. If there were no assignment to the *Result name*, it might be given a value in some other way — for example, by execution of a `read` statement or by a procedure reference.

As an alternative, consider the following function definition, which has no `result` clause in its header statement. The main program in Example 7.8b, without any changes, can use this version of the function. Note that the function result value is assigned to the function name. This method is prohibited for directly recursive functions.

```
! Example 7.8c. (Function without result clause in header)
  real function Clip (X)
     ! This function returns the value of its argument, except that
     ! it returns 0.0 if the argument is less than 0, and it
     ! returns 1.0 if the argument is greater than 1.
    real, intent (in) :: X
! start function Clip
    if (X < 0.0) then
      Clip = 0.0
    else if (X > 1.0) then
      Clip = 1.0
    else
      Clip = X
    end if
  end function Clip
```

Attributes of the Result Name

The *Result name*, which is the function name if no `result` clause appears in the procedure header, has a type and type properties and may have other attributes. A function may return a simple numerical or logical value, a character string, an array, or a (derived type) structure. A function result may also have the `pointer` attribute.

The type and type properties (`kind` type parameter and character length) may be specified in the function header, for example,

```
character (len = 20) function String (A, B) result (S)
```

Specification of type and type properties may be omitted from the function header if they are declared within the function declaration. However, it is recommended that they be specified in the header because they are more visible in this position.

The only attributes (other than type and type properties) permitted for a function result are `dimension` and `pointer`. These attributes cannot be included with the type specification in the function header; they must be declared in specification statements within the defining program or subprogram. Two alternatives exist:

1. Specify the type and type properties in the function header and specify `dimension` or `pointer` attributes in separate attribute-oriented declaration statements (see Section 1.2) within the function definition.
2. Omit the type specification from the function header and declare the type and type properties along with the `dimension` or `pointer` attributes in a type declaration within the function definition.

The second alternative seems preferable for any function whose result has the `dimension` or `pointer` attribute because these two attributes cannot be declared in the function header. For example:

```
function Tubular (Length, Width) result (X)
  real :: Length, Width, X(3, 3)
```

Similarly, for a function result of character type, it may be preferable to omit the type specification from the function header and to declare the character length of the result along with the type, type properties, and other attributes in a type declaration within the function definition:

```
function Name (N) result (String)
  integer, parameter :: S_Len = 20
  character (len = S_Len) :: String
  integer :: N
```

Derived type function result. The result type may be a (user-defined) derived type (see Section 6.2), in which case the function result variable would be a structure of the derived type (see also Example 7.1). The derived type definition must be accessible in the referencing program or subprogram as part of the interface information for the procedure. It may be inherited from the host program, as illustrated in Example 7.9, or it may be imported from a module. (For an external function of derived type, the type must be made accessible with an explicit interface in one of the ways discussed in Appendix D.6.) A derived type defined internally within the function subprogram would not be accessible in the referencing program or subprogram.

EXAMPLE 7.9 In the following program, the derived type specification for the function result is shown in the function header. As an alternative, the type could be omitted from the function header and declared inside the function definition.

```
! Example 7.9.
  program Thanks_John
    type :: New_Type
      real :: A, B
    end type New_Type
    type (New_Type) :: X
! start program Thanks_John
    print *, Analysis (3.1416)
  contains
    type (New_Type) function Analysis (Radians) result (Theta)
      real, intent (in) :: Radians
      Theta % A = Radians
      Theta % B = 2.0 * Radians
    end function Analysis
  end program Thanks_John
```

7.3 Exercises

1. Study the subroutine `Find` and the main program `Condense` in Example 7.6. Suppose that this program is provided with data consisting of all zeros, except that the 31st data item is 36.70, the 48th item is 17.24, and the 92nd item is 531.16. What results will be printed?

2. Rewrite the main program `Condense` to perform an operation similar to the subroutine `Find` in Example 7.6a by means of the intrinsic function `Pack` (see Appendix A). Note that `Pack` does not record the location at which each element was found.

3. Study the subroutine `Reverse` and the main program `Test_3` in Example 7.7. Suppose that this program is provided with each of the following sets of data:

	L	B_i (i = 1 to L)					
Set 1:	6	1.0	2.0	3.0	4.0	5.0	6.0
Set 2:	4	1.0	2.0	3.0	4.0		
Set 3:	5	9.5	7.6	5.2	3.2	1.0	

a. In each case, what values will A_i and A_{n+1-i} have, after the reference to `Swap_It` has been executed, when the value of i equals $n/2$?

b. In each case, what results will be printed?

4. Rewrite the main program `Test_3` to perform the same operation as `Reverse` in Example 7.7a by means of array section notation (with negative increment).

5. Write a main program that will read an array `A` of 10 real values and that will then read a pair of integers i and j and call `Swap_It` to exchange A_i and A_j.

6. Study the function `Clip` and the main program `Clip_Test` in Example 7.8. What results will be printed if the main program and procedures are executed with each of the following sets of input data?

	A	B	C
Set 1:	-2.0	0.5	2.0
Set 2:	0.5	-2.0	2.0
Set 3:	0.3	0.5	3.0

7. Rewrite the main program `Clip_Test` to perform the same operation as `Clip` in Example 7.8a by means of the intrinsic functions `Max` and `Min` (see Appendix A).

8. Cube root: Write a function to compute the cube root of a real argument by Newton's method. Starting with `Q` = 1.0, evaluate the expression

```
(2.0 * Q + R / (Q * Q)) / 3.0
```

where `R` is a given real argument. If this expression has almost the same value as `Q`, return this value as the cube root of `R`. Otherwise, assign this expression value as the next value of `Q`, and repeat the calculation. (Problem: What is meant by "almost the same value"?)

9. Write a function definition appropriate to each of the following descriptions:

a. Given a value of `X`, `Flag` returns the absolute value of `X` if that value does not exceed 1.0; if the absolute value of `X` is greater than 1.0, however, the value of `Flag` is 1.0.

b. Given a value of `X` and a value of `Y`, `Quad` returns the integer value 1, 2, 3, or 4 according to the quadrant in which the point `(X, Y)` lies: 1 if `X` is positive or zero and `Y` is positive or zero; 2 if `X` is negative and `Y` is positive or zero; 3 if `X` is negative and `Y` is negative; 4 if `X` is positive or zero and `Y` is negative.

c. Large returns the largest value in List (a vector of N elements) that does not exceed the given value K. If every element of the linear array exceeds K, Large returns the value of K itself. Assume that N does not exceed 100. For example, if $List_1$ through $List_4$ contain the values (12, 75, 14, -9) and the value of K is 39, then the value of Large (List, 4, K) will be 14. However, if the List values are (42, 59, 105, 72) and K is 39, the same expression will have the value 39.

d. TriSum returns the sum of values of array elements $Check_{i,j}$ above the main diagonal (that is, the sum of all those elements for which $i > j$).

10. Euclid's algorithm. The following algorithm for finding the greatest common divisor of a pair of integers, I1 and I2, is attributed to the Greek mathematician Euclid (c. 300 B.C.):

    1. Divide I1 by I2, ignoring the quotient and saving the remainder. (Hint: Use the intrinsic function Modulo.)
    2. If the remainder is zero, then I2 is the greatest common divisor.
    3. Otherwise, return to step 1 to divide I2 by this remainder. (To keep the notation straight, assign I2 to I1 and the remainder to I2, before returning to step 1.)

    a. Write a function Euclid with two integer parameters, I1 and I2, whose value is the greatest common divisor of I1 and I2.

    b. Write a main program to read two integers, find their greatest common divisor (using the function Euclid), and print the result.

11. Root finding by the bisection, or midpoint, method:

    1. Fun is a function of a single argument, X. If the sign of the function value at X = A is opposite to the sign of the function at X = B, then proceed to step 2; otherwise, stop. (Hint: The signs are opposite if the value of the expression Fun (A) * Fun (B) is less than zero.)
    2. Repeat steps 3 through 5 at most 20 times. (If the loop exit has not occurred by the time the iteration has been traversed 20 times, stop.)
    3. Set the value of C to the average of the values of A and B, and compute Fun (C).
    4. If the absolute value of Fun (C) is less than 0.001, exit from the loop (and print the value of C as the approximate root).
    5. If Fun (C) has the same sign as Fun (A), assign the value of C to the variable A; otherwise, assign the value of C to the variable B; in either case, continue the iteration.

7.4 RECURSIVE PROCEDURES (Optional)

A Fortran 90 subroutine or function may be declared to be *recursive*, which means that the procedure is permitted to refer to itself. In other words, a recursive subroutine may call itself, and a recursive function definition may contain a reference to its own name (as a procedure name) in an expression. A procedure may be *indirectly* recursive: Procedure A may refer to procedure B which refers back to A (either directly or via a further chain of references). Unless it is declared as recursive, a Fortran procedure must not refer to itself either directly or indirectly.

The program pattern for a recursive subroutine definition is

> `recursive subroutine` *Subroutine name* `(` *Dummy argument list* `)`
> ⋮
> `end subroutine` *Subroutine name*

Except for the keyword `recursive`, the header statement for a recursive subroutine definition is the same as for a nonrecursive one. The keyword is required both for directly recursive subroutines and for indirectly recursive subroutines.

The keyword `recursive` must appear in the header statement for a recursive function definition, either before or after the *Type*. A separate *Result name* (in a `result` clause) is required for directly recursive functions and is recommended for indirectly recursive functions as well (and, in fact, for all function definitions):

> `recursive` *Type* `function` *Function name* `(` *Dummy argument list* `) &`
> `result (` *Result name* `)`
> ⋮
> `end function` *Function name*

EXAMPLE 7.10 Recursion can be useful for *reversing* a linear sequence. The following program reads a list of integers from a file and applies recursion to print them in reverse order. The method may be described as follows:

> To reverse-print a list of integers, reverse-print a list that consists of all except the first integer and then print the first integer.
>
> However, to reverse-print an empty list, do nothing.

Several features of this problem description are typical of recursive problem definitions:

1. The method for performing a *list of tasks* ("reverse-print a list of integers") is described quite differently from the method for performing a *single task* ("print an integer").
2. The way to perform a *single task* ("print an integer") is supposed to be already known or to be directly defined somewhere else.
3. The way to perform a *list of tasks* ("reverse-print a list") is not described explicitly, but is described only in terms of performing a *subset of the same list of tasks* ("reverse-print all except the first").

4. However, the performance of a certain *basic list* ("reverse-print an empty list") is described directly.

```
! Example 7.10. Reverse-print a list of integers.
  program Turnip
    implicit none
    integer :: EoF
! start program Turnip
    open (2, file = "zahlen.txt")
    call Reverse_Print                              ! Reverse-print a list.
  contains
    recursive subroutine Reverse_Print
      integer :: A
  ! start subroutine Reverse_Print
      read (2, *, iostat = EoF) A          ! Read first integer in current list.
      if (EoF == 0) then
        call Reverse_Print                   ! Reverse-print remainder of list.
        print *, A                         ! Print first integer in current list.
      end if
    end subroutine Reverse_Print
  end program Turnip
```

Does it seem surprising that the list is printed in reverse without apparently being stored anywhere? Can you explain how it works? (Hint: See the discussion of activation records in Section 5.6. Note that the recursive subroutine has one local variable. What would happen if A were inherited from the main program block instead?)

Application: Recursive Selection Sort

Dialogue: Sorting a vector

María Flores suggests, "Let's do an example, Cathy. Suppose you want to sort a vector of 12 integers. What sorting method should you use?"

"My teacher told us that *selection* is the simplest sorting method when there are only a few items to sort. She said it's too slow when there are thousands of items, or even several hundred, because the time it takes is proportional to the square of the number of elements."

"Your teacher is right. For larger amounts of data, there are more efficient algorithms, such as *Quicksort*."

"But I don't remember the details of the selection sorting method, Miss Flores."

"The basic idea is easy enough: *First you find the largest item in the vector and swap it with the last item. Then you apply selection sorting to the remainder — all but the last item.*"

"That sounds kind of crazy. To sort all of the items, you have to sort most of them. . . . Wait a minute! It's just recursion."

"So it is. Your main program will set up the vector to be sorted and will call the recursive selection sort subroutine. This subroutine will find the largest element and exchange it with the last element, and it will then call itself recursively to sort most of the vector — all but the last element."

"My teacher says you have to check a recursion carefully to be sure that it will not go on forever."

"In this problem, the unsorted part of the vector gets shorter by one element at each recursive call. When there is only one element left, there is nothing to sort, so you skip the recursive call."

"So, how do I find the largest item?"

"You can use a simple linear search [see Example 5.31]. A better method is to use the intrinsic function `MaxLoc`. However, this particular intrinsic function is a bit clumsy; I have written an extended version that is easier to use [see Example 7.16]. You can use my program, and I will explain it to you later. Just put a `use Max_Loc_Mod` statement in your search subprogram, and then find the largest element with an expression like this:

```
Loc = Max_Loc (Vector)
```

This statement will assign the location of the largest item in `Vector` to `Loc`. Notice that the function name has an underscore to distinguish it from the intrinsic function name `MaxLoc`."

"Let me try it, Miss Flores. . . . The procedure doesn't return a value, so it's a subroutine. I'll call it `Selection_Sort`. I have to put in the keyword `recursive` because it's going to call itself recursively. The unsorted part of the array will be the argument to this subroutine. When I call it from the main program, the unsorted part will be the whole vector. In the recursive call, the unsorted part will be an array section that includes everything in the current argument vector except the last element.

"I don't need to say `implicit none` because it will be an internal procedure. But I have to put `use Max_Loc_Mod` right after the subroutine header.

"Now for the instructions that sort the remaining unsorted part of the vector. . . . They don't need to be executed unless the array has more than one element, so I'll put them in an `if` construct. First, I call `Max_Loc` to put the location of the largest element into `Loc`. Then, I call `Swap_It` — that will be another internal subroutine — to exchange the last element and the element whose subscript is `Big`. Finally, I call `Selection_Sort` recursively. That should do it:

```
 recursive subroutine Selection_Sort (Unsorted)
   use Max_Loc_Mod
   integer :: Loc

! start subroutine Selection_Sort

   if (N > 1) then ! Skip if only one element remains.
     Loc = Max_Loc (Unsorted)          ! Location of largest element
     call Swap_It (Unsorted(N), Unsorted(Loc))
     call Selection_Sort (Unsorted(1: N - 1))           ! Recursion
   end if

 end subroutine Selection_Sort
```

"That's pretty short, actually. Now I'll fix it up with a main program and the Swap_It procedure:

```
subroutine Swap_It (A, B)
  real, intent (in out) :: A, B
  real :: Aux

! start subroutine Swap_It

  Aux = A
  A = B
  B = Aux

end subroutine Swap_It
```

Cathy writes the main program (see Example 7.11) and compiles it along with her procedures `Selection_Sort` and `Swap_it`.

EXAMPLE 7.11

```
! Example 7.11. Selection sort.
  program Variety
    implicit none
    integer, parameter :: MANY = 12
    real :: Vector (MANY)

! start program Variety

    open (1, file = "file_in.txt")
    open (2, file = "file_out.txt")
    read (1, *) Vector
    call Selection_Sort (Vector)
    write (2, *) Vector

    contains

    recursive subroutine Selection_Sort (Unsorted)
      :
    end subroutine Selection_Sort

    subroutine Swap_It (A, B)
      :
    end subroutine Swap_It

    end program Variety
```

The compiler finds three errors:

```
Error: Implicit type for N
Error: Implicit type for UNSORTED
Error: Invalid argument list in reference to UNSORTED at line 26
```

"I forgot to declare `N`. That's easy — I'll put it in the `integer` type declaration with `Loc`. But I don't know what to do about the second error, Miss Flores. I can't declare `Unsorted` because I don't know how big it will be."

"It's an *assumed-shape array*, Cathy. It gets its shape from the actual argument; you just have to declare the rank [see Section 8.2]. While you're at it, you can give it an `intent` attribute. The same array will be returned with its elements changed, so it should be `intent (in out)`:

```
real, intent (in out) :: Unsorted (:)
```

As for the third error message, Fortran thinks `Unsorted` is a function because it is not declared to be an array. But I see one other problem. You never give `N` a value."

"It's supposed to be the number of elements left to be sorted."

"Use the intrinsic function `Size`. It returns the number of elements in an array."

"OK. I think I have it all put together now:

```
   recursive subroutine Selection_Sort (Unsorted)
     use Max_Loc_Mod
     intrinsic Size
     real, intent (in out) :: Unsorted (:)
     integer :: N, Loc

 ! start subroutine Selection_Sort

      N = Size (Unsorted)
      if (N > 1) then             ! Skip if only one element remains
           Loc = Max_Loc (Unsorted)! location of largest element
           call Swap_It (Unsorted(N), Unsorted(Loc))
           call Selection_Sort (Unsorted(1: N - 1))           !
 recursion
      end if

     end subroutine Selection_Sort
```

"You know, Miss Flores, I liked that other version of `Swap_It` that inherits the array [see Example 5.5]. But the sort subroutine is an internal subprogram, and you said Fortran won't let me put another internal subprogram inside it."

"You can put your sort subroutine in a module, Cathy. That will give you one more nesting level."

"That's a good idea. The sort subroutine will be a module subprogram, and `Swap_It` will be an internal subprogram inside it. I'll make a file with the module first, followed by the main program (see Example 7.12)."

EXAMPLE 7.12

```
! Example 7.12a. Selection sort (module).
  module Sel_Sort_Mod
    use Max_Loc_Mod                                   ! Specification part of module
    intrinsic Size
  contains                                               ! Subprogram part of module
    recursive subroutine Selection_Sort (Unsorted)             ! Module subprogram
      real, intent (in out) :: Unsorted (:)                  ! Assumed-shape array
      integer :: N, Loc
  ! start subroutine Selection_Sort
      N = Size (Unsorted)
      if (N > 1) then                           ! Skip if only one element remains.
        Loc = Max_Loc (Unsorted)                     ! Location of largest element
        call Swap_It (N, Loc)
        call Selection_Sort (Unsorted(1: N - 1))                         ! Recursion
      end if
    contains
      subroutine Swap_It (I, J)                              ! Internal subprogram
        ! Obtains Unsorted by inheritance from host subprogram.
        integer, intent (in) :: I, J
        real :: Aux
    ! start subroutine Swap_It
        Aux = Unsorted(I)
        Unsorted(I) = Unsorted(J)
        Unsorted(J) = Aux
      end subroutine Swap_It
    end subroutine Selection_Sort
  end module Sel_Sort_Mod
```

```
! Example 7.12b. Selection sort (main program).
  program Variety
    use Sel_Sort_Mod
    implicit none
    integer, parameter :: MANY = 12
    real :: Vector (MANY)
! start program Variety
    open (1, file = "file_in.txt")
    open (2, file = "file_out.txt")
    read (1, *) Vector
    call Selection_Sort (Vector)
    write (2, *) Vector
  end program Variety
```

Application: Quicksort

We have examined programs for the selection sort method (Examples 7.11 and 7.12) and for a variant of the insertion sort method (Examples 5.22 and 6.29). These two methods are simple and easy to use, and they are not too slow for small amounts of data: It can be shown that the expected number of comparisons required for either method is proportional to the square of the number of items to be sorted.

For sorting thousands of items, however, a much more efficient method is Quicksort, for which the expected number of comparisons is proportional to $n \cdot \log n$ where n is the number of items.[7] A version of the algorithm is included here for reference. For short sublists, Quicksort switches to a simple method, such as insertion or selection, to reduce overhead. Some experimentation may be undertaken to determine an optimum value for the maximum simple sort size, which will depend somewhat on how eYciently the simple sort is implemented.

EXAMPLE 7.13

```
! Example 7.13. BGA Fortran Quicksort.
  module BGA
    implicit none
    intrinsic Size
  contains
    subroutine Quick_Sort (List)                             ! Module subprogram
      real, dimension(:), intent (in out) :: List           ! Assumed-shape array
  ! start subroutine Quick_Sort
      call RQS (1, Size (List))              ! Call recursive internal subroutine.
    contains
      recursive subroutine RQS (Left_End, Right_End)      ! Internal to Quick_Sort
          ! Inherit List from module subprogram.
        integer, intent (in) :: Left_End, Right_End
        integer, parameter :: Max_Simple_Sort_Size = 6               ! Magic number
        integer :: I, J
        real :: Chosen
    ! start subroutine RQS
        if (Right_End < Left_End + Max_Simple_Sort_Size) then
          call Simple_Sort (Left_End, Right_End)        ! Sort short lists simply.
```

[7] For an excellent version of Quicksort, with a detailed explanation, see Brainerd, Goldberg, and Adams, *Programmer's Guide to Fortran 90* (New York: McGraw-Hill, 1990), p. 149. Examle 7.13 is a slight modification of this version.

```
      else                                          ! Continue with Quick_Sort algorithm.
        Chosen = List((Left_End + Right_End) / 2)
        I = Left_End - 1; J = Right_End + 1
        do
          do                          ! Scan List from left until List(I) >= Chosen.
            I = I + 1; if (List(I) >= Chosen) exit
          end do
          do                          ! Scan List from right until List(J) <= Chosen.
            J = J - 1; if (List(J) <= Chosen) exit
          end do
          if (I < J) then
            call Swap_It (I, J)                                ! List(I) <=> List(J)
          else if (I = J) then
            I = I + 1; exit                                    ! Exit with I > J
          else
            exit
          end if
        end do
        if (Left_End < J) call RQS (Left_End, J)                        ! Recursion.
        if (I < Right_End) call RQS (I, Right_End)
      end if
    end subroutine RQS
    subroutine Swap_It (I, J)                              ! Internal to Quick_Sort
      ! Swap_It List(I), List(J).
      ! Inherit List from module subprogram.
        ⋮
    end subroutine Swap_It
    subroutine Simple_Sort (Vector)                        ! Internal to Quick_Sort
      ! Sort Vector by insertion or selection method.
        ⋮
    end subroutine Simple_Sort
  end subroutine Quick_Sort
end module BGA
```

7.5 DATA TYPE ENCAPSULATION (Advanced)

A new data type may be *encapsulated* in a module. That is, the derived type — the arrangement of data for structures of the new type — is defined in the module, and operations on the new type are defined there as well.

Encapsulated operations may be defined by functions in the usual way, as illustrated in Examples 7.1 and 7.2. In those examples, multiplying numbers of the new type requires a call to the function `Mult_Polar`:

```
P3 = Mult_Polar (P1, P2)
```

A cleaner solution is to *extend* standard operators such as +, *, and = (the assignment operator) so that they can be applied to objects of the new type to produce the expected results. After operator extensions for the new type have been defined, operations with the extended operators can be written in the usual *infix* form:

```
P3 = P1 * P2
```

Extending Standard Operators

As part of an encapsulated data type, any of the following standard ("intrinsic") Fortran 90 operators can be extended so as to be applicable to objects of a new type:

```
+       -      *      /      **      //
.not.  .and.  .or.   .eqv.  .neqv.
==      /=     <      <=     >       >=
```

Any of the traditional relational operators (see Appendix D.2) can also be extended in the same way. The significance of extended operators, when applied to the new type, is defined in the same module where the type is defined.

For each operator to be extended, an *interface block* is created, which contains the name of a function subprogram (in the same module) that defines the operation to be performed.[8] The function must have one or two dummy arguments with the `intent (in)` attribute. The assignment operator can also be extended, but the implementation differs in certain details. The defining procedure must be a subroutine with two dummy arguments, the first with `intent (out)` and the second with `intent (in)`. Further details appear in Chapter 12 of the *Fortran 90 Handbook.*[9]

---

[8] This use of interface blocks is completely independent from that described in Section 8.6 and in Appendix D.6, whose purpose is to supply interface information concerning the dummy arguments and function result of an external procedure.

[9] J. C. Adams et al., *Fortran 90 Handbook* (New York: McGraw-Hill, 1992), chap. 12.

Application: Polar Complex Numbers with Standard Operators

Example 7.1 partially implements an encapsulated data type for complex numbers represented in polar form. The following example extends that implementation.

EXAMPLE 7.14 The module in this example defines the new data type `Polar` and creates the following functions and operators:

The type conversion function `Make_Polar` for constructing a `Polar` object from two real numbers

The type conversion functions `Amplitude` and `Phase` for extracting parts of a `Polar` object as real numbers

Extended +, -, *, and / operators to add, subtract, multiply, and divide a pair of `Polar` objects

An extended ** operator to raise a `Polar` value to a real power

A program or subprogram with a `use` statement for the module obtains access to interface information for the type conversion functions.

In contrast to Example 7.1, this module does not permit users to convert between `Polar` and Fortran-style complex numbers. The functions `F_Complex` and `P_Complex`, which perform such conversions, are now kept `private` for use only by the addition and subtraction operators. A procedure that uses the module must create objects of the new type from real expressions with `Make_Polar`.

The specification part of the module begins with a `private` attribute declaration that hides the operator extension functions and the functions that convert from `Polar` to Fortran style. The definition for the derived type `Polar` follows; its two real components, `R` and `Theta`, are declared `private` and are not accessible from outside the module. The `public` functions `Amplitude` and `Phase` are provided for extracting copies of the separate parts of a `Polar` object.

The subprogram part of the module consists of subprograms defining the three public type conversion functions, the five private operator extension functions, and the two private conversion functions. Notice that the addition and subtraction extension functions use `F_Complex` and `P_Complex`: The simplest way to add and subtract `Polar` numbers is to first convert them to Fortran-style complex numbers.

```
! Example 7.14. Encapsulated Polar data type.
 module Ursa
   implicit none
   private Add_Polar, Sub_Polar, &
      Mult_Polar, Div_Polar, Exp_Polar, F_Complex, P_Complex
   type :: Polar
     private
     real :: R
     real :: Theta
   end type Polar
   interface operator (+)
     module procedure Add_Polar
   end interface
   interface operator (-)
     module procedure Sub_Polar
   end interface
   interface operator (*)
     module procedure Mult_Polar
   end interface
   interface operator (/)
     module procedure Div_Polar
   end interface
   interface operator (**)                          ! Note: Second operand is real.
     module procedure Exp_Polar
   end interface
  contains
   type (Polar) function Make_Polar (Amplitude, Phase) result (P)
     real, intent (in) :: Amplitude, Phase
  ! start function Make_Polar
     P % R = Amplitude
     P % Theta = Phase
   end function Make_Polar
   real function Amplitude (P) result (A)
     type (Polar), intent (in) :: P
  ! start function Amplitude
     A = P % R
   end function Amplitude
   real function Phase (P) result (T)
     type (Polar), intent (in) :: P
  ! start function Phase
     T = P % Theta
   end function Phase
```

```
! The remaining module procedures are private.
    type (Polar) function Add_Polar (P1, P2) result (P)
    type (Polar), intent (in) :: P1, P2
! start function Add_Polar
    ! Convert to Fortran complex, add, and convert back.
    P = P_Complex (F_Complex (P1) + F_Complex (P2))
  end function Add_Polar

  type (Polar) function Sub_Polar (P1, P2) result (P)
    type (Polar), intent (in) :: P1, P2
! start function Sub_Polar
    ! Convert to Fortran complex, subtract, and convert back.
    P = P_Complex (F_Complex (P1) - F_Complex (P2))
  end function Sub_Polar

  type (Polar) function Mult_Polar (P1, P2) result (P)
    type (Polar), intent (in) :: P1, P2
! start function Mult_Polar
    ! Multiply amplitudes and add phases.
    P % R = P1 % R * P2 % R
    P % Theta = P1 % Theta + P2 % Theta
  end function Mult_Polar

  type (Polar) function Div_Polar (P1, P2) result (P)
    type (Polar), intent (in) :: P1, P2
! start function Div_Polar
    ! Divide amplitudes and subtract phases.
    P % R = P1 % R / P2 % R
    P % Theta = P1 % Theta - P2 % Theta
  end function Div_Polar

  type (Polar) function Exp_Polar (P1, R2) result (P)
    ! Note: Second argument is real.
    type (Polar), intent (in) :: P1
    real, intent (in) :: R2
! start function Exp_Polar
    ! Exponentiate amplitude and multiply phase.
    P % R = (P1 % R) ** R2
    P % Theta = (P1 % Theta) * R2
  end function Exp_Polar

  complex function F_Complex (P) result (Bear)
    ! Convert polar to Fortran-style complex.
    intrinsic Real, Sin, Cos, Cmplx
    type (Polar), intent (in) :: P
    real :: X, Y
```

```
! start function F_Complex
    X = P % R * Cos (P % Theta)
    Y = P % R * Sin (P% Theta)
    Bear = Cmplx (X, Y)
  end function F_Complex
  type (Polar) function P_Complex (Z) result (S)
    ! Convert Fortran-style complex to polar.
    intrinsic Abs, AImag, ATan2, Real
    complex, intent (in) :: Z
! start function P_Complex
    S % R = Abs (Z)
    S % Theta = ATan2 (AImag (Z), Real (Z))
  end function P_Complex
end module Ursa
```

```
program Driver
  use Ursa
  implicit none
  real :: Deg = 57.2957795130
  real :: A1, F1, A2, F2
  type (Polar) :: P1, P2, P3
! start program Driver
  do
    print *, "␣Please␣enter␣Amplitude␣and␣Phase␣(degrees)␣of"
    print *, "␣two␣polar␣numbers.␣To␣stop,␣enter␣0,0,0,0␣"
    read *,  A1, F1, A2, F2
    if (A1 == 0) exit
    P1 = Make_Polar (A1, F1 / Deg); P2 = Make_Polar (A2, F2 / Deg)
    print *, Amplitude (P1), Phase (P1), Amplitude (P2), Phase (P2)
    P3  = P1 + P2
    print *, "␣Sum:␣", Amplitude (P3), Phase (P3) * Deg
    P3 = P1 * P2
    print *, "␣Product:␣", Amplitude (P3), Phase (P3) * Deg
    P3 = P1 ** 3.0
    print *, "␣Cube:␣", Amplitude (P3), Phase (P3) * Deg
  end do
end program Driver
```

Execution of the program in Example 7.14 with typical input values produces the following results:

```
Please enter Amplitude and Phase (degrees) of
two polar numbers. To stop, enter 0,0,0,0
2.0  30.0  0.5  60.0
2.0000000  0.5235988  0.5000000  1.0471976
Sum:  2.4458232 35.8667412
Product:  1.0000000 90.0000000
Cube:  8.0000000 90.0000000

Please enter Amplitude and Phase (degrees) of
two polar numbers. To stop, enter 0,0,0,0
1.0  0.0  1.0  90.0
1.0000000  0.0000000E+00  1.0000000  1.5707963
Sum:  1.4142137 45.0000000
Product:  1.0000000 90.0000000
Cube:  1.0000000  0.0000000E+00
```

Application: Encapsulated Stack Data Type

EXAMPLE 7.15 The following program implements an encapsulated stack data type stored as an array. Alternatively, the operations can be implemented with linked list storage (see Section 6.3).

```
! Example 7.15. Encapsulated stack data type with array storage.
 module Stack_Module
 ! Specification part of module
   implicit none
   type :: Element_Type
     integer :: Key
     integer :: Sequence
   end type Element_Type
   type :: Stack_Type
     private
     integer :: Current_Size
     type (Element_Type), pointer, dimension(:) :: Space
   end type Stack_Type
   integer, private :: Max_Size
 ! Procedure part of module
 contains
   subroutine Create_Stack(S_Ptr, N)
     type (Stack_Type), pointer :: S_Ptr
     integer, intent (in) :: N
```

```
! start subroutine Create_Stack
    allocate (S_Ptr)
    allocate (S_Ptr % Space(N))
    Max_Size = N
    S_Ptr % Current_Size = 0
  end subroutine Create_Stack

  subroutine Destroy_Stack(S_Ptr)
    type (Stack_Type), pointer :: S_Ptr
! start subroutine Destroy_Stack
    S_Ptr % Current_Size = 0
    deallocate (S_Ptr % Space)
    deallocate (S_Ptr)
  end subroutine Destroy_Stack

  logical function Push (S_Ptr, Element) result (OK)
    type (Stack_Type), pointer :: S_Ptr
    type (Element_Type), intent (in) :: Element
    integer :: N

! start function Push
    N = S_Ptr % Current_Size + 1
    OK = (N <= Max_Size)
    if (.not. OK) return
    S_Ptr % Space(N) = Element
    S_Ptr % Current_Size = N
  end function Push

  logical function Pop (S_Ptr, Element) result (OK)
    type (Stack_Type), pointer :: S_Ptr
    type (Element_Type), intent (out) :: Element
    integer :: N

! start function Pop
    OK = Peek (S_Ptr, Element)
    if (.not. OK) return
    S_Ptr % Current_Size = S_Ptr % Current_Size - 1
  end function Pop

  logical function Peek (S_Ptr, Element) result (OK)
    type (Stack_Type), pointer :: S_Ptr
    type (Element_Type) , intent (out) :: Element
    integer :: N

! start function Peek
    N = S_Ptr % Current_Size
    OK = (N > 0)
    if (.not. OK) return
    Element = S_Ptr % Space(N)
  end function Peek

end module Stack_Module
```

```
! Main program
 program Lab_Prog
   use Stack_Module
   implicit none
   integer, parameter :: Many = 6
   type (Element_Type) :: Element = Element_Type (99, 0)
   integer :: Op, Push_Sequence = 1
   type (Stack_Type), pointer :: Stack
! start program Lab_Prog
   call Create_Stack (Stack, Many)
   do
     print *, "␣Please␣enter␣Operation:␣"
     print *, "␣0␣to␣quit;␣1␣to␣push;␣2␣to␣pop;␣3␣to␣peek.␣"
     read *, Op
     select case (Op)
     case (0)
       print *, "␣Operation␣0␣means␣quit.␣"
       exit
     case (1)
       print *, "␣Please␣enter␣value␣to␣push.␣"
       read *, Element % Key
       Element % Sequence = Push_Sequence
       Push_Sequence = Push_Sequence + 1
       if (.not. Push (Stack, Element)) then
         print *, "␣Error:␣Push␣failed.␣"
         exit
       end if
     case (2)
       if (.not. Pop (Stack, Element)) then
         print *, "␣Error:␣Pop␣failed.␣"
         exit
       else
         print *, "␣Popped:␣ ", Element % Key, Element % Sequence
       end if
     case (3)
       if (.not. Peek (Stack, Element)) then
         print *, "␣Error:␣Peek␣failed.␣"
         exit
       else
         print *, "␣Peeked:␣", Element % Key, Element % Sequence
       end if
```

```
    case default
      print *, Op, "␣is␣not␣a␣valid␣operation.␣"
    end select
  end do
  do while (Pop (Stack, Element))
    print *, "␣Left␣on␣stack:␣", Element % Key, Element % Sequence
  end do
  call Destroy_Stack (Stack)
end program Lab_Prog
```

7.6 USER-DEFINED GENERIC PROCEDURES (Optional)

Application: Extended MaxLoc *and* MinLoc *Functions*

In Section 5.3, we noted certain annoyances with the intrinsic functions `MaxLoc` and `MinLoc`. For argument arrays of rank 1, these functions return an array of rank 1 rather than a scalar. (Several other similar functions, such as `All` and `Count`, return a scalar result when the argument is a vector.) Furthermore, these two functions as well as `MaxVal` and `MinVal` are not applicable to argument arrays of character type. As an example of user-defined generic procedures, we now consider how to extend these intrinsic functions.

We first investigate the creation of functions similar to `MaxLoc` and `MinLoc`, but specialized for use with vector arguments so that they return a scalar result instead of a rank-1 array. The following example shows only the functions that locate the *largest* element in a vector; in practice, another almost identical set of statements would be added to the module for locating the smallest element.

A procedure must specify the type of each dummy argument (either in a type declaration, or implicitly as described in Appendix D.1). Therefore, we must create separate functions for an integer vector argument and for a real vector argument. However, we can give these two functions the same name; that is, we can create a *generic* function that will accept either an integer vector or a real vector, in the same way as the generic intrinsic procedure `MaxLoc` accepts either an integer array or a real array.

As in Section 7.5, we place the separate functions in the procedure part of a module. In the specification part, we create an interface block and give it the *generic name* that is to be used to reference either of the specific functions. The body of this interface block consists of a *list* of the specific module procedure names that may be substituted for the generic name.

Fortran must be able to *resolve* a generic procedure reference (to uniquely select one of the specific procedures) based *only* on the number of arguments and on the type, kind type parameter, and rank of each argument.[10] In Example 7.16, the actual argument type is different in each of the specific procedures. The generic function name is `Max_Loc`, and the specific names are `I_Max_Loc` (for integer vectors) and `R_Max_Loc` (for real vectors).

The body of each of these two specific procedures is simple except for the handling of special cases when the argument vector has size 0 or when an optional mask argument is present. The most important step is to call the intrinsic function `MaxLoc`, storing the result in a local vector of size 1 and then returning the vector element as a scalar result.

We now see that it is easy to add to the list a third specific procedure, `S_Max_Loc`, for finding the largest of a vector of strings. The body of this third specific procedure is quite different from the first two, as it contains a loop that performs a linear search of the vector of strings.

We add one further facility to the module in order to extend the existing generic intrinsic function `MaxVal` (which requires an array argument of integer or real type) to accept a vector of strings as an additional argument category. This last procedure does not create a new generic function name; instead, it extends the interpretation of an existing generic intrinsic function name. We could not have extended `MaxLoc` in this manner because a reference to a function named `MaxLoc` with an integer argument of rank 1, for example, would not be able to distinguish between the existing intrinsic function and one that we might attempt to define.

---

10 Selection based on the number of arguments involves further complications due to the possibility of optional and keyword arguments (see Section 8.7). This question is discussed in detail in the *Fortran 90 Handbook* (Adams et al., op. cit.), p. 538.

EXAMPLE 7.16

```
! Example 7.16. Generic vector maximum and minimum.
 module Max_Loc_Mod
   implicit none                            ! Specification part of module
   intrinsic All, Any, Len, MaxLoc, Present, Shape, Size
   integer :: R(1)
   interface Max_Loc
     module procedure I_Max_Loc, R_Max_Loc, S_Max_Loc
   end interface
   interface MaxVal                        ! Same as intrinsic function name
     module procedure S_Max_Val
   end interface
 contains                                   ! Subprogram part of module
   integer function I_Max_Loc (Vector, Mask) result (Ans)
     integer, intent (in), dimension(:) :: Vector
     logical, intent (in), optional, dimension(:) :: Mask      ! See Section 8.7.
 ! start function I_Max_Loc
     if (Size (Vector) > 0) then
       if (Present (Mask)) then
         if (All (Shape (Vector) == Shape (Mask)) .and. Any (Mask)) then
           R = MaxLoc (Vector, Mask = Mask)
         else
           R = 0
         end if
       else
         R = MaxLoc (Vector)
       end if
     else
       R = 0
     end if
     Ans = R(1)
   end function I_Max_Loc
   integer function R_Max_Loc (Vector, Mask) result (Ans)
     real, intent (in), dimension(:) :: Vector
       :                                               ! Similar to I_Max_Loc
   end function R_Max_Loc
```

```
  integer function S_Max_Loc (Vector, Mask) result (Ans)
    character (len = *), intent (in), dimension(:) :: Vector
    logical, intent (in), optional, dimension(:) :: Mask      ! See Section 8.7.
    character (len = Len (Vector)) :: String
    logical, dimension(Size(Vector)) :: M
    integer :: Loop
! start function S_Max_Loc
    if (Present (Mask)) then; M = Mask; else; M = .TRUE.; end if
    R = 0
    String = "␣"
    do Loop = 1, Size (Vector)
      if (M(Loop) .and. (Vector(Loop) > String)) then
        R = Loop; String = Vector(Loop)
      end if
    end do
    Ans = R(1)
  end function S_Max_Loc
  function S_Max_Val (Vector, Mask) result (Ans)
    character (len = *), intent (in), dimension(:) :: Vector
    character (len = Len (Vector)) :: Ans
    logical, intent (in), optional, dimension(:) :: Mask       ! See Section 8.7
    integer :: Loc
  ! start function S_Max_Val
    if (Present (Mask)) then
      Loc = S_Max_Loc (Vector, Mask)
    else
      Loc = S_Max_Loc (Vector)
    end if
    if (Loc > 0) then
      Ans = Vector(Loc)
    else
      Ans = "␣"
    end if
  end function S_Max_Val
end module Max_Loc_Mod
```

EXAMPLE 7.17 The following trivial driver program may be used to test the module `Max_Loc_Mod`.

```
! Example 7.17. Test drive Max_Loc_Mod.
  program Driver
    use Max_Loc_Mod
    implicit none
    character (len = 3), dimension(3) :: Data
! start program Driver
    Data(1) = "a b"
    Data(2) = "a a"
    Data(3) = "aaa"
    print *, S_Max_Loc (Data), MaxVal (Data)
  end program Driver
```

Execution of the program in Example 7.17 produces the following output:

```
3 aaa
```

EXAMPLE 7.18 As a further test of the module, let's employ the selection sort module from Example 7.12. For variety, the type and length of the sort vector have been changed to `character (len = 20)`.

```
! Example 7.18. Selection sort (compare Example 7.12).
  module Sel_Sort_Mod
    use Max_Loc_Mod                               ! Specification part of module
  contains                                           ! Subprogram part of module
    recursive subroutine Selection_Sort (Unsorted)          ! Module subprogram
      character (len = 20), intent (in out) :: Unsorted (:)  ! Assumed-shape array
      integer :: N, Loc
  ! start subroutine Selection_Sort
      N = Size (Unsorted)
      if (N > 1) then                         ! Skip if only one element remains.
        Loc = Max_Loc (Unsorted)                     ! Location of largest element
        call Swap_It (N, Loc)
        call Selection_Sort (Unsorted(1: N - 1))                       ! Recursion
      end if
    contains
      subroutine Swap_It (I, J)                              ! Internal subprogram
        ! Obtains Unsorted by inheritance from host subprogram.
        integer, intent (in) :: I, J
        character (len = 20) :: Aux
```

```
    ! start subroutine Swap_It
        Aux = Unsorted(I)
        Unsorted(I) = Unsorted(J)
        Unsorted(J) = Aux
      end subroutine Swap_It

    end subroutine Selection_Sort

  end module Sel_Sort_Mod
```

```
  program Variety
    use Sel_Sort_Mod
    implicit none
    integer, parameter :: MANY = 200
    integer :: Loop, EoF, N
    character (len = 20) :: Vector (MANY)

! start program Variety
    open (1, file = "simply.txt")
    open (2, file = "file_out.txt")

    do Loop = 1, MANY
      read (1, *, iostat = EoF) Vector(Loop)
      if (EoF < 0) exit
    end do

    N = Loop - 1
    call Selection_Sort (Vector(1: N))

    do Loop = 1, N
      write (2, *) Vector(Loop)
    end do

  end program Variety
```

Chapter 8 Procedure Arguments

8.1 OVERVIEW

Key Concepts Related to Procedure Arguments

1. Each *dummy argument* that appears in the header statement of a procedure definition must be the name of a *variable,* which may be a scalar variable, an array variable, or a structure of any type. A dummy argument must not be an array element designator, a structure component designator, or a substring designator.
2. Each *actual argument* used in any reference to the procedure is an *expression*, which may be a constant or a variable name. (Fortran 90 variable names include whole array names and whole structure names as well as array element designators and structure component designators.) For a dummy argument that is given a value during execution of the procedure, the corresponding actual argument must be a variable name.
3. Except for optional and keyword arguments (Section 8.7), the number of actual arguments in the procedure reference should agree with the number of dummy arguments in the procedure header. Except for keyword arguments, the correspondence between dummy and actual arguments depends on their respective *positions* in the argument list. The names of the actual arguments may be different from the names of the corresponding dummy arguments.
4. The *type,* `kind` *type parameter,* and *rank* (number of dimensions) of each actual argument must match those of the corresponding dummy argument. The procedure definition must include a length specification for each dummy argument of character type and a shape specification for each dummy argument array, even though length and dimension specifications for the actual arguments must also appear in the referencing procedure.

   As described in Sections 8.2 and 8.3, the length of a character dummy argument or the shape (extent along each dimension) of a dummy argument array may be left partially unspecified; the actual length or shape is then *assumed* (taken) from the length or shape of the corresponding actual argument.

In traditional Fortran programs, explicit character lengths and explicit array shapes are declared for the dummy arguments. In some cases (see Sections 8.2 and 8.3 and Appendices D.6 and E.4), special rules permit actual arguments whose length or shape is different from that of the dummy argument.

5. A procedure may have no arguments, one argument, or more than one argument. If there are no arguments, a `function` statement (in a procedure definition) *must* include empty parentheses; in a `subroutine` statement, the empty parentheses are *optional*. Thus, the first statement of a procedure definition may have any of the following forms (among others):

   `subroutine` *Subroutine name* `(` *Dummy argument list* `)`
   `subroutine` *Subroutine name* `()`
   `subroutine` *Subroutine name*
   `recursive subroutine` *Subroutine name* `(` *Dummy argument list* `)`
   Type `function` *Function name* `(` *Dummy argument list* `)`
   Type `function` *Function name* `()`
   Type `function` *Function name* `(` *Dummy argument list* `) &`
     `result (` *Result name* `)`
   Type `function` *Function name* `() result (` *Result name* `)`
   `recursive` *Type* `function` *Function name* `(` *Dummy argument list* `) &`
     `result (` *Result name* `)`

Input Arguments and Output Arguments: `intent`

It is recommended that an `intent` attribute be declared for each dummy argument in a procedure (except for pointers, which cannot have an `intent` attribute). This attribute may be specified in a type declaration (between the type designator and the double colon) or in a separate attribute-oriented `intent` statement. It has one of three forms:

```
intent (in)
intent (out)
intent (in out)
```

Here is an example:

```
real :: Argument
intent (in out) :: Argument
real, intent (in) :: FT, CT
```

Note the following points:

1. If the `intent` attribute has the value `in`, the dummy argument must not be given a value within the procedure. The matching actual argument in the referencing procedure may be a variable name, a constant, or an expression that contains one or more operators.

2. If the `intent` attribute is `out` or `in out`, the corresponding actual argument must be a variable name; that is, it must not be a constant or any other expression except a variable name.
3. If the `intent` attribute is `out`, the procedure must give the dummy argument a value before using it. That is, the procedure must be written as if the dummy argument value is undefined when execution of the procedure begins.
4. If the `intent` attribute is `in out`, the corresponding actual argument must have a defined value when execution of the procedure begins.
5. If no `intent` attribute is declared, the procedure may use the dummy argument value or may give it a value during execution of the procedure. If the procedure gives a value to the dummy argument, the corresponding actual argument must not be a constant or any other expression except a variable name. If the procedure does not give the dummy argument a value before using it, the corresponding actual argument must have a defined value when execution of the procedure begins.

If a dummy argument (with no declared `intent` attribute or with `in out` or `out` as its `intent` attribute) is given a value during execution of the procedure, that value becomes the value of the actual argument when the procedure terminates.

Implementation of the `intent` attribute is discussed in Section 8.8.

Array Elements as Actual Arguments

When an array element is an actual argument, the subscript expression is evaluated at the time the procedure is referenced. The subscript value does not change during execution of the subroutine or function, even if the procedure changes the value of some variable appearing in the subscript expression. The subscript will not be evaluated again until the next time the procedure is referenced.

EXAMPLE 8.1 The following subroutine `Find` compares a value `X` with each element `A(K)` until it finds `A(K) < X`, and it returns the value of `K` thus determined.

```
! Example 8.1. Find the first element of A that is smaller than X.
  program Subscription
    implicit none
    intrinsic Size
    integer, parameter :: SIZE = 20
    real, dimension(SIZE) :: B = 0.0, C = 1.0
    integer :: I = 5

! start program Subscription
    call Find (B(I), C, I)
    print *, I

  contains

    subroutine Find (X, A, K)
      real, intent (in) :: X
      real, dimension(:), intent (in) :: A
      integer, intent (out) K
```

```
! start subroutine Find
    do K = 1, Size (A)
      if (A(K) < X) return
    end do
  ! The value of K is Size(A) + 1 if this point is reached.
  end subroutine Find
end program Subscription
```

Although the variable K in the subroutine of Example 8.1 corresponds to the actual argument variable I, the identity of the argument variable B(I) does not change when the value of K changes. The array element B(I), corresponding to the dummy argument X, is selected on the basis of the value of I at the time of execution of the call statement.

8.1 Exercise

1. Show how to accomplish the same result as in Example 8.1 with intrinsic functions instead of the internal procedure (subroutine) Find. Assume that the elements are in order. (Hint: To find the first element, use MinLoc with a mask argument that is the whole-array expression (A < X).)

8.2 ARRAYS AS DUMMY ARGUMENTS

Arrays in a Procedure

A dummy argument array is an *explicit-shape* array, an *assumed-size* array, or an *assumed-shape* array.

1. Explicit-shape and assumed-size arrays are considered obsolete (see Appendix D.6). An explicit-shape dummy argument array, just as in traditional Fortran, is one whose shape is completely specified by declarations in the procedure definition.[1] An explicit-shape array may be a fixed-size array or an adjustable array. An assumed-size

[1] The disadvantage of explicit-shape dummy arguments is that the shape of the corresponding actual argument array must *separately* be completely specified in the program or subprogram from which the procedure is referenced, and there is no way to ensure that these shape specifications agree. According to the traditional Fortran view, an actual argument is simply the beginning address of a collection of bits or bytes whose type, dimension, and other attributes are not permanently attached to the object but are specified locally (for the corresponding dummy argument) within the procedure.

array is like a fixed-size array except that the upper bound for its last dimension is not specified.

2. Use of the Fortran 90 assumed-shape array feature is strongly recommended. The shape of an assumed-shape dummy argument array is *assumed* (taken) from the actual argument array. (Note the difference between assumed shape and assumed size.)

Besides dummy argument arrays, a procedure may, of course, have local arrays. It may also inherit other arrays from a host program or subprogram or import arrays from modules. *Fixed-size* local arrays in a procedure, just as in a main program, are those declared with constant expressions for upper bounds and for any lower bounds that are not omitted. *Automatic* local arrays (which may appear in a procedure, but not in a main program) are described in Section 8.4; such arrays are declared with dimension bound expressions (specification expressions) involving one or more *variables* that have defined values at procedure entry. *Deferred-shape* arrays may also appear in a procedure; such arrays are either allocatable arrays (see Section 5.6) or pointer targets (see Section 6.3) in heap storage.

Assumed-Shape Arrays

It is recommended that all dummy argument arrays be specified as *assumed-shape* arrays. Fortran 90 can treat such an argument as a complete array object, rather than as a sequence of elements that happen to occupy adjacent storage. However, many existing programs employ explicit-shape arrays, which are described Appendix D.6.

An assumed-shape array is a dummy argument array whose name, type (and subtype), and rank are declared in the procedure, but whose shape (extent along each dimension) is left unspecified. The dimension attribute specification, which may appear in the type declaration, contains a colon for each array dimension; thus, the rank is the *number of colons* in the dimension specifier — for example,

```
real, dimension(:, :) :: Data_Array                ! Rank is 2.
```

Recall that the shape of an array involves the *size* (extent) along each dimension, but not the precise upper and lower subscript bound values. Each lower bound is 1 by default, but a different lower bound may be specified. The declaration for an assumed-shape array may specify *lower bounds* for each dimension, leaving the upper bounds to be determined:

```
real, dimension(0:, 0:) :: Data_Array
```

At each procedure reference, the dummy array will *assume* (take on) the shape of the corresponding actual argument array. The lower subscript bounds of the dummy argument array are taken from the assumed-shape declaration or are 1 by default; the upper subscript bounds are determined from these lower bound values along with shape information for the actual argument. The actual argument may be a whole array or an array section. If the procedure does not change the value of the dummy argument, the actual argument may be an array-valued expression.

An assumed-shape array may be a dummy argument in an internal procedure with the referencing program unit as its host or in a module procedure imported by the referencing procedure. If an assumed-shape array is a dummy argument in an external procedure, the referencing program unit may contain an *interface block* (see Appendix D.6) for the external procedure. In any case, the referencing program unit must have explicit access (see Section 7.2) to interface information for the procedure where an assumed-shape array appears as a dummy argument.

EXAMPLE 8.2 In the following program, the first time `Frobenius_Norm` is referenced, the shape of the dummy argument array `A` will be 40 by 40; the second time, the shape of `A` will be 4 by 4.

```
! Example 8.2. Assumed-shape arrays.
  program Schwarzkopf
    implicit none
    intrinsic Sum
    integer, parameter :: BIG = 40, JIG = 4
    real, dimension(BIG, BIG) :: Wig
    real, dimension(JIG, JIG) :: Fig
    external Frobenius_Norm

! start program Schwarzkopf
    read *, Wig
    print *, Frobenius_Norm (Wig)
    read *, Fig
    print *, Frobenius_Norm (Fig)

  contains

    real function Frobenius_Norm (A) result (Total)
      real, intent (in), dimension(:) :: A
      intrinsic Sum

  ! start function Frobenius_Norm
      Total = Sum (A ** 2)
    end function Frobenius_Norm

  end program Schwarzkopf
```

EXAMPLE 8.3 We have already seen some examples with assumed-shape arrays, including the Crout elimination algorithm in Example 5.25, part of which is reproduced here.

```
! Example 8.3. Solve linear system by Crout method.
 module Crout_Elimination
   implicit none
 contains
   subroutine Solve (A, B, X)
     intrinsic Size, MatMul, Dot_Product
     real, intent (in) :: A(:, :), B(:)          ! Assumed-shape array arguments
     real, intent (out) :: X(:)
     real, allocatable :: LU(:, :), W(:)              ! Allocatable local arrays
     integer :: N, M
 ! start subroutine Solve
     ! Determine problem size; allocate work space and copy A.
     N = Size (A, Dim = 1)                    ! Extent of A along first dimension
     allocate (LU(N, N), W(N))
     :
     deallocate (LU, W)
   end subroutine Solve
 end module Crout_Elimination
```

Transition Tip

- Change all dummy argument arrays in internal procedures and module procedures to assumed-shape arrays.

8.2 Exercises

In your answers to the following exercises, dummy argument arrays should be assumed-shape arrays wherever possible.

1. Define a subroutine `Norm` that computes the square root of the sum of the squares of all the elements in a vector `V`. The subroutine returns this result as the value of a dummy argument named `Total` and sets the value of the logical dummy argument `Flag` to false if `Total` is smaller than 10^5; `Flag` is set to true otherwise. Note that you can use elementwise array multiplication (as described in Section 5.2; compare Example 8.2) to compute a vector-valued expression containing the squares of the elements of `V`. Then you can use the array intrinsic function `Sum` to add the elements of this vector. As an alternative, you can use the array intrinsic function `ScaPr` to compute the scalar product of `V` with itself.

2. Define a function with a dummy argument array of rank 2 (a matrix) and with a result of logical type. The result value should indicate whether or not the matrix is symmetric. (Hint: If the matrix is not square, it cannot be symmetric. Use the array intrinsic function `Shape` to find the dimensions of the matrix and then set the result to false if the two extents are different. Otherwise, apply `All` to a whole-array expression that compares the matrix with its `Transpose`.)

3. These exercises demonstrate the role of scalar products in matrix multiplication.

   a. Write a program that uses the array intrinsic function `ScaPr` to compute the product of two matrices. The element in the `I`th row and `J`th column of the product matrix is the scalar product of the `I`th row of the first matrix and `J`th column of the second matrix. Note that the array sections `A(I, :)` and `A(:, J)` have rank 1 (as discussed in Section 4.2).

   b. Use the array intrinsic function `MatMul` to more easily compute the product of two matrices. Write a complete program to read the elements of two matrices, compute their product with `MatMul`, and print the elements of the product matrix.
   Use the following data:

`Matrix_1` and `Matrix_2`

Set 1:

$$\begin{bmatrix} 1.0 & 2.0 & 3.0 \\ 5.0 & 7.0 & 4.0 \\ 6.0 & 5.0 & 3.0 \end{bmatrix} \qquad \begin{bmatrix} -11.0 & 15.0 & -13.0 \\ 9.0 & -15.0 & 11.0 \\ -2.0 & 4.0 & 3.0 \end{bmatrix}$$

Set 2:

$$\begin{bmatrix} 1.0 & 2.0 & 3.0 & 4.0 & 5.0 \\ 1.6 & 4.1 & 5.2 & 3.1 & 1.5 \\ 1.0 & -1.0 & 1.0 & -1.0 & 1.0 \end{bmatrix} \qquad \begin{bmatrix} 1.0 & 7.3 \\ 1.0 & 2.4 \\ 1.0 & 1.6 \\ 1.0 & 1.5 \\ 1.0 & 9.7 \end{bmatrix}$$

8.3 DUMMY ARGUMENTS OF CHARACTER TYPE

A dummy argument in a procedure may be the name of a variable of character type. An *assumed-length* character dummy argument is declared with an asterisk as its length specifier; it is recommended that dummy arguments of character type be declared in this way. It is also recommended that dummy argument arrays of character type (as well as other types) be declared with assumed shape.

An assumed-length character argument is analogous to an assumed-shape array argument: The character dummy argument assumes the length of the corresponding actual argument. For example, the declaration

```
character (len = *) :: String
```

may appear in a procedure where `String` is a dummy argument. The length of the dummy argument will then be determined by the length of the actual argument used in the reference to the procedure.

An assumed-shape dummy argument array of assumed-length character strings, which is the recommended style, might be declared as follows:

```
character (len = *), dimension(:, :) :: String_Array
```

Transition Tip

- Change all dummy argument character strings in internal procedures and module procedures to assumed-length strings.

8.4 AUTOMATIC ARRAYS AND CHARACTER STRINGS

An automatic array is not a dummy argument, but its `dimension` declaration expressions contain the names of one or more variables that are dummy arguments, are inherited from the host, are imported from a module, or are `common` variables (see Appendix E.3). The values of the dimension bounds are determined at the time of procedure entry and are not affected if one of the controlling variables is changed during execution of the procedure. Space for the array is allocated as part of the activation record (see Section 5.6) for the procedure.

Similarly, a character string that is not a dummy argument may be an automatic string. Its length may be determined at the time of procedure entry from variables in the length declaration that can be evaluated at procedure entry.

An automatic array or string cannot have the save attribute and cannot be initialized. Space for such a variable is reserved as part of the activation record.[2] The amount of space to be reserved is determined, at the time of procedure entry, from the current values of variables in the dimension or length declaration. Such variables must have a defined value at the time of procedure entry, so they must be inherited or imported variables, dummy arguments, or variables in `common`.

Note that a function result variable may be an automatic array or an automatic character string.

Automatic Versus Allocatable Local Arrays

Sometimes (as we shall see in Example 8.6) we have a choice between automatic local arrays and allocatable local arrays. There is often reason to prefer automatic arrays because their memory management is stack based. However, the size of an automatic ar-

[2] Some processors allocate heap space for automatic objects. Since the program has no explicit control over this space, the distinction has little practical importance.

ray that is to bc stored in the activation record must be established, at the time of procedure entry, from the values of variables that are dummy arguments or are otherwise known at entry time.

Allocatable arrays require heap storage management, which can be more complicated. However, the allocatable array facility is more general, and it is applicable in many situations when automatic arrays are not adequate. The size of an allocatable array can be determined, during execution of the procedure, from an input variable value or by some other calculation. As another example, the actual allocation of a particular allocatable array might be made to depend upon the presence of some optional argument (see Section 8.7).

Specification Expressions

In a procedure, an expression that specifies the bounds of an automatic array or the length of an automatic character variable is not required to be a constant. A more general *specification expression* is permitted, so long as all parts of the expression have defined values that are accessible at the time the procedure is referenced. The following rules apply:

1. A specification expression may be a constant expression (see Section 1.3).
2. A specification expression may include names of inherited or imported variables, dummy argument variabless, or `common` variables. Such variables must have defined values at the time of procedure entry.[3]
3. A specification expression may include certain references to intrinsic functions, including scalar intrinsic functions whose arguments and results are of integer or character type, as well as other intrinsic functions with constant expressions as actual arguments. Also permitted are inquiry functions including character length, array shape or size, numerical inquiries such as the radix of the real number representation model, and `kind` subtype inquiries including `Selected_Int_Kind` or `Selected_Real_Kind`.

In particular, an intrinsic inquiry function such as `Size` may appear in a specification expression with an assumed-shape array as its argument. Thus, the shape declaration for an automatic array (which may be the result variable in a function) can be made to depend upon the shape of a dummy argument. Similarly, an assumed-length character string dummy argument may determine the length of a local variable or a function result of character type.[4]

[3] There are exceptions. The values of some intrinsic inquiry functions depend only upon the *attributes* of their arguments and thus do not require defined argument *values*.

[4] Specification expressions are generally more restrictive than initialization expressions (see Section 1.3). However, an assumed-shape array or an assumed-length string is not permitted as an argument to an inquiry function in an initialization expression.

In the following statements, the shapes of the function result G, the automatic local array Y, and the allocatable array Z are all based on the shape assumed by B from its corresponding actual argument array:

```
    function A (B) result (G)
      implicit none
      intrinsic Size
      real, intent (in), dimension(:) :: B
    ! Assumed-shape argument array
      real, dimension(Size (B)) :: G, Y
    ! Automatic result and local arrays
      real, allocatable, dimension(:) :: Z
    ! Allocatable local array
      integer :: SB
  ! start function A
      SB = Size (B)
      allocate (Z(SB))
      G = B
        :
    end function A
```

EXAMPLE 8.4 In the following program, note the use of an expression as the length specifier for `Third`. The last statement in this program *concatenates* (joins) the two character strings called `First` and Second and assigns the result to `Third`. (See Section 6.1 for a description of string concatenation.)

```
! Example 8.4. Constant expressions.
 program Comment
   implicit none
   integer, parameter:: L1 = 12, L2 = 16
   character (len = L1) :: First
   character (len = L2) :: Second
   character (len = L1 + L2) :: Third
! start program Comment
   print *, "␣Please␣enter␣a␣", L1, "-character␣string.␣"
   read *, First
   print *, "␣Please␣enter␣a␣", L2, "-character␣string.␣"
   read *, Second
   Third = First // Second
   print *, Third
 end program Comment
```

EXAMPLE 8.5 The following program employs an automatic array to provide working space for a procedure that exchanges two designated rows of a given array. The vector `Auxiliary_Row` is a (local) automatic array with the same number of elements as a row of the input array.

```
! Example 8.5. Automatic array to save a copy of the dummy argument.
  program Algebra
    implicit none
    intrinsic Size
    integer, parameter :: N = 4, M = 5
    real :: Source_Array(N, M)
! start program Algebra
    read *, Source_Array
    do
      read *, I, J
      if (I == 0) stop
      call Row_Swap (Source_Array, I, J)
      print *, Source_Array
    end do
  contains
    subroutine Row_Swap (A, Row_1, Row_2)
      real, intent (in) :: A(:, :)
      integer, intent (in) :: Row_1, Row_2
      real, dimension(Size (A, Dim = 2)) :: Auxiliary_Row
  ! start subroutine Row_Swap
      Auxiliary_Row = A(Row_1, :)
      A(Row_1, :) = A(Row_2, :)
      A(Row_2, :) = Auxiliary_Row
    end subroutine Row_Swap
  end program Algebra
```

EXAMPLE 8.6 The Crout elimination algorithm in Example 5.25 (see also Example 8.3) might be recast to use automatic local arrays instead of allocatable local arrays and to use adjustable arrays instead of assumed-shape arrays as dummy arguments. Either of these changes could be made without the other.

```
! Example 8.6. Solve linear system by Crout method.
  subroutine Solve (A, B, X, N)
    intrinsic Size, MatMul, Dot_Product
    integer :: N
    real, intent (in) :: A(N, N), B(N)                ! Adjustable array arguments
    real, intent (out) :: X(N)
    real, allocatable :: LU(N, N), W(N)                   ! Automatic local arrays
! start subroutine Solve
    :
  end subroutine Solve
```

8.5 POINTERS AS DUMMY ARGUMENTS (Optional)

An actual argument or a dummy argument may have the `pointer` or `target` attribute. The only restriction is that an actual argument must have the `pointer` attribute if the corresponding dummy argument has the `pointer` attribute. Several cases must be considered:

1. If an actual argument to a procedure is currently the target of one or more pointers, the procedure does not have access to the pointers. In particular, there is no way for the procedure to allocate or deallocate any such pointers. Any changes to the dummy argument modify only the actual argument (the target object).
2. If a dummy argument has the `target` attribute, when procedure execution begins it is not allocated or associated with any local pointer or dummy argument pointer in the procedure. Furthermore, any such association that may be established during procedure execution becomes undefined upon exit from the procedure. Even if a pointer and its target are passed as separate actual parameters, the procedure cannot recognize (or destroy) the association between them. If a procedure with a target dummy argument is neither an internal procedure nor a module procedure, an interface block may be required in the calling program (see Appendix D.6).
3. When an actual argument has the `pointer` attribute, Fortran must determine whether to transmit the *pointer* or its current *target* to the procedure. Fortran makes this determination by observing whether the dummy argument is a pointer: If the dummy argument is a pointer, the effective actual argument is the pointer itself; if not, the effective actual argument is the target. Explicit interface information is required so that the correct choice can be made: If the procedure is neither an internal procedure nor a module procedure, an interface block may be required in the calling program (see Appendix D.6).

4. When a dummy argument has the `pointer` attribute, at the beginning of execution of the procedure it is given the same target (if any) as the actual argument. If the pointer is changed (allocated, deallocated, nullified, or pointer-assigned) during execution of the procedure, the actual argument pointer reflects the change. A dummy argument with the `pointer` attribute must not have a declared `intent` attribute because Fortran cannot determine whether the attribute applies to the pointer or to its target.

Application: Recursive Linked List Traversal

Linked List Search with `do while`

Suppose that a simple linked list has been created, in the manner illustrated by Example 6.32 (Section 6.3). We assume that the `Next` pointer component of the final list element has been nullified. The first part of the following program is the same as that of Example 6.32. Steps have been added, after the list is created, to perform a linear search of the linked list, comparing the `Name` component of each list element with the character string `New_Name`. When the search succeeds or the end of the linked list is reached, a message is printed to indicate the result of the search.

EXAMPLE 8.7

```
! Example 8.7. Make linked list and search for New_Name.
  program Literate
    implicit none
    intrinsic Associated
    integer, parameter :: S_LEN = 20, LIMIT = 3

    type :: Box_Type
      character (len = S_LEN) :: Name
      type (Box_Type), pointer :: Next
    end type Box_Type

    type (Box_Type), pointer :: Root, Temp
    integer :: Loop
    character (len = S_LEN) :: New_Name = "␣"

! start program Literate
    nullify (Root)

    do Loop = 1, LIMIT
      allocate (Temp)
      read *, Temp % Name                ! Read to Name component of new structure.
      Temp % Next => Root        ! Copy Root to pointer component of new structure.
      Root => Temp                                       ! Copy new pointer to Root.
    end do
```

```
  read *, New_Name
  call Look_Up (Root)
contains
  subroutine Look_Up (Current_Ptr)
    type (Box_Type), pointer :: Current_Ptr
! start subroutine Look_Up
    do while (Associated (Current_Ptr))       ! Do while Current_Ptr is not NIL.
      if (New_Name == Current_Ptr % Name) then
        print *, New_Name, "⊥Found.⊥"
        return
      else                                                        ! Keep looking.
        Current_Ptr => Current_Ptr % Next                   ! Pointer assignment
        cycle                                         ! Next iteration of while loop
      end if
    end do
    print *, New_Name, "⊥Not⊥found.⊥"
  end subroutine Look_Up
end program Literate
```

In Example 8.7, the subroutine `Look_Up` begins with `Root` as the value of `Current_Ptr`. The `do while` loop searches along the linked list until it reaches the final `NIL` (disassociated) pointer. At each step, it compares the `Name` component of `Current_Ptr⊙` to the string `New_Name`. If the strings match, the search terminates; otherwise, the search advances by assigning the `Next` (pointer) component of `Current_Ptr⊙` to `Current_Ptr`.

Insertion in a Linked List

If we insert the items in the same sequence as in Example 6.32, the `Name` fields will be in alphabetical order. Now suppose we want to insert a new item in the list, keeping the list in alphabetical order. We change the subroutine `Look_Up` so that it exits from the loop when `New_Name` is smaller than the `Name` component of `Current_Ptr⊙` (see Figure 8.1). If `New_Name` were in the list, we would have found it prior to this point.

FIGURE 8.1. Finding the insertion point in a linked list.

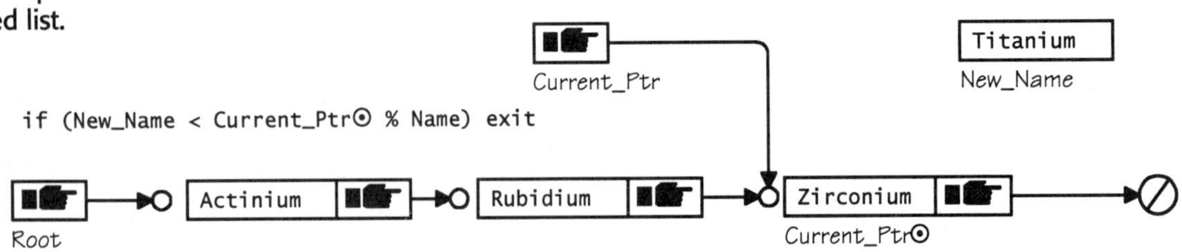

We want to insert New_Name in its proper position, just ahead of Current_Ptr⊙. Our first attempt, shown in the following example, is not successful.

EXAMPLE 8.8

```
! Example 8.8. Link new item to copy of pointer.
  subroutine Look_Up (Current_Ptr)
    type (Box_Type), pointer :: Current_Ptr, New_Item
! start subroutine Look_Up
    do while (Associated (Current_Ptr))          ! Do while Current_Ptr is not NIL.
      if (New_Name == Current_Ptr % Name) then
        print *, New_Name, "␣Found.␣"
        return
      else if (New_Name < Current_Ptr % Name) then
          ! Search has gone beyond insertion point.
        exit                                                  ! Go to INSERT step.
      else                                                        ! Keep looking.
        Current_Ptr => Current_Ptr % Next                     ! Pointer assignment
        cycle                       ! Continue with next iteration of while loop.
      end if
    end do
      ! INSERT                                           ! Insert new item into list.
    print *, New_Name, "␣Not␣found.␣"
    allocate (New_Item)
    New_Item % Name = New_Name                      ! Copy pointers to link new item.
    New_Item % Next => Current_Ptr
    Current_Ptr => New_Item                          ! This program does not work. ☹
  end subroutine Look_Up
```

The program in Example 8.8 does not work correctly because it links the newly allocated list item to a *copy* of the pointer where it should be inserted. Figure 8.2 illustrates this process (the dotted line shows the previous target of Current_Ptr).

FIGURE 8.2. The newly allocated item is linked to a copy of the pointer where it should be inserted.

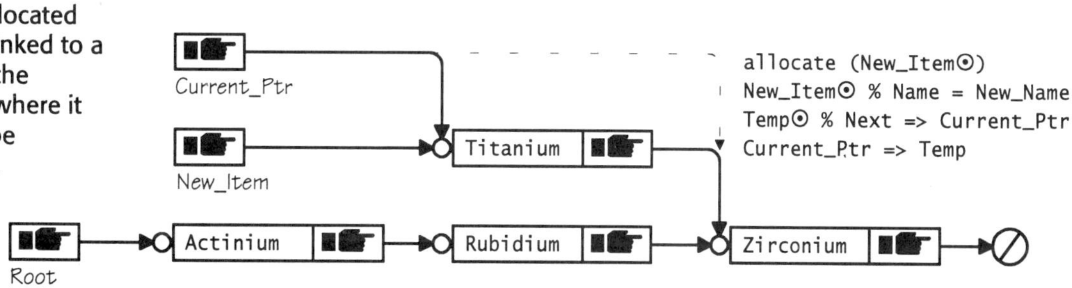

Many textbooks on data structures present exceedingly inelegant solutions to this problem, involving extra items at the head of the list and additional pointers to the list item that precedes `Current_Ptr⊙`. However, there is a simple and elegant method for traversing a linked list by moving along the sequence of actual pointers instead of copying them.[5] The method is much the same as in Example 8.8, except that the do while loop is replaced by a *recursive* procedure whose argument is an *actual pointer* in the linked list instead of a copy.

EXAMPLE 8.9

```
! Example 8.9. Link new item to actual pointer.
  recursive subroutine Look_Up (Current_Ptr)
    type (Box_Type), pointer :: Current_Ptr, New_Item
! start subroutine Look_Up
    if (Associated (Current_Ptr)) then
      if (New_Name == Current_Ptr % Name) then
        print *, New_Name, "⊥Found.⊥"
        return
      else if (New_Name > Current_Ptr % Name) then                ! Keep looking.
        call Look_Up (Current_Ptr % Next)                           ! Recursion
        return
      else          ! New_Name < Current_Ptr % Name. Exit from both if constructs.
      end if
    else                               ! Pointer is NIL. Exit from outer if construct.
    end if
    print *, New_Name, "⊥Not⊥found.⊥"                         ! Insert a new item.
    allocate (New_Item)
    New_Item % Name = New_Name                     ! Copy pointers to link new item.
    New_Item % Next => Current_Ptr
    Current_Ptr => New_Item                      ! Assign to actual argument pointer.
  end subroutine Look_Up
```

[5] See, for example, F. M. Carrano, *Data Abstraction and Problem Solving with C++: Walls and Mirrors,* (Redwood City, Calif.: Benjamin/Cummings, 1995), *pp.* 210–14. However, other authors note that in certain situations this recursive technique can be impractical because of the large amount of activation record space that it requires.

Application: Binary Search Tree

A *binary search tree* is a binary tree in which, at each node, every *key* in the left subtree is smaller than the key at that node and every key in the right subtree is larger than the current key. The following program implements a binary search tree in a manner almost identical to the recursive linked-list program of Example 8.9. Each node in the tree has two pointer components, `Left` and `Right`, instead of the single pointer `Next`. The search goes either to the right if `New_Key` is larger than the `Key` component of `Current_Ptr`⊙ or to the left if `New_Key` is smaller. Insertion occurs only when `Current_Ptr` is found to be disassociated. The procedure `Print_Tree` is also recursive. It prints the entire left subtree, then the current node, and finally the right subtree. Because of the way the tree is constructed, the nodes will be printed in the order of their Key components.

EXAMPLE 8.10

```
! Example 8.10. Binary search tree.
  program Binary_Tree
    implicit none
    intrinsic Associated
    integer, parameter :: S_LEN = 20
    type :: Box_Type
      character (len = S_LEN) :: Key
      type (Box_Type), pointer :: Left, Right
    end type Box_Type
    type (Box_Type), pointer :: Root
    character (len = S_LEN) :: New_Key = "␣"
    integer :: EoF

  ! start program Binary_Tree
    nullify (Root)
    open (unit = 1, file = "simply.txt")

  Input_Loop: &
    do
      read (1, *, iostat = EoF) New_Key
      if (EoF < 0) exit Input_Loop
      call Look_Up (Root)
    end do Input_Loop

  ! This point is reached at end of input file.
  call Print_Tree
```

```
contains
  recursive subroutine Look_Up (Current_Ptr)
    type (Box_Type), pointer :: Current_Ptr, New_Item
! start subroutine Look_Up
    if (Associated (Current_Ptr)) then                      ! Pointer is not NIL.
      if (New_Key == Current_Ptr % Key) then
        print *, New_Key, "␣Found.␣"
      else if (New_Key > Current_Ptr % Key) then
        call Look_Up (Current_Ptr % Right)                           ! Recursion
      else                                       ! New_Key < Current_Ptr % Key
        call Look_Up (Current_Ptr % Left)                            ! Recursion
      end if
      return
    else                          ! Insertion occurs only when Current_Ptr is NIL.
      print *, New_Key, "␣Not␣found.␣"
      allocate (New_Item)
      New_Item % Key = New_Key
      nullify (New_Item % Left)
      nullify (New_Item % Right)
      Current_Ptr => New_Item                    ! Assign to argument pointer.
    end if
  end subroutine Look_Up
  subroutine Print_Tree
! start subroutine Print_Tree
    print *, "␣====BINARY␣SEARCH␣TREE====␣"                     ! Print heading.
    call Print_Subtree (Root)
  end subroutine Print_Tree
  recursive subroutine Print_Subtree (Current_Ptr)
    type (Box_Type), pointer :: Current_Ptr
! start subroutine Print_Subtree
    if (Associated (Current_Ptr)) then
      call Print_Subtree (Current_Ptr % Left)
      print *, Current_Ptr % Key
      call Print_Subtree (Current_Ptr % Right)
    end if
  end subroutine Print_Subtree
end program Binary_Tree
```

8.6 PROCEDURE NAMES AS ARGUMENTS (Optional)

A dummy argument may be a procedure name; the corresponding actual argument must then also be a procedure name. Wherever the dummy argument appears, it represents the procedure whose name appears as the actual argument.

Why might such a feature be useful? Certain operations are performed, in a sense, on a whole function rather than on a particular function value. Common examples are the operations of integrating a given function or finding zeros of a given function. In an application that applies such an operation to only one function, the operation can be defined in terms of a particular function name. If necessary, the name of the operand function can be changed to the name given in the definition of the operation. For example, an integration subprogram might be written to operate on a function named `Func_A`, or a zero-finding subprogram might be written to operate on a function named `Func_B`.

When an application needs to apply the same operation to more than one function — for example, to integrate several different functions, or to find zeros of several different functions — the function name cannot be specified as part of the definition of the operation. Instead, the operation may be defined by a procedure with the operand function name as a *dummy argument.*

Note the following points:

1. A *function name* may be the actual argument corresponding to a dummy argument that is a procedure name. This situation should not be confused with that in which a *function reference*, consisting of the function name with an argument list, appears as an *expression* in an actual argument list corresponding to a dummy argument that is a variable name.
2. Internal procedure names, statement function names (see Appendix D.9), or generic function names[6] are not permitted as actual arguments.
3. If the dummy argument is used as the subroutine name in a `call` statement, the actual argument must be a subroutine name. If the dummy argument is used as a function name in an expression, the actual argument must be the name of a function whose result variable agrees in type, subtype (`kind` parameter), and rank with the corresponding attributes of the actual argument function result.
4. A procedure name dummy argument must not have a declared `intent` attribute.

The most straightforward arrangement is for the actual argument to be the name of an external procedure, with an interface block describing the dummy procedure in the subprogram where the procedure name dummy argument appears. An interface

[6] An intrinsic function that does not have a specific name must not be used as an actual argument. Specific intrinsic function names that are permitted as actual arguments are shown in Appendix A. A specific intrinsic function name that is used as an actual argument must be declared in an intrinsic statement.

block for an external procedure consists essentially of a copy of a portion of the subprogram where the procedure is defined.[7] The required portion includes specifications of the type, type properties, and all other attributes of the *dummy arguments* and of the *function result* (if it is a function). The names of the dummy arguments in the interface block may be different from those in the original procedure, however. Note that an interface block may inherit specifications from a module. (See also Appendix D.6.)

Application: Quadrature (Numerical Integration)

EXAMPLE 8.11 (Compare Exercise 5 of Section 4.1.) Quadrature, or approximate numerical integration, may be applied to a real function of a single real argument, which is supplied as a procedure name argument. The integral may be estimated numerically by dividing the range of integration into small intervals and applying the composite trapezoidal rule (which approximates the integrand function by a straight line over ea-ch interval) or by the composite Simpson's rule (which approximates the integrand function by a parabolic arc over each pair of intervals). Set `Delta_X = (B - A) / Real (N)` for some *even integer* value of `N`, where `A` and `B` are the limits of integration. The integrand function will be evaluated at `X = A +` i `Delta_X`, for $i = 0$ to `N`. We sum values of the integrand function separately for odd and even values of i, excluding the limit values 0 and `N`. (We may employ a single loop in which the index `I` goes from 1 to `N` – 1, and test whether or not `Modulo (I, 2)` is 0.) The approximate integral calculated by the composite trapezoidal rule is then

```
Delta_X * (F(A) + F(B)) / 2.0 + Odd_Sum + Even_Sum
```

and the composite Simpson's rule gives

```
Delta_X * (F(A) + F(B) + 4.0 * Odd_Sum + 2.0 * Even_Sum) / 3.0
```

```
! Example 8.11a. Function to perform quadrature by Simpson's rule.
 module Quadrature_M
   implicit none
   intrinsic Modulo
 contains
   real function Quadrature (Integrand, A, B, N_In) result (Simpson)
     real, external :: Integrand                  ! External attribute declaration
     real, intent (in) :: A, B
     integer, intent (in) :: N_In
     real :: Simpson, X, Delta_X
     integer :: I, N
 ! start function Quadrature
     N = N_In + Modulo (N_In, 2)                  ! Add 1 to N if it is not even.
```

[7] Interface blocks are also used for a completely separate purpose relating to generic functions, generic operators, and generic assignment, as described in Sections 7.5 and 7.6.

```
    Delta_X = (B - A) / Real (N)
    Evens = 0.0
    Odds = 0.0
    do I = 1, N - 1
      X = A + Real (I) * Delta_X
      if (Modulo (I, 2) == 0) then
        Evens = Evens + Integrand (X)
      else
        Odds = Odds + Integrand (X)
      end if
    end do
!   Trapezoid = Delta_X * &
!     (0.5 * (Integrand(A) + Integrand(B)) + Odd_Sum + Even_Sum)
    Simpson = Delta_X * &
      (Integrand(A) + Integrand(B) + 4.0 * Odds + 2.0 * Evens) / 3.0
  end function Quadrature
end module Quadrature_M
```

In Example 8.11a, the first dummy argument to the function `Quadrature` is a dummy procedure. Note that the `external` attribute (described later in this section) or an explicit interface is required in the subprogram in which the procedure name is an *actual* argument. For a dummy procedure, the `external` declaration is often the better choice. Example 8.11a illustrates the `external` statement, and Example 8.12a illustrates the `interface` block.

`Quadrature` invokes the dummy function `Integrand` several times — which causes invocation of whatever actual function currently corresponds to the dummy function. The program in Example 8.11a might be used to integrate either of the following functions.

```
! Example 8.11b.
! Fourth-degree polynomial test for Quadrature.
  real function Poly_4 (Z) result (A)                    ! External subprogram
    implicit none
    real, intent (in) :: Z
! start function Poly_4
    A = 17.3 + Z * (23.4 + Z * (137.0 + Z * (64.2 - Z)))
  end function Poly_4
```

```
! Gaussian distribution test for Quadrature.
  real function Distribution (Z) result (B)              ! External subprogram
    implicit none
    real, intent (in) :: Z
! start function Distribution
   B = Exp (-X ** 2)
  end function Distribution
```

The `external` *Attribute for Procedure Name Actual Arguments*

The `external` declaration statement illustrated in Example 8.12 describes a subroutine or function whose name appears as an actual argument. For example, the declaration

```
external Poly_A, Poly_B
```

appears in the main program of Example 8.12c to declare that the two polynomial functions used as actual arguments are defined by external subprograms. When interpreting an actual argument list containing a procedure name, Fortran needs to be informed that the name is that of a procedure and not of a data object. If Fortran can obtain the necessary interface information by other means — for example, if the actual argument procedure is inherited from a module or if it is an external procedure for which an interface block appears — the `external` statement is omitted.

The `external` attribute for one or more *functions* may also be declared in a type declaration, along with the type of the function result variables. The `external` attribute for one or more *subroutines* must be declared in a separate `external` statement because a type declaration is not appropriate for subroutines.

An actual argument may also be the name of an intrinsic function. The foregoing discussion also applies in this case, except that an intrinsic declaration statement appears instead of the external declaration statement.

EXAMPLE 8.12 The bisection, or midpoint, method, finds an approximate root of the equation `Fun(X) = 0` — that is, a value of `X` such that `Fun(X)` is close to zero. Suppose that a pair of argument values `A` and `B` are given initially such that `Fun(A)` and `Fun(B)` have opposite signs. The values of `A` and `B` are replaced by a pair of values that are closer together so that `Fun(A)` and `Fun(B)` still have opposite signs. This step is repeated, decreasing the distance between `A` and `B` each time, until `A` and `B` differ by no more than a specified tolerance, say, 0.001; at this point, the average of the values of `A` and `B` is returned as an approximate root of `Fun(X) = 0`. (Note that we speak of a *root* of the equation or a *zero* of the function.)

The bisection method may be implemented as a main program which assumes that the function to be examined will always have the name `Fun`. If there is never more than one function under consideration, it is always possible to name it `Fun` or whatever specific name the main program expects.

On the other hand, we may wish to develop this method as a general procedure that finds an approximate zero of any function whose name is given as an argument. The procedure will also require as arguments the initial values of `A` and `B` and the tolerance value to be used for accepting the approximate result.

```
! Example 8.12a. Bisection procedure for finding an approximate
!   zero of any real function of one real argument.
  module Zero_M
    implicit none
    intrinsic Abs, Spacing
```

```
  real function Zero (Fun, A_In, B_In) result (C)
    real, intent (in) :: A_In, B_In
    interface                             ! Interface block for dummy function Fun
      function Fun (T) result (R)
        real :: R
        real, intent (in) :: T
      end function Fun
    end interface
    integer, parameter :: Max_Div = 20
    real :: A, B
! start function Zero
    A = A_In; B = B_In
    FA = Fun (A); FB = Fun (B)
    if (FA * FB > 0.0) then      ! Check for error in initial values of A and B.
      print *, "␣Improper␣A␣and␣B␣values.␣"
    else                 ! Subdivide the (A, B) interval as many as Max_Div times.
      do Loop = 1, Max_Div
        C = 0.5 * (A + B); FC = Fun (C)
        if (Abs (A - B) <= 100.0 * Spacing (A)) exit
        if (FC * FA > 0.0) then
          A = C
        else
          B = C
        end if
      end do
    end if
  end function Zero
end module Zero_M
```

In Example 8.12a, the first dummy argument of Zero represents the function whose approximate zero is to be found. An interface block is given for the dummy procedure to indicate that it is a function and to give the attributes of the function result and of its dummy argument. The corresponding actual argument in any reference to Zero must be the name of a procedure defined by a function definition that is available to Fortran. The argument attributes and result attributes of the actual argument function must match those declared in the interface block.

To use Zero, we first define one or more functions whose zeros are to be found. Each such function must be capable of being matched to the interface block for the dummy function Fun in Zero. Thus, it must have a single argument of real type and must return a value of real type so that a proper reference will be made when statements such as FA = Fun (A) are executed (with the actual function substituted for the dummy

Fun). For example, we might be interested in two different polynomials that are defined by the following external function program units:

```
! Example 8.12b.
! First test polynomial for Zero.
  real function Poly_A (Z) result (A)                          ! External subprogram
    implicit none
    real, intent (in) :: Z
! start function Poly_A
    A = 17.3 + Z * (23.4 + Z * (137.0 + Z * (64.2 - Z)))
  end function Poly_A
```

```
! Second test polynomial for Zero.
  real function Poly_B (Z) result (B)                          ! External subprogram
    implicit none
    real, intent (in) :: Z
! start function Poly_B
   B = -102.4 + Z * (51.2 + Z * (25.6 + Z))
  end function Poly_B
```

We may then use the following main program that calls Zero to find a zero of either of these functions.

```
! Example 8.12c. Find zeros of Poly_A and Poly_B.
  program George
    use Zero_M
    external Poly_A, Poly_B          ! Procedures that appear as actual arguments
! start program George
    RTA = Zero (Poly_A, 0.0, 100.0)
    RTB = Zero (Poly_B, 0.0, 100.0)
    print *, RTA, RTB
  end program George
```

The function Zero and the two polynomial functions Poly_A and Poly_B must be furnished to Fortran with the main program in Example 8.12c. The first reference to Zero asks for a zero of Poly_A between 0 and 100, within a tolerance of 100.0 * Spacing (A), which is a bit more than the difference that might occur due to roundoff error. The second reference to Zero specifies similar conditions for finding a zero of Poly_B. The print statement in the main program then displays the approximate zeros.

8.6 Exercise

1. Write a main program that uses the trapezoidal rule module (Example 8.11a) to find the approximate integral from 0.0 to 1.0, with 100 integration steps, for each of the external functions Poly_A, Poly_B, and the intrinsic function Sin.

8.7 OPTIONAL AND KEYWORD ARGUMENTS (Advanced)

Any dummy argument of a procedure may be declared to be *optional*. The actual arguments may include a *keyword* that matches a dummy argument name in the explicit interface. Both of these features are especially useful for calling a routine that has a long list of dummy arguments, not all of which are required at every reference to the routine.

EXAMPLE 8.13

```
! Example 8.13. Optional arguments.
  program Invoker
    implicit none
    intrinsic Present
    integer :: X
! start program Invoker
    call Me_Madam (X, Third = 22)
    print *, X
  contains
    subroutine Me_Madam (First, Second, Third)
      integer, optional, intent (in) :: Second
      integer, intent (out) :: First
      integer, intent (in) :: Third
      integer :: Local
  ! start subroutine Me_Madam
      if (Present (Second)) then
        Local = Second
      else
        Local = 1234.5
      end if
      First = Local * Third
    end subroutine Me_Madam
  end program Invoker
```

Note the following points:

1. No special action is required to specify that a particular dummy argument may be referred to by a keyword, but the procedure interface must be explicit (see Appendix D.6). This requirement is automatically satisfied for internal procedures and for module procedures.

2. Any actual argument that appears without a keyword is associated by position, in the traditional way. All positional arguments *in a particular actual argument list* must precede all keyword arguments. Thus, an actual argument list may consist of some positional arguments (required or optional, but without skipping any positions), followed by a mixture (in any order and entirely in keyword form) of the remaining required arguments along with those remaining optional arguments that are needed in this particular procedure reference.
3. An external procedure (see Appendix D.6) requires an explicit interface when it is called with a keyword argument or with a missing optional argument.

EXAMPLE 8.14 The next two examples illustrate optional arguments.[8]

```
! Example 8.14. Keyword arguments.
  program Kingdom
    implicit none
! start program Kingdom
    ! All three of the following function references are equivalent.
    print *, Series_Sum (400, 700, 100.0, 0.1)
    print *, Series_Sum (D = 0.1, M = 400, N = 700, S = 100.0)
    print *, Series_Sum (400, 700, D = 0.1, S = 100.0)
  contains
    real function Series_Sum (M, N, S, D) result (Series_Sum_Result)
      integer, intent (in) :: M, N
      real, intent (in) :: S, D
      integer :: Loop
  ! start function Series_Sum
      Series_Sum_Result = 0.0
      do Loop = M, N
        Series_Sum_Result = Series_Sum_Result + S + D * real (Loop)
      end do
    end function Series_Sum
  end program Kingdom
```

A procedure with optional dummy arguments may use the intrinsic function `Present` (see Appendix A) to determine whether a particular optional dummy argument appears in the actual argument list at the current invocation of the procedure. Note that an omitted optional argument must not be referenced during execution of the procedure. Therefore, all references to optional arguments should appear inside `if` blocks (or similar protected sections of the program) controlled by a test based on `Present`.

[8] Examples 8.14 and 8.15 are adapted from Brainerd, Goldberg, and Adams, *Programmer's Guide to Fortran 90* (New York: McGraw-Hill, 1990), pp. 104–06.

EXAMPLE 8.15

```
! Example 8.15. Optional arguments and the intrinsic function Present.
  program Discretion
    implicit none
    intrinsic Present
! start program Discretion
    ! All of the following function references are equivalent.
    print *, Series_Sum (0, 700, 100.0)                 ! D assumes default value.
    print *, Series_Sum (0, 700, S = 100.0)             ! D assumes default value.
    print *, Series_Sum (N = 700, S = 100.0)      ! M and D assume default values.
    print *, Series_Sum (D = 0.1, S = 100.0, N = 700)   ! M assumes default value.
  contains
    real function Series_Sum (M, N, S, D) result (Series_Sum_Result)
      integer, intent (in), optional :: M
      integer, intent (in) :: N
      real, intent (in) :: S
      integer, intent (in), optional :: D
      integer :: Temp_M, Loop
      real :: Temp_D
  ! start function Series_Sum
      if (Present (M)) then
        Temp_M = M
      else
        Temp_M = 0
      end if
      if (Present (D)) then
        Temp_D = D
        else
          Temp_D = 0.1
        end if
      Series_Sum_Result = 0.0
      do Loop = Temp_M, N
        Series_Sum_Result = Series_Sum_Result + S + Temp_D * real (Loop)
      end do
    end function Series_Sum
  end program Discretion
```

8.8 IMPLEMENTATION OF ARGUMENTS (Optional)

During execution of a procedure, most Fortran 90 processors provide storage space in an *activation record* (see Section 5.6) for data objects that "belong to" the procedure — that is, for dummy arguments (values or references), local variables, and function results. However, local objects with the `save` attribute are stored *statically* along with global `common` data, and dynamic data objects including allocatable arrays and pointer targets are stored in a *heap*.

As it compiles each procedure, Fortran designs the layout for the activation record: It determines the amount of space required and establishes the position of each data object *relative to* the activation record. The computer code generated by the compiler refers to each data object by this relative position within the activation record for the procedure.

Although the size and the arrangement of an activation record are established by the compiler, no storage is actually allocated for it until the procedure is invoked during execution of the program. As a step toward initiating execution of a procedure, Fortran allocates the amount of space required for the activation record on an *activation record stack*. During execution of the procedure, all references to dummy argument or local variable values (except static objects and heap objects) cause information to be stored in or retrieved from the activation record. When execution of the procedure terminates, the space occupied by the activation record is released for possible further use by other procedures that may be invoked later.

The activation record for each procedure also includes space for some "system" information. Included, first of all, are a few items of information that permit the execution sequence to return to the proper point in the referencing procedure when the procedure terminates. The activation record for an internal procedure or module procedure requires one additional item of system information — a pointer to the activation record of the host program or subprogram that permits reference to data inherited from the host.

Attributes of Dummy Arguments and Function Results

A function result has a type and may have `kind` and character length type properties as well as array shape (`dimension`) and `pointer` attributes. It may be an assumed-length character string. It may be recursive.

A dummy argument that is a variable name has a type and may have `kind` and character length type properties as well as array shape (`dimension`), `intent`, `optional`, `pointer`, and `target` attributes. It may be an assumed-length character string or an assumed-shape array. A dummy argument that is a procedure name may have the `optional` attribute and may have an explicit interface.

Type properties and attributes of a function result and of dummy argument data objects may be specified by declarations in the procedure, in any of the usual forms. Type and type properties, but not `dimension` and `pointer` attributes, may be declared in a function header statement. Such declarations, either in the function header or in separate declarations, may include specification expressions (Section 8.4).

The `intent` *Attribute*

An `intent` attribute may be declared for a dummy argument, unless it has the `pointer` attribute (see Section 6.3) or is a procedure name argument.

The `intent (in)` attribute value corresponds roughly to "call by value" in some other programming languages. Most modern Fortran 90 implementations will provide space in the activation record for the *value* of a dummy argument for which this attribute value is declared, unless it is a large array. The value of the actual argument will be copied to the activation record when the procedure is invoked. References to the dummy argument within the procedure will access the activation record copy and will not have to refer back to the original value in the referencing procedure. Efficiency will be gained if there are many references to the dummy argument.

The `intent (in out)` attribute value corresponds roughly to "call by reference" in some other programming languages. The corresponding actual argument must be a variable name (which may be an array or array element, a structure or structure component, or a substring); Fortran will test this condition if interface information is available.

Two diVerent implementation models for `in out` arguments are possible. One is the traditional Fortran implementation, according to which a *reference* to the actual argument is passed to the procedure and stored in the activation record, as just described. Equivalent, except in unusual cases, is the *copy-in, copy-out* implementation.[9] With this implementation, the actual argument value is "copied in" and stored in the activation record when execution of the procedure begins, and the value stored in the activation record when execution terminates is "copied out" and stored as the value of the actual argument. During execution, the dummy argument is treated as a local variable. This copy-in, copy-out implementation is almost never adopted for a dummy argument that is an array.

A possible implementation for a dummy argument whose `intent` attribute is `out` is to treat it as a local variable (initially undefined) and to "copy out" the value from the activation record to the actual argument when execution of the procedure terminates. The reference implementation is also possible and is adopted by most processors for dummy arguments that are arrays.

If the `intent` attribute is `in out` or `out`, the corresponding actual argument must be a variable name; that is, it must designate storage to which the value can be assigned. The actual argument must not be a constant or any expression other than a variable name. (An implementation that copies the value from the activation record to the ac-

---

[9] Exceptional situations are those that involve *aliasing*, such as two different dummy arguments that correspond to the same actual argument variable.

tual argument has nowhere to put the value of a constant or of an expression that is not a variable name.) Fortran prohibits a constant or an expression that contains operators as the actual argument for a dummy argument whose intent is `in out` or `out`, and it will check this restriction if the necessary interface information is available.

If no `intent` attribute is declared, the effect is that of the traditional reference implementation: A reference or an assignment to the dummy argument is, in effect, a reference or an assignment to the corresponding actual argument. The actual argument must have a defined value if the dummy argument is assumed to have a value when execution of the procedure begins. It must be a variable name if the dummy argument is assigned a value within the procedure; a constant or an expression other than a variable name will lead to the same consequences that we reviewed earlier.

Array Arguments

For a dummy argument that is an array, many Fortran processors store an *address* in the activation record. Even if the dummy argument array is declared with the `intent (in)` attribute, processors usually choose not to provide space for the entire array argument in the activation record. If the dummy argument is an explicit-shape or assumed-size array, the address stored in the activation record is that of the base element.

The usual implementation model for assumed-shape dummy arrays involves a *descriptor* that contains type, shape, and location information for the actual argument array. The address of this descriptor is stored in the activation record.

Implementation of Recursion

Procedures, including internal procedures, may be *recursive*. A recursive procedure is one that invokes itself either directly or indirectly (by means of other intermediate procedures).

EXAMPLE 8.16 The following program calculates binomial coefficients as the ratio of factorials. (This method works only for rather small numerical values; compare Examples 4.22 and 7.4. A numerically superior method for calculating binomial coefficients, which does not use factorials, is Pascal's triangle; see Example 5.28.)

```
! Example 8.16. Calculate binomial coefficients as ratios of factorials.
  program Binomial
    implicit none
    integer :: N, R
! start program Binomial
    read *, N, R
    print *, "␣N␣=␣", N, "␣R␣=␣", R
    print *, "␣C␣=␣", Factorial (N) / (Factorial (R) * Factorial (N - R))
  contains
```

```
  recursive integer function Factorial (K) result (Value)
    integer, intent (in) :: K
! start function Factorial
    if (K <= 1) then
      Value = 1
    else
      Value = K * Factorial (K - 1)                       ! Recursive call
    end if
  end function Factorial
end program Binomial
```

The function Factorial is invoked from the main program three times during execution of the second print statement in Example 8.16. Each time the function is invoked from the main program, it may be invoked again recursively from within the function itself, depending upon the value of K, before the execution sequence returns to the main program at the point of the reference.

At each call to Factorial, a new activation record for the procedure is created on the central stack. Each record has space for the dummy argument value, K, and the result, Value. The activation record also has space for information that would be needed to locate the activation record of the host (which would be required for inherited names) and for execution sequence control information that permits execution to resume at the proper point when execution of the procedure ends.

Let's watch what happens during execution of this program. First of all, space is set aside for the values of the two main program variables, N and R. Execution of the main program begins with the read statement.

Suppose that the input values obtained by the read statement in the main program are 3 for N and 2 for R. Execution of the print statement begins and soon reaches the point of the function reference Factorial (N). At this point, a copy of the activation record for Factorial is created on the central stack (see Figure 8.3).

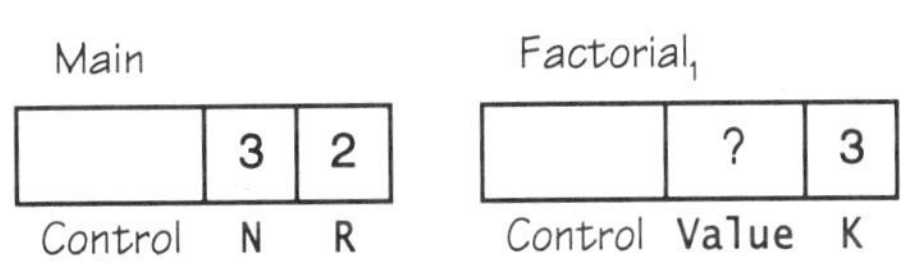

FIGURE 8.3. Activation records for main program and procedure *Factorial* (first copy).

The execution sequence control information is stored in the activation record, directing that termination of the procedure should be followed by further evaluation of the expression in the print statement in the main program. The value of N, which is 3, is copied to the activation record and becomes the value of the dummy argument K.

Execution of the procedure now begins; since (K <= 1) is false, the expression K * Factorial (K - 1) will be evaluated and assigned to Value. During evaluation of this expression, a recursive invocation of `Factorial` is required. A new copy of the activation record for `Factorial` is created on the central stack (see Figure 8.4).

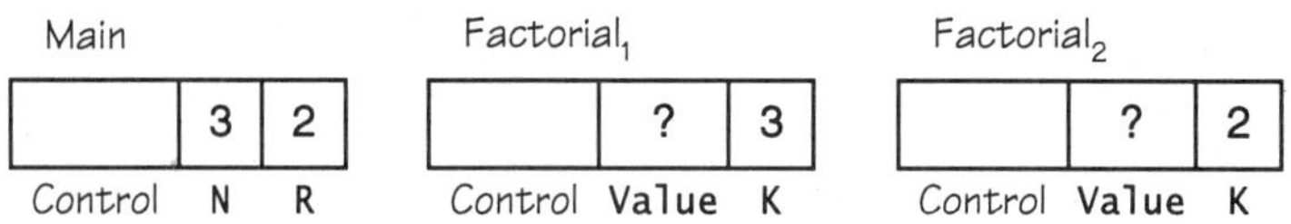

FIGURE 8.4. Second copy of activation record for *Factorial*.

The execution sequence control information is stored in the activation record, indicating the assignment statement in the procedure (at its first invocation). The value of the actual argument, `K - 1`, is computed from the value of `K` in the first activation record for `Factorial`. This value, 2, is copied to the second activation record for `Factorial` as the value of the dummy argument `K`.

The procedure now requires another recursive evaluation of `Factorial` with the actual argument value 1. A third copy of the activation record for `Factorial` is created. Control information is stored to indicate that execution should return to the second invocation of the procedure when this third invocation terminates. Since `(K <= 1)` is now true, `Value` is set to 1 (see Figure 8.5).

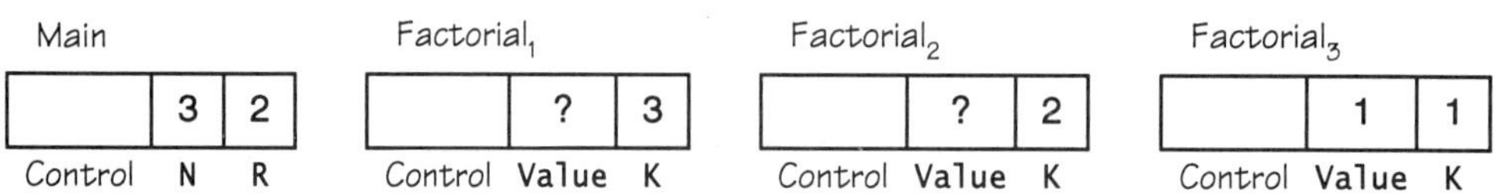

FIGURE 8.5. Third copy of activation record for *Factorial*.

This third invocation of `Factorial` terminates; the result value is returned to the referencing expression in the second invocation, and the third activation record is deleted. Execution now resumes in the middle of the expression `K * Factorial (K - 1)` in the second invocation. The result value, 1, is multiplied by the value of `K` from the second activation record. The value 2 still exists in this position, having been saved on the central stack. So the expression evaluation can be completed, giving the value 2, which is assigned to `Value`, the result of the second invocation of `Factorial` (see Figure 8.6).

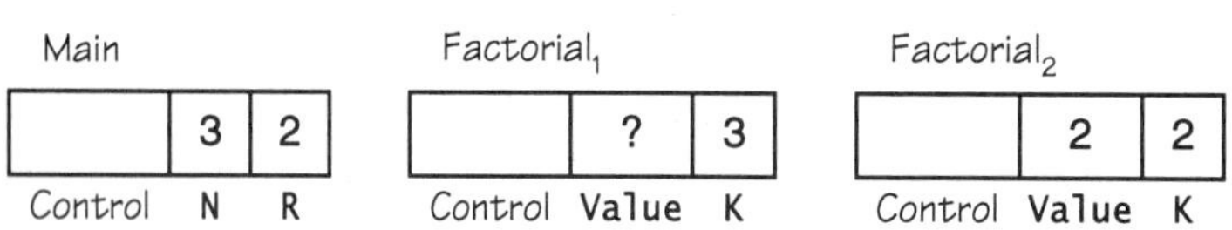

FIGURE 8.6. Result from third invocation of *Factorial*.

The second activation record is now deleted. The result 2 from the second invocation of `Factorial` is returned to the first invocation and multiplied by the value of `K` from the activation record for the first invocation, which is 3. The product is 6, which becomes the result value from the first invocation (see Figure 8.7).

FIGURE 8.7. Final value of *Factorial*.

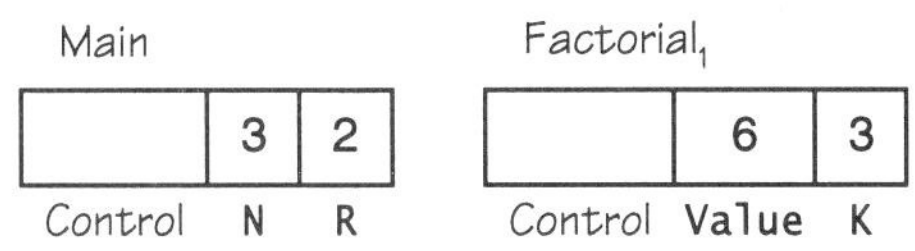

This result is returned to the referencing expression in the main program, and the first activation record for `Factorial` is deleted from the central stack, leaving only the main program activation record, as Figure 8.8 shows.

FIGURE 8.8. Final state of main program activation record.

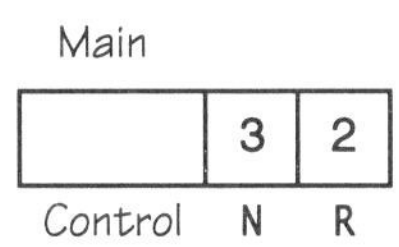

Similar steps take place, invoking `Factorial` with actual argument values 2 and 1, to complete the evaluation of the expression in the `print` statement in the main program. Each time `Factorial` is invoked, either from the main program or from the procedure, a new activation record is created on the central stack. Each time the procedure terminates, the result value is passed to the referencing procedure and the latest activation record is deleted. Finally, the main program terminates and its activation record is also deleted, leaving the central stack empty.

Assignment to Dummy Arguments or Host Variables

A procedure may assign a value to a dummy argument variable (unless its `intent` attribute is declared to be `in`). This value will be stored as the value of the corresponding actual argument, which should be a variable in the procedure from which the procedure was referenced. The referencing procedure may be a previous invocation of a recursive procedure, or it may be a different procedure altogether. The activation record model maintains an indication of the specific activation record in which the actual argument variable belongs: It is the activation record that was effective at the time of the reference that contained the actual argument variable name.

Fortran encounters a slight complication when a reference is made to an inherited object or to an object in a module that is imported into the referencing procedure. The compiler must take into account the fact that such an object is not located in the activation record of the current procedure, but is in the activation record of the host program or subprogram or of the imported module.

Part V
INPUT AND OUTPUT

Chapter 9 describes the extensive input and output features of Fortran, including *formatted sequential external* data transfer, *direct access* transfer, *unformatted* transfer, and transfer to and from *internal* files.

A Fortran `read`, `write`, or `print` statement specifies the direction of data transfer (in or out). In the most important case — formatted data transfer to or from an external file with sequential access — the input or output statement also specifies a *format* and may specify a *unit* (an external device to or from which data is to be transmitted). The format specifier may be an *asterisk* denoting list-directed formatting, a *character expression* whose value is a string containing a sequence of *format codes*, or a *statement label* that designates a separate `format` statement. If there is no unit specifier, a *default device* is determined by the processor; if present, the unit specifier is an *integer expression* indicating a specific external device or an *asterisk* denoting the default device. An input or output statement may also specify the traditional *advancing* (record-oriented) style of input or output or the alternative *nonadvancing* form, as well as the *exception handling* to be applied in case an error, end-of-file, or end-of-record condition occurs during data transfer.

The unit specified in a Fortran input or output statement must be *connected* to a *file* before data transfer can begin. The connection has certain *properties* that may be established by default or by execution of an `open` statement; the `inquire` statement returns connection property values. Other file manipulation statements are `close`, `end file`, `rewind`, and `backspace`.

Chapter 9
Input and Output

9.1 FORTRAN INPUT AND OUTPUT

Control Information for Data Transfer

As we have seen, Fortran input and output are processes whereby data is transferred (in either direction, between internal computer storage and various external devices) during execution of `read`, `write`, and `print` statements. Fortran needs three items of information to control the basic characteristics of this data transfer, and in some cases it needs two additional items of information. Data transfer characteristics that are specified by control information include the following:

1. The direction of data transfer (input or output)
2. The external device, or unit, to or from which data is to be transferred
3. The format description that specifies conversion between the computer-oriented internal form of data and its representation as a character string on the external device (not required for unformatted input and output; see Section 9.5)
4. (Optional) Positioning action that is to occur at the end of data transfer: advancing, if the file on the external device is to be repositioned to the end of the current record; nonadvancing, if the file position is to remain in its place within the current record
5. (Optional) Exception handling to be performed in the event of an end-of-file, end-of-record, or error condition during data transfer

Control information may be given either in a *short-form* `read` or `print` statement without a control list or in a *long-form* `read` or `write` statement with a control list. In either form, an input list or output list is also required (see Section 9.2) to describe data items to be transferred.

Direction of Transfer

The direction of transfer is determined by the initial keyword in the statement. The keyword `read` denotes *input,* while `write` or `print` denotes *output.* The distinction between `write` and `print` is purely historical; in particular, there is no relation between the keyword and whether or not the external device is an actual printer. The keyword `print` always appears in a short-form output statement, and `write` always appears in a long-form output statement; `read` appears in input statements of both forms.

External Device

Fortran identifies each external device in a processor-dependent manner with a unique integer value called a *unit number*. A given unit number represents the same device in the main program and in all of its modules and subprograms; thus, unit numbers may be said to have *global scope*.

A short-form input or output statement does not explicitly specify a unit; a *default* device for input or output is determined by the processor. In the most common case, the default input device is the terminal keyboard into which the user types data for direct entry to the computer, and the default output device is the monitor screen of the same terminal. Sometimes, the default output device is a printer.

Note that some operating systems, such as UNIX, permit *redirection* of input or output. When a Fortran program specifies the default unit, commands at the operating system level (see Section P.6) may designate a different input or output unit without program text modification or recompilation.

The control list in a long-form input or output statement must include a *unit specifier* that is either an *integer expression* indicating a specific external device or an *asterisk* denoting the default input or output device. The devices designated by an asterisk unit specifier are the same as the default devices for short-form input and output statements. (See more about the unit specifier in Section 9.5.)

Fortran transfers data to or from *files* that are composed of *records* (see Section 9.2). A sequential file that has been written by a Fortran program ends with an end-of-file indicator, which is called an *endfile record* because Fortran must process it in much the same way as a normal record in order to detect an end-of-file condition. However, the actual physical form of the end-of-file indicator does not necessarily resemble that of a normal record.

Format

A format must be specified in either a short-form or long-form statement for formatted input or output. This specifier may be an *asterisk*, which (as we have seen) designates *list-directed formatting*. The alternative is *explicit formatting*, controlled by a *format description* that is a character string consisting of a sequence of format codes. If the format specifier is a *character expression*, the format description is the value of the expression; if the format specifier is a *statement label*, the format description is contained in a statement with that label. (See also Sections 9.3 and 9.5 and Appendix B.)

Positioning at End of Data Transfer

With the traditional record-oriented style of input and output, Fortran positions the file between records as the last step in each `read` or `write` operation. The Fortran 90 term for this record-oriented positioning is *advancing* data transfer. With *nonadvancing* data transfer, on the other hand, the file position does not change after data transfer but may remain positioned within a record, and a subsequent input or output statement may transfer additional data to or from the same record. (See also Section 9.2.)

Advancing transfer is the default. Nonadvancing transfer requires the control list specifier `advance = "NO"`. Advancing transfer will be selected if there is no control list, a control list without any `advance =` specifier, or a control list with the specifier `advance = "YES"`.

If nonadvancing transfer is specified, the control list may also contain a *size specifier.* After nonadvancing input, a count of the characters transferred is stored as the value of an integer variable that is named in the size specifier. This count includes only those characters that are transmitted under the control of *data* format codes (see Appendix B.8).

Exception Handling

Exception handling cannot be specified without a control list. The necessary information may be given in either of two forms:

1. The control list may contain an exception specifier of the form `iostat =` *Integer variable.* The *Integer variable* is to be set at the end of execution of the input or output statement to a value that indicates whether or not any exceptional conditions have occurred.
2. The control list may designate one or more *statement labels* to which control will be transferred in case Fortran encounters an input or output error, an end-of-file condition, or an end-of-record condition.

Execution of the program is aborted if an exception occurs for which no exception handling is provided. Each of the statement label specifiers covers one of the three exceptions; the exception specifier covers all three. An exception specifier may be present in addition to any of the label specifiers. For example, if an end-of-file condition occurs during execution of a statement that contains both an exception specifier and an end-of-file branch label, control will be transferred to the designated label *and* the integer variable in the exception specifier will be set to indicate that the end of file has been detected.

Fortran gives a priority order to the exceptions: If an error is detected, the end-of-file condition and the end-of-record condition are ignored. If an end-of-record condition occurs (which is possible only for nonadvancing input), an end-of-file condition cannot occur during execution of the same statement.

EXAMPLE 9.1

```
! Example 9.1. Exception handling.
  program Unusual
    implicit none
    integer :: Code, Input_Data
! start program Unusual
    do
      read (*, *, iostat = Code, err = 7) Input_Data      ! Note statement label 7.
      if (Code < 0) stop "␣End␣of␣input␣file."
      print *, Input_Data
    end do
7   continue  ! Execute this statement if an error condition is detected
    print *, "␣Error␣code:␣", Code
  end program Unusual
```

Input and Output Statement Forms

When the format is the only item of control information that is needed, a simple short-form input or output statement (without a control list) is appropriate:

> `read` *Format* , *Input list*
> `print` *Format* , *Output list*

The *Format* specifier is either an asterisk that denotes list-directed formatting or a character expression or statement label that denotes explicit formatting (see Section 9.3). *Input list* items in the `read` statement are names of variables whose values are to be read; *Output list* items in the `print` statement are expressions whose values are to be written. A short-form statement cannot specify a unit (other than the processor default), nonadvancing transfer, exception processing, or unformatted input and outpu (see Section 9.5).

A long-form input or output statement (with a control list) can include additional control information such as a *Unit* specifier, a nonadvancing input or output specifier (see Section 9.2), or an exception specifier (see Section 9.2). The long-form input and output statements are as follows:

> `read (` *Control list* `)` *Input list*
> `write (` *Control list* `)` *Output list*

The first position in a *Control list* is reserved for the *Unit* specifier that indicates the external device to or from which the input data is to be transferred. The *Unit* specifier is an integer expression or an asterisk. An asterisk as the *Unit* specifier signifies that the device to be used is the same processor-dependent default device that is associated with the `print` statement or with the short-form `read` statement. For example:

```
read (*, *) I, Code, Str, Bugle, DPVar
read (*, fmt = *) I, Code, Str, Bugle, DPVar
read (unit = *, fmt = *) I, Code, Str, Bugle, DPVar
```

Besides the *Unit* specifier in the first position and the *Format* specifier in the second position, a *Control list* may contain optional specifiers (in any order) to describe positioning after data transfer or exception handling (see Section 9.2).[1]

Positioning at end of data transfer:
- *Advance* specifier
- *Size* of nonadvancing input

Exception handling:
- *Exception* specifier (`iostat`)
- *Error branch* specifier
- *End-of-file branch* specifier
- *End-of-record branch* specifier

Here are some statements with positioning and exception specifiers:

```
read (*, *, advance = S, Size = N) Whole_Array
read (*, *, iostat = EoF) Rate, Hours
read (3, *, advance = "NO", eor = 371, iostat = EoF) C
```

We note the following differences between the short and long statement forms.

1. The *Control list* in a long-form statement must specify a *Unit* and a *Format*. (The *Format* specifier is omitted for unformatted input and output; see Section 9.5.) A short-form statement must specify a *Format*; a processor-dependent default *Unit* is assumed.
2. The *Control list* in a long-form statement must be enclosed in parentheses and is not followed by a comma. The *Format* specification in a short-form statement is not enclosed in parentheses and must be followed by a comma unless the *Input list* or *Output list* is empty.
3. The keywords `read` and `write` appear in long-form input and output statements; short-form statements employ the keywords `read` and `print`.
4. The *Input list* or *Output list* in a short-form statement is identical to that in a long-form statement.

---

[1] A *Control list* must include a *Unit* specifier; a *Control list* for *formatted* input or output must also contain a *Format* specifier. Section 9.5 describes the following additional *Control list* features: The *Unit* specifier and the *Format* specifier may appear in any position if they are written in keyword form as unit = *Unit* and fmt = *Format*. A *Control list* for *unformatted* input or output omits the *Format* specifier. An optional *Record number* may be specified for direct access. See also Appendix D.11 for a description of the namelist specifier.

5. A short-form statement can designate only the processor-dependent default input and output devices. A long-form can specify any input or output device (including either of the default devices, which are designated by an asterisk unit specifier).

EXAMPLE 9.2

```
! Example 9.2. Control list examples.
  program C_List
    implicit none
    real :: A = 1.5, C = 2.6, Y = 3.7
    integer :: Code, B, X, Z
! start program C_List
    write (*, *, advance = "NO") A, B, C
    read (*, *, iostat = Code) X, Y, Z
    write (*, *) X + Y + Z
  end program C_List
```

In the long-form `read` and `write` statements in Example 9.2, the first two positions in each *Control list* are the *Unit* specifier and the *Format* specifier. In each of these input and output statements, the *Unit* specifier is an asterisk designating the default input or output device — the same external device that would be called for in a short-form `read` statement or a `print` statement. The second asterisk in each of these statements, in the *Format* specifier position, indicates list-directed formatting. The *Unit* and *Format* specified by the asterisks in these long-form statements are therefore the same as for the simpler statements

```
print *, A, B, C
read *, X, Y, Z
print *, X + Y + Z
```

The positioning specifier `advance = "NO"` in the first `write` statement in Example 9.2 states that the output file is *not* to be advanced to a new record after A, B, and C have been written to the file. Thus, the second `write` statement will append additional data to the same output record.

The exception specifier `iostat = Code` causes Code to be given a value upon completion of the `read` statement, indicating whether or not any exceptional conditions occurred during input. Such conditions could include errors during the input process or detection of an attempt to read past the end of the input file. If `advance = "NO"` were also specified in the same statement, the exception specifier might also indicate an attempt to read beyond the end of the current record.

9.2 DATA TRANSFER

Records

The information on a file is subdivided into *records*. A record corresponds roughly to a line on a terminal screen or to a printed line. From the viewpoint of a Fortran program, the structure (length and arrangement) of a record is established at the time the record is written. The structure of unformatted records (see Section 9.5) is processor-dependent, since the amount of space required on the external unit depends on the representation of data by the processor.

In preparing a program to write records and then read those same records, a program designer needs very little understanding of their actual structure. However, the records may be read or written by a different Fortran program, by a program in some other programming language (such as Cobol, Ada, or C++), by a text editor, or even on a different computer. In these cases, the designer of a Fortran program that uses these records must understand their structure in detail so that the *Input list* or *Output list* and the *Format* specification can be prepared properly.

Formatted Records

A formatted record is composed of characters. These characters may include letters, digits, and special symbols. They need not be limited to the characters of the Fortran 90 character set but may include any characters that the processor can recognize. Typically, the length of a formatted record may be a few characters or as many as a few hundred.

List-directed formatting produces records whose lengths depend in some ways upon the processor and thus are not entirely predictable. Explicitly formatted records, however, consist of a sequence of characters whose length is completely specified by the rules of Fortran.

If the pad property of the connection is yes (see Section 9.4), input proceeds as if the actual record were "padded" with any blanks that might be required to satisfy the *Input list* and the *Format* specification. However, if the pad property is no, formatted input must respect the actual length of the records. The default pad property is yes.

Record Length

For each external device, the records have a definite maximum size (number of characters). The examples in this chapter assume that the default input device can transmit records of at least 132 characters.

The length of a formatted record may be zero — for example, a record produced by a list-directed or explicitly formatted `write` statement with an empty *Output list* or a record written when the format scan encounters two consecutive slashes (see

Appendix B.8). A record whose length is zero is still recognized as a record by the Fortran input process.

A formatted record may have been prepared by some means other than execution of a Fortran program. In any case, it consists of some fixed number of characters.

For unpadded input, the record length required to satisfy the *Input list* must not exceed the actual record length — it is impossible to read from a record more characters than have been written there. For example, a record of zero length would have to be read by a statement with no list, with a format containing two consecutive slashes, or in some other way that does not require any transmission of data from the record. It is legitimate, however, to read fewer characters than a record contains.

The Input or Output List

The form of the *Input list* or *Output list* is the same whether it appears in a short-form `read` or `print` statement or in a long-form `read` or `write` statement. Also, the form of the list does not depend on whether format control is list-directed or explicit.

Each item in any input or output list may designate a variable or an implied `do` loop. Recall that a variable may be a whole array or structure, a substring, an array element, an array section, or a structure component. If it is a structure, its ultimate components (see Section 6.2) must not have the `pointer` attribute (see Section 6.3). An output list item may also be an expression, including a constant. (A restriction on array sections with vector subscripts as input list items is mentioned in Section 5.2.) Substring names as list items introduce no special difficulty (some examples of such use appear in Section 6.1).

If there are two or more list items, they must be separated by commas. In a short-form input or output statement, the comma following the *Format* specifier is omitted if there are no list items. The same list may contain items of integer, real, character, and other types; consider the following example:

EXAMPLE 9.3

```
! Example 9.3. Input and output lists with items of different types.
  program Lists
    implicit none
    real :: X, B, D, P(100), A(100)
    integer :: I = 2, J(100, 100), K = 5, L = 9
! start program Lists
    read *, X, B, D, P(14), J(I, K), J(25 * I - 4), A(K + 1), Pay, A(2 * L)
    print *, X, B, D, P(14), J(I, K), J(25 * I - 4), A(K + 1), Pay, A(2 * L)
  end program Lists
```

Each input list item designates a specific variable for which values are to be assigned. Constants — and expressions in general — are prohibited as input list items because they are not associated with objects to which values can be assigned. However, output lists may include constants and expressions, as the following example illustrates:

```
print *, &
   X + B, -1, P(14) + 1.0, .TRUE., X < B, "Here" // "␣it␣is.␣"
```

An input or output list is scanned from left to right during data transmission. For example, the following list might appear in an input statement:

```
X, A(I), I, P(I)
```

Assume that the value of I has been previously set to 2, and that the third data value encountered in the default input unit is 6. After the first two input data values have been read and assigned to X and to A(2), the value of I will be changed to 6 when the third data value is read. Thus, the fourth data value will be assigned to P(6) and not to P(2). This example illustrates the particular importance of relative list position when an integer variable appearing in the list is also used as a subscript in the same *Input list*.

An implied do loop has the following form (as indicated in Section 5.4):

(*Sublist* , *Index* = *Initial value* , *Limit* , *Increment*)

Any item that can appear in an input or output list, including an inner implied do loop, can also appear in the *Sublist* of an implied do loop. The *Index*, *Initial value*, *Limit*, and *Increment* are subject to the same rules that apply to indexed do loops (see Section 5.4) and are interpreted in an analogous manner. The increment, if omitted, is given the default value 1. Control parameters for an inner implied do loop may depend upon those of an outer implied do loop. An example is J in the following loop:

```
((A(I, J), I = 1, J), J = 1, 5)
```

An input or output list item may specify transfer of a whole array or of an array section. For formatted input or output, a *separate* format code is required for *each element* of an array or array section of intrinsic type (except complex, which requires two format codes per element). When an array name appears without a subscript as an input or output list item, it represents the whole array (in the standard Fortran array element sequence; see Section 5.2). Likewise, an array section designator in an input or output list represents all elements of the array section.

An input or output list item may specify transfer of a whole structure. For formatted input or output, a *separate* format code is required for *each ultimate component* of a structure (each component of intrinsic type that results from recursively decomposing any components that are arrays or structures; see Section 6.2). Components are transmitted in the order of their appearance in the derived type definition. A structure that is mentioned in an input or output list must not have any pointers as ultimate components.

EXAMPLE 9.4

```
! Example 9.4. Whole arrays, array sections, and structures as list items.
  program Hologram
    implicit none
    type :: Small
      integer :: I, J
      character (len = 5), dimension(3) :: Word
    end type Small
    type :: Big
      integer :: Count
      type (Small), dimension(8) :: Data
    end type Big
    type (Big) :: A
    integer, dimension(5, 2, 4) :: X
! start program Hologram
    read *, A
    print *, A % Count, A % Data(3)
    read *, X
    print *, X(2: 4, :, 3)
  end program Hologram
```

In the program of Example 9.4, the first `read` statement reads the whole array `A`, which consists of the integer `Count` and the array `Data` made up of 8 structures of type `Small`. Each of these structures consists of two integers and an array named `Word` that holds three strings of length 5. Thus, the input record must contain (in the correct sequence) a total of 17 integers and 120 characters. The first `print` statement prints the `Count` component of `A` as a single integer, followed by the two integers and the array of three strings from the third element of the array `A % Data`. The second `read` statement reads all 40 elements of the array `X` (in the standard Fortran array element sequence), and the print statement displays an array section consisting of six elements.

Sample input and output data might appear as follows:

Input:

```
999
1 1 aaaaa bbbbb ccccc
2 2 ddddd eeeee fffff
3 3 ggggg hhhhh iiiii
4 4 jjjjj kkkkk lllll
5 5 mmmmm nnnnn ooooo
6 6 ppppp qqqqq rrrrr
7 7 sssss ttttt uuuuu
8 8 vvvvv wwwww xxxxx

 1  2  3  4  5
 6  7  8  9 10
11 12 13 14 15
16 17 18 19 20
21 22 23 24 25
26 27 28 29 30
31 32 33 34 35
36 37 38 39 40
```

Output:

```
999 3 3 ggggghhhhhiiiii
22 23 24 27 28 29
```

Nonadvancing Input and Output

In the absence of any directions to the contrary, Fortran input and output always positions the input or output file at the end of the last record to or from which information has been transferred. This record-oriented style of input and output is not always convenient — it would often be preferable to stop data transfer in the middle of an input or output record and to continue later with the remainder of the same record.

Instead of this default, or *advancing*, file-positioning style, an input or output statement may request a *nonadvancing* style, whereby the file position remains unchanged at the end of data transfer. Thus, the file position may remain within a record after the input or output statement has been executed. It is possible to write a record by a sequence of nonadvancing transfers followed by a final advancing transfer to complete the record.

Nonadvancing data transfer cannot be specified in a short-form `read` or `print` statement because it requires a control list. Furthermore, nonadvancing data transfer is permitted only with explicitly formatted input or output; it is incompatible with list-directed input and output. Permitting list-directed nonadvancing input or output would be a possible Fortran processor extension to the language, but in the input case there is potential conflict between the end-of-record condition and the concept that list-directed input values can be freely distributed over multiple records. Nonadvancing input or output is also incompatible with unformatted, direct access, or internal file input and output (see Section 9.5) and is prohibited with `namelist` input or output (see Appendix D.11) as well.

EXAMPLE 9.5

```
! Example 9.5. Nonadvancing data transfer.
  program Non_Advancing
    character (len = *), parameter :: S ="supercalifragilisticexpialidocious"
! start program Non_Advancing
    write (*, *) "␣Line␣1.␣"
    write (*, "(A)", advance = "NO") "␣###␣"
    write (*, "(A)", advance = "NO") S( 1:  7)
    write (*, "(A)", advance = "NO") "␣###␣"
    write (*, "(A)", advance = "NO") S( 8: 17)
    write (*, "(A)", advance = "NO") "␣###␣"
    write (*, "(A)", advance = "NO") S(18: 27)
    write (*, "(A)", advance = "NO") "␣###␣"
    write (*, "(A)", advance = "NO") S(28: )
    write (*, *)
    write (*, *) "␣Line␣3.␣"
    write (1, *) "␣Line␣1.␣"
    write (1, "(A)", advance = "NO") "␣###␣"
    write (1, "(A)", advance = "NO") S( 1:  7)
    write (1, "(A)", advance = "NO") "␣###␣"
    write (1, "(A)", advance = "NO") S( 8: 17)
    write (1, "(A)", advance = "NO") "␣###␣"
    write (1, "(A)", advance = "NO") S(18: 27)
    write (1, "(A)", advance = "NO") "␣###␣"
    write (1, "(A)", advance = "NO") S(28: )
    write (1, *)
    write (1, *) "␣Line␣3.␣"
  end program Non_Advancing
```

Execution of the program in Example 9.5 produces the following result:

```
Line 1.
### superca ### lifragilis ### ticexpiali ### docious
Line 3.
```

Statement Form

Specification of advancing versus nonadvancing input or output appears in the *Control list* of a `read` or `write` statement. The keyword `advance` = must be followed by a character expression whose value is YES or NO: The value YES requests the traditional record-oriented (advancing) style; NO requests partial-record (nonadvancing) style. If this keyword does not appear (or if there is no control list), the default is advancing.

Two other specifiers are permitted only in a control list that specifies nonadvancing input. The *Size* specifier, of the form `size` = *Integer variable*, returns a count of the characters read; the *End-of-record branch* specifier, of the form `eor` = *Label*, detects end-of-record exceptions.

File Position

The principal difference between advancing and nonadvancing input or output is the positioning of the file after data transfer. The essence of nonadvancing input and output is to "freeze" the file position immediately after the last character transferred. Since nonadvancing input and output must transfer data to or from *formatted* records, position within a record is measured in characters.

In standard Fortran terminology, when a file is positioned within a record, that record is the *current record*. There is no current record when the file is positioned between records, before the first record of the file, or after the last record of the file (which may be the endfile record). There is always a *preceding record* unless the file has no records or is positioned within or just before the first record. There is always a *next record* unless the file has no records or is positioned within or just after the last record.

Format rescan and slash editing (Appendices B.7 and B.8) are processed in the same way for nonadvancing as for advancing input or output. The remaining portion of the current record is skipped, and the file is positioned at the beginning of the next record, which becomes the current record. Explicitly formatted input or output of more than one record with a single input or output statement is impossible without format rescan or slash editing.

After data transfer, if no error condition or end-of-file condition has occurred, the file is positioned as follows:

1. Advancing input or output positions the file after the record just read or written; that record becomes the preceding record and there is no longer a current record.
2. Nonadvancing input or output simply freezes the file position.

End of record. An end-of-record condition occurs when a nonadvancing input statement attempts to read from a position beyond the end of the current record. When this condition occurs, Fortran positions the file after the current record. If there is an *Exception* specifier, Fortran sets the designated *Integer variable* to a processor-dependent negative integer value different from the end-of-file value; and if there is an *End-of-record branch* specifier, control is transferred to the designated *Label*. If the pad property of the file connection is yes (see Section 9.4), blank characters are supplied to satisfy the *Input list*.

For example, suppose that a record contains 10 characters. If 10 characters are read by a nonadvancing `read` statement (with no slash or T format code and no format rescan; see Appendices B.7 and B.8), the position after data transfer is still within that record. If an attempt is made to read an 11th character, an end-of-record condition occurs and the file is positioned between records.

Prepositioning. If the previous statement was advancing, the file is necessarily positioned between records and no change in position is required prior to data transfer. If the previous statement was nonadvancing and an end-of-record condition did not occur, the file is positioned within the record last written and there is a current record. In either case, Fortran 90 positions the file prior to data transfer (either advancing or nonadvancing) according to the following rules:

1. If there is a current record, the file position is not changed.
2. For input, if there is no current record, there must be a next record (which may be the endfile record). The file is positioned at the beginning of the next record, which becomes the current record.
3. For output, if there is no current record, a new record is created as the next record. The file is positioned at the beginning of this new record, which becomes the current record.

These rules imply that when nonadvancing data transfer is followed by advancing data transfer, the advancing transfer begins at the next character position beyond where the nonadvancing data transfer left off. Thus, a sequence of nonadvancing transfers followed by an advancing transfer will continue reading or writing the same record (assuming, for input, that the record is long enough) and will end the current record after the advancing transfer.

Character Count

The control list of a nonadvancing input statement may contain a *Size* specifier of the form `size =` *Integer variable*. When execution of the statement terminates (either normally or with an end-of-record condition), the designated integer variable becomes defined with a count of the characters transferred by data format codes during execution of the current input statement. Blanks added for padding and characters transferred by nondata format codes (see Appendix B.8) are not counted. Note that, in the case of slash editing or format rescan, the count may include characters from more than one record.

Exception Handling

The *Control list* of a long-form input or output statement may contain an *Exception* specifier, an *Error branch* specifier, an *End-of-file branch* specifier, and an *End-of-record branch* specifier to permit detection of exceptional conditions. (Note that the *End-of-record branch* specifier is permitted only in a nonadvancing `read` statement.) These specifiers have the following forms:

An *Exception* specifier is `iostat` = *Integer variable*
An *Error branch* specifier is `err` = *Label*
An *End-of-file branch* specifier is `end` = *Label*
An *End-of-record branch* specifier is `eor` = *Label*

Each processor defines its own set of *error conditions*. An *end-of-file condition* occurs during input if the end of the input file is reached before transfer of data specified by the list can be completed. An *end-of-record condition* occurs during nonadvancing input if the end of the current input record is reached before transfer of data specified by the list can be completed.

An exception code will be assigned to the *Integer variable* in the *Exception* specifier on completion of the input or output operation. This exception code value will be

Zero if the operation was completed normally
Positive if an error condition has occurred
Negative if the operation was a sequential input operation and no error has occurred, but an end-of-file condition was detected during the operation
Negative, with a value different from the end-of-file value, if the operation was a nonadvancing input operation and no error or end-of-file condition has occurred, but an end-of-record condition was detected during the operation

The *Labels* given in the *Error branch*, *End-of-file branch*, and *End-of-record branch* specifiers must refer to executable statements in the same procedure. Control will be transferred to the designated label if the corresponding condition is detected.

9.2 Exercises

1. Find the Fortran language errors in the following input and output lists:

   a. `print *, A, B, C, (D(I) I = N, M)`

   b. `print *, John Jackson, 14.35. X(1)`

   c. `read *, L, Jill, Johnnie, Jacob(I), I = 1, N`

   d. `print *, (A(I), I = 1, 1, 500, 1)`

   e. `read *, 4, 16, 20`

   f. `read *, Able, X, Baker, (Y(2, J), J = 3.9(`

   g. `read *,`

h. `print *, *`

i. `print *, -SqRt(C ** 2 + B ** 3) / 4,0`

j. `print *, (B(I), I = 1, K, C (3), I = 1, K), D, E`

k. `read *, N, B, B, (A(I), I = 1, N), "A⊥=". A`

l. `print *, A`

2. Construct *input lists* that assign values to the sequences of array elements described as follows:

   a. All elements of a vector `T` having even subscripts up to 50

   b. All elements in the third column of an 8 by 7 array called `Check`

   c. All elements in the first row, followed by all elements in the sixth row, of the same 6 by 5 array called `R`

3. Construct short-form input or output statements, with list-directed formatting for each of the following:

   a. Read the elements A_1 through A_n inclusive, preceded by the value of n.

   b. Print all the elements of the fourth row of an `M` by `N` array called `C`.

   c. Print all elements of the `L`th column of an `N` by `N` array named `D`.

   d. Read pairs of elements for the last two columns of the 8 by 9 array `Q`.

   e. Print the 4 by 4 array called `Criss_Cross`; the elements are to be ordered by columns. (That is, print all elements of column 1, then all elements of column 2, and so on.)

   f. Given n, read pairs, each consisting of an element of the vector `A` having an odd subscript $(1, 3, 5, \ldots, 2n - 1)$ followed by an element of the vector `B` having an even subscript $(2, 4, 6, \ldots, 2n)$.

   g. Print the odd rows of an `M` by 5 array called `Crazy`.

4. Analyze the following nested implied `do` loop in detail to determine the sequence of subscript values represented (you may wish to make a sketch of a 4 by 3 matrix):

```
((Matrix(I, J), I = J, 4), J = 1, 3)
```

5. Given a knight located at the point K_{ij} near the center of a chessboard, print the contents of all eight locations to which the knight is permitted to move. (That is, the value of i may increase or decrease by 2 while the value of j increases by 1, or vice versa.)

9.3 THE FORMAT SPECIFIER

The format specifier in either a long-form or a short-form input or output statement may have one of three representations, each of which we shall consider further:

1. It may be an asterisk indicating that the arrangement of the external data depends only on the items in the input or output list (and upon the processor).
2. It may be a character expression — that is, a literal character constant (in the input or output statement itself) or a named constant defined elsewhere, the name of a character variable, or some other character expression. The character string that results from evaluating this expression describes the format of the external data.
3. It may be a statement label that refers to a `format` statement containing a format description.

Asterisk Format Specifier (List-Directed Formatting)

An asterisk format specifier indicates list-directed formatting, which is adequate for input in most situations and for output in applications where the precise appearance of the results is not important. On the other hand, for formal reports and other kinds of output where the printed data must be arranged in columns or in some other precise form, list-directed format control is inadequate.

Data items for list-directed input are arranged in "free form" on input data records. Consecutive items are separated by one or more consecutive blanks or by a comma. Values may appear anywhere in the data record. A blank character, a comma, or the end of a record must not be embedded within a single input data value of integer, real, or logical type.

A pair of commas with no data value between them indicates a "null" input data item. (There may be spaces between the commas, but no digits or other characters that represent data.) An input list item that corresponds to a null data item remains unchanged in value; if it has not been previously assigned a value, it remains undefined.

Free-Form Data for List-Directed Input

Note the following points:

1. An input data item of integer type is an optional sign followed by a string of digits.
2. An input data item of real type is an optional sign followed by a string of digits that may contain a decimal point, followed by an optional exponent. The exponent, if present, may have any of several forms. The most complete form consists of the letter E followed by a plus or minus sign, followed by an integer constant. Either the E or the sign may be omitted, but not both, since there must be some indication that an exponent is present. The letter D may be used instead of E for editing input fields corresponding to either real or double-precision input items.

3. An input data item of complex type consists of a pair of real items (of any acceptable form) enclosed in parentheses and separated by a comma.
4. An input data item of logical type may be an uppercase or lowercase `T` or `F`.
5. An input data item of character type may be a character constant delimited by quotation marks or by apostrophes. If it does not contain any blank, comma, or slash characters, it may be undelimited; that is, it may be written without enclosing quotation marks or apostrophes. (A data item consisting entirely of one or more blanks must be delimited.) As a further restriction, an undelimited input data item must not begin with a quotation mark, an apostrophe, or an integer constant and an asterisk; and the item cannot cross a record boundary. Undelimited character items that violate these rules might be confused with other list-directed forms.

Execution Sequence for List-Directed Input and Output

Execution of a `read` statement assigns input data values in sequence to the variables in the *Input list*. The sequence of data values from the input record must correspond exactly to the sequence of variables in the list. Several data values may be included in a single record; it is not necessary to fill the records.

Execution of a `write` or `print` statement transmits values of the expressions in the *Output list*, in sequence, to an external device such as the terminal screen or to an output file. The exact appearance of the data on the output device may vary from one Fortran processor to another, but the output record is terminated at the end of data transfer. (Nonadvancing data transfer with list-directed formatting is not permitted.)

Explicit Format Control

Appendix B explains in detail the individual format codes (officially known as *format edit descriptors*) that control explicit formatting. These codes are combined into a format specifier that may be written as a character expression or as a separate labeled statement. Each format code describes the details of transmission of one or more items of information to or from the external device.

When the format specifier is very simple, consisting of only a few format codes, it is often preferable to write it directly in the input or output statement as a literal constant character expression. Textbook exercises and examples are often simple enough to justify this treatment. Most of the explicitly formatted input and output examples in this text employ a character constant format code.

In actual applications, which often contain longer and more complicated format specifiers, the labeled statement form is usually preferable. With most Fortran processors, separate `format` statements are translated by the compiler to a form that can be manipulated quickly and easily during the input or output process, but character expression format specifiers must be analyzed during program execution. Furthermore, a given `format` statement may be used with several input or output statements, but it needs to be analyzed only once.

Character Expression Format Specifier

The format specifier may be a character expression in the input or output statement. In simple cases, a format specifier may be a literal character constant, as the following example illustrates.

EXAMPLE 9.6

```
! Example 9.6. Format specification with literal character constants.
  program Literal
    implicit none
    real :: A, B, C
    integer :: J, K
! start program Literal
    read "(3␣G12.0,␣2␣I3)", A, B, C, J, K                ! Short-form input statement
    read (*, "(3␣G12.0,␣2␣I3)" ) A, B, C, J, K            ! Long-form input statement
  end program Literal
```

Either of the read statements in Example 9.6 will read the five data items A, B, C, J, and K using the format description "(3␣G12.0,␣2␣I3)". Note that the first of these is a short-form statement and the second is a long-form statement. In the first statement, the parentheses enclosing the format description are inside the apostrophes that delimit the character constant; they should not be confused with the parentheses that delimit the control list in the long-form `read` statement.

Instead of a literal character constant, a format specifier may be the name of a character string, often a named constant, that contains the format description. A format specifier may also be a character expression of any form, including a scalar variable, an array, or a substring. One way of rewriting Example 9.6, with a reference to an initialized character variable, is shown in Example 9.7. An initialized variable, a named constant, or some other character expression might have a slight advantage over a literal constant in the case of a short format that is used in several input or output statements.

EXAMPLE 9.7

```
! Example 9.7. Format specification with an initialized character variable.
  program Refer
    implicit none
    real :: A, B, C
    integer :: J, K
    character (len = *) :: F14 = "(3␣G12.0,␣2␣I3)"
! start program Refer
    read F14, A, B, C, J, K
    read (*, F14) A, B, C, J, K
  end program Refer
```

A format description that is not a constant may be useful when certain characters within it will need to be changed during execution of the program — for example,

```
F14(2:2) = 5
```

The `format` Statement

The format specifier in an input or output statement may be the statement label of a `format` statement in the same procedure. A `format` statement has the form

Label `format` *Format description*

The *Format description* is, in effect, an undelimited character constant that can be analyzed by the compiler. Some processors more easily recognize a format specification in this form and are able to apply improved optimization techniques. Furthermore, in some cases where the format specification includes many quotation marks and apostrophes, the lack of an outer delimiter is an advantage.

The *Format description* consists of a parenthesized list of format codes. Each format code describes the details of transmission of one or more items of information to or from the external device.

EXAMPLE 9.8

```
! Example 9.8. Format specification with a format statement.
  program Statement
    implicit none
    real :: A, B, C
    integer :: J, K

! start program Statement
    read 14, A, B, C, J, K
    read (*, 14) A, B, C, J, K
14  format (3 G12.0, 2 I3)
  end program Statement
```

A labeled `format` statement may be placed at any convenient point among the program statements (see Appendix C). Each `format` statement may be placed immediately after the first input or output statement that refers to it, or `format` statements may be grouped near the beginning or end of the program or subprogram. A `format` statement must not be repeated within a procedure, even if there is more than one reference to it. The `format` statement *Label* may be referenced as a *Format* specifier in an input or output statement of either the short form or the long form. In Example 9.8, the same format description used in Examples 9.6 and 9.7 appears in a labeled `format` statement.

9.4 FILES (Advanced)

Processors that execute Fortran programs vary widely in their ability to perform complicated input and output operations, especially those that involve a number of different external devices. The Fortran language includes capabilities that can be adapted to the requirements of many different processors. Central to these capabilities in the Fortran language is the concept of a *file*. A file is an external source from which data may be obtained or an external destination to which it may be sent. (See also the discussion of formatted internal data transfer in Section 9.5.)

Data cannot be transferred to or from a file until the file is *connected* to the program. The principal purposes of file connection are to designate a *unit number* to be used by the program in referring to the file and to establish certain properties that affect the ways in which data can be transferred to or from the file.

A file may be *preconnected* by Fortran before execution of the program begins, or it may become connected as a result of the execution of an `open` statement:

1. Every Fortran program has access to two preconnected files, which are the special default input and output files. The default input file is automatically designated for a short-form `read` statement or for a long-form `read` statement whose *Control list* includes an asterisk as the unit specifier. The default output file is automatically designated for a `print` statement or for a `write` statement that includes an asterisk as the unit specifier. Both the default input file and the default output file are formatted sequential files. A Fortran processor may provide additional preconnected files.
2. A file may become connected as a result of the execution of an `open` statement.

A file may preexist — that is, it may be known to Fortran before execution begins — or it may be created by the program during execution. A file may be created by execution of an `open` statement; a preconnected file may also be created by execution of the first statement that transfers data to the file. A preexisting file must either have a name or be preconnected.

A file connection may be terminated by execution of a `close` statement that specifies the unit to which the file is connected. Fortran automatically closes any connections that remain at the end of program execution.

Because unit numbers are global in scope, an `open` statement or a `close` statement for a unit may appear in the main program or in any of its modules or subprograms, and will create or terminate the connection to that unit for all parts of the executable program.

Connection Properties

At the time a unit becomes connected to a file (either by preconnection or by execution of an `open` statement), the following properties may be established:

1. An *access method*, sequential or direct, is always established. (Direct access is described in Section 9.5.)
2. A *form*, formatted or unformatted, is established for a connection to a preexisting file or to a file that is created at the time it becomes connected. For a preconnected, preexisting file, the form is established by the preconnection. For a preconnected file that is not preexisting, the form may be established either by the preconnection or by the statement that creates the file. (See Section 9.5 for unformatted input and output.)
3. A *record length* may be established. If the access method is direct, the connection establishes a record length, which is the length of each record of the file. If the access method is sequential, the record length is optional and (if established) is the maximum length of records in the file. The record length is an integer value measured in characters if the file is formatted and in processor-dependent units if the file is unformatted.
4. A *blank significance* property, zero or null (see Appendix B.9), is established for a connection if the form is formatted. This property has no effect on output. For a preconnected file, the property is established by the preconnection.
5. A *permanence* property, temporary or permanent, specifies disposition of the file when the connection is terminated. If the permanence property is temporary, the file will be deleted (will cease to exist) when the connection is terminated. For a preconnected file that does not exist, the permanence property is temporary. For a preconnected file that exists, the permanence property is established by the preconnection.
6. An *initial position*, rewind, append, or as is, specifies initial positioning of the file during execution of the `open` statement. A new file will be positioned at its initial point. A file that already exists will be positioned at its initial point if the initial position is rewind or at its terminal point (or just prior to the endfile record, if any) if the initial position is append. If the file already exists and the initial position is as is, the position will remain unchanged during execution of the `open` statement.
7. An *action* property, read, write, or read write, specifies which kinds of data transfer statements are permitted. The `write`, `print`, and `end file` statements are permitted only if the action property is write or read write; `read` statements are permitted only if the action property is read or read write.
8. A *delimiter*, apostrophe, quote, or none, is permitted in an `open` statement only if the form for the connection is formatted. It applies only to output and specifies the delimiter to be used for character strings written with list-directed formatting or `namelist` formatting (see Appendix D.11).
9. A *pad* property, yes or no, is permitted in an `open` statement only if the form for the connection is formatted. It applies only to input and specifies whether or not the required record length, based on the *Input list* and the *Format* specification, is permitted to exceed the actual length of the record on the input file. If the property is yes, input proceeds as if the actual record were "padded" with blanks if required by

the *Input list* and *Format* specification. If the property is no, the required record length must not exceed the actual record length.

The open *Statement*

An open statement designates the unit number and establishes the connection properties for a file that is not preconnected. The statement consists of the keyword open followed by a *Control list* (Section 9.1), which is a list of specifiers enclosed in parentheses.

The *Control list* in an open statement must include a *Unit* specifier, which must not be an asterisk or an internal file designator. Unless the permanence property is temporary, the list must also include a *File name* specifier. This specifier has the form file = *Character expression*, where the value of *Character expression* is a file name that is acceptable to the processor. The list of specifiers may also include an *Exception* specifier and an *Error branch* specifier, which have the same form as those described in Section 9.2. The following optional specifiers are also permitted:

1. access = *Character expression*, where the value of *Character expression* is SEQUENTIAL or DIRECT. This specifier establishes an access method for the connection. If this specifier is omitted, the default access method is sequential.
2. form = *Character expression*, where the value of *Character expression* is FORMATTED or UNFORMATTED. This specifier establishes a form for the connection. If this specifier is omitted, the default form is formatted if the access method is sequential and unformatted if the access method is direct.
3. recl = *Integer expression*, where the value of *Integer expression* is positive. This specifier must appear only if the access method is direct, and it establishes a record length for the connection.
4. blank = *Character expression*, where the value of *Character expression* is NULL or ZERO. This specifier is permitted only if the form is formatted, and it establishes a blank significance property (see Appendix B.9) for the connection. The blank significance property is null by default if the specifier is omitted.
5. status = *Character expression*, where the value of *Character expression* is OLD, NEW, SCRATCH, REPLACE, or UNKNOWN. This specifier establishes a permanence property for the connection. The permanence property is permanent if the value is OLD, NEW, or REPLACE; it is temporary if the value is SCRATCH, and it is processor dependent if the value is UNKNOWN. The value of *Character expression* must not be SCRATCH if a *File name* specifier appears in the open statement. The default permanence property is processor dependent.

   The status specifier has other effects upon the execution of the open statement. If the value of *Character expression* is OLD, the file must already exist; if it is NEW, the file must not already exist. If the value is REPLACE and the file does not already exist, it is created; if it already exists, it is deleted and a new file with the same name is created. When the file is closed, or at the end of execution of the program, it will cease to exist if its permanence property is temporary.

6. `position` = *Character expression*, where the value of *Character expression* is REWIND, APPEND, or ASIS. This specifier establishes an initial position for the connection. The default initial position is as is.
7. `action` = *Character expression*, where the value of *Character expression* is READ, WRITE, or READWRITE. This specifier establishes an action property for the connection. The default action property is read write.
8. `delim` = *Character expression*, where the value of *Character expression* is APOSTROPHE, QUOTE, or NONE. This specifier is permitted only if the form is formatted, and it establishes a delimiter for the connection. The default delimiter is none.
9. `pad` = *Character expression*, where the value of *Character expression* is YES or NO. This specifier is permitted only if the form is formatted, and it specifies a pad property for the connection. The default pad property is yes.

Some examples of `open` statements are as follows:

```
open (unit = 6, file = "My_Data.bin", form = "UNFORMATTED")
open (unit = J, file = "My_Input.txt")
open (unit = J, file = "My_Input.txt", action = "READ")
open (unit = 31, access = "DIRECT", recl = 720)
```

The `close` *Statement*

Note that `close` statements are not required in most Fortran programs: When the program terminates normally, all connected units will automatically be closed. For large data processing tasks, however, or in other situations where files must be closed considerably earlier than the time of program termination, `close` statements may be needed.

A `close` statement consists of the keyword `close` followed by a parenthesized list of specifiers, which must include in an external *Unit* specifier and may include an *Exception* specifier, an *Error branch* specifier, and a `status` specifier of the form `status` = *Character expression,* where the value of *Character expression* is KEEP or DELETE — for example,

```
close (5)
close (iostat = Code, unit = 5, status = "DELETE")
```

The value of *Character expression* must not be KEEP if the permanence property of the connection is temporary.

Execution of a `close` statement terminates the connection between the specified external unit and the file to which it is connected. If the unit is not connected to a file, the `close` statement has no effect. After execution of a `close` statement, the unit may be reconnected to the same file or to a different file. If the file has a name, it may be reconnected to the same unit or to a different unit. If the file is not named, there is generally no way to identify it in order to reconnect it after it has become disconnected.

If the `status` specifier is KEEP, the state of existence of the file remains unchanged. If this specifier is DELETE, the file ceases to exist. If the specifier is omitted, the file ceases to exist if its permanence property is temporary; otherwise, its state of existence remains unchanged.

At termination of execution of an executable program, except due to an error condition, all connected units are implicitly closed with the `status` specifier `KEEP` if the permanence property is permanent or with the `status` specifier `DELETE` if the permanence property is temporary.

The `inquire` *Statement*

An `inquire` statement consists of the keyword `inquire` followed by a *Control list*, which must include either an external *Unit* specifier or a *File name* specifier, but not both. (See also the variant `inquire` statement described in Section 9.5 that provides information concerning a given output list.) The *Control list* may include an *Exception* specifier (`iostat`), an *Error branch* specifier, and any of the specifiers in the following list:

`exist` = *Logical variable*	`recl` = *Integer variable*
`opened` = *Logical variable*	`nextrec` = *Integer variable*
`number` = *Integer variable*	`blank` = *Character variable*
`named` = *Logical variable*	`position` = *Character variable*
`name` = *Character variable*	`action` = *Character variable*
`access` = *Character variable*	`read` = *Character variable*
`sequential` = *Character variable*	`write` = *Character variable*
`direct` = *Character variable*	`readwrite` = *Character variable*
`form` = *Character variable*	`delim` = *Character variable*
`formatted` = *Character variable*	`pad` = *Character variable*
`unformatted` = *Character variable*	

If a *File name* specifier is given, the `inquire` statement relates to the specified named file. If no file having the specified name exists, the variables named in the `named`, `name`, `sequential`, `direct`, `formatted`, and `unformatted` specifiers become undefined. If `opened` becomes false, the variables named in the `access`, `form`, `recl`, `nextrec`, `blank`, `position`, `action`, `read`, `write`, `readwrite`, `delim`, and `pad` specifiers become undefined. If a *Unit* specifier is given and the specified unit is not connected to a file, the variables named in the `named`, `name`, `access`, `sequential`, `direct`, `form`, `formatted`, `unformatted`, `recl`, `nextrec`, `blank`, `position`, `action`, `read`, `write`, `readwrite`, `delim`, and `pad` specifiers become undefined. If the access property is sequential, the variables named in the `recl` and `nextrec` specifiers become undefined. If the form property is unformatted, the variables named in the `blank`, `delim`, and `pad` specifiers become undefined.

The variable named in the `exist` specifier becomes true if a *File name* specifier is given and a named file with the specified name exists or if a *Unit* specifier is given and the specified unit exists; otherwise, the variable becomes false.

The variable named in the `opened` specifier becomes true if a *File name* specifier is given and the specified file is connected to a unit or if a *Unit* specifier is given and the specified unit is connected to a file; otherwise, the variable becomes false. If the variable named in the `opened` specifier becomes true, the variable named in the `number` specifier is assigned the value of the unit number to which the named file is connected; otherwise, the variable is assigned the value –1.

The variable named in the `named` specifier becomes true if the file is a named file; otherwise, the variable becomes false. If the variable named in the `named` specifier becomes true, the variable named in the `name` specifier is assigned the name of the file (which is not necessarily the same as the name given in the *File name* specifier).

The variable named in the `access` specifier is assigned `"SEQUENTIAL"` or `"DIRECT"` according to the access method of the connection. If there is no connection, the variable becomes undefined. The variables named in the `direct` and `sequential` specifiers are each assigned `"YES"`, `"NO"`, or `"UNKNOWN"`, indicating whether or not the particular access method is included among the set of allowed access methods for the file (or whether this information cannot be determined).

The variable named in the `form` specifier is assigned `"FORMATTED"` or `"UNFORMATTED"` according to the form for the connection. If there is no connection or if the connection is to a file that does not exist and for which no form has been established, the variable becomes undefined. The variables named in the `formatted` and `unformatted` specifiers are each assigned `"YES"`, `"NO"`, or `"UNKNOWN"`, indicating whether or not the particular form is among the set of allowed forms for the file (or whether this information cannot be determined).

The variable named in the `recl` specifier is assigned the record length for the connection (measured in characters for formatted records and in processor-dependent units for unformatted records) if the access method is direct.

If the access method is `"DIRECT"`, the variable named in the `nextrec` specifier is assigned a value 1 greater than the record number of the last record read or written (if any). If the file is connected but no records have been read or written since it was connected, the variable is assigned the value 1.

The variable named in the `blank` specifier is assigned `"NULL"` or `"ZERO"` according to the blank significance property of the connection.

The variable named in the `position` specifier is assigned `"REWIND"`, `"APPEND"`, or `"ASIS"` according to the initial position for the connection if the file has not been repositioned since the connection was established; otherwise, the variable is assigned a processor-dependent value.

The variable named in the `action` specifier is assigned `"READ"`, `"WRITE"`, or `"READWRITE"` according to the action property of the connection. The variables named in the `read`, `write`, and `readwrite` specifiers are each assigned `"YES"`, `"NO"`, or `"UNKNOWN"`, indicating whether or not the particular action is among the set of allowed actions for the file (or whether this information cannot be determined).

The variable named in the `delim` specifier is assigned `"APOSTROPHE"`, `"QUOTE"`, or `"NONE"` according to the delimiter for the connection. If there is no connection, the variable becomes undefined.

The variable named in the pad specifier is assigned "YES" or "NO" according to the pad property of the connection.

Note that the inquire statement does not provide a way to determine the permanence property of the connection.

The end file *Statement*

The end file statement applies only to output. Executing this statement sets the end-of-file indicator at the next record position on a sequential file. An end file statement has the form

```
end file Unit
```

The keyword end file may be written as one word or two (see Appendix C.1). The *Unit* designates the specific external unit that is connected to the file on which the end-of-file indicator is to be set. An end file statement may also have a *Control list,* which, if present, must contain a *Unit* specifier and may also contain an *Exception* specifier and an *Error branch* specifier (of the form described in Section 9.2). Some examples of end file statements are as follows:

```
end file 17                              ! Without control list
end file (17)                               ! With control list
end file (iostat = Code, unit = 17)
end file (unit = NEW)
```

Note that, after execution of an end file statement, the file is positioned after the end-of-file indicator; the file must then be repositioned by a backspace or rewind statement before further data transfer can be accomplished. Note also that execution of an end file statement creates the file if it does not already exist.

An end-of-file indicator is set automatically at the current file position by execution of a backspace, rewind, or close statement on a sequential file, if the most recent data transfer statement referring to the file was a write or print statement and the file has not been repositioned.

File Positioning with rewind *and* backspace

A file connected for sequential access consists of a sequence of (zero or more) records, which may be followed by an end-of-file indicator. Explicit file positioning occurs by execution of a rewind statement, a backspace statement, or an open statement that establishes an initial position property for the connection. Implicit file positioning occurs during execution of a read, write, print, or end file statement.

Rewind

The rewind statement positions a file at its initial point — that is, at the beginning of the first record of the file. A rewind statement may have the form

```
rewind Unit
```

The *Unit* designates the specific external unit that is connected to the file to be rewound. A `rewind` statement may have a *Control list*, which, if present, must contain a *Unit* specifier and may also contain an *Exception* specifier and an *Error branch* specifier (of the form described in Section 9.2). Some examples of `rewind` statements are as follows:

```
rewind 8                                  ! Without control list
rewind (8)                                   ! With control list
rewind (iostat = Code, unit = 8)
```

Backspace

If the file is positioned after a record or after the end-of-file indicator, execution of a `backspace` statement repositions it before the same record or before the end-of-file indicator. If the file is positioned within a record, it is repositioned before the current record. If the file is already at its initial point, this statement has no effect. The `backspace` statement may have the form

backspace *Unit*

The *Unit* designates the specific external unit that is connected to the file to be repositioned. A `backspace` statement may have a *Control list*, which, if present, must contain a *Unit* specifier and may also contain an *Exception* specifier and an *Error branch* specifier (of the form described in Section 9.2). Some examples of `backspace` statements are as follows:

```
backspace 8                               ! Without control list
backspace (8)                                ! With control list
backspace (iostat = Code, unit = 8)
```

Input Positioning

Let us suppose that a file has been connected to unit 7 for sequential access. The file contains several records and an end-of-file indicator and is to be used for input. If a rewind initial position property for the connection was not established by preconnection or by the `open` statement, we should give the command

```
rewind 7
```

to rewind the file on unit 7.

Suppose that several `read` statements are then executed.

1. If the file is unformatted, each `read` will advance the file by one record.
2. If the file is formatted, each *advancing* `read` statement will advance the file by one record, plus additional records that are read when a slash is encountered in the format or when rescan occurs. At the end of execution of each advancing `read` statement, the file is positioned at the end of the record just read.

3. Each *nonadvancing* `read` from a formatted file will advance the file when a slash is encountered in the format or when rescan occurs, and the position remains within the current record at the end of execution of the statement.

Now let us suppose that the end-of-file indicator is encountered during execution of a `read` statement whose control list contains an exception specifier. The file is then positioned following the end-of-file indicator, and an indication of the end-of-file condition is returned to the program. At this point, no further data transfer is possible until the file has been repositioned. For example, another `rewind` will again position the file at its initial point; a `backspace` will reposition the file just before the end-of-file indicator.

Output Positioning

Now consider a file that is to be used for sequential output. Suppose that this file is connected to unit 13; it contains no records and no end-of-file indicator. Again, we begin by positioning the file at its initial point. If a rewind initial position property for the connection was not established by preconnection or by the `open` statement, we should give the command

```
rewind 13
```

to rewind the file on unit 13.

Suppose that several `write` statements are then executed.

1. If the file is unformatted, each `write` will add one record to the file.
2. If the file is formatted, each *advancing* `write` statement will add at least one record, plus additional records if a slash is encountered in the format or if rescan occurs, and will then position the file at the end of the record just written.
3. A *nonadvancing* `write` statement will add a new record when a slash is encountered in the format or when rescan occurs, but will not end the record after data transfer.

After the desired data has been transmitted to the file, the statement `end file 13` may be executed to append an end-of-file indicator following the last record written. If the last data transfer was a nonadvancing `write`, the partial record is closed before the end-of-file indicator is appended. After the `end file` statement has been executed, the file is positioned after the end-of-file indicator, and no further data transfer is permitted until the file has been repositioned. For example, another `rewind` will again position the file at its initial point; a `backspace` will reposition the file just before the end-of-file indicator.

If we omit the `end file` statement after the last write, and if no further data transfer intervenes, an end-of-file indicator will be appended to the file automatically when it is closed (either explicitly by a `close` statement or implicitly at the end of program execution).

Summary of Sequential File Positioning

- A sequential file may be used for both input and output. A series of `read` statements may be executed to position the file at the end of a particular record; `write` statements may then be used to add new data to the file beyond that point. The last record written on a sequential file becomes the last record of the file; any records that were previously present on the file beyond that point are lost when a new record is written.
- An end-of-file indicator may be written to the file either explicitly (by execution of an `end file` statement) or implicitly (when the file is repositioned after a `write` operation). A `read` operation that moves the file position past this indicator must include an *Exception* specifier or an *End-of-file branch* specifier; the `status` variable will then be set, or the indicated control transfer will take place (or both).
- Data transfer is prohibited while a file is positioned beyond the end-of-file indicator as a result of a `read` or an `end file` operation. A `backspace` may be executed to reposition the file ahead of the end-of-file indicator, or a `rewind` may be executed to reposition the file at its initial point, after which further input and output operations may take place.

EXAMPLE 9.9 The following program rewrites all records of a preexisting file beyond a certain point. Suppose that each record of the file consists of a single character string. The program reads records from the file until it encounters the first record to be replaced, or until it reaches the end of the file. Then it backspaces the file and writes additional records.

```
! Example 9.9. Replacing the last part of an existing file.
  program Placer
    implicit none
    integer, parameter :: S_Len = 20
    character (len = S_Len) :: Key, String
! start program Placer
    read *, Key
    open (2)       ! Access is sequential, and form is formatted, by default.
    do
      read (2, "(A)", iostat = EoF) String
      if ((String == Key) .or. (EoF < 0)) exit
    end do
    backspace (2)
    do
      read *, String
      if (String == "⊥") exit
      write (2, "(A)" ) String
    end do
  end program Placer
```

9.5 ADDITIONAL INPUT AND OUTPUT FEATURES (Optional)

Keyword Form for Unit and Format Specifiers

In a *Control list*, as we have seen, a *Unit* specifier must always be present. It has the form

`unit =` *Device*

or simply

Device

If the keyword `unit =` is omitted, the *Unit* specifier must be the first item in the *Control list*. The *Device* code may be an integer expression or an asterisk (see Section 9.1).

The *Format* specifier must be present for formatted input or output. It has either of the forms

`fmt =` *Format*

or simply

Format

The keyword `fmt =` may be omitted only if the keyword in the *Unit* specifier is also omitted; in this case the *Format* specifier must be the second item in the *Control list*. The *Format* code may have any of several forms (as described in Section 9.3).

Direct Access Input and Output

The connection of a file to a unit has an access method, which is sequential or direct (see Section 9.4). Sequential access has been illustrated in all examples so far.

Direct access means that records may be accessed in an arbitrary sequence. Each record of a file connected for direct access has a unique record number, which is established when the record is written and does not change. An input or output statement for direct access must include a *Record number* to indicate which record is to be read or written.

Records may be read or written in any order. There is no way to delete a record, but a record may be rewritten. Nonadvancing input or output (see Section 9.2) with direct access is not permitted. The concept of "end of file" does not apply to direct access.

We have seen that the length of each record of a sequential file is established when the record is written. In contrast, all records of a direct access file have the same length, which is established at the time the file is connected.

A file connected for direct access is implicitly positioned during execution of a `read`, `write`, or `print` statement. Prior to data transfer, the file is positioned at the beginning of the record specified in the *Control list*, and data transfer takes place to or from this record. More than one record may be read or written during formatted data transfer (if a slash format code is encountered or if rescan occurs). The record numbers of the additional records follow consecutively after the number specified in the *Control list*.

A `read`, `write`, or `print` statement for direct access must have a *Control list* so that it can specify a record number. This specifier has the form

rec = *Record number*

The keyword `rec` must not be omitted. The *Record number* is an integer expression with a positive value, designating a record to or from which information is to be transferred.

Some examples of direct access input and output statements are as follows:

```
write (3, "(5⊥G⊥16.8)", rec = 176) I, Code, String_1, &
  Bugle, Prism
read (unit = 7, fmt = 57, rec = 176) X, Y, A(2), A(4)
write (7, fmt = *, rec = 176) X, Y, A(2), A(4)
```

EXAMPLE 9.10 Suppose that unit 3 is currently connected for direct access. We wish to read some information from the default input unit and write it at record 176 on unit 3.

```
! Example 9.10. Direct access input and output.
  program Copy
    implicit none
    integer :: I, Code
    complex :: Bugle, Prism
    character (len = 10) :: String_1
! start program Copy
    read *, I, Code, String_1, Bugle, Prism
    write (3, "(5⊥G⊥16.8)", rec = 176) I, Code, String_1, Bugle, Prism
  end program Copy
```

In Example 9.10, there are two statements for input and output. The `read` statement appears without a *Control list*; therefore, data is to be found on the default input unit. This unit and the default output unit are always preconnected for *sequential* input or output. No *Unit* specifier is required, and the *Format* specifier consists of an asterisk to designate list-directed input (see Section 9.3). This statement does not include a *Record number* (which would be permitted only for direct access) nor any of the other optional specifiers. A *Control list* would be required for specifying any input or output control information other than *Unit* and *Format*.

The `write` statement designates unit 3 and the character constant format `"5⊥G⊥16.8"`. Presence of a *Record number* indicates that access to unit 3 is direct rather than sequential. Again, no status or error specifiers are included.

Unformatted Input and Output

The connection of a file to a unit has a form which is formatted or unformatted (see Section 9.4). *Unformatted* files usually correspond to so-called binary files, whereas formatted files correspond to text files. Formatted data transfer has been illustrated in all examples so far.

Unformatted records contain information in a processor-dependent form that is obtained by transferring data to and from internal storage without any editing or other transformation. The external representation of the data corresponds exactly to its internal representation. Thus, unformatted data transfer is more efficient because the data is merely copied between the external device and the internal storage of the computer. Formatted records, on the other hand, are composed of characters representing data values; a formatted record corresponds to a printed line. Conversion is needed between the internal form of the data and its representation on the file.

A derived type value (structure) is treated as a whole. It is not equivalent to a list of its ultimate components because Fortran has considerable leeway with regard to the actual storage of structure components.

A disadvantage of unformatted records is that they are unsuitable for communication with humans unless further processing is applied to convert between the internal representation and a form readable by humans. Furthermore, unformatted files are not portable: Records written by one Fortran processor are not necessarily readable by some other Fortran processor. Unformatted data transfer is intended for creation of "temporary" files that are meant to be read back into the same system from which they were written.

An input or output statement for unformatted data transfer must not include a format specifier (see Section 9.3). An input or output list for unformatted data transfer has the same structure as for formatted data transfer.

Each unformatted `read` or `write` statement transfers exactly one record. The input list of an unformatted `read` statement must agree with the output list that was used when the record was written, except that two real values may correspond to one complex value of the same `kind`.

EXAMPLE 9.11

```
! Example 9.11. Unformatted data transfer.
  program Unformatted
    implicit none
    real :: A(2)
    integer :: J(3)
    logical :: Flag
    type :: Person
      character (len = 20) :: Name
      integer :: Age
    end type Person
    type (Person) Author
```

```
! start program Unformatted
   read *, A, J, Flag, Author
   open (unit = 1, form = "UNFORMATTED", file = "temp", status = "SCRATCH")
   write (1) A, J, Flag, Author
     :
   read (1) A, J, Flag, Author
   print *, A, J, Flag, Author
  end program Unformatted
```

Formatted Internal Data Transfer

Formatted *internal* data transfer changes the representation of data without actually transmitting it to or from an external device.

Formatted external data transfer includes two separate processes: the change in representation of data between its internal form and its external form, and the transmission of the data to or from the external device. For formatted input, data in the form of a string of characters is transmitted from the external device to a "buffer" that is inside the computer but is inaccessible to the Fortran program; it is then converted from character string form to the form required by the internal representation (integer, real, logical, or character, for example) and is thus made available for further processing. Formatted output reverses these steps: Internally represented data is converted to a character string in an internal buffer and is then transmitted to the external device.

We see that Fortran includes a hidden facility. Since it is capable of formatted input and output, Fortran can convert data under format control between an internal representation and a character string that humans can read. It would seem useful to separate this facility from the process of transmitting data (without any conversion) between the buffer and the external device. Actually, all that is needed is a way to make a buffer accessible to the Fortran program.

Accordingly, the Fortran input and output statements for formatted data transfer are extended to permit specification of an *internal* buffer (an internal character string) instead of an external device. Rather than an integer expression or asterisk in the *Unit* specifier position of the *Control list*, the name of a character variable (which may be an array, an array element, or a substring) designates the buffer or "internal file." The characters in the buffer are treated as a single record, except that if the buffer is a character array, the array elements are treated as a sequence of records.

In most respects, the buffer is used for internal data transfer as if it were a formatted sequential external device. However, note that a statement that calls for internal data transfer must not specify list-directed formatting or nonadvancing transfer. External data transfer with respect to the same buffer is possible. Such data transfer may be unformatted or list directed, or it may have any other properties that are appropriate for the external device to or from which the data is to be transferred. Assignment statements or other statements may also refer to the character data in the buffer.

EXAMPLE 9.12 Suppose that each record on the default input device contains 79 characters. The first character is either a blank or a C. If it is a blank, the 2nd through 79th characters consist of 13 six-digit real fields. If the first character is a C, the remaining 78 character positions contain arbitrary Fortran or non-Fortran characters that are to be copied to a line printer.

```
! Example 9.12. Formatted internal data transfer.
 program Uniform
   implicit none
   character (len = 79) :: Buffer
   real, dimension(13) :: Z
   integer :: N = 0, EoF
! start program Uniform
   do
     read (*, "(A 79)", iostat = EoF) Buffer          ! External input (formatted)
     if (EoF /= 0) exit
     if (Buffer(1 : 1) == "C") then
       print *, Buffer(2 : )                                   ! External output
     else if (Buffer(1: 1) = "⊥" then
       read (unit = Buffer, fmt = "(1X,⊥13⊥F6.3)") Z       ! Internal data transfer
       call Calc (Z, Result)
       print *, Result
     else
       print *, "⊥Column⊥1⊥is⊥not⊥blank⊥or⊥C⊥at⊥record⊥number⊥", N
     end if
     N = N + 1
   end do
 contains
   subroutine Calc (Z, Result)
     intrinsic Sum
     real :: Z(13), Result
 ! start subroutine Calc
     Result = Sum (Z ** 2)                                     ! Typical function
   end subroutine Calc
 end program Uniform
```

The first `read` statement in Example 9.12 calls for formatted external input to a character variable named `Buffer`:

1. If the first character position of this variable contains C, the remaining characters are printed; that is, they are transmitted to the default output device (the only device accessible via the `print` statement) with list-directed formatting (denoted by the asterisk format specifier).

2. If the first character of `Buffer` is not a `C`, the `else` block is executed, which contains a `read` statement for formatted internal data transfer. Data from the buffer is treated as if it were coming from a formatted record on an external device. The data is converted to real internal representation as specified by the format `"(1X, 13 F6.3)"` and stored in the thirteen elements of the array `Z`.

The array `Z` is passed as an actual argument to the subroutine `Calc`, which uses it to obtain the desired `Result` value. This value is then printed with list-directed formatting. The iteration continues with the next record number until all records in the file have been read and processed.

Inquire by Output List

The inquire by output list form of the `inquire` statement does not include a *File name* specifier or a *Unit* specifier. It includes only the specifier

`iolength` = *Integer variable*

and an *Output list*. The *Integer variable* in the `iolength` specifier is assigned a value that would be suitable as a `recl` specifier in an `open` statement specifying unformatted direct access. Here is an example:

```
inquire (iolength = Length) X, Y, String
```

APPENDICES

Appendix A contains detailed specifications for the procedures in the Fortran 90 intrinsic procedure library. It describes inquiry and numerical manipulation functions, conversion and transfer functions, computation functions, the merge function, array functions, and three intrinsic subroutines. The classification scheme in this appendix is adapted from the *Fortran 90 Handbook*.[1]

Appendix B describes format codes for explicitly formatted input and output. These codes constitute a separate language that is needed only for transmission of data in tabular form — for example, for printing data as a formal report.

Appendix C describes modern Fortran 90 free source program form, as well as the traditional Fortran fixed form. Source program features include the Fortran character set, lexical tokens, and placement of program statements.

Appendix D covers features considered obsolete for purposes of this text. These include the features that are listed as obsolescent by the Fortran 90 standard, along with other features whose use is no longer recommended but which will be encountered in existing Fortran programs. Separate sections of this appendix are devoted to implicit type specification, traditional forms for relational operators, the `data` statement, statement labels and `go to`, additional `do` construct forms, external functions and subroutines, alternative entry points for procedures, statement labels as arguments, statement functions, line printers, and additional input and output features (`include`, `namelist`, and Hollerith format).

Appendix E describes storage association, which, for purposes of this text, includes sequence association. Major storage association features are `equivalence` (association within a subprogram), `common` (association between subprograms), and sequence association (for dummy argument arrays). Note that the information in this appendix is included to facilitate reading and maintenance of existing traditional programs; creation of new programs that depend upon storage association is *not* recommended. The enhancements to this feature that Fortran 90 permits — namely, creating "unspecified" storage units and mixing storage units of different categories in a single sequence — are considered especially unfortunate and are not described in full detail.

---

[1] J. C. Adams et al., *Fortran 90 Handbook* (New York: McGraw-Hill, 1992), chap. 13.

Appendix A
Intrinsic Procedure Library

ALPHABETICAL INDEX OF THE FORTRAN INTRINSIC PROCEDURE LIBRARY

Bulleted procedures (marked ▪) are *elemental*. Numbers correspond to item numbers in Sections A.1 through A.6.

Note: The Kind argument in each of the functions AInt, ANInt, Char, Cmplx, Int, Logical, NInt, and Real is optional. If present, it must be an *initialization expression* — that is, it must be a *constant* expression that can be evaluated at compile time. Certain operations are excluded, such as exponentiation to a real power, any intrinsic function that returns a real result, and nonelemental array intrinsics.

Specific names of intrinsic procedures

A generic intrinsic procedure name must not be used as an actual argument. Instead, depending on the argument types that will be permitted when the argument procedure is referenced, a specific name must be chosen from the following table. In this table, argument types are coded as I for integer, R for real, C for complex, D for double precision, and S for character string.

Generic Name	Specific Names
Abs	Abs (R), CAbs (C), DAbs (D)
Cos	ACos (R), DACos (D)
AImag	AImag (C)
AInt	AInt (R), Dint (D)
ANInt	ANInt (R), DNInt (D)
ASin	ASin (R), DSin (D)
ATan	ATan (R), DATan (D)
ATan2	ATan2 (R), DATan2 (D)
Cos	Cos (R), CCos (C), DCos (D)
Conjg	Conjg (C)
CosH	CosH (R), DCosH (D)
Dim	Dim (R, R), IDim (I, I)
DProd	DProd (R, R)
Exp	Exp (R), CExp (C), DExp (D)
Index	Index (S, S)
Len	Len (S)
Log	ALog (R), CLog (C), DLog (D)
Log10	ALog10 (R), DLog10 (D)
Mod	Mod (I, I), AMod (R, R), DMod (D, D)
NInt	NInt (R), IDNInt (D)
Sign	Sign (R, R), DSign (D, D), ISign (I, I)
Sin	Sin (R), CSin (C), DSin (D)
SinH	SinH (R), DSinH (D)
SqRt	SqRt (R), CSqRt (C), DSqRt (D)
Tan	Tan (R), DTan (D)
TanH	TanH (R), DTanH (D)

A.1 INQUIRY AND NUMERICAL MANIPULATION FUNCTIONS

Character Inquiry Function

1. `Len (String)`

Length of a character string.
Argument. `String` must have character type. It may be scalar or array valued.
Result Type, Subtype, and Shape. Scalar of default integer type.
Specific name. `AImag` (complex).
Result Value. The number of characters in `String` if it is scalar or in an element of `String` if it is array valued.

Bit Inquiry Function

2. `Bit_Size (I)`

Number of bits in the Fortran bit model.
Argument. `I` must have integer type.
Result Type, Subtype, and Shape. Scalar of integer type with the same subtype as `I`.
Result Value. The number of bits in the Fortran bit model.

Kind Inquiry Functions

3. `Kind (X)`

Numerical `kind` value for objects with the same subtype as `X`.
Argument. `X` may have any intrinsic type.
Result Type, Subtype, and Shape. Scalar of default integer type.
Result Value. The numerical `kind` value for objects with the same subtype as `X`.

4. `Selected_Int_Kind (R)`

Numerical `Kind` value for an integer data representation that includes all integer values n with $-10^R < n < 10^R$.
Argument. `R` must be scalar and must have integer type.
Result Type, Subtype, and Shape. Scalar of default integer type.
Result Value. The numerical `kind` value for an integer data representation that includes all values n with $-10^R < n < 10^R$, or it is -1 if no such integer representation is available on the processor. If more than one integer representation meets the criterion, the result is the `kind` subtype selector value for that representation with the smallest decimal exponent range, unless there are several such representations, in which case the result is the smallest `kind` value among those representations that meet the criterion.

5. `Selected_Real_Kind ([P] [,R])`

Numerical `kind` value for a real data representation with at least `P` digits of decimal precision and with a decimal exponent range of at least R.

Arguments. At least one argument must be present.

P (optional) must be scalar and must have integer type.

R (optional) must be scalar and must have integer type.

Result Type, Subtype, and Shape. Scalar of default integer type.

Result Value. The numerical `kind` value for a real data representation for which `Precision (X)` is at least P and `Range (X)` is at least R. If no such representation is available on the processor, the result is –1 if the precision is not available, –2 if the exponent range is not available, and –3 if neither is available. If more than one real representation meets the criteria, the result is the `kind` value for that representation with the smallest decimal precision, unless there are several such representations, in which case the result is the smallest `kind` value among those representations that meet the criteria.

Numerical Inquiry and Manipulation Functions

Environmental Inquiry Functions

6. `Digits (X)`

Number of significant digits in the Fortran numeric model for the same type and subtype as the argument.

Argument. X must have integer or real type. It may be scalar or array valued.

Result Type, Subtype, and Shape. Scalar of default integer type.

Result Value. The number of significant digits (with respect to `Radix (X)`) in the Fortran numeric model for the same type and subtype as X.

7. `Epsilon (X)`

A positive number that is almost negligible compared to unity, in the Fortran numeric model for real type and the same subtype as the argument.

Argument. X must be real. It may be scalar or array valued.

Result Type, Subtype, and Shape. Scalar of real type with the same subtype as X.

Result Value. $\texttt{Radix (X)}^{\texttt{1-Digits (X)}}$ in the Fortran numeric model for real type and the same subtype as X.

8. `Huge (X)`

Largest number in the Fortran numeric model for the same type and subtype as the argument.

Argument. X must have integer or real type. It may be scalar or array valued.

Result Type, Subtype, and Shape. Scalar with the same type and subtype as X.

Result Value. $\texttt{Radix (X)}^{\texttt{Digits(X)}}-1$ if X has integer type and $(1 - \texttt{Radix (X)}^{\texttt{-Digits(X)}})$ $*\ \texttt{Radix (X)}^{\texttt{MaxExponent(X)}}$ if X is real, in the Fortran numeric model for the same type and subtype as X.

9. `MaxExponent (X)`

Maximum exponent in the Fortran numeric model for real type and the same subtype as the argument.
Argument. X must be real. It may be scalar or array valued.
Result Type, Subtype, and Shape. Scalar of default integer type.
Result Value. The maximum exponent in the Fortran numeric model for real type and the same subtype as the argument.

10. `MinExponent (X)`

Minimum (most negative) exponent in the Fortran numeric model for real type and the same subtype as the argument.
Argument. X must be real. It may be scalar or array valued.
Result Type, Subtype, and Shape. Scalar of default integer type.
Result Value. The minimum exponent in the Fortran numeric model for real type and the same subtype as the argument.

11. `Precision (X)`

Decimal precision in the Fortran numeric model for real type and the same subtype as the argument.
Argument. X must be real or complex. It may be scalar or array valued.
Result Type, Subtype, and Shape. Scalar of default integer type.
Result Value. `Int ((Digits (X) - 1) * Log10 (Radix (X)))` + k in the Fortran numeric model for real type and the same subtype as the argument, where k is 1 if `Radix (X)` is an integral power of 10 and k is 0 otherwise.

12. `Radix (X)`

Radix (number base) in the Fortran numeric model for the same type and subtype as the argument.
Argument. X must have integer or real type. It may be scalar or array valued.
Result Type, Subtype, and Shape. Scalar of default integer type.
Result Value. The radix (number base) in the Fortran numeric model for the same type and subtype as the argument.

13. `Range (X)`

Decimal exponent range in the Fortran numeric model for the same type and subtype as the argument.
Argument. X must have integer, real, or complex type. It may be scalar or array valued.
Result Type, Subtype, and Shape. Scalar of default integer type.
Result Value.
Case 1: For an integer argument, the result is `Int (Log10 (Huge (X)))`.
Case 2: For a real or complex argument, the result is `Int (Min (Log10 (Huge (X)), -Log10 (Tiny (X))))`.

14. `Tiny (X)`

Smallest positive number in the Fortran numeric model for real type and the same subtype as the argument.

Argument. X must be real. It may be scalar or array valued.

Result Type, Subtype, and Shape. Scalar of real type with the same subtype as X.

Result Value. $\texttt{Radix (X)}^{\texttt{MinExponent(X)-1}}$ in the Fortran numeric model for real type and the same subtype as X.

Numerical Manipulation Functions

15. `Exponent (X)`

Elemental function: Exponent part of the argument in the Fortran numeric model for real type and the same subtype as the argument.

Argument. X must be real.

Result Type. Default integer.

Result Value. If X is nonzero, the result is the exponent part of the representation for X in the Fortran numeric model for real type and the same subtype as X, except that the result is undefined if the exponent is outside the range for default integers. If X is 0, the result is 0.

16. `Fraction (X)`

Elemental function: Fraction part (significand) of the argument in the Fortran numeric model for real type and the same subtype as the argument.

Argument. X must be real.

Result Type and Subtype. Same as X.

Result Value. $\texttt{X * Radix (X)}^{-\texttt{Exponent(X)}}$ in the Fortran numeric model for real type and the same subtype as X. If X is 0, the result is 0.

17. `Nearest (X, S)`

Elemental function: Nearest *different* representable number in a given direction in the Fortran numeric model for real type and the same subtype as the argument.

Arguments.

X must be real.

S must be real and nonzero.

Result Type and Subtype. Same as X.

Result Value. The nearest number distinct from X that is representable by the Fortran numeric model for real type and the same subtype as X, in the direction of the infinity with the same sign as S.

18. `RRSpacing (X)`

Elemental function: Reciprocal of the relative spacing of numbers near the argument value in the Fortran numeric model for real type and the same subtype as the argument.

Argument. X must be real.

Result Type and Subtype. Same as X.
Result Value. $|X * \mathrm{Radix}(X)^{-\mathrm{Exponent}(X)}| * \mathrm{Radix}(X)^{\mathrm{Digits}(X)}$ in the Fortran numeric model for real type and the same subtype as X.

19. `Scale (X, I)`

Elemental function: Multiply X by the Ith power of the radix in the Fortran numeric model for real type and the same subtype as X.
Arguments.
X must be real.
I must have integer type.
Result Type and Subtype. Same as X.
Result Value. $X * \mathrm{Radix}(X)^{I}$ in the Fortran numeric model for real type and the same subtype as X, provided that this result is within range; if not, the result is processor dependent.

20. `Set_Exponent (X, I)`

Elemental function: Number whose fractional part (significand) is the fractional part (significand) of X and whose exponent part is I, in the Fortran numeric model for real type and the same subtype as X.
Arguments.
X must be real.
I must have integer type.
Result Type and Subtype. Same as X.
Result Value. $X * \mathrm{Radix}(X)^{I-\mathrm{Exponent}(X)}$ in the Fortran numeric model for real type and the same subtype as X, provided that this result is within range; if not, the result is processor dependent. If X is 0, the result is 0.

21. `Spacing (X)`

Elemental function: Absolute spacing of model numbers near the argument value.
Argument. X must be real.
Result Type and Subtype. Same as X.
Result Value. $\mathrm{Radix}(X)^{\mathrm{Exponent}(X)-\mathrm{Digits}(X)}$ in the Fortran numeric model for real type and the same subtype as X, provided that this result is within range; otherwise, the result is `Tiny (X)`.

Array Inquiry Functions

22. `Allocated (Array)`

Test whether an allocatable array is currently allocated.
Argument. `Array` must be an allocatable array.
Result Type, Subtype, and Shape. Default logical scalar.
Result Value. The result is true if `Array` is currently allocated, and it is false if `Array` is not currently allocated. The result is undefined if the current allocation status of the array is undefined.

23. `LBound (Array [, Dim])`

All lower bounds or a specified lower bound of an array.

Arguments.

`Array` may have any type, and must be array valued. It must not be a pointer that is currently disassociated or an allocatable array that is not currently allocated.

`Dim` (optional) must be scalar and must have integer type with $1 \le$ `Dim` $\le n$, where n is the rank of `Array`. The corresponding actual argument must not be an optional dummy argument.

Result Type, Subtype, and Shape. The result has default integer type. It is scalar if `Dim` is present; otherwise, it is an array of rank 1 and size n, where n is the rank of `Array`.

Result Value.

Case 1: If `Array` is a whole array or an array structure component and dimension `Dim` of `Array` does not have size 0, `LBound (Array, Dim)` is the lower bound for subscript `Dim` of `Array`. If `Array` is a whole array or an array structure component and dimension `Dim` has size 0 or `Dim` designates the last dimension of an assumed-size array, `LBound (Array, Dim)` is 1. If `Array` is not a whole array or an array structure component, `LBound (Array, Dim)` is 1.

Case 2: The ith component of `LBound (Array)` is `LBound (Array, `i`)`, for $i = 1, 2, \ldots, n$, where n is the rank of `Array`.

24. `Shape (Source)`

Shape of an array or a scalar.

Argument. `Source` may have any type. It may be array valued or scalar. It must not be a pointer that is currently disassociated or an allocatable array that is not currently allocated. It must not be an assumed-size array.

Result Type, Subtype, and Shape. A default integer array of rank 1 whose size is equal to the rank of `Source`.

Result Value. The shape of `Source`.

25. `Size (Array [, Dim])`

Extent of an array along a specified dimension or the total number of elements in the array.

Arguments.

`Array` may have any type and must be array valued. It must not be a pointer that is currently disassociated or an allocatable array that is not currently allocated. If `Array` is an assumed-size array, `Dim` must be present with a value less than the rank of `Array`.

`Dim` (optional) must be scalar and must have integer type with $1 \le$ `Dim` $\le n$, where n is the rank of `Array`.

Result Type, Subtype, and Shape. Scalar of default integer type.

Result Value. The extent of dimension `Dim` of `Array` or, if `Dim` is absent, the total number of elements of `Array`.

26. `UBound (Array [, Dim])`

All upper bounds of an array or the upper bound along a specified dimension.

Arguments.

`Array` may have any type and must be array valued. It must not be a pointer that is currently disassociated or an allocatable array that is not currently allocated. If `Array` is an assumed-size array, `Dim` must be present with a value less than the rank of `Array`.

`Dim` (optional) must be scalar and must have integer type with $1 \le$ `Dim` $\le n$, where n is the rank of `Array`. The corresponding actual argument must not be an optional dummy argument.

Result Type, Subtype, and Shape. The result has default integer type. It is scalar if `Dim` is present; otherwise, it is an array of rank 1 and size n, where n is the rank of `Array`.

Result Value.

Case 1: If `Array` is a whole array or an array structure component and dimension `Dim` of `Array` does not have size 0, `UBound (Array, Dim)` is the upper bound for subscript `Dim` of `Array`. If `Array` is a whole array or an array structure component and dimension `Dim` has size 0, `UBound (Array, Dim)` is 0. If `Array` is not a whole array or an array structure component, `UBound (Array, Dim)` is the number of elements in the given dimension.

Case 2: The ith component of `UBound (Array)` is `UBound (Array,` i`)`, for $i = 1, 2, \ldots, n$, where n is the rank of `Array`.

Pointer Association Status Inquiry Function

27. `Associated (Pointer [, Target])`

Test whether pointer argument is currently associated, whether the pointer is currently associated with the specified target, or whether two pointers are currently associated with the same target.

Arguments.

`Pointer` must be a pointer and may have any type. Its pointer association status must not currently be undefined.

`Target` (optional) must be a pointer or target. If it is a pointer, its pointer association status must not currently be undefined.

Result Type. Default logical type.

Result Value.

Case 1: If `Target` is absent, the result is true if `Pointer` is currently associated with a target and false if it is not.

Case 2: If `Target` is present and is a target, the result is true if `Pointer` is currently associated with `Target` and false if it is not.

Case 3: If `Target` is present and is a pointer, the result is true if both `Pointer` and `Target` are currently associated with the same target and is false otherwise. If either `Pointer` or `Target` is disassociated, the result is false.

Argument Presence Inquiry Function

28. `Present (A)`

Test whether an optional argument is present.
Argument. `A` must be an optional argument of the procedure in which the `Present` function reference appears.
Result Type and Subtype. Default logical scalar.
Result Value. The result is true if `A` is present as an actual argument in the current reference to the procedure in which the `Present` function reference appears; otherwise, it is false.

A.2 CONVERSION AND TRANSFER FUNCTIONS

Conversion Functions

29. `AChar (I)`

Elemental function: Character in a specified position of the ASCII collating sequence. `AChar` is the inverse of the function `IAChar`.
Argument. `I` must have integer type.
Result Type and Subtype. Default character, of length 1.
Result Value. If $0 \le$ `I` ≤ 127, the result is the character in position `I` of the ASCII collating sequence, provided that the processor can represent that character. If the processor cannot represent lowercase letters and `I` corresponds to a lowercase letter, the result is the corresponding uppercase letter.

30. `AImag (Z)`

Elemental function: Imaginary part of a complex number.
Argument. `Z` must be complex.
Result Type and Subtype. Real, with the same subtype as `Z`.
Specific name. `AImag` (complex).
Result Value. If `Z` is (x, y), the result value is y.

31. `AInt (A [, Kind])`

Elemental function: Truncation to a whole number.
Arguments.

`A` must be real.
`Kind` (optional) must be a scalar integer initialization expression.

Result Type and Subtype. The result is real. If `Kind` is present, it specifies the subtype of the result; otherwise, the result has the same subtype as `A`.

Specific names. `AInt` (real), `DInt` (double).
Result Value. `AInt` truncates toward 0, to the next smaller integer in absolute value.

32. `ANInt (A [, Kind])`

Elemental function: Nearest whole number.
Arguments.
A must be real.
`Kind` (optional) must be a scalar integer initialization expression.
Result Type and Subtype. The result is real. If `Kind` is present, it specifies the subtype of the result; otherwise, the result has the same subtype as A.
Specific names. `ANInt` (real), `DNInt` (double).
Result Value. If A is positive, `ANInt (A)` is `AInt (A + 0.5)`; otherwise, `ANInt (A)` is `AInt (A - 0.5)`.

33. `Char (I [, Kind])`

Elemental function: Character in a given position of the processor collating sequence associated with the specified character subtype. `Char` is the inverse of the function `IChar`.
Arguments.
`I` must have integer type with $0 \le$ `I` $\le n-1$, where n is the number of characters in the collating sequence for the specified character subtype.
`Kind` (optional) must be a scalar integer initialization expression.
Result Type and Subtype. Character of length 1. If `Kind` is present, it specifies the subtype of the result; otherwise, the result has default character type.
Specific name. `Char` (character). Must not be used as an actual argument.
Result Value. The character in position `I` of the collating sequence for the specified character subtype. Note that

- `IChar (Char (I, Kind (C)))` must have the value `I` for $0 \le$ `I` $\le n-1$, where n is the number of characters in the collating sequence for the specified character subtype; and
- `Char (IChar (C), Kind (C))` must have the value C for any character C capable of representation in the processor.

34. `Cmplx (X [, Y] [, Kind])`

Elemental function: Convert to complex type.
Arguments.
X must have integer, real, or complex type.
Y (optional) must have integer or real type. It must not be present if X is complex.
`Kind` (optional) must be a scalar integer initialization expression.
Result Type and Subtype. The result is complex. If `Kind` is present, the subtype is that specified by `Kind`; otherwise, the subtype of the result is default complex.
Result Value. If Y is absent and X is not complex, the result is the same as if Y were present with the value 0. If Y is absent and X is complex, the result is the same as if Y were present with the value `AImag (X)`. Note that `Cmplx (X, Y, Kind)` has real part `Real (X, Kind)` and imaginary part `Real (Y, Kind)`.

35. `Conjg (Z)`

Elemental function: Conjugate of a complex number.
Argument. Z must be complex.
Result Type and Subtype. Same as Z.
Specific name. `Conjg` (complex).
Result Value. If Z is (x, y), the result value is $(x, -y)$.

36. `Dble (A)`

Elemental function: Convert to double-precision real type.
Argument. A must have integer, real, or complex type.
Result Type and Subtype. Double-precision real.
Result Value. If A has integer, real, or double-precision type, the result has the same value as A. If A is complex, the result is `Dble (Real (A))`.

37. `IAChar (C)`

Elemental function: Position of a character in the ASCII collating sequence.
Argument. C must have default character type and length 1.
Result Type and Subtype. Default integer.

Result Value. If C is a character in the ASCII collating sequence, the result is the position of C in that sequence, and 0 ≤ `IAChar (C)` ≤ 127. If C is not in the ASCII collating sequence, the result is processor dependent.

Note that the values of relational expression values applied to *`IAChar`* function results are consistent with the lexical comparison functions *LGE*, *LGT*, *LLE*, and *LLT*. For example, if *`LLE (C, D)`* is true then *`IAChar (C) IAChar (D)`* is true, for any two characters *C* and *D* that are representable by the processor.

38. `IBits (I, Pos, Len)`

Elemental function: Subsequence of bits of an integer.
Arguments.

`I` must have integer type.

`Pos` must have integer type and nonnegative.

`Len` must have integer type. It must be nonnegative, and `Pos` + `Len` must be less than or equal to `Bit_Size (I)` in the Fortran bit model.
Result Type and Subtype. Same as `I`.
Result Value. The sequence of `Len` bits in `I` beginning at bit `Pos`, right-adjusted and with all other bits 0, in the Fortran bit model.

39. `IChar (C)`

Elemental function: Position of a character in the processor collating sequence for the character subtype whose `kind` parameter is that of the character.
Argument. C must have character type and length 1. It must be a character capable of representation in the processor.
Result Type and Subtype. Default integer.

Result Value. The position of `C` in the processor collating sequence for the character subtype whose `kind` selector value is `Kind (C)` and is in the range $0 \le$ `IChar (C)` $\le n-1$, where n is the number of characters in the collating sequence.

40\. `Int (A [, Kind])`

Elemental function: Convert to integer type.

Arguments.

`A` must have integer, real, or complex type.

`Kind` (optional) must be a scalar integer initialization expression.

Result Type and Subtype. Integer. If `Kind` is present, the subtype is that specified by `Kind`; otherwise, the result has default integer type.

Result Value.

Case 1: If `A` has integer type, `Int (A)` is `A`.

Case 2: If `A` is real and |`A`| < 1, then `Int (A)` is 0. If `A` is real and |`A`| ≥ 1, then the magnitude of `Int (A)` is the largest integer that does not exceed the magnitude of `A` and the sign of `Int (A)` is the sign of `A`.

Case 3: If `A` is complex, the result is `Int (Real (A))`.

The result is undefined if the processor cannot represent the result with the specified integer subtype.

41 `Logical (L [, Kind])`

Elemental function: Converts between `kind`s of logical.

Arguments.

`L` must be logical.

`Kind` (optional) must be a scalar integer initialization expression.

Result Type and Subtype. Logical. If `Kind` is present, the subtype is that specified by `Kind`; otherwise, the result has default logical type.

Result Value. The result value is that of `L`.

42\. `NInt (A [, Kind])`

Elemental function: Nearest integer.

Arguments.

`A` must be real.

`Kind` (optional) must be a scalar integer initialization expression.

Result Type and Subtype. Integer. If `Kind` is present, the subtype is that specified by `Kind`; otherwise, the result type has default integer type.

Specific names. `IDNInt` (double), `NInt` (real).

Result Value. If `A` > 0, `NInt (A)` is `Int (A + 0.5)`; if `A` ≤ 0, `NInt (A)` is `Int (A - 0.5)`. The result is undefined if the processor cannot represent the result with the specified integer subtype.

43. `Real (A [, Kind])`

Elemental function: Convert to real type.

Arguments.

`A` must have integer, real, or complex type.

`Kind` (optional) must be a scalar integer initialization expression.

Result Type and Subtype. Real.

Case 1: If `A` has integer or real type and `Kind` is present, the subtype is that specified by `Kind`. If `A` has integer or real type and `Kind` is not present, the result has default real type.

Case 2: If `A` is complex and `Kind` is present, the subtype is that specified by `Kind`. If `A` is complex and `Kind` is not present, the subtype is the same as that of `A`.

Result Value.

Case 1: If `A` has integer or real type, the result is equal to `A`.

Case 2: If `A` is complex, the result is the real part of `A`.

Transfer Function

44. `Transfer (Source, Mold [, Size])`

Physical representation of `Source`, with type and subtype of `Mold`.

Arguments.

`Source` may have any type and may be scalar or array valued.

`Mold` may have any type and may be scalar or array valued.

`Size` (optional) must be scalar and must have integer type. The corresponding actual argument must not be an optional dummy argument.

Result Type, Subtype, and Shape. The result has the same type and subtype as `Mold`.

Case 1: If `Mold` is a scalar and `Size` is absent, the result is a scalar.

Case 2: If `Mold` is array valued and `Size` is absent, the result is array valued with rank 1. Its size is as small as possible such that its physical representation is not shorter than that of `Source`.

Case 3: If `Size` is present, the result is array valued with rank 1 and size `Size`.

Result Value. If the physical representation of the result has the same length as `Source`, the physical representation of the result is that of `Source`. If the physical representation of the result is longer than `Source`, the physical representation of the leading part is that of `Source` and the remainder is processor dependent. If the physical representation of the result is shorter than `Source`, the physical representation of the result is the leading part of `Source`. If `D` and `E` are scalar variables such that the physical representation of `D` is at least as long as `E`, then `Transfer (Transfer (E, D), E)` must be the same as `E`. If `D` is array valued and `E` is array valued with rank 1, then `Transfer (Transfer (E, D), E, Size (E))` must be the same as `E`.

A.3 COMPUTATION FUNCTIONS

Numerical Computation Functions

45. `Abs (A)`

Elemental function: Absolute value.
Argument. A must have integer, real, or complex type.
Result Type and Subtype. The same as A, except that the result is real if A is complex.
Specific names. `Abs` (real), `CAbs` (complex), `DAbs` (double), `IAbs` (integer).
Result Value. If A has integer or real type, the result is |A|; if A is complex with value (x, y), the result is $\sqrt{x^2 + y^2}$.

46. `ACos (X)`

Elemental function: Arc cosine (inverse cosine) function.
Argument. X must be real with $-1 \leq X \leq 1$.
Result Type and Subtype. Same as X.
Specific names. `ACos` (real), `DACos` (double).
Result Value. The result value is $\cos^{-1}X$, expressed in radians, in the range 0 ≤ `ACos (X)` ≤ π.

47. `ASin (X)`

Elemental function: Arcsine (inverse sine) function.
Argument. X must be real with $-1 \leq X \leq 1$.
Result Type and Subtype. Same as X.
Specific names. `ASin` (real), `DASin` (double).
Result Value. The result value is $\sin^{-1}X$, expressed in radians, in the range −π/2 ≤ `ASin (X)` ≤ π/2.

48. `ATan (X)`

Elemental function: Arctangent (inverse tangent) function.
Argument. X must be real.
Result Type and Subtype. Same as X.
Specific names. `ATan` (real), `DATan` (double).
Result Value. The result value is $\tan^{-1}X$, expressed in radians, in the range −π/2 ≤ `ATan (X)` ≤ π/2.

49. `ATan2 (Y, X)`

Elemental function: Two-argument arctangent (inverse tangent) function.
Arguments.
Y must be real.
X must be real with the same subtype as Y. If Y is 0, X must not be 0.

Result Type and Subtype. Same as X.
Specific names. `ATan2` (real), `DATan2` (double).
Result Value. The principal value of the *argument* (phase) of the complex number `(X, Y)`, expressed in radians. The result value lies in the range $-\pi <$ `ATan2 (Y, X)` $\leq \pi$. If $X \leq 0$, the result value is `ATan (Y / X)`; if $X < 0$ and $Y \leq 0$, the result value is $\pi -$ `ATan (Y / X)`; if $X < 0$ and $Y > 0$, the result value is $-\pi -$ `ATan (Y / X)`.

50. `Ceiling (A)`

Elemental function: Smallest integer greater than or equal to the argument.
Argument. A must be real.
Result Type and Subtype. Default integer.
Result Value. The smallest integer greater than or equal to A. The result is undefined if the processor cannot represent this value in the default integer type.

51. `Cos (X)`

Elemental function: Cosine function.
Argument. X must be real or complex.
Result Type and Subtype. Same as X.
Specific names. `CCos` (complex), `Cos` (real), `DCos` (double).
Result Value. The result is cos *X*. If X is real, it is expressed in radians. If X is complex, its real part is expressed in radians.

52. `CosH (X)`

Elemental function: Hyperbolic cosine function.
Argument. X must be real.
Result Type and Subtype. Same as X.
Specific names. `CosH` (real), `DCosH` (double).
Result Value. The result is cosh *X*.

53. `Dim (X, Y)`

Elemental function: The difference X – Y if this is positive; otherwise, 0.
Arguments.
X must have integer or real type.
Y must have the same type and subtype as X.
Result Type and Subtype. Same as X.
Specific names. `DDim` (double), `Dim` (real), `IDim` (integer).
Result Value. The result is `Max (X - Y, 0)`.

54. `Dot_Product (Vector_A, Vector_B)`

Dot product (scalar product) of numerical or logical vectors.
Arguments.
`Vector_A` must be numeric (of integer, real, or complex type) or logical. It must be array valued with rank 1.
`Vector_B` must be numeric if `Vector_A` is numeric or logical if `Vector_A` is logical. It must be array valued with rank 1 and must have the same size as `Vector_A`.

Result Type, Subtype, and Shape. If the arguments are numeric, the type and subtype of the result are the same as for the expression `Vector_A * Vector_B`. If the arguments are logical, the result is logical with the same subtype as the expression `Vector_A .and. Vector_B`. The result is scalar.

Result Value.

Case 1: If `Vector_A` has integer or real type, the result is `Sum (Vector_A * Vector_B)`. If the vectors have size 0, the result is 0.

Case 2: If `Vector_A` is complex, the result is `Sum (Conjg (Vector_A) * Vector_B)`. If the vectors have size 0, the result is 0.

Case 3: If `Vector_A` is logical, the result is `Any (Vector_A .and. Vector_B)`. If the vectors have size 0, the result is false.

55. `DProd (X, Y)`

Elemental function: Double-precision real product.

Arguments.

  `X` must have default real type.

  `Y` must have default real type.

Result Type and Subtype. Double-precision real.

Specific name. `DProd` (real).

Result Value. The result is `X * Y`.

56. `Exp (X)`

Elemental function: Exponential.

Argument. `X` must be real or complex.

Result Type and Subtype. Same as `X`.

Specific names. `CExp` (complex), `DExp` (double), `Exp` (real).

Result Value. The result is e^X. If `X` is complex, its imaginary part is expressed in radians.

57. `Floor (A)`

Elemental function: Greatest integer less than or equal to the argument.

Argument. `A` must be real.

Result Type and Subtype. Default integer.

Result Value. The greatest integer less than or equal to `A`. The result is undefined if the processor cannot represent this value in the default integer type.

58. `Log (X)`

Elemental function: Natural (base *e*) logarithm.

Argument. `X` must be real or complex. If `X` is real, it must be positive. If `X` is complex, it must not be 0.

Result Type and Subtype. Same as `X`.

Specific names. `ALog` (real), `CLog` (complex), `DLog` (double).

Result Value. The result is $\log_e X$. If `X` is complex, the result is the principal value with imaginary part ω in the range $-\pi < \omega \leq \pi$. The imaginary part of the result is π only if the real part of `X` is negative and the imaginary part of `X` is 0.

59. `Log10 (X)`

Elemental function: Common (base 10) logarithm.
Argument. X must be real and positive.
Result Type and Subtype. Same as X.
Specific names. `ALog10` (real), `DLog10` (double).
Result Value. The result is $\log_{10} X$.

60. `MatMul (Matrix_A, Matrix_B)`

Product of numeric or logical matrices.
Arguments.

`Matrix_A` must be numeric (of integer, real, or complex) or logical. It must be array valued with rank 1 or 2.

`Matrix_B` must be numeric if `Matrix_A` is numeric or logical if `Matrix_A` is logical. It must be array valued with rank 1 or 2. `Matrix_A` and `Matrix_B` must not both have rank 1. The size of the first (or only) dimension of `Matrix_B` must equal the size of the last (or only) dimension of `Matrix_A`.

Result Type, Subtype, Shape, and Value. If the arguments are numeric, the type and subtype of the result are the same as for the expression `Matrix_A * Matrix_B`. If the arguments are logical, the result is logical with the same subtype as the expression `Matrix_A .and. Matrix_B`. The shape of the result depends on the shapes of the arguments.
Result Value.
Case 1: If `Matrix_A` has shape (n, m) and `Matrix_B` has shape (m, k), the result has rank 2 and shape (n, k); element (i, j) of the result is `Dot_Product (Matrix_A (`*i*`, :), Matrix_B (:, `*j*`))`.
Case 2: If `Matrix_A` has shape (m) and `Matrix_B` has shape (m, k), the result has rank 1 and shape (k); element j of the result is `Dot_Product (Matrix_A (:), Matrix_B (:, `*j*`))`.
Case 3: If `Matrix_A` has shape (n, m) and `Matrix_B` has shape (m), the result has rank 1 and shape (n); element i of the result is `Dot_Product (Matrix_A (`*i*`, :), Matrix_B (:))`.

61. `Max (A1, A2 [, A3] [,... ])`

Elemental function: Maximum value.
Arguments. The arguments must all have the same type, which must be integer or real; they must all have the same subtype.
Result Type and Subtype. Same as the arguments.
Result Value. The largest argument.

62. `Min (A1, A2 [, A3] [,... ])`

Elemental function: Minimum value.
Arguments. The arguments must all have the same type, which must be integer or real; they must all have the same subtype.
Result Type and Subtype. Same as the arguments.
Result Value. The smallest argument.

63. `Mod (A, P)`

Elemental function: Remainder function (remainder from `Int`).

Arguments.

A must have integer or real type.

P must have the same type and subtype as A.

Result Type and Subtype. Same as A.

Specific names. `AMod` (real), `DMod` (double), `DMod` (double).

Result Value. If P is nonzero, the result is `A - Int (A / P) * P`. If P is 0, the result is processor dependent.

64. `Modulo (A, P)`

Elemental function: Modulo function (remainder from `Floor`).

Arguments.

A must have integer or real type.

P must have the same type and subtype as A.

Result Type and Subtype. Same as A.

Result Value. If P is nonzero, the result is `A - Floor (Real (A) / Real (P)) * P`. If P is 0, the result is processor dependent.

65. `Sign (A, B)`

Elemental function: Transfer sign from B to A.

Arguments.

A must have integer or real type.

B must have the same type and subtype as A.

Result Type and Subtype. Same as A.

Specific names. `DSign` (double), `ISign` (integer), `Sign` (real).

Result Value. The result is |A| if B ≥ 0 and −|A| if B < 0.

66. `Sin (X)`

Elemental function: Sine function.

Argument. X must be real or complex.

Result Type and Subtype. Same as X.

Specific names. `CSin` (complex), `DSin` (double), `Sin` (real).

Result Value. The result is sin X. If X is real, it is expressed in radians. If X is complex, its real part is expressed in radians.

67. `SinH (X)`

Elemental function: Hyperbolic sine function.

Argument. X must be real.

Result Type and Subtype. Same as X.

Specific names. `DSinH` (double), `SinH` (real).

Result Value. The result is sinh X.

68. `SqRt (X)`

Elemental function: Square root.
Argument. X must be real or complex. If X is real, it must not be negative.
Result Type and Subtype. Same as X.
Specific names. `CSqRt` (complex), `DSqRt` (double), `SqRt` (real).
Result Value. The result is $\sqrt{X}$. If X is complex, the result is the principal value with nonnegative real part. When the real part of the result is 0, the imaginary part is nonnegative.

69. `Tan (X)`

Elemental function: Tangent function.
Argument. X must be real.
Result Type and Subtype. Same as X.
Specific names. `DTan` (double), `Tan` (real).
Result Value. The result is tan X, with X expressed in radians.

70. `TanH (X)`

Elemental function: Hyperbolic tangent function.
Argument. X must be real.
Result Type and Subtype. Same as X.
Specific names. `DTanH` (double), `TanH` (real).
Result Value. The result is tanh X.

Character Computation Functions

71. `AdjustL (String)`

Elemental function: Adjust left, removing leading blanks and appending trailing blanks.
Argument. `String` must have character type.
Result Type. Character with the same length and subtype as `String`.
Result Value. The same as `String` except that any leading blanks have been deleted and the same number of trailing blanks have been appended.

72. `AdjustR (String)`

Elemental function: Adjust right, removing trailing blanks and inserting leading blanks.
Argument. `String` must have character type.
Result Type. Character with the same length and subtype as `String`.
Result Value. The same as `String` except that any trailing blanks have been deleted and the same number of leading blanks have been inserted.

73. `Index (String, Substring [, Back])`

Elemental function: Starting position of a substring within a string.
Arguments.
`String` must have character type.
`Substring` must have character type with the same subtype as `String`.

Back (optional) must be logical.

Result Type and Subtype. Default integer.

Result Value.

Case 1: If Back is absent or is present with the value false, the result is the smallest positive value of I such that String (I : I + Len (Substring) - 1) = Substring, or 0 if there is no such value. The result is 0 if Len (String) < Len (Substring), and the result is 1 if Len (Substring) is 0.

Case 2: If Back is present with the value true, the result is the largest value of I less than or equal to Len (String) - Len (Substring) + 1 such that String (I : I + Len (Substring) - 1) = Substring, or 0 if there is no such value. The result is 0 if Len (String) < Len (Substring), and the result is Len (String) + 1 if Len (Substring) is 0.

74. Len_Trim (String)

Elemental function: Length of character string, ignoring trailing blank characters.

Argument. String must have character type.

Result Type and Subtype. Default integer.

Result Value. The number of characters remaining after any trailing blanks in String are removed. If all characters in String are blanks, the result is 0.

75. LGE (String_A, String_B)

Elemental function: Test whether a string is lexically greater than or equal to another string, based on the ASCII collating sequence.

Arguments. String_A and String_B must have default character type.

Result Type and Subtype. Default logical.

Result Value. If the strings have unequal length, the result is the same as if the shorter string were extended on the right with blanks to the length of the longer string. If either string contains a character not in the ASCII character set, the result is processor dependent. The result is true if the strings are equal or if String_A follows String_B in the ASCII collating sequence; otherwise, the result is false. Note that the result is true if both String_A and String_B have length 0.

76. LGT (String_A, String_B)

Elemental function: Test whether a string is lexically greater than another string, based on the ASCII collating sequence.

Arguments. String_A and String_B must have default character type.

Result Type and Subtype. Default logical.

Result Value. If the strings have unequal length, the result is the same as if the shorter string were extended on the right with blanks to the length of the longer string. If either string contains a character not in the ASCII character set, the result is processor dependent. The result is true if String_A follows String_B in the ASCII collating sequence; otherwise, the result is false. Note that the result is false if both String_A and String_B have length 0.

77. `LLE (String_A, String_B)`

Elemental function: Test whether a string is lexically less than or equal to another string, based on the ASCII collating sequence.

Arguments. `String_A` and `String_B` must have default character type.

Result Type and Subtype. Default logical.

Result Value. If the strings have unequal length, the result is the same as if the shorter string were extended on the right with blanks to the length of the longer string. If either string contains a character not in the ASCII character set, the result is processor dependent. The result is true if the strings are equal or if `String_A` precedes `String_B` in the ASCII collating sequence; otherwise, the result is false. Note that the result is true if both `String_A` and `String_B` have length 0.

78. `LLT (String_A, String_B)`

Elemental function: Test whether a string is lexically less than another string, based on the ASCII collating sequence.

Arguments. `String_A` and `String_B` must have default character type.

Result Type and Subtype. Default logical.

Result Value. If the strings have unequal length, the result is the same as if the shorter string were extended on the right with blanks to the length of the longer string. If either string contains a character not in the ASCII character set, the result is processor dependent. The result is true if `String_A` precedes `String_B` in the ASCII collating sequence; otherwise, the result is false. Note that the result is false if both `String_A` and `String_B` have length 0.

79. `Repeat (String, NCopies)`

Concatenate several copies of a string.

Arguments.

`String` must be scalar and must have character type.

`NCopies` must be scalar and must have integer type. Its value must not be negative.

Result Type, Subtype, and Shape. Character scalar of length `NCopies * Len (String)`, with the same subtype as `String`.

Result Value. The concatenation of `NCopies` copies of `String`.

80. `Scan (String, Set [, Back])`

Elemental function: Scan a string for any one of the characters in a set of characters.

Arguments.

`String` must have character type.

`Set` must have character type with the same subtype as `String`.

`Back` (optional) must be logical.

Result Type and Subtype. Default integer.

Result Value.

Case 1: If `Back` is absent or is present with the value false and `String` contains at least one character that is in `Set`, the result is the position of the leftmost character of `String` that is in `Set`.

Case 2: If `Back` is present with the value true and `String` contains at least one character that is in `Set`, the result is the position of the rightmost character of `String` that is in `Set`.
Case 3: The result is 0 if no character of `String` is in `Set`.

81. `Trim (String)`

Remove trailing blanks from string.
Argument. `String` must have character type.
Result Type and Subtype. Character with the same subtype as `String`. The length of the result is `Len_Trim (String)`.
Result Value. The same as `String` except that any trailing blanks are removed. If all characters in `String` are blanks, the result has length 0.

82. `Verify (String, Set [, Back])`

Elemental function: Verify that a set of characters contains all the characters in a string by identifying the position (if any) of the first character in a string of characters that does not appear in a given set of characters.
Arguments.
`String` must have character type.
`Set` must have character type with the same subtype as `String`.
`Back` (optional) must be logical.
Result Type and Subtype. Default integer.
Result Value.
Case 1: If `Back` is absent or is present with the value false and `String` contains at least one character that is not in `Set`, the result is the position of the leftmost character of `String` that is not in `Set`.
Case 2: If `Back` is present with the value true and `String` contains at least one character that is not in `Set`, the result is the position of the rightmost character of `String` that is not in `Set`.
Case 3: The result is 0 if every character of `String` is in `Set` or if `String` has length 0.

Bit Computation Functions

83. `BTest (I, Pos)`

Elemental function: Tests whether a bit is 1 or 0.
Arguments.
`I` must have integer type.
`Pos` must have integer type. It must be nonnegative and less than `Bit_Size (I)`.
Result Type and Subtype. Default logical.
Result Value. The result is true if bit `Pos` of `I` is 1 and is false if bit `Pos` of `I` is 0 in the Fortran bit model.

84. `IAnd (I, J)`

Elemental function: Bitwise *and.*

Arguments.

`I` must have integer type.

`J` must have integer type with the same subtype as `I`.

Result Type and Subtype. Same as `I`.

Result Value. The result is `I .and. J` evaluated bitwise, where `I` and `J` are represented according to the Fortran bit model.

85. `IBClr (I, Pos)`

Elemental function: Set a bit to 0.

Arguments.

`I` must have integer type.

`Pos` must have integer type. It must be nonnegative and less than `Bit_Size (I)`.

Result Type and Subtype. Same as `I`.

Result Value. The same as `I` except that bit `Pos`, in the Fortran bit model, is set to 0.

86. `IBSet (I, Pos)`

Elemental function: Sets a bit to 1.

Arguments.

`I` must have integer type.

`Pos` must have integer type. It must be nonnegative and less than `Bit_Size (I)`.

Result Type and Subtype. Same as `I`.

Result Value. The same as `I` except that bit `Pos`, in the Fortran bit model, is set to 1.

87. `IEOr (I, J)`

Elemental function: Bitwise *exclusive or.*

Arguments.

`I` must have integer type.

`J` must have integer type with the same subtype as `I`.

Result Type and Subtype. Same as `I`.

Result Value. The result is `I .neqv. J` evaluated bitwise, where `I` and `J` are represented according to the Fortran bit model.

88. `IOr (I, J)`

Elemental function: Bitwise *or.*

Arguments.

`I` must have integer type.

`J` must have integer type with the same subtype as `I`.

Result Type and Subtype. Same as `I`.

Result Value. The result is `I .or. J` evaluated bitwise, where `I` and `J` are represented according to the Fortran bit model.

89. `Ishft (I, Shift)`

Elemental function: Shift bits to the left or right.

Arguments.

`I` must have integer type.

`Shift` must have integer type. The absolute value of `Shift` must be less than or equal to `Bit_Size (I)`.

Result Type and Subtype. Same as `I`.

Result Value. The result is obtained by shifting the bits of `I`, in the Fortran bit model, by `Abs (Shift)` positions. If `Shift` is positive, the shift is to the left; if `Shift` is negative, the shift is to the right; if `Shift` is 0, no shift is performed. Bits shifted beyond the end of `I` are lost. Zeros are shifted in from the opposite end.

90. `IshftC (I, Shift [, Size])`

Elemental function: Circular shift rightmost bits to the left or right.

Arguments. If `Size` is absent, the effective `Size` value is `Bit_Size (I)`.

`I` must have integer type.

`Shift` must have integer type. The absolute value of `Shift` must be less than or equal to the effective `Size` value.

`Size` (optional) must have integer type. `Size` must be positive and must not exceed `Bit_Size (I)`.

Result Type and Subtype. Same as `I`.

Result Value. The result is obtained by shifting the `Size` rightmost bits of `I`, in the Fortran bit model, circularly by `Abs (Shift)` positions. If `Shift` is positive, the shift is to the left; if `Shift` is negative, the shift is to the right; if `Shift` is 0, no shift is performed. No bits are lost. The unshifted bits are unaltered.

91. `Not (I)`

Elemental function: Bitwise *not*.

Argument. `I` must have integer type.

Result Type and Subtype. Same as `I`.

Result Value. The result is `.not. I` evaluated bitwise, where `I` is represented according to the Fortran bit model.

A.4 MERGE FUNCTION

92. `Merge (TSource, FSource, Mask)`

Elemental function: Choose alternative value according to a mask.

Arguments.

`TSource` may have any type.

`FSource` must have the same type and subtype as `TSource`.

`Mask` must be logical.

Result Type and Subtype. Same as `TSource`.

Result Value. `TSource` where `Mask` is true and `FSource` everywhere else.

A.5 ARRAY FUNCTIONS

Array Reduction Functions

93. `All (Mask [, Dim])`

Determine whether all values are true in `Mask` along dimension `Dim`.

Arguments.

`Mask` must be logical and array valued.

`Dim` (optional) must be an integer scalar with $1 \le$ `Dim` $\le n$, where n is the rank of `Mask`. The corresponding actual argument must not be an optional dummy argument.

Result Type, Subtype, and Shape. The result is logical with the same subtype as `Mask`. It is scalar if `Dim` is absent or if `Mask` has rank 1; otherwise, the result is an array of rank $n - 1$, and the shape of the result is the shape of `Mask` with dimension `Dim` omitted.

Result Value.

Case 1: The result is true if all elements of `Mask` are true or if `Mask` has size 0. The result is false if any element of `Mask` is false.

Case 2: If `Mask` has rank 1, `All (Mask, Dim)` is the same as `All (Mask)`. Otherwise, element $(s_1, s_2, \ldots, s_{\text{Dim}-1}, s_{\text{Dim}+1}, \ldots, s_n)$ of `All (Mask, Dim)` is equal to `All (Mask (`s_1`,` s_2`, ... ,` $s_{\text{Dim}-1}$`, : ,` $s_{\text{Dim}+1}$`, ... ,` s_n`))`.

94. `Any (Mask [, Dim])`

Determine whether any value is true in `Mask` along dimension `Dim`.

Arguments.

`Mask` must be logical and array valued.

`Dim` (optional) must be an integer scalar with $1 \le$ `Dim` $\le$ n, where n is the rank of `Mask`. The corresponding actual argument must not be an optional dummy argument.

Result Type, Subtype, and Shape. The result is logical with the same subtype as `Mask`. It is scalar if `Dim` is absent or if `Mask` has rank 1; otherwise, the result is an array of rank n – 1, and the shape of the result is the shape of `Mask` with dimension `Dim` omitted.
Result Value.
Case 1: The result is true if any element of `Mask` is true. The result is false if all elements of `Mask` are false or if `Mask` has size 0.
Case 2: If `Mask` has rank 1, `Any (Mask, Dim)` is the same as `Any (Mask)`. Otherwise, element $(s_1, s_2, \ldots, s_{\mathrm{Dim}-1}, s_{\mathrm{Dim}+1}, \ldots, s_n)$ of `Any (Mask, Dim)` is equal to `Any (Mask (`s_1`,` s_2`, . . . ,` $s_{\mathrm{Dim}-1}$`, : ,` $s_{\mathrm{Dim}+1}$`, . . . ,` s_n`))`.

95. `Count (Mask [, Dim])`

Count of true elements in `Mask` along dimension `Dim`.
Arguments.
`Mask` must be logical and array valued.
`Dim` (optional) must be scalar and must have integer type with $1 \le$ `Dim` $\le n$, where n is the rank of `Mask`. The corresponding actual argument must not be an optional dummy argument.
Result Type, Subtype, and Shape. The result has default integer type. It is scalar if `Dim` is absent or if `Mask` has rank 1; otherwise, the result is an array of rank n – 1, and the shape of the result is the shape of `Mask` with dimension `Dim` omitted.
Result Value.
Case 1: The result of `Count (Mask)` is the number of true elements of `Mask` or is 0 if `Mask` has size 0.
Case 2: If `Mask` has rank 1, `Count (Mask, Dim)` is the same as `Count (Mask)`. Otherwise, element $(s_1, s_2, \ldots, s_{\mathrm{Dim}-1}, s_{\mathrm{Dim}+1}, \ldots, s_n)$ of `Count (Mask, Dim)` is equal to `Count (Mask (`s_1`,` s_2`, . . . ,` $s_{\mathrm{Dim}-1}$`, : ,` $s_{\mathrm{Dim}+1}$`, . . . ,` s_n`))`.

96. `MaxVal (Array [, Dim] [, Mask])`

Maximum element value in `Array` where `Mask` is true along dimension `Dim`.
Arguments.
`Array` must have integer or real type and array valued.
`Dim` (optional) must be scalar and must have integer type with $1 \le$ `Dim` $\le n$, where n is the rank of `Array`. The corresponding actual argument must not be an optional dummy argument.
`Mask` (optional) must be logical and its shape must be conformable with that of `Array`.
Result Type, Subtype, and Shape. The result has the same type and subtype as `Array`. It is scalar if `Dim` is absent or if `Array` has rank 1; otherwise, the result is an array of rank n – 1, and the shape of the result is the shape of `Array` with dimension `Dim` omitted.
Result Value.
If `Size (Array)` is 0 or if `Mask` is present and has no true elements, the result is the negative number of largest magnitude supported by the processor for the type and subtype of `Array`. Otherwise,
Case 1: The result of `MaxVal (Array)` is the maximum element value in `Array`.

Case 2: The result of `MaxVal (Array, Mask = Mask)` is the maximum element value in `Array` where `Mask` is true.
Case 3: If `Array` has rank 1, `MaxVal (Array, Dim [, Mask])` is the same as `MaxVal (Array [, Mask = Mask])`.
Otherwise, element $(s_1, s_2, \ldots, s_{\mathtt{Dim}-1}, s_{\mathtt{Dim}+1}, \ldots, s_n)$ of `MaxVal (Array, Dim [, Mask])` is equal to `MaxVal (Array (`s_1`, `s_2`, ... , `$s_{\mathtt{Dim}-1}$`, : , `$s_{\mathtt{Dim}+1}$`, ... , `s_n`) [, Mask = Mask (`s_1`, `s_2`, ... , `$s_{\mathtt{Dim}-1}$`, : , `$s_{\mathtt{Dim}+1}$`, ... , `s_n`)] )`.

97. `MinVal (Array [, Dim] [, Mask])`

Minimum element value in `Array` where `Mask` is true along dimension `Dim`.

Arguments.

`Array` must have integer or real type and array valued.

`Dim` (optional) must be scalar and must have integer type with $1 \le$ `Dim` $\le n$, where n is the rank of `Array`. The corresponding actual argument must not be an optional dummy argument.

`Mask` (optional) must be logical and its shape must be conformable with that of `Array`.

Result Type, Subtype, and Shape. The result has the same type and subtype as `Array`. It is scalar if `Dim` is absent or if `Array` has rank 1; otherwise, the result is an array of rank $n - 1$, and the shape of the result is the shape of `Array` with dimension `Dim` omitted.

Result Value.

If `Size (Array)` is 0 or if `Mask` is present and has no true elements, the result is the positive number of largest magnitude supported by the processor for the type and subtype of `Array`. Otherwise,
Case 1: The result of `MinVal (Array)` is the minimum element value in `Array`.
Case 2: The result of `MinVal (Array, Mask = Mask)` is the minimum element value in `Array` where `Mask` is true.
Case 3: If `Array` has rank 1, `MinVal (Array, Dim [, Mask])` is the same as `MinVal (Array [, Mask = Mask])`.
Otherwise, element $(s_1, s_2, \ldots, s_{\mathtt{Dim}-1}, s_{\mathtt{Dim}+1}, \ldots, s_n)$ of `MinVal (Array, Dim [, Mask])` is equal to `MinVal (Array (`s_1`, `s_2`, ... , `$s_{\mathtt{Dim}-1}$`, : , `$s_{\mathtt{Dim}+1}$`, ... , `s_n`) [, Mask = Mask (`s_1`, `s_2`, ... , `$s_{\mathtt{Dim}-1}$`, : , `$s_{\mathtt{Dim}+1}$`, ... , `s_n`)] )`.

98. `Product (Array [, Dim] [, Mask])`

Product of all elements of `Array` where `Mask` is true along dimension `Dim`.

Arguments.

`Array` must have integer, real, or complex type and array valued.

`Dim` (optional) must be scalar and must have integer type with $1 \le$ `Dim` $\le n$, where n is the rank of `Array`. The corresponding actual argument must not be an optional dummy argument.

`Mask` (optional) must be logical and its shape must be conformable with that of `Array`.

Result Type, Subtype, and Shape. The result has the same type and subtype as `Array`. It is scalar if `Dim` is absent or if `Array` has rank 1; otherwise, the result is an array of rank n – 1, and the shape of the result is the shape of `Array` with dimension `Dim` omitted.

Result Value.

If `Size (Array)` is 0 or if `Array` has rank 1 and `Mask` is present and has no true elements, the result is 1 with the type and subtype of `Array`. Otherwise,

Case 1: The result of `Product (Array)` is the product of all elements of `Array`.

Case 2: The result of `Product (Array, Mask = Mask)` is the product of the elements of `Array` where `Mask` is true.

Case 3: If `Array` has rank 1, `Product (Array, Dim [, Mask])` is the same as `Product (Array [, Mask = Mask])`.

Otherwise, element $(s_1, s_2, \ldots, s_{\text{Dim}-1}, s_{\text{Dim}+1}, \ldots, s_n)$ of `Product (Array, Dim [, Mask])` is equal to `Product (Array (`s_1`, `s_2`, ... , `$s_{\text{Dim}-1}$`, : , `$s_{\text{Dim}+1}$`, ... , `s_n`) [, Mask = Mask (`s_1`, `s_2`, ... , `$s_{\text{Dim}-1}$`, : , `$s_{\text{Dim}+1}$`, ... , `s_n`)] ).`

99. `Sum (Array [, Dim] [, Mask])`

Sum of all elements of `Array` where `Mask` is true along dimension `Dim`.

Arguments.

`Array` must have integer, real, or complex type and array valued.

`Dim` (optional) must be scalar and must have integer type with $1 \le$ `Dim` $\le n$, where n is the rank of `Array`. The corresponding actual argument must not be an optional dummy argument.

`Mask` (optional) must be logical and its shape must be conformable with that of `Array`.

Result Type, Subtype, and Shape. The result has the same type and subtype as `Array`. It is scalar if `Dim` is absent or if `Array` has rank 1; otherwise, the result is an array of rank n – 1, and the shape of the result is the shape of `Array` with dimension `Dim` omitted.

Result Value.

If `Size (Array)` is 0 or if `Array` has rank 1 and `Mask` is present and has no true elements, the result is 0 with the type and subtype of `Array`. Otherwise,

Case 1: The result of `Sum (Array)` is the sum of all elements of `Array`.

Case 2: The result of `Sum (Array, Mask = Mask)` is the sum of the elements of `Array` where `Mask` is true.

Case 3: If `Array` has rank 1, `Sum (Array, Dim [, Mask])` is the same as `Sum (Array [, Mask = Mask])`.

Otherwise, element $(s_1, s_2, \ldots, s_{\text{Dim}-1}, s_{\text{Dim}+1}, \ldots, s_n)$ of `Sum (Array, Dim [, Mask])` is equal to `Sum (Array (`s_1`, `s_2`, ... , `$s_{\text{Dim}-1}$`, : , `$s_{\text{Dim}+1}$`, ... , `s_n`) [, Mask = Mask (`s_1`, `s_2`, ... , `$s_{\text{Dim}-1}$`, : , `$s_{\text{Dim}+1}$`, ... , `s_n`)] )`

Array Construction Functions

100. `Pack (Array, Mask [, Vector])`

Pack an array into an array of rank 1 under the control of a mask. Elements of an array may be "gathered" into a vector by `Pack`.

Arguments.

`Array` may have any type and must be array valued.

`Mask` must be logical and its shape must be conformable with that of `Array`.

`Vector` (optional) must have the same type and subtype as `Array` and must have rank 1. If `Mask` is array valued, `Size (Vector)` must not be less than `Count (Mask)`. If `Mask` is scalar with the value true, `Size (Vector)` must not be less than `Size (Array)`.

Result Type, Subtype, and Shape. An array of rank 1 with the same type and subtype as `Array`. If `Vector` is present, the size of the result is `Size (Vector)`. If `Vector` is absent and `Mask` is array valued or is scalar with the value false, the size of the result is the number of true elements in `Mask`. If `Vector` is absent and `Mask` is scalar with the value true, the size of the result is `Size (Array)`.

Result Value.

Case 1: If `Mask` is array valued, let t be the number of true elements in `Mask`. The ith element of the result is the element of `Array` that corresponds to the ith true element of `Mask`, taking elements in standard Fortran array element sequence, for $i = 1, 2, \ldots, t$. If `Vector` is present and has size $n > t$, the ith element of the result is `Vector (`i`)`, for $i = t + 1, \ldots, n$.

Case 2: If `Mask` is scalar with the value false and `Vector` is absent, the result is an array of rank 1 and size 0. If `Mask` is scalar with the value false and `Vector` is present and has size n, the ith element of the result is `Vector (`i`)`, for $i = t + 1, \ldots, n$.

Case 3: If `Mask` is scalar with the value true, let t = `Size (Array)`. The ith element of the result is the ith element of `Array`, taking elements in standard Fortran array element sequence, for $i = 1, 2, \ldots, t$. If `Vector` is present and has size $n > t$, the ith element of the result is `Vector (`i`)`, for $i = t + 1, \ldots, n$.

101. `Spread (Source, Dim, NCopies)`

Replicate an array by adding a dimension.

Arguments.

`Source` may have any type. It may be scalar or array valued. The rank of `Source` must be less than 7.

`Dim` must be scalar and must have integer type with 1 ≤ `Dim` ≤ n, where n is the rank of `Source`.

`NCopies` must be scalar and must have integer type.

Result Type, Subtype, and Shape. An array of the same type and subtype as `Source`, with rank $n + 1$, where n is the rank of `Source`.

Case 1: If `Source` is scalar, the shape of the result is `(Max (NCopies, 0))`.

Case 2: If `Source` is array valued with shape $(d_1, d_2, \ldots, d_{n+1})$, the shape of the result is $(d_1, d_2, \ldots, d_{\texttt{Dim}-1},$ `Max (NCopies, 0)`, $d_{\texttt{Dim}}, \ldots, d_n)$.

Result Value. `NCopies` copies of `Source`, broadcast along dimension `Dim` (as in forming a book from copies of a single page) to form array whose rank is one greater than the rank of `Source`.

Case 1: If `Source` is scalar, each element of the result is `Source`.

Case 2: If `Source` is array valued, element $(r_1, r_2, \ldots, r_{n+1})$ of the result is `Source` $(r_1, r_2, \ldots, r_{\texttt{Dim}-1}, :, r_{\texttt{Dim}+1}, \ldots, r_n)$.

102. `Unpack (Vector, Mask, Field)`

Unpack an array of rank 1 into an array under the control of a mask.

Arguments.

`Vector` may have any type. It must have rank 1. Its `Size (Vector)` must not be less than `Count (Mask)`.

`Mask` must be logical and must be array valued.

`Field` must have the same type and subtype as `Vector` and its shape must be conformable with that of `Mask`.

Result Type, Subtype, and Shape. An array of the same type and subtype as `Vector` and it has the same shape as `Mask`.

Result Value. An array composed of elements of `Vector` "scattered" to specific positions determined by `Mask`. The element of the result that corresponds to the *i*th true element of `Mask`, in standard Fortran array element sequence, is `Vector` (i), for $i = 1, 2, \ldots,$ `Count (Mask)`. The element of the result that corresponds to a false element of `Mask` is the corresponding element of `Field` if `Field` is array valued or `Field` if `Field` is scalar.

Array Reshape Function

103. `Reshape (Source, Shape [, Pad] [, Order])`

Construct an array of a specified shape from the elements of a given array.

Arguments.

`Source` may have any type. It must be array valued. The size of the result is `Product (Shape)`. If `Pad` is absent or has size 0, `Size (Source)` must be greater than or equal to `Product (Shape)`.

`Shape` must have integer type and must be scalar valued with rank 1 and constant size. Its size must be positive and less than 8. It must not have an element whose value is negative.

`Pad` (optional) must have the same type and subtype as `Source`. `Pad` must be array valued.

`Order` (optional) must have integer type and must have the same shape as `Shape`. Its value must be a permutation of $(1, 2, \ldots, n)$, where n is the size of `Shape`. If absent, the result is the same as if it were present with value $(1, 2, \ldots, n)$.

Result Type, Subtype, and Shape. The result has the same type and subtype as `Source`. The shape of the result is the same as the value of the argument `Shape`.
Result Value. The elements of the result, taken in permuted subscript order `Order(1)`, . . . , `Order(`n`)`, are those of `Source` in standard Fortran array element sequence, followed if necessary by those of `Pad` in standard Fortran array element sequence, followed if necessary by additional copies of `Pad` in standard Fortran array element sequence.

Array Manipulation Functions

104. `CShift (Array, Shift [, Dim])`

Perform a circular shift on an array.
Arguments.

`Array` may have any type and must be array valued.

`Shift` must have integer type and must be scalar if `Array` has rank 1; otherwise, it must be scalar or of rank $n - 1$ and must have shape $(d_1, d_2, \ldots, d_{\mathtt{Dim}-1}, d_{\mathtt{Dim}+1}, \ldots, d_n)$, where $(d_1, d_2, \ldots, d_n)$ is the shape of `Array`.

`Dim` (optional) must be scalar and must have integer type with $1 \le$ `Dim` $\le n$, where n is the rank of `Array`. If `Dim` is absent, the result is the same as if it were present with the value 1.

Result Type, Subtype, and Shape. The result has the same type, subtype, and shape as `Array`.

Result Value. `CShift` performs a circular shift on an array expression of rank 1 or performs circular shifts on all the complete sections of rank 1 along a given dimension of an array expression of rank 2 or greater. Elements shifted out at one end of a section are shifted in at the other end. Different sections may be shifted by different amounts and in different directions.

Case 1: If `Array` has rank 1, element i of the result is `Array (1 + Modulo (`i` + Shift -1, Size (Array)))`.

Case 2: If `Array` has rank greater than 1, section $(s_1, s_2, \ldots, s_{\mathtt{Dim}-1}, :, s_{\mathtt{Dim}+1}, \ldots, s_n)$ of the result is `CShift (Array(`s_1`, `s_2`, ..., `$s_{\mathtt{Dim}-1}$`, :, `$s_{\mathtt{Dim}+1}$`, ..., `s_n`), 1, `sh`)`, where sh is `Shift` if `Shift` is scalar or `Shift (`s_1`, `s_2`, ..., `$s_{\mathtt{Dim}-1}$`, `$s_{\mathtt{Dim}+1}$`, ..., `s_n`)` if `Shift` is array valued.

105. `EOShift (Array, Shift [, Boundary] [, Dim])`

Perform an end-off shift on an array.
Arguments.

`Array` may have any type and must be array valued.

`Shift` must have integer type and must be scalar if `Array` has rank 1; otherwise, it must be scalar or of rank $n - 1$ and must have shape $(d_1, d_2, \ldots, d_{\mathtt{Dim}-1}, d_{\mathtt{Dim}+1}, \ldots, d_n)$ where $(d_1, d_2, \ldots, d_n)$ is the shape of `Array`.

`Boundary` (optional) must have the same type and type parameters as `Array` and must be scalar if `Array` has rank 1; otherwise, it must be scalar or of rank $n - 1$ and must have shape $(d_1, d_2, \ldots, d_{\mathtt{Dim}-1}, d_{\mathtt{Dim}+1}, \ldots, d_n)$. `Boundary` may be omitted if `Array` has an intrinsic type, in which case a default `Boundary` value is applied: 0 for integer type, 0.0 for real type, (0.0, 0.0) for complex type, false for logical type, and m blanks for character type with length m.

`Dim` (optional) must be scalar and must have integer type with $1 \le$ `Dim` $\le n$, where n is the rank of `Array`. If `Dim` is absent, the result is the same as if it were present with the value 1.

Result Type, Subtype, and Shape. The result has the same type, subtype, and shape as `Array`.

Result Value. `EOShift` performs an end-off shift on an array expression of rank 1, or performs end-off shifts on all the complete sections of rank 1 along a given dimension of an array expression of rank 2 or greater. Elements are shifted out at one end of a section and copies of a boundary value are shifted in at the other end. Different sections may have different boundary values and may be shifted by different amounts and in different directions.

If $s_{\mathtt{Dim}} + sh$ is between `LBound (Array, Dim)` and `UBound (Array, Dim)`, element $(s_1, s_2, \ldots, s_n)$ of the result is `Array`$(s_1, s_2, \ldots, s_{\mathtt{Dim}-1}, s_{\mathtt{Dim}} + sh, s_{\mathtt{Dim}+1}, \ldots, s_n)$, where sh is `Shift` if `Shift` is scalar or `Shift` $(s_1, s_2, \ldots, s_{\mathtt{Dim}-1}, s_{\mathtt{Dim}+1}, \ldots, s_n)$ if `Shift` is array valued. Otherwise, element $(s_1, s_2, \ldots, s_n)$ of the result is `Boundary`.

106. `Transpose (Matrix)`

Transpose an array of rank 2.

Argument. `Matrix` may have any type and must have rank 2.

Result Type, Subtype, and Shape. An array with the same type and subtype as `Matrix` and with rank 2 and shape (n, m), where (m, n) is the shape of `Matrix`.

Result Value. Element (i, j) of the result is `Matrix` (j, i), for $i = 1, 2, \ldots, n$ and $j = 1, 2, \ldots, m$.

Array Location Functions

107. `MaxLoc (Array [, Mask])`

Location of the largest element of `Array` where `Mask` is true. Location of the first such element if there is more than one.

Arguments.

`Array` must have integer or real type and must be array valued.

`Mask` (optional) must be logical and its shape must be conformable with that of `Array`.

Result Type, Subtype, and Shape. The result has default integer type; it is an array of rank 1, and its size is the rank of `Array`.

Result Value.

Case 1: If `Mask` is present, the result is an array of rank 1 whose element values are the values of the subscripts of an element of `Array`, corresponding to a true element of `Mask`, whose value equals the maximum value of all such elements of `Array`. The ith subscript of the result is between 1 and e_i (inclusive), where e_i is the extent of the ith dimension of `Array`. If more than one such element has the maximum value, the ele-

ment whose subscripts are returned is the first such element taken in standard Fortran array element sequence. If `Size (Array)` is 0 or if every element of `Mask` is false, the result is processor dependent.
Case 2: If `Mask` is absent, the result is the same as `MaxLoc (Array, .TRUE.)`.

108. `MinLoc (Array [, Mask])`

Location of the smallest element of `Array` where `Mask` is true. Location of the first such element if there is more than one.

Arguments.

`Array` must have integer or real type and must be array valued.

`Mask` (optional) must be logical and its shape must be conformable with that of `Array`.

Result Type, Subtype, and Shape. The result has default integer type; it is an array of rank 1, and its size is the rank of `Array`.

Result Value.

Case 1: If `Mask` is present, the result is an array of rank 1 whose element values are the values of the subscripts of an element of `Array`, corresponding to a true element of `Mask`, whose value equals the minimum value of all such elements of `Array`. The ith subscript of the result is between 1 and e_i (inclusive), where e_i is the extent of the ith dimension of `Array`. If more than one such element has the minimum value, the element whose subscripts are returned is the first such element taken in standard Fortran array element sequence. If `Size (Array)` is 0 or every element of `Mask` is false, the result is processor dependent.
Case 2: If `Mask` is absent, the result is the same as `MinLoc (Array, .TRUE.)`.

A.6 INTRINSIC SUBROUTINES

Clock, Date, and Time Subroutines

109. `Date_And_Time ([Date] [, Time] [, Zone] [, Values])`

Date and time in a standard form.

Arguments.

`Date` (optional) must be scalar and must have default character type with length at least 8 in order to contain the complete value; it is an `intent (out)` argument. Its leftmost 8 characters are set to a value of the form *yyyymmdd*, where *yyyy* is the year, *mm* is the month, and *dd* is the day. If no date is available, `Date` is set to blank.

`Time` (optional) must be scalar and must have default character type with length at least 10 in order to contain the complete value; it is an `intent (out)` argument. Its leftmost 10 characters are set to a value of the form *hhmmss.sss*, where *hh* is the hour, *mm* is the minutes, and *ss.sss* is the seconds and milliseconds. If no clock is available, `Time` is set to blank.

`Zone` (optional) must be scalar and must have default character type with length at least 5 in order to contain the complete value; it is an `intent (out)` argument. Its leftmost 5 characters are set to a value of the form ±*hhmm*, where *hh* and *mm* are the time difference with respect to Coordinated Universal Time (UTC, also called *Greenwich Mean Time*) in hours and minutes. If no clock is available, `Zone` is set to blank.

`Values` (optional) must have default integer type with rank 1; it is an `intent (out)` argument. Its size must be at least 8. The values returned in `Values` are as follows:

- `Values (1)` is the year (for example, 1999), or –`Huge (0)` if no date is available
- `Values (2)` is the month, or –`Huge (0)` if no date is available
- `Values (3)` is the day, or –`Huge (0)` if no date is available
- `Values (4)` is the time difference with respect to Coordinated Universal Time (UTC) in minutes, or –`Huge (0)` if this information is not available
- `Values (5)` is the hour, in the range of 0 to 23, or –`Huge (0)` if no clock is available
- `Values (6)` is the minutes, in the range 0 to 59, or –`Huge (0)` if no clock is available
- `Values (7)` is the seconds, in the range 0 to 60, or –`Huge (0)` if no clock is available (note that the seconds value may be 60 for a "leap second")
- `Values (8)` is the milliseconds, in the range 0 to 999, or –`Huge (0)` if no clock is available

110. `System_Clock ([Count] [, Count_Rate] [, Count_Max])`

Data from real-time clock in integer form.

Arguments.

`Count` (optional) must be scalar and must have default integer type; it is an `intent (out)` argument. It is set to a processor-dependent value based on the current value of the processor clock or to –`Huge (0)` if no processor clock is available. The processor-dependent value is incremented by 1 for each clock count until the value `Count_Max` is reached and is reset to 0 at the next count. It lies in the range 0 to `Count_Max` unless no processor clock is available.

`Count_Rate` (optional) must be scalar and must have default integer type; it is an `intent (out)` argument. It is set to the number of clock counts per second or to 0 if no processor clock is available.

`Count_Max` (optional) must be scalar and must have default integer type; it is an `intent (out)` argument. It is set to the maximum value that `Count` can have or to 0 if no processor clock is available.

Bit Copy Subroutine

111. `MvBits (From, FromPos, Len, To, ToPos)`

Elemental subroutine: Copy a sequence of bits from one data object to another.

Arguments.

`From` must have integer type; it is an `intent (in)` argument.

`FromPos` must have integer type and must be nonnegative; it is an `intent (in)` argument. `FromPos` + `Len` must be less than or equal to `Bit_Size (From)` in the Fortran bit model.

`Len` must have integer type and must be nonnegative; it is an `intent (in)` argument.

`To` must be a variable of integer type with the same subtype as `From`; it is an `intent (in out)` argument. `From` may be the same variable as `To`. In the Fortran bit model, `To` is set by copying the sequence of bits of length `Len`, starting at position `FromPos` of `From`, to position `ToPos` of `To`. No other bits of `To` are altered.

`ToPos` must have integer type and nonnegative; it is an `intent (in)` argument. `ToPos` + `Len` must be less than or equal to `Bit_Size (To)` in the Fortran bit model.

Random Number Subroutines

112. `Random_Number (Harvest)`

Generate one pseudorandom number or an array of pseudorandom numbers from a uniform distribution over the range $0 \le x < 1$.

Argument. `Harvest` must be real; it is an `intent (out)` argument. It must be a scalar variable or an array variable. It is set to a pseudorandom number (or numbers) from a uniform distribution over the interval $0 \le x < 1$.

113. `Random_Seed ([Size] [, Put] [, Get])`

Restart or query the pseudorandom number generator used by `Random_Number`.

Arguments. The number of arguments present must be 0 or 1.

`Size` (optional) must be scalar and must have default integer type; it is an `intent (out)` argument. It is set to the number N of integers that the processor uses to hold the seed.

`Put` (optional) must be a default integer array of rank 1 with `Size (Put)` ≤ N; it is an `intent (in)` argument. It is used by the processor to set the seed value.

`Get` (optional) must be a default integer array of rank 1 with `Size (Put)` ≤ N; it is an `intent (out)` argument. It is set by the processor to the current seed.

If no argument is present, the processor sets the seed to a processor-dependent value.

Appendix B
Format Codes for Input and Output

B.1 USING FORMAT CODES

The specific codes (officially called *edit descriptors*) in a format description are, in effect, keywords. For example, the format code letter I indicates that the associated data has *integer* type, while the letters E and F, as well as some other letters, may correspond to data of *real* type.

Fields in a Formatted Record

Each record accessed for formatted data transfer consists of a sequence of characters. Numerical data is represented externally by a string of decimal digits and other characters, while information of logical or character type is represented externally by a sequence of characters of some other appropriate form.

For list-directed data processing, the string representing each data value may be positioned rather freely within the input or output record and is separated from the adjacent data representations by one or more blank spaces and possibly a comma. Under explicit format control, however, the record is more rigidly subdivided into groups of character positions called *fields*; each field holds the characters that represent a single data value of integer, real, logical, or character type.

EXAMPLE B.1 The following specification describes the arrangement of five fields within a record

```
(3 E12.0, 2 I3)
```

The first format code in the specification is 3 E12.0, which means that the first *three* fields (groups of character positions) in the record contain *real* data and that each field is *twelve* characters wide. That is,

3 refers to the first *three* fields in the input record.

E specifies that these fields contain *real* data (E is one of several format codes that may be used with real data).

12.0 specifies that each field is *twelve* characters wide.

The remaining format code, 2 I3, indicates that the next *two* fields contain data of *integer* type in fields *three* characters wide:

2 refers to the next *two* fields of the input record

I specifies that these fields contain data of *integer* type.

3 specifies that each field is *three* characters wide.

Figure B.1 shows how data values might be prepared in 42 character positions of a record to be read with the format description in Example B.1. The data must be prepared in accordance with this description; that is, each of the first three groups of 12 character positions must contain a real constant, and each of the next two 3-character position fields must contain an integer constant.

```
read "(3⊥E12.0,⊥2⊥I3)", A, B, C, I, J
```

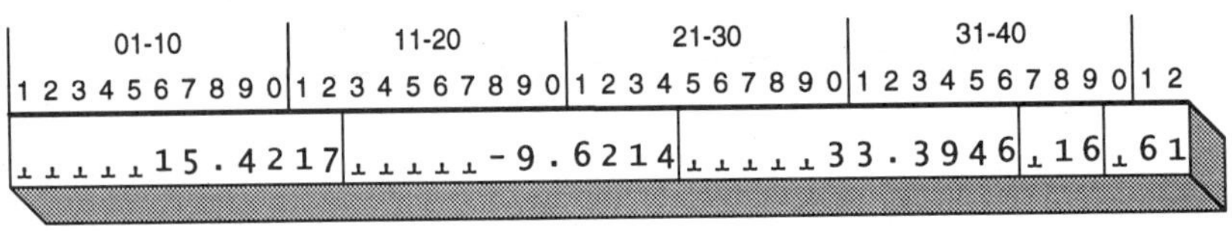

FIGURE B.1. Input fields specified by given format codes.

Interpreting Format Codes

Each format code in a format description includes the following information:

1. A count, indicating the number of consecutive fields to which it corresponds. If there is no integer constant preceding the letter that indicates conversion mode, the count is 1 by default.

2. A conversion mode, indicated by a letter such as E, F, or I, which corresponds to the type of the corresponding input or output list item as well as to the form of the data item in the record.
3. A field width — that is, the number of characters in the record occupied by the field.

Some format codes also include a fourth item of information.

4. A decimal position. For output with real or double-precision conversion modes, the field width is followed by a period and then by another integer constant. For F format codes, this integer specifies the number of digits that will appear to the right of the decimal point; its significance in E output format codes will be discussed later. For real or double-precision input, we use a 0 in this position (except in certain cases that will be discussed later).

For example, in the output format (F10.5, E16.8), the first format code specifies a field for real data that is 10 character positions wide with 5 digits to the right of the decimal point; the second format code specifies a 16-character field for real data.

EXAMPLE B.2

```
write (19, "(1X,␣2␣E16.8␣/␣1X,␣E16.8)") SPos, SNeg, SPos + SNeg
```

Meaning: Transmit, to the output device identified as unit 19, the values of SPos, SNeg, and their sum. The code 1X transmits a blank as the first character of the output record. The values of SPos and SNeg will each be printed according to the code E16.8, which means that they will be printed as real values in fields 16 characters wide. The slash specifies the end of an output record. Since there is further information to be transmitted, a new record will be started. The 1X following the slash, as before, transmits a blank character. Then the value of SPos + SNeg is printed according to the format code E16.8 — that is, in real form, in a field 16 character positions wide.

EXAMPLE B.3

```
read "(I8)", N
```

Meaning: Transmit the value of N from the default input device. The value of N will appear in integer form within the field consisting of the first 8 characters of the record.

EXAMPLE B.4

```
print "(1X,␣E16.8)", Sum
```

Meaning: Print the value of Sum on the default output device in real form in a field 16 characters wide..

EXAMPLE B.5 Sum the positive elements of a vector A that has N elements

```
! Example B.5.
 program Awe_Sum
   implicit none
   intrinsic Sum
   integer, parameter :: MAX = 100
   real, dimension(MAX) :: A = 0.0                              ! Initialize A.
   real :: Total
   integer :: N
! start program Awe_Sum
   read (9, "(I5)") N
   if (N > MAX) stop "␣First␣input␣value␣is␣too␣large.␣"
   read (9, "(E10.0)") A(1: N)
   Total = Sum (A(1: N), Mask = (A(1: N) > 0.0))
   print "(1X,␣E16.8)", Total
 end program Awe_Sum
```

The first read statement obtains the numerical value of N from the first record of the file on input unit 9. This is the total number of elements of the array A that have been prepared as data; it must not be larger than MAX. The second read statement transfers data from unit 9 to all elements of the array section `A(1: N)`. Each element is contained in a separate record on the input file and occupies the first 10 character positions of the record.

The array intrinsic function `Sum` now adds together all elements of the array section `A(1: N)` that correspond to true values of the mask `(A(1: N) > 0.0)`. The sum is assigned as the value of `Total`. The `print` statement sends the value of `Total` to the default output unit (which may be a printer).

EXAMPLE B.6 Sum separately the positive and the negative elements of a vector `A` that has `N` elements

```
! Example B.6.
  program Whole_Sum
    implicit none
    intrinsic Sum
    integer, parameter :: N = 20
    real, dimension(N) :: A
    real :: SPos, SNeg
! start program Whole_Sum
    read (9, "(E10.0)") A
    write (19, "(1X,⊥E15.3)") A
    SPos = Sum (A, Mask = (A > 0.0))
    SNeg = Sum (A, Mask = (A < 0.0))
    write (19, "(1X,⊥2⊥E16.8⊥/⊥1X,⊥E16.8)") SPos, SNeg, SPos + SNeg
  end program Whole_Sum
```

The first `read` statement is immediately followed by a `write` statement that "echoes" the data just read in so that the user can verify that the data is correct. The last output statement, which prints the results of the calculation, is the same as in Example B.2.

B.2 INTEGER INPUT AND OUTPUT

I Format Codes for Integer Output

Figure B.2 and the following table illustrate the format code `Iw` for printing data of integer type.

```
print "(1X,␣I6,␣I5,␣I6,␣I8)", I, J, K, L
```

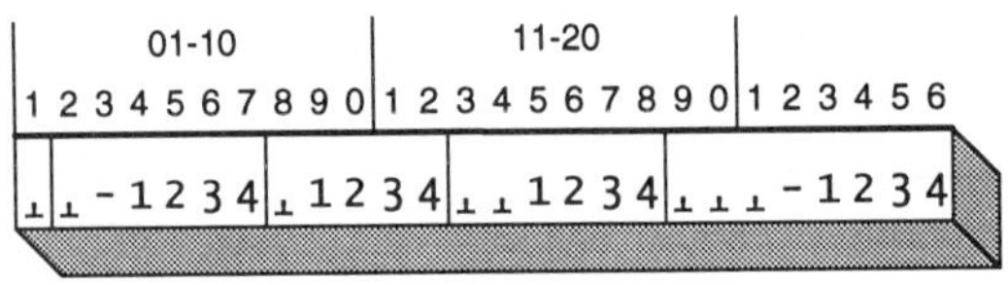

FIGURE B.2.
Integer output.

Integer output			
Integer variable	Internal value	Format code	External appearance
`I`	−1234	`I6`	`␣-1234`
`J`	+1234	`I5`	`␣1234`
`K`	+1234	`I6`	`␣␣1234`
`L`	−1234	`I8`	`␣␣␣-1234`

Note the following points:

1. Integers are printed as far right as possible in the field, and unused space is filled with blank characters. The output value representation always includes at least one digit.
2. If the value is negative, a minus sign is printed immediately to the left of the number. Positive integers (and zero) appear without plus signs.
3. Integers are printed without decimal points.

There is also a format code `Iw.m`, which indicates that at least `m` digits are to appear in the output field, including leading zeros if necessary. Of course, `m` must not be larger than the field width, `w`. Also, by special convention, an entirely blank field will be printed for a zero data value when `m` is 0.

If the output field is not wide enough, it will be filled with asterisks. Programmers should follow the practice of liberally allocating character positions for output to ensure that the field will be wide enough for the largest values of the output data that may be anticipated. Excess field width does no harm and can improve readability.

I *Format Codes for Integer Input*

Some examples of integer input (using format code Iw) are shown in Figure B.3 and in the following table.

```
read "(I3,⊥I4,⊥2⊥I6,⊥I8,⊥I3)", I, J, K, L, M
```

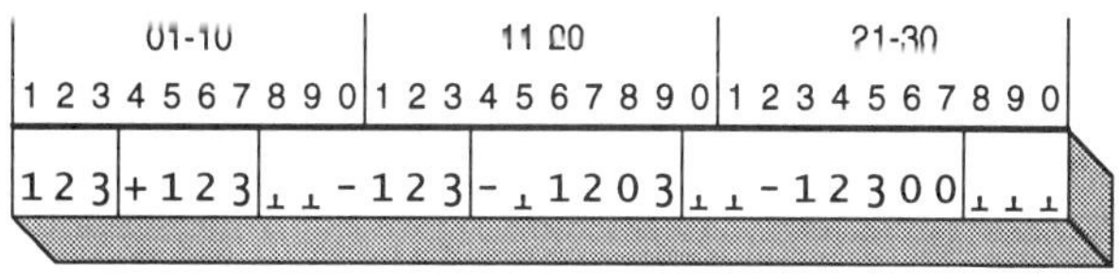

FIGURE B.3.
Integer input.

Integer input			
External appearance	Field width	Format code	Internal value
123	3	I3	+123
+123	4	I4	+123
⊥⊥-123	6	I6	−123
-⊥1203	6	I6	−1203
⊥⊥-12300	8	I8	−12300
⊥⊥⊥	3	I3	0

We note the following points:

1. The data value, in the form of an integer constant (without a decimal point), may appear in the allotted group of character positions (field).
2. The constant need not fill the field and may be preceded by blank character positions. The exact position of the constant within its field is not important. A field that is entirely blank represents a zero value. (On the other hand, a blank field with list-directed input does not represent zero but is treated as a "null" item.)
3. If a plus or minus sign precedes the integer, it may appear anywhere in the field to the left of the first digit. (Plus signs are usually omitted.)

Note also that each processor limits the size of integers. Integer constants as input data items are subject to these same size limitations.

The format code Iw.m may be used for input, but m has no effect.

B, O, *and* Z *Format Codes for Integer Input and Output*

The Bw, Bw.m, Ow, Ow.m, Zw, and Zw.m format codes indicate that the field to be edited occupies w character positions. The corresponding list item must have type integer. The code letter B, O, or Z does not appear in the external field.

The output produced by these format codes is the same as for the I codes except that it is represented as a binary, octal, or hexadecimal number. On input, m has no effect.

An input field must consist of digits that are appropriate to the radix: a binary digit for B format must be 0 or 1; an octal digit for O format must be between 0 and 7; a hexadecimal digit for Z format must be a decimal digit or one of the letters A through F. For example, the integer value 200 in binary is 11001000; in octal, it is 310; in hexadecimal, it is C8. An output statement might be written as follows:

```
print "(B9, O4, Z3)", 200, 200, 200
```

The output record would contain the following sequence of characters:

```
⊥11001000⊥310⊥C8
```

These same characters would be appropriate for an input statement with the same format.

G *Format Code for Integer Input and Output*

The Gw.d and Gw.dEe format codes are permitted with list items of integer type and have the same effect as the Iw format code. The values of d and e in the format code are ignored.

B.3 REAL AND COMPLEX INPUT AND OUTPUT

F *Format Code for Real Output*

The format code Fw.d is used for real output that is to be printed without an exponent. Examples are shown in Figure B.4 and in the following table.

```
print "(1X,␣F10.3,␣F6.0,␣F8.2,␣F5.2,␣F6.3)", A, B, B,
```

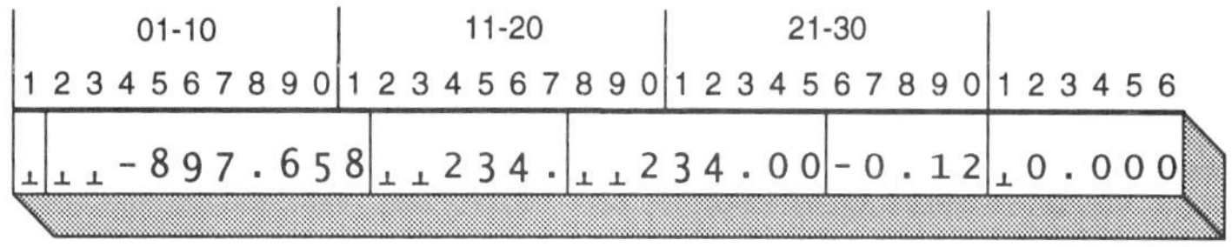

FIGURE B.4. Output of real data without exponents.

Real output with F format code			
Real variable	Internal value	Format code	External appearance
A	−897.6577	F10.3	␣␣-897.658
B	234.	F6.0	␣␣234.
B	234.	F8.2	␣␣234.00
C	−0.12	F5.2	-0.12
H	0.	F6.3	␣0.000

Note the following points:

1. A number need not fill its field. It is printed as far right as possible. To improve readability, we may wish to specify a wider field than is actually required so that blank spaces will appear between adjacent results.
2. A zero may be printed to the left of the decimal point if the output value is positive and less than 1. A zero must be printed if there would otherwise be no digits in the output field.
3. If the value is negative, a minus sign is printed immediately to the left of the number. Positive numbers (and zero) appear without a plus sign.
4. When a number is converted to external form, it is rounded to the least significant digit printed; that is, $0.5 * 10^{-D}$ is added to the absolute value of the number before the unwanted digits are dropped for printing. This rounding is illustrated on the first line of the preceding table.

If the output field is not wide enough, it will be filled with asterisks. Even small numerical values require that w be at least 2 more than d to allow room for printing the decimal point and a digit to its left (which may be 0); negative values require an additional space for the sign. Larger values require still wider fields. Even experienced programmers often have difficulty in estimating the sizes of the results that are to be printed. Division by an unexpectedly small number somewhere in the program, for example, may cause a variable to become far larger in magnitude than was anticipated. If there is any possibility that the field width will be insufficient, an E or G format code is recommended.

D *and* E *Format Codes for Real Output*

The format codes Dw.d, Ew.d, and Ew.dEe are used for real output that is to appear in printed form with an exponent. Examples are shown in Figure B.5 and the following table.

```
print "(1X,␣E15.8,␣2␣E12.4,␣E10.2)", A, B, C, D
```

FIGURE B.5 Output of real data with exponents.

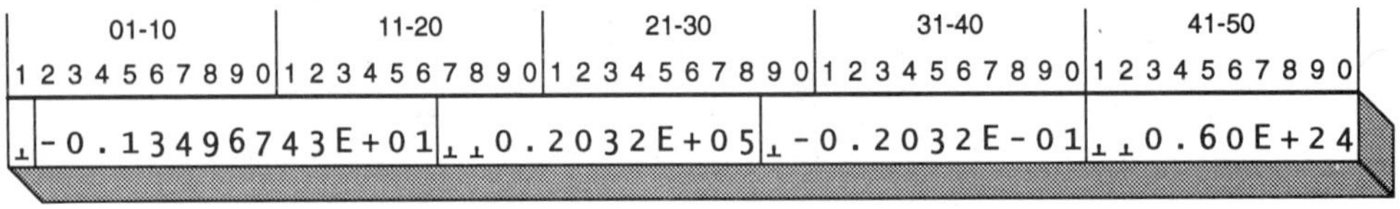

Real output with E format code			
Real variable	Internal value	Format code	External appearance
A	−1.3497643	E15.8	-0.13496743E+01
B	20318.7	E12.4	␣␣0.2032E+05
C	−0.02032	E12.4	␣-0.2032E-01
D	$6.023 \cdot 10^{23}$	E10.2	␣␣0.60E+24

Note the following points:

1. A number need not fill a field. It is printed at the right end of the field; any extra blanks at the left improve readability.
2. The general form for printing results with E conversion is ␣0.xx...xxE±ee where the x's represent the d significant digits and the e's are the digits of the exponent. If the exponent is less than 10, the first exponent digit is 0. The significant digits and the exponent are each printed with a minus sign if negative. No sign is printed if the value printed is positive or zero; however, a positive or zero exponent is always printed with a plus sign.
3. The minimum field width for E format code should be kept clearly in mind. It takes at least seven print positions, besides the d significant digits, to print the complete form. The rule w d + 7 will guarantee enough space for the following:

   Four characters of the exponent — the letter E, the sign, and two numerical digits
   The decimal point
   A zero to the left of the decimal point
   The sign of the value

   An eighth extra character position will guarantee a blank space separating adjacent fields. For display of results having eight significant digits, for example, the format code E16.8 is recommended.
4. As with the F format code, real numbers are rounded during conversion to the external form. Rounding is illustrated on the second and fourth lines of the preceding table.

There is no danger that the field will be not be wide enough if we observe the rule w d + 7. If this rule is not observed, however, the entire output field may be filled with asterisks.

ES *and* EN *Format Codes for Real Output*

The format codes ESw.d and ESw.dEe are the same as the E format codes except that the output field is represented in *scientific notation* with one significant digit to the left of the decimal point. The scale factor has no effect.

The format codes ENw.d and ENw.dEe are the same as the E format codes except that the output field is represented in *engineering notation* with one, two, or three significant digits to the left of the decimal point. The exponent value is always a multiple of 3. The scale factor has no effect.

G *Format Code for Real Output*

The format code Gw.d may be used for real output in a more flexible form. Appearance of an exponent in the printed output will depend on the magnitude of the data value. The G output format produces the more readable appearance of F for data of intermediate size while giving the same protection as E for exceptional data values that are very large or very small. (Fixed-decimal output produced by the F format code is unsatisfactory both for very large data values, which extend too far to the left, and for very small values, whose significant digits are too far to the right. Floating-decimal output generated with the E format code avoids these problems but is less readable.)

If the exponent is between 0 and d (inclusive), the G code gives the effect of F but with the value of w decreased by 4. In other words, the number is printed in the first w - 4 character positions of the output field and is followed by four blanks; the total number of significant digits printed, both to the right and to the left of the decimal point, is always d. If the exponent is negative or is larger than d, however, output conversion identical to Ew.d is performed instead. The E and G formats are compared in the following table:

Comparison of E and G conversion codes for real output		
	External appearance	
Internal value	E11.4 format code	G11.4 format code
−20321.	-0.2032E+05	-0.2032E+05
−8977.	␣-8977.␣␣␣␣	␣-8977.␣␣␣␣
23.40	␣0.2340E+02	␣␣23.40␣␣␣␣
−1.395	-0.1395E+01	␣-1.395␣␣␣␣
−0.1200	-0.1200E+00	-0.1200␣␣␣␣
0.02032	␣0.2032E-01	␣0.2032E-01
−0.02032	-0.2032E-01	-0.2032E-01
0.00004999	␣0.4999E-04	␣0.4999E-04

Format Codes for Real Input

Real input data to be converted with any of the real format codes Fw.d, Ew.d, Ew.dEe, Dw.d, Gw.d, Gw.dEe, ESw.d, ESw.dEe, ENw.d, and ENw.dEe may appear in the input record in any valid real constant form. In particular, it is not necessary to include an exponent for E input conversion or to omit the exponent when the F code is used for input. Examples are shown in Figures B.6 and B.7 and in the table that follows each figure.

```
read "(F10.4,⊥F8.0,⊥F5.3,⊥E13.6,⊥E9.0,⊥E8.4,⊥E8.2)", (A(I), I = 1, 8)
```

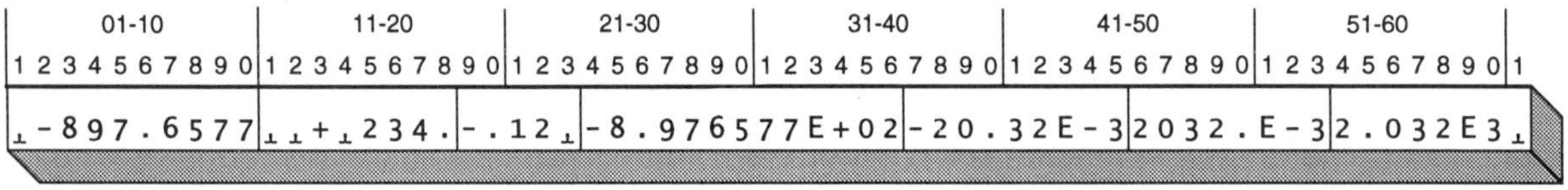

FIGURE B.6. Input of real data with explicit decimal point.

Real input with explicit decimal point in external field		
External appearance	Field width	Internal value
⊥-897.6577	10	−897.6577
⊥⊥+⊥234.	8	+234.
-.12⊥	5	−0.12
-8.976577E+02	13	−897.6577
-20.32E-3	9	−0.02032
2032.E-3	8	+2.032
2.032E3⊥	8	2032.0

```
read "(F10.2,⊥F6.0,⊥F6.3,⊥F4.2,⊥E8.2,⊥E7.0,⊥E9.3,⊥E8.2)", (Z(J), J = 2, 9)
```

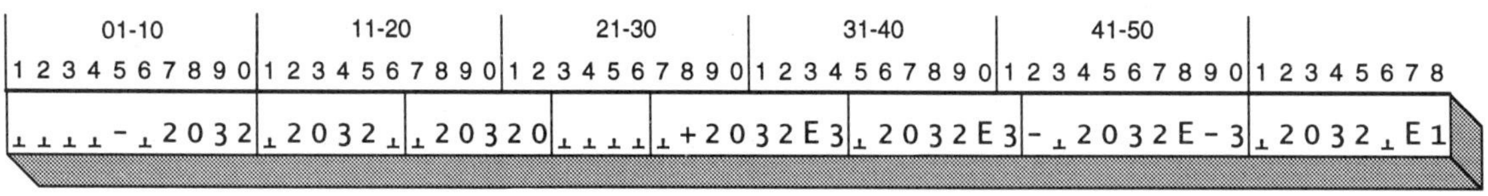

FIGURE B.7. Input of real data without explicit decimal point.

Real input without explicit decimal point in external field			
External appearance	Field width	Decimal position	Internal value
`⊥⊥⊥⊥-⊥2032`	10	2	−20.32
`⊥2032⊥`	6	0	+20320.
`⊥20320`	6	3	+2.032
`⊥⊥⊥⊥`	4	2	0.0
`⊥+2032E3`	8	2	+20320.
`⊥2032E3`	7	0	+2032000.
`-⊥2032E-3`	9	3	−0.002032
`⊥20320E1`	8	2	+2032.

For real input with any of the codes F, E, D, G, ES, or EN, the following observations apply.

1. A plus or minus sign preceding the significant digits may appear anywhere in the field to the left of the first digit. (Plus signs are usually omitted.)
2. The number need not fill the field. A field that is entirely blank represents a zero value. Note that when an exponent appears in the field, it is treated as an integer.
3. If a decimal point appears in the input field, the value of d in the format code is ignored; the actual decimal point overrides the format specification.
4. If a decimal point does not appear explicitly, an implied decimal position is determined by the value of d (counting from the right end of the field, or from the first character position to the left of the exponent if there is one in the field).
5. An exponent may appear in the input record in any of several forms. The most complete form consists of the letter E followed by a plus or minus sign, followed by an integer constant. Either the E or the sign may be omitted, but not both, since there must be some indication that an exponent is present. The letter D may be used instead of E for editing input fields corresponding to either real or double-precision input list items. Some permissible forms for the input constant $0.2032\,10^3$ with format code `E10.4` are as follows:

Input constant forms		
`⊥⊥⊥⊥2032E3`	`⊥⊥2032E⊥03`	`⊥+2032E+03`
`⊥⊥⊥2032E+3`	`⊥⊥2032E+03`	
`⊥⊥⊥2032E03`	`⊥⊥2032E+3`	

Double-Precision Input and Output

Double-precision data for input and output is handled in essentially the same way as real data. The D, E, F, G, ES, and EN format codes can be used for output of double-precision data or for input of data corresponding to a list item of double-precision type.

The external form for input data of double-precision type may be represented using the letter D or E to indicate the exponent; such data may be read with the E, F, or G conversion code. The format code Dw.d, analogous to Ew.d, is also available for use with data prepared with a D exponent; in fact, it will handle any of the external forms permitted for real input.

Double-precision output data produced with the E conversion code will be printed with an E indicating the exponent; the G code may also produce output that contains the letter E to indicate the exponent (depending on the magnitude of the data; see the preceding description of G output conversion). For applications that require a printed D rather than an E to indicate the exponent, the format code Dw.d should be used.

In short, all the D, E, F, and G format codes are interchangeable for input. Any of these codes may be used with list items of real or double-precision type and with input data prepared in any of the forms permitted for real input as well as any of those forms with a D replacing the E to indicate the exponent. For output, any of the D, E, F, and G codes may be used with a list of items of real or double-precision type. Only the appearance of the printed output will be affected by the choice among these codes. There is no difference between Ew.d and Dw.d output except for the printing of the letter E or D with the exponent.

EXAMPLE B.7

```
double precision Fox
Fox = 1.234567890123450D0
print "(1X,␣D22.15)", Fox
```

Appearance of the output:

```
␣0.123456789012345D+01
```

Complex Input and Output

Any of the real format specification codes may be used for input or output of data of complex type, but a pair of numerical fields and a pair of format codes correspond to a single complex variable (or expression) in the input or output list.

EXAMPLE B.8

```
complex Rabbit
Rabbit = (1.234567, 8.901234)
print "(1X,␣2␣E14.7,␣2␣F5.2)", Rabbit, (1.234, 5.678)
```

Appearance of the output:

```
␣0.1234567E+01␣0.8901234E+01␣␣␣␣1.23␣␣␣␣5.68
```

The form of complex data prepared for input under explicit format control differs from the list-directed form. For explicitly formatted input, the data is prepared in the form of two real fields (of any acceptable real form), whereas list-directed input requires a form analogous to that of a complex constant — that is, two real numerical input values separated by a comma and enclosed in parentheses.

B.4 LOGICAL INPUT AND OUTPUT

L Format Code

The format code Lw is used for input or output of data corresponding to list items of logical type. The printed output appears as w – 1 blanks followed by a T or an F. For input, the external field may contain optional blanks and a T or an F (optionally preceded by a period and followed by any characters).

G Format Code for Logical Data

The Gw.d and Gw.dEe format codes are permitted with list items of logical type and have the same effect as the Lw format code. The values of d and e in the format code are ignored.

B.5 CHARACTER INPUT AND OUTPUT

The format codes A and Aw are used with character data. The form Aw specifies a field width for the data in the external record. The first form omits the field width specification; the number of characters transmitted to or from the record is determined by the length of the character string that is referenced by the corresponding item of the input or output list.

A Format Codes for Character Output

We have seen how to annotate printed numerical results by printing words and phrases in the form of comments, titles, or headings. In the examples presented so far, the text was included as a character constant or referenced as a character expression in the output list of a list-directed output statement. The A and Aw format codes provide this same facility, with additional control over the appearance of the output, when explicit formatting rather than list directed formatting is used. A different method, in which the text to be printed is incorporated into the format description, is described later; that method is generally less flexible than the one presented here, in which the text is included in (or referenced from) the output list.

Let us suppose that two numbers, `Err` and `N`, are to be printed along with certain alphanumerical information. Suppose that `Err` is the difference between a computed and an observed value of a function (so that it may properly be called the error) and that `N` is the number of observations used in computing `Err`. Hence, we wish to print a line of the form

```
After xxx trials, the error is yyyyy.yy
```

where xxx is the current value of the integer variable `N` and yyyyy.yy is the current value of the real variable `Err`. If `N` is an integer between 0 and 999 and `Err` is to be printed with the code F9.2, the format specification shown in the following example would be appropriate:

EXAMPLE B.9

```
print "(A6, I4, A17, F9.2)", "⊥After", N, "⊥trials,⊥error⊥is", Err
```

The total width of the four fields printed by this statement is 36 characters. First the 6 characters `⊥After` are transmitted to the default output device; the next 4 characters are the (three-digit integer) value of `N` preceded by a blank; the 17 characters `⊥trials,⊥error⊥is` follow; the final 9 characters are the value of `Err` printed in F9.2 format.

In Example B.9, the length of each character constant to be printed is the same as the width of the corresponding A field. Therefore, the slightly simpler format specification `(A, I4, A, F9.2)` would produce the same output. This latter format also has some flexibility in that it could be used with character constants of different lengths. For example, the same format could be used for printing the total of N data values:

```
print "(A, I4, A, F9.2)", "⊥The⊥total⊥of", M, "⊥values⊥is", Sum
```

This flexibility imposes an additional burden if the various items of output need to be aligned in some manner. It would be necessary to count the characters in each of the character constants to determine the precise locations of the numerical fields that would be printed.

On the other hand, the first format specification (with field widths `A6` and `A17`), along with character constants of lengths 13 and 10, respectively, as in the second `print` statement, will result in truncation and padding of the character data to match the specified field widths. The data specified by the character list item will be truncated from the right or padded with blanks on the left before being transmitted to the output device. (Note that this is not the same as the padding applied during character assignment.) The printed result with

```
print "(A6, I4, A17, F9.2)", &
  "⊥The⊥total⊥of", M, "⊥values⊥is", Sum
```

might appear as follows:

```
⊥The⊥t⊥⊥⊥⊥⊥⊥⊥⊥values⊥is 43210.95
```

The character constant `⊥The⊥total⊥of` is truncated from 13 to 6 characters, and the 10 characters `⊥values⊥is` are padded with 7 additional blanks on the left.

Of course, character constants are not the only source of text for character output. The following examples illustrate explicitly formatted input and output of character variables and expressions as well as constants.

EXAMPLE B.10

```
! Example B.10.
  program Carrot
    implicit none
    real :: Code = 1.2, X = 3.4, Reals = 5.6, Flag = 7.8, Second
    character (len = 7) :: First = "ABCDEFG", Second = "PAYROLL"
! start program Carrot
    print "(2G15.5,⊥A15,⊥2G15.5)", 179.3, X, Second, Code, Reals
    print "(4G15.5,⊥A)", Flag, X, Reals, 2.0, First
    print "(A14)", First // Second
  end program Carrot
```

Result:

```
179.3⊥3.4⊥PAYROLL⊥1.2⊥5.6
7.8⊥3.4⊥5.6⊥2.0⊥ABCDEFG
ABCDEFGPAYROLL
```

EXAMPLE B.11

```
! Example B.11.
  program Radish
    implicit none
    intrinsic Index
    integer :: Loc_1
    character (len = 50), dimension(6) :: Hamlet
! start program Radish
    Hamlet(2) = "Whether⊥'tis⊥nobler⊥in⊥the⊥mind⊥to⊥suffer"
    Loc_1 = Index (Hamlet(2), "the")
    print "(I5, ': ', ⊥A)", Loc_1, Hamlet(2)(Loc_1 + 1: )
  end program Radish
```

Result:

```
⊥⊥⊥⊥4:⊥her⊥'tis⊥nobler⊥in⊥the⊥mind⊥to⊥suffer⊥⊥⊥⊥⊥⊥⊥⊥⊥
```

A Format Codes for Character input

The A and Aw format codes are also used for character input.

EXAMPLE B.12 A chemist prepares data including the symbol for a chemical element and the number of atoms of the element in a certain complex molecule. A program will read the data, look up the symbol in an internal table (using a linear search), and use related data from the table to compute the molecular weight of the molecule. The input statement is written as follows:

```
    read "(A2,⊥I3)", Name, N_Atoms
```

The first two character positions of the input record contain the chemical element symbol, and the next three characters contain the number of atoms.

In Example B.12, if the character variable Name is declared to have length 2, the format specification (A, ⊥I3) would also be appropriate. For input of character data without a field width specification, the number of characters of the input record that will be used is determined by the character length specification for the input list variable.

If a field width is specified but is different from the actual character length of the input list item, the characters read will be padded on the right with blanks or truncated from the left to the length of the list item. Thus, if Name has length 3, the statement

```
read "(A2,␣I3)", Name, N_Atoms
```

along with the following characters in the input record

```
Cu107
```

will result in the characters `Cu␣` being stored as the value of Name. However, if Name were of length 1, the field would be truncated from the left and only the character u would be stored.

Input form

Character values for input with explicit format control are not delimited (enclosed) by quotation marks or apostrophes. This form contrasts with the list-directed form, where delimiters are needed to establish the beginning and end of a character constant in the external record (except for certain simple strings).

The division of records into fields for explicitly formatted input is sufficient to delimit character items. Quotation marks or apostrophes within an input data value are represented by only a single character in the input field.

EXAMPLE B.13 Suppose that we wish to read from an input record the following information:

> The first five (or fewer) characters of the name of a chemical element, Name, such as `␣IRON`, `OXYGE`, or `URANI`
>
> Heat capacity coefficients A, B, and C

Input data could be prepared as shown in Figure B.8. An appropriate input statement is the following:

```
read "(A5,␣3␣G9.4)", Name, A, B, C
```

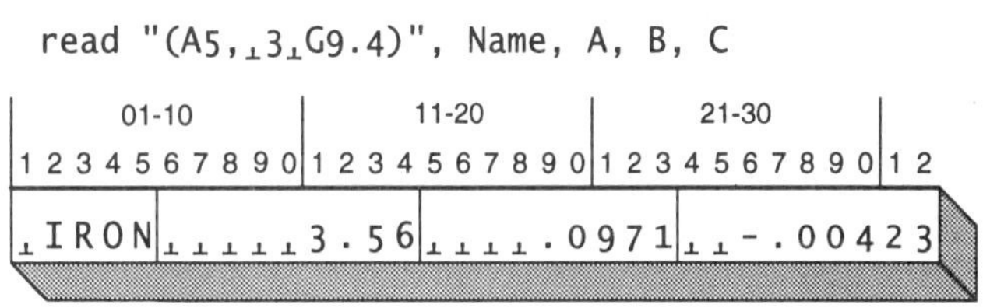

FIGURE B.8. Input fields for Example B.13.

EXAMPLE B.14 The following program reads an arbitrary 50-character position message to be printed out later. A sample data record is shown in Figure B.9

```
character (len = 50) :: Phideaux
read "(A50)", Phideaux
```

`read "(A50)", Phideaux`

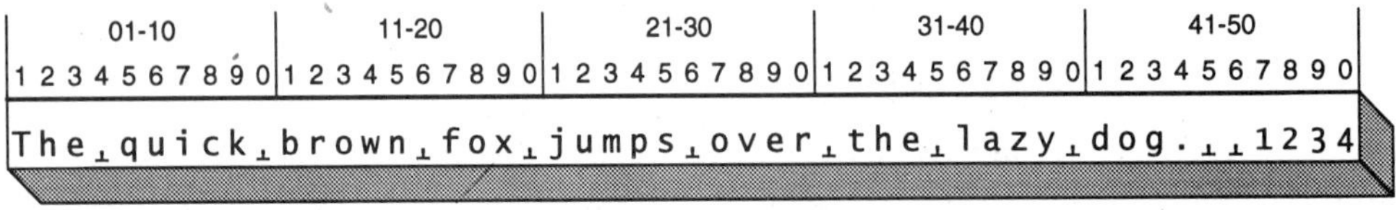

FIGURE B.9. Sample data record for Example B.14.

G Format Code for Character Data

The Gw.d and Gw.dEe format codes are permitted with list items of character type, and have the same effect as the Aw format code. The values of d and e in the format code are ignored.

B.6 FORMAT CODE REPETITION

When two or more adjacent fields of an input or output record are to have identical format codes, it is not necessary (as we have seen) to write out the code for each field separately if they can be combined by means of a repeat count. Thus,

```
G12.4, G12.4, G12.4
```

can also be written as

```
3 G12.4
```

Suppose that we wish to read values for A, B, C, I, and J from a record, as shown in Figure B.10. The real values A, B, and C are to be converted according to G code, and the integer values I and J are to be converted according to I code. The repeat count feature simplifies the format specification "(G12.4, G12.4, G12.4, I3, I3)" to that shown in Example B.15:

```
read "(3⊥G12.4,⊥2⊥I3)", A, B, C, I, J
```

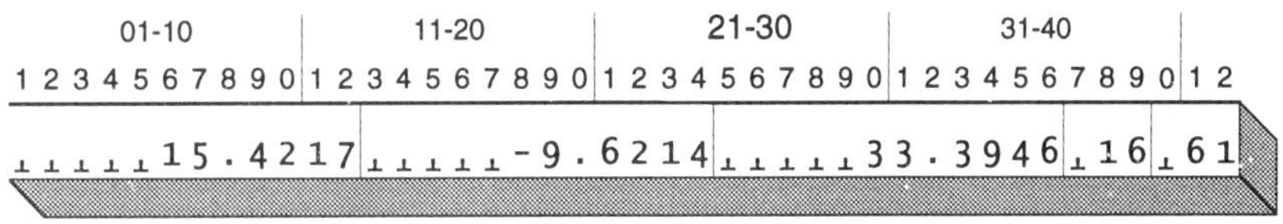

FIGURE B.10. Data for Example B.15.

EXAMPLE B.15

```
read "(3⊥G12.4,⊥2⊥I3)", A, B, C, I, J
```

A group of format codes can be enclosed in parentheses and preceded by a repeat count digit, as the next three examples illustrate.

EXAMPLE B.16 The following two statements are equivalent

```
read "(G12.4,⊥I3,⊥G12.4,⊥I3)", A, I, B, J
read "(2⊥(G12.4,⊥I3))", A, I, B, J
```

EXAMPLE B.17 Suppose that the data shown in Figure B.10 is reorganized so that the integer values appear between the real values. The format specification and the input list in Example B.15 might be rearranged as follows:

```
read "(2⊥(G12.4,⊥I3),⊥G12.4)", A, I, B, J, C
```

EXAMPLE B.18 More complicated patterns of repeated code groups can easily be imagined. In particular, we may have one repeated group of format codes nested within another group. The two following format descriptions are equivalent

```
(2 (I5, I4, I3), F5.2, 2 (I5, I4, I3), F5.2, I6)
(2 (2 (I5, I4, I3), F5.2), I6)
```

B.7 CORRESPONDENCE OF LIST, FORMAT, AND RECORD

During execution of an input or output statement, a correspondence or matching occurs between the items of the input or output list, format codes in the format description, and fields of the input or output record on the external device. In this matching, repeated format codes are counted as matching the proper number of fields. List items such as implied do loops, array sections, and structures may correspond to multiple fields (and to multiple format codes). The list, the format description, and the external record are all *scanned* in parallel during the input or output process, with repetitions as indicated by repeated format codes, implied do loops, and so on.

As we shall see (Appendix B.8), there are also some *nondata* format codes that are associated with a field of the record but do not correspond to any list item. When one of these codes is encountered, the scan of the input or output list is temporarily halted while the scanning process continues with the format description and the external record.

It may happen that there are exactly the same number of list items, format codes, and fields (taking into account the special cases just mentioned). When the last item of the list has been transmitted, the parallel scan will be completed and execution of the input or output statement comes to an end.

Format Longer Than List

Suppose that there are more format codes than list items. In this case, when the list is exhausted and action has terminated, the remaining format codes are ignored. To illustrate, suppose that, as an alternative to Example B.17, we had used the format description

```
(3 (G12.4, I3))
```

with the list

```
A, I, B, J, C
```

This format description suggests a record whose sixth field is three characters wide and contains an integer. Since there are only five items in the list, however, the sixth format code will not be used, and the effect is identical to that of Example B.17.

List Longer Than Format: Format Rescan

Suppose that there are more list items than format codes in the format description. The end of the description always signals the end of a record; therefore, the input or output process must continue to another record in order to complete the list. For instance, suppose that, for Example B.17, we had used the format description

```
(G12.4, I3)
```

which specifies an input record containing only two fields. Since five data items must be read, the format must be *rescanned* to match the remaining items of the list. However, each rescanning corresponds to matching the list items with the fields of a new record. Thus, three records in all must be read before the list can be satisfied. The first record contains values for A and I, the second has values for B and J, and the third has the single value of C.

Extra characters of an input record will be ignored after the fields indicated in the format description have been transmitted. For instance, if only the two fields indicated by G12.4, I3 are to be read from a record, then any characters beyond character position 15 in the record are ignored: It is immaterial whether the record contains additional blanks or other characters or whether the record contains only 15 characters (or any larger number).

In attempting to satisfy an input or output list by rescanning the format description, Fortran does not necessarily return to the very beginning of the format. It returns to a *rescan point*, which is determined as follows:

1. Search backward from the right end of the format description until a right parenthesis *other than* the terminal right parenthesis of the format is encountered. Then find the matching left parenthesis. The rescan begins with this left parenthesis or with the repeat count (if there is one) controlling this left parenthesis.
2. If there are no parentheses inside the outermost pair that delimits the entire format description, the rescan includes the entire format.

In the first of the following examples, the rescan point is near the middle of the format; in the second, the rescan point is at the repeat count that immediately follows the opening right parenthesis of the format.

```
(2 (I5, I4, I3), F5.2, 2 (I5, I4, I3), F5.2, I6)
                       ^ rescan point
(2 (2 (I5, I4, I3), F5.2), I6)
 ^ rescan point
```

Once the rescan point is determined, the format description continues to be rescanned from this point as many times as necessary until the list is exhausted. Note that a new record is started each time rescan occurs.

EXAMPLE B.19 Suppose that we wish to print the computed values of the variables Fee and Foe along with the first N elements of the vector Fum. Values for Fee and Foe are to be printed on the first line, and the elements of Fum are to be arranged three per line. A suitable output statement and format description would be as follows:

```
print "(1X, 2 G10.2 / (1X, 3 G10.4))", Fee, Foe, (Fum(J), J = 1, N)
!                     ^ rescan point
```

In Example B.19, the first two data items, Fee and Foe, will be printed according to the format code G10.2. The slash indicates the end of a record (which would be the end of a line if the record were printed). Only 21 characters of the first record have been specified, so the remainder of this record will be blank. The next record is described by the format description (1X, 3 G10.4), which will be used in printing the first three elements of the array Fum. Since this is the last parenthesized group in the format, the rescan point will be at the beginning of this group. Thus, the format code (1X, 3 G10.4) will be used repeatedly until all of the first N elements of Fum have been printed, three per line. If N is not a multiple of 3, the list will be exhausted during the middle of a scan of this repeated format group; the output process will then terminate, ignoring the remaining format codes.

B.8 NONDATA FORMAT CODES

In addition to the format codes that correspond to list items, there are other *nondata* editing codes — also called *control codes* — for purposes such as specifying the position of a field within the external record or printing a fixed sequence of characters (independent of the output list). They do not match any list item and do not cause the values of any program variables to be transmitted.

Codes for Positioning

Skipped character positions

When one or more characters of an input record are to be ignored or skipped or when one or more blank characters are to be inserted into an output record, we can designate this group of character positions as a field to be skipped by incorporating in the format description the code wX, where w is the width of the field — that is, the number of character positions to be skipped. Here w must be an unsigned integer constant. Note that an X format code is not needed to cause the remainder of an input record (to the right of the last field of interest) to be skipped or to cause the remainder of a printed line (to the right of the last data value printed on the line) to be left blank.

In many instances, it is simpler to widen a numerical field than to introduce an extra skipped field. For example, if we wish to print five blank character positions followed by a five-digit integer, we could use either the pair of format codes 5X, I5 or the single code I10. These two formats will have the same effect, except that the code I10 will avoid problems due to field overflow that could occur if the integer to be printed were unexpectedly larger than five digits.

Tabular format

Character positions can also be skipped in a slightly different way, analogous to the use of the tabulation key on a typewriter. This feature is invoked by means of the format code Tw, which changes the sequence of processing a record of input or output such that the wth character of that record is the next one to be transmitted.

This feature is especially attractive with columnar data output. A format such as

```
(T20, F7.3)
```

could be used with the format

```
(T20, "HEADING")
```

for example, to guarantee that the characters printed by the two formats will be properly aligned vertically. This feature is helpful for preparing complicated columnar tables or graphs.

Whereas Tw acts as an *absolute* tab operation and resets the current character position to w, the *relative* tab codes TLw (tab left) or TRw (tab right) move the current position left or right by w characters from the current position. Note that the effect of TRw is identical to that of wX.

The new character position resulting from the T, TL, TR, and X format codes becomes effective only when the next actual data transfer occurs. For instance, TR999 editing during input from a short record does not cause an error unless an attempt is made to actually transfer data from the new position. Similarly, TR does not increase output record length unless data is subsequently written to the record.

Tabular format codes in Fortran 90 are subject to the *left tab limit,* which is defined as the current file position at the beginning of execution of each `read` or `write` statement. If data transfer proceeds into another record, the left tab limit is redefined as the leftmost position of that record. A TL format code that would attempt to reposition farther left moves only to the left tab limit. The Tw format code sets the current position w spaces to the right of the left tab limit.

Suppose that the first 10 characters of a 100-character record have been transferred by nonadvancing input or output. A new `read` or `write` statement for the same unit is executed, with TL5 as the first format code. (Any amount of intervening input or output could have taken place on other units.) It is possible, in conformance with the Fortran standard, that Fortran has already physically transferred the 10 characters as instructed by the first statement and is physically unable to move the current position into the part of the record whose transfer is already complete. At the beginning of execution of the second statement, the left tab limit is set at the current position, following character position 10. Therefore, the TL5 format code has no effect.

Multiple-Record Formats

We have seen that a format description may describe the fields of more than one record either when a slash is included among the format codes or when rescan occurs. For either input or output, the slash indicates that transmission of the current record is to cease and a new record is to be started.

When consecutive slashes appear in the format description, as in

```
(1X, 3 G10.2 // (1X, 4 G10.4))
```

the first slash causes termination of the first output record. Since the format has not been exhausted, transmission of a second output record is initiated; however, the second slash immediately terminates this second record. The effect is to transmit the second record as an empty record. (On a printer, a blank line would be printed.) Again, since the format has not been exhausted, transmission of a third output record is initiated, and this record is generated according to the format (1X, 4 G10.4), beginning with a one-character position skipped field. If there are more than seven list items, the format will be rescanned and successive records will use the format (1X, 4 G10.4) again. Note that no list item corresponds to a skipped field — that is, to an X format code — so four list items will be transmitted each time the format is rescanned.

The number of records read or written by a formatted output statement can be determined from the following rule:

> A new record is read or written each time a slash is encountered in the format and each time a format rescan occurs. Unless the statement contains a control list with the specifier advance = "NO", a new record is read or written at the completion of execution of the statement (even if the input or output list is empty).

Thus, the occurrence of *n* consecutive slashes results in *n* – 1 empty output records or skipped input records, except that the occurrence of *n* slashes at the beginning or end of a format description causes *n* empty records or skipped records. A complete format description consisting only of *n* slashes causes *n* + 1 empty records or skipped records (even if *n* is 0).

The Format Description as a Source of Text

Suppose that we have a number of output statements in a program, all with different lists of items to be printed, but with the same text to accompany the items in each of the different lists. For example, the program might contain the following statements.

EXAMPLE B.20

```
! Example B.20.
  program Texas
    implicit none
    integer :: I1, I2, L1, L2, Last, Loc
    real :: W1, W2, Final
! start program Texas
    read *, I1, L1, W1, I2, L2, W2, Last, Loc, Final
    print "(2␣I4,␣G16.8)", "␣After␣event␣number␣", I1, &
      "␣the␣largest␣element␣is␣at␣location␣", L1, "␣and␣its␣weight␣is␣", W1
        ⋮
    print "(2␣I4,␣G16.8)", "␣After␣event␣number␣", I2, &
      "␣the␣largest␣element␣is␣at␣location␣", L2, "␣and␣it␣weight␣is␣", W2
        ⋮
```

```
    print "(2␣I4,␣G16.8), "␣After␣event␣number␣", Last, &
      "␣the␣largest␣element␣is␣at␣location␣", Loc "␣and␣its␣weight␣is␣", Final
  end program Texas
```

The repeated text may be removed from the individual output lists and placed in the format description, as the following example shows.

EXAMPLE B.21

```
! Example B.21.
  program Florida
    implicit none
    integer :: I1, I2, L1, L2, Last, Loc
    real :: W1, W2, Final
! start program Florida
    read *, I1, L1, W1, I2, L2, W2, Last, Loc, Final
    print 24, I1, L1, W1
    print 24, I2, L2, W2
    print 24, Last, Loc, Final
24  format ("␣After␣event␣number␣", I5, &
      "␣the␣largest␣element␣is␣at␣location␣", I5, &
        "␣and␣its␣weight␣is␣", E15.7)
  end program Florida
```

Execution of these statements with the revised format description has the same effect as Example B.20.

Text to be transmitted directly from the format description to an output device may be specified either by a *character constant format code* or by the H format code described in Appendix D.11. These codes do not correspond to any item in the output list. Each time such a format specification is encountered during output processing, the prescribed text is copied to the output record directly from the format itself. These format codes cannot be used for input.

Character constant format code

A character constant within an output format specification causes transmission of the character constant value directly to the output device. The character constant is delimited, as usual, by quotation marks or by apostrophes.

Some caution is necessary when a character constant format code appears in a character constant format description. If the format description is delimited by quotation marks, the format code should be delimited by apostrophes.

A more confusing situation occurs when the text in a character constant format code includes a quotation mark or an apostrophe to be printed. For example, we might wish to print

```
␣␣2␣isn't␣␣3
```

specifying the integers 2 and 3 as numerical constants in the output list but obtaining `isn't` from a character constant format code.

EXAMPLE B.22 If the format description is delimited by quotation marks, we may delimit the character constant format code with apostrophes and double the inner apostrophe, as follows:

```
print "(1X,␣I3,␣'␣isn''t',␣I3)", 2, 3
```

The actual format specification, `(1X, I3, '␣isn''t', I3)`, contains a character constant format code delimited by apostrophes, so the inner apostrophe must be doubled.

EXAMPLE B.23 We can eliminate the extra delimiter level with a separate `format` statement

```
   print 26, 2, 3
26 format (1X, I3, "␣isn't", I3)
```

The separate `format` statement in Example B.23 may be more readable than the named character constant in Example B.22. Note that the format designator in a `format` statement is, in effect, an undelimited character string.

Processing at the End of a List: Colon Format Code

While executing an input or output statement, Fortran scans the list, the format description, and the record in parallel. If it arrives at the end of the input or output list when the format scan is at the final right parenthesis or when the next format code is one associated with a list item (such as `I`, `E`, `F`, `G`, or `A`), execution of the input or output statement is terminated at that point. If the next format code is a *nondata* code (such as slash, `X`, `T`, or character constant) that does not require a list item, execution will continue except in the following two cases:

1. Format processing continues through nondata codes only until the final right parenthesis of the format description is encountered — no rescan will occur after the list has been exhausted.
2. If a colon format code is encountered after the list has been exhausted, the parallel scan terminates and execution of the input or output statement ceases. This format code, consisting simply of a colon within the format description, therefore indicates that any nondata format codes that follow are to be effective only if the list is not exhausted.

The nondata format codes whose effect can be suppressed at the end of an input or output list are tabs, slashes, and character constants. Note that character constant format codes are permitted only for output.

EXAMPLE B.24

```
! Example B.24.
  program Sigmoid
    implicit none
    real, dimension(72) :: A
! start program Sigmoid
    print "(4(: '␣I␣=␣', I3, '␣A(I)␣=␣', G16.8))", (I, A(I), I = 1, N)
  end program Sigmoid
```

Careful study of Example B.24 reveals that the repeated format group will be scanned four times before the end of the format description is reached. Therefore, when N is not a multiple of 4, the characters ␣I␣=␣ would be printed after the last A_i value if the colon were not included in the format.

Processing an Empty Input or Output List

If the list is empty initially, nondata format codes will be processed in accordance with the rules just given. (Tab and slash format codes may be encountered during input processing; these same codes as well as character constant format codes may occur during output.) An input or output list is effectively empty if its only items are zero-trip implied do loops or zero-sized array sections. (However, an empty string as a list item requires a data format code.)

Output statements with empty lists are often used for printing messages, titles, and headings or for skipping one or more lines without calling for the display of the values of any variables. The associated format description will not contain any of the codes that need to be associated with a list item. Empty input lists may also be used for positioning or other editing of input records without data transmission — for example, to skip an input record.

EXAMPLE B.25 An output statement with an empty list would have either of the following forms. Note that there is no comma following the format specification in the short form when there is no list

```
print Format
write ( Control list )
```

Suppose we wish to print the three headings Rate, Hours, and Pay above three columns of numbers in a table. Each column will be 15 character positions wide, with an extra 5 character positions to the left of the first character position. We also wish to skip two lines after printing the headings (see Figure B.11). Thus, the following are appropriate output statements and format descriptions:

EXAMPLE B.26

```
print "(T17,⊥'Rate',⊥T31,⊥'Hours',⊥T48,⊥'Pay'⊥//)"
print "(5X,⊥F15.2,⊥I15,⊥F15.2)", Rate, N_Hours, Pay
```

```
print "(T17,⊥'Rate',⊥T31,⊥'Hours',⊥T48,⊥'Pay'⊥//)"
print "(5X,⊥F15.2,⊥I15,⊥F15.2)", Rate, N_Hours, Pay
```

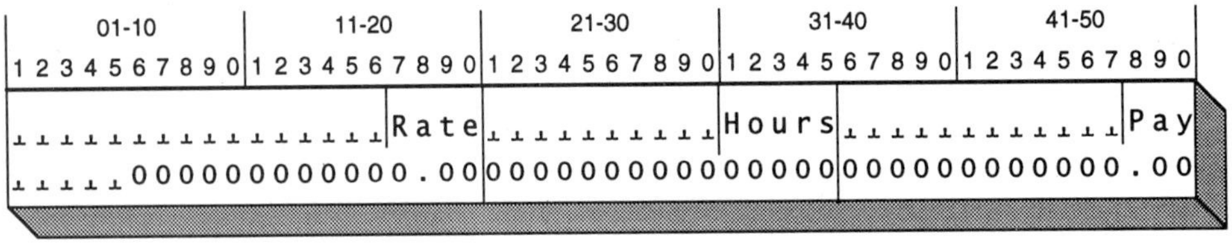

FIGURE B.11. Data for Example B.26.

EXAMPLE B.27 To print the message `Check data again.` we could use the following statement:

```
print  "('Check⊥data⊥again.')"
```

EXAMPLE B.28 To print the title `The Automatic Change Maker` (preceded by 26 blanks) on a line at the top of the page and then skip four lines, we could use the following statement:

```
print "('1', 26X, 'The⊥Automatic⊥Change⊥Maker' ////)"
```

B.9 CONTROL FORMAT CODES

Control format codes include the codes S, SP, SS, and kP covered in this section, as well as the colon format code and the codes BN and BZ that have been discussed previously.

Control of Optional Output Plus Sign

An output field produced by I, F, E, EN, ES, D, or G editing includes an optional sign in the position immediately to the left of the numerical digits representing the value. The sign must appear if the numerical value is negative, but the processor has some leeway in case it is positive. For example, the processor may choose to suppress the sign of a positive value that would otherwise be too large for the designated field width, while printing plus signs on smaller positive numbers.

At the beginning of execution of each Fortran output statement, the printing of these plus signs is entirely subject to the option of the processor. However, an S, SP, or SS format code may appear anywhere in the format description to control sign printing. The control specified by such a format code remains effective until another S, SP, or SS code is encountered in the format scan.

An SP format code specifies that "optional" plus signs are to be printed, and an SS code indicates that they are to be suppressed. The S code restores the processor option.

These codes do not have any effect if they are encountered in a format description for input.

Scale Factor Control

The kP format code specifies the scale factor, k, which is an optionally signed integer constant. The value of the scale factor in effect at the beginning of execution of an input or output statement is zero. The effective value of the scale factor changes only when a kP format code is encountered during the format scan.

Input

During input editing, the scale factor affects only fields without an explicit exponent, during F, E, EN, ES, D, or G format conversion. An input field for one of these format codes is converted as though it were followed by the exponent –k. For example, with a 2P scale factor in effect, an input field three character positions wide containing the characters 123 would represent 1.23 as an internal value. An input scale factor can be used with a data field that is too narrow to hold an explicit decimal point or exponent.

Output

During output editing, the scale factor affects all F, E, and D format conversions, as well as those G conversions that are equivalent to E. It has no effect on EN or ES output conversion. The effect of ES output editing is the same as that of applying the scale factor 1P to the corresponding E format code.

For F output editing, the scale factor is added to the exponent of the internal data value. For example, with the format 2P, F6.3 and the internal value 2.3402, the number 234.02 would be printed. This feature might be useful for conversion of units — for example, when a length measured in meters is to be printed in centimeters.

For E or D output editing, the scale factor must be greater than $-d$ and must not exceed $d + 1$, where d is the decimal position specified in the E or D format code. If $-d < k \leq 0$, there will be exactly $|k|$ leading zeros and $d - |k|$ significant digits after the decimal point. If $0 < k \leq d + 1$, there will be exactly k significant digits to the left of the decimal point and $d - k + 1$ significant digits to the right of the decimal point (thus, a total of $d + 1$ significant digits in the output field). The output exponent is adjusted to produce a correct representation of the magnitude of the output data value. For example, the value 23.401 with format code `E11.4` would be printed as `⊥0.2340E+02`, but with scale factor `1P` it would print as `⊥2.3402E+01`.

For G editing, the effect of the scale factor depends on whether the G format code is actually interpreted as F or as E. This choice is made before considering the scale factor. If the exponent would be between 0 and d (inclusive), the F interpretation is used, and the scale factor is ignored. If the exponent (before considering scale factor) would be negative or larger than d, the E interpretation is used, and the scale factor is applied to determine the number of leading zeros after the decimal point.

The following table presents some examples of E, ES, and G output conversion with various scale factor values:

Effect of scale factor on real output with E and G format codes

Internal value	External appearance					
	E11.4 or 0P,E11.4 format code	ES11.4 or 1P,E11.4 format code	G11.4 or 0P,G11.4 format code	-1P,G11.4 format code	1P,G11.4 format code	5P,G11.4 format code
−20320.	-0.2032E+05	-2.0320E+04	-0.2032E+05	-0.0203E+06	-2.0320E+04	-20320.E+00
−8977.1	-0.8977E+04	-8.9771E+03	⊥-8977.⊥⊥⊥⊥	⊥-8977.⊥⊥⊥⊥	⊥-8977.⊥⊥⊥⊥	⊥-8977.⊥⊥⊥⊥
23.402	⊥0.2340E+02	⊥2.3402E+01	⊥⊥23.40⊥⊥⊥⊥	⊥⊥23.40⊥⊥⊥⊥	⊥⊥23.40⊥⊥⊥⊥	⊥⊥23.40⊥⊥⊥⊥
−1.3954	-0.1395E+01	-1.3954E+00	⊥-1.395⊥⊥⊥⊥	⊥-1.395⊥⊥⊥⊥	⊥-1.395⊥⊥⊥⊥	⊥-1.395⊥⊥⊥⊥
−0.12003	-0.1200E+00	-1.2003E-01	-0.1200⊥⊥⊥⊥	-0.1200⊥⊥⊥⊥	-0.1200⊥⊥⊥⊥	-0.1200⊥⊥⊥⊥
−0.020321	-0.2032E-01	-2.0321E-02	-0.2032E-01	-0.0203E+00	-2.0321E-02	-20321.E-06
0.020321	⊥0.2032E-01	⊥2.0321E-02	⊥0.20321E-01	⊥0.0203E+00	⊥2.0321E-02	⊥20321.E-06
0.000049991	⊥0.4999E-04	⊥4.9991E-05	⊥0.4999E-04	⊥0.0500E-03	⊥4.9991E-05	⊥4.9991.E-09

This table demonstrates that the scale factor has no effect on G editing when the exponent (before considering the scale factor) would be in the range for which F conversion is used. It also illustrates the fact that when the E interpretation is used for G editing, the effect is the same (for any scale factor value) as if the corresponding E format code were specified.

One other interesting observation can be made from this table. An E format code (or a G format code that is applied as an E format code) causes output of one more significant digit when the scale factor has a positive value (up to the limit, d + 1), as compared to a zero scale factor. In particular, a scale factor value of 1 (or ES format code) produces output in the "classical" scientific notation, with exactly one significant digit to the left of the decimal point and d significant digits to the right. Also, the number of significant digits is decreased when the scale factor is negative.

Control of Blank Characters in Input Fields

In the era when most computer input was prepared on punched cards, Fortran decreed that any blank character within an input field was to be treated as a zero character during formatted input conversion, which was supposed to reduce the number of keystrokes during data entry in certain cases. However, this convention was later found to be rather troublesome. In particular, it requires care to ensure that an integer input data item (or an integer exponent on a real data item) is positioned at the extreme right of its input field. For this reason, among others, an alternative rule was later established, to the effect that blank characters within input fields should be ignored. Fortran now provides a means for selecting between these two alternatives.

When an external device is made available for input of data to a Fortran program (for example, by execution of an `open` statement), a *blank significance property* is established for the connection if the form property of the connection is formatted. The blank significance property of a connection is either zero or null.

At the beginning of execution of each formatted input statement in the Fortran program, the blank significance property reverts to that of the connection. While execution of the statement continues, the currently effective blank significance property can change only when a `BN` or `BZ` format code is encountered during the format scan. The blank significance property and the `BN` and `BZ` format codes have no effect on output.

The `BN` format code specifies that any blanks appearing within a field on formatted input are "treated as null characters" (ignored). The `BZ` format code specifies that blanks are "treated as zeros." For example, with `BZ` in effect, an integer field containing the characters `123␣␣` is interpreted as 12300, and a real input data field containing `1.23E+2␣` is interpreted as `1.23E20`. With `BN` in effect, the resulting values are `123` and `1.23E2`, respectively.

Appendix C
Source Program Form

A Fortran program may be written either in *free source form* or in the traditional Fortran *fixed source form*. Each *program unit* (main program, module, external subprogram, or block data program unit) must consistently follow either free source form rules or fixed source form rules, but complete program units of the two forms may be combined. Some Fortran processors do not permit mixing the two forms in one file.

In the following descriptions, certain special rules apply to *character strings*. For purposes of this appendix, a character string is an explicit constant of character type or the characters that follow H in the H (Hollerith) edit descriptor that is described in Appendix D.11.

Fortran character set

Fortran statements (including specifications and instructions) are composed from characters in the Fortran character set, which consists of 26 uppercase (capital) and lowercase letters, the digits 0 through 9, the blank (space), and the following 21 special characters:

A standard Fortran processor is not required to support lowercase letters. If it does accept lowercase letters, however, it must treat them exactly like uppercase letters (except in character data). This text assumes that your Fortran processor accepts lowercase letters; if it does not, you will have to convert all of the lowercase letters in the examples to upper case.

The special characters have a variety of purposes, which we shall encounter as we proceed. For example, the asterisk denotes multiplication, and the slash indicates division. It is especially important to note the distinction between similar characters such as 0 (digit *zero*) and O (letter *oh*), or among 1 (digit *one*), l (letter *ell*), and I (letter *eye*).

Fortran recognizes the difference between uppercase and lowercase letters in character data, but in all other contexts Fortran makes no distinction. Thus, you may write keywords, variable names, or other names in upper case, in lower case, or in a mixture of the two cases. Fortran does not distinguish between alternative forms such as `ALPHA` and `Alpha` (or even `aLPHA`, `aLpHa`, etc.). To avoid confusion, however, you should write each name consistently. In this textbook, names of variables, constants, and procedures (including intrinsic procedures) are written with an initial uppercase letter. Long names composed of several words often include underscores, and names often include interior uppercase letters, as the following examples illustrate:

```
This_name_contains_underscores
This_Is_A_Longer_Name
```

Keywords may be written entirely in lower case, although Fortran does not require this style convention.

Comments and character data may contain Fortran characters or any other characters that the processor is able to represent.

Lexical tokens

In a Fortran program, characters are grouped into *lexical tokens* that are then further grouped into *lines* and *statements*. A lexical token is one of the following:

A name
A keyword
An explicit constant
A statement label
An operator (such as +, >=, or //)
A delimiter (such as a left or right parenthesis)

A name or a keyword consists of one or more letters, digits, and underscore characters. There must not be more than 31 characters, and the first character must be a letter.

A keyword has the same appearance as a name, but Fortran recognizes that in certain contexts it has special significance. Fortran keywords are not *reserved words*. The characters that comprise a keyword (such as `if`, `end`, or `dimension`) could also be used as a name (but this practice is not recommended). The following perfectly legal Fortran statement is confusing — to say the least:

```
if (Then > Else) print *, Read  ! ☹
```

In the examples in this book, all keywords are written entirely in lower case and all names are capitalized.

Placement of program statements

In general, all declarations except `format` statements must precede the executable statements of a program unit.

<table>
<tr><td colspan="2">program statement, module statement,
subroutine statement, function statement, or block data statement</td></tr>
<tr><td>use statements</td><td rowspan="5">format statements
entry statements</td></tr>
<tr><td>implicit none statement</td></tr>
<tr><td>implicit statements
named constant specifications</td></tr>
<tr><td>named constant specifications
data statements
derived type definitions
interface blocks
type declaration statements
statement function statements
specification statements</td></tr>
<tr><td>executable statements and constructs
data statements</td></tr>
<tr><td colspan="2">contains statement</td></tr>
<tr><td colspan="2">internal subprograms or module subprograms</td></tr>
<tr><td colspan="2">end statement</td></tr>
</table>

The following suggested statement sequence will satisfy the requirements of Fortran in simple cases:

1. Program unit header (`program`, `module`, `subroutine`, `function`, or `block data` statement)
2. `use` directives
3. `implicit none` directive
4. Specifications for named constants used in other specifications
5. Derived type definitions
6. Type declaration and specification statements, including named constant specifications
7. Executable statements
8. `contains` statement
9. Internal procedure definitions
10. `end` statement

Additional rules summarized in the following table *prohibit* certain kinds of statements in some positions.

Prohibited statements	Prohibited positions
Derived type definition or interface block	`block data`
`contains` statement	Internal subprogram, interface body, or `block data`
`use` statement	`block data`
`format` statement, executable statement, or statement function	Module specification part, interface body, or `block data`
`data` statement	Interface body
`entry` statement	Main program, internal subprogram, module specification part, interface body, or `block data`

C.1 FREE SOURCE FORM

Blank characters are significant. A blank character must not appear within a lexical token. A blank must appear between adjacent names, keywords, explicit constants, or labels.

Certain keywords — namely, any keyword beginning with `end`, as well as `go to`, `else if`, `block data`, `double precision`, `in out`, and `select case` — may be regarded either as one lexical token or as two tokens. The following are keywords that *must* be written as two separate lexical tokens:

`case default`	`do while`
`implicit` *Type*	`implicit none`
`interface assignment`	`interface operator`
`module procedure`	`recursive function`
`recursive subroutine`	`recursive` *Type*
Type `function`	*Type* `recursive`

A free-form source program line may be entirely blank, or it may contain up to 132 characters. Fortran ignores any characters on a free-form line beyond character position 132.

A blank line, or a line whose first nonblank character is an exclamation point, is a *comment line*. A line that is not a comment line may contain a *trailing comment*: An exclamation point on the line (except in a character string) marks the beginning of a trailing comment, which continues to the end of the line. Characters on a comment line or in a trailing comment provide valuable documentation, but they have no effect on the execution of the program. Characters that are not in the Fortran character set may appear in a comment or in a character string.

A line that is not a comment line is a *continuation line* if the preceding noncomment line has an ampersand as the last nonblank character that is not part of a trailing comment; otherwise, it is an *initial line*. A line must not have an ampersand (with or without a trailing comment) as its only nonblank character. The first noncomment line in a program unit is an initial line.

The first nonblank character on a continuation line may be an ampersand. When it is necessary to continue a single lexical token over the end of a line, the ampersand character at the end of the line must be matched by an ampersand as the first nonblank character of the continuation line. When a character string is broken at the end of a line, there must be no trailing comment.

A *composite line* consists of characters from an initial line or from an initial line and one or more consecutive continuation lines (which may be interspersed with comment lines). Ignoring trailing comments, interspersed comment lines, characters following an ampersand that denotes continuation, and an initial ampersand on a continuation line with the blank characters that precede it, the remaining characters of the initial line and any continuation lines are joined to form the composite line.

A composite line may contain a single statement. However, Fortran permits two or more statements in the same composite line. Semicolons separate multiple statements of a composite line. A statement label may follow a semicolon; it must be followed by one or more blanks to separate it from the statement. Consider this example:

```
Temp = X;  X = Y;  Y = Temp                        ! Exchange X and Y.
if (I == 0) go to 1;  I = 0;  1 continue
```

The portion of a composite line that contains any one statement must not extend over more than 39 continuation lines.

Comment lines may precede the first statement of a program unit. Lines following the end statement of a program unit are not part of that program unit.

C.2 FIXED SOURCE FORM

A program unit may be written in the traditional Fortran fixed source form. Two nontraditional features, trailing comments and multistatement lines (as described in the following paragraphs), may also appear in a fixed-form program unit. As in free form, names may be as long as 31 characters and may contain underscores.

A line in fixed source form consists of exactly 72 characters. The compiler ignores any characters on a fixed-form line beyond character position 72.

Blank characters are not significant in free source form. A blank character may appear within a lexical token, and has no effect except in a character string.

A line is a *comment line* if any of the following conditions holds:

1. The line contains only blank characters.
2. Character position 1 contains the letter C or an asterisk.
3. The first nonblank character on the line is an exclamation point and is not in character position 6.

A line that is not a comment line may contain a *trailing comment*: An exclamation point on the line (except in a character string) marks the beginning of a trailing comment, which continues to the end of the line. Characters on a comment line or in a trailing comment provide valuable documentation, but they have no effect on the execution of the program. Characters that are not in the Fortran character set may appear in a comment or in a character string. (Note that trailing comments are permitted in Fortran 90 fixed source form but not in traditional Fortran programs.)

A line that is not a comment line is a *continuation line* if there is a character other than a blank or zero in character position 6; otherwise, it is an *initial line*. The first noncomment line in a program unit must be an initial line. Note that an exclamation point or a semicolon in character position 6 of a line indicates that the line is a continuation line and has no other significance.

Character positions 1 to 5 of an initial line either are blank or contain a statement label. Character positions 1 to 5 of a continuation line must be blank.

A *composite line* consists of characters from an initial line or from an initial line and one or more consecutive continuation lines (which may be interspersed with comment lines). Characters from positions 7 to 72 (except trailing comments) of the initial line and of any continuation lines are joined to form the composite line.

A composite line contains one or more statements. Semicolons separate multiple statements of a composite line. A statement following a semicolon in a fixed-form composite line must not be labeled. (Note that multistatement lines are permitted in Fortran 90 fixed source form but not in traditional Fortran programs.) Consider this example:

```
Temp = X;  X = Y;  Y = Temp                          ! Exchange X and Y.
```

The portion of a composite line that contains any one statement must not extend over more than 19 continuation lines.

A composite line that contains an end statement must consist only of an initial line. A statement that is not an end statement and that extends over more than one line must not appear to be an end statement when continuation lines are ignored.

Comment lines may precede the first statement of a program unit. Lines following the end statement of a program unit are not part of that program unit.

C.3 COMPATIBLE TEXT

Text prepared in accordance with the following rules is compatible with both fixed source form and free source form. In particular, such text could appear in a file that is intended for possible reference from `include` lines in either fixed-form or free-form program units.

1. Treat blanks as being significant.
2. Confine statement labels to character positions 1 to 5 and statements to character positions 7 to 72.
3. Begin each comment line with an exclamation point as the first nonblank character, but not in character position 6.
4. To continue a statement, place an ampersand in character position 73 and another ampersand in character position 6 of the next noncomment line.

Trailing comments and multistatement lines are permitted in either source form.

It is not difficult to write a program that will scan fixed-form text and automatically convert comments and continuation lines to conform to rules 3 and 4. It is necessary to do only the following: Delete any characters in positions beyond 72. Change any asterisk or C found in character position 1 (indicating a comment) to an exclamation point. When any character other than a blank or a zero appears in position 6 of a noncomment line (indicating fixed-form continuation), change it to an ampersand and append an ampersand in position 73 of the preceding noncomment line. Fixed-form program text already conforms to rule 2.

Many fixed-form programs are written as though blanks were significant. Most programmers put blanks between adjacent names, keywords, explicit constants, or labels; they do not put blanks within a name, a keyword, a noncharacter explicit constant, a label, an operator, or a delimiter. For example, `do` statements in most fixed-form programs are not written in a compressed style such as `do30i ....` Converting the comments and continuation lines, as described, would transform such programs into compatible form.

However, fixed-form programs that do not treat blanks as being significant are considerably more difficult to transform into compatible form. A suitable tool for this more general situation would include the equivalent of a Fortran lexical analyzer that does not rely on significant blanks.

Appendix D Obsolete Features

D.1 IMPLICIT TYPE SPECIFICATION

Type Declarations

As has been recommended, a subprogram may contain type declaration statements to specify the data types of individual variables and constants. An `implicit none` statement in the subprogram (or in its host) instructs Fortran to require type declarations for all data objects, including function results.

Type declaration statements in the examples in this book have the following forms:

> *Type name* :: *List of names*
> *Type name* (*Properties*) *Attributes* :: *List of names*

Such a declaration asserts that all names in the *List* are names of variables of the designated *Type*. The *Type name* may be followed by a parenthesized list of *Properties* that include a `kind` subtype selector and, for character type, a length specifier, as illustrated by Example D.1. Array dimension bounds and other attributes may also be specified in a type declaration.

EXAMPLE D.1

```
integer, parameter :: R = Kind (0.0), LONG_R = Kind (0.0D0)
integer, parameter :: DEFAULT_I = Kind (0), L_STR1 = 5, L_STR2 = 7
real :: Large, X, Prune, Number, J22, Q
real (kind = LONG_R) :: Iron, Naper, Kilos, J, Tape
real, dimension(3: 3) :: Work_Space
double precision :: X, Y, Z
integer :: Big, Small, Left, Right, M
integer (kind = DEFAULT_I) :: A, B, I
logical :: Switch, Metric, Count, Trad_Real
complex (kind = R) :: A, B, C
character (len = L_STR1) :: Able, Baker, Item
character (len = L_STR2) :: Table
type (Table), pointer :: Root
```

A subprogram may have as many type declarations as are required. The same name must not be explicitly declared more than once (even if the same data type and other specifications are given).

Declarations that do not specify a `kind` subtype selector are interpreted as declaring the *default* `kind` for the particular data type. The default `kind` for real type is the same as traditional single precision. A `double precision` type declaration must not give a `kind` parameter value. A `character` type declaration that does not contain length information declares the default length, which is 1.

Declared Implicit Type Specification

The `implicit` Statement

An abbreviated form is available for declaring that all names beginning with a designated letter (or letters) have a particular data type (as well as `kind` and character length parameters). While this usage is not recommended, it is described here because you are likely to encounter it in existing Fortran programs.

In its usual form, the `implicit` statement consists of the keyword `implicit` followed by a list, each of whose items consists of a type name followed by a parenthesized sublist of initial letters, specifying that names having those initial letters are to have that data type — for example,

```
implicit integer (I, J, K), real (A, B, X, Y)
```

Fortran considers uppercase and lowercase letters as equivalent. Note that the initial letters in the examples are written in upper case for consistency with the convention used for names throughout this text.

An `implicit` statement may specify a user-defined type:

```
implicit integer (I, J, K), type (New_Type) (X, Y, Z)
```

A range of letters may also be specified. A pair of letters in alphabetical order, separated by a minus sign (regarded as a hyphen), is interpreted as including all letters between those mentioned. Thus, the following two statements are equivalent:

```
implicit complex (U, V, W, X, Y, Z)
implicit complex (U - Z)
```

Once a letter has appeared in an `implicit` statement or has been included within a range of letters, it must not appear again in an `implicit` specification.

Type property specifiers — that is, a real subtype (`kind`) selector or a character length specifier — may appear in parentheses following the data type name. These specifiers, as well as the type, then apply to names having the designated initial letters:

```
integer, parameter :: Low = Selected_Real_Kind(6)
implicit real (kind = Low) (A, B, C, D), character (len = 5) (Q - S)
```

An `implicit none` statement must not appear in a subprogram that contains any other `implicit` statements. In an internal procedure or module procedure, the implicit type rules of the host (which may be `implicit none`) are inherited and become the default implicit rules of the procedure, but these default implicit rules may be modified by `implicit` statements in the procedure.

Here are some examples.

1. The pair of declarations

```
implicit integer (A, B, C, D)
implicit real (M), complex (E, F, Z), character (len = 5) (Q)
```

   proclaim that names beginning with the letters A, B, C, or D refer to data of integer type; those beginning with M are real. Names beginning with E, F, or Z refer to complex data; and those beginning with Q refer to character strings of length 5.

2. An `implicit` statement might declare that all names beginning with the letters C, X, Y, or Z refer to data of complex type:

```
implicit complex (kind = Default_Real) (C, X - Z)
```

3. The following `implicit` statement asserts that variables whose names begin with P, Q, or R have integer type, while variables whose names begin with S have character type with length 20:

```
implicit integer (P - R), character (len = 20) (S)
```

   In a subprogram that contains this `implicit` statement, variables named `P23K`, `Result`, `Quidley`, `Pool`, and `Random_Value` would have integer type, while variables named `String_1`, `Strongly_Recommended`, `S`, and `Sam_I_Am` would have character type with length 20.

Explicit type declarations may appear in a program or subprogram that contains `implicit` statements. An explicit type declaration may refer to a name that begins with one of the letters specified in an `implicit` declaration; the explicit type specification supersedes the implicit typing. It is permissible to declare a name to have the same data type that would have been specified implicitly. For example, if both of the following statements (and no other type declarations or `implicit` statements) were included in a subprogram

```
implicit real (I)
integer :: Index
```

all variables in the program beginning with the letter `I` would have default real type as specified by the `implicit` statement, except that the particular variable named `Index` would have integer type according to the explicit type declaration for this name.

The same observation applies if the explicitly declared name consists of a single letter:

```
implicit real (I)
integer :: I
```

The name I is the name of an integer variable, while all other variables beginning with the letter I are real.

As another example, the following statements might appear in the same subprogram:

```
implicit complex (M, Q - Z)
real :: L, M, Z
character (len = 5) :: P, Q, R
```

The first statement declares that all names beginning with the letter M or with any letter of the alphabet between Q and Z (inclusive) refer to data of complex type unless a name beginning with one of those letters appears in an explicit type declaration. The `real` and `character` explicit type declarations do not apply in general to all names beginning with certain letters, but only to the specific one-letter names given in the declaration. These explicit type declarations therefore do not modify the implicit rules — all names that begin with M, Z, Q, or R retain their implicit types, except for those individual one-letter names that are explicitly mentioned.

Here is another example:

```
implicit double precision (D, T)
double precision :: A, Beta, Q(6, 10), M
```

These statements declare that A, Beta, M, and Q, as well as all names beginning with D or T, refer to values of double-precision type.

Implicit attributes other than type

Data type including derived types (structured data types), `kind`, and character length are the only attributes that can be declared implicitly. The other attributes, which cannot be declared implicitly, are as follows:

- Accessibility (`public` or `private`)
- `intent (in, out, in out)`
- `dimension` (array rank and shape)
- `save`
- `pointer`, `target`, and `allocatable`
- `external` and `intrinsic` (procedures)
- `common`, `equivalence`, and `sequence` (storage association attributes)

Initialization cannot be declared implicitly; it must be specified in a type declaration or in a `data` statement.

Implicit character type declaration

An `implicit` statement may declare an implicit character type and length for names beginning with certain letters. For example,

```
implicit character (len = 16) (A - C)
```

specifies that names beginning with the letter A, B, or C refer to a character variable of length 16. (All names covered by one `implicit character` declaration have the same length.) Of course, an explicit type declaration can specify a different type or a different character length for certain names beginning with these same letters — for example,

```
implicit character (len = 16) (A - C)
real Billy, Axe, B
character (len = 3) Abel, C
```

If all three of these declarations appear in the same program, the two explicit type declarations override the implicit specification: `Billy`, `Axe`, and `B` are real variables; `Abel` and `C` are character variables of length 3; and all other names beginning with A, B, or C represent character variables of length 16.

Default Implicit Type Specification

A reader who faithfully follows the recommendations of this textbook may be surprised to encounter existing Fortran programs that contain no data type declarations at all. This practice may have been justified for programs written in early versions of Fortran, in which almost all variables had either real or integer type. With the richer data type repertoire (including user-defined data types) and the introduction of longer names in Fortran 90 and in view of increasing emphasis on program correctness, it is no longer acceptable to write programs without declaring each name individually.

One simple reason is that spelling errors are common. If a statement in the program assigns a value to the variable `Acceleration` and an expression in a subsequent statement references a name misspelled as `Acelleration`, the latter reference will obviously not address the former variable. With full explicit type declaration, enforced by the appearance of an `implicit none` statement in every main program, module specification part, external subprogram, and block data subprogram, Fortran would presumably discover the misspelled name during compilation. (If a misspelling changes one valid name into another valid name, the compiler will not complain unless there is some other inconsistency in the usage of these names.)

However, thousands of lines of Fortran programs have been written without type declarations. The rules of implicit typing are presented here so that you can understand such programs when you encounter them.

In the absence of any explicit or implicit type declaration that applies to a name (in a subprogram without an `implicit none` statement), its data type is determined according to the following default implicit type rules:

1. If the first character of the name is one of the letters I, J, K, L, M, or N, the data type is integer (with default `kind`).
2. If the first character of the name is any letter other than I, J, K, L, M, or N, the data type is real (with default `kind`).
3. There is no default implicit typing for any data types other than default integer and default real. Variables of data types other than integer and real (logical, character,

complex, double-precision, and derived types) and those of real and integer types with nondefault subtypes must have their data types specified either by a declared implicit type specification or by an explicit type declaration.

Thus the default rules have the same effect as the `implicit` statement

```
implicit real (A - H, O - Z), integer (I - N)
```

except that the latter precludes other `implicit` statements in the same subprogram. According to the default rules, the following variables have integer type:

```
I15      J24K     Ike      Loop     Kim
J123T    Mass     N_Y_1    N        L3
Last     Kount
```

And, the following variables are of real type:

```
Temp     XX       F55      P3_ZK    Result
Alpha    A        X        Total    Count
```

A subprogram may contain `implicit` statements that do not cover all letters of the alphabet. For example, if the only `implicit` statement in a particular subprogram is

```
implicit complex (M, Q - Z)
```

default implicit type rules apply to the remaining letters. Thus, the letters `I` through `L` and `N` continue to imply integer type, and all other letters will continue to imply real type.

EXAMPLE D.2

```
! Example D.2. Combination of declared implicit and default implicit typing.
  program Conquest
    implicit complex (M, Q - Z)
    integer :: M, Q, V = 0, Z = 3
    real :: Lone_Mountain, Mississippi = 1.234, Zelda
    character (len = 5) :: Pine_Tree, Quips, Rapunzel
! start program Conquest
    read *, M, Q, Lord, Mary
    Amazon = 1.2 * Mississippi
    King = Lord + 3
    Queen = Mary
    print *, King, Lord, M, Q, V, Z                        ! Integer type
    print *, Amazon, Lone_Mountain, Mississippi, Zelda        ! Real type
    print *, Mary, Queen                                   ! Complex type
    print *, Pine_Tree, Quips, Rapunzel                  ! Character type
  end program Conquest
```

The implicit declaration in Example D.2 causes all names beginning with the letter `M` or with any letter of the alphabet between `Q` and `Z` (inclusive) to refer to data of complex type unless a name beginning with one of those letters appears in an explicit type declaration. The `integer`, `real`, and `character` explicit type declarations apply to the specific names that appear in the declaration. Thus, you apply the default implicit type rules to determine the data types of the variables not otherwise covered: `Amazon` is real, while `King` and `Lord` are integer variables. The implicit declaration applies to `Queen` and `Mary`. The `integer`, `real` and `character` type declarations supersede both the implicit declaration (in the case of `M`, `Q`, `V`, `Z`, `Mississippi`, `Zelda`, `Quips`, and `Rapunzel`) and the default implicit rules (in the case of `Lone_Mountain` and `Pine_Tree`).

Alternative Declaration Forms for Strings

Some variant forms for array declarations have already been described in the text. There are also several alternative syntactic forms for declaring character length. In the following list, the first form is the one used in this text; the others are some of the more useful variants. In the last form, *Length* must be an integer literal constant; specification expressions are permitted in the other forms. The last two forms, with the asterisk, are permitted only for the default subtype. The second form is permitted for default subtype or when a `kind` = specifier *follows* the *Length value* specifier.

```
character (len = Length value ) :: List
character ( Length value ) :: List
character * ( Length value ) :: List
character * Length :: List
```

As another alternative, the length can be specified in the *List*, in either the entity-oriented or the attribute-oriented form. Here are some examples:

```
character (len = 7) :: A, B
character (7) :: A, B
character * 7 :: A, B
character :: A * 7, B * 23
```

In a declaration for an array of character strings, any of the variant array declaration forms may be combined with any of the variant character length forms — for example,

```
character * 7, dimension(17) :: A, B
character :: A(10) * 5
```

D.2 TRADITIONAL FORMS FOR RELATIONAL OPERATORS

Fortran 90 defines the symbolic forms `==`, `/=`, `<`, `<=`, `>`, and `>=` as alternatives to the traditional forms provided by previous Fortran versions. These traditional forms and their symbolic equivalents are as follows:

Traditional notation	Symbolic notation	Meaning
`.eq.`	`==`	Is equal to
`.ne.`	`/=`	Is not equal to
`.lt.`	`<`	Is less than
`.le.`	`<=`	Is less than or equal to
`.gt.`	`>`	Is greater than
`.ge.`	`>=`	Is greater than or equal to

D.3 THE `data` STATEMENT

Initial values for a list of variables may be declared in a separate `data` statement. It is not necessary for all of the variables in the list to have the same data type (or other attributes). The general form of this declaration is

`data` *List of variables* / *List of constants* /

The *List of variables* consists of names of variables (separated by commas). The *List of constants* provides the corresponding values, which may be explicit constants, named constants, or structure constructors, but must not be expressions. In this context, a numerical constant with a sign is considered to be a *signed constant* rather than an expression.

The data type of each name in the *List of variables* must agree with the type of the corresponding constant when either has type character or logical. A constant of any numerical type (integer, real, double precision, or complex) may correspond to a variable of any numerical type; data type conversion will occur automatically, if necessary, in the same manner as for mixed-type assignment.

The length of a character variable in the *List of variables* need not match that of the corresponding character constant. The constant will be extended with blanks on the right or truncated from the right, if necessary (as for assignment), to match the length of the character variable.

A sequence of identical constants in the *List of constants* may be replaced by an integer *repeat count* followed by an asterisk and a single copy of the constant. The effect of Example 1.1 could be obtained with `data` declarations, as shown in Example D.3.

EXAMPLE D.3

```
! Example D.3. Initial value in data statement.
  program Initial_4
    implicit none
    real :: R, S, T, U, V, W
    integer :: Mt, Nobody
    data R, T, U, W, Mt / -9.25, 5.9, 2 * 0.0, 14 /
! start program Initial_4
    read *, S, V, Nobody
    print *, R, S, T, U, V, W
    print *, Mt, Nobody
  end program Initial_4
```

Nondecimal Representation of Integers

You can write an integer constant in a `data` statement with radix (number base) 2, 8, or 16 instead of 10. Special syntax is provided so that these forms can be recognized. The letter `B` (for *binary*, radix 2), `O` (for *octal*, radix 8), or `Z` (for *hexadecimal*, radix 16) is followed by a string of digits enclosed in quotation marks or apostrophes. The digits must be appropriate to the radix: A binary digit must be `0` or `1`; an octal digit must be between `0` and `7`; and a hexadecimal digit must be a decimal digit or one of the letters `A` through `F`. For example, the integer value 200 might be written as `B"11001000"`, as `O"310"`, or as `Z"C8"`. For small integer values, the interpretation of these constants is obvious, but larger values can affect the sign of the result in a nonportable way; therefore the meaning of such constants is not specified in the Fortran standard.

Fortran input and output facilities permit reading or writing of integers in these same three alternative radix forms. That is, an internal integer value may be represented externally in a binary, an octal, or a hexadecimal form. (See the discussion of B, O, and Z format codes in Appendix B.2.)

Implied do *Loops in* data *Statements*

EXAMPLE D.4 An implied do loop may be used in a data statement in the same way as in an input or output list (see Sections 6.2 and 6.1)

```
data (A(I), I = 1, 5) / 5.1, 6.2, 7.3, 8.4, 9.5 /
```

The list of items consists of a single implied do loop that designates all the elements A(1) through A(5). The parameters (initial value, limit, and increment) must be integer constant expressions. Thus, the implied do loop

```
(A(I), I = J, M)
```

would be invalid even if values for J and M were specified in preceding data statements.

EXAMPLE D.5 A repeat count notation is acceptable within the list of constants

```
data R, (S(I), I = 1, 7), T / 4.4, 5 * 1.5, 2.5, 2 * 21.7 /
```

Five identical values of 1.5 are declared for S(1) through S(6); also, both S(7) and T are given the value 21.7.

EXAMPLE D.6 Implied do loops may be nested. In this example, the limit of the inner loop is I, which is the index variable for the outer loop

```
data ((K(I, J), J = 1, I), I = 1, 8) / 36 * 1 /
```

The lower triangular portion of the vector K is initialized with ones.

In a data statement, the parameters of the outermost implied do loop must be integer constant expressions. However, those of the inner loop may also involve integer variables that appear as parameters in the outer list of the same nest.

D.4 STATEMENT LABELS AND go to

Although the go to statement can lead to difficulties, it is a powerful and flexible construct — perhaps too powerful and flexible. Lacking such statements as `if-then-else` and `exit`, older versions of Fortran required go to statements to bridge the gap. This statement permits an arbitrary deviation of the execution sequence from that provided by any of the "structured" control constructs that have been discussed up to this point.

A go to statement requires that a specific point in the program be designated, at which execution is to continue. For this purpose, *statement labels* are provided.

Statement Labels

A label consists of one or more digits written at the left of a statement.[1] A label must not contain more than five digits, and at least one of the digits must be nonzero. Here are some statements with labels:

```
10      J = J + 1
4       read *, A, B
7231    continue
73      if (X > Y) XgY = .TRUE.
3       XgY = X > Y
```

Two labeled statements in the same program or subprogram must not have the same label. A statement label in a subprogram may be the same as a label in the host; Fortran treats them as independent labels.

Any Fortran statement except the *Dependent statement* of a simple `if` statement may be labeled. However, it is recommended that statement labels be avoided except where they are absolutely necessary.

The go to Statement

The go to statement has the form

go to *Label*

Note that the keyword go to may be written with or without a blank between go and to (see Appendix C.1). This statement specifies that the sequence of execution of the statements of the program is to be interrupted, and that the next statement to be executed is the one with the specified label — for example,

---

[1] In free source form (Appendix C.1), a label is the first lexical token of a labeled statement. (Note that no unlabeled Fortran statement begins with a digit.) The statement label must be separated from the next lexical token by at least one blank character. In fixed source form (Appendix C.2), a label occupies character positions 1 to 5 of an initial line.

```
go to 10
```

The labeled statement must appear in the same procedure as the `go to` statement that refers to it and may either precede or follow the `go to` statement. Two or more `go to` statements in the procedure may refer to the same statement label.

A labeled statement may appear in any of the *Blocks* of an `if`, a `case`, or a `do` construct. However, it is required that any `go to` statement referring to a labeled statement *inside* a block must be in the same block. A `go to` that transfers control into a block from outside the block (even from another block in the same construct) is prohibited. However, the final statement of a construct (`end if`, `end select`, or `end do`) may be labeled, and a `go to` within any block of the same construct (but not outside the construct) may refer to it.[2]

`go to` *as the Dependent Statement in a Simple* `if`

As noted previously, when the *Dependent statement* in a simple `if` is a control statement (such as an `exit` statement), executing the dependent statement when the *Condition* is true will interrupt the execution sequence. If the *Dependent statement* is not a control statement, no such interruption takes place; the statement that follows the simple `if` statement will be executed in its normal execution sequence. We now see that a `go to` statement appearing as the *Dependent statement* in a simple `if` will also interrupt the execution sequence when the *Condition* is true.

The `continue` *Statement*

A `continue` statement is simply

```
continue
```

and is usually written with a label — for example,

```
876     continue
```

Inasmuch as few labels are needed in Fortran 90 programs, `continue` statements should likewise rarely be needed. The `continue` statement has no effect on the execution of a program — it is most often employed as a placeholder for a label. A labeled `continue` statement can mark a point in the program where a label is needed, but where no particular computational action is desired. Some programmers prefer to follow the rule that all labeled statements are `continue` statements. An unlabeled `continue` statement is permitted, although such a statement would have little purpose.

Most often, a `continue` statement is the terminal statement of a traditional indexed `do` construct that is written in the label form (see Appendix D.5). Such `do` constructs will be found in existing programs, but it is recommended that loops in new programs be written with the nonlabel `do` form.

---

[2] Branching to an `end if` statement from outside the `if` construct is on the official "obsolete features" list.

Other Statements for Explicit Sequence Control

Computed go to

The *computed* go to statement provided an efficient multi-way branching mechanism, based on the value of an integer expression, in traditional versions of Fortran that did not have a case construct. Although case is a superior construct for achieving the same effect, the computed go to is still found in Fortran programs. It has the following form:

go to (*List of statement labels*) [,] *Integer expression*

The comma following the parenthesized list is optional. Each statement label in the list refers to a labeled statement in the same procedure.

Execution of a computed go to statement results in a branch to the first statement label in the list if the value of the *Integer expression* is 1, to the second statement label in the list if the value of the *Integer expression* is 2, and so on. For example,

```
go to (30, 42, 50, 9), K
```

results in a jump to the statement labeled 30 if the value of K is 1, to statement 42 if K is 2, to 50 if K is 3, and to 9 if K is 4.

If the value of the *Integer expression* is less than 1 or greater than the number of labels in the list, none of the branches is selected. Instead, control proceeds to the statement immediately following the computed go to.

Arithmetic if

Note: Arithmetic if is listed as obsolescent by the Fortran 90 standard.

As an alternative to the computed go to for three-way branching, some traditional Fortran programs employ the *arithmetic* if statement. This statement branches to one of three labels on the basis of an arithmetic expression (of real or integer type) whose value is negative, zero, or positive. The arithmetic if statement has the following form:

if (*Expression*) $Label_1$, $Label_2$, $Label_3$

Note that a jump to one of the three labels always occurs. Of course, any two of the labels may be the same. For example,

```
if (SqRt (X) - Root) 20, 40, 30
```

results in a branch to one of the three labels, depending upon whether the value of the expression SqRt (X) – Root is negative, zero, or positive. Thus, the effect is the following: If SqRt (X) is less than Root, branch to statement 20; if it is equal, branch to statement 40; and if it is greater, branch to statement 30.

D.5 ADDITIONAL do CONSTRUCT FORMS

Labeled Form of do Construct

All three of the do constructs (do while, simple do, and indexed do) described in Chapter 4 have the following nonlabeled form:

```
[ Construct name : ] do [ , ] Loop control
   Block
end do
```

A labeled form is also permitted, with two variations.

1. The construct may be closed with a labeled end do statement:

```
[ Construct name : ] do Label [ , ] Loop control
   Block
Label   end do
```

2. Alternatively, the construct may be closed with a labeled continue statement:

```
[ Construct name : ] do Label [ , ] Loop control
   Block
Label   continue
```

This form, when the *Construct name* is omitted and the *Loop control* is that of an indexed do, is in fact the traditional Fortran do loop form. The comma after the *Label* is optional, as it is in all do constructs.[3]

One point must be noted: A transfer to the terminal statement of the construct — for example, execution of a go to statement that specifies the label of the terminal statement — will properly cause execution to continue with the next traversal of the block; it has the same effect as a cycle statement. A transfer to the do statement at the head of the construct, however, is a transfer outside the block; it will cause repetition of the entire do construct from the beginning, including a new initialization of the loop control.

Whereas it is permissible to jump from a point within a do block to a point outside or to transfer from one point in the block to another (including transfer to a labeled terminal statement), it does not make sense to jump into a do block from a point outside. Such a jump would not permit the loop control to be initialized and executed correctly.

[3] The optional comma is included in examples of the labeled do form in this section of the appendix. In traditional Fortran programs with labeled do constructs and nonsignificant blanks, the comma is useful as a separator.

Indexed do *with Real Parameters*

Note: Indexed do with real parameters is listed as obsolescent by the Fortran 90 standard.

Fortran permits an indexed do statement with real expressions for the parameters *Index variable*, *Initial value*, and *Increment*. Numerical uncertainty may be introduced in the calculation of the trip count expression

1 + Floor ((*Limit* – *Initial value*) / (*Increment*))

Therefore, the precise number of repetitions is not always exactly predictable when these parameters are not integers. More consistent and nearly equivalent results can be obtained with integer parameters.

As an example, consider the statement

```
do X = 0.1, 3.1, 0.5
```

which will cause the loop to be traversed with the sequence of X values 0.1, 0.6, 1.1, 1.6, 2.1, 2.6, 3.1. The trip count calculation begins with the evaluation of (3.1 – 0.1) / (0.5), which gives 6.0; the next lower integer is 6, and we add 1 to find that the loop will be executed 7 times, as expected. Or will it? Many computers represent decimal fractions with a slight error; thus, the value of (3.1 – 0.1) may turn out to be slightly less than 3.0, in which case the quotient would be smaller than 6.0. If this happens, the final traversal of the loop with 3.1 as the value of X will not occur.

In general, then, the only proper uses of real and double-precision indexed do parameters are in cases where it is immaterial whether or not the loop is executed precisely the correct number of times. Integer parameters are appropriate where predictable results are required. For example, the do statement just mentioned could be replaced as follows:

```
do IX = 1, 31, 5
  X = 0.1 * Real (X)
```

Action Statement as a do *Construct Terminator*

Note: Action statement as a do construct terminator is listed as obsolescent by the Fortran 90 standard.

Fortran permits most other statements to replace continue in the label form of the do construct; any statement other than continue, such as an assignment statement or an input or output statement, is called an *action statement*. If the *Block* contains a go to (or other control transfer statement) referencing a labeled action statement at the end of a do construct, the action statement will be executed as part of the block before the update step begins.

Although this usage is no longer recommended, it appears in many traditional Fortran programs. The program transformations explained in the following discussion can make such programs more readable.

Nested Loops with a Common Terminal Statement

Note: Nested loops with a common terminal statement is listed as obsolescent by the Fortran 90 standard.

Another practice that is permitted by the rules of Fortran, but leads to obscure program structure, is the use of a single label (and thus a common terminal statement) for two or more do constructs in a nest. For example, the following is permitted:

```
   do 20, Row = 1, 6
     do 20, Col = 1, 6
       if ( . . . ) go to 20
        :
20     Total = . . .
```

Although this usage is no longer recommended, it appears in many traditional Fortran programs. Many programmers will at some time encounter a program that has been written disregarding (or in ignorance of) this recommendation. Thus, it is helpful to know how such a program will be interpreted according to Fortran rules. We obtain the correct interpretation if we view the labeled terminal statement as part of the innermost do construct of the nest.

The following simple transformations modernize program form and greatly improve readability without affecting program execution:

1. Insert extra end do statements after the labeled statement, one for each indexed do statement that refers to this common label.
2. Remove the label from the indexed do statements, but leave unchanged any other statements (such as go to statements) that refer to the label.

This transformation converts the program in the preceding example to the following form, whose correct interpretation is the same as that of the original nest:

```
   do Row = 1, 6
     do Col = 1, 6
       if ( . . . ) go to 20
        :
20     Total = . . .
     end do
   end do
```

The offending label no longer affects loop control; it is now merely the point of reference of the go to statement, which causes a transfer of control from one point in the innermost block to another. (If there were no remaining references to the labeled statement, the label could be removed to make the program more readable.)

This same way of viewing the terminal statement of a do loop also gives the proper interpretation in case the terminal statement is a control statement. Note that it also gives the correct answer to the question, From which points in the nest is it permissible to jump to the terminal statement? Since the terminal statement belongs to the innermost loop, a jump to that statement from an outer loop in the nest would be prohibited.

D.6 EXTERNAL FUNCTIONS AND SUBROUTINES

Independent program units with restricted data sharing have long been a feature of the Fortran language. Except for two mechanisms, argument passing and `common` storage (see Appendix E.3), data cannot be exchanged among external program units or between an external program unit and the main program.

Even for data that is shared through these mechanisms, Fortran has traditionally provided access to data values only in the form of a raw computer representation; the type, properties, and attributes of the data are not actually shared, but must be specified separately in each program unit. This independence of specifications is perhaps excessive and has some undesirable effects:

1. In a large program, many specification statements may need to be duplicated in several different program units, and all copies must be updated when a change is made.
2. Programming tricks are encouraged, such as giving a shared data item a different type or different dimensions in separate program units.

It is recommended that external subroutines and external functions be converted to internal or module procedures. A small subprogram or one that shares substantial amounts of data with a procedure that references it may be converted to an internal subprogram. Other external program units may be converted to modules (singly or in groups) simply by enclosing them between `module` and `end module` statements. For large libraries, tools are available to generate an interface block for each external procedure. These interface blocks may then be packaged into one or more modules that are imported into the procedures that use the library.

An exception to this recommendation applies to procedures whose names are used as actual arguments corresponding to dummy arguments that are procedure names. The most straightforward programming practice is to make the actual argument an external procedure, with an interface block (describing the dummy procedure) in the subprogram where the procedure name dummy argument appears.

External Procedures

An external procedure is a subroutine or function defined by an external subprogram in a separate program unit that is not a part of any host. An external subprogram has the same form as a module subprogram. It begins with a `subroutine` or `function` statement. If it contains internal subprograms, a `contains` statement must be placed between the end of the procedure and the first internal subprogram. The subprogram ends with an `end`, `end subroutine`, or `end function` statement. This statement follows the `end` statement of the last internal subprogram (if any) that it contains.

Procedure interface

Traditionally, Fortran did not provide modules or internal procedures. External subroutines and functions in separate program units were the only means of program subdivision (except for the rudimentary statement function facility described in Appendix D.9). Note that Fortran processes each program unit separately. For example, while compiling an external procedure reference in the main program, it has no access to the declarations in the external procedure.

Fortran 90 modules and internal procedures have access to additional information at the point of a procedure reference; this additional information can be supplied for external subprograms in the form of an interface block.

Automatic explicit interface. Fortran 90 obtains the necessary interface information *automatically* in the following cases:

1. When a procedure imports a module with a `use` statement, it obtains access to information specified within the module.
2. The required information is also automatically available for referencing an internal procedure from within the host subprogram or a module procedure from other procedures within the host module.
3. Information concerning procedures in the Fortran intrinsic library (Appendix A) is available to the Fortran compiler as required.
4. For a directly recursive reference from a procedure to itself, the required specifications are available: Fortran has all the information it needs to permit a procedure to reference itself.

Default implicit interface. Interface information is not automatically available for external procedures. We say that the interface to an external procedure is *implicit by default*.

In simple cases, an implicit interface may be adequate. If the external procedure reference does not involve any of a certain list of modern features (see Interface block discussion that follows), it is only necessary to coordinate specifications in the referencing program or subprogram with those in the procedure. This must be done manually; most Fortran processors do not analyze the specifications to detect inconsistencies.

For a reference to an external function, a type declaration for the external function name must be included in the program or subprogram where the reference appears.[4] The type declaration must agree with the type of the *Result name* established in the function definition.

[4] If no interface information or function type declaration is provided in the referencing procedure, the function reference expression will be given an implicit type based on the function name, as described in Appendix D.1.

It is recommended that the `external` attribute also be declared for the function name, in the case of an implicit interface:

```
complex, external :: F_Complex
```

Dummy argument types, character string lengths, and array shapes must also be coordinated for both external functions and external subroutines. The most straightforward practice (which is recommended) is to make sure that the specifications of all actual arguments agree exactly with those of the corresponding dummy arguments. However, interface independence implies the possibility of argument alignment based on sequence association (see Appendix E.4) rather than on precise argument matching.

Interface block. An explicit interface is required if a procedure reference involves any of the modern Fortran features listed next. As already noted, the required explicit interface is automatically provided for reference to an internal procedure or to a module procedure. For external procedure reference, however, the only alternative is to provide this information in the form of an *interface block* in the referencing procedure (or in a module from which it is imported), which describes the arguments of the external procedure, as well as the result value if it is a function.

An interface block for an external procedure consists essentially of a copy of a portion of the subprogram where the procedure is defined.[5] The required portion includes specifications of the type, type properties, and all other attributes of the *dummy arguments* and of the *function result* (if it is a function). The names of the dummy arguments in the interface block may be different from those in the original procedure, however. Note that an interface block may inherit specifications from a module.

Conditions that require explicit interface (and thus require an interface block for an external procedure reference) include the following:

If the external procedure is a function and its result variable is an array, a pointer, or a character string whose length is determined during execution of the procedure

If any dummy argument of the external procedure is a pointer, a pointer target, or an assumed-shape array (one whose shape will be assumed from the actual argument array)

If the external procedure has an optional dummy argument or is referenced with an argument keyword

An interface block is also *permitted* whenever it is not *required*. It is recommended that any program or subprogram containing a reference to an external procedure contain (or import) an interface block for the procedure.

If several procedures make reference to the same external procedure, this alternative has the disadvantage that the interface information must be copied into each subprogram that invokes the procedure. (The `include` feature described in Appendix D.11,

[5] Interface blocks are also used for a completely separate purpose relating to generic functions, operators, and assignment, as described in Sections 7.5 and 7.6.

may simplify the copying of specification information.) Particular care is required in the presence of implicit type specification (see Appendix D.1) to ensure that types are applied consistently in all procedures where the interface information is used.

Copying may be avoided by placing the interface block in a module and importing it as required. However, this method has little advantage over defining the *entire procedure* in a module, unless the complete text of the procedure definition is not available. There are some cases in which this latter situation might occur. For instance, the procedure might be in a library for which the source text is not available. Or, in a program development environment at a certain stage, references to a particular unimplemented procedure might appear only in program branches whose execution is currently inhibited.

Traditional Array and String Argument Forms

Fixed-size, adjustable, and assumed-size dummy argument arrays

In traditional Fortran programs, prior to the advent of assumed-shape dummy argument arrays, only fixed-size, adjustable, and assumed-size dummy argument arrays were provided. The basic difficulty with these dummy argument arrays stems from the fact that the shape of the corresponding actual argument array must *separately* be completely specified in the program or subprogram from which the procedure is referenced, and there is no way to ensure that these shape specifications agree. In fact, the corresponding actual argument is permitted to be an array element (related to the dummy argument by *sequence association*) instead of an array.

Recall the following definitions:

1. A *fixed-size* array has dimensions that do not change. The dimension bounds in the array declaration are numerical constants, named constants, or constant expressions. They contain no variables except those that are permitted in specification expressions — for example, variable arguments to inquiry functions.
2. An *adjustable* array is a dummy argument array whose dimension declaration expressions contain one or more variables. These must have defined values at the time of procedure entry; hence, they must be imported, inherited, passed as arguments, or in `common` storage. The values of the dimension bounds for an adjustable array are determined by evaluating the variables in the declaration expressions at the time of procedure entry.
3. An *assumed-size* array is a fixed-size dummy argument array or an adjustable dummy argument array whose last dimension bound is to be determined from the actual argument array. The upper bound of the last dimension is specified as an asterisk. (Note the difference between *assumed size* and *assumed shape.*)

The features considered obsolete are illustrated by the following declarations.

```
function A (C, D, E, F, N) result (G)
  implicit none
  integer, parameter :: K = 17
  real, intent (in) :: C(K)                    ! Fixed-size array
  real, intent (in) :: D(N)                    ! Adjustable array
  real, intent (in) :: E(K, *)                ! Assumed-size array
  real, intent (in) :: F(N, *)                ! Assumed-size array
  integer, intent (in) :: N
    :
 end function A
```

The function A has array dummy arguments C, D, E, and F and a scalar dummy argument N. C is a fixed-size array because its dimension bound is a constant. D is an adjustable array because its dimension bound is a dummy argument. E and F are assumed-size arrays because the last dimension bound is an asterisk. (The first bound for E is fixed and for F is adjustable.)

Argument association for these arrays is based on the standard Fortran array element sequence. Fortran associates the actual argument with the *base element* of the dummy argument array — that is, with the first element in the standard sequence. Elements of the dummy argument array are located, in relation to the base element, according to the shape specification for the dummy argument array. This argument passing mechanism is simple, but the programmer must ensure that the actual array in the referencing procedure provides adequate storage space for the dummy array in the procedure.

It is suggested here that the actual array corresponding to an explicit-shape dummy argument array be declared with precisely matching dimensions. Although this practice is recommended, certain special effects can be achieved by relaxing this rule. As one example, the corresponding actual argument may be an *array element.* The effective actual argument is then a sequence of array elements, in standard Fortran array element sequence, with the designated actual argument element as the base element of the sequence. (See also Appendix E.4.)

Fixed-size arrays as dummy arguments. In the shape specification for a fixed-size dummy argument array, the upper and lower bounds for each dimension are given by constant expressions, which are specification expressions that *do not* contain any variables, but may include operators and certain intrinsic functions that the Fortran compiler is able to evaluate.

Adjustable arrays as dummy arguments. An adjustable dummy argument array differs from a fixed-size dummy argument array in only one way: The specification expression in the upper or lower bound for some dimension *does* contain a variable. However, the following rules must be observed:

1. An adjustable array must be a dummy argument.
2. Each subscript expression must be a specification expression. Recall that variables in a specification expression must be imported from a module, be inherited from a host program or subprogram, or appear in the procedure as a dummy argument or in a common statement (see Appendix E.3). Each such variable must have a defined value at the time the procedure is referenced.
3. The corresponding actual argument array must be a fixed-size array — or, in a hierarchy of procedures, the actual argument array may correspond to a fixed-size array at some higher level.

In practice, the principal difference between adjustable arrays and assumed-shape arrays is that the declaration for an adjustable array specifies the dimension information *explicitly*. From a philosophical viewpoint, a much more important difference between the two mechanisms is that they represent two quite different views of the nature of an array object. Fortran handles an adjustable array as a *sequence of storage units* whose initial point is given by the actual argument array or array element and whose shape is established by dimension information in the procedure. An assumed-shape array, however, is viewed as a *complete, self-contained array object* whose shape is passed to the procedure in a natural way. One consequence is that an assumed-shape array dummy argument can correspond to an actual argument that is an array section or other array object that does not necessarily occupy contiguous storage. The assumed-shape array mechanism sacrifices the possibility of cute tricks, such as inventing a completely new shape for the dummy argument array in blissful independence of the actual argument shape (see Appendix E.4).

EXAMPLE D.7 In the following program, the first reference to `Frobenius_Norm` will assume that the dummy argument array `A` is 40 by 40; the second time, `A` will be assumed to be 4 by 4. The current value of `N` is used for locating the specific elements of `A` that are needed in each case.

```
! Example D.7.
  program Schwarzkopf
    implicit none
    intrinsic Sum
    integer, parameter :: BIG = 40, JIG = 4
    real, dimension(BIG, BIG) :: Wig
    real, dimension(JIG, JIG) :: Fig
    external Frobenius_Norm
! start program Schwarzkopf
    read *, Wig
    print *, Frobenius_Norm (Wig, BIG)
    read *, Fig
    print *, Frobenius_Norm (Fig, JIG)
contains
    real function Frobenius_Norm (A, N) result (Total)
      real, intent (in), dimension(N, N) :: A
      integer, intent (in) :: N
  ! start function Frobenius_Norm
      Total = Sum (A ** 2)
    end function Frobenius_Norm
  end program Schwarzkopf
```

Assumed-size arrays as dummy arguments. A `dimension` attribute specification has three separate effects, only two of which apply to assumed-size arrays (note the difference between *assumed size* and *assumed shape*):

1. It informs Fortran that the name is an array name and establishes the rank of the array. Thus, it "authorizes" appearance of the array name, along with the specified number of subscript expressions, to form an array element name.
2. It specifies the sequential arrangement of the array elements (the *array shape*) and thus permits Fortran to locate a particular array element. The specification gives values that are needed for the standard Fortran array element sequence formula.
3. It determines the total number of elements and hence the total amount of space (the *array size*) to be reserved for the array.

Only the first two of these effects apply to an assumed-size dummy array. Operations that require knowledge of the total number of array elements, such as whole-array input and output, are not permitted for assumed-size arrays.

An assumed-size dummy argument array is permitted in a procedure when the total number of elements does not need to be specified. The function Frobenius_Norm in Example D.7 does not actually make any use of the fact that the matrix A contains 1600 elements. The declaration for A is needed only to establish that A is an array and to establish the element sequence.

EXAMPLE D.8 The function does not need to know the number of columns of A

```
! Example D.8.
  function Frobenius_Norm (A, N) result (Total)
    real :: Total
    real, intent (in), dimension(N, *) :: A
    integer, intent (in) :: N
    intrinsic :: Sum
! start function Frobenius_Norm
    Total = Sum (A(1: N, 1: N) ** 2)
  end function Frobenius_Norm
```

Generally, we can leave unspecified the upper subscript range bound for the last dimension in the definition for any explicit-shape dummy argument array by writing an asterisk in the place of this last upper subscript bound expression.

```
real, dimension(40, *), intent (in) :: A
real, dimension(N, *), intent (in) :: A
real, dimension(*) :: X
```

Since this bound has no effect on the arrangement of the array elements, it is not needed except when the procedure must specify the total number of elements in the array.

We see that an assumed-size dummy argument array has a specified rank and shape, except that the total number of elements is not specified. Thus, assumed-size arrays cannot be used in procedures that need definite array size information. For example, when the name of a whole dummy argument array appears in an input or output list (in the procedure), indicating that the entire array is to be transmitted, data transmission is controlled by the array declaration in the procedure and requires knowledge of all subscript range bounds. Fortran would be unable to correctly interpret the statement

```
print *, A
```

if it were added to the function definition in Example D.7 unless the declaration for A is modified to provide an explicit upper bound for the second dimension.

Fixed-size and adjustable character dummy arguments

Much of the preceding discussion of fixed-size and adjustable dummy argument arrays applies, after appropriate adjustment of terminology, to fixed-size and adjustable character dummy arguments. (There is no character string counterpart to assumed-size arrays.) Again, the difficulty stems from the fact that the length of the corresponding actual argument must be specified *separately* in the program or subprogram from which the procedure is referenced, and there is no way to ensure that these length specifications agree. The recommended alternative is to use assumed-length strings for all dummy arguments of character type.

Recall the following definitions:

1. A *fixed-length* character variable has constant declared length.
2. An *adjustable* character variable is declared with a length that is a specification expression to be evaluated at the time of procedure entry.
3. An *assumed-length* character variable is a dummy argument character variable for which the length is not specified. At procedure entry, such a character variable assumes the length of the corresponding actual argument.

The features that are considered to be obsolete are illustrated by the following declarations.

```
function A (C, D, N) result (G)
  implicit none
  intrinsic Len
  integer, parameter :: K = 17
  character (len = K), intent (in) :: C
  character (len = N), intent (in) :: D
  integer, intent (in) :: N
end function A
```

The function A has dummy arguments C and D of character type and N of integer type. C is a fixed-length dummy argument because its length specifier is a constant. D is an adjustable dummy argument because its length specifier is a dummy argument.

D.7 ALTERNATIVE ENTRY POINTS FOR PROCEDURES

Some subprograms require two or more rather independent sequences of operations upon some data that is not required in any other subprogram. Traditional Fortran programs, lacking modules and internal procedures, sometimes accomplish this task in an external procedure with more than one starting point. Secondary entries are provided through the use of the `entry` statement, whose general form is

`entry` *Name* (*Dummy arg list*)

Each entry is regarded as defining another procedure within the same subprogram. These separate procedures share all the specifications of the subprogram including variable declarations, derived type definitions, and internal procedure interface information. It is also permissible, although rather dangerous, for these procedures to share some of the same instructions.

An `entry` statement may appear anywhere in an external subprogram or in a module subprogram except within `if`, do, `case`, and `where` constructs. An internal subprogram must not contain an `entry` statement.

An entry *Name* in a procedure must not be the same as any dummy argument name. If the procedure is a subroutine, all entry names are subroutine names; if the procedure is a function, all entry names are function names. If the procedure is recursive, any entry name may be called recursively.

Subroutine Entry

Suppose that an external subroutine reads data into an array, sorts it into a predetermined sequence, and prints the resulting sorted array values. However, for some purposes, it is desirable to use the same subroutine with data that has already been read into the array. We may define the subroutine `InSort` for sorting with input, and we provide a secondary entry named `ArSort` for sorting data that is already in an array.

EXAMPLE D.9

```
! Example D.9. External subroutine with two entry names.
! Call InSort to read an array and sort it.
  subroutine InSort (Array, NMax, N)
    implicit none
    real, dimension(0: NMax - 1), intent (in out) :: Array
    integer, intent (in) :: N
    integer :: EoF
! start subroutine InSort
    do N = 0, NMax - 1
     read (*, "(F10.0)", iostat = EoF) Array(N)
      if (EoF < 0) exit
    end do
    print *, N, "␣values␣have␣been␣read␣into␣Array.␣"
! Call ArSort to sort data already in the array.
  entry ArSort (Array, N)
          :
!        (sort procedure)
          :
    print "(5 G15.6)", (Array(I), I = 1, N)
  end subroutine InSort
```

When the external subroutine in Example D.9 is called using the procedure name `InSort`, execution begins at the first executable statement of the subroutine. After the first `print` statement is executed, the `entry` statement is ignored and execution continues at the point beyond the `entry` statement. When `ArSort` is called, execution begins at the first executable statement after the `entry` statement.

Note that the two entry points may have different argument lists. The call to either name must provide actual arguments corresponding to the particular list for the entry point that is used. For example, `ArSort` does not use `NMax`, so this argument is not included in calls to `ArSort`.

Function Entry

An `entry` statement may have a `result` clause. Each entry is regarded as defining another function. The function result value may be established by giving a value to any *Result name*.

If all entry result names in a function procedure have the same type, kind, and shape as the function result variable, each entry name is an alternative name (alias) for the function result variable. In this case, the result variable may have any intrinsic or derived type and it may be an array or a pointer.

If any of the entry names differs in type, kind, or shape from the function result name, the following two restrictions apply:

1. None of the results may be arrays, pointers, or derived type structures.
2. Either the results must all have default numeric types (any mixture of default integer, default real, double-precision real, and default complex) or they must all have default character type with the same length.

D.8 STATEMENT LABELS AS ARGUMENTS

A Motivation: Exception Handling

In many of the procedures illustrated so far, we have tacitly assumed that the input arguments have "proper" values — that is, values that fall in ranges for which the task to be performed makes sense. For example, a certain subroutine may assume that one of its arguments does not exceed the size of an array. It is presumed that if there is any doubt, the main program will test for improper variable values before using them as actual arguments. If such tests are not made, the results produced by the procedure may be nonsensical and may lead to errors later on.

Other examples arise in the use of common mathematical functions. Intrinsic procedures may require argument values in an acceptable range; for example, `SqRt` may require that its argument value be greater than or equal to zero. The particular action taken when such an error occurs may depend on the processor; in some cases, execution of the program is abruptly terminated.

It would be helpful if either the procedure or the referencing procedure would assume responsibility for checking parameter values and taking appropriate corrective action. In practice, since activation of a function occurs implicitly (in the middle of the evaluation of an expression), it is awkward for the referencing procedure to detect an error that occurs during execution of the function, to take corrective action, and then to resume evaluation of the expression. Alternatives are to check the argument values before executing the statement containing the function reference, to rearrange the entire program to use a subroutine instead of a function, or to attempt corrective action after completing execution of the statement containing the function reference. The third alternative may be particularly awkward if the expression affects the action of a control statement such as `if-then`.

With subroutines, we have a bit more flexibility. The most straightforward approach is to add an extra `Error` argument for error detection purposes. The subroutine assigns one of several values to this argument as a result of tests made in the subroutine. Thus, for each of several distinct conditions, the `Error` argument may be assigned a different value. Upon return to the calling program, a control statement can be executed to direct control to the desired location, where alternative action can be taken.

EXAMPLE D.10 The program in Example 3.10 can be used as the basis for a subroutine to find all roots of a quadratic equation. The main program reads coefficients `C1`, `C2`, and `C3` corresponding to the dummy arguments `A`, `B`, and `C` in the subroutine `Quad`. The subroutine sets values of the argument variables `R1` and `R2` and an "indicator" variable, `Indic`. The subroutine sets this integer dummy argument variable to one of three values:

1. `A` is zero. The given coefficients do not specify a quadratic equation. The values of `R1` and `R2` are set to zero.
2. `A` is not zero, but the discriminant is negative. There are two conjugate complex roots. `R1` is set to the real part; `R2`, to the imaginary part.
3. `A` is not zero, and the discriminant is nonnegative. There are two real roots (which may be equal). `R1` and `R2` are set to the values of these two real roots.

Upon return from the subroutine, the main program takes the appropriate action, based on the value of `Indic`.

```
! Example D.10a. Subroutine to find all roots of a quadratic equation,
! given the coefficients A, B, and C. Sets Indic to 1 if A, B, and C do
! not specify a quadratic equation, to 2 if the equation has two complex
! roots, or to 3 if the equation has two real roots (which may be equal).
  subroutine Quad (A, B, C, R1, R2, Indic)
    implicit none
    real, intent (in) :: A, B, C
    real, intent (out) :: R1, R2
    integer, intent (out) :: Indic
    real :: Part1, Part2, Discriminant
    intrinsic SqRt, Abs, Sign
! start subroutine Quad
    if (A == 0.0) then
      R1 = 0.0
      R2 = 0.0
      Indic = 1
      return
    else                                 ! A is not zero. Find the discriminant.
      Part1 = -B / (2.0 * A)
      Discriminant = B ** 2 - 4.0 * A * C
      Part2 = SqRt (Abs (Discriminant))
      if (Discriminant < 0.0) then     ! Negative discriminant. Roots are complex.
        R1 = Part1
        R2 = Part2
        Indic = 2
        return
      else                             ! For maximum accuracy, force signs to agree.
        Part2 = Sign (Part2, Part1)
        R1 = Part1 + Part2
        if (R1 /= 0.0) then
          R2 = C / (A * R1)
        else
          R2 = Part1 - Part2
        end if ! (R1 /= 0.0)
        Indic = 3
        return
      end if ! (Discriminant < 0.0)
    end if ! (A == 0.0)
  end subroutine Quad
```

Using Alternate Returns

Note: Alternate returns is listed as obsolescent by the Fortran 90 standard. This use of statement labels, like those described in Appendix D.4, can interfere with program comprehension.

A second approach to exception handling involves the use of a statement label as an actual argument. The special "alternate return" form provides that one or more of the dummy arguments of a subroutine (not a function) may consist of merely an asterisk. The corresponding actual argument must be a statement label in the referencing procedure. Within the subroutine, the statement

```
return 1
```

causes a return to the statement label corresponding to the *first* asterisk that appears among the dummy arguments. Similarly,

```
return 2
```

causes a return to the statement label corresponding to the *second* asterisk among the dummy arguments, and so on. Corresponding to an asterisk in the dummy argument position, the actual argument in each `call` statement that references the subroutine must appear as a statement label preceded by an asterisk.

For example, in the subroutine `Quad`, suppose that we replace the pair of statements

```
Indic = 1
return
```

by the statement

```
return 1
```

and similarly delete the other statements that assign values to `Indic`, changing the following `return` statements to `return 2` and `return 3`, respectively. Also, we would rewrite the dummy argument list as

```
(A, B, C, R1, R2, *, *, *)
```

The last three actual arguments in a reference to `Quad` must be statement labels preceded by asterisks, as in the following main program.

```
! Example D.10b. Main program using Quad to find roots of quadratic equation with
! coefficients C1, C2, and C3.
  program Use_Me_Too
    implicit none
    real :: C1, C2, C3, R1, R2
    external Quad                                                   ! Subroutine
! start program Use_Me_Too
    read *, C1, C2, C3
    print *, "⊥Coefficients⊥are:⊥", C1, C2, C3
    call Quad (C1, C2, C3, R1, R2, *10, *20, *30)
    stop
10      print *, "⊥Not⊥a⊥quadratic.⊥"
          stop
20      print *, "⊥Complex⊥roots:⊥", R1, "⊥+⊥or⊥-⊥i⊥", R2
          stop
30      print *, "⊥Real⊥roots:⊥", R1, R2
  end program Use_Me_Too
```

Execution of one of the `return` statements will select the actual statement label (10, 20, or 30) that corresponds to the designated one of the asterisks in the dummy argument list. The designated statement will be executed immediately upon return from the subroutine.

D.9 STATEMENT FUNCTIONS

Whereas a module procedure or an external procedure is defined independently, a *statement function* is defined by a single statement that appears within the referencing procedure. A statement function produces a single scalar result value and is referenced by appearance of the function name, with an argument list, in an expression in the same way as any other function. Thus, a statement function is analogous to an internal function definition containing a single assignment statement.

A statement function definition has the form

Statement function name (*Dummy arg list*) = *Expression*

Although it has the form of an executable assignment statement, such a statement is actually a nonexecutable function definition. Fortran recognizes a statement function definition by the fact that it consists of a name followed by a parenthesized list followed by an assignment operator, and the name does not appear in an array declaration.

The type and type properties of the function result are those of the statement function name, which should be declared in a type declaration in the host procedure (see also Appendix D.1). A statement function result must not have the `dimension` or `pointer` attribute.

Certain restrictions must be observed in defining and referencing statement functions:

1. The form can be used only when the function is simple enough to be defined in a single statement.
2. A statement function is known only within the subprogram in which it is defined. Thus, it cannot be referenced from another subprogram (although, of course, an identical statement function definition can be written as part of another subprogram). A statement function definition is not permitted within an internal subprogram. A statement function name must not be passed as a procedure name argument and must not appear in an `external` statement.
3. The dummy arguments must be scalar variables. The corresponding actual arguments may be variables, constants, or other expressions of matching type and must have defined values when the statement function is referenced. Whole-array expressions are not permitted in a statement function definition.
4. Variables in the defining expression that do not appear in the dummy argument list are inherited from the host subprogram. The current values of those variables in the host subprogram are used in computing the function value.
5. The defining expression may involve intrinsic functions, external or internal functions, or other statement functions; however, if other statement functions are used, they must be defined earlier in the subprogram. That is, a statement function must precede other statement function definitions that refer to it.

EXAMPLE D.11 In the following program, the first read statement obtains values for N and T. The value of N specifies how many data cases follow, and the value of T is used by the statement function SumSq. If the function value is positive, its square root is printed; if it is negative, the square root is not calculated

```
! Example D.11.
program Light_Cone
  implicit none
  real :: X, Y, Z, T, SumSq
  integer :: N, I
  intrinsic SqRt
  SumSq (X, Y, Z) = X ** 2 + Y ** 2 + Z ** 2 - T ** 2 ! Stmt function definition
! start program Light_Cone
  read *, N, T
  do I = 1, N
    read *, A, B, C
    write (*, *, advance = "NO") A, B, C, T
    if (SumSq (A, B, C) >= 0.0) then
      R = SqRt (SumSq (A, B, C))
      print *, R
    end if
  end do
end program Light_Cone
```

D.10 VERTICAL SPACING CONTROL FOR LINE PRINTERS

A Fortran processor may designate certain output devices as *line printers* on which a special form of vertical spacing control will be applied. When records are transmitted to such a device, the first character of each output record is not printed but is used to control vertical spacing during the print operation; the remaining characters actually appear on the printed line. Because there is no portable way for a program to determine in advance whether or not the default output device is such a line printer, the examples in this text have a blank character in the first character position of each output record. This blank character will designate single spacing if it is used as a vertical spacing control character.

The most common spacing code is single line spacing — the line printer advances by one line position *before* the printing takes place. The character code that indicates single line spacing is a blank. We can force a blank in the first character position of an output record in any of several ways. The simplest technique is to make the first code an X code such as 1X or 5X or a tab code. Another possibility is to transmit a blank from the format description (as explained in Appendix B.8). Or, we can widen the first output field to provide it with more than enough character positions to print the required data and its sign. However, this latter method incurs the risk (especially with the I and F output codes) that the data may exceed the expected size and overflow into the vertical spacing control position.

Fortran defines the following standard vertical spacing control characters for line printers:

Desired vertical spacing	Required character code
Single space	␣ (blank)
Double space	0 (zero)
Skip to top of next page	1 (one)
No space (overprint)	+ (plus)

For a line printer, it must be kept in mind that the first character of *each record* controls vertical spacing. The first format code after any slash will correspond to the first field of a new record and will therefore include vertical spacing information. When the format rescan point is other than the beginning of the format description, vertical spacing should be considered again at this point in the format because the first format code after the rescan point will also correspond to the first field of a new record. In Example B.19, we stated that the format

```
(1X, 2 G10.2 / (1X, 3 G10.4))
```

would be suitable. Note that the format code 1X, which will cause one character position to be skipped, has been included at the beginning of the format and again just after the rescan point (after the inner left parenthesis). Thus, each new record will begin a blank character. Since this first character is not printed but controls vertical spacing, the effect is to guarantee that single line spacing will occur just before each line is printed.

For line printing, a character constant may provide vertical spacing control. The character constant format code "␣" would have the same effect as the code 1X — that is, to cause one blank character to be transmitted to the output record. Other control characters, such as 0 to indicate double spacing, can be produced by a character constant format code.

EXAMPLE D.12 The following program will produce double-spaced lines on a line printer (compare Example B.19)

```
! Example D.12.
  program Effort
    implicit none
    integer :: N
    real :: Fee, Fie, Foe
    real, dimension(100) :: Fum
    character (len = *), parameter :: FMT_25 = "('0', 3 G10.2 / ('0', 4 G10.4))"
! start program Effort
      :
    print FMT_25, Fee, Fie, Foe, (Fum(J), J = 1, N)
  end program Effort
```

D.11 ADDITIONAL INPUT AND OUTPUT FEATURES

The `include` feature and `namelist` formatting have long been supported in various forms by many processors, but they are standardized for the first time in Fortran 90. For purposes of this text, however, both of these features are considered obsolete.

The traditional `cH` or Hollerith format code discussed here is generally inferior to the character constant format code described in Appendix B.8.

Incorporating Text into a Source Program with `include`

The following is quoted from the Fortran standard, ISO / IEC 1539 : 1991 (E):

> Additional text may be incorporated into the source text of a program unit during processing. This is accomplished with the `include` line, which has the form
>
> `include` *Char-literal-constant*
>
> The *Char-literal-constant* must not have a `kind` type parameter value that is a named-constant.
>
> An `include` line is not considered a statement.
>
> An `include` line must appear on a single source line where a statement may appear; it must be the only nonblank text on this line other than an optional trailing comment. Thus a statement label is not allowed.

The effect of the `include` line is as if the referenced source text physically replaced the `include` line prior to program processing. Included text may contain any source text, including additional `include` lines; such nested `include` lines are similarly replaced with the specified source text. The maximum depth of nesting of any nested `include` lines is processor dependent. Inclusion of the source text referenced by an `include` line must not, at any level of nesting, result in inclusion of the same source text.

When an `include` line is resolved, the first included statement line must not be a continuation line and the last included statement line must not be continued.

The interpretation of *Char-literal-constant* is processor dependent. An example of a possible valid interpretation is that *Char-literal-constant* is the name of a file that contains the source text to be included.

Input and Output with Namelist Formatting

The control list of a `read`, `write`, or `print` statement may contain a "`namelist` group name" (optionally preceded by "`nml =`") instead of a format specifier. Such a statement does not have an input or output list.

The `namelist` group name must be declared, imported, or inherited by each procedure that uses it in an input or output statement. A `namelist` declaration has the form

`namelist` / *Namelist group name* / *Variable name list*

EXAMPLE D.13 The variables named in the list may include structures, arrays, and array sections, as the following example shows

```
! Example D.13.
  program Names
    implicit none
    real :: A, B, C, V, W, X(5), Y(3)
    namelist / N_List / A, B, C
    namelist / S_List / A, V, W, C, X, Y

! start program Names
    read *, V, W, X, Y
    open (1, file = "nml_data.txt")
    open (2, file = "nml_out.txt")
    read (1, N_List)
    write (2, S_List)
  end program Names
```

Data for `namelist` input begins with an ampersand followed by the `namelist` group name, which must match the group name in the input control list. Next comes a sequence of name–value pairs, ending with a slash. The name in each pair must be one of the variable names listed in the `namelist` declaration. An equals sign separates the name in each pair from the value. The value in each pair is a single input data item, except that the value may consist of a set of data items when the named variable is a structure, an array, or an array section. The data items are separated in the same way as list-directed input items and may include null items and repeat counts.

Output produced with `Namelist` formatting appears on the external file in the same way as list-directed output, except that an ampersand followed by the `namelist` group name will appear at the beginning of the first record written, and each name in the variable name list of the `namelist` statement appears in order followed by an equals sign and then by its value (which is a single data item or a set of items for a structure, an array, or an array section).

Hollerith Format Code

An alternative to the character constant format code described in Appendix B.8 is the `H` format code, also known as Hollerith format code (for punched-card data processing pioneer Herman Hollerith). This code cannot be used for input. The format `cH` (where the *character count* `c` is an integer expressed as a string of decimal digits) causes the `c` characters immediately following the `H` to be transmitted to a field of `c` characters in the output record. For example, the format specification in Example B.21 may be replaced as follows:

```
print "(20H␣After␣event␣number␣,␣I5,␣&
  &␣36H␣the␣largest␣element␣is␣at␣location␣,␣I5,␣&
  &␣19H␣and␣its␣weight␣is␣,␣E15.7)", I1, L1, W1
```

A disadvantage of `H` format code, especially for long strings, is the difficulty of determining the correct value for the character count `c`. A slight advantage is that the string appears in a format statement without a delimiting quotation mark or apostrophe, for example:

```
27  format (1X, 20H␣Don't␣say␣"ain't".␣)
```

The string in this format code would be awkward to express as a delimited character constant because it includes both apostrophes and quotation marks.

Appendix E Storage Sequence and Storage Association

E.1 STORAGE SEQUENCE

Fortran stores data of default numeric types (default integer, default real, double-precision real, default complex, and default logical) in *numeric storage units.* Data of default character type occupies *character storage units*. Certain other data occupies *unspecified storage units*. The traditional Fortran data model is heavily storage-oriented and provides ways of allocating a given *storage sequence* (a sequence of numeric storage units or a sequence of character storage units) to data objects with different names, which are then said to be *associated* by storage association (`common` or `equivalence`) or by sequence association (between actual and dummy arguments).

Numeric Storage Units

The following rules apply to numeric storage units:

1. A nonpointer scalar object of default integer, default real, or default logical type occupies one numeric storage unit.
2. A nonpointer scalar object of double-precision real type or default complex type occupies two numeric storage units. (Note that storage sequences for double-precision complex data are *unspecified*, rather than numerical.)
3. A nonpointer scalar object of a derived type occupies a sequence of numeric storage units if it has the `sequence` attribute and if all of its ultimate components have a type that occupies numeric storage units. Such an object is called a *numeric sequence structure.*
4. A nonpointer array object occupies a sequence of numeric storage units if its elements have a type that occupies numeric storage units.

Character Storage Units

A character string in storage occupies a sequence of character storage units, one for each character of the string. Because of the wide variety of representations for numerical and character data on actual computers, it is extremely difficult to establish universally acceptable conventions for sharing numeric storage units with character storage units. Therefore, Fortran assumes that the two forms of storage are incompatible. In a standard conforming (portable) program, a particular area of storage cannot contain character data at one time and numerical or logical data at another time.

The following rules apply to character storage units:

1. A nonpointer scalar object (a *string*) of default character type occupies a sequence of character storage units. The number of storage units is the *length* of the string.
2. A nonpointer scalar object of a derived type occupies a sequence of character storage units if it has the `sequence` attribute and if all of its ultimate components have default character type. Such an object is called a *character sequence structure*.
3. A nonpointer array object of default character type occupies a sequence of character storage units. Each element of a character array may occupy more than one character storage unit. All the elements of a character array are combined into a single storage sequence. Thus, the total number of character storage units occupied by a character array is found by multiplying the length of each element by the total number of array elements.

Unspecified Storage Units

Objects of nondefault subtypes (`kind` type parameters) and certain derived types that do not meet the requirements for numeric or character storage units may comprise a storage sequence under certain circumstances:

1. A nonpointer scalar object of integer, logical, complex, or character type, with a nondefault subtype, occupies an unspecified storage unit. A nonpointer scalar object of real type, with a subtype other than default real or double-precision real, occupies an unspecified storage unit. (An object of complex type with double-precision real subtype *does not* occupy four numeric storage units.)
2. A nonpointer scalar object of a derived type occupies one unspecified storage unit if it has the `sequence` attribute but it is neither a numeric sequence structure nor a character sequence structure.
3. The unspecified storage units for different combinations of types and subtypes are incompatible.

Storage Association

For purposes of explanation, assume that you have numbered all of the different incompatible unspecified storage units that appear in a given program, including intrinsic types that have nondefault subtypes and derived types that have the `sequence` attribute. You now have numeric storage units, character storage units, and various unspecified storage unit categories $U_1, U_2, \ldots, U_n$.

A sequence of objects of any mixture of these types occupies a sequence of storage units of the corresponding categories. Two sequences of objects with the same number of storage units of each category, in the same order, may become associated by `common` or `equivalence` storage association. For example, two associated sequences might each consist of 100 numeric storage units, followed by 144 storage units of category U_1, followed by 1024 character storage units, followed by 7 storage units of category U_2.

Note that pointers and derived type structures cannot participate in storage association (via `common` or `equivalence`) unless they have the `sequence` attribute. A derived type with the `sequence` attribute, if it contains one or more ultimate components with the `pointer` attribute, is eligible for `common` but not for `equivalence` storage association.

Constructing and maintaining different sequences of objects that are to be associated is an exceedingly difficult and error-prone process. Except for the most trivial applications, it is recommended that the objects in any two associated storage sequences have identical names and attributes.

Nevertheless, it is sometimes necessary to analyze a sequence of numeric, character, and unspecified storage units that has been constructed in ignorance (or in defiance) of judicious programming methodology, so some slightly more difficult examples are included here. These examples are limited to sequences of the forms permitted in earlier versions of Fortran and illustrate numeric storage sequences that mix arrays and scalars as well as character sequences that mix different lengths. Unspecified storage units and combinations of numeric storage units with character storage units are permitted by Fortran 90 and are explained in the text but are not illustrated in the examples.

E.2 LOCAL STORAGE ASSOCIATION

The `equivalence` Declaration

The `equivalence` declaration permits association of storage sequences *locally*, within a single subprogram. The `equivalence` facility operates by creating an *alias*; that is, by causing two or more names to refer to the same object. Specifically, the same storage units are reserved for the separate names. Other Fortran features, including some uses of pointers, can also cause aliasing.

It is now recognized that `equivalence` and other forms of aliasing are detrimental to good program style. As Lou Glassy has pointed out,[1] "[Fortran] **`equivalence`** is useful for three things: saving memory, cheating the type system, and creating aliasing bugs. Modern computers have more than 4K words of memory; the intrinsic type conversion functions [and `Transfer`; see Appendix A.2] provide an explicit way to change the type of data; we can live without aliasing bugs."

One difficulty with aliasing is that certain compiler optimizations are effective only under the assumption that any specific area of storage is referred to by a single name, within the scope (set of program statements) over which the name is associated with that area of storage. A programmer can become confused by an alias even more easily than a compiler. Consider the following example:

EXAMPLE E.1

```
! Example E.1.
  program Alias
    implicit none
    real :: X, Y
    equivalence (X, Y)
! start program Alias
    X = 3
    Y = -17
    print *, X
  end program Alias
```

We expect the assigned value of `X` in Example E.1 to be maintained until execution of the `print` statement, and appearance of the output value –17 is a bit surprising. But `X` and `Y` are different names for the same storage unit because of the **`equivalence`** declaration, and this surprising output is, in fact, produced.

Although most uses of `equivalence` can be expressed more suitably in Fortran 90 with allocated arrays or by other means, many existing traditional Fortran programs contain `equivalence` declarations. An `equivalence` declaration informs Fortran that certain groups of names are to be considered synonymous — for example, `N` and `Number`; B_1 and `Bone`; and `Hrs`, `Hours`, and `Time`. The following declarations achieve this objective:

```
equivalence (N, Number)
equivalence (B(1), Bone)
equivalence (Hrs, Hours, Time)
```

[1] Lou Glassy, "Tiny Ninety: A Subset of F90 for Beginning Programmers," *Fortran Journal* (4:3) May/June 1992.

These three declarations may be combined into one:

```
equivalence (N, Number), (B(1), Bone), (Hrs, Hours, Time)
```

All the names enclosed in a given set of parentheses form an *equivalence class.* Any number of such equivalence classes can be created in a single declaration. Within one equivalence class, the order is immaterial.

The names in each equivalence class may be array element names, but the subscripts must be initialization expressions. Thus, in the second example, B(I) could not have been used (unless I were a named constant).

Equivalence between elements of two different arrays implies a correspondence among other elements of the two arrays. Thus, the declarations

```
implicit none
real, dimension(10) :: B, C
equivalence (B(1), C(1))
```

will cause array elements B_1, B_2, . . . , B_{10} to occupy the same storage units as C_1, C_2, . . . , C_{10}. Note that the relationship thus established for elements B_1 and C_1 automatically establishes the relationship between B_2 and C_2, between B_3 and C_3, and so on.

In this particular case, the equivalenced elements are the base elements of the two arrays — that is, the element specified by the lowest subscript value in the declared range for each dimension, which is the first element in the standard Fortran array element sequence. In such a case, the array names (without a subscript) may be declared equivalent:

```
equivalence (B, C)
```

Again, the same effect would be achieved by the declaration

```
equivalence (B(3), C(3))
```

It may be noted that array elements with subscript values smaller than that mentioned in the `equivalence` declaration are also made equivalent. When an element of one array appears in an equivalence class with an element of another array, the storage units occupied by all elements of the two arrays are automatically made to correspond on the basis of their position in the standard Fortran array element sequence.

It is not necessary that equivalenced arrays have the same rank or the same shape. For example, suppose that P is a 3 by 4 array (of rank 2), Q is a vector of length 9, and R is a 2 by 6 array (of rank 2). Appropriate declarations would be as follows:

```
implicit none
real, dimension(3, 4) :: P
real, dimension(12) :: Q
real, dimension(2, 6) :: R
equivalence (P, Q, R)
```

Equivalence among Different Types

A particularly dangerous programming practice permitted by Fortran, which will be found in some existing programs, is creation of an alias among variables of different types.

The variables named in an equivalence class are permitted to have different types as long as the storage units they occupy are compatible. It must be kept in mind that real, integer, and logical scalar variables of default `kind` each occupy a single numeric storage unit and that double-precision and default complex scalar variables each occupy two consecutive storage units. Default character variables occupy character storage units and so can be combined with one another in an equivalence class (if string length is taken into account), but objects that occupy character storage units must not be combined with those that occupy numeric storage units.

As an example, suppose that we wish to store integers in column 8 of a real array named `Harry`. We can do so if an array of type integer — say `Jerry` — is declared to be equivalent to a portion of the real array `Harry`. We can then use the array name `Jerry` when we wish to manipulate elements of column 8, but we will use the array name `Harry` when we manipulate elements in any of the other columns. If `Harry` is a 5 by 18 array, then suitable declarations might be as follows:

```
implicit none
real, dimension(5, 18) :: Harry
integer, dimension(5) :: Jerry
equivalence (Harry(1, 8), Jerry)
```

Partial Equivalence

Partial overlap of arrays is permitted. Consider the following example:

```
implicit none
real, dimension(10) :: D, E, F
double precision :: A
real, dimension(2, 4) :: S
complex, dimension(4) :: Z, C
equivalence (D(4), E(2), F, A), (F(3), S(2,2)), (Z, E), (E(4), C)
```

In the first equivalence class, the vectors D, E, and F partially overlap. Next, we see that the third element of F is aligned with the fourth element of S. The double-precision variable A occupies the same storage units as F_1 and F_2.

Each element of a complex array consists of two real data items, the first of which is the real part and the second of which is the imaginary part of the complex element. Partial equivalence may be used to relate two complex arrays in such a way that an element of one is associated with parts of two elements of the other. A real array may also be included in the same equivalence class. In this example, the first (base) element of E is aligned with the real part of Z_1. Taking into account the sequence of storage units occupied by the complex array Z, we can ascertain that E_4 is aligned with the imaginary part of Z_2. Another equivalence class prescribes that E_4 (and thus also the imaginary part of Z_2) is aligned with the real part of C_1. The relationship among the variables is illustrated by the diagram in Figure E.1.

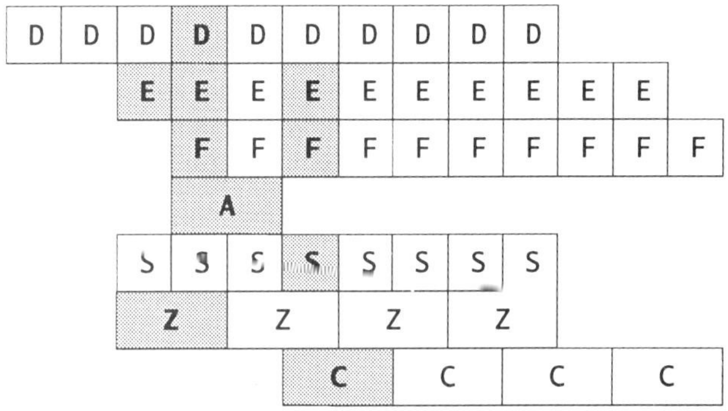

FIGURE E.1. Partial equivalence among real, double-precision, and complex variables.

Names of default character variables, including arrays and substrings, may appear in an equivalence class to specify sharing of character storage units. Recall that a particular area of storage cannot contain character data at one time and numerical or logical data at another time; therefore numeric storage units must not be combined with character storage units in an equivalence class.

A substring name in an equivalence class specifies the position within a string that will determine the equivalence relations among the variables and array elements of character type. The specified character storage position is the first character of the designated substring. Consider the following example:

```
implicit none
character (len = 10) :: A
character (len = 6), dimension(3) :: B
character (len = 1), dimension(12) :: C
character (len = 4), dimension(2) :: D
equivalence (A(8:8), B(2)(6:), C(3), D(2)(3:))
```

The relationship among the variables is illustrated in Figure E.2.

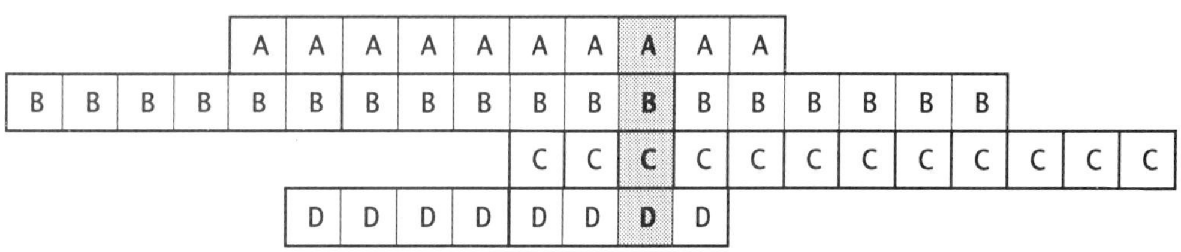

FIGURE E.2. Partial equivalence among character strings.

E.3 STATIC STORAGE ASSOCIATION

The common Declaration

The Fortran 90 module facility provides an excellent way to create *global* data objects and to specify all of their attributes at a single point in the text of a program. Lacking such a feature, traditional versions of Fortran require independent specification of a global storage sequence in each subprogram from which objects from the sequence are to be referenced. Large traditional Fortran programs often contain very long lists of variables to be shared between subprograms. In many such programs, several subprograms contain identical lists. The incorporation of this list into the separate subprograms is managed by `include` directives, but Fortran must repetitively analyze each copy of the long list as it processes each subprogram. One advantage of the newer facility is that Fortran needs to analyze the global definition only once and can incorporate the *processed* definition (which may consist of symbol table information) into various subprograms under control of `use` statements.

Some examples are given here to illustrate the traditional Fortran `common` feature, including numeric storage sequences with a mixture of arrays and scalars as well as character storage sequences with a mixture of different lengths.

Two or more independent subprograms may each include a statement of the form

`common` *List of variables*

Numeric, character, and unspecified storage units are *statically* allocated for the listed variables in the order of their appearance within the list.

EXAMPLE E.2

```
implicit none
real, dimension(10, 5) :: B
common A, B, C, D
```

The type declaration specifies that `B` is an array of 50 numeric storage units. The `common` declaration specifies that the first 53 storage units of a certain block of static storage are to be allocated by Fortran in the following pattern: The first storage unit is allocated to `A`, the second through fifty-first storage units are allocated to `B(1, 1)` through `B(10, 5)`, and the fifty-second and fifty-third storage units are allocated to `C` and to `D`.

Any of the subprograms that contains a `common` statement may store information in the storage units in the block or may retrieve information from those storage units. The *List of variables* need not be identical in the `common` statements of the various subprograms. The correspondence between variable names and storage units is *positional*, depending only upon the sequence of variable names in the list and the number of storage units required for each variable.

A dummy argument name in a procedure must not appear in a `common` declaration in the same procedure (although an actual argument in the referencing subprogram may be a `common` variable). The reason is that Fortran would not know in such circumstances whether to find the designated data value or address in the activation record for the procedure (according to the usual method for dummy arguments), or in static storage.

The following example shows how we might redefine the subroutine `Reverse` and the associated main program `Test_3` in Example 7.7 to use `common` declarations and eliminate the arguments. Note that `common` declarations are required both in `Reverse` and in the main program. Although the names listed in the two declarations are not the same, their positional correspondence in relation to the sequence of storage units in the `common` region achieves the desired matching.

EXAMPLE E.3 The subroutine `Reverse` reverses the first `N` elements of the assumed-shape array `A`. A procedure containing a reference to `Reverse` must specify an array and the value to be associated with `N` in the actual argument list

```
! Example E.3. (Main program)
! Main program to test Reverse.
  program Test_3
    implicit none
    intrinsic Min
    common L, B
    integer, parameter :: S = 200
    real, dimension(S) :: B
    integer :: L, I, EoF
! start program Test_3
    open (1, file = "zahlen.txt")
    do
      read (1, *, iostat = EoF) L, (B(1: Min (L, S)))
      if (EoF < 0) stop "␣End␣of␣data␣file.␣"
      if (L > S) stop "␣Too␣much␣input␣data.␣"
      print *, "␣Input:␣", L, B(1: L)
      call Reverse
      print *, "␣Output:␣", B(1: L)
    end do
  end program Test_3
```

```
! External subroutine to reverse the first N elements of an array A.
  subroutine Reverse
    implicit none
    common N, A
    real, dimension(200) :: A
    integer :: N
    integer :: Loop
! start subroutine Reverse
    if (N > 200) stop "⊥N⊥is⊥too⊥large.⊥"
    do Loop = 1, N / 2
      call Swap_It (Loop, N + 1 - Loop)
    end do
  contains
    subroutine Swap_It (J, K)                     ! Internal subprogram inherits A.
      integer, intent (in) :: J, K
      real :: Temp
  ! start subroutine Swap_It
      Temp = A(J); A(J) = A(K); A(K) = Temp
    end subroutine Swap_It
  end subroutine Reverse
```

Note that the names in the common declarations agree in type, even though the names themselves may differ. For instance, the first storage unit in this block of static storage contains a number stored in the integer internal representation, while the next 200 are stored in the real representation.

For example, an external procedure might declare

```
implicit none
real, dimension(20) :: X
real, dimension(3, 3) :: Trial
real :: Able
real, dimension(4) :: Crow
integer, dimension(6) :: Items
integer :: Code
common X, Trial, Able, Crow, Items, Code
```

The main program could contain the declarations

```
implicit none
real, dimension(34) :: Array
integer, dimension(2, 2) :: List
integer :: I, J, K
common Array, List, I, J, K
```

In each case, the storage sequence consists of 34 storage units allocated to real data, followed by 7 storage units of integer type. The reconfiguration of the arrays is specified for each subprogram independently. Of course, complicated rearrangements such as the one illustrated here can lead to programs that are difficult to understand, so they should usually be avoided.

Storage for common *Sequences*

The block of static storage consists of a single sequence of storage units, which is allocated to variables as specified in the common declarations in each of the subprograms. The common declaration in each subprogram establishes the arrangement of this storage sequence.

Corresponding positions in the storage sequence, in all subprograms, must agree with regard to the *storage unit category*. Thus, the sequence might consist of 100 numeric storage units, followed by 512 character storage units, followed by 3 unspecified storage units for a certain globally defined derived type. This arrangement is permitted if all subprograms that define the sequence conform to this same description. Within a numeric or character storage unit subsequence, the subprograms are permitted to specify different allocations of the storage units.

Named and Unnamed common *Blocks*

In some programs, the static storage allocated to variables listed in common declarations may be treated as a single block; in others, the programmer may wish to create several smaller blocks, giving each block a separate name. For example, it may be desirable to specify one block for character variables and another block for variables that occupy numeric storage units.

Separate named common blocks may also be desirable when some subprograms share data that is of no concern to others. In Example E.4 (given shortly), a block designated by the name S is shared by the main program and subprogram A, another block called T is shared by the main program and subprogram B, and a third unnamed block is shared by all three subprograms.

It is a rule of good programming practice that access to any data object should be restricted to those program regions that require it. For example, subprogram B makes no reference to the data in block S, so block S is not mentioned in subprogram B and is therefore inaccessible.

The declaration for a named common block has the following general form:

common / *Block name* / *List of variables*

The declaration for an unnamed common block has the following general form:

common *List of variables*

There is no type associated with the *Block name*. The main program and its subprograms may refer to any number of named common blocks, plus a single unnamed block.

In some ways, the unnamed block may be viewed as a named block whose name is an empty string.

A *Block name* is a *global name*: The same name may appear in declarations for a given block in two (or more) subprograms from which the data in that block is to be referenced. The names of the individual variables and arrays in the block may be different. For example, in one subprogram a certain storage unit may be occupied by the variable named `Able`, while in another subprogram the same storage unit may be occupied by the third element of an array called `Baker`. Although the names in the *List of variables* in the two subprograms need not be identical, their position within the *sequence of storage units* in the block establishes the desired correspondence among the variables.

In all subprograms using the same *named* `common` block, the same block size must be maintained; that is, in each subprogram the total number of storage units required for the *List of variables* in a given block must agree. This requirement is not imposed on the *unnamed* block, which is one of the important differences between named and unnamed blocks.

EXAMPLE E.4

```
! Example E.4.
  program Main
    implicit none
    real :: A, B, X(50), P(100)
    common A, B, X
    common / S / P
      :
  end program Main
```

```
  subroutine A
    implicit none
    real :: AA, BB, XX(20), R(10, 10)
    logical :: F, G, H(10)
    common AA, BB, XX
    common / S / R
    common / T / F, G, H
      :
  end subroutine A
```

```
  function B () result (Z)
    implicit none
    real, intent (in) :: Z
    real :: A, B3, Dummy(30), Tim(5, 4), Q(4, 3)
```

```
    common A, B3, Dummy, Tim
    common / T / Q
      ⋮
  end function B
```

In Example E.4, static storage is provided for the following variables.

For the main program:

Unnamed block: A, B, and X_1 to X50

Block S: P_1 to P_{100}

For procedure A:

Unnamed block: AA, BB, and XX_1 to XX_{20}

Block S: $R_{1,1}$ to $R_{10,10}$

Block T: F, G, and H_1 to H_{10}

For procedure B:

Unnamed block: A, B3, and $Tim_{1,1}$ to $Tim_{5,4}$, where $Tim_{1,1}$ occupies the same storage unit as X_{31} in the main program

Block T: $Q_{1,1}$ to $Q_{4,3}$

Note that the *unnamed* block does not need to have the same length in all procedures. The unnamed block in procedure A is considerably shorter than that in the main program.

Also note that, in order to achieve the desired match between the elements of Tim in subprogram B and X in the main program, an extra array, Dummy, has been inserted in the common declaration in the procedure to occupy the 30 storage units that are not referred to in the subroutine.

EXAMPLE E.5

```
  implicit none
  common / S67 / A, B, C, K1
```

Variables A, B, C, and K1 are assigned, in the order listed, to the storage units in a common block named S67. Imagine that this declaration appears in a procedure called Sub6, which communicates with another called Sub7. The corresponding variables in the latter procedure are named TA, TB, TC, and Ind. The declaration needed in Sub7 is therefore

```
common / S67 / TA, TB, TC, Ind
```

Data Initialization in common *Blocks*

Occasionally, we may wish to initialize, in a type declaration or in a `data` statement (see Appendix D.3), values for certain variables that are listed in a `common` declaration. Our first inclination might be to declare the initial value in an arbitrary one of the subprograms in which the variable appears. However, two restrictions must be observed. First, initial values may be declared for variables (and array elements) in a named `common` block, but not for those in an unnamed block. Second, initialization of a variable in a named block must take place in a separate special subprogram called a *block data program unit.*

This program unit contains only declarations; no executable statements may be included. It may be recognized by its header statement, which is simply

```
block data
```

or

block data *Program unit name*

To illustrate, suppose that, in Example E.4, we wish to initialize the array elements P_1, P_3, and P_{10} in named block S and the scalar variable F and the array element H_5 in block T. A suitable `block data` program unit might be the following:

```
block data Initials
  implicit none
  real, dimension(100) :: P
  logical :: F = .TRUE., G
  logical, dimension(10) :: H
  common / S / P
  common / T / F, G, H
  data P(1), P(3), P(10) / 2.0, 3.0, 4.0 /
  data H(5) / .FALSE. /
end block data Initials
```

Note that any variable that is to be initialized in the `block data` program unit must appear in a `common` declaration for a named block. Furthermore, the size of each `common` block listed in the `block data` program unit must agree with its size in the other subprograms that mention this named block.

Interaction of common *and* equivalence *Declarations*

It is permissible for a variable or an array name to appear both in a `common` declaration and in an `equivalence` declaration in the same program. However, some restrictions must be observed in order to avoid difficulties when the `equivalence` causes an implied lengthening of the `common` block.

1. An unnamed common block may be lengthened only in the direction of increasing positional value. For example, suppose that real variables A, B, and C are placed in the first three storage units in accordance with the declaration

```
common A, B, C
```

Now suppose that D(1), the base element of a real vector of length 3, is declared equivalent to B:

```
implicit none
real :: A, B, C
real, dimension(3) :: D
common A, B, C
equivalence (B, D(1))     ! Valid (forward) extension of block
```

The three elements of D occupy the second, third, and fourth positions of the common sequence, thus extending the block in the forward direction. In contrast, to declare D(3) equivalent to B would imply extension of the block in an invalid direction:

```
implicit none
real :: A, B, C
real, dimension(3) :: D
common A, B, C
equivalence (B, D(3)) ! Invalid (backward) extension of block
```

The second and third elements of D occupy the first two positions of the common sequence, but the first element of D cannot be accommodated without extending the block backward, which is not permitted.

2. Concerning named common blocks, remember that identically named blocks in two or more subprograms must have the same length. Hence, extension of such a region is permissible only if corresponding adjustments are made in all named common declarations in other subprograms that designate the same *Block name*.

3. Within a given subprogram, no two variables or array names may be declared equivalent if both names also appear in common declarations (for the same block or different blocks). Such a practice would imply a contradictory relationship:

```
implicit none
real :: A, B, C
common A, B, C
equivalence (A, C)                          ! Invalid equivalence
```

The equivalence statement specifies the impossible requirement that the first and third positions of the common block occupy the same storage.

E.4 SEQUENCE ASSOCIATION FOR ARRAY ARGUMENTS

Storage Space for Explicit-Shape Dummy Argument Arrays

For explicit-shape dummy argument arrays, the traditional implementation is still employed by most Fortran processors to improve efficiency and to ensure compatibility with older Fortran programs. In this implementation, Fortran does not set aside any separate space to hold the elements of a dummy argument array. The space must be provided by the actual argument array. The actual array elements are not moved to the procedure; rather, a base address is transmitted. This information is used by the procedure to locate the elements of the actual array.

The `dimension` declaration in the procedure "authorizes" use of the dummy array name along with the designated number of subscript expressions. The shape information that appears in this declaration establishes the sequence of the elements of the dummy array according to the standard Fortran array element sequence formula. The Fortran rule, that the value of each subscript expression must lie within the declared subscript range bounds, applies only with regard to the array shape declaration in the same procedure, except that an assumed-size dummy argument array obtains its final dimension bound (declared with an asterisk) from the actual argument array.

A dummy argument array may be smaller, but must not be larger, than the actual argument array. For example, corresponding to the actual array `Wig` with 1600 elements, the dummy array `A` could be declared in the procedure as

```
real, dimension(40: 5) :: A
```

but not as

```
real, dimension(40: 50) :: A
```

Strictly speaking, this restriction applies not to the declaration in the procedure but to the statements that actually refer to elements of the dummy array. Thus, the dummy array could be declared as

```
real, dimension(40: 50) :: A
```

with no ill effects as long as only the first 40 columns — that is, the first 1600 elements — of `A` are used by the procedure. However, some processors will provide assistance in ensuring array size conformance if the dummy array bounds are kept within the bounds of the actual array.

Reconfiguring a Dummy Argument Array

The rank (number of dimensions) and the extent in each dimension need not agree between an explicit-shape dummy argument array and the corresponding actual argument array as long as the actual array provides sufficient space for all elements of the dummy array. Such *reconfiguration* of explicit-shape dummy argument arrays should be avoided, except where it is absolutely necessary, since in most cases it leads to programs that are difficult to understand and to modify. Array sections and other modern array features, properly understood, provide superior constructs for almost all applications. The subject is discussed here principally for the benefit of those who must read older Fortran programs and determine the meaning of statements that imply array reconfiguration. Nevertheless, array reconfiguration introduces no great difficulty for Fortran, which merely applies the array declaration to the dummy argument in the procedure where it appears, independently of any declaration for a corresponding array in a different subprogram.

When an explicit-shape array name appears as a dummy argument in a procedure, the corresponding actual argument must be an array name or an array element name. A reference to the procedure transmits the address of the base element of the actual argument array or the address of the designated array element. The procedure uses this address to refer to the base element of the dummy argument array.

For example, the procedure might contain the declaration

```
real, dimension(12, 12) :: A
```

while the referencing subprogram declares

```
real, dimension(16, 9) :: Wig
```

Thus, each array consists of 144 elements.

It must be emphasized that the subscript sequence for an explicit-shape dummy argument array and for its actual argument array are independently determined from the array declarations in each subprogram. In effect, the standard array element sequence formulas are applied separately in the procedure and in the referencing subprogram. Thus, the array element named `Wig(1, 2)` in the referencing subprogram is the 17th element in the storage sequence for the array, but the same storage unit would be called `A(5, 2)` in the procedure since the dummy argument array `A` has only 12 elements in each column.

The same array, `Wig`, could also be used as an actual argument for some other procedure to correspond to a dummy array declared as

```
real, dimension(144) :: Vector
```

or as

```
real, dimension(3, 6, 8) :: Block
```

The 17th element of `Vector` would be named simply `Vector(17)`, but the correspondence between elements of `Wig` and those of `Block` is more difficult to determine. (The 17th element of `Block` is called `Block(2, 6, 1)`.)

As a special case of array reconfiguration, an *array element name* may be used as an actual argument when the dummy argument is an explicit-shape array name. For example, suppose that the subroutine `Fix_It` contains a vector declared as

```
integer, dimension(100) :: List
```

and the main program has an array named `Space` with more than 100 elements:

```
integer, dimension(120) :: Space
```

We may now call `Fix_It` from the main program, using `Space(17)` as an actual argument. The subroutine views this as the base element of a fictitious actual argument array. The argument as seen from the subroutine is a vector of length 100 (because of the declaration in the subroutine), consisting of the elements `Space(17)`, `Space(18)`, . . ., `Space(116)` — that is, the 100 elements of the array `Space` beginning with the element specified as the actual argument. Any element from `Space(1)` through `Space(21)` could be properly used as the actual argument because there are at least 100 elements in the storage sequence that begins with any of these elements.

As another example, suppose that `Work` is a 5 by 7 rectangular matrix. We have a subroutine `Calculate`, which requires an explicit-shape vector (array of rank 1) as its argument, and we want to apply `Calculate` to the third column of `Work`. Since the elements of a column of `Work` occupy consecutive storage units in the storage sequence for the array, the five elements in a column of the array can be treated by `Calculate` as though they formed a five-element vector. We may call `Calculate`, using as the actual argument the *first element* of the desired column of `Work`:

```
call Calculate (Work(1, 3))
```

Because of the way in which an array storage sequence is defined, we can use a column (but not a row) of a matrix as an actual argument to a procedure that expects a vector.

Now suppose that there is a subroutine, `Grind`, which requires an argument that is a 5 by 5 square matrix. Again, the main program contains the 5 by 7 matrix `Work`. We can pass the last five columns of `Work` to the subroutine by specifying `Work(1, 3)` as the actual argument.

More complicated is the fact that we can, in effect, form a 5 by 5 square matrix from any 25 consecutively stored elements of `Work`. The actual argument specifies the first of these elements; the subroutine `Grind` will assume that they form a 5 by 5 matrix (because of the declaration in the subroutine) stored in conventional order, beginning with the specified element.

Still more complicated is a situation in which only a portion of the actual argument array is processed by the procedure. Let the function `Frobenius_Norm` be defined as follows:

EXAMPLE E.6

```
! Example E.6.
  function Frobenius_Norm (A, N) result (Total)
    real :: Total
    real, dimension(40, 40), intent (in) :: A
    integer, intent (in) :: N
    intrinsic :: Sum
    integer :: I, J
! start function Frobenius_Norm
    Total = Sum (A(1: N, 1: N) ** 2)
  end function Frobenius_Norm
```

Now suppose that `Frobenius_Norm` is referenced from the expression

`X = Frobenius_Norm (Wig(7,3), 4)`

The procedure will compute the sum of the elements in the upper left-hand 4 by 4 submatrix of the dummy argument array. This array has columns of length 40 because of the declaration in the function definition. Therefore, the first 4 columns occupy 160 storage units, of which positions 1, 2, 3, 4, 41, 42, 43, 44, 81, 82, 83, 84, 121, 122, 123, and 124 are referenced by the procedure if `N` is 4. Thus, the elements of `Wig` that will be involved in the calculation are the elements in those positions *relative* to the actual argument array element `Wig(7,3)`.

Other examples are possible involving arrays with specified lower subscript bounds other than 1.

Explicit-shape Dummy Arrays of Default Character Type

For a dummy argument that is an explicit-shape array or an assumed-size array of default character type, the actual argument may be a character array, a character array element, or a character array element substring. All characters in all elements of the dummy argument array form a single sequence of characters: The last character in an array element is immediately followed by the first character of the following array element. The lengths of dummy and actual array elements need not agree, but the actual array must be big enough for the sequence implied by the declaration for the dummy argument array.

Answers to Selected Exercises

P.1 Exercises

1. Comment lines are 1 and 4. Statement lines are: specifications, lines 2 and 3; instructions, lines 5 and 6.

P.2 Exercises

1. Possible answers:
   a. `real :: Area, Length, Width`
   b. `real :: Average, First, Second, Third, Count = 3.0`
   c. `real :: Voltage, Current, Resistance`
   d. `real :: Energy, Mass, Square = 2.0, Speed_Of_Light = 2.99792458E8`
2. Possible answers:
   a. `Area = Length * Width`
   b. `Average = (First + Second + Third) / Count`
   c. `Voltage = Current * Resistance`
   d. `Energy = Mass * Speed_Of_Light ** Square`

P.3 Exercises

1. a. Possible answer:

```
! Section P.2, Exercise 1a. The area of a rectangle is
!   obtained by multiplying its length by its width.
  program Rectangle
    implicit none
    real :: Area, Length, Width
! start program Rectangle
    print *, "␣Please␣enter␣the␣length␣and␣width␣&
      &of␣a␣rectangle.␣"
    read *, Length, Width
    Area = Length * Width
    print *, "␣The␣area␣is:␣", Area
  end program Rectangle
```

   c. Possible answer:

```
! Section P.2, Exercise 1c.
!   Voltage is current times resistance.
  program Ohms_Law
    implicit none
    real :: Voltage, Current, Resistance
```

```
! start program Ohms_Law
    print *, "␣Please␣enter␣current␣and␣resistance.␣"
    read *, Current, Resistance
    Voltage = Current * Resistance
    print *, "␣The␣voltage␣is:␣", Voltage
  end program Ohms_Law
```

P.4 Exercises

1. Possible answer:

```
! Section P.4, Exercise 1.
  program Rectangle
    implicit none
    real :: Area, Length, Width
    integer :: Loop, Limit = 3
! start program Rectangle
    do Loop = 1, Limit
      print *, "␣Please␣enter␣the␣length␣and␣width␣of␣a␣rectangle.␣"
      read *, Length, Width
      Area = Length * Width
      print *, "␣The␣area␣is:␣", Area
    end do
  end program Rectangle
```

3. Possible answer:

```
! Section P.4, Exercise 3. Trade the values 1 and 2.
  program Trade_1
    implicit none
    integer :: I
! start program Trade_1
    print *, "␣Please␣enter␣1␣or␣2.␣"
    read *, I
    print *, "␣Thank␣you.␣␣You␣have␣entered:␣", I
    I = 3 - I
    print *, "␣Your␣value␣was␣changed␣to:␣", I
  end program Trade_1
```

P.5 Exercises

1. Possible answer:

```
! Section P.5, Exercise 1. Temperature converter.
  program Con_Temp
    implicit none
    real :: Fahr, Cels
! start program Con_Temp
    Fahr = Temp_F ()
    Cels = Temp_C (Fahrenheit_Temp)
    call Output (Fahr, Cels)
  contains
```

```
  real function Temp_F () result (FT)
    print *, "⊥Please⊥enter⊥the⊥Fahrenheit⊥temperature.⊥"
    read *, FT
  end function Temp_F
  real function Temp_C (FT) result (CT)
    real, intent (in) :: FT
    real, parameter :: SCALE = 1.8, OFFSET = 32.0
    CT = (FT - OFFSET) / SCALE
  end function Temp_C
  subroutine Output (FT, CT)
    real, intent (in) :: FT, CT
    print *, FT, "⊥deg.⊥F⊥=⊥", CT, "⊥deg.⊥C⊥"
  end subroutine Output
end program Con_Temp
```

3. Possible answer:

```
! Section P.5, Exercise 3. Temperature converter
 program Con_Temp
   implicit none
   real :: Fahr, Cels
! start program Con_Temp
   Fahr = Temp_F ()
   Cels = Temp_C (Fahrenheit_Temp)
   call Output (Fahr, Cels)
 contains
   subroutine Temp_F ()
     print *, "⊥Please⊥enter⊥Fahrenheit⊥temperature.⊥"
     read *, Fahr
   end subroutine Temp_F
   subroutine Temp_C ()
     real, parameter :: SCALE = 1.8, OFFSET = 32.0
     Cels = (Fahr - OFFSET) / SCALE
   end subroutine Temp_C
   subroutine Output
     real, intent (in) :: FAHR, CELS
     print *, FAHR, "⊥deg.⊥F⊥=⊥", CELS, "⊥deg.⊥C⊥"
   end subroutine Output
 end program Con_Temp
```

1.2 Exercises

1. Not valid; contain digit followed by nondigit: `Oscilloscope`; `1234S`; `7g46h`; `1Z2`; `0Oo`; `1Iii`.
   Not valid; contain characters not permitted in variable or constant: `N/4`; `G46$`.
3. Not valid; contains digit followed by nondigit: `2EAx`.
   Not valid; contain characters not permitted in variable or constant: `X$`; `X&Y`; `Two's_Complement`; `My_Dog's_Name`.
   Not valid; has more than 31 characters: `An_Even_Longer_Variable_Name9012`.

1.3 Exercises

1. ID, valid Fortran name: `Love; Ijk; Hate; X3; Land_Scape; Police_Man; Computer; Kite; Biter; Miter; A1B2`

   RC, valid Fortran real constant: `123.4; 3.; 3.00000; 0.00003`

   IC, valid Fortran integer constant: `123; 1234`

   N, none of these; contains digit followed by nondigit: `1A2B`

   N, none of these; contain characters not permitted in variable or constant: `$1.98; I*J*K; 3*X; 123,400.000`

3. `3.08    5.224    300000    .0000291    9.9    10000.0`
5. `1.0E6    8.0E-6    4.321E2    3.14E-1`
7. Possible answers:
   - b. `real :: New_Vol, Old_Vol, Old_Pressure, New_Pressure, Old_Temp, New_Temp`
   - c. `real :: Celsius, Fahrenheit, Offset = 32.0, Scale = 1.8`

1.4 Exercises

1.
```
real :: Total = 0.0
integer :: Count = 0
```

1.5 Exercises

1. (9.0, 9.0)

2.1 Exercises

1. Possible answer:
```
New = W; W = X; X = Y; Y = Z; Z = New
```

2.2 Exercises

1. Valid Fortran assignment statements:
   - a. `RP = 2.0 * (RL + RW)`
   - d. `L = I + J + K`
3. a. 0.75 b. 27.0 c. 6.75
5. a. real, −3.0 b. real, 1.0 c. real, 12.0 d. real, 11.0 e. real, 8.0 f. real, 0.0

2.3 Exercises

1.
   - a. `R = A + Real (I)`
   - b. `W = Real (I) - 1.3 + Real (J)`
   - c. `K = Real (2 / 3) * 6.6`
   - d. `I = Real (123456789) + B`
   - e. No coercion
3. `5.0`

5. Possible answer:

```
! Section 2.3, Exercise 5. Spherical coordinates.
 program Globe
   implicit none
   real :: R, Theta, Phi, X, Y, Z
! start program Globe
   print *, "␣Please␣enter␣X,␣Y,␣Z.␣"
   R = SqRt (X ** 2 + Y ** 2 + Z ** 2)
   Theta = ATan2 (Y, X)
   Phi = ATan2 (X ** 2 + Y ** 2, Z)
   print *, R, Theta, Phi
   X = R * Cos (Theta) * Sin (Phi)
   Y = R * Sin (Theta) * Sin (Phi)
   Z = R * Cos (Phi)
   print *, X, Y, Z
 end program Globe
```

7. a. `A * Sin (Theta - T)`
   b. `Sin (Y / SqRt (X ** 2 + Y ** 2))`
   c. `Tan (Theta)`
   d. `Sin (2.0 * Pi * L)`
   e. `Sin (ATan2 (SqRt (A ** 2 + B ** 2), Abs (C)))`
9. `print *, Floor (1.57, 0.18), Modulo (1.57, 0.18)`
15. a. `Modulo (N - 1, 12) + 1`
    b. `Second_Minute = Modulo (First_Minute + More - 1, 12) + 1`

2.4 Exercises

1. See Section P.5 exercises.

3.1 Exercises

1. b. Possible answer (partial):

```
if (X > Y) then
  X_Rank = "larger␣"; Y_Rank = "smaller"
else if (X < Y) then
  X_Rank = "smaller"; Y_Rank = "larger␣"
else
  X_Rank = "equal␣␣"; Y_Rank = "equal␣␣"
end if
```

3. Possible answer:

```
! Section 3.1, Exercise 3.
!   Current is voltage divided by resistance.
  program Ohms_Law
    implicit none
    real :: Voltage, Current, Resistance
```

```
! start program Ohms_Law
  print *, "␣Please␣enter␣voltage␣and␣resistance.␣"
  read *, Voltage, Resistance
  if (Resistance /= 0.0) then
    Current = Voltage / Resistance
    print *, "␣The␣current␣is:␣", Current
  else
    print *, "␣Resistance␣must␣not␣be␣zero.␣"
  end if
end program Ohms_Law
```

5. Possible answer (partial):

```
if (X < 0.0) then
  Sign_Of_X = -1
else if (X = 0.0) then
  Sign_Of_X = 0
else
  Sign_Of_X = 1
end if
```

7. a. `(C > D) .or. (.not. (A + B < D))`
   b. `A < 99.0 .or. B < 99.0`
   c. Correct as it stands.
   d. `A == B`
   e. `A == 1 .or. A == 2`
   f. `X >= J`

9. a. `(X > Y) .and. ((F < 2) .or. (G == 4))`
   b. `(X > 0.0) .and. (X < 3.0 * A)`
   c. `(P > X) .or. (P > Y) .or. (P > Z)`
   d. `(A /= B) .and. ((C /= G) .and. (C /= H) .and. (C /= J))`
   e. `Abs (F) <= (3.0 * G)`
   f. `((A >= 1) .and. (A <= 8)) .and. ((B >= 1) .and. (B <= 8))`
   g. `((A >= 1) .and. (A <= 8)) .and. ((B < 1) .or. (B > 8))`
   h. `((X > 4) .and. (Y < 5)) .or. ((X < 5) .and. (Y > 4))`
   i. `SqRt ((X2 - X1) ** 2 + (Y2 - Y1) ** 2) > &`
      `SqRt ((X3 - X1) ** 2 + (Y3 - Y1) ** 2)`
   j. `((A < 0.0) .and. (B < 0.0)) .or. ((A >= 0.0) .and. (B >= 0.0))`
   k. `((A == 0.0) .or. (B == 0.0)) .and. (.not. ((A == 0.0) .or. (B == 0.0)))`

13. a. `Max (Length_1, Length_2)`
    b. `Sign_Of_X = Sign (0.5, X) - Sign (0.5, -X)`
    c. `print *, Abs (A)`

3.2 Exercises

1. Possible answer (partial):

```
select case (Litmus * 10)
  case (: 45)
    print *, "␣The␣litmus␣is␣red.␣"
```

```
    case (83 :)
      print *, "␣The␣litmus␣is␣blue.␣"
    case default
      print *, "␣The␣litmus␣is␣purple.␣"
  end select
```

3.

		Value of I			
		0	1	2	3
a.	Value of 3 − I	3	2	1	0
b.	Result from Example 3.5.	1	2	1	1
c.	Result from Example 3.9.	0	2	1	3
d.	Result from Example 3.14	0	2	1	3
e.	Result from Example 3.21.	0	2	1	3

5. NDays will be 31 (the default case).
7. Possible answer (partial):

```
select case (NInt(Sign(1.0, X)))
  case (1)
    Sign_Of_X = 1.0
  case (-1)
    Sign_Of_X = -1.0
  case default
    Sign_Of_X = 0.0
end select
```

3.3 Exercises

1. a. `Merge ("AM", "PM", Time > 0.0 .and. Time <= 12.0)`
   b. `Merge (X, Y, X < Y)`
   c. `Merge (366, 365, Modulo (Year, 4) == 0)`
   d. `Merge (1, 2, I == 2)`

3.4 Exercises

1. `Merge ("X", "Y", Big_X)`
3. `((A + B) > C) .or. ((X + Y) == Z)`
7. Possible answer:

```
! Section 3.4, Exercise 7.
  program X_Or_Y_1
    implicit none
    real :: X, Y
! start program X_Or_Y_1
    print *, "␣Please␣enter␣values␣for␣X␣and␣Y.␣"
    read *, X, Y
    print *, "␣The␣proposition␣'X␣exceeds␣Y'␣is:␣", X > Y
  end program X_Or_Y_1
```

4.1 Exercises

1. a. `do I = 1, N`
   b. `do I = 1, N - 1`
   c. `do Jolly = 12, 62`
   d. `do I = 1, N`
   e. `do I = 1, N`

3. Possible answer:

```
! Section 4.1, Exercise 3. Divisors of an integer.
  program Dividend
    implicit none
    integer :: N, Loop
! start program Dividend
    print *, "␣Think␣of␣a␣number.␣"
    read *, N
    do Loop = 1, Floor (SqRt (Real (N)))
      if (Modulo (N, I) == 0) print *, I, N / I
    end do
  end program Dividend
```

5. Possible answer:

```
! Section 4.1, Exercise 5. Quadrature.
  program Quad
    implicit none
    intrinsic Selected_Real_Kind, Real, Modulo
    intrinsic Exp
    integer, parameter :: P = 12, K = Selected_Real_Kind (P)
    integer :: N, I
    real (kind = K) :: A, B, Delta_X, X, Evens, Odds, Pi, Ans
! start program Quad
    do
      print *, "␣N?␣"
      read *, N
      if (N < 1) exit
      if (Modulo (N, 2) /= 0) N = N + 1
      print *, "␣A?,␣B?␣"
      read *, A, B
      Delta_X = (B - A) / Real (N, Kind = K)
      Evens = 0.0
      Odds = 0.0
      do I = 1, N - 1
        X = A + Real (I, Kind = K) * Delta_X
        if (Modulo (I, 2) == 0) then
          Evens = Evens + F (X)
```

```
      else
        Odds = Odds + F (X)
      end if
    end do
    Trapezoid = Delta_X * (0.5 * (F (A) + F (B)) + Odds + Evens)
    Simpson = Delta_X &
      * (F (A) + F (B) + 4.0 * Odds + 2.0 * Evens) / 3.0
    print *, Trapezoid, Simpson
  end do
contains
  real function F (X) result (R)
    real (kind = K), intent (in) :: X
! start function F
    R = Exp (-X ** 2)                     ! Or use another expression.
  end function F
end program Quad
```

4.3 Exercises

1. Possible answer:

```
! Section 4.3, Exercise 1. Nth root by Newton's method.
  program Newt_Root
    implicit none
    intrinsic Abs
    real :: X, Root = 1.0          ! Use 1.0 as first guess for Root.
    real, parameter :: TOLERANCE = 1.0E-5
    integer :: N, Loop
    integer, parameter :: Max = 20
! start program Newt_Root
    print *, &
    "⊥Please⊥enter⊥N⊥and⊥the⊥number⊥whose⊥Nth⊥root⊥is⊥wanted.⊥"
    read *, N, X
    if (N <= 0) stop
    X = Abs (X)                               ! X must be nonnegative.
    do Loop = 1, Max
      if (Abs (Root ** N / X - 1.0) > TOLERANCE) exit
      if (Loop = Max) stop "⊥Slow⊥convergence.⊥"
      Root = ((N - 1) * Root + X / (Root ** (N - 1))) / N
    end do
    print *, "⊥Nth⊥root⊥of:⊥", X, "⊥is:⊥", Root
  end program Newt_Root
```

4.4 Exercises

1. For set 1 (K = 6, L = 3), the statement will be executed 18 times and the final value of `Total` will be 13.0. For set 2 (K = 4, L = 5), the statement will never be executed and the final value of `Total` will be 0.0 .

4.5 Exercises

1. Possible answer:

```
! Section 4.5, Exercise 1. Total of data values from file.
  program Totem
    implicit none
    integer :: EoF
    real :: Next_Item, Total = 0.0
! start program Totem
    open (2, file = "zahlen.txt")
    do
      read (2, *, iostat = EoF) Next_Item
      if (EoF < 0) exit
      Total = Total + Next_Item
    end do
    print *, Total
  end program Totem
```

3. Possible answer:

```
! Section 4.5, Exercise 3. Sequence check of input values.
  program Butterfly
    implicit none
    integer :: Record_Number = 1, Count = 0, EoF
    real :: Next_Item, Previous
! start program Butterfly
    open (2, file = "butterfl.txt")
    do
      read (2, *, iostat = EoF) Next_Item
      if (EoF < 0) exit
      if (Record_Number > 1) then
        if (Next_Item < Previous) then
          print *, Record_Number, Next_Item, Previous
          Count = Count + 1
        end if
      end if
      Record_Number = Record_Number + 1
      Previous = Next_Item
    end do
    print *, "⊥Number⊥of⊥sequence⊥errors:⊥", Count
  end program Butterfly
```

5.1 Exercises

1. a. `integer, dimension(8, 8) :: Chess`
   b. `complex, dimension(7, 10) :: D`
   c. `real, dimension(13) :: X, Y, Z`
      `integer, dimension(39) :: J`
   d. `integer, dimension(13) :: Newton` `! Or real`
3. a. `Beta(J)`
   b. `Alpha(J + 2)`
   c. `Gamma(2 * J - 1)`
4. `real, dimension(5, 4, 17) :: Carton`
6. a. 6 b. 61 c. 9.15 d. 16.14 e. −12.69 f. 7

5.2 Exercises

1. a. Rank 1; shape (3); size 3.
   b. Rank 1; shape (5); size 5.
   c. Rank 1; shape (12); size 12.
   d. Rank 1; shape (3), size 3.
   e. Rank 1; shape (6); size 6.
   f. Rank 2; shape (3, 3); size 9.
   g. Rank 1; shape (6); size 6.
   h. Rank 3; shape (3, 6, 3); size 54.
   i. Rank 3; shape (3, 6, 9); size 162.
   j. Rank 4; shape (2, 2, 2, 2); size 16.
   k. Rank 7; shape (0, 2, 2, 2, 2, 2, 2); size 0.
3. possible answer:

```
  Section 5.2, Exercise 3. Sequence of musical notes.
  program Melody
    implicit none
    logical :: First = .TRUE.
    integer :: Sequence(25, 25) = 0, EoF
    integer :: Next, Prev
! start program Melody
    open (2, file = "notedata.txt")
    do
      read (2, *, iostat = EoF) Next
      if (EoF < 0) exit
      if (.not. First) Sequence (Next, Prev) = &
        Sequence (Next, Prev) + 1
      First = .FALSE.
      Prev = Next
    end do
    print *, "␣Number␣of␣sequence␣errors:␣", Count
  end program Melody
```

5. `Tax(3: 22) = Tax(: 20); Tax(:2) = 0.0`
7. `A = B`

5.3 Exercises

1. Possible answer:

```
integer function Find_Last_Neg (A, Value) result (Last_I)
! implicit none                        ! Omit if Find is internal.
  intrinsic Size, MaxLoc
  real, intent (in), dimension(:) :: A
  real, intent (out) :: Value
  integer :: I, Temp(1)
  integer, dimension (Size (A)) :: Numbers, Mark
! start function Find
  Numbers = (/ (I, I = 1, Size (A)) /)
  Mark = Merge (Numbers, 0, A < 0.0)
  Temp = MaxLoc (Mark)
  Last_I = Temp(1)
  Value = A(Last_I)
end function Find_Last_Neg
```

3. Possible answer:

```
subroutine Summit (Array, Row_Sums, Col_Sums, Grand)
  implicit none
  intrinsic Shape, Size
  real, intent(in) :: Array(:, :)
  real, intent (out) :: Row_Sums(:), Col_Sums(:), Grand
  integer, dimension(2) :: S
! start subroutine Summit
  S = Shape (Array)
  if ((Size (Row_Sums) /= S(1)) .or. &
    (Size (Col_Sums) /= S(2))) stop "⊥Shape⊥error.⊥"
  Row_Sums = Sum (Array, Dim = 2)
  Col_Sums = Sum (Array, Dim = 1)
  Grand = Sum (Array)
end subroutine Summit
```

5. The product of a 5 by 0 matrix and a 0 by 7 matrix is a 5 by 7 matrix all of whose elements have the value 0.0.

5.4 Exercises

1. Possible answer:

```
! Section 5.4, Exercise 1.
!   Absorption and reflection at the surface of a metal.
  program Refractory
    implicit none                                   ! directive
    intrinsic Abs, AImag, ATan2                    ! (Optional)
    real :: Pi, Lambda = 598.3, Alpha(3), Y(3), R(3)
    complex :: N(3)
    integer :: I
```

```
! start program Refractory
   Pi = ATan2 (0.0, -1.0)
   print *, Lambda
   N(1) = (.04, 2.4)       ! Complex index of refraction for Sodium
   N(2) = (1.5, 5.3)          ! Complex index of refraction for Tin
   N(3) = (3.7, 5.4)      ! Complex index of refraction for Gallium
   Alpha = 4.0 * Pi * AImag (N) / Lambda   ! Absorption coefficient
   Y = 1.0 / Alpha                                      ! Skin depth
   R = Abs ((N - 1.0) / (N + 1.0)) ** 2                ! Reflectance
   print "(3 G9.3, A, G9.3, A, G9.3)", &            ! See Appendix B.
     (N(I), Alpha(I), "␣Depth:␣", Y(I),   "␣Reflectance:␣", R(I), &
       I = 1, 3)
     end program Refractory
```

3. Possible answer:

```
! Section 5.4, Exercise 3: Digital adder for logical arrays.
  program Adder
    implicit none
    integer, parameter :: Length = 4
    logical :: A(Length), B(Length), C(Length + 1), &
      Temp = .FALSE.
    integer :: Loop
! start program Adder
    print *, "␣A,␣B?␣"
    read *, A, B
    do Loop = 1, Length
      C(Loop) = Sum_3 (A(Loop), B(Loop), Temp)
      Temp = Carry (A(Loop), B(Loop), Temp)
    end do
    C(Length + 1) = Temp
    print *, C
  contains
    logical function Sum_3 (X, Y, Z) result (Q)
      logical, intent(in) :: X, Y, Z
  ! start function Sum_3
      Q = X .neqv. (Y .neqv. Z)
    end function Sum_3
    logical function Carry (X, Y, Z) result (Q)
      logical, intent(in) :: X, Y, Z
  ! start function Carry
      Q = (X .and. Y) .or. (X .and. Z) .or. (Y .and. Z)
    end function Carry
  end program Adder
```

5. The following simple method requires $m \cdot n$ comparisons.

```
do I = 1, M
```

```
    do J = 1, N
      if (A(I) == B(J)) print *, I, J, A(I, J)
    end do
  end do
```

A more complicated method, which would be faster for large arrays, is to sort each array by an $n \cdot \log n$ method such as Quicksort and then watch for duplicates while merging the two arrays.

6.1 Exercises

1. Possible answer:

```
! Section 6.1, Exercise 1.
  program Payroll
    implicit none
    character (len = 20) :: Name
    real :: Rate, Hrs, Pay
! start program Payroll
    open (2, file = "payrolin.txt")
    do
      read (2, *, iostat = EoF) Name, Rate, Hrs
      if (EoF < 0) exit
      Pay = Rate * (Hrs + 0.5 * Max (0.0, Hrs - 40.0))
      print *, Name, Rate, Hrs, Pay
    end do
  end program Payroll
```

5. a. `"quick␣brown␣fox"`
   b. `"The␣quick␣brown␣fox␣jumps"`
   c. `"over␣the␣lazy␣dog."`
   d. `"own␣fo"`

7. a. `Longer = List_1 // List_2 // List_3`
   b. `Longer(8:8) = "A"`
   c. `List_2 = Longer(6: 9)`

15. Possible answer (partial):

```
character (len = L), dimension (N) :: Array
do Loop = 1, N
  if (Array(Loop) = Test) exit
end do
print *, Loop
```

17. `Count (Checker == "XX")`

19. `RMC = Count (Checker == "RM")`
    `RKC = Count (Checker == "RK")`
    `BMC = Count (Checker == "BM")`
    `BKC = Count (Checker == "BK")`

21. Possible answer (partial):

```
Len = Length (String)
Min = 0
do Loop = 1, Len
  Loc = Index (String(Min + 1: ), "␣")
  if (Loc == 0) exit                        ! No more blank characters.
  Min = Min + Loc
  print *, "␣Blank␣character␣found␣at:␣", Min
  N_Loc = Verify (String(Min + 1: ), "␣")
  if (N_Loc == 0) exit                   ! No more nonblank characters.
  Min = Min + N_Loc
  print *, String(Min), "␣Nonblank␣character␣found␣at:␣", Min
end do
```

6.3 Exercises

1. The list will be a circular list consisting only of the latest new item at any time. Pointer assignment to Root makes "garbage" of the item previously linked to Root.

7.3 Exercises

1. 31 36.70 48 17.24 92 531.16

3.

	A_i	A_{n+i-1}	Printed results					
Set 1:	4.0	3.0	1.0	2.0	3.0	4.0	5.0	6.0
Set 2:	2.0	3.0	1.0	2.0	3.0	4.0		
Set 3:	5.2	5.2	9.5	7.6	5.2	3.2	1.0	

5.

```
use Reverse_M
  ⋮
read *, A
read *, I, J
call Swap_It (I, J)
```

7.

```
Almost = Max (0.0, Min (1.0, X))
```

9. a.

```
Flag = Min (Abs (X), 1.0)
```

c.

```
if (Any (List <= K)) then
  Large = MaxVal (List, Mask = (List <= K))
else
  Large = K
end if
```

10.
```
! Section 7.3, Exercise 10. Euclid's algorithm.
 program Main
   integer :: P, Q
! start program Main
   read *, P, Q
   print *, Euclid (P, Q)
 contains
   integer function Euclid (I1, I2) result (GCD)
     integer, intent (in) :: I1, I2
 ! start function Euclid
     do
       Remainder = Modulo (I1, I2)
       if (Remainder == 0) then
         GCD = I2; return
       else
         I1 = I2
         I2 = Remainder
       end if
     end do
   end function Euclid
 end program Main
```

8.1 Exercises

1. See Section 5.3, Exercise 1. Modify as follows:

```
Mark = Merge (Numbers, 0, A < X)
Temp = MinLoc (Mark)
```

8.2 Exercises

1.
```
 subroutine Norm (V, Total, Flag)
   intrinsic SqRt, Sum
   real, intent (in) :: V
   real, intent (out) :: Total
! start subroutine Norm
   logical, intent (out) :: Flag
   Total = SqRt (Sum (V * V))
   Flag = Total >= 1.0E5
 end subroutine Norm
```

3. a.
```
do I = 1, Size (A, Dim = 1)
  do J = 1, Size (B, Dim = 2)
    Product (I, J) = ScaPr (A(I, :), B(:, J))
  end do
end do
```

8.6 Exercises

1. Possible answer:

```
program Trapezoids
  use Quadrature_M
  implicit none
  intrinsic Sin
  real, parameter :: A = 0.0, B = 1.0
  real, parameter :: N = 100
! start program Trapezoids
  print *, Quadrature (Poly_A, A, B, N)
  print *, Quadrature (Poly_B, A, B, N)
  print *, Quadrature (Sin, A, B, N)
end program Trapezoids
```

9.2 Exercises

1. Possible answers:
   a. `print *, A, B, C, (D(I), I = N, M)`
   b. `print *, John Jackson, 14.35, X(1)`
   c. `read *, L, Jill, Johnnie, (Jacob(I), I = 1, N)`
   d. `print *, (A(I), I = 1, 500, 1)`
   e. Constants are not permitted in an input list.
   f. `read *, Able, X, Baker, (Y(2, J), J = 3, 9)`
   g. `read *`
   h. `print *`
   i. `print *, -SqRt(C ** 2 + B ** 3) / 4.0`
   j. `print *, (B(I), C (3), I = 1, K), D, E`
   k. `read *, N, B, A`
   l. Correct as it stands.
3. a. `read *, N, (A(I), I = 1, N)`
   b. `print *, C(4, :)`
   c. `print *, D(:, L)`
   d. `read *, (Q(I, 8), Q(I, 9), I = 1, 8)`
   e. `print *, Criss_Cross`
   f. `read *, (A(2 * I - 1), B(2 * I), I = 1, N)`
   g. `print *, Crazy (1: : 2, :)`
5.
```
print *, K(I - 2, J - 1), K(I - 2, J + 1), K(I - 1, J - 2), &
  K(I - 1, J + 2), K(I + 2, J - 1), K(I + 2, J + 1), &
  K(I + 1, J - 2), K(I + 1, J + 2)
```

Index

NOTE: features marked ☠ in the index are considered obsolete in this text.